THE LAW OF DEFAMATION AND THE INTERNET

SECOND EDITION

by

MATTHEW COLLINS

BA, LLB (Hons), PhD

Barrister, Owen Dixon Chambers, Melbourne

OXFORD

UNIVERSITY PRESS

OXFORD

UNIVERSITY PRESS

Great Clarendon Street, Oxford OX2 6DP

Oxford University Press is a department of the University of Oxford.
It furthers the University's objective of excellence in research, scholarship,
and education by publishing worldwide in

Oxford New York

Auckland Cape Town Dar es Salaam Hong Kong Karachi
Kuala Lumpur Madrid Melbourne Mexico City Nairobi
New Delhi Shanghai Taipei Toronto

With offices in

Argentina Austria Brazil Chile Czech Republic France Greece
Guatemala Hungary Italy Japan South Korea Poland Portugal
Singapore Switzerland Thailand Turkey Ukraine Vietnam

Oxford is a registered trade mark of Oxford University Press
in the UK and in certain other countries

Published in the United States
by Oxford University Press Inc., New York

© Matthew Collins 2005

The moral rights of the author have been asserted
Database right Oxford University Press (maker)

Crown copyright material is reproduced under Class Licence
Number C01P0000148 with the permission of OPSI
and the Queen's Printer for Scotland

First published 2005

British Library Cataloguing in Publication Data

Data available

Library of Congress Cataloging in Publication Data

Data available

Typeset by RefineCatch Limited, Bungay, Suffolk
Printed in Great Britain
on acid-free paper by
Ashford Colour Press Ltd., Gosport, Hants.

ISBN 0–19–928182–3   978–0–19–928182–4

3 5 7 9 10 8 6 4 2

100 640183

FOREWORD

Over the past few years the Internet has conferred huge benefits on us all but, inevitably, it has been open also to largely ungovernable abuses. Most notoriously, of course, there has been the spread of child pornography. It has been exploited too for the undermining of the values embodied in Article 8 of the European Convention on Human Rights through intrusions upon personal privacy and the often casual 'trashing' of personal reputations.

So far, communications via the Internet have been treated by common lawyers as though they are rather like seaside postcards sent by conventional means: see eg *Dow Jones & Company Inc v Gutnick* (2002) 210 CLR 575. That is because so far, judges have no other language for addressing them. They can only resort to the rather crude tool of analogy. It is possible, I imagine, to draw analogies between satellites and stagecoaches, but they are unlikely to advance greatly the sum of human knowledge.

Fortunately for those who commit their thoughts to the Internet, or have them so committed by others, it can at least be said that notions of privilege, public interest, and fair comment have moved on apace since the distant days when judges had, by using similar analogies, to grapple with the novelty of telegrams. As Brett J observed in *Williamson v Freer* (1874) LR 9 CP 393, 395:

> It is like the case of a libel contained in a post-card. It was never meant by the legislature that these facilities for postal and telegraphic communication should be used for the purpose of more easily disseminating libels.

The truth is, of course, that the developers of the technology in the nineteenth century were no more thinking of libel or contempt than were those of the late twentieth. They simply provided facilities for communicating information and ideas more widely and more quickly. They changed the environment in which we live.

Where the environment changes only by degrees analogies can be helpful. One can learn gradually to cope. From time to time, however, there is a quantum leap. The environment is simply transformed. Analogies are no longer of any use because the Internet is not like anything else. The common law has been left standing.

Some analogies are overtaken more quickly than others. Even in the 1960s Lord Denning could explain the means of proving 'general bad reputation', for mitigating damages, by reference to the village constable. How is that homely figure supposed to help in the global 'village' in which we all now live? Or take the thorny and now common pitfalls of jurisdiction. When a communicator with something to say addresses his mail to England, or presents himself at customs in Dover in readiness for his lecture tour, he knows that he is voluntarily submitting himself to the jurisdiction of the English courts. Yet there is no obvious analogy with someone who puts his ideas onto the world wide web or his own web site. He is potentially exposed to a multiplicity of suits, and uncertain outcomes, throughout the world. There is no single set of laws or even principles recognized as of universal applicability.

What is plainly required is an international convention identifying generally applicable rules governing, for example, responsibility for publication and republication, jurisdiction and limitation, as well as providing for common defences. Needless to say, that is pie in the sky. For the foreseeable future, those who provide Internet facilities, and those who avail themselves of their services, must continue to hack their respective paths though a thicket of domestic laws and international conventions often in conflict with one another—but to which they may find themselves vulnerable at any moment. Those who communicate news and opinions, or indeed any information, need to be able to make at least an informed assessment of the risks to which they are subjecting themselves, if necessary with the assistance of legal advice. At present they can do little more than take a leap in the dark.

Practitioners called upon to advise them in their unenviable plight, and judges required to sort out the consequences, must therefore turn gratefully to Dr Collins' pioneering and scholarly work. He has successfully identified and ana-lysed the nature of the legal problems to be confronted and the absurdities to which they often give rise. His guidance is wise and useful. In the Foreword to the first edition, four years ago, Lord Bingham came to the prescient conclusion that it would not be the last. What he could not then have foreseen was how, in such a short space of time, this impressive store of knowledge was to be rendered indispensable. Dr Collins deserves our thanks and our congratulations.

David Eady
4 June 2005

PREFACE

The Internet is a vast repository of information and opinion, from the sober and authoritative, to the scurrilous and unreliable. Its benefits are manifold and manifest. The public interest demands that regulation of the Internet be kept to a minimum, so that the potential of this instantaneous, global medium of communication can be fully harnessed. Abrogation of regulation, however, is neither realistic nor desirable. Ubiquity and ease of access invite abuse. Where damaging material is published online, its consequences are not artificially quarantined in a cyberspace; they are felt offline as surely as if the material had been published in a book or newspaper, or broadcast by radio or television.

This text is concerned with exploring how the law attempts to reconcile online freedom of expression with the need to provide a remedy where that freedom is abused by the publication of material which unjustifiably damages or destroys reputations. While principally addressed to an audience of practitioners and students in the United Kingdom, and secondarily in Australia, the text attempts to survey relevant authorities in other jurisdictions, including most importantly the United States and Canada.

Since the publication of the last edition, there have been a number of significant legal developments. The Electronic Commerce (EC Directive) Regulations 2002 (UK) have commenced operation, strengthening considerably the hand of Internet intermediaries who unwittingly host, cache, or carry defamatory material. Courts in the United Kingdom, the United States, Australia, and Canada have had to decide, in a range of circumstances, whether to assume jurisdiction over foreigners who have published defamatory material via the Internet. The Human Rights Act 1998 (UK), which incorporates the rights in the European Convention on Human Rights into the domestic law of the United Kingdom, and decisions of the European Court of Human Rights interpreting that Convention, have created new impetus for the evolution of common law defamation principles.

In this edition, apart from updating the text to deal with those and other developments, there are two further major changes. First, Part VI, which deals with principles of private international law, has been expanded and restructured. There are now separate chapters dealing with grounds of jurisdiction, principles of *forum non conveniens*, choice of law rules in the United Kingdom, choice of law rules in Australia, and methods of proof of foreign law. The new structure will make it easier for readers to identify points of relevance or interest.

Secondly, the coverage and analysis of relevant aspects of American law has been substantially augmented. American online publishers are increasingly called upon to defend defamation actions abroad arising out of material uploaded in the United States but having consequences elsewhere. The warm reception the first edition received in the United States convinced me that American practitioners, publishers, and students with an interest in this area of the law need and want to understand how courts in the United Kingdom and Australia deal with defamation actions generally, and more specifically with questions of intermediary liability, jurisdiction, and choice of law. At the same time, however, a consequence of the proliferation of defamation actions against American publishers abroad is that practitioners in the United Kingdom and Australia need to understand that American sensibilities are confronted by systems of law which accord relatively more significance to the right to reputation, and relatively less significance to freedom of expression, than their own.

When writing a text dealing with a rapidly developing area of law such as that with which this book is concerned, it is impossible to settle on an entirely satisfactory deadline. Shortly before the manuscript for this edition was due to be delivered, the European Court of Human Rights delivered its judgment in *Steel and Morris v United Kingdom*, and a Grand Chamber of the European Court of Justice delivered its judgment in Case C–281/02, *Owusu v Jackson*. It has been possible to incorporate the likely implications of those decisions into this edition. On the other hand, at the time of publication, moves were afoot in Australia to replace the current tangle of inconsistent State and Territory defamation laws with a national law, or national co-operative laws. At the time of writing the outcome and timing of those moves was impossible to predict with any confidence.

I have attempted to state the law on the basis of materials available to me in March 2005 and, of course, am to blame for all errors and omissions.

MATTHEW COLLINS

Owen Dixon Chambers
Melbourne
March 2005

ACKNOWLEDGEMENTS

I was struck in putting together this edition by the extent to which Professor Sally Walker's knowledge of the law of defamation, and in particular her profound understanding of its historical emergence, structure, and interconnections with other areas of the law, has informed my own understanding. I am deeply grateful to her. I also wish to acknowledge the editors and staff at Oxford University Press, for their professionalism and attention to detail.

Immersion in research and writing commitments for a text of this kind involves sacrificing evenings and weekends, and an almost maniacal obsession with the subject matter which, unsurprisingly, is not entirely shared by others. For various reasons, including providing at different times willing sounding boards, sympathetic ears, practical assistance, and forbearance, I thank Paul Bangay, my parents Robyn and John Collins, Mark Dean, Natalie Hickey, Jason Waple, and Alex Wolff. Finally, my partner Leonard Vary merits special thanks; more than anything else his support sustained me through the completion of this edition.

CONTENTS—SUMMARY

CONTENTS

Contents

VII OTHER SOURCES OF LAW

TABLE OF CASES

European Court of Justice

TABLE OF STATUTES

Northern Territory

TABLE OF REGULATIONS AND RULES

TABLE OF TREATIES AND EUROPEAN LEGISLATION

ABBREVIATIONS

1st cir	United States Court of Appeals, first circuit
2d cir	United States Court of Appeals, second circuit
3d cir	United States Court of Appeals, third circuit
4th cir	United States Court of Appeals, fourth circuit
5th cir	United States Court of Appeals, fifth circuit
6th cir	United States Court of Appeals, sixth circuit
9th cir	United States Court of Appeals, ninth circuit
10th cir	United States Court of Appeals, tenth circuit
A 2d	Atlantic Reporter, second series (USA)
AC	Appeal Cases (UK)
AC	Appellate Court (USA)
ACT	Australian Capital Territory
ACTR	Australian Capital Territory Reports
ACTSC	Australian Capital Territory Supreme Court, media neutral citation
AD	Supreme Court, Appellate Division (USA)
ALJR	Australian Law Journal Reports
All ER	All England Law Reports
All ER Rep	All England Law Reports, reprint
ALR	Australian Law Reports
App Cas	Appeal Cases (England)
AR	Alberta Reports (Canada)
ATPR	Australian Trade Practices Reports
Az	Arizona (USA)
BCLR (4th)	British Columbia Law Reports, fourth series (Canada)
Beav	Beavan's Reports (England)
Bing	Bingham's Reports (England)
Bing NC	Bingham's New Cases (England)
BR	Broadcasting Reports (Australia)
BSA	Broadcasting Services Act 1992 (Cth)
C & K	Carrington and Kirwan's Reports (England)
C & M	Carrington & Marshman's Reports (England)
C & P	Carrington & Payne's Reports (England)
Ca	California (USA)
CA	Court of Appeals (USA)
Cal App 4th	California Appellate Reports, fourth series (USA)
Cal Rptr 2d	California Reporter, second series (USA)
Cal Rptr 3d	California Reporter, third series (USA)

CB	Common Bench Reports (England)
CD	United States District Court, Central Division
CDA	Communications Decency Act, 47 USC (1996) (USA)
Ch	Chancery Law Reports (England)
CLJ	Current Law Journal (Malaysia)
CLR	Commonwealth Law Reports (Australia)
CM & R	Crompton, Meeson & Roscoe's Reports (England)
CPC (4th)	Carswell's Practice Cases, fourth series (Canada)
CPD	Common Pleas Division Reports (England)
CPR	Civil Procedure Rules (England and Wales)
Cr & J	Crompton & Jervis' Exchequer Reports (England)
Cro Eliz	Croke's King Bench Reports (England)
Ct	Connecticut (USA)
Cth	Commonwealth of Australia
D	Dunlop Bell & Murray's Session Cases (Scotland)
D	United States District Court
DC	District of Columbia (USA)
DC cir	United States Court of Appeals, District of Columbia circuit
DLR	Dominion Law Reports (Canada)
DLR (3d)	Dominion Law Reports, third series (Canada)
DLR (4th)	Dominion Law Reports, fourth series (Canada)
DPA	Data Protection Act 1998 (UK)
EB & E	Ellis, Blackburn & Ellis' Queen's Bench Reports (England)
ECHR	European Convention on Human Rights and Fundamental Freedoms
ECR	European Court Reports
ED	United States District Court, Eastern District
EHRR	European Human Rights Reports
EMLR	Entertainment and Media Law Reports (UK)
ER	English Reports
Esp	Espinasse's Nisi Prius Reports (England)
EWCA Civ	Court of Appeal of England and Wales, Civil Division, media neutral citation
EWHC	High Court of England and Wales, media neutral citation
F & F	Foster & Finlayson's Reports (England)
F	Fraser's Session Cases (Scotland)
F	Federal Reporter (USA)
F 2d	Federal Reporter, second series (USA)
F 3d	Federal Reporter, third series (USA)
F Supp	Federal Supplement (USA)
F Supp 2d	Federal Supplement, second series (USA)
FCA	Federal Court of Australia, media neutral citation
FCR	Federal Court Reports (Australia)
Fl	Florida (USA)
FLR	Federal Law Reports (Australia)
FSR	Fleet Street Reports (UK)

H & C	Hurlstone & Coltman's Exchequer Reports (England)
H & N	Hurlstone & Norman's Exchequer Reports (England)
HCA	High Court of Australia, media neutral citation
HKLRD	Hong Kong Law Reports and Digest
HLC	House of Lords Cases (UK)
HRA	Human Rights Act 1998 (UK)
Il	Illinois (USA)
KB	King's Bench Reports (England)
La	Louisiana (USA)
LJCP	Law Journal Reports, Common Pleas (England)
LJKB	Law Journal Reports, King's Bench (England)
LJQB	Law Journal Reports, Queen's Bench (England)
Lloyd's LR	Lloyd's List Law Reports (UK)
Lloyd's Rep	Lloyd's Reports (UK)
LR Ex	Law Reports, Exchequer (England)
LR PC	Law Reports, Privy Council
LR QB	Law Reports, Queen's Bench (England)
LT	Law Times Reports (England)
M	Macpherson's Session Cases (Scotland)
M & W	Meeson & Welsby's Exchequer Reports (England)
Md	Maryland (USA)
Me	Maine (USA)
Media L Rep	Media Law Reporter (USA)
Mn	Minnesota (USA)
Mo	Missouri (USA)
Mod	Modern Reports (England)
Mood & R	Moody & Robinson's Nisi Prius Reports (England)
ND	North Dakota (USA)
ND	United States District Court, Northern District
NE 2d	North Eastern Reporter, second series (USA)
NJ	New Jersey (USA)
NSR (2d)	Nova Scotia Reports, second series (Canada)
NSW	New South Wales (Australia)
NSWCA	New South Wales Court of Appeal, media neutral citation (Australia)
NSWLR	New South Wales Law Reports (Australia)
NSWR	New South Wales Reports (Australia)
NSWSC	New South Wales Supreme Court, media neutral citation (Australia)
NT	Northern Territory (Australia)
NW 2d	North Western Reporter, second series (USA)
NY	New York (USA)
NY	New York Reports (USA)
NY 2d	New York Reports, second series (USA)
NYS 2d	New York Supplement, second series (USA)
NZCA	New Zealand Court of Appeals, media neutral citation
NZLR	New Zealand Law Reports

OAC	Ontario Appeal Cases (Canada)
Oh	Ohio (USA)
OR (3d)	Ontario Reports, third series (Canada)
P	Probate Division Reports (England)
P 3d	Pacific Reporter, third series (USA)
Pa	Pennsylvania (USA)
PD	Probate, Divorce, and Admiralty Division Reports (England)
QB	Queen's Bench Reports (England)
QBD	Queen's Bench Division Reports (England)
Qd R	Queensland Reports (Australia)
Qld	Queensland (Australia)
R	Rettie's Session Cases (Scotland)
Russ	Russell's Chancery Reports (England)
S Ct	Supreme Court Reporter (USA)
SA	South Australia
SALR	South Australian Law Reports
SASC	South Australian Supreme Court, media neutral citation
Sask R	Saskatchewan Reports (Canada)
SASR	South Australian State Reports
SC	Session Cases (Scotland)
SC	Superior Court (USA)
SC	Supreme Court (USA)
Scott	Scott's Common Pleas Reports (England)
SCR	Supreme Court Reports (Canada)
SD	South Dakota (USA)
SD	United States District Court, Southern District
SE 2d	South Eastern Reporter, second series (USA)
SJ	Solicitors' Journal (England)
SLR	Singapore Law Reports
SLT	Scots Law Times (Scotland)
So 2d	Southern Reporter, second series (USA)
SR (NSW)	State Reports (New South Wales) (Australia)
Stark	Starkie's Nisi Prius Reports (England)
SW 2d	South Western Reporter, second series (USA)
Swans	Swanston's Chancery Reports (England)
Tas	Tasmania (Australia)
Tas R	Tasmanian Reports (Australia)
Tas SR	Tasmanian State Reports (Australia)
TLR	Times Law Reports (England)
Tn	Tennessee (USA)
TPA	Trade Practices Act 1974 (Cth)
Tx	Texas (USA)
UCQB	Upper Canada Queen's Bench Reports, new series
UK	United Kingdom
US	United States Reports

Va	Virginia (USA)
Vic	Victoria (Australia)
VLR	Victorian Law Reports (Australia)
VR	Victorian Reports (Australia)
VSC	Victorian Supreme Court, media neutral citation (Australia)
VSCA	Victorian Court of Appeal, media neutral citation (Australia)
Wa	Washington (USA)
WA	Western Australia
WAR	Western Australian Reports
WASC	Western Australian Supreme Court, media neutral citation
WASCA	Western Australian Court of Appeal, media neutral citation
Wash 2d	Washington Reports, second series (USA)
Wash App	Washington Appellate Reports (USA)
WD	United States District Court, Western District
Wi	Wisconsin (USA)
WL	Westlaw citation
WLR	Weekly Law Reports (England)
WN	Weekly Notes (England)
WWR	Western Weekly Reports (Canada)
Wy	Wyoming (USA)

PART I

THE INTERNET REVOLUTION

1

GENERAL INTRODUCTION

A. The Internet

The Internet is, at its core, a medium of instantaneous, long-distance communi-   **1.01**
cation. It makes communicating with a thousand, or a million, people no more
difficult than communicating with a single person. For the first time, it brings
mass communication to the masses: anyone with a computer and an Internet
connection can utilize its potential. It facilitates communication in any combination of writing, sounds, and pictures. It knows no geographical boundaries: any
Internet user can communicate globally, with a potentially limitless audience.

While other media of communication may have some of these qualities, their
confluence in the Internet is unique. The Internet represents a communications
revolution.

As the Internet makes instantaneous global communication available to so
many people, it has the potential to create new communities united by common
interest, rather than geography. It is a medium which celebrates and encourages
free speech and the exchange of ideas.

B. Defamation via the Internet

The law of defamation is the imperfect mechanism by which the law attempts to   **1.02**
reconcile the competing interests of freedom of expression and the protection of
individual reputation. The cause of action is potentially enlivened where

3

defamatory matter is published of and concerning a claimant. Published matter will be defamatory if it conveys an imputation that tends to lower the claimant in the estimation of right-thinking members of society generally, or cause others to shun or avoid the claimant, or expose the claimant to hatred, contempt, or ridicule. A publication may be in any form capable of signifying meaning, including the written and spoken word, symbols, pictures, visual images, and gestures.

1.03   Before the invention of the printing press, publications overwhelmingly occurred in a single place and at a single point in time, and had limited audiences. Successive technological advances have increased the potential for permanent and multi-jurisdictional publications.

1.04   The Internet increases dramatically the potential for multi-jurisdictional defamation. Defamatory matter published via the Internet may have a global audience of indeterminate size, and a devastating impact on the reputation of its target. The legal implications of defamatory matter published via the Internet are complicated by the global nature of the medium. What constitutes actionable defamation in one jurisdiction may be entirely lawful in another.

C. Sources of Law

1.05   This book contains a systematic analysis of how the rules of civil defamation law apply, or are likely to apply, to material published via the Internet.

Authorities in relation to the application of principles of defamation law to matter published via the Internet are emerging in a gradual and piecemeal fashion. In a great many instances, it is still necessary to explain or predict the law by reference to authorities decided in non-Internet contexts, or to have regard to the law of foreign jurisdictions, particularly the United States.

This book is written for a primary audience of lawyers and students in the United Kingdom, and for a secondary audience in Australia.

The rules of civil defamation law in the United Kingdom and Australia each have a common law heritage. In some areas, however, those rules are now developing in different ways.

United Kingdom

England

1.06   The cause of action for defamation arises as a matter of common law in England (which, for the sake of simplicity, in this book includes Wales). The common law has, however, been modified in a number of important respects by the Defamation Acts of 1952 and 1996. Specific procedural rules and directions have been prescribed for defamation actions.[1]

Scotland

Although in most respects similar to English defamation law, the principles of **1.07** defamation law differ somewhat in Scotland. An effort has been made throughout the text to identify the major differences as they arise.

The indulgence of Scottish readers is sought in relation to two matters. First, English terminology has generally been preferred in this book. For example, 'claimant' or 'plaintiff' are used instead of 'pursuer', 'defendant' instead of 'defender', 'tort' instead of 'delict', 'publication' instead of 'communication', 'justification' or 'truth' instead of '*veritas*', and 'injunction' instead of 'interdict'. Secondly, except where Scottish law differs from English law, relevant principles have been illustrated primarily by the citation of English or Australian cases.

Northern Ireland

In Northern Ireland, the common law is subject to the Defamation Act (North-ern Ireland) 1955 and the Defamation Act 1996. As with Scots law, an attempt has been made to identify relevant differences for Northern Irish readers as they arise.

European influences

The direction of civil defamation law in the United Kingdom is now heavily **1.09** influenced by the jurisprudence of the European Court of Human Rights, by reason of the domestic implementation of the European Convention on Human Rights and Fundamental Freedoms (ECHR) in the Human Rights Act 1998.

In addition, jurisdictional issues, which arise frequently in the context of Inter-net-defamation disputes, are subject not just to common law principles, but also to Council Regulation 44/2001 of 22 December 2000 ('the Brussels Regula-tion'),[2] and the Brussels and Lugano Conventions ('the Conventions'), on juris-diction and the enforcement of judgments in civil and commercial matters. Analysis of the application of the Brussels Regulation and the Conventions to civil defamation cases involving material published via the Internet is an important objective of this book.

---

[1] See Civil Procedure Rules, Pt 53, Practice Direction 53, and the Pre-action Protocol for Defamation.
[2] [2001] OJ L12/1.

1.10 The law of the European Union is also relevant in a further way to cases in the United Kingdom involving material published via the Internet. The Directive of the European Parliament and Council on Electronic Commerce[3] prescribes rules as to the liability of Internet intermediaries who participate in the publication of defamatory material which they did not create. The Directive has been transposed into the domestic law of the United Kingdom by the Electronic Commerce (EC Directive) Regulations 2002. Those regulations will require close analysis.[4]

Australia

Common law and statute

1.11 Australia presently suffers from not having uniform civil defamation laws. Jurisdictional differences abound between the States and Territories. The cause of action for defamation arises as a matter of common law in South Australia, Victoria, Western Australia, and the Australian Capital Territory.[5] It arises out of legislation in New South Wales, Queensland, Tasmania, and the Northern Territory.[6] It is codified in Queensland and Tasmania.

Federal influences

1.12 Defamation law in Australia has also had to adapt to conform to the freedom to discuss government and political matters which is implied in Australia's federal Constitution. Australia's federal structure also affects the content of the jurisdiction and choice of law rules which apply where defamatory publications span more than one State or Territory. Matters which are unique to the Australian legal environment will be dealt with, where appropriate, throughout the text.

Law reform

1.13 At the time this edition went to print, there was the tantalizing prospect that the Australian States might soon pass uniform defamation laws, or that the Commonwealth might enact a Defamation Act which would apply throughout Australia to most publications, including all Internet publications. If either of those proposals come to pass, Australian defamation law will be, in many respects, dramatically simplified.

---

[3] Directive 2000/31/EC of the European Parliament and of the Council of 8 June 2000 on certain legal aspects of information society services, in particular electronic commerce, in the internal market [2000] OJ L178/1 ('Directive on Electronic Commerce').

[4] See chapter 17.

[5] The common law rules have been substantially modified in the ACT by Chapter 9 of the Civil Law (Wrongs) Act 2002 (ACT).

[6] The relevant legislation are the Defamation Act 1974 (NSW), the Defamation Act 1889 (Qld), the Defamation Act 1957 (Tas), and the Defamation Act 1938 (NT).

A shared common law heritage

The similarities between the rules of civil defamation law in the United King-   **1.14**
dom and Australia greatly exceed the differences. The decided cases of each
country are frequently cited in the courts of the other. Australian legislation
borrows from that in the United Kingdom, and vice versa. When existing rules
are applied in a new context, such as that of the Internet, it is helpful to draw on
a broad and international base of legal analysis.

It is hoped that, by analysing the law as it applies in both the United Kingdom
and Australia, this book will satisfy practitioners and students in both countries,
and encourage the law to develop in similar ways in each place.

2

THE INTERNET

A. A Brief History of the Internet

Computer networks and the origins of the Internet

It seems almost quaint now to reflect on a world before computer networks **2.01** began to proliferate; when personal computers, let alone their predecessors, stood alone, unable to interconnect, to transfer information among them, and to share software. Yet computer networking only began in earnest in the late 1960s, beginning an inexorable march towards ubiquity that continues today.

Local area networks

Networking technology began with the development of local area networks **2.02** (LANs) of computers, interconnected usually by coaxial cable, in individual government and university departments, and businesses. LAN hardware enables each individual computer in the network to communicate and to share software, by permitting the transfer of data from computer to computer. LANs are ultimately limited by geography: the cables connecting each computer in the network can be only so long. The interconnectability of different LANs is limited by the existence of a vast array of different LAN technologies, not all of which are compatible. Some LAN technologies only work with particular types of computer. Different LAN technologies might be chosen by different users because of their speed, or cost.

Wide area networks

2.03   By the late 1960s, the technology for connecting geographically distant computers had developed, leading to the emergence of the first wide area networks (WANs). Usually, each computer in a WAN is connected to the network by a modem which sends signals along a long-distance transmission line, such as a telephone line or cable. At the centre of a WAN is a dedicated computer which receives and sends signals from individual computer to individual computer in the network. The central computer receives and distributes each signal.

ARPANET

2.04   From the early 1960s, the United States' Department of Defense funded research into the interconnection of computers through the Advanced Research Projects Agency (ARPA). ARPA developed its own WAN, known as ARPANET, and explored connecting computers using satellite and radio transmission technology. The internetwork, or internet, created by the connection of different LANs and WANs to ARPANET became known as the Internet project.[1]

One of the aims of the Internet project was to create a computer network which would enable communication to continue, even if part of the network was unavailable, lost, or destroyed. This was seen as being particularly important by the United States' Department of Defense, as a means of maintaining essential communications in times of war. ARPANET was therefore designed so that there were always at least two alternative routes between each of the constituent networks.

The Internet began as, and remains in essence, a WAN. The constituent parts of the WAN are other WANs, LANs, and individual computers.

---

[1] There are several well-written histories of the Internet. Four of the best are Douglas Comer, *The Internet Book* (2nd edn, 1997); Steven Miller, *Civilizing Cyberspace* (1996); Rob Kitchin, *Cyberspace* (1998); James Gillies and Robert Cailliau, *How the Web was Born* (2000). The online resource Hobbes' Internet Timeline (<http://www.zakon.org/robert/internet/timeline/>) is an authoritative repository of information about the history of the Internet.

The growth of the Internet

ARPANET grew at a steady pace: in December 1969, four networks were connected; this number rose to 111 networks by March 1977.[2] Data was first sent from one computer to another on 29 October 1969.

2.05

From as early as 1971, users of ARPANET were able to exchange electronic mail messages.[3] By 1973, the first non-American computer networks connected to ARPANET.[4]

TCP/IP

The technology used in different LANs and WANs is not always compatible, so ARPA researchers in the early 1970s created software designed to enable communication between incompatible systems. Known as the TCP/IP Internet Protocol Suite (TCP/IP), the software had two primary elements: internet protocol (IP) software, which enabled basic communication between incompatible systems, and transmission or transfer control protocol (TCP) software, which regulated the order in which packets of information were sent and reassembled via the Internet.

2.06

By about the mid-1980s, TCP/IP had become the standard software throughout the computer industry for interconnecting incompatible networks.

Evolution of the modern Internet

From the late 1970s, the American National Science Foundation (NSF) funded the establishment of the Computer Science Network (CSNET), which was designed to reach and connect all computer scientists in the United States. In the early to mid-1980s, the NSF encouraged computer science departments connected to CSNET to use TCP/IP software to connect to the Internet.[5]

2.07

By about 1985, it had become clear that the ARPANET WAN did not have the capacity to continue to expand for much longer. From 1986, the NSF created a new and more substantial WAN known as NSFNET, which in 1988 replaced ARPANET as the backbone WAN of the Internet.[6] ARPANET finally ceased

2.08

---

[2] Kitchin (n 1 above) 30.

[3] ibid; Hobbes' Internet Timeline (n 1 above). Gillies and Cailliau (n 1 above) 32 claim that the first e-mail message was sent in 1972.

[4] Kitchin (n 1 above) 32, Hobbes' Internet Timeline (n 1 above), and Gillies and Cailliau (n 1 above) 51–3 agree that the first non-American networks to connect to ARPANET were in London and Norway, using a combination of satellite and line connections. Gillies and Cailliau (ibid) 36 note that computers in Hawaii, Alaska, Japan, Australia, and California began communicating using radio and satellite technology in the same year.

[5] Comer (n 1 above) 64; Kitchin (n 1 above) 35; Gillies and Cailliau (n 1 above) 78–9.

[6] Comer (n 1 above) 68; Miller (n 1 above) 46.

operating in 1990.[7] NSFNET was jointly built and maintained by the NSF and the computer manufacturer, International Business Machines Corporation (IBM), a long-distance telephone company, MCI, Inc (MCI), and an organization based in Michigan named Merit Network, Inc (Merit).[8]

2.09 In 1990, IBM, MCI, and Merit formed a company called Advanced Networks and Services, Inc (ANS), which upgraded and managed NSFNET until it was finally retired in April 1995. NSFNET and the plans for its future development into an American National Information Infrastructure (NII) are what was originally meant by references to the 'information superhighway'.[9]

2.10 Since 1995, most Internet backbone traffic has been routed through interconnected networks operated primarily by large telecommunications companies.

In 1995, MCI developed a high-performance WAN known as vBNS.[10] vBNS is a high-speed backbone WAN available mainly to American scientific and research institutions meeting criteria specified by the NSF. Another high-speed backbone WAN known as the Abilene Internet2 network was developed by American universities and research laboratories from 1998.[11]

2.11 From the mid-1970s, groups in several European countries had used TCP/IP to connect some of their own LANs and WANs.[12] In 1991, a European group developed EBONE. EBONE became the main backbone WAN for European connections to the Internet.[13] Similar backbone WANs emerged elsewhere.

2.12 In Australia, the largest backbone WAN providing access to the Internet is a descendent of AARNET, which was originally funded in 1988 by the Australian Vice-Chancellors' Committee (AVCC) and the Commonwealth Scientific and Industrial Research Organization (CSIRO).[14] Most of the infrastructure constituting AARNET was sold to Telstra Corporation Ltd in 1995.

---

[7] Kitchin (n 1 above) 36; Gillies and Cailliau (n 1 above) 45; Hobbes' Internet Timeline (n 1 above).

[8] Comer (n 1 above) 68.

[9] Comer (ibid) 306; Gillies and Cailliau (n 1 above) 265. 'Information superhighway' is also used colloquially to refer to the Internet itself. The expression was coined by the then American Vice President Al Gore.

[10] vBNS means 'very high-performance Backbone Network System': <http://www.vbns.net>.

[11] <http://www.internet2.edu>.

[12] The first such network was CYCLADES, a French network, which began in November 1973. Networks were later established in other European countries. The most successful was the French network Minitel, which began in 1981, and grew to become the largest electronic mail system the world had then seen: see Kitchin (n 1 above) 32. On the development of computer networking in Europe generally, see Gillies and Cailliau (n 1 above) 47–90.

[13] Comer (n 1 above) 76–7.

[14] Berny Goodheart and Frank Crawford, *Oz Internet* (1995) 36–44.

Phenomenal growth

The Internet has experienced phenomenal growth. The estimated number of **2.13**
Internet users has grown from about 26 million in December 1995 to about
813 million in September 2004.[15] The capacity of the Internet is currently
4,294,967,296 computers. High growth rates seem likely to continue for some
time yet.

The United Kingdom and Australia each rank near the top of the tables of
countries with the highest total number of Internet connections (see Table 1),
and the highest proportion of the population connected to the Internet (see
Table 2 below). In absolute terms, the United States has easily the highest total
number of Internet connections.

Table 1. Countries with the highest number of Internet users (as at February 2005)

1	United States	197.9 million
2	China	94 million
3	Japan	66.68 million
4	Germany	46.46 million
5	United Kingdom	35.31 million
6	South Korea	31.6 million
7	Italy	28.61 million
8	France	25.05 million
9	Canada	20.45 million
10	Brazil	18.66 million
11	India	18.48 million
12	Spain	14.10 million
13	Australia	13.41 million
14	Mexico	12.25 million
15	Taiwan	11.6 million

Source: <http://www.internetworldstats.com>

B. How the Internet Works

Interconnected computers

A network of networks

Although conceptually the Internet seems like an enormous single computer **2.14**

---

[15] Reliable statistics on Internet usage can be found at <www.nua.ie/surveys> and <http://www.internetworldstats.com>.

Table 2. Countries with the highest proportion of the population connected to the Internet (as at February 2005)

1	Sweden	74.3%
2	Hong Kong	69.9%
3	United States	66.8%
4	Netherlands	66.2%
5	Iceland	66.1%
6	Australia	65.4%
7	Canada	63.8%
8	South Korea	63.3%
9	Denmark	62.4%
10	Switzerland	61.6%
11	Singapore	60.2%
12	United Kingdom	59.0%
13	Liechtenstein	57.3%
14	Germany	56.2%
15	Bermuda	54.0%

Source: <http://www.internetworldstats.com>

network, it is in reality a network of computer networks. The connecting networks include LANs, WANs, and WAN backbones.[16]

Internet service providers

2.15 Government departments, universities, corporations, groups, and individuals connect to the Internet in a number of ways. Most connect by subscribing to an Internet service provider (ISP).

The main American ISPs began as providers of self-contained computer network services which later expanded to provide subscribers with access to the Internet. They are sometimes known in American parlance as bulletin board systems or services (BBSs), reflecting their origins primarily as places where messages could be exchanged and commented upon by subscribers.

Some large ISPs operate high-speed Internet backbones. Smaller ISPs typically provide Internet access by interconnecting to a high-speed Internet backbone owned and operated by another ISP. Subscribers might be individuals with a personal computer, which becomes part of the ISP's WAN through the use of a modem and telephone line or cable. Other subscribers might be the operators of LANs or WANs, such as businesses, which connect to the ISP's WAN through

---

[16] There are many authoritative texts on how the Internet works. Some accessible examples include Comer (n 1 above); Alan Freedman, Alfred Glossbrenner, and Emily Glossbrenner, *The Internet Glossary and Quick Reference Guide* (1998) and Preston Gralla, *How the Internet Works* (4th edn, 1998).

the use of a dedicated cable. Wireless access to the Internet is rapidly gaining in popularity, using a variety of technologies.

The transfer of information

Digital signals

Material is communicated via the Internet by the transfer of digital signals from one computer to another. The signal might carry a message, as in the case of electronic mail or bulletin board postings; detailed textual, audio, visual, or audiovisual information, as in the case of information posted on the world wide web; or computer programs or files, as in the case of file transfer protocol (FTP). **2.16**

Signals are transferred around single LANs and WANs in packets, or units of data. Each packet is allocated a 'header', which identifies the sending computer, and the intended recipient computer, using numbers allocated by the network. Packet transfer is almost instantaneous in most networks. Networks use a mechanism known as packet switching to ensure that all computers wanting to send packets across a network have fair access to the available resources. In essence, packet switching technology forces each computer on the network wishing to send a packet to take turns. When a recipient computer receives network packets, it reassembles them. In the simple case of an electronic mail message, the recipient computer constructs the message by reassembling the network packets sent by the sending computer.

IP datagrams

Sending signals around the Internet involves the transfer of packets between interconnected networks which may themselves be incompatible. Transfer is achieved through the use of dedicated computers or devices, and TCP/IP software. Every computer with Internet capability must therefore have TCP/IP software loaded onto it. Such software is typically bundled into the programs for Internet browsers and electronic mail. **2.17**

A sending computer with a signal destined for another computer located somewhere on the Internet will divide the signal into packets capable of being transferred over the Internet, known as datagrams or IP datagrams. Each IP datagram contains a unit of data which might be a constituent part of any type of digital signal, from a text message, to computer program files or audio, visual, or film data.

Routers

Networks interconnect with other networks via special-purpose devices called routers. The primary purpose of the router is to send packets of data from one network to another, and to receive packets of data destined for a computer **2.18** within the home network of the router. A router can potentially connect to any number of different LANs, WANs, or WAN backbones.

The sending computer transfers the IP datagrams to the router of the network to which the sending computer is a part. In the case of an individual who connects to the Internet via a modem and telephone line or cable, the datagrams will typically be sent to a router maintained by the sender's ISP.

Internet addresses

Assignment

2.19   Each computer attached to the Internet has a unique numeric representation, known as an IP address. Whenever a new network connects to the Internet, it is assigned a unique set of IP addresses by the relevant Internet authority.[17] Those addresses are then distributed by the operator of the network to individual computers. Individual computers might be allocated a 'static', or permanent, IP address by the network operator, or a 'dynamic', or different IP address each time the computer connects to the network. IP addresses are a number in a form such as 123.45.67.89.

Computer users are also allocated names. For example, the name 'jack@networka.co.uk' might represent the computer operated by 'Jack' on the Network A computer network, which is connected to the Internet. In this example, Network A has been allocated the designation 'networka' by the organization which administers the '.co.uk' domain. The Network A network operator would have assigned Jack the designation 'jack'.

Domain name servers

2.20   The sending computer processes the destination address of the IP datagrams. To establish the precise address, the computer sends a signal to a computer called a domain name server, which is a computer containing details of other networks which are connected to the Internet. The domain name server will typically be operated by an ISP or the operator of a backbone WAN. If the domain name server recognizes the location of the recipient's network, it sends details of the relevant address back to the sending computer. If the domain name server does not recognize the location of the recipient's network, it will send a signal to another domain name server, and so on, until the location and address are

---

[17] 'Top level generic' domain names, ie those with suffixes such as '.com', '.net', and '.org', are administered by ICANN, the Internet Corporation for Assigned Names and Numbers: <http://www.icann.org>. The '.uk' domain is administered by Nominet UK: <http://www.nominet.org.uk>. The Australian equivalent is .au Domain Administration Ltd (auDA), which regulates domain names with the '.au' suffix: <http://www.auda.org.au>.

identified. The process of identifying destination addresses is entirely auto-mated, and usually almost instantaneous.

Delivery of messages

The sending computer sends IP datagrams to the router of the network   **2.21**
to which the sending computer is attached. That router examines the address
to which the datagrams are to be sent, and forwards them on to the next
network along an available path to that address. If two or more paths lead
to the address, the IP datagrams are sent via the shortest path. The IP
datagrams are then transferred from network to network, until they reach their
destination.

Because the sending computer's signals have been divided into IP datagrams,
they have to be reassembled, in the correct order, before they can be deciphered
correctly by the recipient computer. The orderly and reliable delivery of IP
datagrams is achieved by the operation of TCP software. When an IP datagram
is sent from any router along the path from one computer to another,
the router's internal clock mechanism starts. When the IP datagram arrives
at the next router on the path to the recipient computer, that router sends
an acknowledgement signal back to the previous router. If that acknowledgement has not been received within the time expected by the previous router,
a copy of the IP datagram is sent again. The TCP software varies the time
the router expects it to take for an acknowledgement to be received based on
the distance the IP datagram must travel, the capacity of the link between the
routers and the amount of other IP datagram traffic moving to and from
the router. If any router on the path receives a duplicate IP datagram, it discards
the second and subsequent copies. If an IP datagram cannot be delivered to
a router on the path to the recipient computer for any reason, the TCP software
will cause a copy of the IP datagram to be sent on an alternative route to the
recipient computer.

Figure A shows a simplified example of how signals might travel from one
computer to another via the Internet.

C. Some Consequences

Intermediaries

Every communication, from the simplest e-mail message to the most compli-   **2.22**
cated interactive web page, passes as a series of IP datagrams through a number
of intermediate networks en route from sender to recipient.

The operators of these intermediate networks will typically be ISPs, the operators of business networks, or the operators of WAN backbones. For any given Internet communication, there will be two categories of intermediary. First,

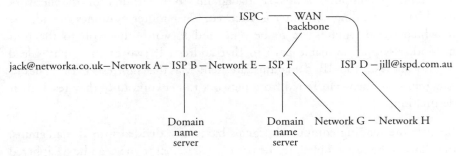

Figure A. A simplified journey through the Internet

This diagram shows a simplified example of how a signal might be transferred over the Internet from Jack (jack@networka.co.uk) to Jill (jill@ispd.com.au):

1. Jack's computer is part of Network A, which might be, for example, a LAN operated by Jack's employer. Network A subscribes to ISP B, which provides the computers in Network A with Internet access. Jill subscribes to ISP D, which provides her with Internet access. ISP C, ISP D, and ISP F have direct, high-capacity links to the WAN backbone. They are likely to be large ISPs, The WAN backbone would also be connected to many other ISPs and networks not shown on the diagram.

2. Jack's computer sends a signal to the nearest domain name server, which is operated by ISP B, asking it to identify the precise address of Jill's computer. Jack's computer divides Jack's message into IP datagrams and attaches headers identifying, among other things, this address. It then sends the IP datagrams to the router for Network A. If the domain name server for ISP B had not known the address of Jill's computer, it might have sent a signal to the domain name server operated by ISP F, via network E and ISP F, to see whether it knew the address, and so on.

3. There are three possible routes from Jack's computer to Jill's computer. The routes are as follows:

   Route 1: Network A → ISP B → ISP C → WAN backbone → ISP D (five intermediaries).
   Route 2: Network A → ISP B → Network E → ISP F → WAN backbone → ISP D (six intermediaries).
   Route 3: Network A → ISP B → Network E → ISP F → Network G → Network H → ISP D (seven intermediaries).

4. The router for network A transfers the IP datagrams constituting Jack's message via the shortest route. Each router along the route sends an acknowledgement that the IP datagram has been received. If an acknowledgement is not received within the time expected, a further copy of the IP datagram will be sent via the same or an alternative route. The signals could get through to Jill's computer via a longer route even if, for example, ISP C and the WAN backbone were congested or had broken down.

5. Once each of the IP datagrams has been received by Jill's computer, they are reassembled in the correct order by TCP software, and deciphered in a form that Jill can read.

there will be those intermediaries through whose computer systems a communication must pass en route from one computer to another.[18] Secondly, there will be other intermediaries through whose computer systems a communication may pass, depending on the route taken by a particular communication.[19] The roles played by different kinds of intermediaries are expanded upon in chapter 14.

The way in which signals travel around the Internet has a number of consequences.

Communications travel via indeterminate routes

First, users of the Internet will almost never know the precise route or routes the IP datagrams have travelled on their journey to a computer screen.[20] Internet communications travel to and from indeterminate points, via indeterminate routes. There will nearly always be more than one possible route from one computer to another, involving different intermediaries. Different IP datagrams constituting a single message might travel different routes to the same destination.

2.23

Interception

Secondly, because signals transferred via the Internet pass through a variety of different computer networks en route from sender to recipient, interception will often be possible and undetectable. Interception might even occur in a country other than that from which the signal emanated, or for which it was intended. A range of steps can be taken to increase the security of Internet communications.

2.24

Anonymity

Thirdly, users of the Internet can readily conceal or distort almost any aspect of their identity. They can hide, if they wish, behind an impenetrable cloak of anonymity. Alternatively, by obtaining access to someone else's Internet connection, an Internet user can assume the identity of that other person. An Internet user who is bent on anonymously publishing a defamatory message can do so with little difficulty, at virtually no risk of being identified and called to account.[21]

2.25

---

[18] In Figure A eg Jill gains access to the Internet via ISP D, which is likely to be a commercial ISP to which she subscribes. Every communication originating from Jill's computer must pass through ISP D's computer system, regardless of its destination. Jack's computer is part of Network A which might be eg a LAN operated by Jack's employer. Network A is connected to the Internet via ISP B. Every communication originating from Jack's computer must therefore pass through the computer systems operated by Network A and ISP B.

[19] In Figure A, Jack's message might pass, depending on the actual route taken, through computer systems operated by ISP C, Network E, ISP F, Network G, Network H, and the WAN backbone.

[20] William Mitchell, *City of Bits* (1995) 8: 'you can find things in [the Internet] without knowing where they are'.

[21] cf paras 5.33–5.41.

D. How the Internet is Used

2.26   Understanding the history of the Internet, and the way in which the technology operates, provides a basis for understanding the manner in which defamatory material can be published via the Internet. There are three main ways in which the Internet is used for the purposes of communication.

E-mail and analogous communications

2.27   Electronic mail, or 'e-mail', is the most used Internet facility. It enables text messages, and messages incorporating sound, pictures, or computer files, to be conveyed, almost instantaneously, from any computer which is connected to the Internet, to any other computer which is connected to the Internet, anywhere in the world.

Sending an e-mail message

2.28   The sender composes a message using an e-mail application program. The program prompts the user to fill in a number of fields, such as the recipient's address, the title for the message, and the message itself. After the sender has directed the computer to dispatch the message, it will be transferred to the recipient's computer via the Internet in the way described earlier. Usually, the message will be stored in a server in the recipient's network, or a server in the network of the recipient's ISP, so that the recipient can transfer a copy of the message to his or her computer when convenient. There are also a number of world wide web-based e-mail services which enable users to send and collect their e-mail messages by visiting a web page. Messages are retrieved from a server maintained by the operator of that page.

Receiving an e-mail message

2.29   Recipients of e-mail messages are notified by their e-mail application program that a message has arrived for them. Typically, e-mail application programs will provide some form of audible notification, such as a beep, and display the sender's name or address, and the title of the message. The recipient then 'opens' the e-mail message by directing the computer to display the message which corresponds with any given name, address, and title.

E-mail messages are in many ways analogous to letters: messages appear to reach the recipient's computer in much the same way as letters are delivered to a household mailbox. Indeed, the e-mail lexicon is largely the same as that of paper-based delivery systems. E-mail messages are retrieved from an 'in-box' or 'mailbox'; messages are 'sent' and 'received'; recipients' details are electronically stored in 'address books'; graphical icons in e-mail application programs depict stamped letters and mailboxes.

E-mail messages are not, however, physical objects capable of delivery in the same way as letters. Rather, an e-mail message is a series of packets of data transferred from computer to computer. Upon delivery, the pieces of data are reconstructed by computer software so that the recipient sees, on a screen, a message which resembles the message as it was depicted on the sender's computer screen.

The route taken by an e-mail message is usually indeterminate

On its route from the sender's computer to the recipient's computer, an e-mail **2.30** message passes through a succession of network routers, located potentially in a number of different places. It is possible that a single e-mail message sent down the street might have passed through networks in another country, or several other countries, on its almost instantaneous journey from sender to recipient.

Typically, Internet users receive their e-mails by logging in via a modem to the mail server maintained by a network operator or ISP. The user can be anywhere in the world; a simple e-mail message sent to a person who lives down the street might be opened by that person using a laptop computer in an airport lounge on the other side of the world. The sender of the e-mail message will have no way of knowing or controlling the place where the e-mail message will be retrieved and read.

Multiple copies of each e-mail message may have been created

Along its route, each e-mail message is likely to have been copied or stored, **2.31** without any direct human intervention, in at least the sender's computer, the recipient's computer, and the networks maintained by the intermediaries who provide both the sender and the recipient with their access to the Internet.[22] Copies of the constituent IP datagrams will also be stored, at least transiently, in any intermediate computer system through which the message has passed en route.[23] If all IP datagrams constituting a single message happen to have passed along only one route, the message may be capable of being intercepted in its entirety at any point on the route.

E-mail messages may have any number of recipients

An e-mail message can be sent to a single recipient, or any number of recipients, **2.32** with equal ease. The sender of an e-mail message can nominate any number of addressees. The e-mail application program automatically generates the

---

[22] In Figure A, copies of Jack's message to Jill are likely to have been stored in Jack's computer, Jill's computer, and computers maintained by Network A, ISP B, and ISP D.

[23] In Figure A, depending on the route or routes taken by the IP datagrams, copies of the constituent parts of Jack's message to Jill may have been stored in computers maintained by ISP C, the WAN backbone, Network E, ISP F, Network G, and Network H.

requisite number of copies of the message without further human intervention. Lists of addressees are known as mailing lists. Mailing lists may be created by individuals. Centralized mailing lists may be maintained by network operators, ISPs, or others.

Similarly, recipients can republish e-mail messages to further recipients with ease. E-mail application programs have a 'forward' function designed expressly for this purpose. An e-mail message intended for a single recipient can thus quickly find a much wider audience, all around the world.[24]

Instant messaging

2.33   Senders of e-mails do not necessarily know when their messages will be read. A variant of traditional e-mail, known as 'instant messaging', overcomes this limitation. Instant messaging systems enable subscribers to identify whether particular persons are currently logged on to the Internet. If so, messages can be sent instantly to those persons, with the knowledge that the messages will probably come to their attention more quickly than traditional e-mail.

Instant messaging services can also be used to communicate via voice, in much the same way as a telephone conversation, and by video, in much the same way as a video-conference. Instead of sending instant messages by text, users connect a 'webcam' and a microphone to their computers. Voice and video messages are broken down into IP datagrams, transferred, and reassembled by the recipient's computer.

Bulletin board postings and analogous group communications

2.34   Bulletin boards are a second way in which the Internet is used for the purposes of communication. Internet bulletin boards are analogous to their physical counterparts. They enable computer users to participate in exchanges with others, by viewing messages posted for others to read, and by contributing messages of their own. Bulletin boards are typically devoted to specific topics of common interest to their subscribers, or to a geographic community.[25]

USENET

2.35   Bulletin boards operate on the Internet in a number of ways. The first widely used bulletin board service on the Internet was the USENET, or netnews service, which continues to enable computer users to contribute to discussions on

---

[24] Some e-mail application programs provide the sender with the ability to 'encode' a message so that it cannot be further copied. Such functions are of limited practical use, however, as they do not prevent recipients from manually retyping such messages before forwarding them on to a wider audience, or from printing the messages and republishing them in paper form.

[25] See generally Comer (n 1 above) 159–71.

tens of thousands of 'newsgroup' topics. Other bulletin board services are operated by individual computer networks via, for example, world wide web sites.

Boards may be moderated or unmoderated

Some bulletin boards are moderated. In a moderated bulletin board, messages **2.36** contributed by computer users may be reviewed by the operator of the bulletin board before being made accessible to other users. Alternatively, the operator of the bulletin board may reserve the right to remove messages on any number of grounds. Control over what messages are made accessible to the users of the bulletin board might be exercised manually by a nominated person. Alternatively, software may be used to screen messages automatically so as, for example, to exclude messages which contain words which the operator has deemed irrelevant or unacceptable. By contrast, in unmoderated bulletin boards, no control is exercised over which messages become accessible to computer users.

Posting a bulletin board message

Computer users wishing to contribute messages to a bulletin board create the **2.37** message in much the same way as they would create an e-mail message. Instead of addressing the message to a specific recipient, the message is addressed to the bulletin board server or operator. Some bulletin boards are freely accessible to all Internet users. Other bulletin boards are accessible only to registered or paying subscribers.

Reading bulletin board postings

Users of a bulletin board typically see the title of each message which has been **2.38** placed on the bulletin board on their computer screen, in much the same way as they would see the title of an e-mail message sent specifically to them. If users wish to see the content of any particular message, they transfer the message from the bulletin board server to their own computer. Transfer can occur manually, by the user reviewing the titles of available messages, or automatically, using software which the user has configured to transfer all messages of a nominated type.

Multiple copies of each posting are created

Copies of each message posted on a bulletin board are therefore stored on the **2.39** bulletin board server or servers, with additional copies created for each user who requests a specific message. Depending on the subject matter and size of the bulletin board, copies of messages may have been transferred to servers or individual computers in a large number of countries. The operators of each of these servers are intermediaries involved in the communication of the messages.

People who lodge messages on a bulletin board may have no way of knowing or effectively controlling who might access those messages, or where they are located.

Because of the large number of messages which are posted on bulletin boards, it is customary for bulletin board operators to remove messages from the bulletin board periodically, by deleting them, or otherwise making them inaccessible to users. Back-up copies of deleted messages may, or may not, have been retained by the bulletin board operator.

Chat rooms

2.40   The popularity of bulletin boards has spawned a series of analogous forms of communication, including chat rooms and Internet Relay Chat (IRC). A form of instant messaging, they allow computer users to exchange messages via a computer in a way which is analogous to a conversation. As each message is typed onto the sender's screen, or almost immediately after, the message appears on the screen of a recipient, or the screens of each member of a group of recipients. Chat rooms have rapidly become a very popular form of Internet communication.

The world wide web and analogous information services

Indexing the Internet

2.41   The Internet enables computer users to retrieve information stored on a vast number of interconnected computers. Finding information on remote computers was largely the domain of the computer literate until 1992, when the world wide web ('www', or 'the web') was created. Before the creation of the web, finding the address of information stored on computers connected to the Internet was difficult.[26] Unless users knew the address of the computer on which the information they sought was stored, they were reliant on 'browsing' systems such as 'gophers'. Gophers are, essentially, interconnected series of indexes of the contents of various Internet addresses. Gophers have many limitations and have become for all practical purposes obsolete as a result of the popularity of the web.[27]

Hyperlinks

2.42   The web is a service which interconnects information stored in a particular way on many Internet servers. To the user, a web site is a series of 'pages' of information maintained by the operator of a participating computer or computer network, and contributed by a vast number of content providers, including

---

[26] Miller (n 1 above) 50.
[27] Gophers became widely available in 1991: Kitchin (n 1 above) 38. For descriptions of gophers and their operation, see Comer (n 1 above) 192–5; Gralla (n 16 above) 119–21; Freedman, Glossbrenner, and Glossbrenner (n 16 above) 177.

individuals, groups, corporations, and governments. Web pages are also known as hypertext documents, because they have been constructed using the computer language known as HyperText mark-up language (HTML).[28] Hypertext documents contain links (hyperlinks) to other hypertext documents stored on the same computer, or on other computers connected to the Internet, anywhere in the world. Hyperlinks typically appear on a user's screen in bold, coloured, or underlined text, or as a graphical icon. By clicking a mouse pointer on a hyperlink, the user is transferred automatically to the linked hypertext document. The system by which the transfer occurs is known as the HyperText Transport Protocol (HTTP).[29]

Linking and framing

Hyperlinks take two broad forms. Ordinary linking involves a simple hyperlink from one web page to another. The Internet user, upon following the hyperlink, is transported to the new page. Linking is said to be 'shallow' if the user is transported to another party's homepage. 'Deep linking', by contrast, occurs when the user is transported to some page on another party's web site other than that party's homepage.   **2.43**

The second form of linking is 'framing'. 'Framing' usually involves the inclusion of a hyperlink on a web page which, when followed, causes another party's web content to be displayed within a 'frame' on the original web page. Unlike ordinary linking, the Internet user does not leave the original web site upon following the hyperlink. Framing can also be automatic; that is, a web page might be constructed so that content from different web sites is simultaneously displayed, in separate frames, on the user's screen.

Web page content

Web sites may contain information which is purely textual. More commonly, however, web sites incorporate colour, pictures, and sound. The development of interfaces such as CGI[30] and Java[31] has enabled web sites to incorporate   **2.44**

---

[28] See eg Comer (n 1 above) 215–29; Gralla (n 16 above) 143–5; Freedman, Glossbrenner, and Glossbrenner (n 16 above) 195.

[29] See eg Gralla (n 16 above) 144–5; Freedman, Glossbrenner, and Glossbrenner (n 16 above) 195–6.

[30] CGI (Common Gateway Interface) technology enables Internet users, via hyperlinks, to submit information to, and activate computer programs on, remote computers. The activated computer program could have almost any purpose, from performing a calculation of the current value of a shareholding, to causing an audiovisual commercial to play on the user's computer screen. See generally Comer (n 1 above) 240–4; Gralla (n 16 above) 209–11; Freedman, Glossbrenner, and Glossbrenner (n 16 above) 59.

[31] Java is a tool which enables the creation of highly dynamic web pages, incorporating animation and sound. Java web pages, when activated, are known as 'applets': see Comer (n 1 above) 245–8; Gralla (n 16 above) 197–203; Freedman, Glossbrenner, and Glossbrenner (n 16 above) 3–4, 219–21.

highly dynamic and interactive information, such as forms, video images, and music.

Web sites are maintained by countless government departments, universities, corporations, groups, and individuals, all around the world. The operator of each web site determines what information will be included in each web page and in so doing contributes to the diversity of information available to Internet users. Web pages are generally accessible from any computer connected to the Internet, anywhere in the world. Web page owners will generally not know who has accessed the information on their web page, or where they are located,[32] although it will often be possible to build up a profile of Internet users who have accessed a particular web site or page.[33]

Some web sites operate on a subscription basis. Subscription web sites are accessible only by persons authorized by the site operator. Typically subscribers are allocated a username and password by the site operator which enables them to log onto the site. Subscription sites may be free, requiring nothing more than registration on the part of the subscriber, or paid, requiring a one-off or periodic payment by the subscriber to the site operator. Operators of subscription web sites will be able to identify much more precisely the people who have accessed information on the site.

Web pages may incorporate highly sophisticated audiovisual information. It is possible, for example, to view news stories, television programmes, music clips, and movies via the Internet. Many radio stations 'broadcast' simultaneously over the Internet, enabling Internet users to hear radio programmes instantaneously from stations around the world.

Audiovisual information may be available 'on demand'; that is, at any time chosen by Internet users, or only at a time or times chosen by the provider of the information, in much the same way as 'live' television or radio broadcasts. The information may be available on a 'streamed' basis, which involves the constituent IP datagrams being progressively transferred and played in a 'stream' from the sending computer to the recipient's computer, or by downloading the information as a file which can be stored in the recipient's computer and played any number of times at leisure.

Browsers

2.45 A user accesses the web using software known as a browser. Browsers enable users to visit any web page by following a series of hyperlinks, or by typing in the address of the page.

---

[32] See further paras 3.02–3.03.
[33] See para 5.11.

URLs

To computer users, web page addresses are names which usually begin with the **2.46** prefix 'http://www.', signifying a hypertext document on the world wide web. Web addresses are also known as uniform resource locators (URLs). Each page of a web site has its own URL. A URL contains, among other information, the domain name of the computer on which the web page is located.[34]

When a user asks the browser to display information on a particular web page, the user's computer sends a signal in the manner described earlier to the server on which the web page is located. The server on which the web page is located sends back to the user the information necessary to display the requested web page. The user's browser then displays the requested page. If the user clicks a mouse pointer on a hyperlink, the browser sends a signal to the server at the URL for the linked web page. That server then sends back to the user's computer the information necessary to display that web page, and so on.[35]

Caching

When an Internet user visits a web page, the information contained on that **2.47** page is transferred to the user's computer. Copies of the IP datagrams which constitute the web page might be stored, at least temporarily, in computers along the route from the web page server to the user's computer. As with e-mail messages, the IP datagrams can be copied by and stored in a number of computers en route, in a number of countries, without any human intervention.

'Caching' is a mechanism used to enable Internet content to be transmitted and displayed more efficiently. Internet material is 'cached' if it is temporarily stored in a bank or reserved section of computer memory for the purpose of enabling the material to be quickly retrieved at a later time. There are two common forms of caching.

First, ISPs may temporarily cache commonly visited web pages or bulletin boards hosted elsewhere on the Internet in their own computer systems so that they may be transmitted more efficiently to subscribers. The ISP's computer system will typically update cached material regularly and automatically. Cached material is able to be transmitted more efficiently to subscribers because it takes less time to transmit the constituent IP datagrams from the ISP's computer system than to request and obtain copies of the IP datagrams from the original host of the material. The frequency with which cached material is updated, and the nature and extent of the cached material, will vary from ISP to

---

[34] See eg Comer (n 1 above) 201–13; Gralla (n 16 above) 168–71; Freedman, Glossbrenner, and Glossbrenner (n 16 above) 351.
[35] See eg Gralla (n 16 above) 165–7.

ISP. Similar forms of caching may be carried out by the operators of other computer networks, such as businesses and government departments.

Secondly, when an Internet user visits a web page, a copy of that web page may be cached in the user's own computer. When the user wishes to return to a previously visited web page, the user's browser may, depending on settings chosen by the user, check to see if the page has been cached and, if so, retrieve the cached page. Users can request the browser to obtain an updated version of the web page from the original host by clicking on the browser's 'refresh' or 'reload' button. The extent to which material is cached and the period for which it is cached can be varied by adjusting settings in the browser.

Search engines

2.48   Finding the URL of useful web pages has been greatly facilitated by the development of commercial search engines. Search engines contain extensive indexes of the contents of other web pages. Users access a search engine from the web site maintained by the operator of the search engine. Users ask the search engine to display a summary of all web pages within its index which contain words specified by the user. The summary will contain a hyperlink to the indexed web pages.

Interactivity

2.49   Web sites which are mere repositories of information are known as 'passive' web sites. Many web sites, however, have a degree of interactivity. Interactivity may assume any number of forms. Many web pages, for example, invite users to send messages to the site operator, so that they can be reviewed or even incorporated into the web page. Such interactions manifest themselves in, among other things, personal and classified advertising, 'visitor books' and 'graffiti walls'. As with bulletin boards, the display of submitted messages may be either moderated, or unrestricted.

FTP

2.50   Web sites can also be used as a platform for transferring files and programs from one computer to another using a method known as file transfer protocol (FTP).[36] FTP can be used for, among many other things, downloading audio or audiovisual files containing songs or video clips.

---

[36] See Comer (n 1 above) 173–82; Gralla (n 16 above) 127–31; Freedman, Glossbrenner, and Glossbrenner (n 16 above) 172.

E. A Glimpse into the Future

Predicting future technological developments is an exercise which, when the future comes, one is likely to regret having undertaken. Nonetheless, some likely short- to medium-term developments of Internet technology can be predicted with reasonable assurance. **2.51**

Speed and reliability

First, the speed with which Internet communications can be achieved will continue to increase. Nearly all communications will ultimately be perceived by human users as being effectively instantaneous. The reliability of instantaneous Internet communications will also increase. Speed and reliability will increase both as a function of improved bandwidth of Internet connections through greater use of high-capacity fibre-optic cables and other technologies, and as a function of faster computer microprocessors and modems.[37] **2.52**

Sounds and pictures

Secondly, the extent to which sound and pictures are incorporated into Internet communications will continue to increase. The quality of video images and sounds capable of being transferred via the Internet will be comparable to that stored on compact and digital video discs or delivered via digital broadcasting services. **2.53**

More and more community groups and individuals, among others, are likely to establish web sites which are much like radio or television stations, able to reach a potentially vast audience, without the start-up costs of broadcasting stations, or the difficulties associated with obtaining access to scarce public broadcast radio frequencies.[38]

Allied to these developments, it is likely that the predominantly text-based nature of Internet communication will continue to be replaced, in time, with greater voice and video communication. Depending on the purpose and content of the communication, users may prefer the spoken word or video images to typescript.

Convergence and ubiquity

Next, there will be greater convergence of the Internet with other technologies. **2.54**

---

[37] For a fascinating insight, see George Gilder, *Telecosm* (2000).
[38] The technology underlying the transfer of audio and audiovisual signals via the Internet is explained in Gralla (n 16 above) 217–27.

Some television stations, for example, have followed the lead of many radio stations by making the programmes they broadcast available for instantaneous, or later, viewing and listening on Internet web sites. That trend is set to continue. Television screens increasingly double as computer monitors. Internet content may be available from other platforms, such as subscription television services. Ultimately, from the consumer's perspective, it is likely to become impossible to distinguish between content delivered via television or radio broadcasting, and content delivered via the Internet. The day is likely to come when consumers will be able to listen to any piece of music, or watch any video programme of their choosing on demand, leading to the substantial demise of traditional music shops and video stores.

Similarly, there is likely to be greater convergence of the Internet and telecommunications. It is already possible to conduct voice and video-conferences via the Internet at a cheaper cost than via commercial telecommunications carriers. As the technology becomes quicker, and more reliable, it seems inevitable that more traditional telecommunications functions will be carried out using the Internet. Voice and video-conferences will potentially be able to include any number of participants.

Allied to these developments, the rapid adoption of wireless systems for the delivery of Internet content promises users the ability to be always on, and on everywhere; able to send and receive e-mail and other messages, and to access and contribute to content on the world wide web using a variety of devices such as mobile telephones, digital assistants, and laptop computers without the need to be physically connected to a network.

Commercialization

2.55 Finally, the commercialization of the Internet will continue. Internet users are already able to select and purchase almost every kind of goods and services over the Internet. The variety of goods and services will no doubt continue to increase over time, as will the sophistication of the manner in which they are offered. Some goods and services are delivered via the Internet itself: purchasing music and video programmes, sharebroking services, and professional advice, are examples.

Cyberspace

2.56 Where Internet technology will ultimately lead is a matter well beyond the scope of this text.[39] A common theme of many visions of the future is the

---

[39] For three thought-provoking visions of the future, see Miller (n 1 above) 1–18, Kitchin (n 1 above) generally, and Gilder (n 37 above) especially Part 5.

convergence of the Internet with virtual reality technologies, creating a true 'cyberspace' in which people located anywhere in the world can interact as if they were in the same room. Taken to its extreme, cyberspatial theorists imagine a computer generated world in which all human senses are stimulated, and otherwise impossible human interactions are facilitated.[40]

---

[40] See eg Mitchell (n 20 above) 19; Miller (n 1 above) 1.

3

ISSUES FOR DEFAMATION LAW

A. Why the Internet is a Communications Revolution

Five characteristics define how the Internet differs from other media of communication. **3.01**

Geographical indeterminacy

First, the Internet places at the fingertips of any person with a computer and a connection to the Internet, anywhere in the world, the ability to communicate instantaneously with a potentially vast global audience. **3.02**

Before the Internet, communications emanated from determinate locations, and had audiences which were capable of being defined in geographic terms. Even mass communications, such as television and radio broadcasts, have a defined and geographically limited audience reach. By contrast, communication on the Internet is characterized by the transfer of signals from computers in indeterminate locations, to other computers in indeterminate locations, via routes which are indeterminate. Even a simple e-mail message, sent to a person who lives across the street, might in fact be viewed by that person logging on to a server from the other side of the world.[1]

---

[1] See para 2.30.

Relevance to civil defamation law

3.03   These matters are relevant in a number of ways to civil defamation law. Most obviously, they affect whether particular courts have jurisdiction to hear and determine a defamation proceeding arising out of the publication of material via the Internet and, if so, which law or laws should be applied.[2]

The global nature of the medium may also affect the operation of some of the defences to defamation law. For example, the places in which defamatory material has been published may be relevant in determining whether the material related to a matter of 'public interest' for the purposes of the defence of fair comment.[3] Places of publication may also affect the availability of statutory defences of justification in some Australian jurisdictions.[4] Defendants may be deprived of the ability to rely on a defence of privilege where defamatory material is published in multiple jurisdictions via the Internet.[5]

Finally, the global nature of the Internet and the resultant potential for multi-jurisdictional defamation raises the question whether the existing remedies available in defamation proceedings in the United Kingdom and Australia are adequate to vindicate the reputations of claimants defamed in material published via the Internet.[6]

Intermediaries

3.04   As explained earlier, intermediaries are involved in every Internet publication.[7] In most cases, an Internet publication will have passed through a number of computer systems, each operated by a different intermediary, on its path from one computer to another.

The unique nature of Internet intermediaries

3.05   Intermediaries are involved in some other forms of communication. For example, postal services and telecommunications carriers are, in a sense, intermediaries involved in the process of communication by letter or telephone.

Internet intermediaries, however, differ in two important respects from postal services and telecommunications carriers. First, the signals constituting an Internet publication will often be stored in computer systems maintained by intermediaries for days, months, or years. They are not like telephone calls,

---

[2] See chapters 25–29.
[3] See chapter 9.
[4] New South Wales, Queensland, Western Australia, Tasmania, and the Australian Capital Territory; see paras 8.15–8.18.
[5] See chapters 10–12.
[6] See chapters 20–24.
[7] See para 2.22.

which occur transiently, or letters which, once delivered, have passed entirely from the control of the postal service.

Secondly, some intermediaries, at least, have the means of monitoring the communications they host or carry, either manually, or through the use of computer software. Although it would be impracticable, given the sheer volume of material communicated via the Internet, for intermediaries to review manually every e-mail message, bulletin board posting, and web page they host or carry, they do have the theoretical ability to do so. In this respect, they are unlike telephone carriers, which could hardly be expected to monitor every telephone call, or postal services, which could hardly open and read every letter they deliver.

Relevance to civil defamation law

Common law. For defamation law, the role of intermediaries gives rise to a number of questions: **3.06**

- Have communications been 'published' to intermediaries, simply because they have passed through their computer systems en route from sender to recipient?[8]
- Where a defamatory e-mail is intercepted by an intermediary en route from the author to the defamed person, is the author of that material potentially liable in respect of publication to the intermediary?[9]
- Are intermediaries 'publishers' of the material which passes through their computer systems?[10]
- If so, are intermediaries able to avoid liability by relying on any statutory defences, or the common law defence of innocent dissemination?[11]
- Could intermediaries be liable for failing to remove defamatory material on their computer systems, once it has been brought to their attention?[12]
- Are intermediaries imputed with the state of mind of the primary author of defamatory material? For example, could the defences of fair comment or qualified privilege be defeated as against an intermediary if the claimant shows that the intermediary does not hold the opinion, or believe in the truth of what has been expressed by the primary author?[13] Could exemplary damages be awarded against an intermediary having regard to the state of mind of the primary author?[14]

---

[8] See paras 5.01–5.04.
[9] See paras 5.05–5.09.
[10] See chapter 15.
[11] See chapters 16–19.
[12] See paras 15.15–15.24 and chapters 16–19.
[13] See paras 9.17–9.19, 9.22–9.26 (fair comment), and 11.42 (qualified privilege).
[14] See para 21.12.

- When addressing each of these questions, is there a relevant distinction between different types of intermediaries?[15]

3.07 **Statutory defences: United Kingdom.** In addition to each of these matters, questions relating to the liability of Internet intermediaries in the United Kingdom have been complicated by factors including uncertainties about:

- the operation of the defences in regulations 17–19 of the Electronic Commerce (EC Directive) Regulations 2002 ('Electronic Commerce Regulations');[16]
- whether the provisions relating to intermediaries in the Electronic Commerce Regulations have effectively transposed the corresponding provisions in the European Parliament and Council's Directive on Electronic Commerce;[17]
- the operation of the defence in section 1 of the Defamation Act 1996 ('the section 1 defence'):[18] and
- the interplay between the section 1 defence and the common law defence of innocent dissemination.[19]

3.08 **Statutory defences: Australia.** In Australia, in addition to the issues already outlined, there is the further question of the application of clause 91 of Schedule 5 to the Broadcasting Services Act 1992 (Cth), a provision which provides a measure of protection to Internet intermediaries from liability under criminal and civil law in respect of material they host or carry.[20] Perhaps inadvertently, that provision has added to the complexity of issues concerning the liability of Internet intermediaries arising out of the publication of defamatory material via the Internet in Australia.

Republication

3.09 To a greater extent than with any other medium, recipients of material published via the Internet are able to republish that material, with minimal effort, to any number of recipients. Some material and information, by its nature, is highly likely to be republished in this manner. Most Internet users will be familiar with the way in which topical e-mails and jokes, for example, can quickly spread among large numbers of people in many countries.

Material published to a small audience via the Internet can thus easily be republished to a wider audience, in any number of geographic locations.

---

[15] Relevant distinctions will be noted as they arise.
[16] See chapter 17.
[17] See paras 17.32–17.34.
[18] See chapter 16.
[19] See paras 18.06–18.07.
[20] See chapter 19.

Relevance to civil defamation law

For the purposes of defamation law, the ready ability to republish material   **3.10**
published via the Internet gives rise to issues such as:

- whether the original author of an Internet publication can be liable for the consequences of its republication;
- whether any effective steps can be taken to minimize the risk of becoming so liable; and
- the circumstances in which Internet users might be liable for republishing material which they did not create.[21]

While not unique to the Internet, these questions are likely to assume greater importance in cases involving defamatory Internet publications than in cases involving other communication media.

Hyperlinks

Fourthly, the Internet differs from other media of communication by reason of   **3.11**
the way in which material can be cross-referenced by hyperlink. It is possible, by
following hyperlinks, to 'jump', seamlessly and almost instantaneously, from
one web page to another, even though, physically, the different web pages might
be stored on different computers in different countries. Hyperlinks can also
connect threads of discussion in a bulletin board. They can be embedded in e-
mail messages or bulletin board postings to enable the recipient to jump
immediately to another message, posting, or web page. No other medium
provides the level of flexibility offered by the Internet.

Another familiar phenomenon for Internet users is the hyperlink from a prominent web page, or from an e-mail message or bulletin board posting, to an
obscure web page, which can have the effect of elevating the obscure to the
notorious in a remarkably short period of time.

Relevance to civil defamation law

Hyperlinks have the effect of blurring the distinction between where one publi-   **3.12**
cation ends, and the next begins. This gives rise to the question whether
material contained in a hyperlinked publication can be used to qualify the
meaning of the words in a publication. For example, a web page which bears a
defamatory meaning, but does not identify anyone, might contain a hyperlink
to a further web page which contains extrinsic identifying material.[22]
Alternatively, a web page which names someone, but is not defamatory, might

---

[21] See paras 5.18–5.23.
[22] See paras 6.03–6.05.

contain a hyperlink to a further web page which does defame the named person.[23] A third possibility is that material contained on a hyperlinked web page might provide the foundation for a *Polly Peck* defence or, in some jurisdictions, a defence of contextual justification.[24]

Another question for defamation law is whether web page owners might potentially be liable for defamatory material on another person's web page, if that material is accessible from their web pages by hyperlink, or conversely whether the author of defamatory material on a web page might be liable for publications arising out of others establishing links to that material from, or framing that material on, their own web pages.[25]

Different forms of publication

3.13 Finally, the Internet is an extremely flexible medium of communication, enabling material to be published in a variety of forms, including words, pictures, text, and sound. The Internet can, depending on the way in which it is used, resemble a television, radio, telephone, video-conferencing facility, newspaper, personal letter, bulletin board, or group discussion. Some material published via the Internet is available indefinitely; other material only transiently.

Relevance to civil defamation law

3.14 For the purposes of defamation law, the form which an Internet publication assumes may determine whether that publication, if defamatory, constitutes libel or slander, a distinction which remains relevant in England, Northern Ireland, and some Australian jurisdictions.[26]

The different forms assumed by Internet publications may also be relevant to the meaning of the publication. Some web pages, for example, have a reputation for sobriety and accuracy, while others are sensational and unreliable. People might be expected to devote different amounts of time to, and to draw different kinds of inferences from, different forms of Internet publication.[27] Some features which are unique to the Internet, such as 'emoticons'—typed symbols which simulate tone of voice or facial expression—might also affect the meaning of an Internet publication.[28] The form in which defamatory material is published via the Internet may also affect the measure of damages, including

---

[23] See paras 7.13–7.17.
[24] See paras 8.07–8.14.
[25] See paras 5.24–5.32.
[26] See chapter 4.
[27] See paras 7.11–7.12.
[28] See para 7.19.

aggravated and exemplary damages, to which a successful claimant is entitled.[29]

The form of Internet publication chosen by a defendant may also be relevant to the operation of some of the defences to defamation law. In some cases, for example, might publication to the world via a web page disentitle a defendant to the defences of fair comment[30] or privilege,[31] even though those defences would have succeeded if the same material had been published in an e-mail message to carefully confined addressees? Might publication via the Internet, in some cases, give rise to the inference that the defendant was actuated by malice, because the medium chosen for the publication of the defamatory material was calculated to inflict the maximum possible damage to the defamed person?[32]

B. A Framework for Analysis

It can be seen, then, that the way in which the Internet works, and is used, raises a very substantial number of questions for the operation of the rules of civil defamation law. As Lord Bingham put it in his foreword to the first edition of this text, 'almost every concept and rule in the field, familiar to students, scholars, practitioners and judges around the world, has to be reconsidered in the light of this unique medium of instant worldwide communication'. Those concepts and rules will be examined in the succeeding chapters.   **3.15**

The approach which has been adopted is a systematic analysis of the cause of action for defamation, its defences and remedies, and the rules relating to jurisdiction and choice of law. The application or likely application of the rules of civil defamation law is explained or predicted by reference to the forms of Internet publications discussed in chapter 2 and the unique characteristics identified above.

The cause of action for defamation

Part II contains an analysis of how the libel/slander distinction, and the elements of the cause of action for defamation, would apply, or be likely to apply, to material published via the Internet.   **3.16**

---

[29] See paras 21.02 (general damages), 21.11 (aggravated damages), and 21.14 (exemplary damages).
[30] See chapter 9.
[31] See chapters 10–12.
[32] See paras 9.18–9.26, 11.39–11.44.

General defences

3.17   Part III explains the application, or likely application, of the major defences to the cause of action for defamation to material published via the Internet. The way in which the defences of justification, fair comment, absolute privilege, and qualified privilege, as well as the other available defences, might apply to material published via the Internet is explained and predicted.

Liability of Internet intermediaries

3.18   Part IV concerns the issue of the extent to which Internet intermediaries might be liable for hosting, caching, or carrying defamatory material which they did not create. It analyses common law principles of publication and the defence of innocent dissemination, and relevant legislation in both the United Kingdom and Australia.

Remedies

3.19   The remedies available to successful claimants in civil defamation actions are the subject of Part V. The blunt nature of the traditional remedies, when applied to defamatory Internet publications, means that lateral solutions, which might afford claimants more effective means of vindicating their reputations, must be considered. Also considered is whether defamation judgments from United Kingdom or Australian courts will be enforceable in foreign jurisdictions, and in particular the United States, where a preponderance of Internet connections are located. Finally, some alternatives to civil defamation law are briefly canvassed.

Jurisdiction and choice of law

3.20   Questions of jurisdiction and choice of law are likely to arise frequently in defamation proceedings arising out of the publication of material via the Internet. The global nature of the medium means that, in most cases, material will have been published in a multitude of jurisdictions. The jurisdiction of domestic courts in the United Kingdom and Australia to hear and determine defamation proceedings arising out of Internet publications, the operation of *forum non conveniens* and choice of law rules, and the methods of proving the content of applicable foreign law, are the subject of Part VI.

Other sources of law

3.21   Finally, Part VII examines two other sources of law which will often be relevant in actions arising out of the publication of defamatory Internet material. Chapter 30 contains an overview of the jurisprudence of the European Court of Human Rights concerning the intersection between the European Convention on Human Rights and civil defamation law, and considers the potential impact of the Human Rights Act 1998 (UK) on defamation actions in the United Kingdom.

Chapter 31 is concerned with the regulation of defamation via the Internet in the United States. It examines some of the key differences between American defamation law and Anglo-Australian defamation law, and contains detailed expositions of the way in which the liability of Internet intermediaries for hosting or carrying defamatory material has been resolved in the United States, and of the circumstances in which American courts will assert jurisdiction over non-residents in relation to material published via the Internet.

Appendices

Glossary

A glossary of common Internet terms appears after chapter 31.   **3.22**

Appendix

The Appendix contains a collation of selected legislative provisions relating to   **3.23**
the liability of Internet intermediaries in the United Kingdom, Australia, and
the United States.

PART II

THE CAUSE OF ACTION FOR DEFAMATION

4

LIBEL OR SLANDER?

A. Introduction

General principles

The distinction between libel and slander

Libel and slander emerged historically as distinct causes of action developed by **4.01** different courts.[1] The distinction between libel and slander turns on the form of the publication. Libel is defamation published in some permanent form; slander is oral defamation, or defamation published in some transient form.[2] Where written material is read out, it has been held to be libel, not slander, at least if the

---

[1] See *Jones v Jones* [1916] 2 AC 481, 489–92; *Meldrum v Australian Broadcasting Co Ltd* [1932] VLR 425, 430–2; Patrick Milmo and WVH Rogers, *Gatley on Libel and Slander* (10th edn, 2003) ('Gatley') para 3.7; John Fleming, *The Law of Torts* (9th edn, 1998) 601.
[2] *Monson v Tussauds Ltd* [1894] 1 QB 671, 692 (Lopes CJ): 'Libels are generally in writing or printing, but this is not necessary; the defamatory matter may be conveyed in some other permanent form. For instance, a statue, a caricature, an effigy, chalk marks on a wall, signs, or pictures may constitute a libel.' See also *Meldrum v Australian Broadcasting Co Ltd* [1932] VLR 425, 432 (Cussen ACJ), 443 (Lowe J).

audience understands that the material is being read out.[3] In England, subject to minor exceptions,[4] legislation deems words spoken in the course of a performance of a play to be published in permanent form.[5]

Some Australian authorities apply a 'mode of publication' test to differentiate between libel and slander. Under that test, slander is material communicated by word of mouth; all other modes of publication are libel.[6]

The policy underlying the distinction between libel and slander may be that written, or permanent, publications have a greater capacity to cause harm than oral, or transient, publications.

Relevance of the distinction

4.02   At common law, libel is actionable per se; slander is actionable, with limited exceptions, only on proof of special damage.[7] All forms of defamation are actionable in Scots law, however, without proof of special damage.[8]

In most Australian jurisdictions, the distinction between libel and slander has been abolished[9] or rendered irrelevant by legislation which deems slander to be actionable even in the absence of special damage.[10] The common law

---

[3] *Forrester v Tyrell* (1893) 9 TLR 257, 257; *Meldrum v Australian Broadcasting Co Ltd* [1932] VLR 425, 443 (Lowe J). In the *Meldrum* case, a majority of the Full Court of the Supreme Court of Victoria preferred the view that a radio broadcast is slander, regardless of whether it involves the reading of written material: 435 (Mann J), 438–9 (McArthur J); Lowe J, 443, would have followed *Forrester*. The judge at first instance in *Meldrum*, Cussen ACJ, would also have followed *Forrester*. [1932] VLR 425, 432. *Meldrum* appears still to be good law in Victoria: *Wainer v Rippon* [1980] VR 129, 132.
[4] Theatres Act 1968 (UK), s 7 (not applicable in Scotland). The exceptions include rehearsals and performances on a domestic occasion in a private dwelling. Plays which are performed for the sole or primary purpose of being recorded, broadcast, or included in a programme service (within the meaning of the Broadcasting Act 1990) are also excluded. Any record of such performances will however be in permanent form. Broadcasts of such performances will be deemed to be in permanent form by reason of the Broadcasting Act 1990 (UK), s 166: see paras 4.06–4.11.
[5] Theatres Act 1968 (UK), s 4(1). 'Play' is given an expansive meaning, including 'any dramatic piece, whether involving improvisation or not' and 'ballet': s 18(1).
[6] *Meldrum v Australian Broadcasting Co Ltd* [1932] VLR 425, 435 (Mann J): 'for spoken words slander only will lie', 438–9 (McArthur J): 'The distinction lies solely, in my opinion, in the mode of publication.'
[7] See eg *Lumby v Allday* (1831) 1 Cr & J 301, 305; *Allsop v Allsop* (1860) 5 H & N 534, 537, 538–9, 539; 157 ER 1292; *Jones v Jones* [1916] 2 AC 481, 490, 499–500, 506. See generally Gatley (n 1 above) para 3.6 and ch 4; Fleming (n 1 above) 600–10; Michael Gillooly, *The Law of Defamation in Australia and New Zealand* (1998) 97–9.
[8] JM Thomson, *Delictual Liability* (1994) 207; Francis McManus and Eleanor Russell, *Delict* (1998) 302. Where the defamatory statement is communicated only to the pursuer, however, only solatium damages are recoverable: see para 5.02.
[9] Queensland: Defamation Act 1889 (Qld), ss 5(1) and 7; Tasmania: Defamation Act 1957 (Tas), ss 6 and 9(1).
[10] New South Wales: Defamation Act 1974 (NSW), s 8; Northern Territory: Defamation Act 1938 (NT), s 2; Australian Capital Territory: Civil Law (Wrongs) Act 2002 (ACT), s 125.

distinction remains relevant, however, in Victoria, South Australia, and Western Australia.

Slanders which are actionable per se include words imputing that the claimant has committed a crime punishable by imprisonment,[11] imputing that the complainant has a contagious or infectious disease, disparaging the claimant in a profession or trade,[12] or imputing sexual immorality on the part of a female.[13]

Special damage

Special damage means pecuniary loss or loss capable of assessment in money terms.[14] Examples of forms of special damage include loss or refusal of employment and general loss of business.[15] There must be a causal link between the slander and the special damage which is not too remote.[16]   **4.03**

The United States

In most States of the United States, libel is only actionable per se if the offending material is defamatory on its face. Special damage must generally be proved where the material is only defamatory by reason of extrinsic facts known to some readers.[17]   **4.04**

The Internet

Where persons are defamed in material published via the Internet, but cannot   **4.05**

---

[11] cf Wrongs Act 1958 (Vic), s 8 and Civil Liability Act 1936 (SA), s 5: 'indictable offence'.

[12] See also Defamation Act 1952 (UK), s 2; Defamation Act (Northern Ireland) 1955, s 2.

[13] See Slander of Women Act 1891 (UK), s 1 (England); Wrongs Act 1958 (Vic), s 8; Civil Liability Act 1936 (SA), s 5.

[14] *Chamberlain v Boyd* (1883) 11 QBD 407, 412, 415; *Chakravarti v Advertiser Newspapers Ltd* (1998) 193 CLR 519, 558–9.

[15] *Sterry v Foreman* (1827) 2 C & P 592; 172 ER 270; *King v Watts* (1838) 8 C & P 614; 173 ER 642; *Chakravarti v Advertiser Newspapers Ltd* (1998) 193 CLR 519, 559.

[16] *Lynch v Knight* (1861) 9 HLC 577, 600; 11 ER 854 (Lord Wensleydale): 'to make the words actionable, by reason of special damage, the consequence must be such as, taking human nature as it is, with its infirmities, and having regard to the relationship of the parties concerned, might fairly and reasonably have been anticipated and feared would follow from the speaking of the words, not what would reasonably follow, or we might think ought to follow'. See also *Chamberlain v Boyd* (1883) 11 QBD 407, 412 (Lord Coleridge CJ): the alleged damage must be 'the natural and probable result of the words complained of', 413 (Brett LJ): 'the direct and probable result of the words'; *Taylor v Hamilton* [1927] SASR 314, 317 (Napier and Richards JJ): 'The plaintiff in a case of this kind does not discharge the onus of proving actual damage by evidence which fails to establish the requisite probability that the words complained of did bring about, or at least contribute in some appreciable degree to, the result tendered as the actual damage.'

[17] Note also that in America, private defamation plaintiffs may recover only such damages as are sufficient to compensate them for 'actual injury', except where actual malice is proved, at least where the defamatory statement involves no matters of public concern: *Gertz v Robert Welch, Inc*, 418 US 323 (1974), 349–50; cf *Dun & Bradstreet, Inc v Greenmoss Builders, Inc*, 472 US 749 (1985), 760–1; see para 31.04.

prove that they have suffered special damage, they will therefore only be able to succeed in defamation proceedings under the law of England, Northern Ireland, and some Australian States[18] if their cause of action is one of libel, rather than slander. Whether defamatory Internet publications are libel or slander is therefore a question of some importance.

Complexities arise in applying the tests to some modern forms of communication. A tape recording, for example, is in permanent form, but conveys spoken words. A film or television programme may convey both spoken words and material in other forms, including writing and pictures.[19] A radio or television programme may or may not be recorded in permanent form.[20]

The classification of material published via the Internet as libel or slander is complicated by the flexibility of the Internet as a medium. Internet communications can resemble television or radio programmes, newspapers, letters, noticeboards, telephone conversations, or video-conferences. Some forms of Internet communication are in permanent form, others are transient; some involve the spoken word, others do not. A further complication is the potential operation of broadcasting legislation in both the United Kingdom and Australia which deems some modern forms of defamatory publication to be libel rather than slander.

To determine whether defamatory Internet publications are libel or slander it is necessary first to consider whether they are deemed by legislation to be libel. Where deeming provisions do not apply, the common law tests will determine whether the publication is to be treated as libel or slander.

B. United Kingdom Legislation

Section 166(1) of the Broadcasting Act 1990

4.06   Section 166(1) of the Broadcasting Act 1990 (UK) applies in England and Northern Ireland.[21] It provides that:

---

[18] Victoria, South Australia, and Western Australia.

[19] Films, including the accompanying soundtrack, were held to be libel in *Youssoupoff v Metro-Goldwyn-Mayer Pictures Ltd* (1934) 50 TLR 581; cf *Wainer v Rippon* [1980] VR 129 (at common law, a television programme is slander). See also *Gorton v Australian Broadcasting Commission* (1973) 1 ACTR 6, 8; *Amalgamated Television Services Pty Ltd v Marsden* (1998) 43 NSWLR 158, 166.

[20] Although under Australian legislation, radio and television broadcasts of matters relating to a political subject or current affairs must be recorded and retained by broadcasters for at least six weeks from the date of broadcast, and longer in certain cases: Broadcasting Services Act 1992 (Cth), Sch 2, cl 5 (commercial media); Australian Broadcasting Corporation Act 1983 (Cth), ss 79A, 79B (ABC); Special Broadcasting Service Act 1991 (Cth), ss 70A, 70B (SBS).

[21] Broadcasting Act 1990 (UK), ss 166(4), 204(3). The provision does not extend to Scotland: s 166(5).

For the purposes of the law of libel and slander (including the law of criminal libel so far as it relates to the publication of defamatory matter) the publication of words in the course of any programme included in a programme service shall be treated as publication in permanent form.

This provision does not appear to have been judicially applied. There is little doubt, however, that where the provision applies, it has the effect of deeming the publication, if defamatory, to be libel, rather than slander.[22]

Whether section 166(1) applies to material published via the Internet turns on whether the publication of material in e-mail messages, bulletin board postings, or web pages amounts to the 'the publication of words in the course of any programme included in a programme service'.

Programmes and programme services

'Programme' is defined in section 202(1) as including 'an advertisement and, in relation to any service, includes any item included in that service'. 'Programme service' is defined in section 201(1) as: **4.07**

any of the following services (whether or not it is, or it requires to be, licensed under this Act), namely—
> (aa) any service which is a programme service within the meaning of the Communications Act 2003;[23]
> (c) any other service which consists in the sending, by means of an electronic communications network (within the meaning of the Communications Act 2003), of sounds or visual images or both either—
>> (i) for reception at two or more places in the United Kingdom (whether they are so sent for simultaneous reception or at different times in response to requests made by different users of the service); or
>> (ii) for reception at a place in the United Kingdom for the purpose of being presented there to members of the public or to any group of persons.

'Electronic communications network' is defined in section 32 of the Communications Act 2003 (UK) to mean, relevantly, 'a transmission system for the conveyance, by the use of electrical, magnetic or electro-magnetic energy, of signals of any description'. Internet communications are conveyed by the use of electrical, magnetic, or electro-magnetic energy, and are thus transmitted by electronic communications networks within the meaning of this definition and for the purposes of section 201(1)(c) of the Broadcasting Act 1990 (UK).

---

[22] An equivalent provision has been so interpreted in Australia: see para 4.12.
[23] The Communications Act 2003 (UK), s 405 defines 'programme service' to mean a television programme service, the public teletext service, an additional television service, a digital additional television service, a radio programme service, or a sound service provided by the BBC.

Internet services

4.08 Many Internet services will be 'programme services' within the meaning of section 201(1)(c). Such services generally consist in the sending, by means of an electronic communications network, of sounds or visual images or both. Bulletin board postings and web pages will generally be sent for reception at two or more places in the United Kingdom, as will e-mail messages with two or more recipients in the United Kingdom.

Further, as the definition of 'programme' in section 202(1) encompasses all items included in such services, it seems likely that all forms of Internet communication, apart from those which are not sent for reception at two or more places in the United Kingdom, will satisfy the description of a 'programme included in a programme service' for the purposes of section 166(1).

By this process of reasoning, many Internet publications will be deemed by section 166(1) as having been published in permanent form and will therefore, if defamatory, constitute libel.

Ordinary e-mail messages

4.09 Ordinary e-mail messages sent only to one United Kingdom recipient, or only to recipients outside the United Kingdom, will not be deemed to have been published in permanent form by section 166(1), because they will not have been sent via a 'programme service' within the meaning of section 201(1). Similarly, instantaneous forms of Internet communication, such as instant messaging, Internet Relay Chat, telephone and video-conferencing services will also fall outside the scope of section 166(1), except where there are two or more recipients of the communication in the United Kingdom. In all such cases, whether the communications are libel or slander will depend on the application of the common law test.

Summary

4.10 In summary, section 166(1) of the Broadcasting Act 1990 (UK) has the effect of deeming many Internet communications to have been published in permanent form. Where those communications are defamatory, they will constitute libel, rather than slander, in England and Northern Ireland. The common law test remains relevant, however, in respect of some forms of Internet communication including, most importantly, ordinary e-mail messages, and instantaneous forms of Internet communication, other than where there are two or more recipients in the United Kingdom.

Northern Ireland

4.11 In Northern Ireland, section 1 of the Defamation Act (Northern Ireland) 1955 provides that 'for the purposes of the law of libel and slander, the broadcasting of words by means of wireless telegraphy shall be treated as publication in permanent form'. This provision has the effect of deeming defamatory radio and television broadcasts to be libel, rather than slander, in Northern Ireland.

The provision will have limited application to defamatory material communicated via the Internet. In the first place, most online material is currently communicated via telephone lines and cables, rather than wirelessly, although wireless technologies are rapidly increasing in popularity and coverage. When users 'connect wirelessly' to the Internet, they typically use a wireless technology, such as wireless broadband, Wi-Fi, or WAP, to connect to the network of an intermediary, which provides subscribers with Internet access using its network of telephone lines or cables. Material communicated via the Internet is thus highly unlikely to be communicated entirely using wireless telegraphy. Secondly, for reasons developed below in the discussion of analogous Australian legislation, it may be that material published via the Internet is only 'broadcast' where that material is in the nature of a television or radio programme.[24]

C. Australian Legislation

In Australia, section 206 of the Broadcasting Services Act 1992 (Cth) ('the BSA') provides that 'For the purposes of the law of defamation, the broadcasting or datacasting of matter is taken to be publication of the matter in a permanent form.' **4.12**

Section 206 has been interpreted as deeming defamatory radio and television programmes to be libel for the purposes of Australian defamation law.[25] Whether section 206 applies to Internet publications depends on whether those publications amount to the 'broadcasting or datacasting of matter'.

Broadcasting

Four reasons can be advanced in support of the conclusion that material published via the Internet does not amount to the 'broadcasting of matter', except where the material is in the nature of a television or radio programme. **4.13**

---

[24] See paras 4.12–4.23.
[25] *Wainer v Rippon* [1980] VR 129, 135; *Gorton v Australian Broadcasting Commission* (1973) 1 ACTR 6, 8.

Legislative guidance

4.14 First, although the BSA does not define 'broadcasting',[26] the predecessor to that Act, the Broadcasting Act 1942 (Cth) ('the 1942 Act'), defined 'broadcast' as 'broadcast by radio or televise'.[27] The 1942 Act thus limited the concept of broadcasting to material delivered by means of radio or television transmission.

This limitation was imported into the definition of the term 'broadcasting service' in section 6(1) of the BSA. That definition is of importance because it determines whether a particular service falls within the regulatory regime established by the BSA. A 'broadcasting service' is:

> a service that delivers *television programs or radio programs* to persons having equipment appropriate for receiving that service, whether the delivery uses the radiofrequency spectrum, cable, optical fibre, satellite or any other means or a combination of those means, but does not include:
>
> (a) a service (including a teletext service) that provides no more than data, or no more than text (with or without associated still images); or
> (b) a service that makes programs available on demand on a point-to-point basis, including a dial-up service; or
> (c) a service, or a class of services, that the Minister determines, by notice in the Gazette, not to fall within this definition.[28]

4.15 Although the matter is not beyond doubt, it appears that the legislature intended to limit the concept of 'broadcasting' for the purposes of section 206 of the BSA to the delivery of material in the nature of television or radio programmes, whether by television or radio transmission or otherwise. Had the legislature intended a more expansive definition of 'broadcasting' for the purposes of section 206, it might have been expected to define the term in a way which differentiated it from the definition of 'broadcast' in the 1942 Act and 'broadcasting service' in the BSA. The use of the words 'television programs or radio programs' in the definition of 'broadcasting service' seems to suggest that the legislature intended to confine 'broadcasting' to the delivery of television programmes and radio programmes.[29]

Distinction between broadcasting services and Internet carriage services

4.16 Secondly, Parliament has drawn a distinction in the BSA between 'broadcasting

---

[26] Nor can any assistance in determining the meaning of the term be derived from the explanatory memorandum to the Broadcasting Services Bill 1992 (Cth).

[27] cf the definition of 'broadcast' in the Broadcasting Act 1990 (UK), s 202(1): 'broadcast' means 'broadcast by wireless telegraphy'; cf also the Defamation (Northern Ireland) Act 1955, s 1, discussed in para 4.11.

[28] Broadcasting Services Act 1992 (Cth), s 6(1), emphasis added.

[29] cf Australian Broadcasting Authority, *Investigation into the Content of Online Services: Report to the Minister for Communications and the Arts* (1996) 45, which concluded that '[i]n a sense, when a user/content creator makes information or entertainment services publicly accessible online it could be said that they have "broadcast" the material.'

services' and 'Internet carriage services' which would appear to be inconsistent with the view that all Internet services are a form of broadcasting.[30] Under the BSA, 'Internet carriage services' are services which carry communications by means of guided or unguided electromagnetic energy between two or more points, at least one of which is in Australia, and which enable 'end-users' to access the Internet.[31] The regime established in the BSA for the regulation of broadcasting services is separate from the regime established for the regulation of Internet carriage services.

Dictionary definitions

Thirdly, dictionary definitions of 'broadcast' tend to support, although not conclusively, the view that broadcasting involves transmissions by means of radio or television, and that broadcasting does not extend to most forms of Internet communication.[32]

4.17

Nature of Internet messages

Finally, most Internet communications, such as e-mail messages, bulletin board postings, and web pages, are not disseminated widely in the same way as ordinary television or radio programmes. E-mail messages and bulletin boards generally have defined addressees, whereas ordinary television or radio programmes are available to anyone with a television or radio set. Web pages are only disseminated when an Internet user types the address for the page into a browser, or clicks on a hyperlink for that page, whereas ordinary television or radio programmes are available simply by turning on a television or radio set. Generally speaking, Internet users cause the dissemination of Internet content, whereas broadcasters cause the dissemination of television and radio programmes. Much Internet content is interactive, whereas ordinary television and radio programmes are not.

4.18

These distinctions are, however, imperfect. In the case of on-demand television and radio services, for example, programmes are disseminated at the instigation

---

[30] ibid, 42–4, 46–7.

[31] The concept of 'Internet carriage services' was introduced into the BSA by the Broadcasting Services Amendment (Online Services) Act 1999 (Cth): see Broadcasting Services Act 1992 (Cth), s 216B and Sch 5, cl 3. An 'Internet carriage service' means a 'listed carriage service that enables end-users to access the Internet'. A 'listed carriage service' has the same meaning as in the Telecommunications Act 1997 (Cth). Under that Act, a 'listed carriage service' means, in effect, a service for carrying communications by means of guided or unguided electromagnetic energy between two or more points, at least one of which is in Australia: Telecommunications Act 1997 (Cth), ss 7, 16.

[32] See eg *The New Shorter Oxford English Dictionary* (1993); *The Australian Concise Oxford Dictionary* (2nd edn, 1992); *The Macquarie Dictionary* (3rd edn, 1998); cf Australian Broadcasting Authority (n 29 above) 45; Broadcasting Act 1990 (UK) s 202(1): ' "broadcast" means broadcast by wireless telegraphy'.

of the user, rather than the broadcaster. Large bulletin boards are similar in some respects to subscription television and radio services, in the sense that they are accessible on demand by subscribers. Television and radio services are increasingly interactive, much like material available via the Internet.

Summary

4.19   Although the matter is far from certain, there is thus a basis for concluding that most material published via the Internet is unlikely to constitute the 'broadcasting of matter' for the purposes of section 206 of the BSA, except where that material is in the nature of a television or radio programme.

Television and radio programmes are increasingly available via the Internet. For example, it is possible to watch current news broadcasts or listen to radio programmes from, among many others, CNN, the BBC World Service, or the Australian Broadcasting Corporation, via the Internet. Such programmes are in the nature of television and radio programmes and may, therefore, fall within the description of 'broadcasting of matter' in section 206 of the BSA.

4.20   The conclusion that material in the nature of television or radio programmes delivered via the Internet amounts to the 'broadcasting of matter' is not affected by the fact that services delivering those programmes will usually be excluded from the definition of 'broadcasting service' in section 6(1) of the BSA, by reason of paragraph (b) of that definition. Most Internet services are services which make 'programs available on a point-to-point basis' and therefore fall outside the scope of the definition of 'broadcasting service'.[33] That conclusion is supported by a determination of the Minister for Communications gazetted on 27 September 2000, pursuant to section 6(1) of the BSA, that services that make television or radio programmes available via the Internet are not 'broadcasting services' for the purposes of the BSA.

Paragraph (b) of the definition and that determination, however, impose a limit only on the 'services' which are regulated by the BSA. It is difficult to see how they could be said to limit the meaning of the word 'broadcasting'.[34] It is likely therefore that defamatory television and radio programmes available via the Internet are libel by virtue of section 206, even where they are excluded from the definition of 'broadcasting service' by reason of paragraph (b) of the definition in section 6(1) of the BSA.

4.21   A different conclusion was reached by a single judge of the Western Australian Supreme Court in *Mickelberg v 6PR Southern Cross Radio Pty Ltd.*[35] The

---

[33] Australian Broadcasting Authority (n 29 above) 45–8.
[34] ibid.
[35] (2001) 24 WAR 187.

defendant had broadcast a radio interview which was allegedly defamatory of the plaintiff. The audio content of the interview was also made available on demand from the defendant's web site. Hasluck J was inclined to the view that, to the extent that it was available via the Internet, the interview did not amount to broadcasting of matter. Hasluck J's reasoning, however, was based on an analysis of the meaning of the term 'broadcasting service' (which does not appear in section 206) rather than the meaning of the words 'broadcasting of matter'. Hasluck J seems to have treated section 206 as though it deems 'broadcasting services' to be publication in a permanent form, whereas the definition deems 'broadcasting of matter' to be so published. On appeal, a Full Court of the Western Australian Supreme Court, without determining the matter, appears to have doubted the correctness of Hasluck J's conclusion.[36]

A different conclusion was also reached by a single judge of the Ontario Superior Court of Justice in *Bahlieda v Santa*,[37] a case concerning whether placing material on a web site constitutes a 'broadcast' for the purposes of section 1(1) of the Libel and Slander Act 1990 (Ontario). That section defines 'broadcasting' to mean: **4.22**

> the dissemination of writing, signs, signals, pictures and sounds of all kinds intended to be received by the public either directly or through the medium of relay stations, by means of,
>
> > (a) any form of wireless radioelectric communication utilizing Hertzian waves, including radiotelegraph and radio telephone, or
> > (b) cables, wires, fibre-optic linkages or laser beams,
>
> and 'broadcast' has a corresponding meaning.

By section 5(1) of the Libel and Slander Act 1990,

> [n]o action for libel in a newspaper or in a broadcast lies unless the plaintiff has, within six weeks after the alleged libel has come to the plaintiff's knowledge, given to the defendant notice in writing, specifying the matter complained of, which shall be served in the same manner as a statement of claim or delivering it to a grown-up person at the chief office of the defendant.

By section 6 of the same Act,

> [a]n action for a libel in a newspaper or in a broadcast shall be commenced within three months after the libel has come to the knowledge of the person defamed, but, where such an action is brought within that period, the action may include a claim for any other libel against the plaintiff by the defendant in the same newspaper or the same broadcasting station within a period of one year before the commencement of the action.

---

[36] *Mickelberg v 6PR Southern Cross Radio Pty Ltd* [2002] WASCA 270, para 44.
[37] (2003) 64 OR (3d) 599.

The plaintiff brought a defamation action against the defendant in the Ontario Superior Court of Justice arising out of material published on the defendant's web site. The defendant brought an application before Pierce J for summary dismissal of part of the plaintiff's claim on the ground that the plaintiff had not given the notice required by section 5(1) or commenced her action within the time required by section 6 of the Libel and Slander Act. The question for Pierce J was whether the placing of material on a web site constituted a 'broadcast' for the purposes of the Libel and Slander Act.

Pierce J concluded that the placing of the material on the defendant's web site did constitute a 'broadcast'. She said:

> The purpose of broadcasting definition [*sic*] is to single out information which is transmitted to mass audiences, where maximum harm to reputation can be done. Traditionally, this involved radio and television . . .

> The court must recognize and give effect to the purpose of the Act, including the mischief it seeks to ameliorate. In this Act, that harm is widespread damage to reputation when a mass audience receives defamatory material. That is the rationale for applying particular rules to broadcasting that do not apply to other forms of defamatory communication. It is the reason for the notice period, and the limitation found in sections 5 and 6 . . .

> The Internet, sometimes more than traditional broadcast media, reaches a mass audience. It uses the same infrastructure common to radio and television, as set out in the Act. I conclude therefore, that placing material on the Internet, via a web site, where it may be accessed by a large audience, constitutes broadcasting with the meaning of the Libel and Slander Act.

As the plaintiff had not given the notice required by section 5(1) or commenced her action within the time required by section 6 of the Libel and Slander Act, the action was statute-barred. Pierce J said that her conclusion was not affected by the fact that the matter complained of had continued to be accessible on the defendant's web site well after the date of first publication, because time runs under Ontario law (unlike English law) from the date the libel came to the attention of the defamed person.

On appeal, the Ontario Court of Appeal overturned Pierce J's decision, and remitted the matter for further hearing. The court noted that expert opinion differed as to whether, among other things, Internet publications involve 'broadcasts' within the meaning of the Libel and Slander Act 1990. The court held that Pierce J was in error in disposing of the matter summarily, observing that '[s]ummary judgment applications are not a substitute for trial and thus will seldom prove suitable for resolving conflicts in expert testimony particularly those involving difficult, complex policy issues with broad social ramifications'.[38]

---

[38] *Bahlieda v Santa* (2003) 233 DLR (4th) 382.

The same provisions of the Libel and Slander Act 1990 were reviewed by a **4.23** differently constituted court of the Ontario Court of Appeal in *Weiss v Sawyer*.[39] The defendant had written, among other things, an allegedly defamatory letter which was published in the print and online editions of *Realms* magazine. The plaintiff failed to give the notice required by section 5(1) of the Libel and Slander Act. Armstrong JA, with whom Catzman and Weiler JJA agreed, dismissed the plaintiff's action in so far as it concerned the letter, on the basis that the word 'newspaper'[40] in section 5(1) was broad enough to encompass a newspaper which is published on the Internet.[41] In view of that conclusion, it was unnecessary for the court to express a view about whether the online edition of *Realms* constituted a 'broadcast' within the meaning of the Libel and Slander Act.[42]

Datacasting

Whether the publication of material via the Internet might amount to the **4.24** 'datacasting of matter' raises further complications. 'Datacasting' is not defined in the BSA. A 'datacasting service', however, means a service that delivers certain kinds of content 'to persons having equipment appropriate for receiving that content, where the delivery of the service uses the broadcasting services bands'.[43] The 'broadcasting services bands' are that part of the radiofrequency spectrum that has been designated under section 31 of the Radiocommunications Act 1992 (Cth) as being primarily for broadcasting services and referred to the Australian Broadcasting Authority for planning.[44] 'Datacasting licensees' will be allowed to 'datacast', among other things, ordinary electronic mail and Internet content.[45]

It seems clear enough that 'datacasting' involves the transmission of information via the radiofrequency spectrum. Where Internet content is delivered via an ordinary telephone line or cable, therefore, it will not amount to datacasting. It would seem to be arguable, however, that where Internet content is delivered via the radiofrequency spectrum, as in the case of wireless broadband, Wi-Fi, and WAP services, it might amount to 'datacasting' for the purposes of section 206 of the BSA. As section 206 refers only to 'datacasting', and not to 'datacasting

---

[39] (2002) 217 DLR (4th) 129.
[40] 'Newspaper' is defined in Libel and Slander Act 1990 (Ontario), s 1(1), to mean 'a paper containing public news, intelligence, or occurrences, or remarks or observations thereon, or containing only, or principally, advertisements, printed for distribution to the public and published periodically, or in parts or numbers, at least twelve times a year'.
[41] (2002) 217 DLR (4th) 129, para 24.
[42] ibid, para 26.
[43] Broadcasting Services Act 1992 (Cth), s 6(1); see also Sch 6.
[44] ibid, s 6(1).
[45] ibid, Sch 6, cl 1.

services', this conclusion would seem to follow regardless of whether the content is delivered via the broadcasting services band part of the spectrum.

Summary

4.25 In summary, except where the Internet is used as a means for delivering material in the nature of television and radio programmes, or where Internet content is delivered via the radiofrequency spectrum, the common law tests will determine whether defamatory Internet publications are libel or slander in those Australian jurisdictions where the distinction remains relevant, namely Victoria, South Australia, and Western Australia.

D. Internet Publications at Common Law

4.26 Although broadcasting legislation in both the United Kingdom and Australia deems some Internet communications to be in permanent form and therefore, if defamatory, libel rather than slander, the common law tests remain relevant in England, Northern Ireland, Victoria, South Australia, and Western Australia in relation to some forms of Internet communication.

How Internet communications are published

4.27 Whatever the nature of the communication, each Internet publication travels from computer to computer as a series of IP datagrams which are likely to have been stored in a number of intermediate computers along the route from sender to recipient.[46]

E-mail messages

4.28 In the case of e-mail messages, the sending computer, the recipient network's mail server, and the recipient's computer, at least, are likely to have retained copies of the messages.[47] The messages can be reviewed at will by the recipient.

Bulletin board postings

4.29 In the case of bulletin board postings, copies are likely to have been stored on, at least, the sender's computer, the bulletin board server, and the computer of each user who has requested a copy of the individual posting.[48] Again, the user is able to review individual postings in much the same way as an e-mail message.

---

[46] See generally paras 2.16–2.18, 2.22.
[47] See para 2.31.
[48] See para 2.39.

Web pages

In the case of web pages, copies of the constituent datagrams will have been stored on the host computer, and probably also the computer of each person who visits the web page. Copies may also be stored in some or all of the intermediate computers en route from the host to the visitor.[49] The user's computer will usually cache the web page in its memory, at least temporarily, so that the user may recall and display the page on the computer screen even after disconnecting from the Internet.   **4.30**

File transfer

Where audio or audiovisual information has been downloaded using FTP or another method by an Internet user, it will usually be stored in the user's computer, able to be reviewed much like a tape or video recording.   **4.31**

Most defamatory Internet publications constitute libel, not slander

Internet publications are therefore often in a permanent form. They may be reviewed on demand at the leisure of the recipient, in much the same way as a reader may delve again and again into a book, or a newspaper. Applying the form of publication test, defamatory Internet publications would thus generally be libel, not slander, at common law.   **4.32**

Most Internet communications, being text- or graphics-based, are not communicated by word of mouth. The mode of publication test, therefore, also leads to the conclusion that most defamatory Internet publications are libel, not slander.

This result is consistent with the policy seemingly underlying the common law: defamatory Internet publications will often have considerable capacity to cause harm, and certainly greater capacity than the usual slanderous forms of communication. This capacity is exacerbated by the ready ability to republish defamatory Internet material to a wide and geographically diverse audience and by the ability of computer users to print out defamatory material, or to store it indefinitely in electronic form.   **4.33**

Three forms of Internet communication merit special consideration, because they are used for the purposes of more transient communication.

---

[49] See para 2.47.

Special cases

Television and radio programmes available via the Internet

4.34   As noted above, where defamatory material in the nature of television and radio programmes is available via the Internet, it is probably deemed by the broadcasting legislation in England, Northern Ireland, and Australia to be published in a permanent form, and thus, libel rather than slander.[50] Examples include television programmes and radio programmes available by accessing the web site of a television station or radio station, irrespective of whether the programmes are available at a time determined by the provider of the programme, or the recipient of the programme.[51]

Instant messaging, Internet Relay Chat and multiple user domains

4.35   Instant messaging, Internet Relay Chat, and chat rooms[52] are forms of Internet communication typically involving textual exchanges somewhat analogous to a spoken conversation. Such exchanges may or may not involve the spoken word or video communication. Participants in such exchanges can review the textual component of the exchange by scrolling up and down the screen. The entire communication may be able to be printed out, stored indefinitely, or forwarded electronically to other participants. All of these factors suggest that such exchanges, if they contain defamatory material, will be libel rather than slander at common law. In England and Northern Ireland, such exchanges are deemed to be libel by reason of section 166(1) of the Broadcasting Act 1990 (UK) where the communication is sent to two or more recipients in the United Kingdom.[53] In Australia, they may be deemed to be libel if delivered wirelessly via the radiofrequency spectrum.[54]

Internet telephone and video-conferencing services

4.36   The Internet can also be used in ways analogous to telephone and video-conferencing services; that is, for the purpose of instantaneous audio or audio-visual communication. As with all Internet communications, these services each involve the transfer of IP datagrams from computer to computer. Copies of the datagrams are likely to have been made and stored, at least transiently, in a number of intermediate computers en route from party to party. On the other hand, these communications involve primarily the spoken word. Although instantaneous audio or audiovisual Internet communications might technically

---

[50]   See paras 4.06–4.11 (England and Northern Ireland), 4.13–4.24 (Australia).
[51]   cf *Mickelberg v 6PR Southern Cross Radio Pty Ltd* [2002] WASCA 270, para 44.
[52]   See para 2.40.
[53]   See paras 4.06–4.11.
[54]   See para 4.24.

be capable of being reconstructed from stored IP datagrams after the event, such reconstruction is unlikely and will often be impossible.

Instantaneous audio or audiovisual communication via the Internet is, from the recipient's point of view, a transient form of communication, much like a telephone conversation, or a video-conference. Such communications would, if defamatory, be likely to be treated as slander, not libel, at common law. In England and Northern Ireland, however, where such communications are made to two or more recipients in the United Kingdom, they will be deemed to be libel by reason of section 166(1) of the Broadcasting Act 1990 (UK).[55] Where such communications are delivered wirelessly via the radiofrequency spectrum, they will probably be deemed to be libel in Australia by reason of section 206 of the BSA.[56]

---

[55] See paras 4.06–4.11.
[56] See para 4.24.

5

PUBLICATION

A. General Principles

The concept of publication

Liability in defamation law attaches to the publication of defamatory material of **5.01** and concerning a claimant. Publication[1] occurs when a person intentionally or negligently takes part in or authorizes the communication of material.[2] Published material can include the written or spoken word, pictures and sounds,

---

[1] The term 'communication' is preferred in Scots law.
[2] Patrick Milmo and WVH Rogers, *Gatley on Libel and Slander* (10th edn, 2003) ('Gatley') para 6.3; John Fleming, *The Law of Torts* (9th edn, 1998) 594–5; Michael Gillooly, *The Law of Defamation in Australia and New Zealand* (1998) 75: material is published by every person who 'intentionally or negligently plays any role in the publication process'. A clear statement of this general rule appears in *Webb v Bloch* (1928) 41 CLR 331, 363–6.

or even conduct bearing some defamatory meaning.[3] Each person who publishes defamatory material is potentially liable.

Communication to a third party

5.02   In all parts of the United Kingdom and Australia, other than Scotland, material is published, for the purpose of civil defamation law, if it is communicated to some person other than the person defamed.[4] In Scotland, communication only to the defamed person is sufficient. In such a case, however, the defamed person may only recover an award of solatium; that is, damages for insult. Communication to a third party is required before damages for actual economic loss are recoverable.[5]

Outside Scotland, communication only to the defamed person may be sufficient where that person is under a duty to communicate the material to another, or where such communication is not out of the ordinary and should reasonably have been anticipated.[6] An example is the case of a trade union secretary who was defamed in a meeting requisition notice sent only to him, but which he was required to distribute to members of the committee by the rules of the union.[7] Another example might be where an employee is under a moral obligation in the course of a job interview to answer questions about the reasons for leaving his previous job, where to do so requires him to repeat a defamatory statement made only to him by his previous employer.[8] In such cases, however, a defence of qualified privilege will usually be available to the defendant, except where the claimant can prove that the defendant was actuated by malice.[9]

Publication in a form capable of being understood

5.03   For publication to occur, the person to whom material is communicated must be capable of understanding it. Material in a foreign language is not published,

---

[3] Gatley (n 2 above) paras 3.1–3.5; Fleming (n 2 above) 602. See also Defamation Act 1952 (UK), s 16(1); Defamation Act (Northern Ireland) 1955, s 14(1): 'Any reference in this Act to words shall be construed as including a reference to pictures, visual images, gestures and other methods of signifying meaning'; Defamation Act 1974 (NSW), s 9(1): 'matter' includes any 'report, article, letter, note, picture, oral utterance or other thing'.

[4] *Pullman v Walter Hill & Co, Ltd* [1891] 1 QB 524, 527, 529, 530; *Powell v Gelston* [1916] 2 KB 615, 619; *Jones v Amalgamated Television Services Pty Ltd* (1991) 23 NSWLR 364, 367; Defamation Act 1889 (Qld), s 5(2); Defamation Act 1957 (Tas), s 7.

[5] *Mackay v M'Cankie* (1883) 10 R 537; *Ramsay v MacLay & Co* (1890) 18 R 130.

[6] *Theaker v Richardson* [1962] 1 All ER 229, 238; *Collerton v MacLean* [1962] NZLR 1045, 1049; *Jones v Amalgamated Television Services Pty Ltd* (1991) 23 NSWLR 364, 368–70.

[7] *Collerton v MacLean* [1962] NZLR 1045, 1049–50.

[8] *Jones v Amalgamated Television Services Pty Ltd* (1991) 23 NSWLR 364, 368–70. In that case, Hunt J refused to strike out the plaintiff's statement of claim, noting that his case was 'arguable'.

[9] ibid, 371. The duty-interest form of qualified privilege is discussed in chapter 11.

for the purposes of defamation law, unless it is communicated to some person capable of understanding that language.[10]

Internet publications

Proof that Internet communications have been published is therefore not usually a difficult task. Every e-mail message which has been received and seen by a recipient, other than the person defamed, who is capable of understanding it, has been published. So too has every message posted on a bulletin board and every web page which is accessible to computer users, if it can be proved that any third person capable of understanding it has displayed and seen the message or web page on a computer screen.[11] The claimant bears the burden of proof. That burden will generally be discharged by proving that at least one person, other than the claimant, saw, read, or heard the communication. In the case of generally accessible web pages and bulletin boards with many subscribers, it may be inferred that publication has occurred.[12]

5.04

Where, however, an e-mail message has not been read by any person other than its author and the defamed person, or a web page, although technically accessible, has not been visited by any person other than its author and the defamed person, then publication will not have occurred, except in Scotland.

By analogy with the foreign language cases mentioned above,[13] the communication of defamatory Internet material in a non-readable form, such as computer code, will not ordinarily constitute publication. Publication only occurs where the material is in a form capable of being understood by humans, and is in fact read, seen, or heard by someone other than the defamed person.[14]

B. Unintentional Publication

General principles

Liability does not attach to unintentional publishers of defamatory material, unless the publication is a direct cause or a natural and probable consequence of

5.05

---

[10] *Jones v Davers* (1596) Cro Eliz 496; 78 ER 747; *Price v Jenkings* (1601) Cro Eliz 865; 78 ER 1091; Fleming (n 2 above) 593.

[11] See eg *Rindos v Hardwick* (Supreme Court of Western Australia, Ipp J, 31 March 1994).

[12] Publication of bulletin board postings was apparently inferred, for example, in *Godfrey v Demon Internet Ltd* [2001] QB 201.

[13] See para 5.03.

[14] Except in Scotland, where publication only to the defamed person, in a form capable of being understood by that person, suffices: see para 5.02.

their conduct or, in all the circumstances, they should reasonably have anticipated publication.[15]

5.06   A letter sent directly to the defamed person is not published merely because it is intercepted and read by a third person, unless it was reasonably foreseeable that it would have been opened and read by some such person.[16] The nature of the publication is, however, relevant; it has been held that it is reasonably foreseeable that defamatory material on a postcard to the defamed person will be read by third persons.[17]

Unauthorized interception of Internet material

Private e-mails

5.07   Internet communications will often be capable of being intercepted and read by third parties.[18] Whether such interception is reasonably foreseeable will be a question of fact. Interception of a defamatory e-mail, sent only to the defamed person, at a private, as opposed to a business, e-mail address, is probably no more foreseeable than interception of a sealed letter, sent only to the defamed person, at a private mailbox. The sheer volume of Internet communications makes it inherently unlikely that any given e-mail will be intercepted and read en route from sender to recipient. Furthermore, the unauthorized interception of e-mails may constitute a criminal offence.[19]

Business e-mails

5.08   The position may well be different with respect to business e-mails. Many businesses have policies to the effect that the proprietor or a nominee may monitor and read e-mails sent by or to staff. Such policies are common and well publicized. In many businesses, e-mails may be accessible not only by the addressee, but also by other persons authorized by the addressee, such as colleagues and assistants. It may therefore be reasonably foreseeable that e-mails sent to individuals at business addresses might be intercepted. If so, such e-mails

---

[15] *Weld-Blundell v Stephens* [1920] AC 956, 975–6, 983, 986–91; *Coulthard v South Australia* (1995) 63 SASR 531, 555–6.

[16] Such as a clerk: *Pullman v Walter Hill & Co, Ltd* [1891] 1 QB 524, 527 (Lord Esher MR): 'if the writer of a letter locks it up in his own desk, and a thief comes and breaks open the desk and takes away the letter and makes it [*sic*] contents known, I should say that would not be a publication'; *Powell v Gelston* [1916] 2 KB 615, 619 (Bray J): 'where to the defendant's knowledge a letter is likely to be opened by a clerk of the person to whom it is addressed the defendant is responsible for the publication to that clerk'.

[17] *Sadgrove v Hole* [1901] 2 KB 1, 5, 6.

[18] See para 2.24.

[19] Regulation of Investigatory Powers Act 2000 (UK), s 1; Telecommunications (Interception) Act 1979 (Cth), s 7.

are probably indistinguishable from letters sent to businesses where a clerk has been deputed to open them.[20]

Hackers

By contrast, the unauthorized interception and reading of e-mails by, for example, computer hackers, should not be treated as being reasonably foreseeable, just as it is not reasonably foreseeable that letters will be illicitly opened.[21] Again, the sheer volume of Internet communications favours this conclusion, as does the existence of legislation in both the United Kingdom and Australia prohibiting the interception of communications transmitted by means of telecommunications systems.[22]

5.09

C. Issues Arising out of Multiple Publications

Place and time of publication

Material is published at the time when, and in the place where, it is received. Each copy of a book or newspaper is thus a separate publication, as is each reception of a television or radio broadcast.[23] Each separate publication of the same material potentially gives rise to a distinct cause of action.[24]

5.10

---

[20] *Pullman v Walter Hill & Co, Ltd* [1891] 1 QB 524, 528 (Lord Esher MR): 'If the letter had been directed to the plaintiffs in their private capacity, in all probability it would not have been opened by a clerk. But mercantile firms and large tradesmen generally depute some clerk to open business letters addressed to them. The sender of the letter had put it out of his own control, and he had directed it in such a manner that it might possibly be opened by a clerk of the firm to which it was addressed.'

[21] *Pullman v Walter Hill & Co, Ltd* [1891] 1 QB 524, 527; *Powell v Gelston* [1916] 2 KB 615, 619–20.

[22] Regulation of Investigatory Powers Act 2000 (UK), s 1; Telecommunications (Interception) Act 1979 (Cth), s 7.

[23] Letters, newspaper articles, other written material: *Pullman v Walter Hill & Co, Ltd* [1891] 1 QB 524; *Hebditch v MacIlwaine* [1894] 2 QB 54, 61; *Joseph Evans & Sons v John G Stein & Company* 1904 12 SLT 462; *Lee v Wilson* (1934) 51 CLR 276, 287; *Bata v Bata* [1948] WN 366; *McLean v David Syme & Co Ltd* (1970) 72 SR (NSW) 513, 519–20, 528; *Shevill v Presse Alliance SA* [1995] 2 AC 18, 41; *Shevill v Presse Alliance SA* [1996] AC 959, 983. Radio and television broadcasts: *Jenner v Sun Oil Co Ltd* [1952] 2 DLR 526, 535–7 (radio broadcast originating in the United States published in Ontario where it was heard); *Gorton v Australian Broadcasting Commission* (1973) 1 ACTR 6, 7 (television broadcast published in each place where it is seen).

[24] *Pullman v Walter Hill & Co, Ltd* [1891] 1 QB 524, 527; *Webb v Bloch* (1928) 41 CLR 331, 363; *Gorton v Australian Broadcasting Commission* (1973) 1 ACTR 6, 7; *Berezovsky v Michaels* [2000] 2 All ER 986, 993; *Godfrey v Demon Internet Ltd* [2001] QB 201, 208–9; *Gutnick v Dow Jones & Co Inc* (2002) 210 CLR 575, paras 44, 64, 124; *Loutchansky v Times Newspapers Ltd (Nos 4 and 5)* [2002] QB 783, para 57.

In the United States, by contrast, a 'single publication' rule generally applies, so that only one cause of action may be brought in respect of all publications of the same material: see further para 13.22.

Arguments that different rules should apply to material published via the Internet, having regard to its global and geographically indeterminate nature, and the spectre of Internet publishers being exposed to the risk of defamation actions in every corner of the globe, have not found favour in England or Australia.[25] Each receipt of a defamatory e-mail message or bulletin board posting, and each display of a defamatory web page, is thus a separate publication, in respect of which a distinct cause of action potentially arises.[26]

In Figure A (page 18), Jack's e-mail message has passed through at least five, and up to seven, different computers on its route to Jill's computer. The message travelled as a series of IP datagrams. The message is unlikely to have been displayed and seen on all of the computers along the route, at least in a form capable of being understood by a human reader, except where some person has deliberately caused the message to be displayed in such a form.

The number of computers through which the message has passed is therefore not to the point; it is the number of computers on which the message has been displayed and seen that determines how many separate publications of the message have occurred.

Human agents might cause messages passing through computer networks within their control to be displayed for any number of reasons. Returning to the example, Jack's employer, the operator of Network A, might use a software screening program which scans messages for certain key words, and then notifies some nominated person that the message should be reviewed before being forwarded to a destination outside Network A. The operator of Jill's ISP, ISP D, might have configured its computer system so that some nominated person is notified of and can view, for example, any message from nominated computers, any message from a computer which exceeds a certain size, or any message which might carry a computer virus. In all of these cases, if the message is displayed and seen along the route from sender to recipient, it has been published, for the purposes of defamation law, to the person who sees the message.

---

[25] See esp *Loutchansky v Times Newspapers Ltd (Nos 4 and 5)* [2002] QB 783: adoption of an American-style single publication rule rejected (see also para 13.22); *Dow Jones & Co Inc v Gutnick* (2002) 210 CLR 575: single publication rule rejected (see para 13.22); location of web servers or uploading as determinant of the place of publication rejected.

[26] *Lee Teck Chee v Merrill Lynch International Bank Ltd* [1998] 4 CLJ 188 (Malayan High Court) (print and online editions of newspapers); *Godfrey v Demon Internet Ltd* [2001] QB 201, 208–9 (bulletin board postings); *Loutchansky v Times Newspapers Ltd (Nos 4 and 5)* [2002] QB 783 (online archives); *Dow Jones & Co Inc v Gutnick* (2002) 210 CLR 575 (subscription web site); *Harrods Ltd v Dow Jones & Co Inc* [2003] EWHC 1162, para 36 (web pages); *King v Lewis* [2004] EWHC 168, para 15; *King v Lewis* [2005] EMLR 4, para 2 (postings published when downloaded).

Estimating the number of publications

Determining how many people might have displayed and seen an Internet 5.11
publication on a computer screen will often be difficult, just as it is difficult to
know how many people have read a particular edition of a newspaper, or seen a
particular television programme. In cases of mass publication involving the
broadcast or print media, it is usually possible to estimate the number of viewers
or readers by adducing evidence of the audience reach and average ratings for a
radio or television programme, or the number of copies of a newspaper or book
printed and in circulation.

Various tools may be available to estimate the approximate number of persons
who might have displayed and seen a particular Internet publication. E-mail
messages have a finite number of original addressees; laborious investigations
through the addressees themselves, or perhaps the ISPs of the addressees, may
yield information about the extent to which the message has been published.
Bulletin board postings will usually have a primary audience reach of the number of subscribers to the bulletin board, which might be able to be ascertained
from the bulletin board operator or operators. Internet content hosts will usually have the technical ability to identify how many 'hits' a particular web page
has had, or to identify the IP address of each Internet user who has visited the
page and the time spent by each such user browsing the page.[27] It will thus often
be possible to develop a sophisticated profile of the extent to which particular
Internet content has been published. In the context of defamation proceedings,
a claimant might need to seek this information by the use of procedural tools
such as disclosure (discovery),[28] pre-action disclosure,[29] non-party disclosure,[30]
witness summonses (subpoenas),[31] and further information (interrogatories).[32]

Web sites with multiple pages

In *Buddhist Society of Western Australia Inc v Bristile Ltd*,[33] a Full Court of the 5.12
Western Australian Supreme Court held that separate letters and other material
on the same web site constitute separate publications, at least where the constituent parts of the web site have a different 'substantive identity', form, and
purpose.[34] The court also noted that in its 'electronic existence', each part of the

---

[27] The number of 'hits' might not be the same as the number of persons who have seen the web
page, however. A separate hit will be recorded each time a person accesses the web page, even if he
or she has accessed the same page previously.
[28] In England, see Civil Procedure Rules, Pt 31.
[29] ibid, r 31.16.
[30] ibid, r 31.17.
[31] ibid, Pt 34.
[32] ibid, Pt 18 and r 53.3.
[33] [2000] WASCA 210.
[34] ibid, para 10.

web site was a separate file.[35] It appears, therefore, that each web page on a site will ordinarily constitute a separate publication. Where the constituent parts do not have a distinct substantive identity, as (perhaps) in the case of a 'headline' connected by hyperlink to a separate web page containing the text of an article, however, it may be arguable that the two web pages form part of the same publication.

The defendant in the *Buddhist Society* case had pleaded, in respect of the whole of the material on its web site, the Australian expanded qualified privilege defence for the discussion of government and political matters ('the *Lange* defence').[36] The Full Court upheld the decision of the judge at first instance to strike out that part of the defendant's defence. The *Lange* defence could not succeed in respect of the whole web site, because one of the letters on the web site clearly had nothing to do with the discussion of government and political matters. The effect of the court's decision is that defendants in such cases must plead separate defences to each separate publication making up a web site.

Defamation proceedings

5.13   At common law, subject to issues of jurisdiction and choice of law,[37] a defamed person may sue in respect of all claims arising out of the same defamatory material in the one proceeding.[38] It will ordinarily be an abuse of process to issue more than one proceeding in respect of different publications of the same defamatory material.[39]

D. Publishers

General principles

5.14   At common law, persons who intentionally or negligently take part in or author-ize the publication of defamatory material are potentially as responsible for publication as if they were the original author.[40] Where more than one person

---

[35] ibid.

[36] ie the defence established by the High Court in *Lange v Australian Broadcasting Corporation* (1997) 189 CLR 520: see paras 11.22–11.26.

[37] See chapters 25–29.

[38] Gatley (n 2 above) para 6.2; *Meckiff v Simpson* [1968] VR 62, 63–4, 69; *McLean v David Syme & Co Ltd* (1970) 72 SR (NSW) 513, 519–21, 528; *Dow Jones & Co Inc v Gutnick* (2002) 210 CLR 575, para 36 (Gleeson CJ, McHugh, Gummow, and Hayne JJ).

[39] ibid. This principle is reflected in legislation in New South Wales: Defamation Act 1974 (NSW), s 9(3).

[40] For a useful discussion of this general principle, see *Webb v Bloch* (1928) 41 CLR 331, 363–6.

takes part in or authorizes the publication, each person is liable for the whole of the damage caused to the claimant.[41]

In non-Internet contexts, liability has been extended beyond the authors of defamatory material to all those who composed the material, editors, media proprietors, and printers. Such persons can be said to have taken part in or authorized publication to the extent necessary for legal liability. Liability is not excused by the fact that the publisher has merely passed on or permitted the publication of defamatory material without endorsement.[42]

The Internet

Liability would clearly extend in an Internet context to persons who played **5.15** some part in the creation or preparation of defamatory material by, for example, editing or otherwise contributing to the content of the material, or the uploading of the content.[43] Operators of bulletin boards who edit messages before they are posted are one obvious example. Such persons will need to rely on a defence if they are to avoid liability for the consequences of a defamatory publication for which they are responsible as publishers.

Intermediaries. More difficult, however, is whether intermediaries of Internet **5.16** publications, who play no part in the creation or preparation of defamatory material, but are involved in making that material available to Internet users, might be considered publishers of that material. That matter will be addressed in chapter 15.

Republication, linking, and framing. Another difficult question is the extent **5.17** to which liability might attach in cases where Internet material is republished or repeated, or where material is only published as a result of 'linking' and 'framing'.

E. Republication and Repetition

General principles

At common law, each republication of defamatory material gives rise to a new **5.18** cause of action.[44] Where it is intended or known that published material will be

---

[41] *London Association for Protection of Trade v Greenlands Ltd* [1916] 2 AC 15, 31; *Broome v Cassell & Co Ltd* [1972] AC 1027, 1063–4; *Bryanston Finance Ltd v de Vries* [1975] QB 703, 730–1; *XL Petroleum (NSW) Pty Ltd v Caltex Oil (Australia) Pty Ltd* (1985) 155 CLR 448, 459–60, 466. Publishers may, however, seek contribution against each other: see paras 21.21–21.24.
[42] *Truth (NZ) Ltd v Holloway* [1960] 1 WLR 997 (PC), 1002–3.
[43] See eg *Ezzo v Grille* [2004] NSWSC 522.
[44] See eg *Buchanan v Jennings* [2004] EMLR 22, para 12.

conveyed to persons other than its original recipients, the original publisher will be liable for the damage caused by all such further publications.[45] So too where the recipient of the original publication is under a moral duty to repeat it, or where the repetition is a natural and probable consequence of the original publication, as where a person gives an interview to a media organization.[46] The person responsible for conveying the defamatory material further will also be liable as an original publisher, subject to the availability of a defence.[47] The original publisher of defamatory material will not, however, be liable for the republication of the material if the republication is too remote or constitutes a *novus actus interveniens* breaking the chain of causation between the original publication and the damage suffered by reason of the republication.[48]

The review cases

5.19   The application of these principles to the repetition or republication of Internet material can best be explored by considering first two cases involving somewhat similar facts. In *Slipper v British Broadcasting Corporation*,[49] the plaintiff claimed that he was defamed in a television programme produced and broadcast by the defendant. After it was broadcast, the programme was extensively reviewed in a number of national newspapers. The issue was whether the defendant could be held liable for the repetition of the allegedly defamatory statements in the subsequent newspaper reviews. The Court of Appeal held that the question was one which should be put to the jury.

The court held that the potential liability of the original publisher in respect of repetitions of the allegedly defamatory material in the newspaper reviews

---

[45] On the compatibility of this principle with the right to freedom of expression in Art 10 of the European Convention on Human Rights, see para 30.44.

[46] *Speight v Gosnay* (1891) 60 LJQB 231, 232; *Ratcliffe v Evans* [1892] 2 QB 524, 530; *Sims v Wran* [1984] 1 NSWLR 317, 320; *Slipper v British Broadcasting Corporation* [1991] 1 QB 283; *Selecta Homes and Building Co Pty Ltd v Advertiser-News Weekend Publishing Co Pty Ltd* [2001] SASC 140, paras 94–7, 175; *McManus v Beckham* [2002] EMLR 40. In the latter case, Laws LJ described the 'natural and probable cause' formula as 'inapt even as a figurative description of the relationship that needs to be shown between D's slander and the further publication if D is to be held liable for the latter'. Laws LJ went on to say that the test is one of foreseeability: D will be responsible for the consequences of a further publication if he or she foresaw, or ought reasonably to have foreseen, that the further publication would probably take place: ibid, 900; cf *Palmer Bruyn & Parker Pty Ltd v Parsons* (2001) 208 CLR 388, paras 63–80.

[47] *Truth (NZ) Ltd v Holloway* [1960] 1 WLR 997 (PC) 1002–3; *Stern v Piper* [1997] QB 123, 128–30, 137; *Wake v John Fairfax & Sons Ltd* [1973] 1 NSWLR 43, 50; *Selecta Homes and Building Co Pty Ltd v Advertiser-News Weekend Publishing Co Pty Ltd* [2001] SASC 140, paras 96, 175.

[48] *Ward v Weeks* (1830) 7 Bing 211; *Weld-Blundell v Stephens* [1920] AC 956; *Shendish Manor Ltd v Coleman* [2001] EWCA Civ 913, paras 47–50. See also *Campbell v News Group Newspapers Ltd* [2002] EMLR 43, 977.

[49] [1991] 1 QB 283.

depended on ordinary tortious principles of causation and remoteness of damage.[50] Stocker LJ expressed the questions raised as follows:

> (i) Did the reviews reproduce the sting of the libel? This is a question of fact for the jury. (ii) Did the defendants invite such reviews? The answer to this question depends upon the facts concerning all the circumstances in which the preview was given to the press and, again, is a matter of fact for the jury. (iii) Did the defendants anticipate that such reviews would repeat the sting of the libel? It is at this point that the issue of natural and probable consequence or foreseeability arises.[51]

Similar issues fell for consideration in *Williams v John Fairfax Group Pty Ltd.*[52] The case concerned whether the publisher of a newspaper could be held liable in respect of the damage caused when a defamatory restaurant review which had appeared in the newspaper was read out by a radio announcer. The plaintiffs argued that the repetition of the review on the radio was a natural and probable consequence of its original publication, having regard to the notoriety of the reviewer and the manner in which the review had been written.[53] Hunt J of the New South Wales Supreme Court refused a strike-out application by the defendants, holding that it was open to the jury to conclude, applying normal tortious principles of causation and remoteness,[54] that the repetition of the review by the radio announcer was a natural and probable consequence of its original publication. Hunt J said:

5.20

> Not all articles published in the newspaper are to be considered in the same way. The report of the usually fatuous remarks made by a visiting US television 'celebrity' would in most cases be unlikely to be repeated. On the other hand, I would think that repetition of the sting of a published exposé would clearly be foreseeable. It is not infrequently that newspapers claim responsibility for having first raised matters which have subsequently become publicly debated issues . . .
>
> In my view, it would arguably be open to a jury to find that the repetition of the matter complained of in the present case, as originally published, was foreseeable. That is the very purpose of a restaurant review: if one person suggests to another that they attend the plaintiffs' restaurant, it is obviously foreseeable that the second will refer to and repeat the sting of the newspaper review as a consideration to be taken into account in the decision to be made . . .
>
> [The radio announcer's] comments may . . . be considered a review of . . . the

---

[50] ibid, 296–7, 299–301, 301–2.

[51] ibid, 296.

[52] [1991] Aust Defamation Reports ¶51,035.

[53] The review was by a prominent Sydney restaurant reviewer and was particularly scathing. The reviewer described the meal as the 'most bizarre' he had ever had in a restaurant. He described a member of the restaurant staff as a 'soap addict smoking couch potato' and related how two pink lorikeets had escaped from a birdcage and dive-bombed his table during the meal. He described a mural displayed in the restaurant as being of 'singular awfulness'. Before reading the review on air, the radio announcer described it as one of the reviewer's 'famous, or shall we say notorious, dump jobs on a restaurant'.

[54] *Williams v John Fairfax Group Pty Ltd* [1991] Aust Defamation Reports ¶51,035, 42,090–1.

restaurant review. In my opinion, it would arguably be open to a jury to conclude that such a review was the very kind of thing which was likely to happen as a result of the original publication. It was the manner in which the second defendant wrote his restaurant review, and perhaps also his notoriety as a restaurant critic, that arguably generated the very risk that people would talk about what he had written and the way in which he goes about reviewing restaurants.[55]

Republication of Internet material

5.21   Internet publications are easily republished to a wide and geographically diverse audience. Some publications are, by their nature, likely to be republished. Most Internet users will know how frequently this occurs, whether the communication be some topical joke, workplace gossip, or important information. In one notorious incident, a British lawyer forwarded an e-mail message from his girl-friend to six of his friends, as a means of gloating about his apparent sexual prowess. Within days the e-mail had circulated the globe and had been forwarded to millions of people.[56]

The forwarding of e-mail messages or bulletin board postings is the most common way in which material is republished via the Internet. Another common way in which republication occurs is by 'cutting and pasting' material from a web page, e-mail message, or bulletin board posting and then forwarding it to others.

5.22   As a general rule, it can probably be safely assumed that the more salacious the material, the more likely it is that it will be republished. Further, the very purpose of publishing material on a web page, or in a bulletin board posting, will often be to reach a wide and geographically diverse audience. It seems likely therefore that in many cases republication will be a natural and probable consequence of the original publication of material via the Internet. Republication will also often be foreseeable in the case of e-mail messages. One would think, for example, that republication was a perfectly natural and probable consequence in the case of the vainglorious lawyer just discussed.

As the review cases suggest, however, each case will turn on its own facts. The state of mind of the original author will be a relevant factor, as will the objective nature of the original material. Contribution rights as between the original author and the party republishing the material may also be a common feature in such cases.[57]

5.23   Having regard to normal tortious principles of causation and remoteness, it

---

[55] ibid, 42,091–2.
[56] Sam Lister, 'Lover in Trouble over Mail Ego', *The Times* (London, UK) 15 December 2000.
[57] See paras 21.21–21.24.

would seem likely that various steps could be taken by persons who publish defamatory material via the Internet to limit potential exposure to liability in respect of republications. Some e-mail programs, for example, have a function which enables the user to prevent an outgoing message from being copied and forwarded by recipients. Such functions are probably effective in most cases in preventing the republication of e-mail messages; recipients who attempt to forward such messages will be prevented by their computer from doing so. Such functions are not, however, perfect; depending on the particular e-mail program used, there might be nothing to prevent the recipient from printing a hard copy of the message and distributing it further in that form, or from copying the text into a new e-mail message and then sending it on to further recipients.

Whether the use of a function which is intended to prevent the republication of e-mail messages is sufficient to prevent an original publisher from being liable for unauthorized republication will be a question of fact. Evidence of the use of such a function would seem to be compelling evidence in most cases that the original publisher did not intend or know that the message would be republished. It is likely that republication in such cases is not a natural and probable consequence of the original publication.

F. Linking and Framing

Introduction

Different questions arise where material comes to be published by reason of **5.24** linking or framing.[58] Suppose a web page, which does not contain any defamatory material, contains a hyperlink to another web page which does contain defamatory material. The defamatory material will be published to all people who visit the first web page and follow the hyperlink to the second web page. The potential liability in such cases of both the original author and the linking party does not appear to have been the subject of any reported cases.

Hyperlinks are the synapses connecting different parts of the world wide web. Without hyperlinks, the web would be like a library without a catalogue: full of information, but with no sure means of finding it.

Almost every web page contains hyperlinked information, so that content is endlessly connected to other content. The usefulness of hyperlinks reaches its zenith in search engines, which generate lists of hyperlinks to web pages on related topics all around the web in a fraction of a second.

---

[58] For an explanation of these terms, see para 2.43.

Another feature of hyperlinks is their ability to elevate the obscure to the notorious in a remarkably short period of time. Many people have personal web sites that have never been seen by anyone other than themselves and their families. But if a popular web site were to include a link to such a site, the site might suddenly receive a vast number of hits from Internet users all around the world.

Liability of the linking or framing party

General principles

5.25 It seems likely that people who link defamatory content to or frame defamatory content on their web pages would be treated as 'publishers' of that material for the purposes of defamation law generally where and to the extent that publications occur by reason of people following the link or viewing the content through the frame. The linking or framing party has taken part in or authorized the publication of the defamatory material to those people who have followed the link or viewed the content through the frame.[59] In principle, this conclusion should hold even where the content of the linked or framed material has changed since the time the link was created. Liability is more likely to turn on whether the linking or framing party can establish a defence than on a negation of publication. If the linking or framing content contains material which operates as an 'antidote' to the defamatory 'bane' of the linked or framed page, it may be that the publication as a whole is deprived of its defamatory meaning.[60]

Whether, in the United Kingdom, linking or framing parties who do not know and have no reason to believe that by linking to or framing another's web page they have caused or contributed to the publication of a defamatory statement might be able to avail themselves of the defence in section 1 of the Defamation Act 1996 is discussed in chapter 16.[61]

Liability of the original author

5.26 At common law, the authors of defamatory web pages are likely to be publishers of the additional publications resulting from people following links from third-party web pages or viewing the defamatory material through a frame on third-

---

[59] *Truth (NZ) Ltd v Holloway* [1960] 1 WLR 997 (PC) 1002–3; *Stern v Piper* [1997] QB 123, 128–30, 137; *Wake v John Fairfax & Sons Ltd* [1973] 1 NSWLR 43, 50; but cf *Carter v British Columbia Federation of Foster Parents Association* (2004) BCLR (4th) 123, paras 51–9 (British Columbia Supreme Court).

[60] See paras 7.13–7.17.

[61] See paras 16.20–16.21. The common law defence of innocent dissemination is unlikely to be available in such cases, because the linking party will not satisfy the definition of a 'subordinate distributor': see para 18.03 and *Thompson v Australian Capital Television Pty Ltd* (1996) 186 CLR 574, discussed in detail in chapter 18 (see especially paras 18.16 and 18.18).

party web pages. There do not appear, however, to be any authorities in any jurisdiction on this subject.

There may be scope in the United Kingdom for arguing, in an appropriate case, that holding an author of defamatory material liable for unintended publications occurring solely as a result of a third party linking to or framing the material without the authority of the author, is incompatible with the right to freedom of expression in Article 10 of the European Convention on Human Rights.[62]

Ordinary linking cases

The principles governing republication and repetition[63] are not directly analo- **5.27**
gous to linking cases. Internet users who follow ordinary links are transported to the original author's web page. That page is then published to them, in the form intended by the original author. The person who has provided the ordinary link has not repeated the defamation in the same way as the person who reviews a television programme[64] or repeats a restaurant review.[65] Properly understood, ordinary linking cases do not involve the repetition or republication of material: the link is merely the route by which the Internet user comes to visit the web page in the first place.

Framing cases

Although the technology is more complicated, it seems most likely that the **5.28**
same position obtains in relation to framed content. Where material is framed, the framed content is composed and displayed on the user's screen directly; that is, the user's computer is directed by the framing site to download content from both the framing and the framed sites, and the user's screen then simultaneously displays the content from both sites. The Internet user is simultaneously connected to both the framing page and the framed page.[66]

See para 30.44.
[63] See paras 5.18–5.23.
[64] *Slipper v British Broadcasting Corporation* [1991] 1 QB 283.
[65] *Williams v John Fairfax Group Pty Ltd* [1991] Aust Defamation Reports ¶51,035.
[66] See eg Edward Cavazos and Coe Miles, 'Copyright on the WWW: Linking and Liability' (1997) 4 Richmond Journal of Law and Technology 3; Matt Jackson, 'Linking Copyright to Homepages' (1997) 49 Federal Communications Law Journal 731; Maureen O'Rourke, 'Fencing Cyberspace: Drawing Borders in a Virtual World' (1998) 82 Minnesota Law Review 609; cf *Futuredontics, Inc v Applied Anagramics, Inc* (9th cir, 23 July 1998), a copyright case in which the defendant argued that a frame is like a lens which enables Internet users to view the material on the framed site. The plaintiff, on the other hand, argued that framing involved the creation of a derivative work; that is, a reproduction of content from the plaintiff's web page, combined with a frame created by the defendant. The court held that it was not able to determine which view was correct.

Analysis

5.29   A better analogy for linking and framing cases is that of the publisher of a defamatory television programme which attracts more viewers than usual because of an advance newspaper review. Although there do not appear to be any authorities on the point, in such a case, the publisher of the programme would clearly be liable in respect of all publications of the programme, including additional publications which would not have occurred but for the newspaper review. By broadcasting a defamatory television programme, the publisher has no means of knowing or controlling how many people will tune in, and can scarcely complain that the programme has been more widely received than expected.

5.30   By analogy, in most linking and framing cases, the author of a defamatory web page will be liable in respect of all publications of that page, including additional publications which occurred only because of the inclusion of the hyperlink or frame on another person's web page. As with a television broadcast, a person who publishes material on an ordinary web page does not know and cannot control the extent of publication. Such a person must accept the risk that the material may reach a wide and geographically diverse audience by reason of others establishing links from or inserting frames on their own web pages. While linking and framing may give rise to legitimate claims for infringement of intellectual property rights or other causes of action, it is difficult to see why additional publications arising out of people linking to a web page or viewing a web page through a frame should not be treated as publications by the original author for the purposes of defamation law.[67]

Limiting liability

5.31   Web page owners can take steps to prevent others from effectively linking to or framing their sites through the use of encryption technology which prevents the site from being accessible to unauthorized persons. Web sites to which people subscribe and are allocated passwords are examples of sites to which links or frames will not generally be effective.

It may also be that if the owner of a web page had expressly purported to prohibit others from linking to or framing particular defamatory content, it could be argued that any publications arising out of a prohibited link or frame might amount to unintentional publication.[68] Such an argument would appear to stand uncertain prospects of success.[69]

---

[67] Provided that this outcome does not violate Art 10 of the European Convention on Human Rights: see para 30.44.
[68] See paras 5.05–5.09.
[69] See n 16 above.

Finally, there may also be scope for arguments about contribution in cases where the vast majority of publications come about by reason of Internet users following a hyperlink.[70]

Alternative analysis

If the above analysis is incorrect, and the proper analogy in cases involving defamatory linked or framed content is that of republication or repetition,[71] then it could surely be argued that any person who establishes a web site impliedly invites and authorizes other Internet users to establish a link from their own web sites, provided that to do so does not infringe any legal rights, such as intellectual property or fair trading rights. Hyperlinks are a fundamental part of the infrastructure of the web. They are the means by which web pages are indexed and organized. Without them, the usefulness of the web would be significantly diminished.[72] In many, if not most cases, the establishment of links to defamatory material on the web is entirely foreseeable. At the same time, on this analysis, it may be that Internet users could limit their potential liability for additional publications of defamatory material by discouraging or prohibiting others from establishing links to their web pages. The use of encryption technologies, or a clear statement to the effect that others may not link to or frame a particular web page, might be appropriate means of limiting potential exposure.

5.32

G. Tracing the Source of a Defamatory Publication

The allure of anonymity

Internet users can, if they so desire, publish defamatory material to the world at large with little or no risk of being identified or traced. Web-based services enable e-mail accounts to be freely opened in false names or 'noms de web'. Material can be posted anonymously to bulletin boards or web sites from Internet cafés, where users pay a small fee for access to a computer which cannot be traced back to them. Many companies, particularly in the United States, offer web hosting services, which enable Internet users to establish and maintain web sites without having to disclose their true names or addresses.

5.33

Even where it is possible to identify the author of defamatory material, he or she may be a person of straw, wholly unable to meet and unlikely to comply with an adverse defamation judgment.

---

[70] See paras 21.21–21.24.
[71] See paras 5.18–5.23.
[72] See paras 2.42, 3.11.

In these circumstances, it is little wonder that defamed persons look to hold Internet intermediaries liable for material hosted, cached, or carried by them. The intermediary may offer the best hope of having the offending material removed from the Internet. The intermediary may be the only deep pocket worth suing. In other words, the intermediary may be the only available and viable defendant.

Tracing protocols

5.34 While it is possible for Internet users to take steps to secure their anonymity, for most ordinary users, the greater problem arising out of Internet use is an absence of privacy. In the vast majority of cases, Internet users send e-mails, post bulletin board messages, or upload material to web sites from traceable computers. Each computer connected to the Internet has a unique numeric address.[73] That numeric address will be attached to each message sent from a particular computer. In the case of Internet users who gain access to the Internet via a commercial ISP, the ISP will generally have the technical ability to monitor how each subscriber uses the Internet, and to trace any given communication back to the computer from which it was sent. In the case of Internet users who are connected to the Internet via an employer's computer system, tracing is likely to be even easier. Legislation such as the Data Protection Act 1998 (UK) and the Privacy Act 1988 (Cth) offer some limited protection against invasions of privacy.[74]

5.35 Some associations of Internet intermediaries have published protocols dealing with the traceability of illegal conduct on the Internet. The London Internet Exchange, LINX, for example, has published a 'Best Current Practice' protocol.[75] Adherence to that protocol would in many instances enable persons who use the Internet for unlawful purposes to be identified. While acknowledging the importance of respecting the privacy of Internet users, the policy underlying the protocol is to enable 'misuse, once detected, to be rooted out'. The protocol seems to assume that Internet intermediaries should monitor the activities of their subscribers for the purpose of dealing with, among other things, 'unsolicited bulk messaging' (spam), 'hacking', 'scams', and 'frauds'. The protocol does not deal explicitly with the circumstances in which Internet intermediaries would be justified in disclosing the identity of their subscribers to third parties. It makes no mention of monitoring Internet use for defamatory publications, and contains no recommendations as to what should happen if defamatory publications are detected.

---

[73] See para 2.19.
[74] See para 24.06–24.10.
[75] <http://www.linx.net/noncore/bcp/traceability-bcp.html>.

Compelling intermediaries to disclose the identity of their subscribers

Norwich Pharmacal proceedings

In *Norwich Pharmacal Co v Commissioners of Customs and Excise*,[76] the House of **5.36**
Lords held that in certain circumstances an independent action for discovery
(disclosure) may be brought against a person for the purpose of obtaining
information about the identity of a wrongdoer. *Norwich Pharmacal* proceedings
will only lie where the person against whom discovery is sought has in some way
facilitated the wrongdoing, and where the discovery is necessary to enable the
wrongdoer to be identified.[77] The applicant need not have a maintainable cause
of action against the person from whom discovery is sought.[78] An order for
discovery might, however, be declined in the interests of justice where, for
example, discovery would involve divulging a third party's secret or confidential
information, or breaching a statutory prohibition. Ordinarily, the costs of the
Norwich Pharmacal proceedings are borne by the applicant.[79]

The circumstances in which proceedings may be brought to identify a defendant have been prescribed in some Australian States and Territories.[80]

Totalise Plc v Motley Fool Ltd

Norwich Pharmacal proceedings were issued against two Internet intermediaries **5.37**
as a means of uncovering the identity of the anonymous author of defamatory
bulletin board postings in *Totalise Plc v Motley Fool Ltd*.[81] In that case, the
claimant sought an order against two defendants to compel them to disclose all
material in their possession which might lead to the identification of 'Zeddust',
an anonymous contributor of defamatory material of and concerning the claimant to bulletin boards hosted by the defendants. The defendants had refused the
claimant's request that they provide any material which might identify Zeddust,
on the basis that compliance with the claimant's request would contravene the
Data Protection Act 1998 (UK). One of the defendants also refused to comply
with the claimant's request in reliance on its terms and conditions, which

---

[76] [1974] AC 133.
[77] ibid, 175, 188, 195–7, 205–6.
[78] ibid.
[79] ibid, 176, 190, 199, 207. The circumstances in which *Norwich Pharmacal* proceedings may
be brought in England are not affected by the Civil Procedure Rules: see r 31.18. The pre-action
disclosure provisions of the Civil Procedure Rules are only available if, among other things 'the
respondent is likely to be a party to subsequent proceedings': ibid, r 31.16(3)(a).
[80] Supreme Court Rules 1970 (NSW), Pt 3, r 1; Supreme Court (General Civil Procedure)
Rules 1996 (Vic), r 32.03; Rules of the Supreme Court 1971 (WA), O 26A, r 3; Supreme Court
Rules 1937 (ACT), O 34A, r 3; Supreme Court Rules (NT), r 32.03. There are no equivalent
rules in Queensland, South Australia, or Tasmania, but it is clear that *Norwich Pharmacal* proceedings may be issued in those States: see eg *Re Pyne* [1997] 1 Qd R 326.
[81] [2001] EMLR 29; appeal on the question of costs successful [2002] EMLR 20.

guaranteed to protect the privacy of its subscribers. In addition to those arguments, at the hearing the defendants sought to rely on section 10 of the Contempt of Court Act 1981, which provides that courts may not require a person to disclose 'the source of information contained in a publication for which he is responsible, unless it be established to the satisfaction of the court that disclosure is necessary in the interests of justice or national security or for the prevention of disorder or crime'.

Owen J of the English High Court granted the relief sought, observing that to do otherwise 'would be to give the clearest indication to those who wish to defame that they can do so with impunity behind the screen of anonymity made possible by the use of web sites on the Internet'. Owen J ordered the defendants to pay the claimant's costs, on the basis that 'it was perfectly plain from the outset that the postings on both web sites were highly defamatory and that, accordingly, the claimant was the victim of a sustained campaign amounting to an actionable tort'.

5.38 One of the defendants, Interactive Investor Ltd, appealed on the question of costs. The Court of Appeal allowed the appeal, observing that:

> *Norwich Pharmacal* applications are not ordinary adversarial proceedings, where the general rule is that the unsuccessful party pays the costs of the successful party. They are akin to proceedings for pre-action disclosure where costs are governed by Part 48.3 CPR. That rule, we believe, reflects the just outcome and is consistent with the views of Lord Reid and Lord Cross in the *Norwich Pharmacal* case. In general, the costs incurred should be recovered from the wrongdoer rather than from an innocent party. That should be the result, even if such a party writes a letter to the applicant asking him to draw to the court's attention matters which might influence a court to refuse the application. Of course such a letter would need to be drawn to the attention of the court. Each case will depend on its facts and in some cases it may be appropriate for the party from whom disclosure is sought to appear in court to assist. In such a case he should not be prejudiced by being ordered to pay costs.[82]

The court concluded that ordinarily in *Norwich Pharmacal* applications, the applicant should be ordered to pay the costs of the party making the disclosure, including the costs of making the disclosure. The court said that there may be cases where the circumstances require a different order, but they do not include cases where:

- the party required to make the disclosure had a genuine doubt that the person seeking the disclosure was entitled to it;
- the party was under an appropriate legal obligation not to reveal the

---

[82] [2002] EMLR 20, para 29.

information, or where the legal position was not clear, or the party had a reasonable doubt as to the obligation;

- the party could be subject to proceedings if disclosure was voluntary;
- the party would or might suffer damage by voluntarily giving the disclosure; or
- the disclosure would or might infringe a legitimate interest of another.[83]

The court was satisfied that it was appropriate for Interactive to have declined to comply with the claimant's request in the absence of a court order, noting that the claimant's application was by no means assured of success. A judge might have refused disclosure of the identity of the author of the postings on the ground that they 'were visibly the product of a deranged mind or were so obviously designed merely to insult as not to carry a realistic risk of doing the claimant quantifiable harm'.[84] The court went on:

> We also believe that it is legitimate for a party, such as Interactive, who reasonably agrees to keep information confidential and private to refuse to voluntarily hand over such information. That we believe was applicable to this case . . . The position could have been different, if they were in some way implicated or involved in the wrongful act.[85]

Other means of ascertaining the author of a defamatory Internet publication

United Kingdom and Australia

Other means of ascertaining the author of defamatory Internet publications **5.39** have been adopted in cases in both the United Kingdom and Australia. *Takenaka (UK) Ltd v Frankl*,[86] for example, was a case involving various e-mail messages defamatory of the claimants which had been sent under the false name 'Christina Realtor' using a Hotmail address. After 'months and expensive litigation', involving *Norwich Pharmacal* proceedings against various ISPs and Hotmail, the claimants tracked down the defendant as the likely author of the e-mail messages. The defendant denied having written the e-mails. The parties agreed to submit a computer to which the defendant had had access to an expert for examination.[87] The expert produced a lengthy report which concluded that, on the balance of probabilities, the defendant had sent the offending e-mail messages. The expert found traces of the Christina Realtor e-mails in the computer. He also noted that the defendant had sent e-mail messages under his own name from the computer a matter of minutes before or after each of the offend-

---

[83] ibid, para 30.
[84] ibid, para 27.
[85] ibid, para 28.
[86] English High Court, 11 October 2000, Alliott J.
[87] See Civil Procedure Rules, r 35.7.

ing messages had been sent. Alliott J of the English High Court accepted the expert's report and entered judgment for the claimants. The Court of Appeal refused to grant leave to appeal.[88]

5.40   Yet another approach was taken in the Western Australian case *Resolute Ltd v Warnes*.[89] The applicants sought to identify the author of defamatory statements on a web page apparently maintained by a group known as the 'Preston shareholder action group'. Proceedings were brought against the defendant, who had been identified in a newspaper report and in unrelated court proceedings as a member or representative of that group. The applicants sought an order that the defendant attend before the court for the purpose of being examined in relation to the identity of the author of the defamatory statements, as well as an order that the defendant give discovery of documents relating to the author's identity.[90] Templeman J granted the relief sought by the applicants.

United States

5.41   A different mechanism has been used to achieve substantially the same result in the United States; namely the commencement of proceedings against a 'John Doe' defendant—being the anonymous author of defamatory material posted on a bulletin board or web page—followed by issuing a subpoena against the relevant intermediary to obtain material which uncovers John Doe's identity.[91]

There are, however, limits on John Doe proceedings. In one notable case, the plaintiff commenced proceedings anonymously against five unknown defendants. The plaintiff claimed the unknown defendants had made defamatory and disparaging misrepresentations about it in Internet chat rooms. After commencing the proceedings, the plaintiff sought to subpoena America Online, Inc with a view to forcing it to reveal the identity of the unknown defendants. The Supreme Court of Virginia refused to allow the plaintiff to do so anonymously.[92]

More recently, in *Melvin v Doe*, the Supreme Court of Pennsylvania held that, subject to certain limits, the First Amendment to the United States' Constitu-

---

[88] For a more orthodox example of how a claimant can establish that a defendant was the author of anonymous postings, see *Vaquero Energy Ltd v Weir* (2004) 352 AR 191 (Alberta Court of Queen's Bench).

[89] [2000] WASC 35.

[90] Under the Rules of the Supreme Court 1971 (WA), O 26A, r 3.

[91] There are many examples, including *Xircom, Inc v Doe* (SC Ca, 14 June 1999); *Hvide v Doe* (Third District Court of Appeals, Florida, 16 October 2000); *America Online, Inc v Nam Tai Electronics, Inc*, 571 SE 2d 128 (SC Va, 2002) (Californian order for out-of-state discovery in a John Doe case enforceable in Virginia).

[92] See *America Online, Inc v Anonymous Publicly Traded Company*, 542 SE 2d 377 (SC Va, 2001).

tion guarantees a right to engage in anonymous political speech, and that an order compelling anonymous defendants to identify themselves may trespass on that right.[93] In another case, an appellate court in New Jersey held that a plaintiff was not entitled to an order which would lead to uncovering the identity of an anonymous defendant who had made nine allegedly defamatory postings without first establishing that actual harm resulted from the postings.[94]

The bringing of John Doe proceedings may be purely symbolic. Plaintiffs may choose to commence such proceedings so as to obtain some collateral benefit by being seen to respond to damaging material posted anonymously on bulletin boards or on web pages. In one instance, a company issued proceedings against more than one hundred defendants, identifying only one by name.[95] The mere fact of bringing the action may have the effect of silencing critics and quelling rumours.[96]

---

[93] 575 A 2d 42 (SC Pa, 2003). The court held that an order to uncover the identity of the anonymous defendants should not be made without considering whether the First Amendment required the plaintiff—in that case, a judge—to establish a prima facie case of actual economic harm.

[94] *Dendrite International, Inc v Joe Doe, No 3*, 775 A 2d 756 (SC NJ, 2001).

[95] See the discussion in Lyrissa Lidsky, 'Silencing John Doe: Defamation and Discourse in Cyberspace' (2000) 49 Duke Law Journal 855, 878–81 of proceedings brought by Hitsgalore.com.

[96] ibid, 880–2.

6

IDENTIFICATION

A. General Principles

The concept of identification

A defamatory publication is actionable only at the suit of a person identified by **6.01** the material. To constitute identification, the material must be 'of and concerning' the person.[1] Most obviously, material identifies a person where that person is named, or identified by title.[2]

Identification by name or title

Where a person is referred to by name or title in an Internet publication, he or **6.02** she is identified to all those to whom publication occurs. It is irrelevant that the recipients of the publication have no knowledge of the person referred to.[3]

---

[1] *Knupffer v London Express Newspaper Ltd* [1944] AC 116, 121, 123.
[2] See eg *Jones v E Hulton & Co* [1909] 2 KB 444, 454, 477; *Consolidated Trust Co Ltd v Browne* (1948) 49 SR (NSW) 86, 89; *Mirror Newspapers Ltd v World Hosts Pty Ltd* (1979) 141 CLR 632, 639, 643.
[3] *E Hulton & Co v Jones* [1910] AC 20, 24; *Mirror Newspapers Ltd v World Hosts Pty Ltd* (1979) 141 CLR 632, 639.

B. Identification of Persons not Referred to by Name or Title

General principles

Extrinsic material

6.03 A publication can identify a person even though the person is not referred to by name or title, if it contains material which would lead people acquainted with the person to believe that he or she was the person referred to.[4]

Evidence that people with special knowledge understood a publication to refer to a particular person is admissible, and failure to lead such evidence can be fatal to the action.[5] Evidence of extrinsic facts which constitute the special knowledge should also be adduced.[6] The test is, however, an objective one: whether the ordinary reasonable person, with knowledge of the extrinsic facts, and in the class of persons to whom the material is published, would have reasonably understood the publication to refer to the unnamed person.[7]

6.04 Where a publication does not refer to a person by name or title, but the person is so identified in a subsequent publication by the same publisher, the subsequent publication is an extrinsic fact capable of proving that the prior publication is of and concerning the person.[8] Similarly, where a person is not referred to by name or title in a publication, but the publication points to another publication containing the extrinsic facts necessary to identify the person referred to, the first publication may sufficiently identify the person for the purposes of defamation law.[9]

The Internet

6.05 These principles are capable of being applied to Internet publications. An e-mail message or bulletin board posting which invites the reader to visit a certain web

---

[4] *Knupffer v London Express Newspaper Ltd* [1944] AC 116, 119, 122, 125; *David Syme & Co v Canavan* (1918) 25 CLR 234, 238.

[5] *Morgan v Odhams Press Ltd* [1971] 1 WLR 1239; *Fullam v Newcastle Chronicle & Journal Ltd* [1977] 1 WLR 651, 655, cf 659; *Raul Amon International Pty Ltd v Telstra Corporation Ltd* [1998] 4 VR 798; *Consolidated Trust Co Ltd v Browne* (1948) 49 SR (NSW) 86, 89; *Shendish Manor Ltd v Coleman* [2001] EWCA Civ 913; *Channel Seven Sydney Pty Ltd v Parras* [2002] NSWCA 202, paras 52–8 (indirect evidence may be sufficient, for example, where the plaintiff was contacted by people in response to what they read in a publication which did not refer to the plaintiff).

[6] *Knupffer v London Express Newspaper Ltd* [1944] AC 116, 121, 125; *Mirror Newspapers Ltd v World Hosts Pty Ltd* (1979) 141 CLR 632, 641–2.

[7] *Morgan v Odhams Press Ltd* [1971] 1 WLR 1239, 1246, 1254–5, 1269–70; *David Syme & Co v Canavan* (1918) 25 CLR 234, 240.

[8] *Hayward v Thompson* [1982] QB 47, 60, 72–3; *Baltinos v Foreign Language Publications Pty Ltd* (1986) 6 NSWLR 85, 89, 97. See also *Chase v News Group Newspapers Ltd* [2002] EWHC 2209.

[9] *Baltinos v Foreign Language Publications Pty Ltd* (1986) 6 NSWLR 85, 97–8.

page to learn the identity of some person may adopt or incorporate the identifying information in the web page so that the e-mail message or bulletin board posting itself is of and concerning the person for the purposes of defamation law.

A hyperlink in an e-mail message, bulletin board posting, or web page may also be sufficient to adopt or incorporate extrinsic identifying material contained in the linked web page. For example, suppose that a web page contained the statement 'Migrants victims of rapacious con-men: click here for more details',[10] and that by clicking a mouse-pointer, the reader was directed by hyperlink to another web page, containing details of the alleged activities and the names of the alleged con-men. It seems likely that regard could be had to the second web page on the issue of whether the persons named on that page had been identified by the statement on the first web page.

C. Unintended Identification

Internet publications have the potential to reach a great many people in geographically diverse locations. There is consequently a very real risk that the use of a person's name on a web page or in a bulletin board posting will inadvertently identify others with the same name. Similarly, there is a very real risk that where a fictitious name is used in an Internet publication, that name will coincide with the name of a real person.

6.06

Applying traditional common law principles, the fact that the publisher did not intend to identify a person is not relevant. Accordingly, a publication naming a fictitious character might be of and concerning a real person bearing the same name.[11] A publication which is intended to refer to a named person might be of and concerning any other person who shares that name.[12]

In *O'Shea v MGN Ltd*,[13] Morland J of the English High Court held that this principle of strict liability violated the guarantee to freedom of expression in Article 10 of the European Convention on Human Rights. The case concerned the publication of a photograph of a woman bearing a resemblance to the claimant in an advertisement for a pornographic web site. The claimant alleged

---

[10] In *Baltinos*, ibid, the headline 'Migrants victims of rapacious con-men' appeared in the *Greek Herald*, together with a recommendation that readers view a story on the subject on a television programme that evening. The plaintiff was named in the television programme, though not in the *Greek Herald*.

[11] *E Hulton & Co v Jones* [1910] AC 20.

[12] Three Scottish cases best illustrate this point: *George Outram and Company v Reid* (1852) 14 D 577; *Morrison v John Ritchie and Company* (1902) 4 F 645; *Wragg v DC Thomson and Company Ltd* 1909 2 SLT 315.

[13] [2001] EMLR 40.

that she was identified by the photograph. Morland J held that the attribution of liability in those circumstances placed an impossible burden on the defendant and served no pressing social need. The traditional rule was therefore inconsistent with, and had to yield to, Article 10, which prevailed by reason of the Human Rights Act 1998 (UK).[14]

D. Group Defamation

6.07 Defamation law provides no remedy to groups who are vilified in a publication, unless it can be shown that the publication sufficiently identifies individual members of the group.[15] This will be possible where the nature of the group is such that any reference to it is a reference to each of the members, or where the nature of the publication is such that it points to one or more specific members of the group.[16] Internet publications which defame the members of a mailing list, or those who post messages to a particular bulletin board, are examples of situations in which each member of the defamed group might be able to maintain an action, at least where the group in question is small.

E. Relevance of the Nature of the Publication

6.08 The nature of the publication is relevant in determining whether it identifies a person.[17] Thus 'far-fetched inferences'[18] and 'a certain amount of loose thinking'[19] might be expected of the reader of a newspaper article, while more 'cautious and critical analytical care' might be expected of the reader of a book.[20]

---

[14] See also para 30.43.

[15] eg *Knupffer v London Express Newspaper Ltd* [1944] AC 116; *Macphail v Macleod* 1895 3 SLT 91; *David Syme & Co v Canavan* (1918) 25 CLR 234; *Dowding v Ockerby* [1962] WAR 110, 119; *Taylor v Network Ten (Perth) Pty Ltd* [1999] WASC 264; *Jackson v TCN Channel Nine Pty Ltd* [2001] NSWCA 108.

[16] *Knupffer v London Express Newspaper Ltd* [1944] AC 116, 119–21, 121–2, 123, 124; *Browne v Thomson & Co* 1912 SC 359, 363; *Mann v Medicine Group Pty Ltd* (1992) 38 FCR 400, 402–3, 413; *Butler v Southam Inc* (2001) 197 NSR (2d) 97, paras 71–9 (Nova Scotia Court of Appeal).

[17] It is also relevant in determining whether a defamatory meaning has been conveyed: see paras 7.11–7.12.

[18] *Morgan v Odhams Press Ltd* [1971] 1 WLR 1239, 1244.

[19] ibid, 1245.

[20] ibid, 1254. Lord Reid noted in the same case, 1245: 'The publishers of newspapers must know the habits of mind of their readers and I see no injustice in holding them liable if readers, behaving as they normally do, honestly reach conclusions which they might be expected to reach. If one were to adopt a stricter standard it would be too easy for purveyors of gossip to disguise their defamatory matter so that the judge would have to say that there is insufficient to entitle the plaintiff to go to trial on the question whether that matter refers to him, but the ordinary reader with perhaps more worldly wisdom would see the connection and identify the plaintiff with consequent damage to his reputation for which the law would have to refuse him reparation.'

Internet publications are likely to be perceived in a number of ways. The sens-   **6.09**
ible reader of information posted on an authoritative web site is thus likely to be
more cautious and critically analytical than the reader of messages posted in
rapid succession in the course of Internet Relay Chat. Identification based on
inference and speculation will, as a general rule, be more readily inferred from
information posted on a sensational web site, than an authoritative one. The
sensible, but hasty, reader of messages posted to a bulletin board with a reputation for scurrilous gossip is more likely to understand a message to refer to some
unnamed person, based on inference and speculation, than the more careful
average reader of a special-purpose bulletin board with a reputation for sobriety
and veracity.[21]

---

[21] See eg *Steele v Mirror Newspapers Ltd* [1974] 2 NSWLR 348, 364 (Hutley JA): 'A sensible
but hasty reader may appear a contradiction in terms, but the authorities have made him the
standard. The extrinsic facts which enable the identification to take place do not have to coincide
exactly with the facts detailed in the defamatory matter, as a reasonable reader will not expect
perfect accuracy. In this regard greater latitude appears to be allowed if the material is published in
a sensational newspaper as contrasted with one with a reputation for sobriety and veracity.'

7

DEFAMATORY MEANING

A. Tests of Defamatory Meaning

The tests

In addition to establishing that material has been published, and that it is 'of **7.01** and concerning' them, claimants in defamation actions must prove that the material bears a defamatory meaning.[1] Except in cases where a publication bears only a direct and literal meaning, the claimant in a defamation action pleads the 'imputations' borne by, or the gist of, the published words.

---

[1] In Scots law, there is no cause of action for defamation unless, in addition, the defamatory statement is false, and has been communicated with malice; that is, with the intention of causing injury. Each of these latter requirements is, however, presumed where the statement complained of is defamatory. The onus is on the defender to rebut the presumption of falsity by pleading a defence of *veritas* (justification): *Mackellar v Duke of Sutherland* (1859) 21 D 222, 227–9 (Clerk LJ). It seems that the presumption of malice is irrebuttable: see eg Kenneth Norrie, *Defamation and Related Actions in Scots Law* (1995) 8, 79; JM Thomson, *Delictual Liability* (1994) 211–13. Malice must, however, be affirmatively pleaded by the pursuer in a case where 'qualified privilege would properly be inferred from the narrative which would be bound to appear in the summons': *Pearson v Educational Institute of Scotland* 1997 SC 245, 252; *Quilty v Windsor* 1999 SLT 346, 354. In relation to the elements of the cause of action for defamation in Scots law generally, see Norrie, ch 2; Thomson, 205–13; Francis McManus and Eleanor Russell, *Delict* (1998) 303–14.

7.02 At common law, a publication bears a defamatory meaning if the imputations borne by the words used:

- 'tend to lower the plaintiff in the estimation of right-thinking members of society generally';[2]
- are likely 'to injure the reputation of another, by exposing him to hatred, contempt or ridicule';[3] or
- '[tend to make] the plaintiff be shunned and avoided and that without any moral discredit on her part'.[4]

Right-thinking members of society generally

7.03 Authorities on the meaning of the first test substitute phrases such as 'reasonable people generally',[5] 'ordinary reasonable [readers or] viewers',[6] '[people of] fair average intelligence',[7] 'ordinary decent folk in the community, taken in general',[8] or 'hypothetical referees'[9] for the expression 'right-thinking members of society generally'.

Moral disparagement

7.04 The defamatory imputation must be disparaging, that is express or imply some blame or morally discreditable conduct by the claimant to constitute a lowering of the claimant in the estimation of right-thinking members of society. By contrast, where exposure to contempt or ridicule, or the 'shun or avoid' test is relied on to found defamatory meaning, no such conduct need be expressly or impliedly attributed to the claimant.[10]

---

[2] *Sim v Stretch* [1936] 2 All ER 1237, 1240.

[3] *Parmiter v Coupland* (1840) 6 M & W 105, 108; 151 ER 340, 340. Scots law treats statements which expose the pursuer to hatred, contempt, or ridicule, but which do not satisfy the other tests of defamatory meaning, as falling outside the scope of defamation law. Where such statements are made, however, the pursuer may have a cause of action for 'verbal injury': see para 24.03.

[4] *Youssoupoff v Metro-Goldwyn-Mayer Pictures Ltd* (1934) 50 TLR 581, 587.

[5] *Skuse v Granada Television Ltd* [1996] EMLR 278, 286.

[6] ibid, 288.

[7] *Slayter v Daily Telegraph Newspaper Co Ltd* (1908) 6 CLR 1, 7 (Griffith CJ).

[8] *Gardiner v John Fairfax & Sons Pty Ltd* (1942) 42 SR (NSW) 171, 172 (Jordan CJ).

[9] *Reader's Digest Services Pty Ltd v Lamb* (1982) 150 CLR 500, 506 (Brennan J).

[10] *Berkoff v Burchill* [1996] 4 All ER 1008, 1013, 1020; *Norman v Future Publishing Ltd* [1999] EMLR 325; *Boyd v Mirror Newspapers Ltd* [1980] 2 NSWLR 449, 452–3; *Brander v Ryan* (2000) 78 SASR 234, 245–6 (Lander J).

Shun or avoid

The 'shun or avoid' test appears to be limited to imputations that a person is insane,[11] or that a woman has been raped.[12]   **7.05**

Queensland and Tasmania

In Queensland and Tasmania, the tests for defamatory meaning are prescribed   **7.06**
by legislation. The Queensland provision defines defamatory matter as an imputation:

> concerning any person, or any person's family, whether living or dead, by which the reputation of that person is likely to be injured, or by which the person is likely to be injured in the person's profession or trade, or by which other persons are likely to be induced to shun or avoid or ridicule or despise the person.[13]

This definition broadly follows the common law, with the exception that imputations injuring persons in their profession or trade need not express or imply blame or morally discreditable conduct to be defamatory.[14]

B. Ascertaining the Meaning of a Publication

General principles

A publication may be defamatory in its natural and ordinary meaning, or   **7.07**
because the words used are defamatory in the light of extrinsic facts, and so bear a 'true' or 'legal' innuendo meaning. In a defamation action, it is for the judge to determine whether the words used are capable of bearing a defamatory meaning.[15] Whether the words do in fact convey a defamatory meaning is a question of fact for the jury in jury trials, and for the judge in cases of trial by judge alone.[16]

---

[11] See eg *Morgan v Lingen* (1863) 3 LT 800, 801 (Martin B): 'a statement in writing that a lady's mind is affected, and that seriously, is without explanation *primâ facie* a libel'.

[12] See eg *Youssoupoff v Metro-Goldwyn-Mayer Pictures Ltd* (1934) 50 TLR 581, 587 (Slesser LJ): 'One may, I think, take judicial notice of the fact that a lady of whom it has been said that she has been ravished, albeit against her will, has suffered in social reputation and in opportunities of receiving respectful consideration from the world.'

[13] Defamation Act 1889 (Qld), s 4(1). The Tasmanian definition differs only slightly: Defamation Act 1957 (Tas), s 5.

[14] *Hall-Gibbs Mercantile Agency Ltd v Dun* (1910) 12 CLR 84; *Sungravure Pty Ltd v Middle East Airlines Airliban SAL* (1975) 134 CLR 1, 10–11 (Gibbs J), 21 (Mason J).

[15] cf Defamation Act 1996 (UK), s 7: 'the court shall not be asked to rule whether a statement is arguably capable, as opposed to capable, of bearing a particular meaning or meanings attributed to it'.

[16] *Jones v Skelton* [1963] 1 WLR 1362, 1370; *Amalgamated Television Services Pty Ltd v Marsden* (1998) 43 NSWLR 158, 165.

Natural and ordinary meaning

7.08   At common law, the natural and ordinary meaning of published material is the meaning which an ordinary person would attribute to the material, based only on the words used and generally known facts.[17] In determining the natural and ordinary meaning of published material, the ordinary person is assumed to have a greater capacity for implication than the lawyer,[18] including the ability to read between the lines, and to indulge in loose thinking.[19] Reasonable readers are, however, neither naïve, nor unduly suspicious, nor avid for scandal.[20] Inferences which the ordinary person would draw from the published material based on generally known facts are relevant to a determination of the natural and ordinary meaning of the material. Such inferences are known as 'false' or 'popular' innuendo meanings.

As the test is an objective one, evidence as to how the words used were actually understood by the recipients of a publication is irrelevant in determining the natural and ordinary meaning conveyed.[21]

True or legal innuendo meaning

7.09   Where a publication conveys a defamatory meaning only to persons with knowledge of extrinsic facts, it is said to bear a 'true' or 'legal' innuendo meaning. For example, the statement that a person frequently visits the web page 'http://www.pixtures.co.uk/' is not defamatory in its natural and ordinary meaning, but if that web page is known to some recipients as a site containing graphic pornographic images,[22] then the statement may convey to those recipients the true or legal innuendo meaning that the person is a pervert.

7.10   Where in a defamation action an imputation borne by a publication is a true or legal innuendo, the extrinsic facts said to cause the actual words to convey a defamatory meaning must be pleaded, and evidence of them led, if the action is

---

[17] On the use of words such as 'alleged', 'suggested', and 'apparently', and the attributed repetition of another's defamatory allegations, see *Shah v Standard Chartered Bank* [1999] QB 241 and the authorities cited therein.

[18] *Lewis v Daily Telegraph Ltd* [1964] AC 234, 277; *Amalgamated Television Services Pty Ltd v Marsden* (1998) 43 NSWLR 158, 165.

[19] *Morgan v Odhams Press Ltd* [1971] 1 WLR 1239, 1245, 1254; *Steele v Mirror Newspapers Ltd* [1974] 2 NSWLR 348, 364; *Amalgamated Television Services Pty Ltd v Marsden* (1998) 43 NSWLR 158, 165.

[20] *Gillick v Brook Advisory Centres* [2001] EWCA Civ 1263; *Mark v Associated Newspapers Ltd* [2002] EMLR 38.

[21] *Hough v London Express Newspaper, Ltd* [1940] 2 KB 507, 515; *Toomey v Fairfax* (1985) 1 NSWLR 291, 301–2.

[22] The web page <http://www.pixtures.co.uk/> is not intended to refer to any actual web page.

to succeed.[23] At common law, it is no defence that the publisher did not know of the extrinsic facts.[24]

Relevance of the nature of the publication

General principles

As with identification,[25] the nature of the publication is relevant to the meaning conveyed by the words used. Where the reader of a book might form an impression of meaning after poring over the words used in some detail, the casual viewer of a television show is forced to form quick impressions of the meaning conveyed.[26] The average viewer of an authoritative television news service will ordinarily analyse the content more cautiously and critically, but be less inclined to draw far-fetched inferences, than the viewer of a sensational current affairs programme with a reputation for gossip and rumour.

7.11

Application to the Internet

As a general rule, it seems likely that the sensible reader will spend more time on, and analyse more closely, an authoritative web site than a sensational one. The same can probably be said of special-purpose bulletin boards used exclusively by persons sharing some common interest, as opposed to general-purpose bulletin boards with a reputation for trading in gossip and rumour. The extent to which the nature of the publication affects the meaning borne by the words used is a question of fact.[27]

7.12

Bane and antidote

General principles

As a matter of legal fiction, published material is taken to have only one natural

7.13

---

[23] *Lewis v Daily Telegraph Ltd* [1964] AC 234, 281 (Lord Devlin).
[24] *Berkoff v Burchill* [1996] 4 All ER 1008, 1018; *Nicholson v Seidler* (1990) 5 BR 363, 365. It might be argued, however, that holding publishers liable in respect of defamatory meanings which they did not intend to convey, and which were conveyed only by reason of extrinsic facts known to some recipients, but not the publishers themselves, violates the guarantee of freedom of expression in Art 10 of the European Convention on Human Rights: see para 30.44.
[25] See paras 6.08–6.09.
[26] *Amalgamated Television Services Pty Ltd v Marsden* (1998) 43 NSWLR 158, 165–6.
[27] See eg *Vaquero Energy Ltd v Weir* (2004) 352 AR 191 (Alberta Court of Queen's Bench), para 17: 'E-mails are easy to send and can be sent anonymously in the sense that readers cannot know who the author is and that person's motives for sending the e-mail. To take an example, if a defamatory article is published about someone in a newspaper with a well-known political bias, a reader can take that into account. Because an e-mail is anonymous, a reader is not readily able to discount comments that are made. There is a greater risk that the defamatory remarks are believed'; *Barrick Gold Corporation v Lopehandia* (2004) 71 OR (3d) 416 (Ontario Court of Appeal), para 38 (Blair JA): 'the Internet is not a traditional medium of communication. Its nature and manner of presentation is evolving.'

and ordinary meaning at common law.[28] Whether qualifications ('the antidote') in a publication are capable of overcoming a defamatory sting ('the bane'), so as to deny the words used as a whole any defamatory meaning, is a question of fact to be assessed by the standard of the ordinary, reasonable, fair-minded reader, listener, or viewer. Publication of a denial will not of itself be an antidote sufficient to neutralize a defamatory bane.[29] A publication which advances and then purports to dispel a defamatory allegation will only be acquitted of any possible defamatory meaning in the 'very clearest of cases'.[30]

7.14   It has been held that in determining the meaning conveyed by a newspaper article, recourse is to be had to the entire article, not just the headline or accompanying photographs, even though some ordinary readers of a newspaper might not go to the text itself to form an impression of the meaning conveyed.[31] On the other hand, as Callinan J of the Australian High Court put it in *John Fairfax Publications Pty Ltd v Rivkin*:

> It is true that an article has to be read as a whole. But that does not mean that matters that have been emphasized should be treated as if they have only the same impact or significance as matters which are treated differently. A headline, for example, expressed pithily and necessarily incompletely, but designed to catch the eye and give the reader a predisposition about what follows may well assume more importance than the latter . . . Layout may create its own impression . . . The order in which matters are dealt with can be significant. The capacity of the first paragraph of an article, the 'intro', to excite the reader's attention is a matter upon which editors place store. The language employed is also of relevance . . . The intrusion of irrelevant information may raise questions as to the meaning intended to be, and actually conveyed . . . True it may be that readers may take an article or articles on impression, but the fact that they may do so is likely to have the consequence that ideas and meanings conveyed by graphic language will create the strongest impressions. Of course publishers are entitled to use colourful and seductive language, but in using it they may run the risk of seducing readers into believing only what is colourful and on occasions scandalous, rather than the facts conveyed by straight reportage.[32]

Application to the Internet

7.15   The application of these principles to Internet publications may lead to results which differ from those in cases involving other forms of publication. Web sites

---

[28] *Slim v Daily Telegraph Ltd* [1968] 2 QB 157, esp at 171–5; *Charleston v News Group Newspapers Ltd* [1995] 2 AC 65, 71–3, 73–4. As the Privy Council observed in *Bonnick v Morris* [2003] 1 AC 300, 309, the common law approach is 'highly artificial, given the range of meanings the impugned words sometimes bear'.
[29] *Mark v Associated Newspapers Ltd* [2002] EMLR 38.
[30] *Jameel v Times Newspapers Ltd* [2004] EMLR 31, 674 (Sedley LJ); *John Fairfax Publications Pty Ltd v Rivkin* (2003) 201 ALR 77, para 26 (McHugh J, dissenting as to the result).
[31] *Charleston v News Group Newspapers Ltd* [1995] 2 AC 65, 70–3, 74.
[32] (2003) 201 ALR 77, para 187; see also para 26 (McHugh J, dissenting as to the result).

maintained by media organizations, for example, commonly consist of a web page which contains a series of headlines, connected by hyperlinks to the text of the associated articles, which will be contained on separate web pages. The Internet user who wishes to read the associated article must take some affirmative step, such as clicking a mouse-pointer on the hyperlink. Similarly, recipients of e-mail messages and bulletin board postings may see the title of the message or posting on their screens, but have to take some further step to display the message or posting itself. The fact that the associated message or posting might affect the natural and ordinary meaning conveyed by the title would appear to be less relevant than in the case of a newspaper headline or a photograph accompanying a newspaper article. The ordinary, reasonable, fair-minded reader of a web page might not be expected to look, metaphorically, beyond the headline to the text of the article itself.[33]

7.16 Where a hyperlink, or the title to an e-mail message or bulletin board posting, conveys a defamatory meaning, whether recourse may be had to qualifications in the associated text to overcome the defamatory sting will be a question of fact to be determined in each case. It might be expected, for example, that ordinary readers of a web page containing a summary of news articles, and hyperlinks to the articles themselves, will be less likely to take the affirmative step of following the hyperlinks than ordinary readers of a web page containing only headlines, connected by hyperlink to the associated articles. In the first case, a defamatory sting in a summary of an article might not be overcome by qualifications in the article itself, because the ordinary reader might not be expected to read beyond the summary. In the second case, an antidote in the article itself might be more likely to qualify the bane of a headline so as to deny the publication as a whole a defamatory meaning. The ordinary reader may be more likely to look beyond the headline, to the associated article.

7.17 Similarly, ordinary readers are probably more likely to read the text of e-mail messages sent to their personal addresses, than the text of every posting on a large bulletin board. In most cases, it would seem likely therefore that the defamatory sting of a title to an e-mail message could be overcome by adequate qualifications in the text of the message. An antidote in the text of a bulletin board posting, however, might not overcome a defamatory sting in the title to that posting, for the ordinary, reasonable, fair-minded reader might be expected to skim the titles, but not read every posting sent to a bulletin board.

---

[33] *Charleston v News Group Newspapers Ltd* [1995] 2 AC 65, 74 (Lord Nicholls): 'Those who print defamatory headlines are playing with fire. The ordinary reader might not be expected to notice curative words tucked away further down in the article. The more so, if the words are on a continuation page to which a reader is directed.' The leading authorities concerning defamatory headlines and photographs are usefully collated in *Warne v Herald & Weekly Times Ltd* [2000] VSC 210, paras 9–15.

Tone and expression

General principles

7.18 The imputations borne by published words can also depend on the tone used by the publisher.[34] A publication may be so dripping in irony that no ordinary reader would take its contents seriously.[35] Tone of voice and facial expression will sometimes neutralize words which would, if read in print, convey a defamatory meaning.

Emoticons

7.19 Because so much of what is published on the Internet is in print, but otherwise analogous to spoken conversation, computer users have developed a series of typed symbols, called 'emoticons', which are intended to simulate tone of voice or facial expression. Typically used in e-mail messages, bulletin board postings, Internet Relay Chat, chat rooms, and instant messaging, emoticons can be used to neutralize words which would otherwise be defamatory. Some common emoticons are set out in Table 3.[36]

Table 3. Some common emoticons

Emoticon	Meaning
:-)	Smiling face, might be used to convey that something is not to be taken seriously: 'Jane will probably end up convicted of something:-)'
;-)	Winking face, might be used to convey mischief: 'Jane is as guilty as hell;-)'
:-o	Open-mouthed face, might be used to convey surprise: 'They are saying that Jane committed the crime:-o'
:-(	Sad face, might be used to convey dismay or hurt: 'Jane will get a long sentence:-('
:-|	Grim face, might be used to convey seriousness: 'Jane was stupid to think she could get away with it:-|'

Emoticons do not fall within the category of generally known facts which can affect the natural and ordinary meaning of words for the purposes of defamation law. Although analogous to tone of voice or facial expression, they are known only to some members of the Internet-using community. For this reason, their use and meaning are better seen as extrinsic facts which might convey a true or legal innuendo meaning. Where a party to a defamation action intends to rely on an emoticon in determining what imputation is borne by a publication, the

---

[34] See eg *Lewis v Daily Telegraph Ltd* [1964] AC 234, 271.
[35] *Yarwood v Mirror Newspapers Ltd* [1968] 1 NSWR 720, 721 (Moffitt J).
[36] Further emoticons are described in Rob Kitchin, *Cyberspace* (1998) 7.

emoticon and its alleged effect should be pleaded.[37] Whether the use of an emoticon was sufficient in any given case to neutralize an otherwise defamatory publication would be a question of fact.

The standards of society

In the United Kingdom, it seems that an imputation is to be judged by the standards of society generally. An imputation is therefore not defamatory if it only affects a person's reputation within some section of the community.[38]   **7.20**

By contrast, in all Australian jurisdictions, determining whether an imputation bears a defamatory meaning is to be judged by the standards of, at least, an 'appreciable section of the community'.[39] This test acknowledges the diversity of modern Australian culture.[40] There seem to be few limits to the number of definable sections of the community, except perhaps small minorities with 'anti-social standards'.[41] A similar approach prevails in the United States.[42]   **7.21**

Applying the Australian test, the Internet-using population may form a section of the community by which some imputations are to be judged. To say, for example, that 'Jill is a Luddite' might not bear a defamatory meaning by the standards of the average person, while to Internet users it might bear the imputation that Jill is incompetent, or behind the times. If Jill were engaged in the business of selling the latest computers, such imputations may lower her in the estimation of the Internet-using community, expose her to hatred, contempt, and ridicule, or injure her in her profession or trade.[43]

---

[37] *Lewis v Daily Telegraph Ltd* [1964] AC 234, 264, 277–8, 281.
[38] *Tolley v Fry* [1930] 1 KB 467, 479 (Greer LJ); *Leetham v Rank* (1912) 57 SJ 111, 112 (Farwell LJ); Patrick Milmo and WVH Rogers, *Gatley on Libel and Slander* (10th edn, 2003) ('Gatley') para 2.10; cf Norrie (n 1 above) 11–12.
[39] *Middle East Airlines Airliban SAL v Sungravure Pty Ltd* [1974] 1 NSWLR 323, 340 (Glass JA). See also *Hepburn v TCN Channel Nine Pty Ltd* [1983] 2 NSWLR 682, 694 (Glass JA): 'appreciable and reputable section of the community'.
[40] But cf *Reader's Digest Services Pty Ltd v Lamb* (1982) 150 CLR 500, 507 (Brennan J): 'The defamatory nature of an imputation is ascertained by reference to general community standards, not by reference to sectional attitudes. But if the imputation is defamatory according to the standards of the community generally, a particular impact of the defamatory imputation may be proved.'
[41] John Fleming, *The Law of Torts* (9th edn, 1998) 583.
[42] *Peck v Tribune Company*, 214 US 185 (1909), 190 (Holmes J): 'important and respectable part of the community'; Gatley (n 38 above) para 2.12.
[43] See eg the reasoning in *Hepburn v TCN Channel Nine Pty Ltd* [1983] 2 NSWLR 682, 694 (Glass JA): 'Where a television programme has been beamed to a large audience it can be presumed, without special proof, that its viewers will include some who advocate the "right to life" and abhor the destruction of foetuses, whatever the circumstances. In the estimation of such persons the plaintiff [who was called an "abortionist" in the course of the *60 Minutes* television programme] can claim to have been disparaged even if abortionist meant lawful abortionist. If it also meant unlawful abortionist, she can also claim to have been denigrated in the eyes of a different but substantial section of the viewers who support the existing law but do not want it extended.'

Part III

GENERAL DEFENCES

8

JUSTIFICATION

A. Introduction

General principles

In the United Kingdom, and in some Australian jurisdictions,[1] defendants have **8.01** a defence of justification[2] in respect of a defamatory imputation if they prove, on the balance of probabilities, that the defamatory imputation is substantially true.[3]

The policy underlying the defence of justification is that liability should only attach where a deserved reputation has been damaged. Where the truth is told, reputations either cannot be damaged, or are only brought down to their proper

---

[1] Victoria, South Australia, Western Australia, the Northern Territory, and the Australian Capital Territory. The defence of justification at common law continues to apply in Western Australia, as an alternative to the Criminal Code (WA), s 356: *Australian Ocean Line Pty Ltd v West Australian Newspapers Ltd* (1985) 58 ALR 549, 597, citing *West Australian Newspapers Ltd v Bridge* (1979) 141 CLR 535 and *Gobbart v West Australian Newspapers Ltd* [1968] WAR 113; cf *Johnston v Australian Broadcasting Commission* (1993) 113 FLR 307, 312. Although there is a statutory defence of justification in the Australian Capital Territory, it seems the common law defence applies as an alternative: see Civil Law (Wrongs) Act 2002 (ACT), s 138.

[2] In Scotland, the defence of justification is known as '*veritas*'.

[3] See eg *Reynolds v Times Newspapers Ltd* [2001] 2 AC 127, 192.

level.[4] Defamation law is interested only in protecting the reputation which a person deserves to have.[5]

8.02 Statutory defences of justification operate in New South Wales, Queensland, Tasmania, Western Australia, and the Australian Capital Territory. The statutory defences in Western Australia and the Australian Capital Territory operate as alternatives to the common law defence.[6] In Queensland, Tasmania, Western Australia, and the Australian Capital Territory, the statutory defence is established by the defendant proving that the defamatory imputations borne by the published material are substantially true, and also that it was for the 'public benefit' for the matter to have been published.[7] In New South Wales, a defendant proves justification by showing that the defamatory imputations conveyed by the publication are matters of substantial truth,[8] and that they relate to a matter of 'public interest' or are published on an occasion of qualified privilege.[9]

8.03 These general principles are modified in England and Scotland where the published matter conveys imputations concerning 'spent convictions'.[10]

8.04 In extreme cases in the United Kingdom, requiring defendants to bear the burden of proving a defence of justification may contravene the guarantee of freedom of expression in Article 10 of the European Convention on Human Rights, at least where proceedings are brought by a well-resourced claimant against unrepresented defendants of modest incomes and resources, in respect of publications conveying serious allegations of general public interest.[11]

Substantial truth

General principles

8.05 A defendant seeking to rely on the defence of justification in respect of a defamatory imputation must prove that the imputation is substantially

---

[4] *Rofe v Smith's Newspapers Ltd* (1924) 25 SR (NSW) 4, 21–2.
[5] *Plato Films Ltd v Speidel* [1961] AC 1090, 1145.
[6] See n 1 above.
[7] Defamation Act 1889 (Qld), s 15; Defamation Act 1957 (Tas), s 15; Criminal Code (WA), s 356; Civil Law (Wrongs) Act 2002 (ACT), s 127.
[8] Defamation Act 1974 (NSW), ss 7(2), 15: an imputation is a matter of substantial truth if the substance is true or if in substance it is not different from the truth.
[9] ibid, s 15. Qualified privilege is discussed in chapters 11 and 12.
[10] See paras 13.09–13.15. As to proof of convictions generally, see Civil Evidence Act 1968 (UK), ss 11, 13 (England); Defamation Act 1974 (NSW), s 55; Evidence Act 1995 (Cth), ss 5, 157.
[11] *Steel and Morris v United Kingdom* (European Court of Human Rights, 15 February 2005); cf *McVicar v United Kingdom* (2002) 35 EHRR 22; *Jameel v Wall Street Journal Europe Sprl (No 2)* [2005] EWCA Civ 74. See also para 30.25.

true.[12] A defamatory imputation may be substantially true, even though some detail which does not alter or aggravate the character of the imputation may be inaccurate; the test is whether the 'sting' of the imputation has been proved true.[13]

As the intention of the defendant is irrelevant, a genuine belief in the truth of the words published is not sufficient for the defence to succeed, if the defamatory imputation cannot be proved to be true.[14]

Where defendants publish rumours, hearsay, or allegations, or merely repeat the statement of another, it is not sufficient for them to prove that they accurately reported or repeated the original publication. To succeed in a defence of justification, defendants must prove the truth of the subject matter of the original publication. This principle is known as the 'repetition rule'.[15]

To maximize the prospect of later being able to rely on a defence of justification, it is thus important for publishers who are not authors to satisfy themselves that the defamatory imputations borne by material for which they are responsible as publishers are substantially true.

Application to the Internet

In a practical sense, this is likely to be more difficult in many cases for inter-   **8.06**
mediaries of Internet publications, than for publishers in other contexts. Editors of newspapers, for example, will ordinarily know their journalists, and be able to take steps to satisfy themselves of the truth of a proposed news story. Proprietors of newspapers will ordinarily have confidence in the ability of their editors to ensure that published material is accurate. Such relationships of trust do not ordinarily exist between Internet intermediaries and Internet users. Proprietors

---

[12] *Digby v Financial News Ltd* [1907] 1 KB 502, 507; *Sutherland v Stopes* [1925] AC 47, 55, 75, 78–9; *Irving v Penguin Books Ltd* (English Court of Appeal, 20 July 2001) para 20; *Mirror Newspapers Ltd v Harrison* (1982) 149 CLR 293, 302–3; Defamation Act 1974 (NSW), ss 7(2), 15. The same standard appears to apply in Scotland: Kenneth Norrie, *Defamation and Related Actions in Scots Law* (1995) 130.

[13] *Edwards v Bell* (1824) 1 Bing 403; 130 ER 162; *Clarke v Taylor* (1836) 3 Scott 95; 132 ER 252; *Sutherland v Stopes* [1925] AC 47, 56, 81, 95; *Rofe v Smith's Newspapers Ltd* (1924) 25 SR (NSW) 4, 22; *Potts v Moran* (1976) 16 SASR 284, 305–6, 308; *Chase v News Group Newspapers Ltd* [2003] EMLR 11, 227; *Herald & Weekly Times Ltd v Popovic* [2003] VSCA 161, para 306 (Gillard AJA).

[14] *E Hulton & Co v Jones* [1910] AC 20, 23–4.

[15] See eg *Lewis v Daily Telegraph Ltd* [1964] AC 234, 283–4 (Lord Devlin); *Stern v Piper* [1997] QB 123, 135–6; *Shah v Standard Chartered Bank* [1999] QB 241, 261–3; *Mark v Associated Newspapers Ltd* [2002] EMLR 38; *Chase v News Group Newspapers Ltd* [2003] EMLR 11, 228; *Adams v Guardian Newspapers Ltd* 2003 SLT 1058, 1065–6; *Jameel v Times Newspapers Ltd* [2004] EMLR 31, 681. In the latter case some doubt was expressed as to whether the repetition rule applies where a publication asserts no more than that a third party has alleged enough to warrant an investigation of the claimant's activities: ibid, 680–1. See also *Bennett v News Group Newspapers Ltd* [2002] EMLR 39.

of servers on which the web pages of third parties are located, for example, are unlikely to know the Internet users who store material on their servers. Similarly, the operator of a bulletin board is unlikely to know all the people who contribute material to the bulletin board. In many cases, the proprietor of the server, or the operator of the bulletin board, may be located in a different country from the author or contributor.

It may also be difficult in many cases for an Internet intermediary to prove that defamatory imputations are substantially true. The evidence required to prove truth on the balance of probabilities may be peculiarly within the knowledge of the author of the publication, who may be difficult or impossible to trace. The cost involved in an Internet intermediary proving the truth of defamatory imputations may be prohibitive, bearing in mind geographic obstacles, and the cost of coercive procedural tools such as witness summonses (subpoenas) and non-party disclosure (discovery).

Internet intermediaries are likely, however, to be treated by defamation law as publishers of much of the material hosted on or which passes through their computer systems.[16] They will not succeed in a defence of justification simply because they had no view as to the truth or otherwise of the published material.

B. Multiple Imputations

Common law

8.07 At common law, where published material bears more than one imputation, the defendant must prove the truth of each imputation to succeed in a defence of justification.[17] Where a defendant can prove the truth of some, but not all, imputations, the claimant is entitled to recover damages in respect of the imputations which the defendant has not proved true, unless the defendant is able to make out some other defence in respect of those imputations.[18]

United Kingdom and Tasmania

8.08 Statutory defences of 'contextual justification' operate in the United Kingdom and Tasmania.[19] The defences operate in circumstances where defendants

---

[16] See chapter 15.
[17] *Digby v Financial News Ltd* [1907] 1 KB 502, 507 (Collins MR); *Herald & Weekly Times Ltd v Popovic* [2003] VSCA 161, para 306 (Gillard AJA).
[18] *Becker v Smith's Newspapers Ltd* [1929] SASR 469, 471; *Cohen v Mirror Newspapers Ltd* [1971] 1 NSWLR 623, 627, 632–3.
[19] Defamation Act 1952 (UK), s 5 (England and Scotland); Defamation Act (Northern Ireland) 1955, s 5; Defamation Act 1957 (Tas), s 18.

cannot prove that an imputation complained of by a claimant is substantially true if, having regard to other distinct imputations complained of by the claimant which have been proved to be substantially true, that imputation has not materially injured the claimant's reputation.[20] The defendant may, however, only rely on the imputations actually sued on by the claimant. A claimant can effectively prevent a defendant from relying on the defences by pleading only imputations which the defendant will be unable to prove to be true.

New South Wales

A similar, but broader, statutory defence of 'contextual justification' operates in New South Wales. The defendant may rely on the substantial truth of any imputations borne by the published material, regardless of whether they have been sued on by the plaintiff. Defendants have a defence if they prove that, having regard to the substantial truth of any imputations borne by the material, any imputation relied on by the plaintiff which cannot be proved to be true has not further injured the plaintiff's reputation.[21] Both the imputation sued on by the plaintiff, and the imputations relied on by the defendant, must relate to matters of public interest, or be published on occasions of qualified privilege.[22] In determining whether the defence is made out, the court focuses on the facts, matters, and circumstances said to establish the truth of the contextual imputation, rather than on the terms of the contextual imputation itself.[23]

8.09

Lucas-Box **meanings and the** *Polly Peck* **principle**

General principles

Where defendants cannot prove the truth of an imputation pleaded by a claimant, they may nonetheless be able to succeed in a defence of justification if they are able to justify another imputation borne by the same publication which has a 'common sting' with the imputation pleaded by the claimant. Under this principle, commonly known as the '*Polly Peck* principle',[24] the defendant is able to plead that the publication bears some imputation not relied on by the claimant, commonly known as a '*Lucas-Box* meaning'.[25] If the defendant is able to

8.10

---

[20] See eg *Moore v News of the World Ltd* [1972] 1 QB 441, 448; *Cornelius v De Taranto* [2001] EMLR 12, 341.

[21] Defamation Act 1974 (NSW), s 16; *Jackson v John Fairfax & Sons Pty Ltd* [1981] 1 NSWLR 36, 39.

[22] Defamation Act 1974 (NSW), ss 16(2)(a), (b).

[23] *John Fairfax Publications Pty Ltd v Blake* (2001) 53 NSWLR 541, 543.

[24] *Polly Peck Holdings Plc v Trelford* [1986] QB 1000.

[25] *Lucas-Box v News Group Newspapers Ltd* [1986] 1 WLR 147. See also *Prager v Times Newspapers Ltd* [1988] 1 WLR 77; *Cruise v Express Newspapers Plc* [1999] QB 931; *GKR Karate (UK) Ltd v Yorkshire Post Newspapers Ltd* [2000] 2 All ER 931.

establish that the publication bears that imputation, that the imputation is true, and that the imputation has a common sting with the imputation pleaded by the claimant, then the defendant is entitled to succeed in a defence of justification in respect of the imputation pleaded by the claimant.[26] The principle applies only to imputations which have a common sting with an imputation pleaded by the claimant.[27]

Rethinking the Polly Peck *principle*

8.11   In *Chakravarti v Advertiser Newspapers Ltd*,[28] Brennan CJ and McHugh J of the Australian High Court expressed the view that the *Polly Peck* principle is contrary to the basic rules of common law pleading and that defendants should not have a defence of justification in cases where they cannot justify the imputations pleaded by the plaintiff.[29] The remaining three judges expressed no view on the question, although at least two assumed that a defendant was able to plead and justify imputations different from those pleaded and proved by the plaintiff.[30]

8.12   The Victorian Court of Appeal considered the implications of *Chakravarti* in *David Syme & Co Ltd v Hore-Lacy*.[31] A majority of the court adopted a 'pleading rule' that defendants seeking to rely on the *Polly Peck* principle may only plead and seek to justify imputations which are not more serious than, and not substantially different in meaning from, those pleaded by the plaintiff.[32]

Application to the Internet

8.13   The operation of the *Polly Peck* principle, and the New South Wales contextual justification defence, to defamatory material published via the Internet poses no special problems where the defendant wishes to rely on the substantial truth of

---

[26] *Polly Peck Holdings Plc v Trelford* [1986] QB 1000, 1032; *Khashoggi v IPC Magazines Ltd* [1986] 1 WLR 1412, 1416–17; *Carlton Communications Plc v News Group Newspapers Ltd* [2002] EMLR 16.

[27] See also *Bookbinder v Tebbit* [1989] 1 All ER 1169, 1175 (Ralph Gibson LJ): the defendant may only rely on a 'wider meaning or a more general charge' than that pleaded by the claimant where that meaning or charge 'can fairly be gathered from the words used, or from the context'; *US Tobacco International Inc v British Broadcasting Corporation* [1998] EMLR 816; *Cruise v Express Newspapers Plc* [1999] QB 931.

[28] (1998) 193 CLR 519.

[29] ibid, 527–30.

[30] ibid, 543 (Gaudron and Gummow JJ).

[31] [2000] VSCA 24. See also *Herald & Weekly Times Ltd v Popovic* [2003] VSCA 161, paras 301–3 (Gillard AJA).

[32] [2000] VSCA 24, paras 22–4 (Ormiston JA), 58–63 (Charles JA). The Victorian approach has found support in some, but not all, other Australian jurisdictions: see eg *Nationwide News Pty Ltd v Moodie* (2003) 28 WAR 314; *Manock v Advertiser News-Weekend Publishing Co Ltd* (2004) 88 SASR 495; cf *Robinson v Laws* [2003] 1 Qd R 81, para 123; *Whelan v John Fairfax Publications Pty Ltd* (2002) 56 NSWLR 89; *John Fairfax Publications Pty Ltd v Jones* [2004] NSWCA 205, para 80.

imputations borne by material on the same web page, or in the same bulletin board posting or e-mail message, as that complained of by the claimant. More difficult, however, is the question whether defendants should be entitled to avoid liability for a false defamatory imputation contained on a web page, or in a bulletin board posting or e-mail message, by relying on the substantial truth of imputations borne by material contained in a hyperlinked web page, bulletin board posting, or e-mail message.

The contextual justification defence in New South Wales applies only to imput- **8.14** ations contained in the 'same publication'.[33] The *Polly Peck* principle appears to be similarly limited.[34] It seems unlikely that, in most cases, material on a web page, or in a bulletin board posting, or e-mail message, could be said to be contained in the same publication as material which is accessible from that web page, bulletin board posting, or e-mail message by hyperlink.[35]

Suppose, however, that a media organization, D, publishes on a web page a series of headlines, linked by hyperlink to the text of detailed articles. Suppose further that D publishes on that web page a headline which falsely alleges that C is having an affair with X, and that C sues in respect of that allegation. Suppose finally that, in the hyperlinked article attached to the headline, D publishes and can prove that C has had affairs with a dozen other named persons.

Had D's allegations been made in a newspaper article, it is likely that D could have defended the proceedings brought by the claimant by pleading that the imputation borne by the article as a whole is that C is promiscuous and that that imputation is a matter of substantial truth.[36] It is arguable that the same result should follow where the allegations are made in two separate, though hyper-linked, web pages. In each case, the damage to C's reputation is likely to be the same, at least where it can be proved that readers followed the hyperlink to the article itself.

For the purposes of the *Polly Peck* principle, it is at least arguable that D should be entitled to look to the hyperlinked web page 'to aver that in their context the words [in the headline] bear a meaning different from that alleged' by the claimant.[37] Where the defence of contextual justification is relied on in New

---

[33] Defamation Act 1974 (NSW), s 16(1).
[34] *Polly Peck Holdings Plc v Trelford* [1986] QB 1000, 1032 (O'Connor LJ): 'the defendant is entitled to look at the whole publication in order to aver that in their context the words bear a meaning different from that alleged by the plaintiff'.
[35] *Buddhist Society of Western Australia Inc v Bristile Ltd* [2000] WASCA 210, para 10; see para 5.12.
[36] See *Khashoggi v IPC Magazines Ltd* [1986] 1 WLR 1412.
[37] *Polly Peck Holdings Plc v Trelford* [1986] QB 1000, 1032 (O'Connor LJ).

South Wales, D might be able to contend that the two web pages constitute the 'same publication'.

C. Statutory Justification Defences in Australia

'Public benefit' and 'public interest'

8.15   In Queensland, Tasmania, Western Australia, and the Australian Capital Territory, a statutory defence of justification only succeeds where it was for the 'public benefit' for the defamatory matter to have been published.[38] In New South Wales, each defamatory imputation must relate to a matter of 'public interest' or be published on an occasion of qualified privilege.[39] The concepts of 'public benefit' and 'public interest' are closely related; it has been said that 'public benefit will result from the publication of matters of public interest'.[40]

8.16   This additional element to the statutory defences of justification is intended to protect the privacy of defamed persons. A matter is published for the public benefit, or relates to a matter of public interest, only where it 'discusses or raises for public discussion or information matters which are properly of public concern'.[41] A subject may not be properly of public concern if it relates to matters which happened a long time ago.[42] The publication of material concerning the private behaviour of public figures will only be properly of public concern if the behaviour affects the performance of their public duties, or if they have put their private behaviour before the public for its judgment.[43] The fact that a matter panders to a desire for scandal is not sufficient.[44]

Matters of public concern

8.17   Matters which are properly of public concern will vary from place to place. It

---

[38] Defamation Act 1889 (Qld), s 15; Criminal Code (WA), s 356; Defamation Act 1957 (Tas), s 15(b); Civil Law (Wrongs) Act 2002 (ACT), s 127.

[39] Defamation Act 1974 (NSW), s 15(2)(b). An imputation is published under qualified privilege only if it was published on an occasion of qualified privilege and the manner and extent of publication was reasonable having regard to the imputation and to the occasion of qualified privilege: ibid, s 14(1). For a discussion of the occasions of qualified privilege, and the concept of 'reasonableness', see chapters 11 and 12.

[40] *Allworth v John Fairfax Group Pty Ltd* (1993) 113 FLR 254, 263 (Higgins J); cf *Traill v Australian Broadcasting Commission* [1988] Tas R 1, 8 (Nettlefold J): '[whether] "public good", "public benefit" and "public interest" in this context mean the same thing is open to some question'.

[41] *Allworth v John Fairfax Group Pty Ltd* (1993) 113 FLR 254, 263 (Higgins J).

[42] *Rofe v Smith's Newspapers Ltd* (1924) 25 SR (NSW) 4, 22; *Cohen v Mirror Newspapers Ltd* [1971] 1 NSWLR 623, 628.

[43] *Chappell v TCN Channel Nine Pty Ltd* (1988) 14 NSWLR 153, 167.

[44] *Johnston v Australian Broadcasting Commission* (1993) 113 FLR 307, 312.

might be justifiable, for example, to publish some matter of local concern in a local newspaper, but not in a metropolitan or national publication.[45] Similarly, in cases where a publication spans more than one jurisdiction, the defendant will need to prove that the publication was made for the public benefit in each jurisdiction in which that requirement applies. In respect of publications occurring in New South Wales, the publication of the imputation will need to relate to a question of public interest in New South Wales if the defence of justification is to succeed in relation to the publication of material in that jurisdiction.

Application to the Internet

Material published on the world wide web is generally available anywhere in the world. Where the material is of only local public concern, the defence of justification might fail in relation to 'hits' on the relevant web page outside that local area in those Australian jurisdictions where a public benefit or public interest requirement applies. The same result would follow for material of only local public concern posted on a bulletin board where that material is viewed by persons outside the local area.

8.18

For the purposes of determining whether a matter is properly of public concern, the 'public' is the audience receiving the publication. A matter which is properly of concern to the police may thus be justifiable if published only to police officers, but not if it is published to members of the public generally.[46]

A defence of justification is therefore likely to fail in those Australian jurisdictions where a public benefit or public interest requirement applies, where material published on a web page or bulletin board is only properly of concern to some sector of the community, but is received by persons outside that sector.

---

[45] *Tisdall v Hutton* [1944] Tas SR 1, 11, 20–3.
[46] *Crowley v Glissan (No 2)* (1905) 2 CLR 744, 756.

9

FAIR COMMENT

A. Elements of the Defence

In the United Kingdom, and in some Australian jurisdictions,[1] publishers have a   **9.01**
common law defence of fair comment in respect of expressions of opinion,
deductions, inferences, conclusions, criticisms, judgments, remarks, or observations[2] ('comments') where:

- the comment relates to a matter of public interest;
- the comment is based on facts which are stated or indicated in the material;

---

[1] Victoria, South Australia, Western Australia, and the Australian Capital Territory. The common law defence of fair comment continues to apply in Western Australia, notwithstanding the
application of defamation provisions of the Criminal Code (WA) to civil actions: see *Australian
Ocean Line Pty Ltd v West Australian Newspapers Ltd* (1985) 58 ALR 549, 597.
[2] *Clarke v Norton* [1910] VLR 494, 499; *Branson v Bower* [2001] EMLR 32, 807; *Skrine v
Euromoney Publications Plc* [2002] EMLR 15, 288–9.

- those facts are true or absolutely privileged; and
- the comment is fair.

Generally speaking, the defence is not available where the publisher was actuated by malice.[3]

9.02 The policy underlying the common law defence of fair comment is partly to ensure that liability occurs only where deserved reputations are damaged, and partly to recognize the general importance of allowing the free expression of opinion. Thus the publication of a defamatory opinion on a matter of public interest will generally be protected provided that it is fair and honest, and even if it is bold, exaggerated, or violent.[4]

9.03 In Queensland and Tasmania, the defence of fair comment has been codified.[5] In New South Wales and the Northern Territory, aspects of the defence have been codified.[6] In Western Australia, a statutory defence of fair comment operates as an alternative to the common law defence.[7]

B. 'Comment'

General principles

9.04 The defence of fair comment applies only to comments, as opposed to assertions of fact. Material is a comment if the people to whom it is published would consider it to be an expression of opinion.[8] Other than in New South Wales, it is for the jury, in a trial by jury, to decide whether material is a comment, or an assertion of fact.[9] The judge or jury may only consider the publication complained of and the context, including any material indicated in the publication.[10]

---

[3] See paras 9.18–9.26.
[4] *Merivale v Carson* (1887) 20 QBD 275, 281, 284.
[5] Defamation Act 1889 (Qld), s 14; Defamation Act 1957 (Tas), s 14.
[6] Defamation Act 1974 (NSW), ss 29–35; Defamation Act 1938 (NT), s 6A.
[7] Criminal Code (WA), s 355.
[8] *Grech v Odhams Press Ltd* [1958] 1 QB 310, 312–13; *London Artists Ltd v Littler* [1969] 2 QB 375, 398; *Smith's Newspapers Ltd v Becker* (1932) 47 CLR 279, 302.
[9] Although where the material is only reasonably capable of being treated as a statement of fact, or an expression of opinion, the judge may so direct the jury: *Telnikoff v Matusevitch* [1992] 2 AC 343, 351; *Pervan v North Queensland Newspaper Co Ltd* (1993) 178 CLR 309, 317. In New South Wales, the judge decides whether the defendant has made out the pleaded defences: Defamation Act 1974 (NSW), s 7A(4)(a). Juries do not sit in civil defamation actions in South Australia or the Australian Capital Territory.
[10] *Telnikoff v Matusevitch* [1992] 2 AC 343, 351, 356.

Imputations of dishonest or corrupt motives

The current trend in the authorities is towards treating an imputation of dis- **9.05** honest or corrupt motives as comment, at least where recipients of the publication would conclude that the imputation was an inference drawn by the publisher from the facts set out in the publication.[11]

In New South Wales, legislation makes it clear that imputations of dishonour- **9.06** able motives may be treated as comments to which the ordinary defence of comment applies.[12]

C. The Comment Must Relate to a Matter of Public Interest

Matters of public interest

At common law, a comment relates to a matter of public interest if it is of **9.07** concern to the public, in that the public has a legitimate interest in the subject matter of the comment. A comment also relates to a matter of public interest if it is in respect of some matter which has been submitted to the public for its attention and criticism, such as a literary or artistic work.[13] A comment will not relate to a matter of public interest if it concerns the private life of public figures who have not submitted their private lives to the public for its judgment.[14]

In New South Wales, legislation imposes a similar 'public interest' requirement **9.08** on the defence of comment.[15] In Queensland, Tasmania, and the Northern Territory, and in Western Australia in respect of the statutory defence of fair comment, the categories of comment capable of attracting a fair comment defence are prescribed.[16]

---

[11] *Slim v Daily Telegraph Ltd* [1968] 2 QB 157, 171 (dishonesty, insincerity and hypocrisy); *O'Shaughnessy v Mirror Newspapers Ltd* (1970) 125 CLR 166, 174 (Barwick CJ, McTiernan, Menzies and Owen JJ): 'it is not our view that an imputation of dishonesty is always an assertion of fact'; *Rocca v Manhire* (1992) 57 SASR 224, 230 (disgraceful or dishonourable conduct); *Branson v Bower* [2001] EMLR 32; *Keays v Guardian Newspapers Ltd* [2003] EWHC 1565, paras 49–50; cf *Hunt v Star Newspaper Co Ltd* [1908] 2 KB 309, 320.

[12] Defamation Act 1974 (NSW), s 30(4).

[13] *London Artists Ltd v Littler* [1969] 2 QB 375, 391; *Gardiner v John Fairfax & Sons Pty Ltd* (1942) 42 SR (NSW) 171, 173–4; *Bellino v Australian Broadcasting Corporation* (1996) 185 CLR 183.

[14] *Mutch v Sleeman* (1928) 29 SR (NSW) 125, 137.

[15] Defamation Act 1974 (NSW), s 31; see also *Green v Schneller* [2000] Aust Torts Reports ¶81–568, 63,895–7 (Simpson J).

[16] Defamation Act 1889 (Qld), s 14; Defamation Act 1957 (Tas), s 14; Defamation Act 1938 (NT), s 6A; Criminal Code (WA), s 355(1).

Application to the Internet

9.09 The difficulties which publishers of defamatory Internet communications might have in proving that material they published relates to matters of public interest have been explored above in relation to the operation of the 'public benefit' and 'public interest' requirement of the statutory defences of justification in Queensland, Western Australia, Tasmania, the Australian Capital Territory, and New South Wales.[17]

In short, the fair comment defence may fail where a comment published via the Internet is of only local concern, or of concern only to some sector of the community, but is published to persons outside the area of local concern, or to persons who have no legitimate interest in the subject of the comment.

D. The Comment Must be Based on Facts Which are Stated or Indicated in the Material

General principles

9.10 At common law, the defence of fair comment is only proved where the comment is based on facts which are expressly set out, or otherwise indicated, in the published material, unless those facts are easily ascertainable,[18] or are matters of general knowledge.[19] The policy underlying this principle is that 'the public [should] have at least the opportunity of ascertaining for themselves the subject-matter upon which the comment is founded'.[20]

Application to the Internet

9.11 In the case of Internet publications, a comment based on facts which are not expressly stated in the material, but which are accessible by hyperlink or by reference to an URL, would be likely to be treated as being sufficiently indicated in the material. Any reader of the comment is easily able to ascertain the facts on which the opinion is based, as long as the factual material contained in the hyperlinked web page or URL reference remains accessible.

---

[17] See paras 8.15–8.18.

[18] *Kemsley v Foot* [1952] AC 345, 355–6; *Telnikoff v Matusevitch* [1992] 2 AC 343, 352; *Pryke v Advertiser Newspapers Ltd* (1984) 37 SASR 175, 192.

[19] *Hawke v Tamworth Newspaper Co Ltd* [1983] 1 NSWLR 699, 704 (Hunt J): 'contemporary history or general notoriety'; *Sims v Wran* [1984] 1 NSWLR 317, 322. The common law requirement is analogous to the requirement articulated by the European Court of Human Rights in cases concerning the interpretation of Art 10 of the European Convention on Human Rights: see para 30.24.

[20] *Kemsley v Foot* [1952] AC 345, 356 (Lord Porter); *Cheng v Tse Wai Chun Paul* [2000] 3 HKLRD 418, 4; *Herald & Weekly Times Ltd v Popovic* [2003] VSCA 161, paras 268–72.

More difficult, however, is whether the defence could apply to the publication on the Internet of expressions of opinion about obscure matters, or matters of purely local concern, where the facts on which the opinions are based have not been expressly set out or otherwise indicated. For example, a scathing critique of the performance of an English actor in a play in Sydney published on a bulletin board might not be able to attract a defence of fair comment in respect of publications of the bulletin board posting in the United Kingdom, unless the factual basis for the criticism is set out or implicit in the posting.[21] If the factual basis is not set out or implicit, ordinary readers of the posting in the United Kingdom may have no means of judging whether they agree with the opinion expressed in the critique.[22]

E. The Facts on Which the Comment is Based Must be True or Absolutely Privileged

General principles

For the defence of fair comment to succeed at common law, the facts on which the comment is based must be true or absolutely privileged. Categories of facts which are absolutely privileged are discussed below.[23] It is not clear whether, to attract the defence, the comment must pertain to the absolutely privileged occasion, or whether the protection of the defence attaches to any comment based on a fact stated on an absolutely privileged occasion.[24]

9.12

Common law

At common law, in cases where the comment is not based on absolutely privileged facts, each fact on which the comment is based must be proved by the defendant to be true.[25]

9.13

United Kingdom, New South Wales, and Tasmania

By statute in the United Kingdom, and in New South Wales and Tasmania, by

9.14

---

[21] *Kemsley v Foot* [1952] AC 345, 355–6, 361.
[22] See also *Sims v Wran* [1984] 1 NSWLR 317, 322; *Bjelke-Petersen v Burns* [1988] 2 Qd R 129, 131–3; *Pryke v Advertiser Newspapers Ltd* (1984) 37 SASR 175, 192.
[23] See chapter 10.
[24] The competing views and authorities are discussed obiter dicta in *Pervan v North Queensland Newspaper Co Ltd* (1993) 178 CLR 309, 320–4. See also D Payne, 'Fair Comment on Privileged Statements of Fact' (1958) Modern Law Review 674.
[25] *Joynt v Cycle Trade Publishing Co* [1904] 2 KB 292, 298; *Digby v Financial News Ltd* [1907] 1 KB 502, 507–8; *Hunt v Star Newspaper Co, Ltd* [1908] 2 KB 309, 317, 320; *Australian Broadcasting Corporation v Comalco Ltd* (1986) 12 FCR 510, 553–6, 585, cf 598 (Pincus J, who thought that the better view is that the facts, taken as a whole, need to be substantially true). See also Defamation Act 1974 (NSW), s 35.

contrast, the defence will succeed even where some of the facts on which the comment is based cannot be proved to be true if, having regard to those facts which have been proved true, the comment is, in the United Kingdom and Tasmania, fair[26] or, in New South Wales, reasonable.[27] In New South Wales, the facts on which the comment is based need not relate to matters of public interest for the defence of comment to succeed.[28]

Queensland and Tasmania

9.15 Although the matter is not beyond doubt, the better view appears to be that in Queensland and Tasmania defendants are not required to prove that each fact on which their comment is based was published for the public benefit to succeed in a defence of fair comment.[29]

F. The Comment Must be Fair

9.16 A comment will be fair if it could honestly be held by a fair-minded person,[30] even if the opinion is grossly exaggerated or prejudiced,[31] wrong or violent,[32] irrational, stupid, or obstinate,[33] expressed in 'ironical, bitter or even extravagant language',[34] or 'uncourteous, or even offensive or vituperative'.[35]

G. The *Polly Peck* Principle

9.17 Defendants must identify the defamatory meanings which they intend to defend as fair comments.[36] A defendant may rely on a defence of fair comment

---

[26] Defamation Act 1952 (UK), s 6 (England and Scotland); Defamation Act (Northern Ireland), s 6; Defamation Act 1957 (Tas), s 14(2).

[27] Defamation Act 1974 (NSW), s 30(3)(b).

[28] ibid, s 30(2).

[29] *Orr v Isles* [1965] NSWR 677, 690–1, 697–700; *Jones v Skelton* [1963] 1 WLR 1362, 1372–4 (PC); *Gorton v Australian Broadcasting Commission* (1973) 1 ACTR 6, 25; cf *Goldsbrough v John Fairfax & Sons Ltd* (1934) 34 SR (NSW) 524, 534, 545; *Gardiner v John Fairfax & Sons Pty Ltd* (1942) 42 SR (NSW) 171, 173; *Orr v Isles* [1965] NSWR 677, 680–7.

[30] See eg *Silkin v Beaverbrook Newspapers Ltd* [1958] 2 All ER 516; *Reynolds v Times Newspapers Ltd* [2001] 2 AC 127, 193.

[31] *Merivale v Carson* (1887) 20 QBD 275, 281.

[32] ibid, 284; *McQuire v Western Morning News Co, Ltd* [1903] 2 KB 100.

[33] *Turner v Metro-Goldwyn-Mayer Pictures, Ltd* [1950] 1 All ER 449, 463.

[34] *Gardiner v John Fairfax & Sons Pty Ltd* (1942) 42 SR (NSW) 171, 174 (Jordan CJ).

[35] *Godfrey v Thomson* (1890) 17 R 1108, 1114 (Lord M'Laren).

[36] *Control Risks Ltd v New English Library Ltd* [1990] 1 WLR 183, 189 (Nicholls LJ); *Anderson v Nationwide News Pty Ltd* (2001) 3 VR 619, para 58. In England, see also Civil Procedure Rules, Practice Direction 53, para 2.6(1).

in respect of an imputation which is different from an imputation pleaded by a claimant, provided that the defendant's imputation has a 'common sting' with the claimant's imputation, and the defendant establishes all of the elements of the defence in respect of the defendant's imputation.[37] This principle is a variant of the *Polly Peck* principle which applies in relation to defences of justification.[38]

H. Malice

Relevance of malice

Proof by the claimant that the defendant was actuated by malice defeats the defence of fair comment in England and Northern Ireland.[39] **9.18**

In Scots law, it seems that the motive of the defender is irrelevant; the defence of fair comment will be available, even where the defender is actuated by malice, provided that the comment is 'fair', in the sense of being relevant to facts which are truly stated or indicated, or published on an occasion of absolute privilege, and which relate to a matter of public interest.[40] **9.19**

Malice defeats the defence of fair comment in Victoria, South Australia, the Australian Capital Territory and, where the common law defence is relied on, Western Australia.[41] **9.20**

In Queensland, Tasmania, the Northern Territory and, where the statutory defence is relied on, Western Australia, malice probably does not defeat the fair comment defence, although it is a factor relevant to fairness: that is, whether the

---

[37] *Polly Peck Holdings Plc v Trelford* [1986] QB 1000, 1032 (O'Connor LJ). See also *Lloyd v Express Newspapers Plc* [1997] EWCA Civ 1319, paras 18–20 (Bingham MR); *Anderson v Nationwide News Pty Ltd* (2001) 3 VR 619.

[38] See paras 8.10–8.12. The modifications to the *Polly Peck* principle which operate in some Australian jurisdictions (see paras 8.11–8.12) in relation to the defence of justification may apply, by parity of reasoning, where the fair comment defence is relied on: *Anderson v Nationwide News Pty Ltd* (2001) 3 VR 619; *Anderson v Nationwide News Pty Ltd (No 2)* (2002) 3 VR 639; cf *Moir v Flint* [2002] WASC 48, paras 26–8; *Cock v Hughes* [2002] WASC 108, paras 45–6; *Cock v Hughes* [2002] WASC 263, paras 8–9.

[39] *Thomas v Bradbury, Agnew and Co, Ltd* [1906] 2 KB 627, 638; *Broadway Approvals Ltd v Odhams Press Ltd (No 2)* [1965] 1 WLR 805, 822; *Adams v Sunday Pictorial Newspapers (1920) Ltd* [1951] 1 KB 354, 360; *Reynolds v Times Newspapers Ltd* [2001] 2 AC 127, 193.

[40] *Archer v John Ritchie & Company* (1891) 18 R 719, 727; *Godfrey v Thomson* (1890) 17 R 1108, 1115; cf *Wheatley v Anderson* 1927 SC 133, 147.

[41] *Renouf v Federal Capital Press of Australia Pty Ltd* (1977) 17 ACTR 35, 53–4; *Gardiner v John Fairfax & Sons Pty Ltd* (1942) 42 SR (NSW) 171, 173; *Duffield v Arts Council of South Australia Inc* (1981) 27 SASR 540, 541–2; *Australian Broadcasting Corporation v Comalco Ltd* (1986) 12 FCR 510, 559–60.

comment was the defendant's real opinion, or whether the defendant's judgment was distorted.[42]

In New South Wales, the relevance of the motive of the defendant to the availability of a defence of comment is the subject of prescription. Where a comment is that of the defendant, the defence of comment fails if the plaintiff proves that the defendant did not in fact hold the opinion expressed.[43]

Malice defined

9.21   Defendants are actuated by malice where the claimant proves that they do not genuinely hold the opinion they have expressed,[44] or where the opinion is expressed with a dominant malicious motive, such as to injure the claimant.[45] Defendants are not actuated by malice, however, simply because they hold irrational beliefs, so long as those beliefs are genuinely held.[46]

I. Publishing the Comment of Another

9.22   At common law, persons who publish the fair comment of another may rely on the defence of fair comment themselves, provided that they are not actuated by malice.[47]

Defendants who publish the comments of others without genuinely holding the opinions expressed themselves are not for that reason actuated by malice.[48] Accordingly, editors of newspapers will usually have a defence of fair comment in relation to opinions expressed on a letters page, even where they do not hold the views expressed themselves. Similarly, Internet intermediaries who make the

---

[42] *Cawley v Australian Consolidated Press Ltd* [1981] 1 NSWLR 225, 229–37; cf *Renouf v Federal Capital Press of Australia Pty Ltd* (1977) 17 ACTR 35, 53–4, 59. The decision in *Cawley* is to be preferred: the legislation in these jurisdictions does not impose any obligation of 'good faith' on the defendant: see eg Michael Gillooly, *The Law of Defamation in Australia and New Zealand* (1998) 137.

[43] Defamation Act 1974 (NSW), s 32(2).

[44] *Horrocks v Lowe* [1975] AC 135, 149–52; *Renouf v Federal Capital Press of Australia Pty Ltd* (1977) 17 ACTR 35, 54.

[45] *Merivale v Carson* (1887) 20 QBD 275, 281–2, 285; *Lyle-Samuel v Odhams, Ltd* [1920] 1 KB 135, 143; *Horrocks v Lowe* [1975] AC 135, 149–52; *Renouf v Federal Capital Press of Australia Pty Ltd* (1977) 17 ACTR 35, 53–4.

[46] *Horrocks v Lowe* [1975] AC 135, 152; *Renouf v Federal Capital Press of Australia Pty Ltd* (1977) 17 ACTR 35, 54.

[47] *Telnikoff v Matusevitch* [1992] 2 AC 343, 355; cf *Chernesky v Armadale Publishers* (1978) 90 DLR (3d) 321. As to the role of malice in Scots law, however, see para 9.19.

[48] *Telnikoff v Matusevitch* [1992] 2 AC 343, 355; *Pervan v North Queensland Newspaper Co Ltd* (1993) 178 CLR 309, 328–30; *Herald & Weekly Times Ltd v Popovic* [2003] VSCA 161, paras 261–5; cf *Chernesky v Armadale Publishers* (1978) 90 DLR (3d) 321.

comments of others available via their computer systems will not need to hold the opinions expressed themselves.

It would constitute malice, however, if an intermediary knew that the author of a comment did not genuinely hold the opinion expressed.[49]

Malice on the part of employees and agents is, however, imputed to their employers or principals.[50]　**9.23**

By contrast, it appears that the ability of a defendant to rely on a defence of fair **9.24** comment is not affected by the malice of another defendant in respect of a joint publication.[51] This may be important in cases where the publication complained of was communicated via the Internet, and the claimant has sued the author of the publication and any Internet intermediaries who made the material available via their computer systems. Except where there is an employment or agency relationship between the author and the intermediary, the intermediary will not be affected by malice on the part of the author, unless the intermediary was aware that the author did not genuinely hold the opinions expressed, or was actuated by an improper motive.

In New South Wales, the defence of comment fails in respect of the publication **9.25** by a defendant of an employee's or agent's comment if the plaintiff proves that the employee or agent did not actually hold the opinion expressed.[52] Where defendants publish the comment of some person other than themselves, or their employees or agents, however, the defence only fails if the plaintiff proves that the publication was not made in good faith for public information, or for the advancement of education.[53] It appears likely that a plaintiff could prove an absence of good faith by showing that the defendant published the person's comment for some dominant malicious motive, or that the defendant knew that the person did not honestly hold the opinion expressed.

In Queensland, Tasmania, the Northern Territory and, where the statutory defence is relied on, Western Australia, it seems that persons who publish the comment of another may rely on the applicable statutory defence of fair comment themselves, provided that the publication is made in good faith and is objectively fair.[54]

It seems, therefore, that in the United Kingdom and throughout Australia, **9.26**

---

[49] Patrick Milmo and WVH Rogers, *Gatley on Libel and Slander* (10th edn, 2003) para 12.25.
[50] *Egger v Viscount Chelmsford* [1965] 1 QB 248, 265, 266, 269.
[51] ibid, 265, 266, 271–2.
[52] Defamation Act 1974 (NSW), s 33(2).
[53] ibid, s 34(2).
[54] *Pervan v North Queensland Newspaper Co Ltd* (1993) 178 CLR 309, 328–9.

where a defamatory comment is published in an e-mail, or on a bulletin board, or web page, the intermediaries involved in the publication of that comment will generally be unlikely to be treated as being actuated by malice or an absence of good faith, unless it can be proved by the claimant that they knew that the author of the comment did not genuinely hold the opinion expressed.

10

ABSOLUTE PRIVILEGE

A. Common Law

Introduction

The law recognizes certain very limited occasions on which defamatory state-   **10.01**
ments are privileged, even where they are actuated by malice and no other
defence applies. Complete immunity from suit is warranted on these occasions,
having regard to the law's interest in ensuring the effective performance of
important public functions.[1]

Absolutely privileged occasions

Absolutely privileged occasions include statements made in the House by   **10.02**
Members of Parliament in their capacity as members,[2] written or spoken state-

---

[1] See eg *Gibbons v Duffell* (1932) 47 CLR 520, 528.
[2] The privilege derives from the Bill of Rights 1688, art 9 (see 1 Will & Mar sess 2, c 2): 'That
the freedome of speech and debates or proceedings in Parlyament ought not to be impeached or
questioned in any court or place out of Parlyament'; *Ex parte Wason* (1869) LR 4 QB 573; *Gipps v
McElhone* (1881) 2 NSWR 18, 21, 24, 25–6. Statements made by Members of Parliament outside
the House are not accorded absolute privilege; privilege may even be lost if the words are adopted
by the Member by reference outside the House: *Beitzel v Crabb* [1992] 2 VR 121, 128 (Hampel
J); *R v Abingdon* (1793) 1 Esp 226, 228; 170 ER 337, 338; *Buchanan v Jennings* [2004] EMLR
22. In relation to the scope of the privilege, see Defamation Act 1996 (UK), s 13; Parliamentary
Privileges Act 1987 (Cth), s 16; *Prebble v Television New Zealand Ltd* [1995] 1 AC 321; *Hamilton
v Al Fayed* [2001] 1 AC 395; *Rann v Olsen* (2000) 76 SASR 450. In *Adams v Guardian Newspapers
Ltd* 2003 SLT 1058, Lord Reed observed that the law in relation to parliamentary privilege was, in
general at least, the same in Scotland as elsewhere in the United Kingdom.

ments made in the course of judicial and quasi-judicial proceedings[3] by the judge, counsel, parties,[4] witnesses, or jurors,[5] and communications between Ministers of the Crown.[6] Communications between solicitors and their clients,[7] and between husbands and wives[8] may also be absolutely privileged at common law.

10.03　The occasions attracting absolute privilege at common law might be extended in rare cases 'where upon clear grounds of public policy a remedy must be denied to private injury because complete freedom from suit appears indispensable to the effective performance of judicial, legislative or official functions'.[9]

B. Legislation

10.04　Legislation in both the United Kingdom and Australia extends the categories of communication which are the subject of absolute privilege.

---

　[3] Proceedings are quasi-judicial if the tribunal in question exercises 'functions equivalent to those of an established court of justice': *O'Connor v Waldron* [1935] AC 76, 81 (Lord Atkin); *Trapp v Mackie* [1979] 1 WLR 377, 379, 389.

　[4] Parties to civil proceedings enjoy absolute privilege in England, Northern Ireland and Australia, but only qualified privilege in Scots law: *Williamson v Umphray* (1890) 17 R 905, 910–11.

　[5] *Scott v Stansfield* (1868) LR 3 Ex 220 (judges); *Primrose v Waterston* (1902) 4 F 783 (judges); *Williamson v Umphray* (1890) 17 R 905 (judge and jury, counsel and witnesses); *Seaman v Netherclift* (1876) 2 CPD 53 (witnesses); *Munster v Lamb* (1883) 11 QBD 588, 603–5, 608 (counsel); *Rome v Watson* (1898) 25 R 733 (counsel); *Royal Aquarium and Summer and Winter Garden Society v Parkinson* [1892] 1 QB 431, 451 (judges, counsel, witnesses, and parties); *Watson v McEwan* [1905] AC 480, 486 (witnesses); *Marrinan v Vibart* [1963] 1 QB 528, 533–5, 537–8 (statements by police officers to the Director of Public Prosecutions, and in evidence to a court, as well as witnesses, counsel, juries, and judges); *Cabassi v Vila* (1940) 64 CLR 130, 139, 140, 144, 149 (witnesses); *Clyne v New South Wales Bar Association* (1960) 104 CLR 186, 200 (counsel).

　[6] *Chatterton v Secretary of State for India in Council* [1895] 2 QB 189, 191, 194 (communication by an 'official in state' to another official in the course of official duties); *Gibbons v Duffell* (1932) 47 CLR 520, 525–6 (communications between Ministers and the Crown, communications among Ministers, communications between high officers of State and Ministers, and communications between High Commissioners and Prime Ministers).

　[7] *More v Weaver* [1928] 2 KB 520, 526 (Scrutton LJ, with whom Lawrence and Green LJJ agreed); cf *Minter v Priest* [1930] AC 558, 574 (Viscount Dunedin), 586 (Lord Atkin) (who each noted, without deciding the question, that the balance of the older authorities was that such communications attract only qualified privilege). See also *Gibbons v Duffell* (1932) 47 CLR 520, 525 (Gavan CJ, Rich and Dixon JJ): 'How far communications between solicitor and client obtain an unqualified protection is not yet finally settled'; *Clarke v Davey* [2002] EWHC 2342, para 37: 'Doubted though it may have been, *More v Weaver* has not been expressly overruled' (Gray J).

　[8] *Wennhak v Morgan* (1888) 20 QBD 635, 637 (Huddleston B, who held that the question could be decided 'on the common law principle that husband and wife are one'), 639 (Manisty J, who agreed and noted that a contrary result 'might lead to results disastrous to social life'); *Cattanach v Melchior* (2003) 215 CLR 1, 30 (McHugh and Gummow JJ).

　[9] *Gibbons v Duffell* (1932) 47 CLR 520, 528 (Gavan Duffy CJ, Rich and Dixon JJ). See also *Mann v O'Neill* (1997) 191 CLR 204, 213–4, 248, 264; *W v Westminster City Council* [2004] EWHC 2866, para 25.

United Kingdom

The following additional categories of absolute privilege apply in the United Kingdom.   **10.05**

Parliamentary papers

All reports, papers, votes, and proceedings published by, or under the authority   **10.06**
of, either House of Parliament are absolutely privileged.[10] The privilege will
apply where any such material is published via the Internet.

Reports of judicial proceedings

Subject to section 8(6) of the Rehabilitation of Offenders Act 1974 (UK),[11] fair   **10.07**
and accurate[12] reports of proceedings before various courts are absolutely privileged in the United Kingdom, if published contemporaneously with the proceedings.[13] The protection applies to proceedings in any court, tribunal, or
judicial body of the United Kingdom, the European Court of Justice and the
European Court of Human Rights, and any international criminal tribunal
established by the Security Council of the United Nations.[14] Where a report of
proceedings has been postponed by reason of some court order, or the operation
of some statutory provision, then the report will be treated as having been
published contemporaneously if it is published as soon as practicable after publication is permitted.[15]

The absolute privilege afforded to fair reports of court proceedings would apply   **10.08**
to reports published contemporaneously via the Internet.[16] It may be, however,
that such reports would only be protected for a limited period. Suppose that a
report of a court proceeding continued to be accessible from a web page weeks,
months, or years after the conclusion of a proceeding.[17] It would seem likely that
absolute privilege would not protect the publisher in respect of any publication
of the report occurring at a time which is no longer contemporaneous with the
proceeding.[18]

---

[10] Parliamentary Papers Act 1840, s 1.
[11] See para 13.14.
[12] As to the meaning of the expression 'fair and accurate', see para 12.03.
[13] Defamation Act 1996 (UK), s 14(1).
[14] ibid, s 14(3).
[15] ibid, s 14(2).
[16] See also para 10.12.
[17] See Patrick Milmo and WVH Rogers, *Gatley on Libel and Slander* (10th edn, 2003) ('Gatley') para 13.36, wherein it is suggested that 'contemporaneously' means 'as nearly at the same
time as the proceedings as is reasonably possible, having regard to the opportunities for preparation of the report and the time of going to press or of making the broadcast'.
[18] See eg *Loutchansky v Times Newspapers Ltd (Nos 4 and 5)* [2002] QB 783. The defence of
qualified privilege might, however, be available: Defamation Act 1996 (UK), s 15 and Sch 1, Pt I,
para 2: see para 12.06.

Miscellaneous other categories

10.09 Various pieces of legislation afford absolute privilege to a variety of other proceedings and reports.[19]

Australia

Queensland, Tasmania, and New South Wales

10.10 The occasions of absolute privilege have been codified in Queensland[20] and Tasmania.[21] In New South Wales, statutory categories of absolute privilege operate in addition to the common law.[22]

Reports of absolutely privileged occasions

10.11 Legislation in some Australian jurisdictions extends absolute privilege, in limited circumstances, to fair and accurate reports of absolutely privileged occasions.[23] Perhaps most notably, absolute privilege is accorded to fair and accurate reports[24] throughout Australia of proceedings or meetings of the Houses and

---

[19] Relevant legislation are collated in Gatley (n 17 above) para 13.49, and include the Parliamentary Commissioner Act 1967, s 10 (certain communications by and to the Parliamentary Commissioner); Pensions Act 1995, ss 103(2) and 113(2) (certain reports by the Occupational Pensions Authority or Compensation Board); Pension Schemes Act 1993, s 151(7) (certain statements, reports and directions by the Pensions Ombudsman); Health Service Commissioners Act 1993, s 14(5) (certain reports and statements by Health Service Commissioners); Broadcasting Act 1990, s 186(7) (certain reports by the Director General of Fair Trading concerning the activities of the BBC); Courts and Legal Services Act 1990, s 23(5) and 69(2) (certain reports by the Legal Services Ombudsman, and reasons given by the Lord Chancellor, the designated judge or the Director General of Fair Trading in the exercise of certain of their functions); Competition Act 1998, s 57 (certain advice, guidance, notices, directions, and decisions of the Office of Fair Trading). See also Kenneth Norrie, *Defamation and Related Actions in Scots Law* (1995) 101–2.

[20] Defamation Act 1889 (Qld), ss 10–12.

[21] Defamation Act 1957 (Tas), ss 10–12.

[22] Defamation Act 1974 (NSW), s 11, read with ss 17, 17A–17U, 18, and 19.

[23] eg: *Commonwealth*: Parliamentary Privileges Act 1987 (Cth), s 10 accords absolute privilege for fair and accurate reports of proceedings or meetings of a House or a committee of the Commonwealth Parliament, provided that the report is published without adoption by the publisher of the substance of the matter; *Victoria*: Wrongs Act 1958 (Vic), s 4 accords absolute privilege for faithful and accurate reports of proceedings in Victorian courts and coronial inquests, but not including obscene or blasphemous material or reports of proceedings which have not been concluded where the presiding officer has pronounced publication to be improper at that stage; *South Australia*: Civil Liability Act 1936 (SA), s 6 accords absolute privilege to fair and accurate reports by newspaper, radio, or television of proceedings publicly heard before 'any court exercising judicial authority' if published contemporaneously with such proceedings; *Western Australia*: Newspaper Libel and Registration Act 1884 Amendment Act 1888 (WA), s 6 accords absolute privilege to fair and accurate reports in registered newspapers of the proceedings 'in any court of justice' and at 'any State or municipal ceremonial, or at any political or municipal meeting, or at a public meeting'; *Northern Territory*: Defamation Act 1938 (NT), s 5 accords absolute privilege to fair and accurate reports of proceedings publicly heard before 'any court exercising judicial authority' if published contemporaneously with the proceedings.

[24] As to the meaning of 'fair and accurate', see para 12.03.

committees of the Commonwealth Parliament,[25] and to faithful and accurate reports in Victoria of proceedings in Victorian courts.[26]

Publication of absolutely privileged reports via the Internet

For the purposes of civil defamation law, material is published in each jurisdiction where the material is received.[27] Where a report which is absolutely privileged in a jurisdiction is published via the Internet in that jurisdiction, the publisher of the report will be entitled to the benefit of the privilege. The same publisher may not be entitled to the benefit of absolute privilege, however, in respect of publications of the same report occurring in other jurisdictions. For example, a faithful and accurate report of a proceeding in the Victorian Supreme Court published on a web page will be absolutely privileged under Victorian law, in so far as that web page is viewed by persons in Victoria: a plaintiff will not succeed even where the report is defamatory of him or her and was actuated by malice. The plaintiff would be able to succeed in respect of publications of the same web page occurring in England, however; under English law the publication of fair and accurate reports of court proceedings attracts only qualified privilege.[28]

10.12

---

[25] Parliamentary Privileges Act 1987 (Cth), s 10.
[26] Wrongs Act 1958 (Vic), s 4.
[27] See para 5.10.
[28] See paras 12.01, 12.06.

11

THE DUTY AND INTEREST FORM OF QUALIFIED PRIVILEGE

A. Forms of Qualified Privilege

In addition to the defences already discussed, defamation law also recognizes **11.01** occasions of qualified privilege, on which the publication of defamatory matter may be excused, having regard to the 'necessities of social intercourse',[1] provided that the publication is not actuated by malice. The occasions of qualified privilege give rise to two distinct defences:

- the defence of qualified privilege for publications in performance of a duty or interest; and

---

[1] John Fleming, *The Law of Torts* (9th edn, 1998) 622; see also *Toogood v Spyring* (1834) 1 CM & R 181, 193; 149 ER 1044, 1049–50; *Watts v Times Newspapers Ltd* [1997] QB 650, 659; *Reynolds v Times Newspapers Ltd* [2001] 2 AC 127, 193–4; Patrick Milmo and WVH Rogers, *Gatley on Libel and Slander* (10th edn, 2003) ('Gatley') para 14.1.

- the defence of qualified privilege for the publication of fair reports of certain proceedings and of extracts of certain publicly available documents.

A publication which would not be entitled to the benefit of the fair reports form of the defence might nonetheless be entitled to the duty and interest form of the defence.[2]

The duty and interest form of the defence of qualified privilege is the subject of this chapter; the fair reports form of the defence will be considered in the next chapter.

Malice, which is relevant to both forms of qualified privilege, is considered towards the end of this chapter.[3]

B. Performance of a Duty or Protection of an Interest

General principles

11.02 At common law, a defendant who has published defamatory material has a defence of qualified privilege, even if the material is false, if the publication was made in the performance of a legal, social, or moral duty or to protect an interest, to persons with a corresponding duty or interest in receiving that material.[4] The defence is, however, defeated where the claimant proves the defendant was actuated by malice.[5]

11.03 The common law defence is available in the United Kingdom, and in most Australian jurisdictions. A defence of 'qualified protection' has been codified in Queensland and Tasmania.[6] A statutory qualified privilege defence operates in New South Wales, as an alternative to the common law.[7] Statutory modifications also apply to the common law defence in New South Wales.[8]

11.04 Whether a publisher has a moral or social duty to communicate defamatory

---

[2] *Bashford v Information Australia (Newsletters) Pty Ltd* (2004) 204 ALR 193, paras 31–5 (Gleeson CJ, Hayne and Heydon JJ), 127 (Gummow J), 182–5 (Kirby J).

[3] See paras 11.39–11.44.

[4] *Adam v Ward* [1917] AC 309, 334; *Horrocks v Lowe* [1975] AC 135, 149.

[5] *Toogood v Spyring* (1834) 1 CM & R 181, 193; 149 ER 1044, 1049–50; *Adam v Ward* [1917] AC 309, 334.

[6] Defamation Act 1889 (Qld), s 16(1); Defamation Act 1957 (Tas), s 16(1). See paras 11.27–11.30.

[7] Defamation Act 1974 (NSW), s 22; see paras 11.31–11.38. Note that in New South Wales, matter is only published under qualified privilege if it is published on an occasion of qualified privilege (whether under the Defamation Act 1974 or otherwise) and the publication is relevant to the occasion: ibid, s 20(1).

[8] See paras 11.37–11.38.

material is a matter to be determined objectively. Defamatory communications will be protected where they are fairly warranted by any reasonable occasion or exigency, having regard to the standards of the great mass of people of ordinary intelligence and moral principle.[9]

Examples

Examples of situations in which such a duty operates include providing references to potential employers stating the character of some person they propose to engage,[10] and reporting alleged criminal behaviour to the police or an investigatory authority.[11] A publication may be made in the protection of an interest if it is made to protect a defendant's legitimate business or proprietary interests,[12] or to respond to an attack on the defendant's character or conduct.[13] **11.05**

In Scots law, the parties to civil proceedings are entitled to a defence of qualified privilege in respect of statements made by them in the course of the proceedings.[14] In all other parts of the United Kingdom and in Australia, by contrast, such statements are absolutely privileged.[15]

C. Recipients' Corresponding Duty or Interest

General principles

At common law, the duty and interest form of the defence of qualified privilege only operates where each recipient of the defamatory publication has a duty or interest in receiving the publication which coincides with the publisher's duty or interest in making the publication.[16] The interest of each recipient in the publication must be legitimate; the recipient must 'not [be] interested in it as a **11.06**

---

[9] *Mowlds v Fergusson* (1940) 64 CLR 206, 220; *Stuart v Bell* [1891] 2 QB 341, 350.

[10] *Spring v Guardian Assurance plc* [1995] 2 AC 296, 324, 329–30, 346–50; *Reynolds v Times Newspapers Ltd* [2001] 2 AC 127, 194.

[11] See eg *Collins v Cooper* [1902] 19 TLR 118; *Reynolds v Times Newspapers Ltd* [2001] 2 AC 127, 194; *Finn v Hunter* (1886) 12 VLR 656, 660; *Telegraph Newspaper Co Ltd v Bedford* (1934) 50 CLR 632, 661.

[12] *Blackham v Pugh* (1846) 15 LJCP 290, 291–4; *Penton v Calwell* (1945) 70 CLR 219, 242–3, 250.

[13] *Laughton v Bishop of Sodor and Man* (1872) LR 4 PC 495, 504; *Penton v Calwell* (1945) 70 CLR 219, 242–3, 250; *Bass v TCN Channel Nine Pty Ltd* [2003] NSWCA 118. A solicitor may be entitled to a defence of qualified privilege when responding to an attack on behalf of a client: *Baker v Carrick* [1894] 1 QBD 838; *Regan v Taylor* [2000] EMLR 549.

[14] *Williamson v Umphray* (1890) 17 R 905, 910–11.

[15] See para 10.02.

[16] *Adam v Ward* [1917] AC 309, 334; *Watt v Longsdon* [1930] 1 KB 130, 147–8, 152. In New South Wales, it is enough that the publisher believes, on reasonable grounds, that the recipient has the requisite duty or interest: Defamation Act 1974 (NSW), s 21; see para 11.38.

matter of gossip or curiosity, but as a matter of substance apart from its mere quality as news'.[17]

This requirement is simple enough in cases where the publication is limited to an individual, such as the police officer to whom a suspected crime is reported, or the potential employer to whom a professional reference is given, or to a group of people with an obvious common interest, such as the members of a professional association. The requirement is more difficult to fulfil in cases where a publication is made to the public at large. Put another way, the law attaches privilege 'more readily to communications within an existing relationship than to those between strangers'.[18]

Examples

11.07 Mutual duties and interests in receiving publications have been held to exist in a vast number of circumstances, including:

- communications among family members;[19]
- commercial credit inquiries,[20] although perhaps not through credit agencies;[21]
- communications among shareholders of a company in respect of discussions of company affairs;[22]
- communications among members of clubs or associations in respect of the affairs of those clubs or associations;[23]
- communications between landlords and tenants in respect of matters relevant to the tenancy;[24]

---

[17] *Howe v Lees* (1910) 11 CLR 361, 398 (Higgins J). See also *Rumsey v Webb* (1842) C & M 104, 105; *London Association for Protection of Trade v Greenlands, Ltd* [1916] 2 AC 15, 35.

[18] *Kearns v General Council of the Bar* [2003] EMLR 27, 579 (Simon Brown LJ), 583 (Keene LJ): qualified privilege attached to publication to 10,132 members of a professional association; *Bashford v Information Australia (Newsletters) Pty Ltd* (2004) 204 ALR 193: qualified privilege attached to a publication in an occupational health and safety bulletin to which only occupational health and safety managers subscribed.

[19] *Todd v Hawkins* (1837) 8 C & P 88; 173 ER 411; *Adams v Coleridge* (1884) 1 TLR 84.

[20] *Waller v Loch* (1881) 7 QBD 619; *Greenlands, Ltd v Wilmshurst* [1913] 3 KB 507, 546–9; *London Association for Protection of Trade v Greenlands, Ltd* [1916] 2 AC 15.

[21] *Macintosh v Dun* [1908] AC 390 (PC); cf *Watt v Longsdon* [1930] 1 KB 130, 148; Defamation Act 1974 (NSW), s 22(3). The Australian High Court has said that *Macintosh v Dun* does not stand as authority for the proposition that the provision of information for fee or profit deprives a publisher of any qualified privilege to which the occasion of the publication would otherwise be entitled: *Bashford v Information Australia (Newsletters) Pty Ltd* (2004) 204 ALR 193, paras 14–21, 189–90.

[22] *Harris v Thompson* (1853) 13 CB 333; 138 ER 1228; *Lawless v Anglo-Egyptian Cotton and Oil Company* (1869) LR 4 QB 262; *Telegraph Newspaper Co Ltd v Bedford* (1934) 50 CLR 632, 658.

[23] *Duane v Granrott* [1982] VR 767, 782 (trade union); *Kearns v General Council of the Bar* [2003] EMLR 27 (members of the English bar).

[24] *Toogood v Spyring* (1834) 1 CM & R 181; 149 ER 1044.

- communications made by and to electors or candidates or those working for candidates during elections;[25] and
- communications in special purpose subscription bulletins or newsletters.[26]

Publication to uninterested persons

Where publication strays substantially outside the group with a legitimate duty or interest in receiving it, the common law privilege is lost in the United Kingdom and all Australian jurisdictions except New South Wales,[27] even in respect of those publications made to persons who do possess the requisite duty or interest.[28] The privilege will, however, survive publication to uninterested persons if the publication occurs in the ordinary course of business,[29] to trespassers,[30] or perhaps to bystanders to whom the publication is not directed, but by whom it is incidentally seen, provided that the mode of publication was reasonable in the circumstances.[31] Wider latitude appears to be available to defendants where the publication is in response to an attack.[32] In such cases, the publication will be protected where a defendant might honestly and on reasonable grounds have believed that the publication was true and necessary for the purpose of vindicating his or her reputation, even though it in fact was not.[33]

11.08

Application to the Internet

Whether a publication communicated via the Internet is able to attract qualified privilege at common law will thus depend on the circumstances. Where a

11.09

---

[25] *Braddock v Bevins* [1948] 1 KB 580; *Roberts v Bass* (2002) 212 CLR 1, paras 73, 161, 166.

[26] *Bashford v Information Australia (Newsletters) Pty Ltd* (2004) 204 ALR 193.

[27] By reason of the Defamation Act 1974 (NSW), s 20(2), (3): see para 11.37.

[28] eg *Chapman v Ellesmere* [1932] 2 KB 431, 456, 469; *Guise v Kouvelis* (1947) 74 CLR 102, 111–12, 114, cf 122–5. See also *Brown v Croome* (1817) 2 Stark 297; 171 ER 652; *Simpson v Downs* (1867) 16 LT 391; *Standen v South Essex Recorders* (1934) 50 TLR 365; *Morosi v Mirror Newspapers Ltd* [1977] 2 NSWLR 749, 775, 779.

[29] eg where words are printed in the usual way by a printer, or dictated and typed by an employee in the ordinary course of business: *Lawless v Anglo-Egyptian Cotton and Oil Company* (1869) LR 4 QB 262, 269–70; *Boxsius v Goblet Frères* [1894] 1 QB 842; *Edmondson v Birch & Co Ltd* [1907] 1 KB 371.

[30] *Neame v Yellow Cabs (SA) Ltd* [1930] SASR 267, 271.

[31] *Stephens v West Australian Newspapers Ltd* (1994) 182 CLR 211, 263 and the authorities cited therein at n 2; *Makeig v Derwent* [2000] NSWCA 136, paras 34–6; *Roberts v Bass* (2002) 212 CLR 1, para 218 (Hayne J). Gatley (n 1 above) para 14.75, citing *Tench v Great Western Railway* (1873) 33 UCQB 8, gives the example of a notice posted on a board in an office for the attention of a company's employees, which is incidentally seen by some non-employees.

[32] *Hemmings v Gasson* (1858) E B & E 346; 120 ER 537; *Laughton v Bishop of Sodor and Man* (1872) LR 4 PC 495, 504–5; *Loveday v Sun Newspapers Ltd* (1938) 59 CLR 503, 512; *Morosi v Mirror Newspapers Ltd* [1977] 2 NSWLR 749, 780.

[33] *Adam v Ward* [1917] AC 309, 339; *Mowlds v Fergusson* (1940) 64 CLR 206, 214–15; *Loveday v Sun Newspapers Ltd* (1938) 59 CLR 503, 515–16.

person with a duty or interest in communicating certain defamatory material does so via a special-purpose bulletin board, to which only persons with a corresponding duty or interest are permitted to subscribe, it is likely that the privilege would apply. The privilege might survive, in the case of a large number of subscribers, even if a minority did not share the common duty or interest of the others. The same material would not be privileged, however, if it were published on a general-purpose bulletin board or on a web page which is accessible generally to the public, where it could be proved that it was received by persons without the requisite duty or interest.[34]

11.10 Where a person is attacked via the Internet, a reply by that person using the same means of communication will ordinarily be privileged. Sending an e-mail reply to all recipients of an e-mail attack would thus be likely to be protected. Attacked persons might also be entitled to send their reply to any other persons to whose notice they believe the original e-mail attack might have come. Similarly, qualified privilege would be likely to protect a reply to an attack on a bulletin board where the reply is published in a posting on the same bulletin board.

11.11 Where an attack takes place to the world at large on a web page, the attacked person would be likely to be entitled to publish a reply on a web page with substantially the same audience. For example, if an individual attacks another individual on his or her personal web page, a reply on the attacked person's personal web page would be likely to be privileged. A defence of qualified privilege would probably not be available, however, if the reply were published by the attacked person on a web page with a substantially different or larger audience. For example, a reply to an attack on an individual's personal web page, which is likely to have been seen by only a handful of people, would be unlikely to be privileged if published on the web page of a large media organization likely to be viewed by many thousands of people.

D. Publication to the World at Large

Introduction

11.12 The common law requirement that each recipient of a publication have a duty or interest which coincides with that of the publisher therefore imposes significant limitations on the operation of the qualified privilege defence. Generally, only some recipients of mass communications such as newspapers or television

---

[34] See eg *Christian Labour Association of Canada v Retail Wholesale Union* (British Columbia Supreme Court, Rice J, 12 November 2003), paras 22–5, 30–1.

broadcasts, or information posted on general-purpose bulletin boards or web pages, will be likely to have the requisite duty or interest in receiving defamatory material.[35]

The common law has developed, however, in both the United Kingdom and **11.13** Australia, to provide greater protection for the discussion of some subjects of public interest. In the United Kingdom, the principal spurs to development have been the European Convention on Human Rights (ECHR) and the Human Rights Act 1998 (UK) ('the HRA').[36] In Australia, the common law has developed to conform with an implied Constitutional freedom to discuss government and political matters.[37] A third course has been adopted in New Zealand.[38]

United Kingdom: *Reynolds v Times Newspapers Ltd*

Introduction

In *Reynolds v Times Newspapers Ltd*,[39] the House of Lords considered the appli- **11.14** cation of the common law defence of qualified privilege in a case concerning the publication, in a newspaper, of an article concerning a prominent Irish polit- ician. In essence, the plaintiff asserted that the article bore the imputation that he had deliberately and dishonestly misled the Irish Parliament and his Cabinet colleagues by suppressing information concerning the suitability of appointing the Irish Attorney-General to the Presidency of the High Court of Ireland.

The HRA implements in the United Kingdom the rights and freedoms con- **11.15** tained in the ECHR, including the right to freedom of expression set out in Article 10 of the ECHR.[40] The HRA had been passed, but had not commenced operation, at the time *Reynolds* was decided. One of the principal arguments in

---

[35] *Theophanous v Herald & Weekly Times Ltd* (1994) 182 CLR 104, 133 and authorities noted therein at n 98; *Roberts v Bass* (2002) 212 CLR 1, para 215 (Hayne J).

[36] See paras 11.14–11.21 and chapter 30.

[37] See paras 11.22–11.26.

[38] *Lange v Atkinson* [2000] 3 NZLR 385. In that case, the New Zealand Court of Appeal held that a defence of qualified privilege was available to generally published statements made about the actions and qualities of those currently or formerly elected to Parliament and those with immediate aspirations to be members, so far as those actions and qualities directly affect or affected their capacity (including their personal ability and willingness) to meet their public responsibilities. The determination of the matters that bear on that capacity will depend on a consideration of what is properly a matter of public concern rather than of private concern. There is no requirement of 'reasonable care' for the defence of the kind which applies in Australia (as to which, see para 11.25). The case had been remitted to the New Zealand Court of Appeal from the Privy Council (see [2000] 1 NZLR 257), immediately following the House of Lords' decision in *Reynolds v Times Newspapers Ltd*.

[39] [2001] 2 AC 127 ('*Reynolds*').

[40] See para 30.02.

Reynolds, which was ultimately rejected, was that in view of Article 10 of the ECHR and the relevant jurisprudence of the European Court of Human Rights, the common law should develop a generic privilege, available in cases involving the publication of political information.[41]

The decision

11.16   Lord Nicholls, with whom Lords Cooke and Hobhouse expressed full agreement, held that the common law defence of qualified privilege should be available to the press in relation to a broad range of publications concerning subjects of public concern. Lord Nicholls said:

> The press discharges vital functions as a bloodhound as well as a watchdog. The court should be slow to conclude that a publication was not in the public interest and, therefore, the public had no right to know, especially when the information is in the field of political discussion. Any lingering doubts should be resolved in favour of publication.[42]

11.17   In assessing whether the defence should protect the press in a particular case, Lord Nicholls held that the full range of circumstances should be taken into account, including:

> 1. The seriousness of the allegation. The more serious the charge, the more the public is misinformed and the individual harmed, if the allegation is not true. 2. The nature of the information, and the extent to which the subject matter is a matter of public concern. 3. The source of the information. Some informants have no direct knowledge of the events. Some have their own axes to grind, or are being paid for their stories. 4. The steps taken to verify the information. 5. The status of the information. The allegation may have already been the subject of an investigation which commands respect. 6. The urgency of the matter. News is often a perishable commodity. 7. Whether comment was sought from the plaintiff. He may have information others do not possess or have not disclosed. An approach to the plaintiff will not always be necessary. 8. Whether the article contained the gist of the plaintiff's side of the story. 9. The tone of the article. A newspaper can raise queries or call for an investigation. It need not adopt allegations as statements of fact. 10. The circumstances of the publication, including the timing.[43]

Lord Nicholls said this list was not exhaustive, and that the weight to be given to these and any other relevant factors will vary from case to case. He said that in general, a newspaper's unwillingness to disclose the identity of a source should not be held against it.[44]

In the circumstances of the case, Lord Nicholls held that the defence was not

---

[41] See also paras 30.37–30.38.
[42] *Reynolds v Times Newspapers Ltd* [2001] 2 AC 127, 205.
[43] ibid.
[44] ibid.

made out. Although the subject matter of the article was clearly of public concern, the allegations were very serious, were presented as statements of fact, and were published without reference to the plaintiff's considered explanation. In all the circumstances, the public did not have a 'right to know' the information presented.[45]

Lords Steyn and Hope dissented in the result, concluding that the defendant's **11.18** failure to publish the plaintiff's explanation should not be treated, as a matter of law, as precluding it from successfully relying on a defence of qualified privilege.[46]

The effect of Reynolds

The effect of *Reynolds* is to liberalize the circumstances in which publications to **11.19** the public at large will be protected by a defence of qualified privilege in the United Kingdom.[47] Earlier decisions had only occasionally applied the defence in such cases.[48] The approach in *Reynolds* is, broadly, to extend the defence to those cases where the public has a 'right to know', with lingering doubts resolved in favour of permitting publication.[49] Where a publication concerns the conduct of politicians, the privilege is likely to be available 'without too much difficulty'.[50]

The *Reynolds* privilege is 'concerned to provide a proper degree of protection for responsible journalism when reporting matters of public concern'.[51] Responsible journalism is 'the point at which a fair balance is held between freedom of expression on matters of public concern and the reputations of individuals'.[52] The standard expected of responsible journalists is to be applied in a flexible manner having regard to practical realities and without unnecessary or undesirable legalisms or rigidity.[53] A journalist who fails to appreciate that an article will convey a defamatory meaning to ordinary, reasonable readers, and so fails to

---

[45] *Reynolds*, 206.

[46] ibid, 216, 237.

[47] *Reynolds* has been accepted in Scotland: *Adams v Guardian Newspapers Ltd* 2003 SLT 1058, 1070 (Lord Reed).

[48] See eg *Brown v Croome* (1817) 2 Stark 297; 171 ER 652; *Cox v Feeney* (1863) 4 F & F 13; 176 ER 445; *Simpson v Downs* (1867) 16 LT 391; *Purcell v Sowler* (1877) 2 CPD 215; *Allbutt v General Council of Medical Education and Registration* (1889) 23 QBD 400; *Standen v South Essex Recorders* (1934) 50 TLR 365; *Perera v Peiris* [1949] AC 1; *Webb v Times Publishing Co Ltd* [1960] 2 QB 535; *Blackshaw v Lord* [1984] QB 1; *Templeton v Jones* [1984] 1 NZLR 448.

[49] *Reynolds v Times Newspapers Ltd* [2001] 2 AC 127, 205. See also *GKR Karate (UK) Ltd v Yorkshire Post Newspapers Ltd* [2000] 2 All ER 931.

[50] *Reynolds v Times Newspapers Ltd* [2001] 2 AC 127, 235.

[51] *Bonnick v Morris* [2003] 1 AC 300, 309 (PC); *Kearns v General Council of the Bar* [2003] EMLR 27, 582–3.

[52] *Bonnick v Morris* [2003] 1 AC 300, 309 (PC).

[53] ibid.

make further inquiries, may thus be entitled to the benefit of the *Reynolds* privilege if her conduct as a whole constituted responsible journalism.[54]

In ascertaining whether a publication occurs on a privileged occasion, it is not necessary to inquire into the truth or falsity of the publication. Rather, the relevant question is whether, in all the circumstances, the public was entitled to know the particular information without the publisher making further inquiries, having regard to the factors identified by Lord Nicholls.[55] Further, it is clear that only the occasion of the publication may be examined for the purposes of ascertaining whether the privilege is available, not the circumstances 'as they might have appeared to the publishers weeks or months later if they had waited to make further inquiries, or waited to see if further facts came to light'.[56]

Defendants may be able to avail themselves of the privilege by publishing, without attempting verification, both sides to a dispute fully, fairly, and in a disinterested manner, provided that they do not in any way suggest that they are adopting the allegations made by one side or the other.[57] Other than in such neutral reportage situations, however, in seeking to demonstrate that a publication accords with the requirements of responsible journalism, a publisher will generally need to establish that those responsible for the publication believed it was true.[58]

11.20 In *Lange v Atkinson*, the New Zealand Court of Appeal held that the decision in *Reynolds* 'appears to alter the structure of the law of qualified privilege in a way which adds to the uncertainty and chilling effect almost inevitably present in this area of the law'.[59] The court declined to adopt Lord Nicholls' checklist of matters relevant to the existence of an occasion of qualified privilege in the United Kingdom,[60] noting that section 19 of the Defamation Act 1992 (NZ) enabled New Zealand courts to control misuses of the privilege,[61] and that there

---

[54] ibid, 309–10. The English Court of Appeal has yet to consider whether *Bonnick v Morris* represents the law of England and Wales: see *Jameel v Wall Street Journal Europe Sprl (No 2)* [2005] EWCA Civ 74, para 97.

[55] *GKR Karate (UK) Ltd v Yorkshire Post Newspapers Ltd* [2000] 2 All ER 931.

[56] *Loutchansky v Times Newspapers Ltd* [2002] QB 321, para 80 (Brooke LJ), paras 87–8 (Sir Martin Nourse); *Al-Fagih v HH Saudi Research & Marketing (UK) Ltd* [2002] EMLR 13, 236.

[57] *Al-Fagih v HH Saudi Research & Marketing (UK) Ltd* [2002] EMLR 13; cf *Adams v Guardian Newspapers Ltd* 2003 SLT 1058, 1068.

[58] *Jameel v Wall Street Journal Europe Sprl (No 2)* [2005] EWCA Civ 74, paras 27–9.

[59] [2000] 3 NZLR 385, 399.

[60] See para 11.17.

[61] Under the Defamation Act 1992 (NZ), s 19, qualified privilege is defeated where the defendant is predominantly motivated by ill-will towards the plaintiff, or otherwise takes improper advantage of the occasion of publication.

were 'significant differences between the constitutional and political context in New Zealand and the United Kingdom in which this body of law operates'.[62]

Application to the Internet

The factors identified by Lord Nicholls as being relevant to the availability of the defence of qualified privilege in cases involving publication to the public at large are capable of being applied to material published via the Internet. In most instances, those factors will apply in the same way as they would apply to traditional media, such as newspapers and broadcasters. The Internet is, however, a global medium of publication. Matters which are in the public interest in some part of the United Kingdom may not be in the public interest in other parts of the United Kingdom, or in other parts of the world. In some cases, therefore, publishing material on a web page, or on a general-purpose bulletin board with an extensive global readership, may militate against the availability of the defence, because the offending material will have been published to persons who do not have a 'right to know', or an interest in receiving, the information.

11.21

Australia: reasonable discussion of government and political matters

Introduction

In Australia, the High Court has held that each member of the Australian community has an interest[63] in disseminating and receiving 'information, opinions and arguments concerning government and political matters that affect the people of Australia'.[64] The court developed an expanded defence of qualified

11.22

---

[62] [2000] 3 NZLR 385, 399.

[63] *Lange v Australian Broadcasting Corporation* (1997) 189 CLR 520, 571.

[64] ibid. The decision in *Lange* marked a substantial change to the manner in which Australian defamation law protects the discussion of government and political matters. The position prior to *Lange* can be briefly described as follows. In 1992, the High Court recognized for the first time the existence of an implied freedom of communication in relation to public affairs and political discussion: *Nationwide News Pty Ltd v Wills* (1992) 177 CLR 1; *Australian Capital Television Pty Ltd v Commonwealth of Australia (No 2)* (1992) 177 CLR 106. The implied freedom was held to limit the Commonwealth's legislative power. Laws which restricted freedom of communication in relation to public affairs and political discussion were only valid if the restriction was 'necessary to protect other legitimate interests and, in any event, not to an extent which substantially impairs the capacity of, or opportunity for, the Australian people to form the political judgments required for the exercise of their constitutional functions': *Nationwide News*, 51 (Brennan J); see also 77 (Toohey J); *Australian Capital Television*, 143. The High Court developed the implied freedom concept in *Theophanous v Herald & Weekly Times Ltd* (1994) 182 CLR 104. In that case it was held that the implied freedom extended both to State laws and the common law, including the common law of defamation. Publications concerning government and political matters were not actionable where defendants established that they were unaware of the falsity of the material published, that they did not publish the material recklessly and that the publication was reasonable in the circumstances ('the Constitutional defence'): see *Theophanous*, 145, 187–8.

privilege to protect widely disseminated publications[65] discussing such matters, provided that publication is reasonable, and not actuated by malice.[66] The expanded defence is commonly known as the '*Lange* defence'.

The House of Lords declined to adopt the *Lange* defence for the United Kingdom in *Reynolds v Times Newspapers Ltd.*[67] The Australian High Court is yet to consider the application of *Reynolds* in Australia. The New South Wales Court of Appeal has held that *Reynolds* does not change the law for New South Wales.[68]

Government and political matters

11.23　The subjects of discussion which concern government and political matters include the selection, election, and performance of members of federal parliament[69] and of the executive and public service,[70] matters the subject of referenda for the amendment of the Constitution,[71] and the affairs of statutory authorities and public utilities.[72] The privilege is capable of extending to the discussion of government and political matters at a State, Territory, and even local

---

In *Stephens v West Australian Newspapers Ltd* (1994) 182 CLR 211, 234 it was noted that a defendant seeking to rely on the defence of qualified privilege in relation to a publication which discussed government and political matters did not have to allege a duty to publish the matter complained of.

Following *Theophanous* and *Stephens*, the position appeared to be that a defendant seeking to rely on the defence of qualified privilege in cases concerning the discussion of government or political matters had only to prove that the subject of discussion fell within the scope of the implied freedom. A plaintiff wishing to defeat the defence had to prove malice on the part of the defendant. The defence of qualified privilege was thus considerably more attractive for defendants than the Constitutional defence because, to succeed, defendants did not have to prove that they were unaware of the falsity of the material they published, that they had not published the material recklessly, or that the publication was reasonable in the circumstances.

Lange had the effect of overturning the Constitutional defence and limiting the availability of qualified privilege in cases concerning the discussion of government and political matters to cases where the defendant can prove that the publication was reasonable: 572–4. The court noted that the additional elements of the Constitutional defence (want of knowledge of falsity and absence of recklessness) were of little practical significance: 574.

See generally Michael Chesterman, *Freedom of Speech in Australian Law: A Delicate Plant* (2000).

[65]　cf publications made to individuals or defined groups which would be entitled to the benefit of a qualified privilege defence at common law: *Roberts v Bass* (2002) 212 CLR 1, paras 73, 224–5. In such cases the 'reasonableness' requirement does not arise. See also *Herald & Weekly Times Ltd v Popovic* [2003] VSCA 161, para 11.

[66]　*Lange v Australian Broadcasting Corporation* (1997) 189 CLR 520, 572–4.

[67]　[2001] 2 AC 127; see paras 11.14–11.21.

[68]　*John Fairfax & Sons Ltd v Vilo* (2001) 52 NSWLR 373.

[69]　*Lange v Australian Broadcasting Corporation* (1997) 189 CLR 520, 559–60, 571.

[70]　ibid, 561, 567, 571.

[71]　ibid, 561.

[72]　ibid.

government level.[73] The discussion of government and political matters concerning the United Nations or other countries may be protected.[74] Such discussions are protected even during the period between elections.[75]

Limits.   There are many cases concerning the limits of the privilege. Notably,   **11.24**
the privilege has been held not to extend to the discussion of disputes concerning the Australian cycling team,[76] the actions of a company and its officers which had attracted the interest of the Australian Competition and Consumer Commission,[77] the publication of statements made to journalists by police,[78] the publication of a city council's views about the failure of one of its tenants and ratepayers to pay rent,[79] a publication about the use of legal proceedings or the threat of proceedings for the purpose of silencing opponents to the construction of a controversial bridge,[80] or a publication imputing that a magistrate was unfit to hold office and should be removed.[81]

Reasonableness

A publication will generally be reasonable where the publisher had reasonable   **11.25**
grounds for believing any defamatory imputations to be true and took such steps as were appropriate to verify the accuracy of those imputations.[82] The publisher must usually have sought and published a response from the defamed person, unless to do so was impracticable or unnecessary.[83] Failing to disclose the whole of an exchange, and thereby distorting the facts, precludes a finding of reasonableness.[84] Common law malice, to the extent that it is 'not covered under

---

[73] ibid, 571–2; *Brander v Ryan* (2000) 78 SASR 234, 248; *Conservation Council of SA Inc v Chapman* [2003] SASC 398, para 11; cf *John Fairfax Publications Pty Ltd v Attorney-General for the State of New South Wales* (2000) 181 ALR 694, para 87.

[74] *Lange v Australian Broadcasting Corporation* (1997) 189 CLR 520, 571.

[75] ibid, 561.

[76] *Watt v Herald & Weekly Times Ltd* [1998] 3 VR 740.

[77] *International Financing & Investment Pty Ltd v Kent* (Supreme Court of Western Australia, Anderson J, 9 April 1998). Anderson J suggested that if the Chairman of the Australian Competition and Consumer Commission had sued in respect of that part of the publication that referred to him, the publisher might have been entitled to rely on the privilege to defeat that suit.

[78] *Deren v State of New South Wales* [1998] Aust Torts Reports ¶81–463.

[79] *Heytesbury Holdings Pty Ltd v City of Subiaco* (1998) 19 WAR 440.

[80] *Conservation Council of SA Inc v Chapman* [2003] SASC 398.

[81] *Herald & Weekly Times Ltd v Popovic* [2003] VSCA 161, paras 6, 9 (Winneke ACJ), 504–7 (Warren AJA), cf 247–53 (Gillard AJA).

[82] *Lange v Australian Broadcasting Corporation* (1997) 189 CLR 520, 574.

[83] ibid; cf *Brander v Ryan* (2000) 78 SASR 234, 250, in which it was held that it was 'not practicable nor indeed was it necessary in view of the plaintiff's conduct for the defendants to seek a response from the plaintiff' prior to publication. See also *Nationwide News Pty Ltd v Redford* [2001] SASC 198, paras 23, 59–60: unnecessary to obtain a response from the plaintiff before publishing an article reporting on proceedings in Parliament the previous day, at least where the writer did not seek 'to put a particular slant on the article'; the writer's failure to convey a fair impression of what occurred in Parliament, however, was unreasonable.

[84] *Herald & Weekly Times Ltd v Popovic* [2003] VSCA 161, paras 14, 221–9.

the rubric of reasonableness', will defeat the *Lange* defence.[85] Reasonableness is not a concept that can be subjected to 'inflexible categorization'.[86]

The motive of causing political damage to a plaintiff or a political party is not, however, an improper motive that would destroy the *Lange* defence.[87]

Application to the Internet

11.26 Where a defamatory publication concerning Australian government and political matters is made via a bulletin board or web page which is accessible globally, or via an e-mail sent to persons outside Australia, the manner and extent of publication is an additional factor which is relevant to the reasonableness of the publication.[88] In such cases, the defamatory publication may be received by a substantial group of people who do not have the same duty or interest as the people of Australia themselves in receiving information concerning Australian government or political matters. It may be that the qualified privilege defence concerning the discussion of government and political matters should fail in such cases, in accordance with the usual rules applying where a publication is made to persons without the requisite duty or interest in receiving it.[89] While, therefore, a defamatory article in a national newspaper concerning the conduct of a Member of Parliament might be published on an occasion of qualified privilege, the same article published on a web page operated by the newspaper might not be privileged if it is published to a substantial number of people outside Australia with no duty or interest in receiving information concerning Australian government and political matters.

---

[85] *Lange v Australian Broadcasting Corporation* (1997) 189 CLR 520, 574; *Brander v Ryan* (2000) 78 SASR 234, 250; *Roberts v Bass* (2002) 212 CLR 1.

[86] *Rogers v Nationwide News Pty Ltd* (2003) 201 ALR 184, para 30 (Gleeson CJ and Gummow J).

[87] *Lange v Australian Broadcasting Corporation* (1997) 189 CLR 520, 574; *Roberts v Bass* (2002) 212 CLR 1, paras 68 (Gaudron, McHugh, and Gummow JJ), 171–2 (Kirby J).

[88] The 'reasonableness' limitation imposed by the High Court in *Lange* was intended to be similar to the statutory reasonableness limitation to the defence of qualified privilege in s 22 of the Defamation Act 1974 (NSW): see *Lange* (1997) 189 CLR 520, 572–3. The manner and extent of publication is a factor relevant to 'reasonableness' in the s 22 defence: *Wright v Australian Broadcasting Commission* [1977] 1 NSWLR 697, 712; see para 11.33.

[89] See para 11.08.

E. Related Statutory Defences: Queensland, Tasmania, and New South Wales

Queensland and Tasmania

In Queensland and Tasmania, the relevant Defamation Acts[90] each prescribe a broad range of circumstances in which a defence of qualified protection will operate in respect of material published in good faith, including:

11.27

(c) for the protection of the interests of the person who makes the publication, or of some other person, or for the public good;

. . .

(e) for the purpose of giving information to the person to whom it is made with respect to a subject as to which that person has, or is reasonably believed by the person who makes the publication to have, such an interest in knowing the truth as to make the last-mentioned person's conduct in making the publication reasonable in the circumstances;

. . .

(g) in order to answer or refute some other defamatory matter published by the person defamed concerning the person by whom the publication is made or some other person; or

(h) in the course of, or for the purposes, of the discussion of a subject of public interest the public discussion of which is for the public benefit.[91]

Breadth of the statutory protection

These provisions are broad in their scope: section 16(1)(h) in particular extends to the public discussion of matters which involve 'the actions or omissions of a person or institution engaged in activities that either inherently, expressly or inferentially invited public criticism or discussion'.[92] The conduct of the plaintiff need not itself be the subject of public interest, provided that the

11.28

---

[90] Defamation Act 1889 (Qld), s 16(1); Defamation Act 1957 (Tas), s 16(1).

[91] Defamation Act 1957 (Tas), s 16(1). The categories in the Defamation Act 1889 (Qld), s 16(1) are materially identical, with the exception of s 16(1)(h) which establishes a defence:

for the publication of defamatory matter . . .

(h) if the publication is made in good faith in the course of, or for the purposes of, the discussion of some subject of public interest, the public discussion of which is for the public benefit, and if, so far as the defamatory matter consists of comment, the comment is fair.

The reference to 'comment' in this provision does not import the elements of the common law defence of fair comment: a defendant need not establish that the comment is based on facts which are substantially true, and stated or indicated in the material: *Pervan v North Queensland Newspaper Co Ltd* (1993) 178 CLR 309, 324 and authorities cited therein at n 59.

[92] *Bellino v Australian Broadcasting Corporation* (1996) 185 CLR 183, 215 (Dawson, McHugh, and Gummow JJ).

imputations concerning that conduct are published in the course of a discussion concerning the conduct of some other person or institution which invites public criticism or discussion.[93]

Absence of good faith

11.29   The statutory qualified protection defence in section 16(1) is defeated on proof by the plaintiff[94] that the defendant lacked good faith.[95] An absence of good faith will be proved where the publication is not relevant to the occasions of privilege set out in section 16(1) or the manner and extent of the publication exceeds what is reasonably sufficient for the occasion, or where the person by whom the publication is made is actuated by ill-will or any other improper motive, or believes the defamatory matter to be untrue.[96]

Application to the Internet

11.30   Publications communicated via bulletin boards and web pages accessible throughout the world will frequently be likely to exceed what is reasonably sufficient for the purposes of the qualified protection defence in Queensland and Tasmania. Similar considerations will apply as with the common law defence, where a publication is made to persons without any duty or interest in receiving it,[97] although unlike the position at common law, the burden of proving that the publication has exceeded what is reasonably sufficient lies with the plaintiff.

New South Wales

11.31   In New South Wales, in addition to the common law defence of qualified privilege, a statutory defence of qualified privilege applies under section 22 of the Defamation Act 1974 (NSW) in respect of publications where

    (a) the recipient has an interest or apparent interest in having information on some subject;

    (b) the matter is published to the recipient in the course of giving to him information on that subject; and

    (c) the conduct of the publisher in publishing that matter is reasonable in the circumstances.[98]

---

[93] ibid, 221–2.
[94] Defamation Act 1889 (Qld), s 17; Defamation Act 1957 (Tas), s 19.
[95] The requirement of good faith is expressly set out in Defamation Act 1889 (Qld), s 16(1) and Defamation Act 1957 (Tas), s 16(1).
[96] Defamation Act 1889 (Qld), s 16(2); Defamation Act 1957 (Tas), s 16(2).
[97] See para 11.08.
[98] Defamation Act 1974 (NSW), s 22(1).

Breadth of the statutory protection

Recipients have an apparent interest in having information on some subject **11.32**
only if the publisher believes on reasonable grounds that they have that interest.[99] The onus of proving reasonableness is on the defendant.[100] Unlike common law qualified privilege, defendants seeking to rely on section 22 do not
have to prove a duty or interest in making the defamatory publication. The
circumstances in which a defence of qualified privilege under section 22 can
arise are thus considerably broader than those under the common law.

Reasonableness

By section 22(2A) of the Defamation Act 1974 (NSW), a court may take such **11.33**
matters into account as it considers relevant for the purposes of determining
whether the conduct of the publisher was reasonable in the circumstances,
including:

  (a) the extent to which the matter published is of public concern;
  (b) the extent to which the matter published concerns the performance of the
     public functions or activities of the person;
  (c) the seriousness of any defamatory imputation carried by the matter
     published;
  (d) the extent to which the matter published distinguishes between suspicions,
     allegations and proven facts;
  (e) whether it was necessary in the circumstances for the matter published to
     be published expeditiously;
  (f) the sources of the information in the matter published and the integrity of
     those sources;
  (g) whether the matter published contained the substance of the person's side
     of the story and, if not, whether a reasonable attempt was made by the
     publisher to obtain and publish a response from the person;
  (h) any other steps taken to verify the information in the matter published.[101]

Notably, the matters prescribed in section 22(2A) do not include whether
publishers had an honest belief in the truth of their publication.[102]

---

[99] Defamation Act 1974 (NSW), s 22(2).
[100] See eg *Morosi v Mirror Newspapers Ltd* [1977] 2 NSWLR 749, 797; *Wright v Australian Broadcasting Commission* [1977] 1 NSWLR 697, 700; *Barbaro v Amalgamated Television Services Pty Ltd* (1985) 1 NSWLR 30, 44.
[101] See also *Wright v Australian Broadcasting Commission* [1977] 1 NSWLR 697, 700–1, 712; *Lange v Australian Broadcasting Corporation* (1997) 189 CLR 520, 572–5.
[102] Before the insertion of s 22(2A) into the Defamation Act 1974 (NSW) by the Defamation Amendment Act 2002 (NSW), such a belief was critical to the availability of the s 22 defence: see *Morgan v John Fairfax & Sons Ltd [No 2]* (1991) 23 NSWLR 374, 385–6; *Wright v Australian Broadcasting Commission* [1977] 1 NSWLR 697, 712; *Kaiser v George Laurens (NSW) Pty Ltd* [1982] 1 NSWLR 294, 298; *Barbaro v Amalgamated Television Services Pty Ltd* (1985) 1 NSWLR 30, 44.

The manner and extent of publication would also appear to be a relevant matter for the purpose of determining whether the conduct of a publisher was reasonable in the circumstances.[103]

In some circumstances it might be reasonable to publish, without endorsement, a defamatory statement made by another person, even where the publisher does not have a genuine belief in the truth of the publication.[104]

Reasonableness is to be judged, flexibly, by reference to the public interest in freedom of speech and the protection of the plaintiff's reputation. The legitimate commercial interests of a publisher are entitled to some consideration, but only where publishers demonstrate with particularity why their conduct was reasonable having regard to the circumstances in which they make their publications.[105] In some circumstances, it may be unreasonable not to have material examined by a lawyer before publication.[106]

11.34 As with the *Lange* defence, and the statutory defences in Queensland and Tasmania, the defence is unlikely to be available in many cases where defamatory material is published via the Internet.[107] The defence will be likely to fail in those cases where the choice of the Internet as a medium for publication means that the manner and extent of publication has exceeded what is reasonable.

Employees, agents, and strangers

11.35 Where an employer or principal publishes the material of an employee or agent, the section 22 defence will fail if the employee's or agent's conduct has not been reasonable in the circumstances. By contrast, where defendants publish material prepared by some person other than themselves, or their employees or agents, the defence only fails if the decision to publish was not reasonable in the circumstances.[108]

11.36 Internet intermediaries who make the defamatory material of others available via their computer systems will thus not be entitled to the benefit of the section 22 defence unless they can show that their decision to publish was reasonable in the circumstances. Factors which are relevant to the reasonableness of the intermediary's conduct might include the reliability, reputation, and past conduct of

---

[103] *Wright v Australian Broadcasting Commission* [1977] 1 NSWLR 697, 712.
[104] *Makim v John Fairfax & Sons Ltd* [1990] Aust Defamation Reports ¶50,075, 40,526 (circumstances analogous to a common law duty to pass on such statements without endorsement, as to which see para 11.40).
[105] *Rogers v Nationwide News Pty Ltd* (2003) 201 ALR 184, paras 30, 32 (Gleeson CJ and Gummow J).
[106] ibid, paras 133 (Callinan J), 173 (Heydon J).
[107] See paras 11.26, 11.30.
[108] *Morgan v John Fairfax & Sons Ltd [No 2]* (1991) 23 NSWLR 374, 382.

the author of the defamatory material,[109] whether the intermediary was on notice that the defamatory material was likely to be published via its computer system, or the reasonableness of an intermediary publishing material without monitoring or censoring it, having regard to the nature of the Internet and the commercial circumstances of the intermediary.[110]

Publication to uninterested persons

Under section 20(2) of the Defamation Act 1974 (NSW), where material is **11.37** published to a number of recipients, only some of whom have the requisite interest in receiving it, then the defence of qualified privilege will be available in respect of publications to those recipients, but not to other recipients who do not have an interest in receiving the material. Under section 20(3), however, the defence will be available even in respect of publications to recipients without the requisite interest in receiving the publication if the extent of publication is reasonable having regard to the matter published and to the occasion of qualified privilege. This provision applies both to common law and statutory categories of qualified privilege in New South Wales.[111]

Reasonable belief

Finally, under section 21 of the Defamation Act 1974 (NSW), where a defence **11.38** of qualified privilege would be available in respect of some publication if a recipient of the publication bore some character, and the publisher believes at the time of communication, on reasonable grounds, that the recipient does bear that character, then the publisher will be entitled to a defence of qualified privilege. Again, this qualification applies both to the common law, and statutory defences of qualified privilege in New South Wales.

F. Malice

Onus

At common law, proof by the claimant that the defendant was actuated by **11.39** malice will defeat all forms of the defence of qualified privilege, including the fair reports forms of qualified privilege considered in the next chapter.[112] In most cases where qualified privilege is embodied in legislation, the onus to prove

---

[109] *Austin v Mirror Newspapers Ltd* (1985) 3 NSWLR 354, 363 (PC).
[110] cf *Rogers v Nationwide News Pty Ltd* (2003) 201 ALR 184, paras 30, 32 (Gleeson CJ and Gummow J).
[111] cf the general position at common law: see para 11.08.
[112] *Toogood v Spyring* (1834) 1 CM & R 181, 193; 149 ER 1044, 1049–50; *Adam v Ward* [1917] AC 309, 334.

malice or an absence of good faith is on the claimant.[113] Malice requires a determination of the subjective state of mind of the publisher at the time of publication.[114]

Malice defined

11.40   Defendants are actuated by malice in relation to a defamatory publication if they make the publication for some dominant[115] purpose other than that for which the privilege is given, or if they know or believe that what they published is false.[116] Malice may be inferred from a defendant's ill-will, prejudice, bias, recklessness, lack of positive belief in the truth of what is published, or improper motive if there is some ground for concluding that it existed on the privileged occasion and actuated the publication.[117]

The privilege will not be lost, however, where defendants know or suspect a defamatory statement is false if they pass it on, without endorsement, in circumstances where they are under a duty to do so.[118]

Defendants are not actuated by malice merely because they are careless, impulsive, irrational, or prejudiced.[119] A failure to take steps to verify the truth of defamatory allegations may constitute malice, however, if the jury could 'infer that the defendant purposely stopped short in his inquiries in order to avoid ascertaining the truth'.[120]

---

[113] But cf Wrongs Act 1958 (Vic), s 5 (publication in a newspaper or periodical of a fair and accurate report of the proceedings of a municipal council); Constitution Act 1975 (Vic), s 74(3) (abstracts of reports, papers, votes, or proceedings of either House or any committee of the Victorian Parliament); Civil Liability Act 1936 (SA), s 12(3) (extracts from or abstracts of certain reports, papers, votes, or proceedings of the South Australian Parliament).

[114] *GKR Karate (UK) Ltd v Yorkshire Post Newspapers Ltd* [2000] 2 All ER 931.

[115] *Horrocks v Lowe* [1975] AC 135, 149; *Reynolds v Times Newspapers Ltd* [2001] 2 AC 127, 194; *Barbaro v Amalgamated Television Services Pty Ltd* (1985) 1 NSWLR 30, 51; *Roberts v Bass* (2002) 212 CLR 1, para 104 (Gaudron, McHugh, and Gummow JJ).

[116] *Horrocks v Lowe* [1975] AC 135, 149–50; *Reynolds v Times Newspapers Ltd* [2001] 2 AC 127, 194; *Webb v Bloch* (1928) 41 CLR 331, 368; *Roberts v Bass* (2002) 212 CLR 1, see esp paras 62, 75–90, 98 (Gaudron, McHugh, and Gummow JJ), 192 (Kirby J); *Amalgamated Television Services Pty Ltd v Marsden* [2002] NSWCA 419, paras 824–5; *W v Westminster City Council* [2005] EWHC 102.

[117] *Roberts v Bass* (2002) 212 CLR 1, paras 76, 78–9 (Gaudron, McHugh, and Gummow JJ), cf 45 (Gleeson CJ).

[118] *Horrocks v Lowe* [1975] AC 135, 151; *Barbaro v Amalgamated Television Services Pty Ltd* (1985) 1 NSWLR 30, 50; *Roberts v Bass* (2002) 212 CLR 1, para 76 (Gaudron, McHugh, and Gummow JJ).

[119] *Horrocks v Lowe* [1975] AC 135, 150; *Barbaro v Amalgamated Television Services Pty Ltd* (1985) 1 NSWLR 30, 50; *Roberts v Bass* (2002) 212 CLR 1, paras 5, 13 (Gleeson CJ), 103 (Gaudron, McHugh, and Gummow JJ).

[120] *Hansen v Border Morning Mail Pty Ltd* (1987) 9 NSWLR 44, 55. See also *R v Crabbe* (1985) 156 CLR 464, 470; *Roberts v Bass* (2002) 212 CLR 1, para 84 (Gaudron, McHugh, and Gummow JJ) (sheer recklessness or wilful blindness).

Where a claimant proves that a defendant's dominant motive in publishing defamatory material was improper, such as spite or ill-will, the defence will be defeated even where the defendant genuinely believed the defamatory material to be true.[121] Past conduct by the defendant may be admissible to infer malice.[122]

The use by a defendant of extreme or disproportionate language may also lead to an inference that the defendant was actuated by malice, if the 'extremity and exaggeration of the language is explicable only by reference to the existence of ill will in the defendant'.[123]

It has been held in Australia that an object of destroying the election prospects of a candidate, without more, is not an improper motive.[124]

Although malice is presumed in Scots law,[125] a defence of qualified privilege is only defeated where the pursuer affirmatively pleads and proves that the defender was actuated by malice.[126]

Application to the Internet

It may be that, in some cases, malice on the part of a defendant could be inferred from publication via the Internet of defamatory material, on the basis that the defendant's choice of that medium reveals a dominant motive to inflict the maximum possible amount of damage on the claimant's reputation.[127]

11.41

Publishing the statement of another

As with malice in the context of fair comment, employers and principals are imputed with the malice of their employees and agents.[128] A defendant is not,

11.42

---

[121] *Horrocks v Lowe* [1975] AC 135, 149–52.

[122] ibid, 151.

[123] *Calwell v Ipec Australia Ltd* (1975) 135 CLR 321, 332 (Mason J).

[124] *Lange v Australian Broadcasting Corporation* (1997) 189 CLR 520, 574; *Roberts v Bass* (2002) 212 CLR 1, paras 11, 14, 39 (Gleeson CJ), 68 (Gaudron, McHugh, and Gummow JJ), 184 (Kirby J).

[125] See para 7.01 (n 1).

[126] Kenneth Norrie, *Defamation and Related Actions in Scots Law* (1995) 103; JM Thomson, *Delictual Liability* (1994) 216–17; Francis McManus and Eleanor Russell, *Delict* (1998) 323.

[127] In *Green v Schneller* [2000] Aust Torts Reports ¶81–568, 63,905 eg Simpson J of the New South Wales Supreme Court held that malice could be inferred from the manner and extent of publication; in that case, by making defamatory allegations to a television reporter 'in the certain knowledge, and with the obvious intention, that they would be broadcast on a national television programme'. See also *Ross v Holley* (Ontario Superior Court of Justice, Low J, 9 November 2004), para 14: 'The defendant's conduct in asking the recipients of his e-mail to re-disseminate to as many individuals as possible was calculated to cause the plaintiff the maximum embarrassment and professional harm and the defendant was persistent in this.'

[128] *Egger v Viscount Chelmsford* [1965] 1 QB 248, 265, 266, 269; *Roberts v Bass* (2002) 212 CLR 1, paras 181–3 (Kirby J).

however, affected by the malice of another defendant in respect of a joint publication,[129] except where the defendant knows that the other defendant was actuated by malice.[130] Internet intermediaries who make defamatory material prepared by others available via their computer systems will thus not be affected by malice on the part of persons other than their employees and agents, unless they were aware that the author knew or believed the publication was false, or was actuated by an improper motive.

Queensland, Tasmania, and New South Wales

Queensland and Tasmania

11.43 Proof by the plaintiff that the defendant lacked good faith[131] will defeat the statutory defences of qualified protection in Queensland and Tasmania.[132]

New South Wales

11.44 In New South Wales, common law malice defeats the defence in section 22 of the Defamation Act 1974 (NSW).[133] Malice will not defeat a defence of qualified privilege in New South Wales, however, where the imputation complained of is a matter of substantial truth and the manner of publication was reasonable having regard to the imputation and to the occasion of qualified privilege.[134]

---

[129] *Egger v Viscount Chelmsford* [1965] 1 QB 265, 266, 272.
[130] *Australian Broadcasting Corporation v Comalco Ltd* (1986) 12 FCR 510; *Bass v TCN Channel Nine Pty Ltd* [2003] NSWCA 118, paras 114 (Handley JA), 164–6, 171 (Wood CJ).
[131] As to the meaning of 'good faith' in this context, see para 11.29.
[132] See paras 11.27–11.30.
[133] See paras 11.31–11.38.
[134] Defamation Act 1974 (NSW), ss 14, 15(2).

12

THE FAIR REPORTS FORM OF QUALIFIED PRIVILEGE

A. Common Law

Overview

At common law, qualified privilege also protects the publication in certain circumstances of fair and accurate reports of certain judicial and parliamentary proceedings, and extracts from and abstracts of certain publicly available records.[1] Malice defeats the defence.[2] In the United Kingdom, the privilege is subject to

12.01

---

[1] *Kimber v The Press Association, Ltd* [1893] 1 QB 65, 68–9, 73, 75–6; *Cunningham v The Scotsman Publications Ltd* 1987 SLT 698: reports of open court proceedings; *Wason v Walter* (1868) LR 4 QB 73, 93: reports of parliamentary proceedings; *Searles v Scarlett* [1892] 2 QB 56, 60, 63, 64; *Gobbart v West Australian Newspapers Ltd* [1968] WAR 113, 120: reports of material contained in registers kept pursuant to legislation which, by legislation, are open to public inspection. In *Gobbart* it was held that the privilege did not extend to fair reports of affidavits filed with the Supreme Court, because the public inspection of such affidavits was made available as a matter of practice and not by law; cf *Smith v Harris* (Supreme Court of Victoria, Byrne J, 1 December 1995) 29–30 and the authorities cited therein. At common law, fair reports of foreign court proceedings may be entitled to qualified privilege if the proceedings are of 'intrinsic world-wide importance, so that a reasonable man in any civilized country, wishing to be well-informed, will be glad to read it, and would think he ought to read it if he has the time available', or if they have 'special connection with' affairs in the jurisdiction in which the report is published, such that the report is of 'legitimate and proper interest' for readers in that jurisdiction: *Webb v Times Publishing Co Ltd* [1960] 2 QB 535, 563–70 (Pearson J).

[2] Malice is discussed in paras 11.39–11.44.

section 8(6) of the Rehabilitation of Offenders Act 1974.[3] By legislation, certain reports of judicial proceedings now enjoy absolute privilege in the United Kingdom[4] and some Australian jurisdictions.[5]

Protected reports

12.02   To attract the benefit of the fair reports form of qualified privilege, the published material must purport to be a report of the proceedings in question, or a copy of, extract from, or abstract of the record in question. Privilege will be lost where publishers adopt the statements as their own.[6] The written judgments delivered by courts are not 'reports' for the purposes of the defence; they are a part of the proceedings themselves.[7]

'Fair and accurate'

12.03   A report of proceedings will be fair and accurate if it is a substantially accurate summary of what took place in the proceedings, even if the report is very brief.[8] Fairness is assessed objectively by comparing the report with the event it purports to describe.[9] Protection is not lost if errors occur which do not substantially alter the impression that recipients of the publication would have received had they been present at the event described.[10] A report dealing only with some part of proceedings of special interest to recipients may attract the privilege, provided that the report is not 'so tendentious or otherwise so slanted as to make it a distorted report of that part of the proceedings to which it relates'.[11]

---

[3] See para 13.14.

[4] See para 10.07.

[5] See para 10.11.

[6] *Grech v Odhams Press Ltd* [1958] 2 QB 275, 285; *Wake v John Fairfax & Sons Ltd* [1973] 1 NSWLR 43, 50; *Green v Schneller* [2000] Aust Torts Reports ¶81–568, 63,897–8; *Rogers v Nationwide News Pty Ltd* (2003) 201 ALR 184, para 18.

[7] *Rogers v Nationwide News Pty Ltd* (2003) 201 ALR 184, paras 21, 55, 128, 151, 160–2.

[8] *Tsikata v Newspaper Publishing Plc* [1997] 1 All ER 655; *Anderson v Nationwide News Pty Ltd* (1970) 72 SR (NSW) 313, 318 (Asprey JA).

[9] *Anderson v Nationwide News Pty Ltd* (1970) 72 SR (NSW) 313, 324.

[10] *Tsikata v Newspaper Publishing Plc* [1997] 1 All ER 655, 670 (Ward LJ): 'the reporter represents the public – he is their eyes and ears and he has to do his best, using his professional skill, to give them a fair and accurate picture of what he saw or heard'; *Thom v Associated Newspapers Ltd* (1964) 64 SR (NSW) 376, 380; cf *Nationwide News Pty Ltd v Redford* [2001] SASC 198, paras 20, 52: privilege unavailable in relation to a report of parliamentary proceedings which omitted to refer to the plaintiff's refutation of the attack made on him.

[11] *Cook v Alexander* [1974] QB 279, 290; *Nationwide News Pty Ltd v Moodie* (2003) 28 WAR 314, paras 78–9; *Rogers v Nationwide News Pty Ltd* (2003) 201 ALR 184, para 23.

Publication to uninterested persons

At common law, a fair report does not lose the protection of the privilege if it is **12.04** published to persons with no duty or interest in receiving it or if the manner and extent of its publication exceeds what is reasonable. It appears, therefore, that fair reports published via the Internet will not lose the benefit of the privilege at common law by reason of the fact that they are made available globally. It may be, however, that publication via the Internet could, in extreme cases, constitute evidence of malice.[12]

B. Statutory Categories: United Kingdom

Schedule 1 to the Defamation Act 1996

Schedule 1 to the Defamation Act 1996 contains a table of reports and state- **12.05** ments protected by qualified privilege.[13] The privilege only applies to the publication of matters which are of public concern, the publication of which is for the public benefit.[14] The table of protected reports and statements is in two parts.

First part

By Part I of the Schedule, the following reports and statements are the subject of **12.06** ordinary qualified privilege; that is, the following reports and statements will be privileged unless shown to have been made with malice:[15]

- fair and accurate reports of proceedings in public of a legislature anywhere in the world;
- fair and accurate reports of proceedings in public before a court anywhere in the world;[16]
- fair and accurate reports of proceedings in public of a person appointed to hold a public inquiry by a government or legislature anywhere in the world;

---

[12] See para 11.41.

[13] Defamation Act 1996 (UK), s 15 and Sch 1, each of which commenced operation on 1 April 1999. Earlier statutory privileges included the Newspaper Libel and Registration Act 1881, s 2; the Law of Libel Amendment Act 1888, s 4 and the Defamation Act 1952, s 7 and Sch.

[14] Defamation Act 1996 (UK), s 15(3).

[15] Malice is discussed in paras 11.39–11.44.

[16] cf the absolute privilege now afforded to contemporaneous, fair, and accurate reports of public proceedings before United Kingdom courts, tribunals, and judicial bodies, the European Court of Justice, the European Court of Human Rights, and international criminal tribunals established by the Security Council of the United Nations: Defamation Act 1996 (UK), s 14; see para 10.07. Note that the privilege is subject to the Rehabilitation of Offenders Act 1974 (UK), s 8(6): see para 13.14.

- fair and accurate reports of proceedings in public anywhere in the world of an international organization or an international conference;
- fair and accurate copies of or extracts from any register or other document required by law to be open to public inspection;
- notices or advertisements published by or on the authority of a court, or of a judge or officer of a court, anywhere in the world;
- fair and accurate copies of or extracts from matter published by or on the authority of a government or legislature anywhere in the world;[17] and
- fair and accurate copies of or extracts from matter published anywhere in the world by an international organization or an international conference.

Second part

12.07 Qualified privilege is generally available in respect of the publication of reports or statements of the kind mentioned in Part II of the Schedule, provided that the publication has not been made with malice.[18] No defence will be available in respect of such statements or reports, however, where claimants show that they requested that the defendant publish in a suitable manner a reasonable letter or statement by way of explanation or contradiction, and the defendant refused or neglected to do so.[19] The expression 'in a suitable manner' means in the same manner as the publication complained of, or in a manner that is adequate and reasonable in the circumstances.[20] The claimant's request must set out the terms of the letter or statement to be published, not just a demand for an apology and retraction.[21]

12.08 Various reports and statements are identified in Part II of the Schedule, including:

- fair and accurate copies of or extracts from notices issued for the information of the public by or on behalf of a legislature or government of any Member State of the European Union or an international organization or international conference;
- fair and accurate copies of or extracts from documents made available by a court in any Member State of the European Union, or the European Court of Justice or any court attached to that court;
- fair and accurate reports of certain public meetings in the United Kingdom,

---

[17] In relation to qualified privilege for the publication of extracts from or abstracts of reports, papers, votes, or proceedings of the United Kingdom Parliament, see also Parliamentary Papers Act 1840 (UK), s 3 and Defamation Act 1952 (UK), s 9.

[18] Defamation Act 1996 (UK), s 15(1). Malice is discussed in paras 11.39–11.44.

[19] ibid, s 15(2).

[20] ibid.

[21] *Khan v Ahmed* [1957] 2 QB 149.

including meetings of local authorities, justices of the peace, commissions, and tribunals;

- fair and accurate reports of public meetings held in a Member State of the European Union;
- fair and accurate reports of proceedings at general meetings of public companies formed under the law of the United Kingdom, the Channel Islands, the Isle of Man, or Member States of the European Union, and fair and accurate copies of or extracts from documents circulated to members of those companies relating to the appointment, resignation, retirement, or dismissal of directors of those companies;
- fair and accurate reports of the findings or decisions of various associations, including artistic, scientific, religious, educational, commercial, professional, sporting, charitable, and community associations; and
- fair and accurate reports of, or extracts from, any adjudication, report, statement, or notice issued with the authority of the Lord Chancellor (or, in Scotland, the Secretary of State).

Relationship between the statutory categories and the common law

Generally

The breadth of the categories accorded qualified privilege by the Defamation Act 1996 means that, in practice, the Act will usually be relied on to the exclusion of the common law categories of fair and accurate reports, copies, and extracts.[22] The fairness and accuracy of a report will be judged by the common law standards discussed above.[23]   **12.09**

Matters which are not of public concern or for the public benefit

The statutory categories of qualified privilege will, however, be defeated if the publication is of 'matter which is not of public concern and the publication of which is not for the public benefit'.[24] In this respect, the scope of the protection afforded by the statutory categories is less than that available at common law.   **12.10**

Suppose, for example, that a media defendant in the United Kingdom published a report of proceedings in the House of Commons on its web page, and that the report faithfully and accurately set out defamatory statements made by a Member of the House concerning some person's private life. Suppose further that the subject of the report was not a matter of public concern, and was not for the public benefit. In the absence of malice on the part of the defendant, such a   **12.11**

---

[22] See para 12.01.
[23] See paras 12.02–12.03.
[24] Defamation Act 1996 (UK), s 15(4).

report would appear to be privileged at common law.[25] By contrast, the statutory qualified privilege in respect of fair and accurate reports of the proceedings of legislatures[26] would not apply in the same circumstances. In both cases, however, it might be argued that publishing the report using a global medium of publication, such as the Internet, amounted to malice on the part of the defendant.[27]

C. Statutory Categories: Australia

12.12 The scope and extent of the privilege accorded to fair and accurate reports, copies, and extracts has also been defined and extended by legislation in each Australian jurisdiction.[28] In some cases, fair reports are accorded absolute privilege.

12.13 Legislation in some jurisdictions extend qualified, and in some cases absolute, privilege to fair reports of some local government and public meetings,[29] and certain extracts from and abstracts of parliamentary papers[30] and some types of official records.[31]

12.14 In Queensland, Tasmania, and Western Australia,[32] the statutory qualified privil-

---

[25] eg *Wason v Walter* (1868) LR 4 QB 73, 93.
[26] Defamation Act 1996 (UK), s 15(1) and Sch 1, Pt I, para 1.
[27] See para 11.41.
[28] The Parliamentary Privileges Act 1987 (Cth), s 10 accords absolute privilege for fair and accurate reports of proceedings at a meeting of a House or a committee of the Commonwealth Parliament, provided that the report is published without adoption by the defendant of the substance of the matter. Under s 109 of the Constitution, this provision overrides any inconsistent provisions in the laws of the States. The relevant State and Territory legislation include the Defamation Act 1974 (NSW), ss 24, 26, Sch 2, cls 2(1) and 2(5); Defamation Act 1889 (Qld), s 13(1)(a), (c); Civil Liability Act 1936 (SA), ss 6, 7(1)(b); Defamation Act 1957 (Tas), s 13(1)(a), (c), (ca); Wrongs Act 1958 (Vic), ss 3A, 4; Criminal Code (WA), s 354(1), (3); Newspaper Libel and Registration Act 1884 Amendment Act 1888 (WA), s 6; Civil Law (Wrongs) Act 2002 (ACT), ss 128–130; Defamation Act 1938 (NT), ss 5, 6(1)(ba), (c).
[29] Defamation Act 1974 (NSW), ss 24, 26, Sch 2, cl 2(9); Defamation Act 1889 (Qld), s 13(1)(f), (g); Civil Liability Act 1936 (SA), s 7(1)(a), (b) (publications by newspaper, radio, or television only); Defamation Act 1957 (Tas), s 13(1)(g), (h); Wrongs Act 1958 (Vic), s 5; Newspaper Libel and Registration Act 1884 Amendment Act 1888 (WA), s 6; Civil Law (Wrongs) Act 2002 (ACT), s 128; Defamation Act 1938 (NT), s 6(1)(a), (b).
[30] Defamation Act 1974 (NSW), ss 25, 26, Sch 2, cls 3(1), (2); Defamation Act 1889 (Qld), s 13(1)(b); Civil Liability Act 1936 (SA), s 12(3); Defamation Act 1957 (Tas), s 13(1)(b); Constitution Act 1975 (Vic), s 74(3); Criminal Code (WA), s 354(2); Civil Law (Wrongs) Act 2002 (ACT), s 129.
[31] The protected records vary widely from jurisdiction to jurisdiction: see Defamation Act 1974 (NSW), ss 25, 26, Sch 2, cls 3(3)–(7), and s 28; Defamation Act 1889 (Qld), s 13(1)(e); Civil Liability Act 1936 (SA), ss 7(1)(d) (publications by newspaper, radio or television only); Defamation Act 1957 (Tas), ss 13(1)(f); Wrongs Act 1958 (Vic), s 5A; Criminal Code (WA), s 354(5); Civil Law (Wrongs) Act 2002 (ACT), s 129; Defamation Act 1938 (NT), s 6(1).
[32] See the legislation of these jurisdictions cited in nn 28–31 above.

ege fair reports defences are defeated if the defendant is actuated by ill-will to the person defamed or some other improper motive, or where 'the manner of the publication is [not] such as is ordinarily and fairly used in the case of the publication of news'.[33] It seems clear that web sites maintained by news organizations could be described as 'ordinarily and fairly used in the case of the publication of news'. The position is less clear in relation to web sites maintained by individuals or other organizations, bulletin boards, and e-mail messages. The Queensland, Tasmanian, and Western Australian legislation do not limit the availability of the protection based on the appropriateness of the choice of a particular medium in a particular case; rather, the emphasis is on whether the publisher ordinarily and fairly uses that medium for the publication of news.

---

[33] Defamation Act 1889 (Qld), s 13(2); Defamation Act 1957 (Tas), s 13(2)(a); Criminal Code (WA), s 354.

13

OTHER DEFENCES

A. Offer of Amends

United Kingdom

In the United Kingdom, a statutory defence[1] applies where a person who is **13.01** alleged to have published a defamatory statement gives an offer to 'make amends',[2] which is not accepted by the aggrieved party, provided that

the offeror did not know and had no reason to believe that:

- the statement referred to or was likely to be understood as referring to the aggrieved party; and

---

[1] Defamation Act 1996 (UK), ss 2–4. These provisions commenced operation on 28 February 2000, replacing s 4 of the Defamation Act 1952 (UK).
[2] Defamation Act 1996 (UK) 2(1).

- the statement was both false and defamatory of that party.[3]

It is presumed, in the absence of proof to the contrary, that the offeror did not know and had no reason to believe either of these matters.[4] Where the defence is raised, the offeror may not rely on any other defence.[5] The fact that an offer was made may, however, be relied on in mitigation of damages, even in cases where no defence is pleaded, or where the offeror relies on other defences.[6]

13.02   An offer of amends may apply to the publication generally, or be limited to a specific defamatory meaning which the person accepts has been conveyed by the publication.[7] The offer must include an offer to publish a suitable correction and a sufficient apology to the aggrieved party, and to pay such compensation and costs as may be agreed or determined to be payable.[8] An offer to make amends may not be made after serving a defence in defamation proceedings brought by the aggrieved person in respect of the publication.[9] The offer must be in writing, and expressed as having been made under section 2 of the Defamation Act 1996.[10] Where recipients of an offer to make amends accept the offer, they may not bring or continue defamation proceedings against the offeror,[11] but are entitled to enforce the offer.[12]

It is to be expected that 'most sensible claimants will accept unqualified offers to make amends'.[13] There is no cap on the level of compensation a judge might fix where an offer of amends is accepted,[14] but in such cases questions of deterrence may not be of great significance.[15] There is bound to be substantial mitigation if an early, unqualified offer to make amends is made and accepted, and an agreed apology is published, and in such cases the offeror will be entitled to be rewarded in the form of a 'healthy discount' on the damages which might otherwise have been payable.[16]

---

[3] Defamation Act 1996 (UK), s 4(1), (3). The words 'had no reason to believe' have been construed as importing a concept of recklessness; that is, offerors will have reason to believe a statement is false if they are genuinely indifferent as to its truth or falsity, as where they shut their eyes to an obvious truth: *Milne v Express Newspapers Plc* [2004] EMLR 24.

[4] ibid, s 4(3).

[5] ibid, s 4(4).

[6] ibid, s 4(5).

[7] ibid, s 2(2).

[8] ibid, s 2(4). The offer must be to publish the correction and apology 'in a manner that is reasonable and practicable in the circumstances': ibid.

[9] ibid, s 2(5).

[10] In England, see also Civil Procedure Rules, Practice Direction 53, paras 2.11, 3.1–3.3.

[11] Defamation Act 1996 (UK), s 3(2).

[12] ibid, s 3(3)–(10).

[13] *Milne v Express Newspapers Plc* [2004] EMLR 24, para 14.

[14] *Abu v MGN Ltd* [2003] 1 WLR 2001.

[15] *Nail v News Group Newspapers Ltd* [2004] EWCA Civ 1708, para 39.

[16] ibid, paras 41–2. In that case the Court of Appeal, among other matters, upheld a trial judge's decision to award a claimant 50% of the amount he would have awarded had the case

Australia

New South Wales, Tasmania, and the Australian Capital Territory

Similar defences operate in New South Wales and Tasmania.[17] In New South **13.03**
Wales, the defence only applies where, at and before the time of publication, the
publisher exercised reasonable care in relation to the matter in question and its
publication, did not intend the matter in question to be defamatory of the
plaintiff and did not know of circumstances by reason of which the matter in
question was or might be defamatory of the plaintiff.[18] The requirements are
similar in Tasmania.[19]

The offer must be accompanied by a statutory declaration[20] or affidavit[21] spec-
ifying the facts relied upon by the offeror to show that the words were published
innocently. Defendants are not prevented in either New South Wales or Tasmania from relying on other defences in a case where they seek to rely on a defence
of offer of amends.

A similar, but somewhat broader, defence operates in the Australian Capital
Territory.[22] Publishers have a defence in the Australian Capital Territory where
they have made an offer of amends which has not been accepted, provided that:

• the offer was made as soon as practicable after the publisher became aware
  that the matter in question is or may be defamatory;
• at any time before the trial the publisher was ready and willing, on acceptance
  of the offer by the aggrieved person, to perform the terms of the offer; and
• in all the circumstances, the offer was reasonable.[23]

The offer of amends defence in the Australian Capital Territory is broader than
the corresponding defences in the United Kingdom, New South Wales, and
Tasmania, because it is available even to publishers who knew or had reason to
believe that the matter in question was of and concerning the aggrieved person
and was false and defamatory of that person.[24]

---

proceeded to trial with no significant aggravation (such as a plea of justification) and no significant mitigation (such as an apology).

[17] Defamation Act 1974 (NSW), ss 36–45; Defamation Act 1957 (Tas), s 17. The Tasmanian
provision mirrors s 4 of the Defamation Act 1952 (UK).
[18] Defamation Act 1974 (NSW), s 36.
[19] Defamation Act 1957 (Tas), s 17(5).
[20] Defamation Act 1974 (NSW), s 38.
[21] Defamation Act 1957 (Tas), s 17(2).
[22] Civil Law (Wrongs) Act 2002 (ACT), ss 116–122.
[23] ibid, s 121.
[24] cf Defamation Act 1996 (UK), s 4(3); Defamation Act 1974 (NSW), s 36; Defamation Act
1957 (Tas), s 17(5).

Application to Internet intermediaries

13.04 The 'innocence' requirement of the statutory defences of offer of amends which apply in the United Kingdom, New South Wales, and Tasmania may well be able to be proved in many cases by intermediaries of defamatory Internet publications.

Suppose, for example, that an Internet intermediary is sued in respect of defamatory material created by one of its subscribers and stored on its computer system. The United Kingdom defence would potentially be available in those circumstances, so long as the intermediary did not know and had no reason to believe that the material referred to or was likely to be understood as referring to the defamed person, or that the material was both false and defamatory. These requirements are unlikely to present any difficulties for the intermediary, as in most cases it will have had no knowledge of the existence of the material at the time of publication.

13.05 The defence of offer of amends is, however, unlikely to be attractive to Internet intermediaries. The statutory defences discussed in Part IV will generally afford a complete defence to intermediaries in cases where the defence of offer of amends would otherwise be available.[25] An intermediary relying on a defence of offer of amends in the United Kingdom would be prevented from relying on those defences.[26]

B. Apology and Payment into Court

General principles

13.06 In England and Northern Ireland, and in Victoria, Queensland, Western Australia, and Tasmania,[27] defendants have a statutory defence where, following the publication of defamatory material in a newspaper or periodical, they:

- publish a full apology before the commencement of the action or at the earliest opportunity afterwards, which counteracts as far as possible the mischief done by the defamatory publication;[28] and
- pay into court a sum of money by way of amends for the injury sustained by the defamatory publication.

---

[25] See chapters 16, 17, and 19.
[26] Defamation Act 1996 (UK), s 4(4).
[27] Libel Act 1843, s 2 (Lord Campbell's Act) (England and Northern Ireland); Libel Act 1845, s 2 (England and Northern Ireland); Defamation Act 1889 (Qld), s 22; Defamation Act 1957 (Tas), s 23; Wrongs Act 1958 (Vic), s 7; Lord Campbell's Act, s 2 (applicable in WA).
[28] *Lafone v Smith* (1858) 3 H & N 735, 736–7.

Similar defences apply in South Australia, the Australian Capital Territory, and the Northern Territory in respect of a broader range of publications.[29]

In each jurisdiction, the defence is defeated by actual malice or gross negligence.[30]

There is no equivalent defence in New South Wales.

The defence is of fairly limited use to defendants because of the obligation to pay money into court by way of amends. A more attractive option for defendants is to make an offer to settle a claim or a payment into court and plead an apology in mitigation of damages.[31]   **13.07**

Application to the Internet

The defence is unlikely to be available in most cases where defamatory material has been published via the Internet. In England and Northern Ireland, and in Victoria, Queensland, Western Australia, and the Australian Capital Territory, the defence applies only to defamatory publications in a newspaper or periodical. In South Australia, the defence applies only to defamatory publications in a newspaper or periodical, or in a television or radio broadcast.   **13.08**

The defence may be available in England and Northern Ireland, and in each Australian jurisdiction other than New South Wales, where the defamation occurred in the Internet version of a traditional newspaper or periodical. Many newspapers have electronic editions of this nature, which are accessible by visiting a web site maintained by the publisher of the newspaper. Whether a web page which resembles a newspaper or periodical, but which is only published in electronic form via the Internet, could be described as a newspaper or periodical is more difficult. It is not clear whether a court would consider such web pages to fall within the relevant legislation.

There would not appear to be any cogent reason, however, why the defence of apology and payment into court should not be extended to web pages which are, in effect, electronic versions of newspapers or periodicals.[32]

---

[29] Civil Liability Act 1936 (SA), s 10 (any libel in a newspaper or periodical, or in a radio or television broadcast); Civil Law (Wrongs) Act 2002 (ACT), s 133 (any libel); Defamation Act 1938 (NT), s 9 (any action for defamation, where the apology is published in any reasonable publication selected by the plaintiff, or where the defendant has offered to publish such an apology).

[30] See the legislation cited in nn 27, 29 above.

[31] In England, see Civil Procedure Rules, Pt 36; Patrick Milmo and WVH Rogers, *Gatley on Libel and Slander* (10th edn, 2003) para 18.14. In Australia, the better alternative is to serve an offer of compromise and plead an apology in mitigation of damages.

[32] *It's in the Cards Inc v Fuschetto*, 535 NW 2d 11 (CA Wi, 1995) (application for review denied 537 NW 2d 574 (SC Wi, 1995)): electronic bulletin board is not a newspaper, magazine,

C. Spent Convictions and Related Matters

United Kingdom: Rehabilitation of Offenders Act 1974

General principles

13.09   Under the Rehabilitation of Offenders Act 1974 (UK), which applies in England and Scotland,[33] 'rehabilitated persons' in respect of certain criminal convictions are, subject to various exceptions, entitled to be treated as if they had not committed, or been charged with, prosecuted for, convicted of, or sentenced for, the offence the subject of the conviction.[34] In particular, evidence of spent convictions is not admissible in judicial proceedings, and questions may not be asked in such proceedings which relate to a rehabilitated person's past, and which cannot be answered without acknowledging or referring to a spent conviction.[35]

13.10   A 'rehabilitated person' is, in broad terms, a person who has served or otherwise undergone or complied with any sentence imposed in respect of a conviction,[36] and whose conviction has become 'spent' by reason of the passage of a 'rehabilitation period'.[37] Only convictions in respect of which a sentence of no more than thirty months' imprisonment was imposed are capable of becoming spent.[38] The 'rehabilitation period' varies, depending on the nature of the offence, the length of the sentence, and whether the offender was under eighteen years of age.[39] The Act applies to convictions by or before courts both in England and Scotland, and elsewhere.[40]

Exception for defamation actions

13.11   Section 8 of the Rehabilitation of Offenders Act 1974 contains an exception which applies specifically to defamation actions, in cases where the defendant has published an imputation that the claimant committed, or was charged with, prosecuted for, convicted of, or sentenced for, the offence the subject of a spent

---

or periodical for the purposes of Wisconsin defamation legislation; cf *Weiss v Sawyer* (2002) 217 DLR (4th) 129 (Ontario Court of Appeal), para 24: 'newspaper', as defined in the Libel and Slander Act 1990 (Ontario), s 1(1) is sufficiently broad to encompass a newspaper or magazine which is published on the Internet: see para 4.23 (n 40).

[33] The Act does not apply in Northern Ireland: Rehabilitation of Offenders Act 1974 (UK), s 11(3).

[34] ibid, s 4(1).

[35] ibid.

[36] ibid, s 1(2).

[37] ibid, s 1(1).

[38] ibid, s 5(1).

[39] See especially ibid, s 5(2) and Tables.

[40] ibid, s 1(4).

conviction.[41] The general rule is that defendants are entitled in such cases to rely on a defence of justification, fair comment, absolute privilege, or qualified privilege, and to prove such matters as may be necessary to establish those defences,[42] or to rebut an allegation of malice.[43] This general rule is subject, however, to two qualifications.

Malice will defeat a defence of justification.   First, under section 8(5) of the **13.12** Rehabilitation of Offenders Act 1974, malice will defeat a defence of justification in respect of an imputation that the claimant has committed, or been charged with, or prosecuted for, or convicted of, or sentenced for an offence the subject of a spent conviction. Malice is not relevant to the availability of the defence of justification in respect of any other kind of imputation in the United Kingdom.

A publication will be malicious if the defendant was actuated by 'some irrele- **13.13** vant, spiteful or improper motive'.[44] A publication might be actuated by malice where, for example, the defendant's dominant intention was to cause damage to the claimant.[45] The choice of the Internet as the medium for publication of an imputation that a person is guilty of an offence, where the offence is the subject of a spent conviction, might constitute evidence of malice in some cases, having regard to the persons to whom the imputation is likely to be published, and to the global nature of the medium.[46]

Fair and accurate reports of judicial proceedings.   Secondly, where in judicial **13.14** proceedings evidence in relation to an offence the subject of a spent conviction has been ruled inadmissible, any report of those proceedings referring to that evidence will not be entitled to the protection of the privilege which ordinarily protects fair and accurate reports of judicial proceedings.[47]

This exception does not apply, however, to reports of judicial proceedings contained in a bona fide series of law reports which does not form part of any other publication and consists solely of reports of proceedings in courts of law, or to

---

[41] ibid, s 8(1).

[42] ibid, s 8(3).

[43] Section 8(3) appears to be sufficiently broad to enable evidence of spent convictions to be adduced to rebut an allegation of malice in cases where defences of either fair comment or qualified privilege are relied upon. See also s 8(4) which, without limiting the generality of s 8(3), expressly permits such evidence to be adduced in cases where a defence of qualified privilege is relied upon.

[44] *Herbage v Pressdram Ltd* [1984] 2 All ER 769, 772 (Griffiths LJ).

[45] See the discussions of malice in the context of the defence of fair comment: paras 9.18–9.26, and qualified privilege: paras 11.39–11.44.

[46] See para 11.41.

[47] Rehabilitation of Offenders Act 1974 (UK), s 8(6). As to the common law and statutory privileges afforded to fair and accurate reports of judicial proceedings, see paras 10.07 (statutory absolute privilege), 12.01 (common law qualified privilege), and 12.06 (statutory qualified privilege).

reports or accounts of judicial proceedings published for bona fide educational, scientific or professional purposes, or given in the course of any lecture, class, or discussion given or held for any of those purposes.[48]

13.15   It would seem to follow that a report of a judicial proceeding on an ordinary web page would not be entitled to refer to inadmissible evidence of spent convictions. A report on a specialist law web site, on the other hand, might be entitled to refer to such evidence, if the publication was for a bona fide educational or professional purpose, did not form part of any other publication, and contained only reports of proceedings in courts of law or reports or accounts of judicial proceedings. This last limitation is likely to impose a significant limitation on online legal publishers. Most specialist law web sites which reproduce the texts of judgments also contain other material, such as extracts of legislation and commentary. It seems that the exception for bona fide series of law reports will not be available to such publishers.

Australia

13.16   A number of Australian jurisdictions have enacted legislation governing spent convictions and related matters, including quashed and pardoned convictions.[49] None of the Australian legislation contains exceptions for defamation law of the kind which apply in the United Kingdom. In most cases, however, the legislation prescribe exclusions which would ordinarily enable evidence of spent convictions and other matters to be adduced in defamation actions, where necessary for the purpose of establishing a defence.[50]

---

[48]   Rehabilitation of Offenders Act 1974 (UK), s 8(7).
[49]   Crimes Act 1914 (Cth), Pt VIIC; Criminal Records Act 1991 (NSW); Criminal Law (Rehabilitation of Offenders) Act 1986 (Qld); Spent Convictions Act 1988 (WA); Criminal Records (Spent Convictions) Act 1992 (NT).
[50]   eg Crimes Act 1914 (Cth), s 85ZZH(c) (disclosure to a court or tribunal, 'for the purpose of making a decision, including a decision in relation to sentencing'); Criminal Records Act 1991 (NSW), s 16(1) (disclosure in the course of 'proceedings before a court'); Criminal Law (Rehabilitation of Offenders) Act 1986 (Qld), s 4(1) (Act to be construed 'so as not to prejudice any provision of law or rule of legal practice that requires, or is to be construed to require, disclosure of the criminal history of any person'), s 5(3)(b) (convictions and charges not forming part of a person's 'criminal history' may be disclosed in civil proceedings 'if the fact of the conviction or charge is relevant to an issue in the proceedings'); Spent Convictions Act 1988 (WA), s 14(1)(a) (Act does not affect 'the procedure of, or evidence admissible in, proceedings of a court or tribunal that applies the laws of evidence'); Criminal Records (Spent Convictions) Act 1992 (NT), s 15(f) (disclosure 'to or in relation to proceedings before a court'). The defendant may however have committed an offence by disclosing the fact of the plaintiff's conviction. In some cases, it may be an offence to publish a report of proceedings in which a person's spent and other convictions have been disclosed.

D. Expired Limitation Period

Although perhaps not strictly a defence, an expired limitation period operates as **13.17**
a potential bar to a defamation action in both the United Kingdom and
Australia.

The limitation period

United Kingdom

In England and Northern Ireland, defamation actions must be brought no later **13.18**
than one year from the date on which the cause of action accrued.[51] The court
has a broad discretion, however, to extend the limitation period on equitable
grounds, having regard to a number of prescribed factors.[52] Where a claimant is
an infant, or is unsound of mind, time begins to run only when he or she ceases
to be an infant, or ceases to be unsound of mind.[53]

In Scotland, the limitation period for defamation actions is three years from the
date the offending publication first came to the notice of the pursuer.[54] In
calculating time, any period during which the pursuer was under the age of 16
years[55] or of unsound mind is to be disregarded.[56] As in England and Northern
Ireland, courts in Scotland may extend the limitation period on equitable
grounds.[57]

Australia

In most Australian jurisdictions, the limitation period for defamation is six years **13.19**

---

[51] Limitation Act 1980 (UK), s 4A (England); Limitation (Northern Ireland) Order 1989, art
6(2). There are also time limits for the service of claim forms: in England, see Civil Procedure
Rules, r 7.5.

[52] Limitation Act 1980 (UK), s 32A (England); Limitation (Northern Ireland) Order 1989, art
51. The prescribed factors include the length of and the reasons for the delay, the explanation for
any delay between the claimant ascertaining the facts relevant to the cause of action and the
commencement of the action, and the extent to which the delay has made relevant evidence
unavailable or less cogent. The discretion in s 32A is 'largely unfettered'. The discretion is less
likely to be exercised in a case where the claimant was not named in the offending publication, or
where the claimant made no contemporaneous complaint about the publication. Where a solicitor is to blame for the expiry of a limitation period, some account may be taken of the claimant's
right to sue the solicitor: *Steedman v British Broadcasting Corporation* [2002] EMLR 17, 328
(David Steel J).

[53] Limitation Act 1980 (UK), ss 28(1), 38(2) (England); Limitation (Northern Ireland) Order
1989, art 48.

[54] Prescription and Limitation (Scotland) Act 1973, s 18A(1), (4)(b).

[55] Legal Capacity (Scotland) Act 1991, s 1.

[56] Prescription and Limitation (Scotland) Act 1973, s 18A(2).

[57] ibid, s 19A.

from the date on which the cause of action accrued.[58] A reduced period of three years applies in the Northern Territory.[59] In South Australia, the limitation period is six years for libel, but two years for slander.[60] In Western Australia, the limitation period is two years for most forms of slander[61] and twelve months for libels published in newspapers.[62] In the Australian Capital Territory, the limitation period is one year from the date on which the offending material was first published.[63] The circumstances in which limitation periods may be extended vary from jurisdiction to jurisdiction.[64]

Accrual of the cause of action

Cause of action generally accrues on publication

13.20 Generally, the cause of action for defamation accrues on publication. In respect of slanders which are only actionable on proof of special damage, however, the cause of action accrues at the time damage occurs.[65] Most defamatory material published via the Internet will constitute libel, rather than slander.[66]

Relevance of the date of original publication

13.21 As a separate cause of action potentially arises each time defamatory material is read, heard, or seen,[67] the date of the original publication is not generally relevant for the purpose of calculating the limitation period. So, for example, defamatory material originally published years ago, but still accessible via the Internet, may be actionable. A claimant will, however, only be entitled to

---

[58] Limitation Act 1969 (NSW), s 14(1)(b); Limitation of Actions Act 1974 (Qld), s 10(1)(a); Limitation of Actions Act 1936 (SA), s 35(c); Limitation Act 1974 (Tas), s 4(1)(a); Limitation of Actions Act 1958 (Vic), s 5(1)(a); Limitation Act 1935 (WA), s 38(1)(c)(iv).

[59] Limitation Act 1981 (NT), s 12(1)(b).

[60] Limitation of Actions Act 1936 (SA), ss 35(c), 37.

[61] Limitation Act 1935 (WA), s 38(1)(a)(ii).

[62] Newspaper Libel and Registration Act 1884 Amendment Act 1888 (WA), s 5.

[63] Limitation Act 1985 (ACT), s 21B(1). The court must increase the limitation period to two years in cases where it was not reasonable for the plaintiff to have known about the publication within one year from the date of first publication: s 21B(2).

[64] In summary, the running of time is suspended in each Australian jurisdiction during any period when the plaintiff is an infant, or of unsound mind: Limitation Act 1969 (NSW), ss 11(3), 52; Limitation of Actions Act 1974 (Qld), ss 5(2), 29; Limitation of Actions Act 1936 (SA), s 45; Limitation Act 1974 (Tas), ss 2(2), 26; Limitation of Actions Act 1958 (Vic), ss 3(2), 23; Limitation Act 1935 (WA), s 16; Limitation Act 1985 (ACT), ss 8(3), 30; Limitation Act 1981 (NT), ss 4(1), 36. There is a general discretion to extend time limits, similar to that in the United Kingdom, in South Australia, and the Northern Territory, but not the other Australian jurisdictions: Limitation of Actions Act 1936 (SA), s 48; Limitation Act 1981 (NT), s 44.

[65] See para 4.01.

[66] See chapter 4.

[67] See para 5.10.

recover damages in respect of publications occurring within the relevant limitation period.[68]

In Scotland, time runs from the date when the publication or communication in respect of which the action is to be brought first came to the notice of the pursuer.[69] It is not entirely clear how this rule might apply to material published via the Internet. Suppose, for example, that a person is defamed in Scotland by material on an obscure web page. The defamed person knows of the existence of the defamatory material but elects not to sue because the material, though defamatory, has not caused any serious harm. Suppose, however, that ten years later the same web page has become highly popular. The defamatory material gains notoriety throughout Scotland and causes the defamed person serious damage. In such a case, it is arguable that the defamed person's cause of action is statute-barred, because the offending publication first came to the defamed person's notice more than ten years ago.[70] On the other hand, it might be argued that a new publication or communication occurs, and time begins to run afresh, each time the offending web page is accessed.[71] In practical terms, if the former view is correct, such a case would presumably be an appropriate one for the exercise of the court's discretion to extend the time within which an action must be brought.[72]

In the Australian Capital Territory, time begins to run from the date of the original publication.[73]

Single publication

In most American States, a 'single publication' rule applies to prevent a multiplicity of suits arising out of the widespread publication of the same material. In substance, the effect of the single publication rule is that only one cause of action arises out of 'any single publication or exhibition or utterance, such as any one edition or issue of a newspaper or book or magazine or any one presentation to an audience or any one broadcast over radio or television or any

13.22

[68] *Loutchansky v Times Newspapers Ltd (Nos 4 and 5)* [2002] QB 783, 817–18. See also *Duke of Brunswick v Harmer* (1849) 14 QB 185; 117 ER 75: fresh publication seventeen years after the date of the original publication not statute-barred; *Costes v Ministère Public* (Cour d'Appel, Paris, 15 December 1999): a new publication occurs, and time begins to run, each time material on a web site is accessed; *Harris v 718932 Pty Ltd* (2003) 56 NSWLR 276: reprint of a defamatory book gives rise to new causes of action; cf *Dow Jones & Co Inc v Jameel* [2005] EWCA Civ 75, paras 22–4, 56.
[69] Prescription and Limitation (Scotland) Act 1973, s 18A(1), (4)(b).
[70] In the case of a newspaper eg it seems clear that the legislature's intention is that time runs from the date the defamed person first learns of the existence of the defamatory edition of the newspaper, not of any individual copy of that edition.
[71] cf *HM Advocate v Beggs (No 2)* 2002 SLT 139, 145; see para 15.11.
[72] Prescription and Limitation (Scotland) Act 1973, s 19A.
[73] Limitation Act 1985 (ACT), s 21B.

one exhibition of a motion picture'.[74] Where the single publication rule applies, the cause of action accrues, and time begins to run, at the time of the first publication. The single publication rule does not apply to any 'republication' which is 'intended to and actually reaches a new audience', such as a second edition of a book, or publication of a paperback edition of a hard-cover book.[75]

The single publication rule applies to material stored on the Internet,[76] but apparently not where an online publication is 'moved to a different Internet address'.[77]

An approach broadly analogous to the American single publication rule has been adopted in some Canadian decisions.[78]

The English Court of Appeal declined to adopt an American-style single publication rule in *Loutchansky v Times Newspapers Ltd (Nos 4 and 5)*.[79] The court affirmed the principles set out in paragraph 13.21 above, observing that the adoption of a single publication rule would be a 'radical' change to the law of defamation.[80] The court acknowledged that permitting an action to be based on a fresh publication of material originally published long ago was 'at odds with some of the reasons for the introduction of a 12-month limitation period for defamation', but noted that 'the scale of such publication and any resulting damage is likely to be modest compared with that of the original publication'.[81]

In Australia, the High Court declined to adopt a single publication rule in *Dow Jones & Co Inc v Gutnick*.[82] The court was not persuaded by the proposition that the rule that each separate publication of defamatory material via the Internet

---

[74] American Law Institute's Uniform Single Publication Act, adopted in many States of the United States; *Holloway v Butler*, 662 SW 2d 688 (CA Tx, 1983); *Crook v Peacor*, 579 F Supp 853 (ED Mich, 1984).

[75] *Firth v State of New York*, 747 NYS 2d 69 (CA NY, 2002); *Cook v Conners*, 215 NY 175 (CA NY, 1915); *Rinaldi v Viking Penguin*, 52 NY 2d 422 (CA NY, 1981).

[76] *Firth v State of New York*, 747 NYS 2d 69 (CA NY, 2002); *Van Buskirk v The New York Times Co*, 325 F 3d 87 (2d cir, 2003); *Traditional Cat Association, Inc v Gilbreath*, 13 Cal Rptr 3d 353 (CA Ca, 2004).

[77] *Firth v State of New York*, 761 NYS 2d 361 (SC NY, 2003).

[78] *Butler v Southam Inc* (Nova Scotia Supreme Court, Nunn J, 29 December 2000) (partly reversed on other grounds (2001) 197 NSR (2d) 97), para 55: 'I should add, for completeness, that archival material contained on the Internet does not amount to a continual publication nor does it alter the date of publication for the time limitation periods'; *Carter v British Columbia Federation of Foster Parents Association* (2004) 27 BCLR (4th) 123 (British Columbia Supreme Court). Note, however, that these decisions turn on the interpretation of Canadian limitation statutes under which the running of time depends on when the plaintiff became aware of the facts giving rise to the cause of action: Defamation Act 1989 (Nova Scotia), ss 17–19; Limitation Act 1996 (British Columbia), s 6(4)(a).

[79] [2002] QB 783.

[80] ibid 818.

[81] ibid.

[82] (2002) 210 CLR 575.

gives rise to a separate cause of action exposes online publishers to the risk of being sued in a multitude of places every time they upload material to a web server, for a combination of substantive and practical reasons. First, Gleeson CJ, McHugh, Gummow, and Hayne JJ pointed out that there are well-established principles of law to prevent vexation by separate suits involving the same parties and issues.[83] In addition, estoppel principles operate after judgment to prevent a party from re-litigating the same issue in the same or a different forum.[84] The effect of these principles in defamation actions is that where an Australian court has jurisdiction and is not a *forum non conveniens*, the plaintiff may claim a remedy in respect of the worldwide publication of allegedly defamatory material. It will ordinarily be an abuse of process to issue more than one proceeding in respect of different publications of the same material.[85] The fact that causes of action concerning the same material might have accrued in different places is a matter dealt with by the operation of choice of law rules. Secondly, Gleeson CJ, McHugh, Gummow, and Hayne JJ thought that the risk of publishers having to defend defamation actions in every corner of the globe was tempered by three significant practical matters:

• courts will only be likely to award substantial damages in respect of publications occurring in a particular place if the plaintiff has a reputation in that place;[86]

• plaintiffs will be unlikely to sue for defamation unless any judgment they

---

[83] ibid, para 36, citing authorities including *CSR Ltd v Cigna Insurance Australia Ltd* (1997) 189 CLR 345; *Maple v David Syme & Co Ltd* [1975] 1 NSWLR 97, 100–2; *Australian Broadcasting Corporation v Waterhouse* (1991) 25 NSWLR 519, 537 and *Meckiff v Simpson* [1968] VR 62, 65, 69.

[84] The principles include:

• *res judicata*: the principle that where an action has been brought and judgment has been entered in that action, no other proceedings may be maintained on the same cause of action: *Blair v Curran* (1939) 62 CLR 464, 532 (Dixon J); *Jackson v Goldsmith* (1950) 81 CLR 446, 466 (Fullagar J); *Port of Melbourne Authority v Anshun Pty Ltd* (1981) 147 CLR 589, 597 (Gibbs CJ, Mason, and Aickin JJ), 608–9 (Brennan J);

• issue estoppel: the principle that a judicial determination directly involving an issue of fact or law disposes of the issue once and for all, so that it cannot afterwards be raised between the same parties or those who claim through them: *Blair v Curran* (1939) 62 CLR 464, 531 (Dixon J); *Port of Melbourne Authority v Anshun Pty Ltd* (1981) 147 CLR 589, 597 (Gibbs CJ, Mason, and Aickin JJ), 609 (Brennan J); and

• so-called *Anshun* estoppel: the principle that matters which were not raised but which reasonably could and should have been raised in prior proceedings may not be raised in later proceedings: *Port of Melbourne Authority v Anshun Pty Ltd* (1981) 147 CLR 589.

[85] *Meckiff v Simpson* [1968] VR 62, 63–4, 69 (Menhennitt J). See also *Gorton v Australian Broadcasting Commission* (1973) 1 ACTR 6; cf *Dow Jones & Co Inc v Gutnick* (2002) 210 CLR 575, para 202 (Callinan J): 'For myself I would see no immediate reason why, if a person has been defamed in more than one jurisdiction, he or she, if so advised might not litigate the case in each of those jurisdictions.'

[86] *Dow Jones & Co Inc v Gutnick* (2002) 210 CLR 575, para 53 (Gleeson CJ, McHugh, Gummow, and Hayne JJ).

obtain is capable of being enforced in a place where the defendant has assets;[87] and

- 'in all except the most unusual of cases, identifying the person about whom material is to be published will readily identify the defamation law to which that person may resort'.[88]

E. Consent

13.23 It is a defence at common law that the claimant expressly or impliedly consented, in a clear and unequivocal way, to the publication of the defamatory material.[89] The publication must be substantially the same as that to which the claimant consented.[90] This defence operates in the United Kingdom, and in all Australian jurisdictions except Queensland and Tasmania, although in those jurisdictions it is a defence to make a publication in good faith on the invitation or challenge of the defamed person.[91]

13.24 It might be argued that the defence of consent should operate in some cases to prevent intermediaries of Internet publications from recovering where they themselves are defamed by material stored on their computer systems. Intermediaries who host content created by their subscribers which is defamatory of them, for example, might be said to have consented to the publication of that content. The better view, however, would appear to be that any implied consent on the part of such intermediaries to the publication of defamatory material of and concerning them is not sufficiently clear and unequivocal to invoke the operation of the defence except where the intermediary knows of the existence of the defamatory material and fails within a reasonable time to act to prevent its publication or continuing publication.

F. Triviality

13.25 In Queensland and Tasmania, defendants have a defence in respect of the publication of words which were not intended to be read, where they prove that the publication was made on an occasion when, and under circumstances where,

---

[87] *Dow Jones & Co Inc v Gutnick* (2002) 210 CLR 575, 53. See also para 165 (Kirby J).
[88] ibid, para 54.
[89] *Monson v Tussauds Ltd* [1894] 1 QB 671, 691; *Moore v News of the World Ltd* [1972] 1 QB 441, 448; *Loveday v Sun Newspapers Ltd* (1938) 59 CLR 503, 514 (Latham CJ); *Jones v Amalgamated Television Services Pty Ltd* (1991) 23 NSWLR 364, 369.
[90] *Moore v News of the World Ltd* [1972] 1 QB 441, 448; *Frew v John Fairfax Publications Pty Ltd* [2004] VSC 311.
[91] Defamation Act 1889 (Qld), s 16(1)(f); Defamation Act 1957 (Tas), s 16(1)(f).

the person defamed was not likely to be injured.[92] In New South Wales and the Australian Capital Territory, a similar defence applies to all forms of defamatory publication.[93] No equivalent defence operates in the United Kingdom, or in the remaining Australian jurisdictions.

The triviality defence is intended to deter frivolous actions for oral defamation, as in the case of 'jocular statements to a few people in a private home, who know the plaintiff too well to take it seriously'.[94] The defence is 'not limited to publications involving trivial matters or content',[95] but rather to publications which are made on an occasion and under circumstances which are unlikely to cause harm. The 'quality of the circumstances of the publication determines at the moment of publication whether it is or is not actionable'; whether the defamed person in fact suffered harm is not to the point.[96]

Publications communicated via the Internet will usually be intended to be read, and so be excluded from the operation of the triviality defence in Queensland and Tasmania. The defence might, however, apply in appropriate cases to voice or video communications carried out via the Internet, in much the same way as it might apply to telephone conversations.   **13.26**

In New South Wales and the Australian Capital Territory, the triviality defence might apply in appropriate cases to e-mail communications among small groups, or to postings to bulletin boards with only a few members. The defence would be less likely to apply to postings on large bulletin boards, or on generally accessible web pages.[97]

G. Miscellaneous Defences in Scots Law

Statements made *in rixa*

Scots law recognizes a defence in cases where a defamatory statement is spoken *in rixa*: that is, in anger or in the course of an argument.[98] It seems that the   **13.27**

---

[92] Defamation Act 1889 (Qld), s 20; Defamation Act 1957 (Tas), s 9(2). Section 362 of the Criminal Code (WA), which is in similar form, applies only to criminal defamation.

[93] Defamation Act 1974 (NSW), s 13: applies where 'the circumstances of the publication of the matter complained of were such that the person defamed was not likely to suffer harm'. Civil Law (Wrongs) Act 2002 (ACT), s 126 is materially identical.

[94] John Fleming, *The Law of Torts* (9th edn, 1998) 609–10.

[95] *Jones v Sutton* [2004] NSWCA 439, para 13 (Beazley JA).

[96] *Morosi v Mirror Newspapers Ltd* [1977] 2 NSWLR 749, 799; *Chappell v Mirror Newspapers Ltd* [1984] Aust Torts Reports ¶80–691, 68,947; *Jones v Sutton* [2004] NSWCA 439.

[97] See eg *Lang v Willis* (1934) 52 CLR 637, but note 651 (Rich J): a jury might 'take one view of words spoken at a vestry meeting or a meeting of directors, and another of words uttered in the heat of a family squabble or of a quarrel in a shearing shed or a taproom or bar'.

[98] *Christie v Robertson* (1899) 1 F 1155, 1157 (Lord M'Laren); *Hunter v Sommerville* (1903) 11 SLT 70, 71.

defence only applies to the spoken word,[99] and will therefore be of limited relevance in cases involving defamatory Internet publications.

Mere abuse

13.28　A related defence in Scots law operates where the offending words constitute 'mere unmeaning abuse' or 'mere vituperation'.[100] The policy underlying the defence is that abusive or sarcastic language may not contain a reflection on the pursuer's 'moral character or reputation'.[101]

Fair retort

13.29　Finally, Scots law recognizes a defence of 'fair retort', which protects defenders who defame pursuers in answer to an attack.[102] The defence only applies where the retort is relevant, and is defeated where the pursuer affirmatively pleads and proves malice.[103] In practice, the defence may be indistinguishable from the duty and interest form of qualified privilege.[104]

H. Publications without Negligence in the Australian Capital Territory

13.30　A statutory defence operates in the Australian Capital Territory where the published matter, other than any published matter imputing criminal behaviour, was not published negligently.[105] For the purposes of the defence, it is sufficient if the defendant establishes that he or she took reasonable steps to ensure the accuracy of the published matter, and gave the plaintiff a reasonable opportunity to comment on the published matter before it was published.[106] The defence is not defeated by malice.

The defence of publication without negligence has no equivalent in the United

---

[99] Kenneth Norrie, *Defamation and Related Actions in Scots Law* (1995) 150–4; Francis McManus and Eleanor Russell, *Delict* (1998) 315; JM Thomson, *Delictual Liability* (1994) 213–14.

[100] *Cockburn v Reekie* (1890) 17 R 568, 571 (Lord M'Laren); *Hunter v Sommerville* (1903) 11 SLT 70, 70–1.

[101] *Hunter v Sommerville* (1903) 11 SLT 70, 71; Norrie (n 99 above) 154–5.

[102] *Gray v Scottish Society for the Prevention of Cruelty to Animals* (1890) 17 R 1185, 1193–5, 1198, 1200; *Milne v Walker* (1893) 21 R 155; Norrie (n 99 above) 155–6; Thomson (n 99 above) 214; McManus and Russell (n 99 above) 315.

[103] *Gray v Scottish Society for the Prevention of Cruelty to Animals* (1890) 17 R 1185.

[104] See eg *Laughton v Bishop of Sodor and Man* (1872) LR 4 PC 495, 504, cited with approval in *Gray v Scottish Society for the Prevention of Cruelty to Animals* (1890) 17 R 1185, 1197–8; *Penton v Calwell* (1945) 70 CLR 219, 242–3, 250; see paras 11.05, 11.08.

[105] Civil Law (Wrongs) Act 2002 (ACT), s 134(1).

[106] ibid, s 134(2).

Kingdom or any other Australian jurisdiction. It marks a significant departure from the common law tradition of strict liability in defamation cases.[107] Although the incidence of the onus is different, the proposed defence is reminiscent of the American approach in cases involving private plaintiffs. In the United States, private plaintiffs are generally able to recover where they prove that defamatory material of and concerning them has been published, and that the defendant was negligent as to the truth or falsity of the material.[108]

At the time the defence was introduced to Parliament, the Attorney-General for the Australian Capital Territory contended that it would 'provide a new and powerful reason for journalists and publishers to get their stories right'. This is an unsustainable rationale for the defence, which surely relaxes the circumstances in which publishers can be liable. It appears to provide a new and powerful defence to excuse journalists and publishers who get their stories wrong.

---

[107] As to the relationship between defamation and negligence generally, see para 24.04.
[108] *Gertz v Robert Welch, Inc*, 418 US 323 (1974) 349–52; *Dun & Bradstreet, Inc v Greenmoss Builders, Inc*, 472 US 749 (1985) 763. See para 31.07.

PART IV

LIABILITY OF INTERNET INTERMEDIARIES

14

INTERNET INTERMEDIARIES

A. Different Kinds of Intermediaries

14.01 Intermediaries play a central role in the publication of Internet communications. Every Internet communication, whatever its form, passes through a number of intermediate computer systems as a series of IP datagrams en route from one computer to another.[1] Intermediaries typically perform one of three functions in respect of a given communication.

Content hosts

14.02 Intermediaries may be 'content hosts': the operators of computer systems on which Internet content, such as web pages and bulletin board postings, is stored. Content hosts play a part every time the content stored on their computer systems is displayed on the screen of an Internet user, anywhere in the world, because they are the primary storage site for that content.

Mere conduits

14.03 At the other end of the spectrum, intermediaries may be 'mere conduits' in respect of a particular communication: the operators of computer systems

---

[1] See para 2.22.

through which communications happen to pass on their route from one computer to another. These intermediaries are perhaps most analogous to the operators of telecommunications networks: they facilitate the communications of others by operating the equipment by means of which the constituent signals are carried. They do not store the signals on their computer systems for any period longer than is necessary for their transmission to a particular recipient.

Caching

14.04   The third function which intermediaries might perform is to 'cache' Internet content: that is, to store particular content on a temporary basis on their computer systems for the purpose of making the transmission of that information to Internet users more efficient.[2] Intermediaries who 'cache' information are not the same as 'content hosts', because they are not the primary storage site for that information. Nor are they the same as 'mere conduits', because they store particular Internet content for a period longer than is necessary for its transmission to a particular recipient.

B. Publication

14.05   Internet intermediaries will only be liable in respect of defamatory material hosted, cached, or carried by them, but which they did not create, if they are 'publishers' of that material for the purposes of civil defamation law, and if they are unable to avail themselves of some statutory or common law defence. The first of those issues—whether Internet intermediaries are 'publishers' of the material they host, cache, or carry—is the subject of chapter 15.

The analysis in chapter 15 demonstrates that Internet intermediaries who know they are hosting or caching defamatory material are publishers of that material for the purposes of civil defamation law. The position is less clear in relation to Internet intermediaries who are mere conduits in the carriage of defamatory material, and in relation to Internet intermediaries who unwittingly host or cache defamatory material, although it is strongly arguable that even they are publishers for the purposes of civil defamation law, whose liability will turn on whether they can establish a defence.

---

[2] See para 2.47.

C. Defences: United Kingdom

There are three specific defences potentially available under United Kingdom **14.06**
law to Internet intermediaries who publish defamatory material which they did
not create.

Section 1 of the Defamation Act 1996

Section 1 of the Defamation Act 1996, which applies throughout the United **14.07**
Kingdom, is a statutory defence which will afford protection from liability in
many cases to Internet intermediaries involved in the publication of defamatory
material hosted, cached, or carried by them, which they did not create. The
section 1 defence is the subject of chapter 16.

Electronic Commerce (EC Directive) Regulations 2002

The second defence potentially available to Internet intermediaries derives from **14.08**
regulations 17 to 19 of the Electronic Commerce (EC Directive) Regulations
2002 ('Electronic Commerce Regulations'), which substantially came into force
on 21 August 2002. The Electronic Commerce Regulations transpose into the
domestic law of the United Kingdom the Directive of the European Parliament
and Council on Electronic Commerce.[3]

The purpose of the Directive on Electronic Commerce was to harmonize the
legislation and case law of Member States concerning electronic commerce,
encourage the development of cross-border services, and prevent distortions of
competition in the internal European market.[4] The Directive does not of itself
have 'horizontal direct effect'; that is, it does not create rights which may be
enforced as between private parties in the courts of the United Kingdom.[5] It
may, however, in some circumstances, entitle Internet intermediaries found
liable under the defamation law of the United Kingdom to obtain compensation from the United Kingdom itself in proceedings before the European Court
of Justice.[6]

Regulations 17 to 19 of the Electronic Commerce Regulations transpose Art- **14.09**
icles 12 to 15 of the Directive on Electronic Commerce into the law of the
United Kingdom. Those regulations found statutory defences which are potentially available to Internet intermediaries who host, cache, or carry defamatory

---

[3] Directive 2000/31/EC of the European Parliament and of the Council of 8 June 2000 on
Certain Legal Aspects of Information Society Services, in particular Electronic Commerce, in the
Internal Market [2000] OJ L178/1 ('Directive on Electronic Commerce').

[4] ibid, recital 40.

[5] See para 17.29.

[6] See para 17.30.

content which they did not create. The Electronic Commerce Regulations are the subject of chapter 17.

Common law defence of innocent dissemination

14.10   The section 1 defence is a statutory modification of the common law defence of innocent dissemination, which may still be available in limited circumstances to Internet intermediaries who host, cache, or carry defamatory material which they did not create. The common law defence of innocent dissemination is the subject of chapter 18.

D. Defences: Australia

14.11   In Australia, the potential liability of Internet intermediaries for defamatory material hosted, cached, or carried by them depends in part on the operation of a very different statutory defence, namely that described in clause 91 of Schedule 5 to the Broadcasting Services Act 1992 (Cth) ('clause 91 defence'). The clause 91 defence operates in addition to the ordinary rules of defamation law.

Statutory intervention has complicated, rather than clarified, the law in Australia. Determining whether intermediaries are liable in respect of material hosted, cached, or carried by them, but which they did not create, involves considering whether the intermediary is a publisher of the relevant material—see chapter 15—and, if so, whether the intermediary is able to avail itself of:

- the common law defence of innocent dissemination—see chapter 18;
- the clause 91 defence—see chapter 19; or
- the statutory modifications to the common law defence of innocent dissemination which operate in Queensland and Tasmania—see chapter 19.

E. United States

14.12   Internet intermediaries in the United States now enjoy a broad statutory immunity from liability for defamatory material hosted, cached, or carried by them.[7] Because of the very substantial differences between the approaches favoured in the United Kingdom and Australia on the one hand, and the United States on the other, the American authorities must be treated with caution. Nonetheless, the American cases, in particular, provide useful examples against

---

[7] Communications Decency Act, 47 USC (USA), s 230(c) (1996).

which the statutory defences in the United Kingdom and Australia, and the relevant common law principles, can be tested. For that reason, among others, chapter 31 contains a detailed treatment of the American legislation, and the main American decisions, concerning the liability of Internet intermediaries.

15

INTERNET INTERMEDIARIES AND PUBLICATION

A. Introduction

Whether Internet intermediaries, such as Internet content hosts, ISPs, and the **15.01** operators of business networks could be liable for defamatory material hosted, cached, or carried by them, but which they did not create, depends on two questions:

(1) whether they are 'publishers' of that material; and
(2) if so, whether they are able to avail themselves of some defence.

This chapter is concerned with the first of these questions. The succeeding four chapters will consider the statutory and common law defences available to Internet intermediaries.

There are, as yet, few authorities concerning the circumstances in which Inter- **15.02** net intermediaries will be treated as publishers of material they host, cache, or carry, but which they did not create, for the purposes of civil defamation law. The present state of the law can thus best be analysed by considering, first, the authorities decided to date and secondly, by reasoning from authorities concerning contexts analogous to the Internet.

B. Authorities Concerning Internet Publications

Godfrey v Demon Internet Ltd

15.03   The leading authority concerning Internet intermediaries and publication is the decision of Morland J in *Godfrey v Demon Internet Limited*.[1]

Demon Internet is an Internet service provider which provides subscribers with, among other things, access to USENET bulletin boards. On 13 January 1997, an unknown person posted a message which was defamatory of the plaintiff on a bulletin board accessible from Demon Internet's news server. Subscribers to Demon Internet were able to download the offending posting from Demon Internet's news server.

On 17 January 1997, the plaintiff put Demon Internet on notice of the existence of the offending posting, and requested that it be removed. Demon Internet did not remove the posting. The posting remained accessible to Demon Internet subscribers until it was automatically removed from the news server on 27 January 1997.

15.04   Morland J held that Demon Internet was a 'publisher' of the offending posting, concluding:

> In my judgment the defendants [*sic*], whenever they transmit and whenever there is transmitted from the storage of their news server a defamatory posting, publish that posting to any subscriber to their ISP who accesses the newsgroup containing that posting. Thus every time one of the defendants' customers accesses [the relevant newsgroup] and sees that posting defamatory of the plaintiff there is a publication to that customer.[2]

Morland J went on to hold that Demon Internet was not able to avail itself of the statutory defence in section 1 of the Defamation Act 1996 (UK).[3]

Although Demon Internet originally announced that it would appeal Morland J's decision, it subsequently abandoned that intention. Demon Internet ultimately agreed to pay the plaintiff £15,000 damages and £230,000 costs.[4]

---

[1] [2001] QB 201.
[2] ibid, 208–9.
[3] See para 16.19.
[4] In 1998, the same plaintiff settled defamation proceedings brought in the United Kingdom against an Australian ISP, the Melbourne PC Users Group. The action concerned allegations similar to those in the Demon Internet case. Other similar proceedings were brought by the same

Godfrey v Demon Internet Ltd is therefore authority for the proposition that a   **15.05**
bulletin board operator with actual knowledge that defamatory material is
stored on its computer system, at least, is a 'publisher' of that material for the
purposes of civil defamation law.

It is also clear that Morland J thought that Demon Internet would have been a   **15.06**
'publisher' of the offending posting even in the absence of actual knowledge.
Morland J said:

> At common law liability for the publication of defamatory material was strict.
> There was still publication even if the publisher was ignorant of the defamatory
> material within the document. Once publication was established the publisher was
> guilty of publishing the libel unless he could establish, and the onus was upon
> him, that he was an innocent disseminator.[5]

Finally, Morland J expressed the view in obiter dictum that 'mere conduit'   **15.07**
intermediaries, who merely operate computer systems through which material
happens to pass en route from one computer to another, are 'publishers' of that
material at common law. Morland J cited *Lunney v Prodigy Services Co*,[6] an
American decision in which an Internet intermediary was held not to be a
'publisher' of a defamatory e-mail message sent by one of its subscribers. Morland J said:

> In my judgment, at English common law Prodigy would clearly have been the
> publisher of the . . . message and therefore *Lunney v Prodigy Services Co* does not
> assist the defendants.[7]

Applications of *Godfrey v Demon Internet Ltd*

There were, at the time of writing (March 2005) no other authorities in the   **15.08**
United Kingdom or Australia concerning whether Internet intermediaries are
publishers of material hosted, cached, or carried by them for the purposes of
civil defamation law. Morland J's conclusion that online material is published at
the time when it is accessed has, however, been uncritically accepted in a number of other cases.

In *Loutchansky v Times Newspapers Ltd (Nos 4 and 5)*,[8] for example, the Court of   **15.09**

---

plaintiff against defendants in Canada, New Zealand, and the United States: see *Godfrey v Demon Internet Ltd (No 2)* (English High Court, Morland J, 23 April 1999).

[5] [2001] QB 201, 207.

[6] 683 NYS 2d 557 (AD NY, 1998), subsequently affirmed by the New York Court of Appeals: 94 NY 2d 242 (CA NY, 1999); see further paras 15.35, 31.35–31.45.

[7] [2001] QB 201, 212.

[8] [2002] QB 783, 813.

Appeal, without analysis, approved of that conclusion, observing that it was consistent with the old case of *Duke of Brunswick v Harmer.*[9]

In *Harrods Ltd v Dow Jones & Co Inc,*[10] Eady J of the English High Court cited *Godfrey v Demon Internet Ltd* and *Loutchansky v Times Newspapers Ltd* as authority for the proposition that for the purposes of defamation law a separate publication of a web page occurs each time a subscriber 'hits' the relevant page. Eady J cited those decisions again in *King v Lewis,*[11] on that occasion as authority for the proposition that the publication of Internet postings takes place when they are downloaded.

15.10 Callinan J of the High Court of Australia cited *Godfrey v Demon Internet Ltd* with approval in *Dow Jones & Co Inc v Gutnick,*[12] as authority for the propositions that each defamatory publication gives rise to a separate cause of action, and that publication occurs when and where comprehension of defamatory matter occurs.

15.11 Morland J's conclusion has also been applied in a contempt case in Scotland, *HM Advocate v Beggs (No 2).*[13] The panel had been prosecuted for assault, sodomy, and murder. Well before the commencement of his trial, a substantial body of prejudicial material concerning the panel had been published in newspapers and periodicals. Some of that material was still accessible from online archives during the trial. Under the Contempt of Court Act 1981 (UK), a publisher may be liable for contempt in respect of a publication which creates a substantial risk that the course of justice in particular legal proceedings will be seriously impeded or prejudiced, if the proceedings in question are active at the time of the publication.[14] While accepting that the publications in the online archives had been legitimately published at a time when the proceedings against the panel were not active, Lord Osborne, citing *Godfrey v Demon Internet Ltd,* held that it was:

> unrealistic to make a distinction between the moment when the material is first published on the web site and the succeeding period of time when it is available for access on demand by members of the public.[15]

---

[9] (1849) 14 QB 185; 117 ER 75: purchase of a back copy of a periodical seventeen years after its original publication constituted a separate publication in respect of which a defamation suit could be brought; cf *Dow Jones & Co Inc v Jameel* [2005] EWCA Civ 75, paras 22–4, 56.

[10] [2003] EWHC 1162, para 36.

[11] [2004] EWHC 168, para 15. See also the report of the unsuccessful appeal in that case: *King v Lewis* [2005] EMLR 4, para 2.

[12] (2002) 210 CLR 575, 652.

[13] 2002 SLT 139.

[14] Contempt of Court Act 1981 (UK), ss 1–2.

[15] *HM Advocate v Beggs (No 2)* 2002 SLT 139, 145.

Totalise Plc v Motley Fool Ltd

A view seemingly contrary to that taken by Morland J concerning whether   **15.12**
Internet intermediaries are 'publishers' of material created by others was taken
by Owen J at first instance in *Totalise Plc v Motley Fool Ltd*.[16] In that case, in the
course of explaining his conclusion that section 10 of the Contempt of Court
Act 1981 (UK)[17] did not prevent an order being made to compel Internet
intermediaries to disclose material in their possession which might assist in
identifying the anonymous author of defamatory bulletin board postings,
Owen J said:

> I have come to the conclusion that section 10 has no application to the instant
> facts. It is concerned with the protection of a journalist's sources and is directed
> at resolving the tension that may arise between the public interest in a free press
> and in enabling justice to be attained by a party seeking to enforce or protect its
> legal rights. The journalist is responsible at law for the material which he pub-
> lishes. The defendants take no such responsibility. They exercise no editorial
> control. They take no responsibility for what is posted on their discussion boards
> . . . The defendants simply provide a facility by means of which the public at
> large is able publicly to communicate its views. In my judgment, they are not
> responsible for the publication of such material within the meaning of the
> section.

On appeal, the Court of Appeal did not disturb this conclusion.[18]

In so far as the above passage is inconsistent with the decision in *Godfrey v*   **15.13**
Demon Internet Ltd, the latter decision is to be preferred. *Totalise* was, in the first
place, concerned with the meaning of the expression 'publication for which he is
responsible' in section 10 of the Contempt of Court Act 1981 (UK), rather than
with the meaning of 'publication' for the purposes of defamation law. It is
capable of being confined to a decision construing that provision. Secondly,
there is no indication that the court in *Totalise* was referred to *Godfrey*. Thirdly,
for the reasons about to be given, *Godfrey* is consistent with earlier authorities
on the meaning of 'publication' for the purposes of defamation law in other
contexts and should be followed.

The proposition that *Godfrey v Demon Internet Ltd* was correctly decided can be   **15.14**
tested by examining two lines of analogous authorities: cases concerning the
failure of proprietors to remove defamatory material from their property, and
cases concerning intermediaries in non-Internet contexts. It will then be

---

[16] [2001] EMLR 29; see also paras 5.37–5.38.
[17] Section 10 provides 'No court may require a person to disclose nor is any person guilty of
contempt of court for refusing to disclose the source of information contained in a publication for
which he is responsible, lest it be established to the satisfaction of the court that disclosure is
necessary in the interests of justice or national security or for the prevention of disorder or crime.'
[18] [2002] EMLR 20.

possible to express some general conclusions about Internet intermediaries and publication.

C. Failure to Remove Defamatory Material

Byrne v Deane

15.15 In *Byrne v Deane*,[19] a member of a golf club brought defamation proceedings against the two proprietors of the club for failing to remove a notice which was allegedly defamatory of him from a noticeboard within the club. The notice had been placed on the board by a third party without the consent of the proprietors. One of the proprietors was also the secretary of the club. Under the rules of the club, notices could only be posted on the board with the consent of the secretary.

It was held that the proprietors had taken part in the publication of the notice by allowing it to rest on the wall and by failing to remove it,[20] although in the result it was held that the notice was not defamatory of the plaintiff.

15.16 Greer LJ held that the two proprietors

> by allowing the defamatory statement, if it be defamatory, to rest upon their wall and not to remove it, with the knowledge that they must have had that by not removing it it would be read by people to whom it would convey such meaning as it had, were taking part in the publication of it.[21]

15.17 Greene LJ agreed, positing that defendants should be liable for the publication of another's defamatory matter if, having regard to all the facts of the case, the proper inference is that by not removing the defamatory matter, they really made themselves responsible for its continued presence in the place where it had been put.[22] This inference would ordinarily be drawn, unless it would require 'very great trouble and expense' to remove the defamatory matter.[23]

15.18 Slesser LJ thought that only the secretary of the club had published the statement:

> I think having read it, and having dominion over the walls of the club as far as the posting of notices was concerned, it could properly be said that there was some evidence that she did promote and associate herself with the continuance of the

---

[19] [1937] 1 KB 818.
[20] ibid, 829–30 (Greer LJ), 837 (Greene LJ), cf 835–6 (Slesser LJ, who thought that only the secretary of the club was responsible for publication of the notice).
[21] ibid, 830.
[22] ibid, 838.
[23] ibid.

publication in the circumstances after the date when she knew that the publication had been made. But with the male defendant I am unable to see that there was any evidence that he was in any way responsible for the publication.[24]

Morland J applied *Byrne v Deane* in *Godfrey v Demon Internet Ltd*.[25]   **15.19**

Urbanchich v Drummoyne Municipal Council

Greene LJ's judgment in *Byrne v Deane* was approved in Australia by Hunt J of   **15.20**
the New South Wales Supreme Court in *Urbanchich v Drummoyne Municipal Council*.[26] The case concerned posters on bus shelters under the control of one of the defendants, the Urban Transit Authority (UTA). The posters showed a photograph of a number of people wearing Nazi uniforms, including Adolf Hitler. The plaintiff, who was named in words accompanying the photograph, claimed that he was defamed by the posters. The plaintiff had asked the UTA to remove the posters from its bus shelters, but the UTA failed to do so. The posters had apparently been fixed to the bus shelters by a third party.

Hunt J was satisfied that the UTA had 'published' the posters. Hunt J stated the   **15.21**
applicable test in the following terms:

> In a case where the plaintiff seeks to make the defendant responsible for the publication of someone else's defamatory statement which is physically attached to the defendant's property, he must establish more than mere knowledge on the part of the defendant of the existence of that statement and the opportunity to remove it. According to the authorities, the plaintiff must establish that the defendant consented to, or approved of, or promoted, or in some way ratified, the continued presence of that statement on his property so that persons other than the plaintiff may continue to read it—in other words, the plaintiff must establish in one way or another an acceptance by the defendant of a responsibility for the continued publication of that statement.[27]

Hunt J went on to say that the requisite conduct on the part of the defendant   **15.22**
could be established by inference.[28] Hunt J emphasized that the decision whether the inference should be drawn is a question of fact to be determined, in a jury case, by the jury.[29]

Application to the Internet

The *Byrne v Deane* line of authority is clearly capable of supporting the conclu-   **15.23**
sion that Internet intermediaries who know that there is defamatory material on

---

[24] ibid, 835.
[25] [2001] QB 201, 208.
[26] [1991] Aust Torts Reports ¶81–127.
[27] ibid, 69, 193.
[28] ibid.
[29] ibid, 69, 194.

their computer systems, and who have the ability to remove that material, become 'publishers' of the material for the purpose of defamation law if they fail to do so.[30] The proviso that a defendant would not be responsible as a publisher where removing or obliterating the offending material would require 'very great trouble and expense'[31] would not normally have any application in a case involving defamatory material published via the Internet. It will usually be a simple matter for an Internet intermediary to act to remove or disable access to defamatory content stored on its computer system.[32] The additional requirement articulated by Hunt J in *Urbanchich* that the defendant must have 'consented to, or approved of, or promoted, or in some way ratified, the continued presence' of the offending content on its property will presumably be readily established where the claimant has put the defendant on notice of the existence of the offending content and demanded its removal.

15.24   It is difficult to conceive of circumstances, however, in which the *Byrne v Deane* line of authority could apply to transient Internet communications, such as e-mail messages, instant messaging, and chat services.[33] Whether an Internet intermediary could be liable as a 'publisher' in such cases, or in other cases where the intermediary unknowingly participates in the communication of defamatory material, will turn on a consideration of a different line of authorities, namely authorities concerning intermediaries in non-Internet contexts.

---

[30] cf *Carter v British Columbia Federation of Foster Parents Association* (2004) 27 BCLR (4th) 123 (British Columbia Supreme Court), paras 106–9: no responsibility for publication of chat room postings where defendant made reasonable efforts to have them removed.

[31] *Byrne v Deane* [1937] 1 KB 818, 838 (Greene LJ); *Urbanchich v Drummoyne Municipal Council* [1991] Aust Torts Reports ¶81–127, 69,194.

[32] cf the facts in *Zeran v America Online, Inc*, 958 F Supp 1124 (ED Va, 1997), affirmed 129 F 3d 327 (4th cir, 1997), discussed in paras 31.55–31.64.

[33] cf *Bishop v New South Wales* [2000] NSWSC 1042. In that case, Dunford J considered *Byrne v Deane* and *Urbanchich v Drummoyne Municipal Council* in a case concerning whether a school should be held responsible for a defamatory performance by students at a school revue. Dunford J held that because of the transient nature of the performance, the school could only be held responsible if the plaintiff showed that 'at some stage before its conclusion the headmaster had the ability and reasonable opportunity to stop the performance . . . [but] did not do so'. Further, the plaintiff had to show that by not doing so, the headmaster 'consented to, authorized, approved of, adopted or acquiesced in the contents of the performance'. Dunford J directed the jury accordingly. E-mail messages, instant messaging, and chat services are transient in nature; it is unlikely that Internet intermediaries could be held liable following this line of authority. Such intermediaries will generally not have the ability or reasonable opportunity to stop the offending publication; nor could it be said that by failing to do so they consent to, authorize, approve of, adopt, or acquiesce in the contents of the publication.

D. Analogies with Intermediaries in Other Contexts

Postal services

Introduction

On ordinary principles, it might be expected that postal services would be considered the publishers of material they deliver. Postal services are similar to Internet intermediaries in that they take part in the communication of the material they deliver, even though they play no part in the creation of the content of that material, and even though, in practical terms, they may be unable to learn that they are carrying defamatory material, or take any step to prevent its publication.

15.25

Day v Bream

Support for this analysis is found in *Day v Bream*,[34] which was cited by Morland J in *Godfrey v Demon Internet Ltd*. In that case, Patteson J instructed the jury that the defendant, who was responsible for delivering parcels, was prima facie liable for putting the contents of those parcels into publication, and that he was only entitled to be excused from liability upon proving he was ignorant of the contents.[35]

15.26

Statutory immunity

In the United Kingdom, the Post Office enjoys statutory immunity from suit in tort in respect of any loss or damage suffered in connection with the provision of a universal postal service because of, among other matters, anything done or omitted to be done in relation to any postal packet in the course of transmission by post.[36] The legislative protection appears to be broad enough to protect the Post Office from liability in defamation law for delivering defamatory letters. Similarly, in Australia, the postal legislation appears to be broad enough to protect Australia Post from liability in defamation law for delivering defamatory letters,[37] although curiously not if it has provided the sender with a receipt.[38]

15.27

Summary

There are no recent cases in which the Post Office or a private courier service has been sued on the basis that, through their ordinary delivery functions, they took

15.28

---

[34] (1837) 2 Mood & R 54; 174 ER 212.
[35] ibid, 56, 212.
[36] Post Office Act 1969 (UK), s 29(1)(a).
[37] Australian Postal Corporation Act 1989 (Cth), s 34(1).
[38] ibid, s 34(2).

part in or authorized the publication of a defamatory letter. It seems likely, however, that the reasoning in *Day v Bream* remains good law and that, at common law, delivery services are 'publishers' of any defamatory material they deliver. Their liability for defamation law will then depend on the availability of defences.[39]

Telephone carriers

Introduction

15.29 Telephone carriers do not enjoy legislative immunity of the kind extended to postal services in either the United Kingdom or Australia. On ordinary principles, telephone carriers might be considered publishers for the purpose of defamation law, in the sense that they intentionally take part in the communication of the telephone conversations carried by their lines. It is surprising, therefore, that the question of the possible liability of telephone carriers does not appear ever to have been addressed in any reported decision in either the United Kingdom or Australia. Telephone carriers are broadly analogous to Internet intermediaries who act as mere conduits, that is, by operating computer systems by means of which communications are carried from one computer to another.

Telephone carriers in the United States

15.30 ***Anderson v New York Telephone Company.*** In the United States, it has been held that telephone carriers are not publishers of defamatory telephone calls made by their subscribers. In the leading decision, *Anderson v New York Telephone Company*,[40] the plaintiff sued the New York Telephone Company (the NYTC) in respect of defamatory material of and concerning him which was publicly available via a recorded message service operated by Bishop Donald Jackson. Jackson's defamatory message was stored in equipment leased by him from the NYTC. Any person dialling one of two telephone numbers could be connected, via the NYTC's lines, to the recorded message service. Anderson had brought the existence of this material to the attention of the NYTC and been promised by the area manager that he would attempt to have Jackson terminate the recordings.

15.31 The Appellate Division of the New York Supreme Court held that the NYTC was a publisher of the defamatory message. The majority judges said that:

---

[39] An additional statutory provision may be relevant in Tasmania. Under s 7(b) of the Defamation Act 1957 (Tas), proof of publication of non-spoken material requires proof that the person making the publication 'knows, or has the opportunity of knowing, the contents or nature of the document or other thing containing the defamatory matter'. Although there do not appear to be any reported cases on the point, it seems likely that postal and courier services could rely on this provision to deny responsibility for publication in Tasmania, as they ordinarily do not know, and do not have any (practical) opportunity of knowing, the content of the material they carry.

[40] 361 NYS 2d 913 (CA NY, 1974) ('*Anderson*').

a telephone company should be liable to a person defamed by a recorded message transmitted over the company's lines if it were established that the defamatory falsehood was transmitted by the company 'with knowledge that it was false or with reckless disregard of whether it was false or not' . . . There would be no liability and, therefore, no obligation to remove the sender's telephone so long as the telephone company, either because of its own independent investigation into the facts or because of the reliable nature of the source of the broadcast, had a reasonable belief that the material being published was true.[41]

An appeal was allowed by the New York Court of Appeal. The Court of Appeal **15.32** held that publication is dependent on proof that the defendant 'had a direct hand in disseminating the material whether authored by another, or not'.[42] As there had been no direct human participation on behalf of the NYTC in the facilitation of phone calls to Jackson's recorded message service, the NYTC was not a publisher of the offending material. The court compared the NYTC to lessors of typewriters, or photocopying machines, and said that it could not seriously be argued that lessors of such machines were the publishers of defamatory material created by lessees. The court also noted that the NYTC was:

> bound to make its equipment available to the public for any legal use to which it can be put . . . and is privileged under its tariff restrictions to terminate service for cause only in certain prescribed circumstances none of which encompass the subscriber's dissemination of defamatory messages.[43]

The decision of the New York Court of Appeal in *Anderson* is somewhat unsatis- **15.33** factory. First, it is true that telephone carriers differ from postal services in that no direct human intervention is ordinarily involved in facilitating a phone call, whereas direct human intervention is involved in delivering a letter. In practical terms, however, the deliverer of a letter has no more opportunity to learn of its defamatory contents than a telephone carrier has to learn of the defamatory contents of a phone conversation. A distinction based on direct human intervention is intellectually unsatisfying and lacks cogency.

Secondly, the assertion that the NYTC was similar to a lessor of typewriters or photocopying machines is open to question. In so far as the NYTC provided message-recording equipment to Jackson, it was in much the same position as the lessor of a typewriter or photocopier. The NYTC's role in the publication of material by Jackson, however, went further than merely supplying equipment. It also played a direct role in the communication of the defamatory material, by supplying the telephone lines connecting Jackson's equipment to the relevant telecommunications infrastructure. Each time a person telephoned Jackson's

---

[41] *Anderson v New York Telephone Company*, 345 NYS 2d 740 (AD NY, 1973), 747 (Goldman PJ, with whom Cardamone and Simons JJ concurred).
[42] *Anderson*, 361 NYS 2d 913 (CA NY, 1974), 915 (Gabrielli J).
[43] ibid, 915–16.

recorded message service, the call was carried by the NYTC's telephone lines. The NYTC was an intermediary in the publication of Jackson's defamatory messages. Its role in the publication of the defamatory material was considerably greater than that of a mere supplier of typewriters or photocopiers, whose role in the publication of defamatory material ends at the time the equipment is supplied.

Thirdly, the facts of *Anderson* demonstrate that, on occasion, telephone carriers actually know that their lines are being used for the publication of defamatory material. It is difficult to see why, in such cases, the ordinary cause of action for defamation should not apply, so that the telephone carrier is liable for the consequences of publication, unless it is able to make out some defence.

15.34 It is thus strongly arguable that, had *Anderson* been decided by an Anglo-Australian court, the NYTC would have been held to be the publisher of the defamatory messages for the purposes of civil defamation law and that the NYTC would have been liable to Anderson, unless it could make out some defence.[44]

15.35 *Lunney v Prodigy Services Co.*   The principle in *Anderson* has been extended in the United States to an Internet service provider, in a case concerning the transmission of an allegedly defamatory e-mail message. In *Lunney v Prodigy Services Co*,[45] the New York Court of Appeals held that, in relation to the transmission of the e-mail message, the provider's conduct was:

> akin to that of a telephone company, which one neither wants nor expects to superintend the content of its subscriber's conversations. In this respect, an ISP, like a telephone company, is merely a conduit.[46]

The United States Supreme Court declined to hear an appeal from the decision of the New York Court of Appeals, without giving reasons.

Treatment of the American authorities in Anglo-Australian law

15.36 As noted earlier, there do not appear to be any Anglo-Australian authorities on whether telephone carriers are publishers of defamatory telephone conversations carried over their lines.[47]

---

[44] In accordance with the *Byrne v Deane* line of authority: see paras 15.15–15.24. See also Raymond Brown, *The Law of Defamation in Canada* (2nd edn, 1994) 346 (n 44).

[45] 94 NY 2d 242 (CA NY, 1999), affirming 683 NYS 2d 557 (AD NY, 1998); see also paras 31.35–31.45.

[46] On the position of telephone carriers in American defamation law, see also American Law Institute, *Restatement of the Law, Second, Torts 2d* (1976) §581, comment b.

[47] The uncertainty as to the position of telephone carriers is well expressed by Marc McDonald, *Irish Law of Defamation* (1987) 66: 'While common sense might suggest that there should not be liability in [most] cases, it is not clear whether that would be because there is no publication by the utility, or if there is, that it is absolutely privileged, or that it comes within the [innocent dissemination] exception, or is protected by a qualified privilege—which, in the last two cases would mean that liability could be found on some occasions.'

In *Godfrey v Demon Internet Ltd*, Morland J mentioned *Anderson* out of defer-
ence to counsel who had referred the decision to the court. Morland J held,
however, that *Anderson* did not assist the defendant, who 'did not play a merely
passive role. [It] chose to receive the [offending] postings to store them, to make
them available to accessors and to obliterate them.'[48] It is not clear from
Morland J's judgment whether he thought that *Anderson* was good law in
England. Morland J went on to consider *Lunney v Prodigy Services Co* briefly,
concluding that it was inconsistent with English law.[49]

The American authorities do not otherwise appear to have been applied in any   **15.37**
reported decision in the United Kingdom or Australia. The 'direct hand' test in
Anderson does not appear to find any support in the Anglo-Australian
authorities.

The 'facilitation' cases

There is, however, a line of authority arising out of intellectual property cases in   **15.38**
the United Kingdom to the effect that persons who *procure* the commission of
torts are liable jointly and severally with the principal tortfeasor, while persons
who merely *facilitate* the commission of such torts are not exposed to liability.[50]
It is possible that this line of authority might apply to defamation law.[51] If so,
telephone carriers might be mere facilitators of defamatory telephone calls, and
so not capable of being held liable as publishers.

Conclusions

The liability of telephone carriers for facilitating defamatory telephone con-   **15.39**
versations may not have been tested judicially in the United Kingdom or Australia because it has been assumed that such carriers would almost always be able
to rely on a defence, such as the common law defence of innocent dissemination
or its statutory equivalent.[52]

In the absence of any definitive authority to the contrary, it is difficult to see   **15.40**

---

[48] [2001] QB 201, 210. See also *Carter v British Columbia Federation of Foster Parents Association* (2004) 27 BCLR (4th) 123 (British Columbia Supreme Court), paras 99–100, but cf para
105.
[49] [2001] QB 201, 212.
[50] See eg *CBS Songs Ltd v Amstrad Consumer Electronics Plc* [1988] 1 AC 1013, 1058 (breach of
copyright); *PLG Research Ltd v Ardon International Ltd* [1993] FSR 197, 238–9 (infringement of
patent); *MCA Records Inc v Charly Records Ltd* [2002] EMLR 1 (infringement of copyright and
trade mark); *Douglas v Hello! Ltd* [2003] EMLR 29, para 70 (breach of confidence: liability as a
joint tortfeasor will only be imposed where the claimant proves 'concerted action to a common
end').
[51] In *MCA Records Inc v Charly Records Ltd* [2002] EMLR 1, 27 Chadwick LJ observed that the
line of authority applied 'at least in the field of intellectual property'.
[52] These defences are discussed in chapters 16 and 18.

why telephone carriers do not satisfy the ordinary definition of a publisher, namely a person who intentionally or negligently takes part in or authorizes the publication of material. Telephone carriers are essential parts of the process of publication: they actually take part in conveying each publication from one telephone user to another.

In the overwhelming majority of cases, telephone carriers do not know, and have no opportunity of knowing, whether they are facilitating defamatory publications. Nor, in any real sense, do they ordinarily have any way of preventing such publications. In some cases, however, as the facts of *Anderson* demonstrate, telephone carriers will know that their lines are being used for the purpose of communicating defamatory material, and have a real opportunity to prevent continuing publications.

15.41 The conclusion most consistent with authority appears to be that telephone carriers are publishers, whose liability turns on the availability of a defence. In the vast majority of cases, the defence of innocent dissemination or its statutory equivalent will afford complete protection to telephone carriers. In those cases where it can be proved that the telephone carrier knows that its service is being used to publish defamatory material, however, it is difficult to see why on ordinary principles the carrier ought not to be liable, at least if it fails to take reasonable steps to prevent the publication.

If this conclusion is correct, then it follows by analogy that Internet intermediaries are publishers of the material they host, cache, or carry for the purposes of civil defamation law.

E. Conclusions

Intermediaries who know they are hosting or caching defamatory Internet content

15.42 There can be little doubt, based on the decision in *Godfrey v Demon Internet Ltd*,[53] and the *Byrne v Deane* line of authority,[54] that Internet intermediaries who actually know that defamatory material is hosted or cached on their computer systems, but fail to take steps to remove or disable access to that material, are 'publishers' for the purpose of civil defamation law.[55]

---

[53] [2001] QB 201; see paras 15.03–15.07.
[54] [1937] 1 KB 818; see paras 15.15–15.24.
[55] cf *Totalise Plc v Motley Fool Ltd* [2001] EMLR 29; see paras 15.12–15.13.

Mere conduits

Mere conduit intermediaries who carry particular Internet communications   **15.43**
from one computer to another, on the other hand, are analogous to postal
services and telephone carriers in the sense that they facilitate communications,
without playing any part in the creation or preparation of their content, and
almost always without actual knowledge of the content.[56]

In view of Morland J's obiter dictum in *Godfrey v Demon Internet Ltd* and the
authorities concerning postal services and telephone carriers discussed above,
mere conduit Internet intermediaries are nonetheless probably publishers of the
material which passes through their computer systems.[57] Their liability in defamation law will depend on whether they can rely on a defence, the most
important of which are the defences for intermediaries discussed in chapters 16
to 19.

There is, however, an argument that telephone carriers are mere 'facilitators' of
telephone calls and therefore cannot be responsible for the publication of
defamatory telephone calls. If that view is correct, and there is a distinction
between 'publishers' and 'mere facilitators', then there is a strong argument that
mere conduit Internet intermediaries are mere facilitators of Internet publications passing through their computer systems, and therefore not responsible for
publishing them.[58]

In Tasmania, it seems that mere conduit Internet intermediaries will not be
publishers of 'non-spoken' material passing through their computer systems by
reason of section 7(b) of the Defamation Act 1957.[59]

Intermediaries who unknowingly host or cache defamatory content

Finally, Internet intermediaries who host or cache bulletin board postings or   **15.44**
web pages on their computer systems differ in one vital respect from postal
services, telephone carriers, and mere conduit Internet intermediaries: they have
the ability to discover that their computer systems are being used for the

---

[56] *Lunney v Prodigy Services Co*, 683 NYS 2d 557 (AD NY, 1998), 561 (Bracken JP): 'The
evidence in the present record leads to the conclusion that the role played by [the ISP] in
connection with the offensive messages sent under the plaintiff's name is, by far, more analogous
to that of a telephone company than to that of a telegraph company.'
[57] *Godfrey v Demon Internet Ltd* [2001] QB 201, 212; see para 15.07; cf *Lunney v Prodigy
Services Co*, 94 NY 2d 242 (CA NY, 1999); see para 15.35.
[58] See para 15.38.
[59] See n 39 above.

purpose of communicating defamatory material, and to take steps to prevent that material from being published or continuing to be published. They are consequently likely to be treated by defamation law as 'publishers'.[60]

---

[60] *Godfrey v Demon Internet Ltd* [2001] QB 201; see para 15.06; but cf *Totalise Plc v Motley Fool Ltd* [2001] EMLR 29, discussed in paras 15.12–15.13. Other cases in which Anglo-Australian courts would have been likely to have held the intermediaries in question to be publishers on this basis include *Cubby, Inc v CompuServe Inc*, 776 F Supp 135 (SD NY, 1991), discussed in paras 31.12–31.22; *Stratton Oakmont, Inc v Prodigy Services Company*, 1995 WL 323710; 23 Media L Rep 1794 (SC NY, 1995), discussed in paras 31.23–31.34; *Lunney v Prodigy Services Co*, 94 NY 2d 242 (CA NY, 1999), discussed in paras 31.35–31.45 (in so far as it concerned the transmission of allegedly defamatory bulletin board postings); and *Blumenthal v Drudge*, 992 F Supp 44 (D DC, 1998), discussed in paras 31.65–31.73.

16

SECTION 1 OF THE DEFAMATION ACT 1996 (UK)

A. Introduction

Scope of the defence

Section 1 of the Defamation Act 1996 (UK) establishes a defence ('the section 1 defence') which will be available, in many cases, to Internet intermediaries in respect of material hosted, cached, or carried by them, but which they did not create. The section 1 defence is, in effect, a statutory version of the defence of innocent dissemination, modified for modern conditions.[1]   **16.01**

Internet intermediaries will also, in many cases, be able to rely on the defences in regulations 17–19 of the Electronic Commerce (EC Directive) Regulations 2002 (UK) ('Electronic Commerce Regulations'). The Electronic Commerce Regulations, and their relationship to the section 1 defence, are dealt with in chapter 17.

Apart from its potential application to intermediaries, the section 1 defence may

---

[1] The relationship between the s 1 defence and the common law defence of innocent dissemination is discussed in paras 18.06–18.07.

also be available to parties who link to or frame defamatory content on their web pages.[2]

Section 1(1)

16.02   Section 1(1) provides:

> In defamation proceedings a person has a defence if he shows that—
> (a) he was not the author, editor or publisher of the statement complained of,
> (b) he took reasonable care in relation to its publication, and
> (c) he did not know, and had no reason to believe, that what he did caused or contributed to the publication of a defamatory statement.

Section 1(2)

16.03   Section 1(2) defines 'author' to mean 'the originator of the statement, but does not include a person who did not intend that his statement be published at all'. 'Editor' is defined to mean 'a person having editorial or equivalent responsibility for the content of the statement or the decision to publish it'. 'Publisher' means 'a commercial publisher, that is, a person whose business is issuing material to the public, or a section of the public, who issues material containing the statement in the course of that business'.[3]

Section 1(3)

16.04   Under section 1(3) a person is not to be considered the author, editor, or publisher of a statement:

> if he is only involved—
> (a) in printing, producing, distributing or selling printed material containing the statement;
> (b) in processing, making copies of, distributing, exhibiting or selling a film or sound recording . . . containing the statement;
> (c) in processing, making copies of, distributing or selling any electronic medium in or on which the statement is recorded, or in operating or providing any equipment, system or service by means of which the statement is retrieved, copied, distributed or made available in electronic form;
> (d) as the broadcaster of a live programme containing the statement in circumstances in which he has no effective control over the maker of the statement;
> (e) as the operator of or provider of access to a communications system by

---

[2] See paras 16.20–16.21.
[3] The definition of 'publisher' is specific to s 1, and not intended otherwise to modify the meaning of the words 'publication' or 'publish' for the purposes of defamation law: Defamation Act 1996, s 17.

means of which the statement is transmitted, or made available, by a person over whom he has no effective control.

In a case not within paragraphs (a) to (e) the court may have regard to those provisions by way of analogy in deciding whether a person is to be considered the author, editor or publisher of a statement.

Section 1(4)

By section 1(4), employees or agents of authors, editors, or publishers are deemed to be in the same position as their employers or principals to the extent that they are responsible for the content of a statement or the decision to publish it.

16.05

Section 1(5)

Section 1(5) sets out matters to which regard must be had in determining whether persons took reasonable care, or had reason to believe that what they did caused or contributed to the publication of a defamatory statement. The factors are the extent of the person's responsibility for the content of the statement or the decision to publish it, the nature or circumstances of the publication, and the previous conduct or character of the author, editor, or publisher.

16.06

B. Availability of the Defence to Internet Intermediaries

Section 1(1)(a): authors, editors, and publishers

Providers of systems or services

Internet intermediaries who host or cache particular content will often not be considered authors, editors, or publishers of defamatory material stored on their computer systems because their involvement will be limited to the conduct described in section 1(3)(c). Relevantly, their involvement in the publication of particular defamatory material will often be limited to operating or providing a system or service by means of which that material was retrieved, copied, distributed, or made available in electronic form.

16.07

Operators of communications systems

Internet intermediaries who are mere conduits in respect of particular content, and intermediaries who merely cache particular content, will often also not be treated as authors, editors, or publishers by reason of section 1(3)(e): they are the operators of, or the providers of access to, a communications system by means of which the defamatory material is transmitted or made available, by a person over whom they have no effective control. Internet intermediaries who

16.08

host content, on the other hand, by for example operating servers on which web pages or bulletin board postings are stored, would be less likely to be able to rely on section 1(3)(e). In the first place, they will often have effective control over the persons who transmit or make available defamatory material via their computer systems, whether by the terms of the contract under which they agree to host the material or otherwise. Secondly, their role in the transmission of that material extends beyond the mere provision of access to a communications system; typically they provide subscribers with access to storage space on their computer systems on agreed terms, and the means to 'upload' material into that space.

Conduct of the intermediary must be limited

16.09   It should be noted that to satisfy section 1(1)(a), Internet intermediaries will generally need to show that their conduct was limited to that described in one or more of the paragraphs under section 1(3).[4] Where the conduct of the intermediary has involved more than merely 'operating or providing any equipment, system or service by means of which the [offending] statement is retrieved, copied, distributed or made available in electronic form',[5] or operating or providing access to 'a communications system by means of which the statement is transmitted, or made available, by a person over whom he has no effective control',[6] then the intermediary may be an author, editor, or publisher of the statement for the purposes of section 1(1)(a).

16.10   **Editors.**   For example, an Internet service provider who has in place systems for monitoring and censoring the content of material hosted on its servers[7] might be said to be, in fact, a 'person having editorial or equivalent responsibility for the content of the statement or the decision to publish it'.[8] Such an Internet service provider might not be entitled to avail itself of the defence in section 1 of the Defamation Act 1996.

16.11   **Publishers.**   Nor would the defence be available to an intermediary who had commissioned a third party to prepare content which was accessible from the intermediary's own web site. In such a case, the intermediary is probably a 'publisher' of the third party's content, as that term is defined in section 1(2).[9]

---

[4] ibid, s 1(3): 'A person shall not be considered the author, editor or publisher of a statement if he is *only* involved . . .' (emphasis added).

[5] ibid, s 1(3)(c).

[6] ibid, s 1(3)(e).

[7] See eg the facts in *Stratton Oakmont, Inc v Prodigy Services Company*, 1995 WL 323710; 23 Media L Rep 1794 (SC NY, 1995) ('*Stratton Oakmont*'); see paras 31.23–31.34.

[8] Defamation Act 1996, s 1(2) (definition of 'editor').

[9] See eg the facts in *Cubby, Inc v CompuServe Inc*, 776 F Supp 135 (SD NY, 1991) ('*Cubby*'), discussed in paras 31.12–31.22 and *Blumenthal v Drudge*, 992 F Supp 44 (D DC, 1998), discussed in paras 31.65–31.73.

Summary.   In many cases, the availability of the section 1 defence will there-   **16.12**
fore turn on the practices and policies of the Internet intermediary. Nonetheless,
it seems likely that in many cases, Internet intermediaries will be able to show
that they were not the author, editor, or publisher of defamatory material
hosted, cached, or carried by them for the purposes of section 1(1)(a) of the
Defamation Act 1996.

Section 1(1)(b): reasonable care

Introduction

In practice, section 1(1)(b) may give rise to difficulties for some Internet inter-   **16.13**
mediaries seeking to avail themselves of the section 1 defence. Under section
1(1)(b), intermediaries must prove that 'reasonable care' was taken in relation to
the publication of the offending material. In determining whether reasonable
care was exercised, courts are required to have regard to the matters set out in
section 1(5) of the Defamation Act 1996.

Nature or circumstances of the publication

First, it is not clear what is meant by the court's obligation, under section   **16.14**
1(5)(b), to have regard to 'the nature or circumstances of the publication'. The
'nature or circumstances' of Internet publications might be expected to have the
effect of lowering the standard of care expected of an Internet intermediary,
having regard to the volume of material likely to be involved, and the difficulties
involved in effectively monitoring or censoring that material.[10] On the other
hand, a court might conclude that an Internet intermediary is under a higher
obligation to monitor and censor material, having regard to the nature of the
Internet and the way in which it is used, in order to minimize the risk of
defamatory statements being published.[11] The first of these possible interpret-
ations ought to be preferred: Internet intermediaries ought not to have to monitor and censor every publication passing through their computer systems in
order to avail themselves of the section 1 defence. Indeed, the monitoring of

---

[10]   This appears to be the way in which the provision was interpreted by Gray J in a High Court
case involving the BBC and the MORI market research agency: see Sarah Jones and David
Attfield, 'A New Libel Defence for Broadcasters', *The Times*, 6 July 1999, 37. That case involved
whether the BBC was entitled to rely on the s 1 defence in relation to a live radio interview, during
which MORI was allegedly defamed. The case was settled, but Gray J made a ruling during the
trial to the effect that the s 1 defence was intended to expand freedom of expression. Gray J
expressed the view that the use of a 'profanity delay unit', which delayed the transmission of a live
broadcast by seven seconds, was relevant to determining whether the BBC had exercised reasonable care for the purposes of s 1(1)(b).
[11]   The logic employed by Burchett and Ryan JJ in *Thompson v Australian Capital Television Pty
Ltd* (1994) 54 FCR 513, 520; see paras 18.09–18.42, esp para 18.13; cf Art 15 of the Directive on
Electronic Commerce, see paras 17.32–17.34.

some Internet communications by an intermediary may be a criminal offence by reason of the Regulation of Investigatory Powers Act 2000.[12]

Previous conduct or character

16.15 Secondly, it is not clear what is meant by the court's obligation to have regard, under section 1(5)(c), to 'the previous conduct or character of the author, editor or publisher' in determining whether the intermediary has exercised reasonable care.[13] Notably, this provision requires regard to be had to the previous conduct or character of the author, editor, or publisher of the defamatory statement, not to the previous conduct or character of the intermediary. This provision would therefore presumably operate in some circumstances to prevent intermediaries from being able to rely on the section 1 defence in respect of defamatory statements communicated via their computer systems by persons who, by their previous conduct or character, must be taken as being likely to attempt to communicate defamatory statements.[14] This interpretation seems to place an extremely onerous burden on intermediaries, and calls to mind Lord Denning MR's rhetorical exhortation in *Goldsmith v Sperrings Ltd*: 'After all, who is to be the censor? Who is to assess its worth? Who is to inquire how many libel writs have been issued against it? And whether the words were true or the comment fair?'[15]

Policies and practices

16.16 Thirdly, there is an inherent tension between, on the one hand, the intermediary's obligation under section 1(1)(b) to exercise reasonable care and, on the other hand, the requirement that, to satisfy section 1(1)(a), the intermediary be 'only involved' in the publication to the extent set out in section 1(3). Diligent Internet intermediaries who put in place procedures to detect and remove defamatory material from bulletin board postings and web pages might thus be deprived of the protection of the section 1 defence, because they cannot be described as being 'only' involved in the conduct set out in section 1(3)(c) or (e).[16] On the other hand, Internet intermediaries who do not put in place such procedures may satisfy section 1(3)(c) or (e), but be deprived of the

---

[12] See esp s 1. Note that the prohibition does not apply to communications 'broadcast for general reception': s 2(3); or where the sender or recipient of the communication has consented to the interception: s 3(1).

[13] Defamation Act 1996, s 1(5)(c).

[14] Examples might include the facts in *Cubby*, 776 F Supp 135 (SD NY, 1991), discussed in paras 31.12–31.22, and *Blumenthal v Drudge*, 992 F Supp 44 (D DC, 1998), discussed in paras 31.65–31.73. See also paras 17.32–17.33.

[15] [1977] 1 WLR 478, 488 (Lord Denning MR, dissent).

[16] See eg the facts in *Stratton Oakmont*, 1995 WL 323710; 23 Media L Rep 1794 (SC NY, 1995), discussed in paras 31.23–31.34.

protection of the section 1 defence because they have failed to exercise reasonable care.[17]

Section 1(1)(c): knowledge and suspicion

Actual knowledge

Section 1(1)(c) may operate in some cases to prevent an intermediary from relying on the section 1 defence even where the intermediary has acted reasonably and responsibly. Under section 1(1)(c), the section 1 defence must fail unless intermediaries can show that they did not know, and had no reason to believe,[18] that their conduct caused or contributed to the publication of a defamatory statement. The section 1 defence will therefore fail in all cases where intermediaries have been put on notice that their computer systems are being used for the purpose of publishing defamatory material, regardless of the conduct of the intermediary.[19]

16.17

As a matter of policy, it might be thought preferable for courts to have the discretion to excuse intermediaries from liability if they have taken reasonable steps, once they become aware of the existence of the material, such as seeking prompt legal advice as to whether it is defamatory, or attempting, albeit unsuccessfully, to remove the material from their computer systems.[20]

Publication of a defamatory statement

It seems that the section 1 defence will not be available where a defendant knows, or has reason to believe, that the defendant's conduct caused or contributed to the publication of a defamatory statement, even where the defendant has reason to believe that some defence will be available in respect of the publication of that statement, such as a defence of justification, fair comment, or privilege. In this regard the section 1 defence is narrower than the defence for hosts in regulation 19 of the Electronic Commerce Regulations,[21] and probably also the common law defence of innocent dissemination.[22]

16.18

---

[17] See eg the reasoning in *Thompson v Australian Capital Television Pty Ltd* (1994) 54 FCR 513, 520; see paras 18.09–18.42, esp paras 18.13, 18.16–18.17, 18.41; cf *Auvil v CBS '60 Minutes'*, 800 F Supp 928 (ED Wash, 1992); see paras 18.20–18.28, esp paras 18.24–18.25.

[18] The factors relevant to this enquiry are those in s 1(5); see para 16.06.

[19] *Godfrey v Demon Internet Limited* [][2001] QB 201, 206; Lord Chancellor's Department, *Reforming Defamation Law and Procedure: Consultation on Draft Bill* (1995), paras 2.4–2.5. See also Eric Barendt et al, *Libel and the Media: The Chilling Effect* (1997) 8–9. So eg the defence would probably have failed on the facts in *Zeran v America Online, Inc*, 129 F 3d 327 (4th cir, 1997), 331, discussed in paras 31.55–31.64.

[20] cf *Carter v British Columbia Federation of Foster Parents Association* (2004) 27 BCLR (4th) 123 (British Columbia Supreme Court), paras 106–9.

[21] See para 17.25.

[22] See paras 18.04–18.06.

Godfrey v Demon Internet Ltd

16.19   In the first reported decision to consider the section 1 defence in an Internet context, an attempt by an Internet service provider to rely on the defence failed. The Internet service provider had known of the existence of a defamatory bulletin board posting on its news server, but had not taken any action to remove it.[23] The Internet service provider was thus unable to prove the matters required by section 1(1)(c) of the Defamation Act 1996. Its attempted reliance on the section 1 defence was held to be 'hopeless'.[24]

C. Availability of the Defence in Linking and Framing Cases

16.20   Finally, the section 1 defence is unlikely to assist parties who provide links to a defamatory statement from, or who frame a defamatory statement on, their web pages.[25] Although such parties are not the 'author' of the linked or framed statement, and will generally not be the 'publisher' of that statement for the purposes of the section 1 defence,[26] it seems likely that they will generally satisfy the definition of an 'editor' for the purposes of section 1(1)(a), namely a person 'having editorial or equivalent responsibility for the content of the statement or the decision to publish it'. A person who links a defamatory statement to, or frames a defamatory statement on, a web page will generally have editorial or equivalent responsibility for the decision to cause that statement to be published. The inclusion of the link or frame is the relevant decision; without that decision, the statement would not be published to those persons who see or read the defamatory statement as a result of visiting the linking or framing party's web page.[27]

16.21   A further reason why the section 1 defence is unlikely to assist parties who link to or frame a defamatory statement is that linking or framing parties are unlikely in many cases to be able to establish that they took reasonable care in relation to the publication of the defamatory statement,[28] or that they did not know and had no reason to believe that their conduct caused or contributed to the publication of the defamatory statement.[29] Linking or framing others' material to or on

---

[23]   *Godfrey v Demon Internet Limited* [][2001] QB 201; see further paras 15.03–15.07.
[24]   ibid, 212 (Morland J).
[25]   On whether such persons are exposed to potential liability, see paras 5.24–5.32.
[26]   ie by reason of the definition of 'publisher' in s 1(2) of the Defamation Act 1996; see paras 16.03, 16.11.
[27]   cf *Godfrey v Demon Internet Ltd* [][2001] QB 201, 209; see para 15.06. Note that by s 17 of the Defamation Act 1996, 'publication' and 'publish' have the meaning they have for defamation law generally.
[28]   Defamation Act 1996, s 1(1)(b).
[29]   ibid, s 1(1)(c).

a web page involves a decision on the part of the linking or framing party. Where the linked or framed material is defamatory, it has the potential to cause serious damage to the reputation of the defamed person. It does not seem unreasonable, in those circumstances, to hold linking or framing parties to a duty of care to monitor appropriately the content of material that they choose to link to or frame on their own web pages.[30]

In this regard, however, it is notable that the 'previous conduct or character or the author, editor or publisher' is a matter which is to be taken into account in determining whether 'reasonable care' has been exercised, or whether a person 'had reason to believe' that his or her conduct caused or contributed to the publication of a defamatory statement.[31] A person who links to a web page with a reputation for trading in scurrilous gossip might therefore be less likely to be able to rely on the defence than a person who links to a web page which ordinarily does not contain any comments about persons.[32]

The fact that the content of a linked or framed web page has been changed since the time the link or frame was established might also be relevant when inquiring whether the linking or framing party has exercised reasonable care. The duty of care might be more likely to have been discharged where the content of the linked or framed page has changed from being innocuous to being defamatory, and where the linking or framing party can be shown to have regularly monitored the linked or framed content.

---

[30] cf *Thompson v Australian Capital Television Pty Ltd* (1996) 186 CLR 574, discussed in paras 18.09–18.42, see esp paras 18.13, 18.16–18.17, 18.41.

[31] Defamation Act 1996, s 1(5)(c).

[32] As to the significance of the content of a publication to the duty of care owed by a person other than the author, editor, or publisher of defamatory material, see also *Thompson v Australian Capital Television Pty Ltd* (1996) 186 CLR 574, discussed in paras 18.09–18.42; see esp paras 18.13, 18.16, 18.40, 18.47.

17

THE ELECTRONIC COMMERCE (EC DIRECTIVE) REGULATIONS 2002 (UK)

A. Genesis and Scope

Introduction

Since they came into force on 21 August 2002, the Electronic Commerce (EC **17.01** Directive) Regulations 2002 (UK) ('Electronic Commerce Regulations') have defined the circumstances in which Internet intermediaries should be held accountable for material hosted, cached, or carried by them, but which they did not create. The Electronic Commerce Regulations are not limited in their application to defamatory Internet material. They apply equally to intermediaries who host, cache, or carry other illegal material, such as pornography or material which infringes others' intellectual property rights.

The Electronic Commerce Regulations transpose into the law of the United **17.02** Kingdom the Directive on Electronic Commerce, issued by the European

Parliament and Council on 8 June 2000.[1] It was an objective of the Directive on Electronic Commerce to remove 'existing and emerging disparities in Member States' legislation and case law concerning liability of service providers acting as intermediaries' which 'prevent the smooth functioning of the internal market, in particular by impairing the development of cross-border services and producing distortions of competition'.[2] The Directive recognizes that service providers have an obligation, in certain circumstances, to act to prevent or stop illegal activities.[3]

Information society services

17.03 The intermediary provisions of the Electronic Commerce Regulations apply to 'information society services'. An 'information society service' means 'any service normally provided for remuneration, at a distance, by electronic means and at the individual request of a recipient of services'.[4] Commercial Internet intermediaries, such as ISPs, bulletin board operators, and web hosting services will usually satisfy this definition.

Business network operators, on the other hand, will ordinarily not satisfy the definition of an 'information society service', in so far as they are intermediaries in the communication of material sent to or by the employees of the business. Their services as an intermediary are not normally provided 'for remuneration' or 'at a distance'. In addition, they may not always be provided 'at the individual request of a recipient of services'.

Similarly, suppliers of Internet access in places such as public libraries, universities, and schools may fall outside the definition of 'information society services' on the grounds that access is not provided for remuneration, or at a distance, or both.

Where intermediaries do not satisfy the definition of an 'information society service', their liability for material hosted, cached, or carried by them, but which they did not create, will depend on the application of the defence in section 1 of

---

[1] Directive 2000/31/EC of the European Parliament and of the Council of 8 June 2000 on Certain Legal Aspects of Information Society Services, in particular Electronic Commerce, in the Internal Market [2000] OJ L178/1 ('Directive on Electronic Commerce').

[2] Directive on Electronic Commerce, recital 40.

[3] ibid.

[4] Electronic Commerce Regulations, reg 2(1), incorporating Art 2(a) of the Directive on Electronic Commerce. Art 2(a) of the Directive on Electronic Commerce incorporates the definition in Directive 98/34/EC laying down a procedure for the provision of information in the field of technical standards and regulations and of rules on information society services, as amended by Directive 98/48/EC.

the Defamation Act 1996[5] and, perhaps, the common law rules of civil defamation.[6]

Mere conduits, caches, and hosts

The Electronic Commerce Regulations distinguish between intermediaries who   **17.04**
act as 'mere conduits', intermediaries who 'cache' information, and intermediaries who 'host' information.

Intermediaries are categorized for the purposes of the Electronic Commerce Regulations by the role they play in respect of the storage and transmission of particular online communications, rather than by their business characteristics or the nature of their relationships with their customers. The same intermediary may, for example, be a mere conduit in respect of the transmission of an e-mail message sent to or by a customer, a 'cache' for the purposes of web sites visited by the customer, and a host in respect of the customer's own web site.

B. Regulation 17: Mere Conduits

The provision

Regulation 17(1) of the Electronic Commerce Regulations provides: **17.05**

(1) Where an information society service[7] is provided which consists of the transmission in a communication network of information provided by a recipient of the service or the provision of access to a communication network, the service provider[8] (if he otherwise would) shall not be liable for damages or for any other pecuniary remedy or for any criminal sanction as a result of that transmission where the service provider—

(a) did not initiate the transmission;
(b) did not select the receiver of the transmission; and
(c) did not select or modify the information contained in the transmission.

The acts of transmission and of provision of access for the purposes of regula-   **17.06**
tion 17(1) include the automatic, intermediate and transient storage of the information transmitted where it takes place for the sole purpose of carrying out the transmission in the communication network, and provided that the infor-

---

[5] See chapter 16.
[6] See esp chapters 15 and 18.
[7] See para 17.03.
[8] 'Service provider' means any person providing an information society service: Electronic Commerce Regulations, reg 2(1).

mation is not stored for any period longer than is reasonably necessary for the transmission.[9]

Analysis

Ordinary e-mail messages

17.07   Regulation 17 would apply to most intermediaries[10] in so far as they are involved in the communication of ordinary e-mail messages. When e-mail messages are sent by an Internet user, the constituent IP datagrams[11] are typically stored on an automatic, intermediate, and transient basis in the computer systems of each intermediary through which they pass, and are typically deleted automatically by the intermediary's computer system immediately after they have been forwarded to the intended recipient. The intermediary's role in the communication of an e-mail message is thus limited to the transmission of that message. The intermediary does not initiate the transmission, select the receiver of the transmission, or select or modify the information contained in the transmission. Provided that the intermediary deletes the message immediately after it has been forwarded to the intended recipient, it will be entitled to the protection of regulation 17.[12]

For the purposes of regulation 17, Internet service providers may be 'mere conduits' in the transmission of e-mail messages sent to or by their own subscribers. Subscribers may, for example, fail to log on and receive their e-mail messages for days or weeks, during which time those messages will be stored on the computer system of the service provider. Provided that the service provider deletes the messages from its computer system upon ultimate transmission to its subscribers, the service provider would not lose the ability to rely on regulation 17.

Web-based e-mail

17.08   The position is likely to be different for intermediaries who operate web-based e-mail services, such as MSN Hotmail.[13] Such services store e-mail messages sent to their subscribers on their servers on a more permanent basis, so that the messages can be viewed by subscribers from any computer, located anywhere in the world. Rather than being deleted automatically from the intermediary's

---

[9] Electronic Commerce Regulations, reg 17(2).
[10] But see para 17.03.
[11] See para 2.17.
[12] See eg the facts in *Lunney v Prodigy Services Co*, 94 NY 2d 242 (CA NY, 1999), discussed in paras 31.35-31.45, in so far as they concerned the transmission of an allegedly defamatory e-mail message.
[13] See para 2.28.

server upon initial transmission to a subscriber, e-mail messages on web-based e-mail services are usually deleted from the intermediary's server only at the request of the subscriber. As messages sent to web-based e-mail services are not stored only on an 'intermediate' or 'transient' basis, and are frequently stored for a period longer than is reasonably necessary for their transmission, regulation 17 is unlikely to apply. Intermediaries operating these services are probably 'hosts', rather than 'mere conduits', of messages received by subscribers.[14]

Bulletin board postings and web pages

Regulation 17 will usually apply to Internet intermediaries who operate com-   **17.09**
puter systems through which particular bulletin board postings and web pages happen to pass en route from one computer to another, provided that the intermediary does not store the constituent IP datagrams for 'any period longer than is reasonably necessary for the transmission'. The requisite period will probably be very short indeed: it seems likely that to attract the benefit of regulation 17, the intermediary would need to configure its computer system to delete any copies of the relevant datagrams immediately after receiving an acknowledgement that they have been received by the intended recipient. If the datagrams are stored for a longer period, then the intermediary will be likely to be deemed to have 'cached' or 'hosted' them.

Relationship between regulation 17 and the section 1 defence

Mere conduit intermediaries, who merely operate computer systems through   **17.10**
which communications happen to pass en route from one computer to another, will often be able to avail themselves of the defence in section 1 of the Defam-ation Act 1996.[15] There may be circumstances, however, in which the application of the section 1 defence and regulation 17 of the Electronic Commerce Regulations lead to inconsistent outcomes.

Suppose, for example, that C discovers that she is being defamed on a web page maintained by a large news organization on its own servers. Suppose further that she puts her ISP, D, on notice of the existence of the defamatory web page, but D does nothing to prevent the page from continuing to be accessible to its subscribers. Suppose finally that D is not the host of, and has not cached, the web page; it is merely the operator of a computer system through which the offending web page passes when any of D's subscribers look at it.

In the circumstances just described, regulation 17 of Electronic Commerce Regulations would exempt D from liability for damages, pecuniary remedies, or criminal sanctions. For the purposes of regulation 17(1), D has not initiated the

---

[14] ie reg 19 will apply: see paras 17.20–17.26.
[15] See para 16.08.

transmission, selected the receiver of the transmission, or selected or modified any of the information contained in the transmission. D's role has been limited to that described in regulation 17(2), namely 'the automatic, intermediate and transient storage' of the offending web page, 'for the sole purpose of carrying out the transmission in the communication network'.

In these circumstances, however, D could well be unable to avail itself of the defence in section 1 of the Defamation Act 1996 in respect of publications of the offending web page to D's subscribers occurring after D has been put on notice of its existence, because in respect of those publications D will know that, by its conduct, it has caused or contributed to the publication of a defamatory statement.[16] It might also be said that D has failed to exercise reasonable care in relation to the ongoing availability of the defamatory web page.[17] For similar reasons D would probably be unable to avail itself of the common law defence of innocent dissemination, to the extent that that defence remains available in the United Kingdom.[18]

C. Regulation 18: Caching

The provision

17.11 Regulation 18 of the Electronic Commerce Regulations provides:

> Where an information society service[19] is provided which consists of the transmission in a communication network of information provided by a recipient of the service, the service provider[20] (if he otherwise would) shall not be liable for damages or for any other pecuniary remedy or for any criminal sanction as a result of that transmission where—
>
> (a) the information is the subject of automatic, intermediate and temporary storage where that storage is for the sole purpose of making more efficient onward transmission of the information to other recipients of the service upon their request, and
> (b) the service provider—
>
>> (i) does not modify the information;
>> (ii) complies with conditions on access to the information;
>> (iii) complies with any rules regarding the updating of the information, specified in a manner widely recognized and used by industry;

---

[16] Defamation Act 1996, s 1(1)(c). See also *Godfrey v Demon Internet Limited* [2001] QB 201, discussed in paras 15.03–15.07.

[17] Defamation Act 1996, s 1(1)(b); see paras 16.13–16.16.

[18] See paras 18.06–18.07 (relationship between the s 1 defence and the common law defence), 18.50–18.52 (conclusions in relation to the availability of the common law defence to mere conduit intermediaries).

[19] See para 17.03.

[20] See n 8 above.

    (iv) does not interfere with the lawful use of technology, widely recognized and used by industry, to obtain data on the use of the information; and

    (v) acts expeditiously to remove or to disable access to the information he has stored upon obtaining actual knowledge of the fact that the information at the initial source of the transmission has been removed from the network, or access to it has been disabled, or that a court or an administrative authority has ordered such removal or disablement.

Scope

Regulation 18 is intended to protect Internet intermediaries from liability in respect of material for which they are not the primary host, but which they store temporarily on their computer systems for the purpose of enabling the efficient availability of Internet material. Many ISPs and other intermediaries routinely 'cache', or temporarily store, commonly accessed web pages on their computer systems, so that those pages will be more quickly accessible to their subscribers. The cached web pages will then typically be updated automatically on a regular basis by the intermediary. Similar arrangements are adopted in relation to bulletin board postings.[21]   **17.12**

There is a degree of tension among the various requirements in regulation 18. On the one hand, for example, the regulation applies only to information which is stored by the intermediary on an 'automatic' basis. On the other hand, an intermediary seeking to rely on regulation 18 must demonstrate that it has complied with conditions on access to the information and complied with rules regarding its updating. There may be circumstances in which establishing these latter matters requires a degree of intervention by the intermediary which is inconsistent with 'automatic' storage of the information. Conversely, an intermediary who does not intervene in the automatic caching of information by its computer system may find in particular circumstances that it has failed to comply with conditions on access to the information or with any rules regarding the updating of the information, and has thereby lost the benefit of regulation 18.

To maximize the prospect of being able to rely on regulation 18, intermediaries who cache content would be well advised to develop policies and procedures: **17.13**

• setting out how they select and obtain cached content;
• acknowledging that the sole purpose of the caching is to facilitate the efficient onward transmission of the cached content to recipients of the service upon request;
• prohibiting the modification of the content;

---

[21] See generally para 2.47.

- identifying how regularly they update and delete cached content; and
- facilitating the expeditious removal or disabling of access to information in the circumstances identified in regulation 18(b)(v).

Conditions on access to information

17.14 The requirement in regulation 18(b)(ii) that service providers comply with 'conditions on access' to information might operate to prevent service providers from relying on regulation 18 if they cache content from web sites which are not generally accessible, but make that content available generally to their subscribers. For example, suppose an Internet user has subscribed to a specialist online service which makes information accessible only to persons who have paid a fee and been allocated a password. In those circumstances, the provider of the service has imposed conditions on access to information. It seems likely that if an intermediary in the transmission of that information to the Internet user cached the information and made it available to other persons upon their request, the intermediary would be unable to rely on regulation 18, even if the information had been cached by the intermediary on an automatic, intermediate, and temporary basis.

Industry rules

17.15 Examples of rules for the caching of material which are 'widely recognized and used by industry' might include codes of practice or policies developed by Internet associations. There did not appear to be any such codes of practice or policies in place in the United Kingdom at the time of writing (March 2005).

Actual knowledge

17.16 Intermediaries lose the benefit of regulation 18 if they fail to act expeditiously to remove or disable access to cached information upon obtaining 'actual knowledge' of the matters identified in regulation 18(b)(v).

17.17 Regulation 22 of the Electronic Commerce Regulations provides:

> In determining whether a service provider has actual knowledge for the purposes of regulations 18(b)(v) and 19(a)(i), a court shall take into account all matters which appear to it in the particular circumstances to be relevant and, among other things, shall have regard to—
>
> (a) whether a service provider has received a notice through a means of contact made available in accordance with regulation 6(1)(c),[22] and

---

[22] That is, received in accordance with the details of the service provider made available to recipients of the service and any relevant enforcement authority. Those details must be easily, directly, and permanently accessible, and include the service provider's electronic mail address, so as to enable the provider to be contacted rapidly, directly, and effectively: Electronic Commerce Regulations, reg 6(1)(c).

(b) the extent to which any notice includes—

    (i) the full name and address of the sender of the notice;

    (ii) details of the location of the information in question; and

    (iii) details of the unlawful nature of the activity or information in question.

17.18 It is difficult to see how regulation 22 could affect the proper interpretation of regulation 18(b)(v). A service provider loses the benefit of regulation 18 only if the provider has 'actual knowledge' of the matters identified in regulation 18(b)(v). Receipt of a notice of the kind referred to in regulation 22 is no more than an illustration of a circumstance in which a service provider would have such knowledge. There are many circumstances in which service providers could lose the benefit of regulation 18 without receiving a notice of the kind referred to in regulation 22.

It is also difficult to see what use a court might make of regulation 22(b)(i). Whether a service provider knows the full name and address of the sender of the notice is surely irrelevant to whether the service provider has actual knowledge of the matters identified in regulation 18(b)(v). A service provider receiving a notice stating, for example, that a court had ordered the removal of certain information could scarcely deny having actual knowledge of the contents of the notice on the basis that the sender's full name and address was not stated.

The matters identified in regulation 22 appear to be more relevant to determining whether, in all the circumstances, a service provider has acted expeditiously to remove or to disable access to cached information, than to whether the service provider has actual knowledge of the matters identified in regulation 18(b)(v).

Relationship between regulation 18 and the section 1 defence

17.19 As with regulation 17, it is possible that the application of the defence in section 1 of the Defamation Act 1996 and regulation 18 of the Electronic Commerce Regulations could lead to inconsistent outcomes. In the example given in paragraph 17.10, for instance, the ISP, D, may well have stored the offending web page in its computer system to enable it to be more efficiently accessed by subscribers. If D has satisfied the conditions in regulation 18(b), then D cannot be liable for damages, any pecuniary remedy, or any criminal sanction as a result of the transmission of the page. As discussed earlier, however, it is unlikely that D would be able to avail itself of the section 1 defence in respect of publications of the offending web page to D's subscribers occurring after its existence has been brought to D's attention.[23]

---

[23] See para 17.10.

D. Regulation 19: Hosting

The provision

17.20   Regulation 19 of the Electronic Commerce Regulations provides:

> Where an information society service[24] is provided which consists of the storage of information provided by a recipient of the service, the service provider (if he otherwise would) shall not be liable for damages or for any other pecuniary remedy or for any criminal sanction as a result of that storage where—
>
> (a) the service provider—
>
>   (i) does not have actual knowledge of unlawful activity or information and, where a claim for damages is made, is not aware of facts or circumstances from which it would have been apparent to the service provider that the activity or information was unlawful; or
>
>   (ii) upon obtaining such knowledge or awareness, acts expeditiously to remove or to disable access to the information, and
>
> (b) the recipient of the service was not acting under the authority or the control of the service provider.

Hosts

17.21   Regulation 19 is intended to apply to Internet intermediaries who store Internet content, such as web pages and bulletin board postings, on their computer systems. An example of a 'host' is Demon Internet, on the facts in *Godfrey v Demon Internet Ltd*.[25] Regulation 19 would not apply, however, where the author of the particular defamatory content was an agent or employee of the intermediary, because in those cases the author would ordinarily be acting 'under the authority or the control' of the intermediary within the meaning of regulation 19(b). An example of this kind of content might be a gossip column prepared by a third party, but commissioned by an ISP and available from that ISP's home page.[26]

Actual knowledge

17.22   Regulation 19 will not operate to protect hosts from liability where they actually know that unlawful material is stored on their computer systems.

---

[24] See para 17.03.
[25] [2001] QB 201; see paras 15.03–15.07. For other examples, see the facts in *Stratton Oakmont, Inc v Prodigy Services Company*, 1995 WL 323710; 23 Media L Rep 1794 (SC NY, 1995), discussed in paras 31.23–31.34 and *Lunney v Prodigy Services Co*, 94 NY 2d 242 (CA NY, 1999), discussed in paras 31.35–31.45 (in so far as they concerned the transmission of allegedly defamatory bulletin board postings).
[26] See eg the facts in *Blumenthal v Drudge*, 992 F Supp 44 (D DC, 1998), discussed in paras 31.65–31.73. See also *Cubby, Inc v CompuServe Inc*, 776 F Supp 135 (SD NY, 1991), discussed in paras 31.12–31.22.

Regulation 22 identifies matters which a court must take into account in determining whether a service provider has actual knowledge for the purposes of regulation 19(a)(i), namely whether the service provider has received a notice including the full name and address of the sender, details of the location of the information in question, and details of the unlawful nature of the activity or information in question. For the reasons identified in relation to regulation 18, regulation 22 is a curious provision of limited application.[27] Receipt of a notice of the kind referred to in regulation 22 may be sufficient to prove that a service provider has actual knowledge of unlawful activity or information, but a service provider may have the requisite knowledge without receiving such a notice, or by reason of having received a notice which does not have all of the characteristics identified in regulation 22.

Awareness of facts and circumstances

Regulation 19 will also not operate to protect hosts in ordinary defamation actions[28] where they are 'aware of facts or circumstances' from which the existence of the unlawful information 'would have been apparent'.[29] It may be that this expression is similar in scope to the requirement in section 1(1)(c) of the Defamation Act 1996, namely that persons seeking to rely on the section 1 defence have 'no reason to believe' that their conduct caused or contributed to the publication of a defamatory statement. Suppose, for example, that an Internet content host has been tipped off that material attacking the reputation of an individual is contained on a particular web page hosted on its computer system, but the host has no knowledge of the actual material. It seems likely that in such a case the intermediary is 'aware of facts or circumstances from which it would have been apparent to the service provider that the activity or information was unlawful'.

17.23

Negligence

It is not entirely clear whether the expression 'is not aware of facts and circumstances from which it would have been apparent to the service provider that the activity or information was unlawful' in regulation 19(a)(i) is sufficiently broad to impose a duty of care upon hosts to monitor for and censor defamatory material stored on their computer systems.

17.24

The language of regulation 19(a)(i) is different from the language of Article

---

[27] See para 17.18.
[28] ie actions involving 'claims for damages'; see Electronic Commerce Regulations, reg 19(a)(i).
[29] ibid.

14(1)(a) of the Directive on Electronic Commerce, which it purports to transpose. The corresponding expression in Article 14(1)(a) is 'is not aware of facts or circumstances from which the illegal activity or information *is* apparent' (emphasis added). While United Kingdom courts are under an obligation to interpret domestic legislation, such as the Electronic Commerce Regulations, so far as possible, in the light of the wording and the purpose of the Directive they transpose,[30] the words 'would have been apparent' in regulation 19(a)(i) of the Electronic Commerce Regulations connote a conditional meaning which is not conveyed by the words 'is apparent' in Article 14(1)(a) of the Directive on Electronic Commerce.

The significance of the difference between the language of regulation 19(a)(i) and the language of Article 14(1)(a) can best be illustrated by example. Suppose that a subscriber to a particular ISP uploads a scandalous gossip column to his web page every week, and that the web page is stored on the ISP's servers. Suppose further that the column has, notoriously, spawned a number of successful defamation actions in the past. Suppose finally that defamation proceedings are brought against the ISP in relation to an item in the gossip column, but that the ISP had no actual knowledge of the existence of that item until the commencement of the proceedings.

Article 14 of the Directive on Electronic Commerce might be expected to protect ISPs from liability on the facts postulated. While the ISP might have been aware of facts or circumstances from which the existence of the offending item ought to have been apparent, or ought with reasonable diligence to have been apparent, it could not be said that the ISP *was* aware of facts or circumstances from which the existence of the particular item was apparent.

For the purposes of ascertaining whether regulation 19 of the Electronic Commerce Regulations protects the ISP, however, the relevant inquiry is whether the ISP was aware of facts or circumstances from which the existence of the defamatory item 'would have been apparent'. It seems to be at least arguable that it would have been apparent to the ISP that, as items in the column had in the past spawned successful defamation actions, further such items would be likely to be published in the column in the future.

If that interpretation is correct, then intermediaries seeking to rely on regulation 19 may be effectively under an obligation to monitor the material they host, at least where they have a reasonable basis for believing that that material may be defamatory.

---

[30] eg Case 14/83 *Von Colson* [1984] ECR 1891, paras 26–8; Case 79/83 *Harz* [1984] ECR 1921, paras 26–8; Case C–131/97 *Carbonari* [1999] ECR I–1103, para 48; cf Case C–106/89 *Marleasing SA* [1990] ECR I–4135, paras 8–9.

There is, however, a contrary argument. The regulation 19 defence is only defeated where the host is 'aware of facts or circumstances from which it would have been apparent that *the* activity or information was unlawful' (emphasis added). In a defamation case, it might be argued that a host will only be aware of the requisite facts or circumstances if the host has actual knowledge of the existence of *the* material complained of, and actual knowledge of facts or circumstances from which it would have been apparent that *that* material was unlawful. In other words, it might be that mere general awareness on the part of a host that its service is being used for the purpose of publishing defamatory material is insufficient to defeat the operation of the regulation 19 defence.

Suppose, for example, that a host is generally aware that its server contains a great deal of material which is controversial and which attacks the reputations of individuals. Suppose further, however, that the host does not monitor or exercise any editorial control over the material it hosts. It might be argued that the host will be entitled to the benefit of the regulation 19 defence in respect of any particular information on its server, because in respect of *that* information, the host is not aware of facts or circumstances from which it would have been apparent that the information was unlawful.

On balance, however, this interpretation is problematic. There would not appear to be any difference, in substance, between a host with 'actual knowledge of unlawful activity', on the one hand, and, on the other hand, a host with awareness of facts or circumstances from which it would have been apparent that particular information, of which the host was actually aware, was unlawful. Such an interpretation is also difficult to reconcile with the use of the conditional language 'would have been apparent' in regulation 19(a)(i). That language tends to suggest that a host loses the benefit of the regulation 19 defence if the host should have known, having regard to the facts and circumstances of which it was aware, that it was the host of unlawful information, whether the host had actual knowledge of the existence of the information or not.

'Unlawful' information

The publication of defamatory material of and concerning a person is only **17.25** unlawful if there is no defence available to the publisher of the material. It seems, therefore, that mere knowledge on the part of a service provider that defamatory material is stored on its server will not defeat the operation of the regulation 19 defence. Suppose, for example, that a host knows that its server contains information imputing that an individual is guilty of a serious crime, but knows no facts or circumstances bearing one way or the other on the truth or falsity of that imputation. In those circumstances, it seems likely that the host would be entitled to rely on the regulation 19 defence. The host does not have actual knowledge that the information on its server is unlawful, and is not aware of facts or circumstances from which it is or would have been apparent that that information is unlawful.

The regulation 19 defence thus appears to be considerably broader than the section 1 defence, which is defeated where defendants merely know, or have reason to believe, that their conduct caused or contributed to the publication of a 'defamatory statement'.[31]

Removal of material

17.26   Finally, under regulation 19, service providers are not held liable for hosting unlawful material, provided that they act expeditiously to remove or disable access to that material upon obtaining actual knowledge of it, or awareness of facts and circumstances from which the existence of the unlawful material would have been apparent.[32] It is not entirely clear from regulation 19 whether unsuccessful attempts by an intermediary to remove or disable access to the offending material would be sufficient to entitle it to the benefit of an exemption from liability.[33]

The defence in section 1 of the Defamation Act 1996, by contrast, ceases to be available to Internet intermediaries from the time they become aware, or have reason to believe, that their computer systems are being used for the publication of defamatory material.[34]

17.27   The application of the section 1 defence and regulation 19 might therefore lead in some cases to different outcomes. Suppose, for example, that an ISP was put on notice that it was hosting on its computer system a web page containing, arguably, unlawful defamatory material. Suppose further that, within 48 hours, the ISP referred the matter to a defamation lawyer for advice, received advice that the material should be removed, and removed the offending web page from its computer system. Suppose finally that during that forty-eight-hour period, a number of persons viewed the offending web page. The section 1 defence would not protect the ISP in respect of the publications of the web page which occurred during the forty-eight-hour period after the ISP was first put on notice

---

[31]   Defamation Act 1996 (UK), s 1(1)(c); see para 16.18. The common law defence of innocent dissemination may be broader than the s 1 defence for the same reason: see paras 18.04–18.06.

[32]   Electronic Commerce Regulations, reg 19(a)(ii).

[33]   One possible interpretation is that the intermediary is obliged only to 'act expeditiously', not to remove or disable access to the information expeditiously: cf *Carter v British Columbia Federation of Foster Parents Association* (2004) 27 BCLR (4th) 123 (British Columbia Supreme Court), paras 106–9.

[34]   Defamation Act 1996, s 1(1)(c); see paras 16.17–16.18.

of its existence.[35] The regulation 19 defence would, however, be likely to be available, because it could be said that the ISP had acted expeditiously to remove or disable access to the offending web page upon learning of its existence.

E. Injunctions and Other Non-Pecuniary Remedies

The protection afforded to Internet intermediaries by the Electronic Commerce Regulations applies only to potential liability for 'damages', 'pecuniary remedies', and 'criminal sanctions'. Regulation 20(1)(b) provides that nothing in regulations 17, 18, and 19 affects 'the rights of any party to apply to a court for relief to prevent or stop infringement of any rights'.[36] Regulation 20(2) provides that '[a]ny power of an administrative authority to prevent or stop infringement of any rights shall continue to apply notwithstanding regulations 17, 18 and 19'. **17.28**

The Electronic Commerce Regulations therefore do not operate to prevent interim or permanent injunctions from being granted in appropriate cases against Internet intermediaries to restrain them from causing or contributing to the publication of defamatory material. The circumstances in which injunctions will be granted in defamation cases in the United Kingdom are, however, severely limited.[37]

The Electronic Commerce Regulations may also not prevent a claimant from invoking the summary disposal procedure in sections 8 and 9 of the Defamation Act 1996 in an action against an Internet intermediary, for the purpose of seeking orders for the publication by the intermediary of a suitable correction and apology.[38]

F. Vertical Direct Effect of the Directive on Electronic Commerce

General principles

Directives of the European Parliament and Council do not have 'horizontal **17.29**

---

[35] *Godfrey v Demon Internet Ltd* [2001] QB 201; see para 16.19.
[36] Regulation 20 of the Electronic Commerce Regulations transposes Arts 12(3), 13(2), and 14(3) of the Directive on Electronic Commerce. Those articles reserve to courts and administrative authorities in Member States the power to require Internet intermediaries to terminate or prevent 'infringements'.
[37] See chapter 20.
[38] See paras 20.28–20.34.

direct effect'; that is, they do not impose obligations upon private parties, or confer rights which may be enforced against private parties.[39]

Where, however, a Member State fails to transpose a Directive into national legislation, it may in certain circumstances be responsible for the consequences of failing to do so, and liable to pay compensation to private parties.[40] The Directive will have such a 'vertical direct effect' if the result prescribed by the Directive entails the grant of rights to private parties, if it is possible to identify the content of those rights from the provisions of the Directive itself, and if there is a causal link between the breach of the Member State's obligation to transpose the Directive and the harm suffered by the private party.[41]

17.30 If an Internet intermediary were to be found liable under the defamation law of the United Kingdom in circumstances in which it is entitled to be exempted from liability under the Directive on Electronic Commerce, the intermediary might be entitled to recover any damages awarded against it in proceedings against the United Kingdom before the European Court of Justice.[42] That is, in those circumstances, vertical direct effect against the United Kingdom might be given to the Directive on Electronic Commerce.

Liability of negligent hosts

17.31 One example of a circumstance in which an Internet intermediary might be liable under United Kingdom law in circumstances in which it would be entitled to be exempted from liability under the Directive on Electronic Commerce has been explored in paragraph 17.24, arising out of the apparent inconsistency between the language of Article 14(1)(a) of the Directive on Electronic Commerce and the language of regulation 19(a)(i) of the Electronic Commerce Regulations.

---

[39] eg Case 152/84 *Marshall* [1986] ECR 723, paras 46–8; Case C–91/92 *Dori* [1994] ECR I–3325, paras 22–5.

[40] eg Cases C–6 and 9/90 *Francovich* [1991] ECR I–5357, paras 38–41. The obligation arises out of the Treaty Establishing the European Community ('EC Treaty'), Art 249 (formerly Art 189).

[41] ibid, para 40.

[42] Cases C–6/90 and C–9/90 *Francovich* [1991] ECR I–5357, paras 38–41. The entitlement to damages will only arise, however, if the failure to implement the Directive was a 'sufficiently serious' breach of Community law: Cases C–46 and 48/93 *Brasserie du Pêcheur and Factortame* [1996] ECR I–1029; Case C–392/93 *British Telecommunications* [1996] ECR I–1631; Case C–178/94 *Dillenkofer* [1996] ECR I–4845. In summary, a complete failure to implement a Directive would ordinarily give rise to an entitlement to damages. On the other hand, a good faith, but incomplete or misconceived attempt at implementation might not be 'sufficiently serious' as to warrant an order for damages, particularly where the words of the Directive in question are ambiguous or imprecise.

Monitoring obligations

A further possible circumstance in which vertical direct effect might be given to the Directive on Electronic Commerce arises out of the fact that Article 15 of the Directive on Electronic Commerce has not been directly transposed into the domestic law of the United Kingdom.

17.32

Article 15 of the Directive on Electronic Commerce prohibits Member States from imposing a general obligation on providers 'to monitor the information which they transmit or store' or 'a general obligation actively to seek facts or circumstances indicating illegal activity'.[43] Member States may, however, require providers to inform competent public authorities of alleged illegal activities undertaken or information provided by recipients of their service.[44] Member States may also require providers to communicate to the competent authorities, upon request, information enabling the identification of recipients of their service with whom they have storage arrangements.[45] This latter requirement would presumably operate to prevent intermediaries from objecting to responding to *Norwich Pharmacal* proceedings or witness summonses from claimants seeking information as to the author of defamatory material hosted, cached, or carried by the intermediary.[46]

It may be that in order to rely on regulation 19 of the Electronic Commerce Regulations, intermediaries are obliged to monitor the material they host, at least where they have a reasonable basis for believing that that material may be unlawful.[47]

17.33

Similarly, the defence in section 1 of the Defamation Act 1996 may be defeated in some circumstances where Internet intermediaries have failed to monitor material hosted, cached, or carried by them. For example, the obligation to exercise reasonable care in section 1(1)(b) might have the effect, in some cases, of requiring an Internet intermediary to monitor the activities of some Internet users if it is subsequently to rely successfully on the section 1 defence.[48] It might be said, therefore, that the section 1 defence imposes in such cases an obligation on intermediaries actively to seek facts or circumstances indicating illegal activity.

While it cannot be said that regulation 19 of the Electronic Commerce Regulations or section 1 of the Defamation Act 1996 in terms impose any positive

17.34

---

[43] Directive on Electronic Commerce, Art 15(1).
[44] ibid, Art 15(2).
[45] ibid.
[46] See paras 5.36–5.41.
[47] See para 17.24.
[48] See paras 16.14–16.15.

monitoring obligation on Internet intermediaries, their effect may be that intermediaries are exposed to liability if they do not monitor the material they host. Such an outcome is at least arguably contrary to Article 15 of the Directive on Electronic Commerce.

The better view, however, would appear to be that the monitoring which intermediaries seeking to avail themselves of the defences in regulation 19 of the Electronic Commerce Regulations and section 1 of the Defamation Act 1996 might be required to undertake does not constitute a 'general obligation' of the kind contemplated by Article 15 of the Directive on Electronic Commerce. Support for this view can be derived from recital 48 to the Directive, which provides:

> This Directive does not affect the possibility for Member States of requiring service providers, who host information provided by recipients of their service, to apply duties of care, which can reasonably be expected from them and which are specified by national law, in order to detect and prevent certain types of illegal activities.

18

THE COMMON LAW DEFENCE OF INNOCENT DISSEMINATION

A. Introduction

Elements of the defence

The common law relieves defendants who are 'subordinate distributors' of **18.01** defamatory publications from liability upon proof that:

- they did not know that the publication complained of contained a libel;[1]
- they did not know that the publication was of such a character that it was likely to contain a libel; and
- the absence of knowledge was not due to any negligence on their part.[2]

---

[1] See para 18.04.

[2] *Emmens v Pottle* (1885) 16 QBD 354; *Vizetelly v Mudie's Select Library, Ltd* [1900] 2 QB 170. See also *Mallon v WH Smith & Son* (1893) 9 TLR 621; *Martin v Trustees of the British Museum* (1894) 10 TLR 338; *Morrison v John Ritchie and Company* (1902) 4 F 645; *Weldon v 'The Times' Book Company (Ltd)* (1911) 28 TLR 143; *Haynes v De Beck* (1914) 31 TLR 115; *Bottomley v FW Woolworth & Co, Ltd* (1932) 48 TLR 521; *Sun Life Assurance Co of Canada v WH Smith & Son, Ltd* [1933] All ER Rep 432; *Goldsmith v Sperrings Ltd* [1977] 1 WLR 478.

18.02 Proof by a defendant who is a subordinate distributor of these elements is treated in some cases as negating the existence of publication by that defendant.[3] The better view is that, as the burden of proof lies with the defendant, proof of the elements constitutes a defence of innocent dissemination.[4] In a defamation action, it is for the defendant who is a subordinate distributor to plead the existence of the elements of innocent dissemination, failing which publication, if properly pleaded by the claimant, will be presumed.

Subordinate distributors

18.03 Categories of 'subordinate distributors' include newspaper and magazine distributors and vendors,[5] book distributors and libraries,[6] and wholesale newspaper agents.[7] Publishers who are not subordinate distributors are 'the author, printer, or the "first or main publisher of a work which contains a libel" '[8]

---

[3] See eg *Vizetelly v Mudie's Select Library, Ltd* [1900] 2 QB 170, 178 (Vaughan Williams LJ): 'What I understand *Emmens v Pottle* 16 QBD 354 really to decide is that the innocent publication of defamatory matter; ie its publication under such circumstances as to rebut the presumption of any malice, is not a publication within the meaning of the law of libel', 179 (Romer LJ): 'although the dissemination of the work by him was primâ facie publication of it, he may nevertheless, on proof of the before-mentioned facts, be held not to have published it. But the onus of proving such facts lies on him, and the question of publication or non-publication is in such a case one for the jury.' See also *Lee v Wilson* (1934) 51 CLR 276, 288 (Dixon J): 'If, however, the publication is made in the ordinary exercise of some business or calling, such as that of booksellers, newsvendors, messengers, or letter carriers, and the defendant neither knows nor suspects, nor using reasonable diligence ought to know or suspect the defamatory contents of the writing, proof of which facts lies upon him, his act does not amount to publication of a libel.'

[4] *Thompson v Australian Capital Television Pty Ltd* (1996) 186 CLR 574, 586; Colin Duncan, Brian Neill, and Richard Rampton, *Duncan & Neill on Defamation* (2nd edn, 1983) 110; cf Lord Denning MR in *Goldsmith v Sperrings Ltd* [1977] 1 WLR 478, 487–9 who concluded, after having read 'every case cited in the textbooks on this subject', that 'a subordinate distributor has never been held liable to a plaintiff except when prior knowledge of the libel has been brought home to him'. Lord Denning's judgment was heavily influenced by free speech concerns. Lord Denning would have put the burden on the plaintiff to prove that a distributor actually knew, or ought to have known, that the publication contained defamatory material. The other two members of the Court of Appeal criticized Lord Denning for addressing the question of distributor liability at all, it not having been an issue argued before the court: [1977] 1 WLR 478, 508 (Bridge LJ), 500 (Scarman LJ). Scarman LJ noted that Lord Denning 'may, or may not, be right in his view of the law'.

[5] *Emmens v Pottle* (1885) 16 QBD 354; *Mallon v WH Smith & Son* (1893) 9 TLR 621; *Bottomley v FW Woolworth & Co, Ltd* (1932) 48 TLR 521; *Sun Life Assurance Co of Canada v WH Smith & Son, Ltd* [1933] All ER Rep 432 (defence failed on the facts).

[6] *Martin v Trustees of the British Museum* (1894) 10 TLR 338; *Weldon v 'The Times' Book Company (Ltd)* (1911) 28 TLR 143; *Vizetelly v Mudie's Select Library, Ltd* [1900] 2 QB 170 (defence failed on the facts).

[7] *Haynes v De Beck* (1914) 31 TLR 115 (defence failed on the facts, although only nominal damages were awarded, without costs, because there was no 'moral obliquity' on the defendants' part).

[8] Patrick Milmo and WVH Rogers, *Gatley on Libel and Slander* (10th edn, 2003) ('Gatley') para 6.18. See also Eric Barendt et al, *Libel and the Media: The Chilling Effect* (1997) 8.

'Printers under modern technological conditions', who may have no knowledge of the contents of what they print, might be capable of being categorized as subordinate distributors.[9]

Actionability of the defamation

It is not entirely clear whether the common law defence of innocent dissemin- **18.04**
ation will be available to a subordinate distributor who knows that a particular publication contains defamatory material, but believes there is a good defence available in respect of that material, such as a defence of justification, fair comment, or privilege, or has no view one way or the other as to the likely availability of such a defence. Most of the authorities suggest that the defence will be defeated where the subordinate distributor knows that the publication contains a 'libel', as opposed merely to a defamatory statement.[10]

Suppose, for example, that a newspaper vendor knows that the page one article **18.05**
in a particular edition of a newspaper contains material which conveys a defamatory meaning, but also believes (honestly, but incorrectly) that the imputation borne by the material is a matter of substantial truth, and would therefore be the subject of a defence of justification in defamation proceedings. Although the point is certainly not without doubt,[11] it seems likely that the newspaper vendor would be entitled in those circumstances to rely on the common law defence of innocent dissemination to avoid liability, because the vendor did not know that the newspaper contained a libel.

If that analysis is correct, then the common law defence will, in effect, be available to subordinate distributors who know that a particular publication contains defamatory material, so long as they do not know or believe that no defence would be available in respect of that material.[12]

---

[9] *McPhersons Ltd v Hickie* [1995] Aust Torts Reports ¶81–348, 62,498 (Priestley JA); cf *Menear v Miguna* (1997) 33 OR (3d) 223, reversing (1996) 30 OR (3d) 602.

[10] As the authors of Gatley (n 8 above) para 6.26 note, most of the authorities 'speak in terms of the defendant having reason to believe that what he is distributing contains a *libel*', citing *Emmens v Pottle* (1885) 16 QBD 354, 357–8; *Ridgway v Smith* (1890) 6 TLR 275, 276; *Mallon v WH Smith & Son* (1893) 9 TLR 621, 622; *Vizetelly v Mudie's Select Library, Ltd* [1900] 2 QB 170, 176, 180. Other authorities to the same effect include *Weldon v 'The Times' Book Company (Ltd)* (1911) 28 TLR 143; *Haynes v De Beck* (1914) 31 TLR 115; *Bottomley v FW Woolworth & Co, Ltd* (1932) 48 TLR 521; *Sun Life Assurance Co of Canada v WH Smith & Son, Ltd* [1933] All ER Rep 432; *Goldsmith v Sperrings Ltd* [1977] 1 WLR 478, 487–9, cf 505; *Thompson v Australian Capital Television Pty Ltd* (1996) 186 CLR 574, 585–91, cf 596; *McPhersons Ltd v Hickie* [1995] Aust Torts Reports ¶81–348, 62,499, cf 62,498.

[11] See eg Gatley (n 8 above) para 6.26.

[12] *Goldsmith v Sperrings Ltd* [1977] 1 WLR 478, 487 (Lord Denning, who dissented as to the result): 'no subordinate distributor . . . should be held liable for a libel . . . unless he knew or ought to have known that a newspaper or periodical contained a libel on the plaintiff himself; that is to say, that it contained a libel which could not be justified or excused'; cf 505 (Bridge LJ).

Availability of the common law defence in the United Kingdom

18.06   This last point is of significance. The defence in section 1 of the Defamation Act 1996 (UK), which is in effect a modified and modernized version of the common law defence of innocent dissemination, would not be available to newspaper vendors in the circumstances just discussed. The section 1 defence is not available to persons who know that what they did 'caused or contributed to the publication of a *defamatory statement*' (emphasis added).[13]

It is therefore arguable that the common law defence of innocent dissemination continues to operate in the United Kingdom, as an alternative to the defence in section 1 of the Defamation Act 1996. The Act does not expressly abolish the common law defence. As the common law defence may be capable of applying in circumstances where the section 1 defence does not, it may be that it should not be taken to have been impliedly abolished by the Act.[14] It is a well-known principle of statutory construction that common law rights are not to be treated as being overridden by statutory provisions in the absence of clear and unambiguous language.[15]

If that view is correct, then defendants who cannot prove the defence in section 1 of the Defamation Act 1996, because they know that a particular publication contains a defamatory statement, may still be able to rely on the common law defence of innocent dissemination if they have no reason to doubt that there would be a good defence available in respect of the statement, such as a defence of justification, fair comment, or privilege.

18.07   Nonetheless, for most practical purposes, the section 1 defence is now plainly of much greater importance in the United Kingdom than the common law defence. The operation of that defence is the subject of chapter 16.

---

[13]   Defamation Act 1996 (UK), s 1(1)(c).

[14]   cf Gatley (n 8 above) para 6.26, wherein it is argued that s 1 might impliedly abolish the common law defence. The authors of Gatley cite in support of this assertion the statement by the Lord Chancellor, when introducing the Defamation Bill, that the s 1 defence would 'supersede' the common law defence (*Hansard*, House of Lords, 8 March 1996, col 577), and the statement in para 2.6 of the *Consultation on the Draft Bill* (5 May 1995) that the s 1 defence would 'replace and modernize innocent dissemination'. It is submitted, however, that recourse cannot be had to extrinsic statements such as these to ascertain whether Parliament intended to abolish the common law defence of innocent dissemination in the absence of some ambiguity in the meaning of s 1 itself: *Black-Clawson International Ltd v Papierwerke Waldhof-Aschaffenberg AG* [1975] AC 591, 614–15; *Pepper (Inspector of Taxes) v Hart* [1993] AC 593, 630. There would not appear to be any relevant ambiguity in the s 1 defence.

[15]   eg *Ash v Abdy* (1678) 3 Swans 664; 36 ER 1014; *Leach v Rex* [1912] AC 305, 301–11; *Attorney-General v Brotherton* [1992] 1 AC 425, 439, 447.

Availability of the common law defence in Australia

The common law defence of innocent dissemination is available in all Austra-   **18.08**
lian jurisdictions except Queensland and Tasmania, where it has been replaced
by a statutory defence.[16]

B. *Thompson v Australian Capital Television Pty Ltd*

Introduction

There are very few recent cases concerning the application of the common law   **18.09**
defence of innocent dissemination in the United Kingdom or Australia, and
even fewer cases concerning the potential application of that defence in cases
concerning modern media of publication. The leading case in recent years is the
decision of the Australian High Court in *Thompson v Australian Capital Tele-*
vision Pty Ltd.[17] By analogy, the reasoning in *Thompson* provides the clearest
indication of how a court might be likely to treat intermediaries of defamatory
Internet publications in those cases where the common law defence might
apply.

The issue in *Thompson* was whether a television station broadcasting to the   **18.10**
Australian Capital Territory and nearby parts of New South Wales ('Channel 7')
was liable for the publication of the *Today Show*, a live current affairs programme produced by another network in Sydney ('Channel 9'). Channel 7
received and simultaneously telecast the *Today Show* via a receiving station in
Canberra.

The episode of the *Today Show* complained of involved an interview with a
young woman who alleged that the applicant had committed incest with her,
resulting in her becoming pregnant and giving birth when she was fourteen.
The interview had been pre-recorded. The young woman interviewed was a
'self-acknowledged prostitute and drug addict'.[18]

Channel 7 received the *Today Show* under an agreement with Channel 9. The
agreement contained 'no particular terms about its content; and the arrangements made for telecast in the Australian Capital Territory did not provide any
opportunity for Channel 7 to monitor independently the statements made
by those involved'.[19] Channel 9 informed Channel 7 each day of the times

---

[16] See paras 19.39–19.43.
[17] *Thompson v Australian Capital Television Pty Ltd* (1994) 54 FCR 513; (1996) 186 CLR 574
('*Thompson*').
[18] *Thompson* (1994) 54 FCR 513, 516 (Burchett and Ryan JJ).
[19] ibid.

scheduled for commercial breaks, so that Channel 7 could insert its own local advertisements. Otherwise, Channel 7 had no foreknowledge of the content of what was to be broadcast. Channel 7 did not edit, and had no opportunity to edit, the programme before it was broadcast. Channel 9 was in complete control of the content of the *Today Show*.[20] There does not appear from the judgments to have been any evidence that Channel 7 had in fact ever censored the *Today Show* as it went to air.

18.11   The High Court, affirming in this respect the majority judges in the Full Federal Court, unanimously held that Channel 7 was an original publisher of the *Today Show*, and was not able to avail itself of a defence of innocent dissemination.

The appeal of this matter to the High Court primarily concerned a question unrelated to the application of the innocent dissemination defence, namely whether by reaching a settlement with Channel 9 under which Channel 9 paid the applicant $50,000, the applicant had released Channel 7 from liability. On this point, the appeal succeeded. It was held that the release of Channel 9 did not have the effect of releasing Channel 7.[21]

To understand the reasoning underlying the judgments in the High Court on the application of the innocent dissemination defence, it is first necessary to set out how this matter was treated in the Full Federal Court.

Decision of the Full Federal Court

Burchett and Ryan JJ

18.12   Burchett and Ryan JJ held that the defence of innocent dissemination was not available to stations, such as Channel 7, which relay television transmissions. Burchett and Ryan JJ thought that a television broadcaster such as Channel 7 was 'a world away' from the kinds of subordinate distributors to whom the defence of innocent dissemination is available.[22] They held that Channel 7 was an 'original publisher' of the *Today Show*: as the television station intended to publish the programme, it could not plead that it did not know its contents.[23] Burchett and Ryan JJ noted that, as a matter of policy, the defence of innocent dissemination should not be available to stations relaying television transmissions, because 'the originator of defamatory material might be insolvent or, as an overseas entity, [unable] to be sued readily or at all in the courts of this country'.[24]

---

[20]   *Thompson* (1994), 529–30 (Miles J).
[21]   *Thompson* (1996) 186 CLR 574, 581–5, 591, 599–617.
[22]   *Thompson* (1994) 54 FCR 513, 519.
[23]   ibid, 519–20.
[24]   ibid, 520.

Burchett and Ryan JJ went on to hold that, even if the defence were available to   **18.13**
Channel 7, Channel 7 was unable to prove the requisite absence of negligence.
First, Burchett and Ryan JJ said that Channel 7 had accepted the producer of
the *Today Show* as its agent for the purposes of considering the propriety of the
content of the programme. As the producer was aware in advance of the content
of the interview which was broadcast, Channel 7 could not escape the consequences of the producer's knowledge. Secondly, Burchett and Ryan JJ noted
that, by their nature, current affairs programmes such as the *Today Show* are
likely to 'involve comments about persons'.[25] Thirdly, Burchett and Ryan JJ
said:

> It was said that there was no opportunity to monitor the content of the pro-
> gramme between its receipt at the Black Mountain receiver and the telecasting of it
> by Channel 7. If that were inevitably so, it would underline the need to require
> precautions to be taken in connection with the making of the programme. But
> nothing at all was proved to show that there was anything inevitable about it. The
> proof offered went no further than that things were done in that way. Whether it
> was feasible to monitor the programme for possibly defamatory statements was
> simply not explored in evidence. If the defence had otherwise been available, it
> seems to us that it would have failed for the same reason that it failed in *Sun Life
> Assurance Co of Canada*—that the company had not shown that its arrangements
> had involved the exercise of reasonable care towards persons who might be dam-
> aged by defamatory statements, to put the matter in the terms chosen by Greer
> LJ.[26]

Miles J's dissent

Miles J dissented in the Full Federal Court decision in *Thompson*. Miles J   **18.14**
concluded that there was no logical reason why the defence of innocent dissemination should be denied to relays of television broadcasts, and that to deny
the application of the defence would be a 'decision of policy, rather than an
application of judicial reasoning'.[27] Miles J thought that the defence applied on
the facts to Channel 7, noting that:

> The trial judge also found that there was nothing in the evidence to suggest that
> [Channel 9] or [Channel 7] was or ever had been other than an entirely reputable
> television broadcaster. [Channel 7] had no foreknowledge of the content of what
> was to be broadcast and no forewarning that on the day in question the broadcast
> was likely to contain anything defamatory. [Channel 7] had no reason to suspect
> that the programme might contain offending material of the nature contained in
> the libel of the appellant. It might also be observed that although [Channel 7] had

---

[25] ibid.
[26] ibid. The case cited in that passage is *Sun Life Assurance Co of Canada v WH Smith & Son,
Ltd* [1933] All ER Rep 432.
[27] *Thompson* (1994) 54 FCR 513, 532.

the opportunity to view the programme as it was being broadcast (for the purpose amongst others of being alerted to the appropriate moment to insert the local advertising material) there was no suggestion that the circumstances were such that [Channel 7] should have terminated the broadcast once the defamatory nature of the interview began to become apparent.[28]

Decision of the High Court

18.15   In the High Court, four of the five judges concluded that there was no basis for restricting the availability of the innocent dissemination defence to printed material. The innocent dissemination defence was thus held to be available in principle to subordinate distributors of electronic material.[29]

All five judges agreed with Burchett and Ryan JJ, however, that on the facts, Channel 7 was unable to avail itself of the defence. The judges concluded that Channel 7 was an original publisher, not a subordinate distributor, of the *Today Show* and that, in any event, it could not prove the other elements of the defence of innocent dissemination.

Brennan CJ, Dawson, and Toohey JJ

18.16   Brennan CJ, Dawson, and Toohey JJ concluded that, although Channel 7 did not participate in the production of the original material constituting the programme,[30] it was nonetheless Channel 7's own decision to telecast the *Today Show* instantaneously and without monitoring. Channel 7 could not claim to be a subordinate distributor simply because it had chosen to adopt the immediacy of the programme.[31] While asserting that they did not wish to trespass into the question whether the defence was made out, Brennan CJ, Dawson, and Toohey JJ noted that live-to-air current affairs programmes such as the *Today Show* carry a high risk of defamatory statements being made, and that it would be curious if Channel 7 could avoid liability because of the way in which it had arranged its affairs.[32]

18.17   Had Channel 7 been a subordinate distributor of the programme, Brennan CJ, Dawson, and Toohey JJ would have held that the defence of innocent dissemination had not been made out. On this question, Brennan CJ, Dawson, and Toohey JJ gave no reasons, other than adopting the judgment of Burchett and

---

[28] *Thompson* (1994), 529–30.
[29] *Thompson* (1996) 186 CLR 574, 589 (Brennan CJ, Dawson, and Toohey JJ), 594 (Gaudron J). Gummow J did not expressly decide the point, although he appeared to favour Burchett and Ryan JJ's conclusion that the defence is not available in respect of relayed television transmissions: ibid, 619–20.
[30] ibid, 589.
[31] ibid, 590.
[32] ibid.

Ryan JJ in the Full Federal Court.[33] Brennan CJ, Dawson, and Toohey JJ noted, however, that Burchett and Ryan JJ had erred in concluding that Channel 9 was Channel 7's agent for the purpose of considering the propriety of televising the material.[34]

Gaudron J

Gaudron J noted that broadcasters who retransmit material do not necessarily acquire any knowledge of it. Whether they ought to know what is being retransmitted is thus a question to be answered by reference to the circumstances of each case.[35] Gaudron J thought the law should be that persons who publish by 'authorising a communication' should not be treated as subordinate distributors.[36] As Channel 7 had authorized the retransmission of the *Today Show*, it was not a subordinate distributor and so could not rely on the innocent dissemination defence.

18.18

Gummow J

Gummow J asserted that he could discern no error in the application of the innocent dissemination defence by Burchett and Ryan JJ, without giving reasons.[37]

18.19

Auvil v CBS '60 Minutes'

It will be contended shortly that *Thompson* was wrongly decided. It will assist in outlining the basis upon which this contention is made to explain, first, an American decision in a case bearing remarkable factual similarities to *Thompson*.

18.20

Auvil v CBS '60 Minutes'[38] involved the broadcast by three affiliate television stations of an American national current affairs programme, *60 Minutes*, which allegedly defamed the plaintiffs. The affiliate stations had not played any part in the preparation of the programme. *60 Minutes* was aired weekly across the United States at 7pm on Sunday evenings. Due to time differences between the east and west coasts, the programme was transmitted by satellite from New York, three hours before air-time, to the affiliate stations, which were located on the American west coast. During the three hours before the affiliate stations broadcast the programme, they had a contractual right, and the technical capability, to review and censor the programme. They also had some idea of the content of the programme from a telex which was sent to them each week with

18.21

---

[33] ibid, 590–1; see para 18.13.
[34] ibid.
[35] ibid, 594.
[36] ibid, 595–6.
[37] ibid, 618–20.
[38] 800 F Supp 928 (ED Wa, 1992) ('*Auvil*').

brief details of the reports which made up the programme. There was evidence that the affiliate stations had from time to time censored national programmes, although not *60 Minutes*. The affiliate stations had not made any attempt to review the programme complained of.

18.22 The affiliate stations thus differed from Channel 7 in *Thompson* in these respects:

- they received *60 Minutes* three hours before they broadcast it, whereas Channel 7 broadcast the *Today Show* as it received it;
- the affiliate stations had a contractual right to edit *60 Minutes*, whereas Channel 7 had no such right with respect to the *Today Show*;
- the affiliate stations received a telex setting out a brief summary of the content of *60 Minutes*, whereas Channel 7 had no prior notice of the content of the *Today Show*.

In all of these respects, the affiliate stations had considerably more control over the content of *60 Minutes* than Channel 7 had in *Thompson* over the content of the *Today Show*.

18.23 Had *Auvil* been decided by the judges who presided over *Thompson*, there is therefore little doubt that the affiliate stations would have been held to be liable. They would have been original publishers, not subordinate distributors of *60 Minutes*. Even if they had been subordinate distributors of *60 Minutes*, they would not have been able to make out the other elements of the defence of innocent dissemination.

18.24 Nielsen J of the United States District Court for the Eastern District of Washington held that the affiliate television stations were not liable for the defamatory content of *60 Minutes*. Nielsen J concluded, citing Washington common law authority,[39] that the affiliate stations had republished the programme, but only as 'mere conduits'.[40] Under Washington law, such conduits are only liable if they know, or have reason to know, of the defamatory character of the publication complained of.[41] Nielsen J thought that affiliate television stations were part of the 'visual' chain of distribution, akin to booksellers in the print context.[42]

Nielsen J held that the effect of making the affiliate stations liable would be to impose a duty upon them to censor. Nielsen J argued that such a finding would:

---

[39] *Herron v Tribune Publishing Co*, 108 Wash 2d 162 (1987); *LaMon v City of Westport*, 44 Wash App 664 (1986).
[40] *Auvil*, 800 F Supp 928, 932.
[41] ibid, citing *Dworkin v Hustler Magazine, Inc*, 634 F Supp 727 (D Wy, 1986).
[42] ibid.

force the creation of full time editorial boards at local stations throughout the country which possess sufficient knowledge, legal acumen and access to experts to continually monitor incoming transmissions and exercise on-the-spot discretionary calls or face $75 million dollar lawsuits at every turn. That is not realistic.[43]

Having established that the affiliate television stations were 'mere conduits' rather than original publishers, Nielsen J had then to consider whether they knew, or ought to have known, of the defamatory nature of the *60 Minutes* edition complained of. Nielsen J concluded that although the affiliate stations might have known from the telex that the programme complained of would be controversial, there was 'not a hint' that the content would be defamatory.[44] Nielsen J then stated: 18.25

> More than merely unrealistic in economic terms, it is difficult to imagine a scenario more chilling on the media's right of expression and the public's right to know . . . Persons injured by defamatory material are not impaired by limiting conduit liability to those situations where culpability is established. The generating source, which in a national broadcast will generally be the deepest of the deep pockets, may still be called upon to defend.[45]

Nielsen J's judgment was clearly influenced by the jurisprudence underlying the First Amendment to the United States' Constitution, which provides that 'Congress shall make no law respecting an establishment of religion, or prohibiting the free exercise thereof; or abridging the freedom of speech, or of the press . . . .'[46]   18.26

Three points can be made about the differences in reasoning between *Thompson* and *Auvil.* First, in the Full Federal Court in *Thompson*, Burchett and Ryan JJ dismissed the argument that Channel 7 was analogous to a bookshop, noting that Channel 7 was 'a world away' from the kinds of subordinate distributors to whom the defence of innocent dissemination is available under Anglo-Australian law.[47] Burchett and Ryan JJ's view in this respect found favour in the High Court. By contrast, in *Auvil,* Nielsen J expressly likened the affiliate stations to booksellers.[48]   18.27

Secondly, Nielsen J thought that the fact that the affiliate stations had the right and the ability to censor the programme was not sufficient to expose them to liability. Nor was it sufficient that the affiliate stations had, in fact, exercised editorial control over programming in the past. Nielsen J considered it relevant that no effort had been made to review the particular programme complained

---

[43] ibid.
[44] ibid.
[45] ibid.
[46] United States' Constitution (1787), Amendment I (1791).
[47] *Thompson* (1994) 54 FCR 513, 519–20.
[48] *Auvil,* 800 F Supp 928, 932.

of. Nielsen J considered that the feasibility of the affiliate stations reviewing the programme was the relevant factor, not their capacity to do so. This contrasts with the majority view in *Thompson*, which was to the effect that Channel 7 could not avoid liability by choosing to broadcast the *Today Show* immediately and without reviewing its contents.[49]

Thirdly, for Nielsen J, it was not enough that the affiliate stations knew the programme would contain controversial material, as not all controversial material is defamatory. By contrast, in *Thompson*, the majority judges argued that current affairs programmes, by their nature, carry 'a high risk of defamatory statements being made'.[50]

18.28 Curiously, Brennan CJ, Dawson, and Toohey JJ cited *Auvil* in a footnote in their decision in *Thompson*, but without any analysis, or explanation as to how their decision sits with that case.[51]

Analysis

18.29 It is submitted, with respect, that the High Court, and the majority judges in the Full Federal Court, erred in their application of legal principle in *Thompson*, and that the decision in *Auvil* is preferable as a matter of policy.

Channel 7 was a subordinate distributor

18.30 The concept of 'subordinate distributors' appears to derive from the following passage from Romer LJ's judgment in *Vizetelly v Mudie's Select Library, Ltd*:[52]

> The result of the cases is I think that, as regards a person who is not the printer or the first or main publisher of a work which contains a libel, but has only taken, what I may call, a subordinate part in disseminating it, in considering whether there has been publication of it by him, the particular circumstances under which he disseminated the work must be considered.

The contrast in this passage is thus between 'the printer or the first or main publisher of a work' and others.

In a passage in the eighth edition of *Gatley on Libel and Slander*[53] cited and approved in the judgment of Burchett and Ryan JJ,[54] subordinate distributors are distinguished from 'the author, printer, or the "first or main publisher of a work which contains a libel"'.

[49] See eg *Thompson* (1996) 186 CLR 574, 590.
[50] ibid.
[51] ibid, n 76.
[52] *Vizetelly v Mudie's Select Library, Ltd* [1900] 2 QB 170, 180.
[53] Philip Lewis, *Gatley on Libel and Slander* (8th edn, 1981) para 241.
[54] *Thompson* (1994) 54 FCR 513, 516.

It is difficult to see why Channel 7 should have been treated as being analogous to an 'author, printer or the first or main publisher' of the *Today Show*. On the facts, it is clear that the reporters and producers involved in the preparation of the programme, including Channel 9, could not have relied on the defence of innocent dissemination. They were clearly the first or main publishers of the programme. Channel 7 was, however, in quite a different position. It was not involved in the preparation of the programme, and was able in truth to plead that it had no knowledge of its contents.

18.31

In the Full Federal Court, Burchett and Ryan JJ asserted that Channel 7 was 'a world away' from the kinds of subordinate distributors to whom the innocent dissemination defence is available.[55] This assertion should be rejected. An affiliate television station in the position of Channel 7 is the broadcasting equivalent of a newsvendor, library, or bookshop: it is simply a mechanism by which content prepared by others is made available to the public. This was the conclusion reached by Nielsen J, in respect of the affiliate television stations, in *Auvil*.[56]

18.32

Burchett and Ryan JJ also thought it relevant that, without the involvement of Channel 7, the *Today Show* 'may never have been published in [the Australian Capital Territory]'.[57] If this assertion were taken to its logical conclusion, it would lead to absurd results. For example, suppose there was only one newsagent in Australia stocking copies of a particular English newspaper. On Burchett and Ryan JJ's reasoning, the newsagent would be an original publisher, rather than a subordinate distributor, of the newspaper in Australia: a result which would be inconsistent with the authorities and the policy underlying the innocent dissemination defence.

18.33

Thirdly, Burchett and Ryan JJ held, citing *McLeod v St Aubyn*,[58] that a person who 'intends to publish' cannot 'plead as a justification that [he or she] did not know the contents'.[59] *McLeod v St Aubyn* was a criminal contempt case, in which it was held that persons who innocently hand over a newspaper, with no knowledge that it contains anything objectionable, are not guilty of criminal contempt because the newspaper happens to contain scandalous material reflecting on the court.[60] Lord Morris noted by contrast that printers and publishers 'intend to publish, and so intending cannot plead as a justification that [they] did not know the contents'.[61] It seems highly unlikely that, in this passage, Lord

18.34

[55] ibid, 519.
[56] 800 F Supp 928, 932.
[57] *Thompson* (1994) 54 FCR 513, 519.
[58] [1899] AC 549.
[59] *Thompson* (1994) 54 FCR 513, 519–20.
[60] *McLeod v St Aubyn* [1899] AC 549, 562.
[61] ibid.

Morris stated a rule applicable to civil defamation law. No other reported authority suggests that the criminal contempt concept of publication is relevant to determining whether a person is a subordinate distributor. The error in Burchett and Ryan JJ's judgment appears to have been recognized in the High Court judgment of Brennan CJ, Dawson, and Toohey JJ,[62] who note that contempt and defamation cases are not truly analogous.

18.35   In their joint judgment in the High Court, Brennan CJ, Dawson, and Toohey JJ asserted that:

> the nature of a live to air current affairs program carries a high risk of defamatory statements being made. In those circumstances it would be curious if Channel 7 could claim to be a subordinate disseminator because it adopted the immediacy of the program.[63]

18.36   The link sought to be drawn by Brennan CJ, Dawson, and Toohey JJ between the manner in which defendants might choose to operate their business, and whether they are entitled to be categorized as subordinate distributors, should be rejected. Channel 7's decision to telecast the *Today Show* instantaneously is a matter which might be relevant to determining whether Channel 7 ought to have known that the material it published was defamatory, or whether absence of knowledge was due to negligence on its part.[64] It is not, however, a matter which is relevant to determining whether it was a subordinate distributor. That question is resolved by asking whether the defendant is, or is analogous to, the author, or the first or main publisher of a work.

It is difficult to see how Brennan CJ, Dawson, and Toohey JJ could be correct in their assertion that they were not 'trespassing into the second question, namely, whether the defence of innocent dissemination was made out'.[65]

18.37   Gaudron J's articulation of a new test, that persons who 'authorized' the communication are not subordinate distributors, finds no support in any other authorities. In formulating her test, Gaudron J appears to have been influenced by principles of vicarious liability and agency.[66] Gaudron J cites a number of authorities in support of the proposition that employers and agents of the creators of defamatory material are liable for the acts of their employees and

---

[62] *Thompson* (1996) 186 CLR 574, 588, citing *R v Griffiths*, ex p *Attorney-General* [1957] 2 QB 192, 203–4.

[63] ibid, 590.

[64] See eg *Vizetelly v Mudie's Select Library, Ltd* [1900] 2 QB 170, 180; *Mallon v WH Smith & Son* (1893) 9 TLR 621, 622; *Martin v Trustees of the British Museum* (1894) 10 TLR 338, 339; *Weldon v 'The Times' Book Company (Ltd)* (1911) 28 TLR 143, 144; *Haynes v De Beck* (1914) 31 TLR 115, 116.

[65] *Thompson* (1996) 186 CLR 574, 590.

[66] ibid, 595. The potential liability of employers and principals for the defamatory publications of their employees and agents is discussed in chapter 22.

principals.[67] When applying her test, however, Gaudron J states 'There can be no doubt that Channel 7 authorized the retransmission to its viewers by its servants or agents of the material which was defamatory of the appellant. Without its authority, the material would not have been retransmitted.'[68]

If the reference to 'servants and agents' in this passage is intended to be a reference to the producers of the *Today Show*, then Gaudron J has clearly erred. Channel 7 was not the agent or employer of the producers of the *Today Show*.[69]

It seems more likely, however, that Gaudron J intended the reference to 'servants and agents' in the passage just cited to be a reference to the employees and agents of Channel 7 responsible for the retransmission itself. If this is what Gaudron J intended, then she is, with respect, applying a test which should be rejected. There would not appear to be any basis for concluding that employees or agents of Channel 7 should be treated as original publishers of the *Today Show*. Such employees and agents are akin to the employees or agents of news-vendors and libraries. They are not analogous to the printer or first or main publisher of a work.

The decision fails to take into account the public interest in freedom of speech

None of the High Court judgments addressed whether there were reasons of policy why Channel 7 ought not to be liable. In the Full Federal Court, Burchett and Ryan JJ cited in support of their conclusion that the defence of innocent dissemination should not be available to stations which relay television transmissions, the danger that a plaintiff might be left with remedies only against insolvent or foreign defendants. This consideration is, as Burchett and Ryan JJ noted, a matter relevant to legislative reform, and not to the task of applying the existing authorities. It is submitted, however, that Burchett and Ryan JJ's correlative assertion that 'there seems to be no reason in policy why the defence should be available to deny the victim a remedy against a solvent and available defendant which has derived whatever benefit it perceived from transmitting the material' should not be accepted. There are policy reasons for protecting subordinate distributors of defamatory material from liability, not the least of which is limiting liability to those situations where culpability is established, bearing in mind the public interest in freedom of speech.[70] These reasons were cogently expressed in *Auvil* by Nielsen J.[71]

Put another way, Burchett and Ryan JJ's analysis recognizes that it is an

18.38

---

[67] ibid.

[68] ibid, 596.

[69] ibid, 590–1 (Brennan CJ, Dawson, and Toohey JJ).

[70] These policy considerations loom large in the American authorities, discussed in chapter 31.

[71] 800 F Supp 928, 932; see paras 18.24–18.25.

objective of defamation law to protect and vindicate reputation, but fails to balance the public interest in free speech against that objective.

18.39   Whether, as a matter of policy, Channel 7 should have been liable as a party which played no part in the preparation of the programme complained of, and which did not know and had no reason to know whether the programme contained defamatory content, should at least have been addressed. Policy questions are accorded great emphasis in the American authorities, such as *Auvil*, due to the pervasive influence of the First Amendment. In addition, there is direct precedent for a consideration of these questions of policy to the application of the innocent dissemination defence in the judgment of Lord Denning MR in *Goldsmith v Sperrings Ltd*,[72] but that reasoning was not referred to in the High Court judgments.

In the United Kingdom context, to the extent that the common law defence of innocent dissemination survives,[73] it might be argued that holding intermediaries such as affiliate television stations, who play no part in the creation of the material they relay, liable as original publishers serves no pressing social need and thus violates Article 10 of the European Convention on Human Rights (ECHR).[74]

Not all current affairs programmes, by their nature, are likely to contain defamatory material

18.40   Burchett and Ryan JJ contended that current affairs programmes, by their nature, are likely to 'involve comments about persons'. Burchett and Ryan JJ then relied on this assertion to reach the conclusion that the *Today Show* was of a character likely to contain defamatory material. This argument is flawed. Not all comments about persons are defamatory, or likely to be defamatory. As was noted in *Auvil*: 'All defamatory material may be controversial, but the converse is not true.'[75]

In a similar vein, Brennan CJ, Dawson, and Toohey JJ assert that 'the nature of a live-to-air current affairs programme carries a high risk of defamatory statements being made'.[76] With respect, this assertion should not be accepted. As was pointed out by Miles J in the Full Federal Court, there was nothing in the evidence to suggest that Channel 9 had ever been anything other than a reputable television broadcaster.[77] Presumably there was no evidence that the *Today*

---

[72] [1977] 1 WLR 478, 483, 488–9, see para 18.40.
[73] See para 18.06.
[74] See also para 18.41.
[75] See *Auvil*, 800 F Supp 928 (ED Wa, 1992), 932 (Neilsen J).
[76] *Thompson* (1996) 186 CLR 574, 590.
[77] *Thompson* (1994) 54 FCR 513, 529.

Show was anything other than a reputable current affairs programme. The blunt assertion by Brennan CJ, Dawson, and Toohey JJ ignores the fact that some current affairs programmes have a greater reputation for veracity and sober analysis than others, and the fact that some current affairs programmes habitually run stories which attack individuals' reputations, while others do not.

Cogent criticisms of the type of approach adopted in *Thompson* were made by Lord Denning MR in his dissenting judgment in *Goldsmith v Sperrings Ltd*, albeit in a case involving printed material:

> Even though a publication may be contentious and controversial—even though it may be scurrilous and give offence to many—it is not to be banned on that account. After all, who is to be the censor? Who is to assess its worth? Who is to inquire how many libel writs have been issued against it? And whether the words were true or the comment fair? No distributor can be expected to do it. Nor, later on, can a jury. There are some publications, of course, which come within the ban of the criminal law, such as pornographic magazines. But no such ban has hitherto been imposed on newspapers or magazines because they are scurrilous or give offence. Nor should such a start be made now. At any rate, no private individual should be allowed to stifle it—on his own estimate of its worthlessness—or the estimate of his friends and those about him. And he would stifle it—as this case shows—if he were allowed to sue the distributors in libel simply for distributing it, and thus making them afraid to handle it anymore. The freedom of the press depends on the channels of distribution being kept open.[78]

Channel 7's lack of knowledge was not due to negligence

Finally, the Australian High Court judges, by adopting the reasoning of Burchett and Ryan JJ, raised the bar impossibly high in concluding that Channel 7, if it were a subordinate distributor, was nonetheless negligent in not knowing that the programme complained of contained defamatory material. **18.41**

Burchett and Ryan JJ attached importance to the fact that no evidence was led to prove that it was not feasible to monitor the *Today Show* for defamatory statements, and that Channel 7 chose to broadcast the programme instantaneously. Even if such evidence had been led, Burchett and Ryan JJ made it clear that such evidence would only 'underline the need to take precautions . . . in connection with the making of the programme'.[79]

In reaching this conclusion, Burchett and Ryan JJ neglected the sorts of considerations which were treated as highly significant in *Auvil*, namely that to avoid liability, stations such as Channel 7 would need to create 'full time editorial boards . . . which possess sufficient knowledge, legal acumen and access to experts to continually monitor incoming transmissions and exercise on-the-spot

---

[78] *Goldsmith v Sperrings Ltd* [1977] 1 WLR 478, 488.
[79] *Thompson* (1994) 54 FCR 513, 520.

discretionary calls'.[80] These considerations must be relevant to determining the scope of the duty of care owed by subordinate distributors.

Burchett and Ryan JJ's reasoning is also inconsistent with that in a number of earlier English authorities, which took into account the practicalities of monitoring publications for defamatory content, as well as the ability to do so.[81]

It should have been accepted that the duty of care owed by Channel 7 did not extend to an obligation to exercise editorial control over a relayed live transmission of content prepared by Channel 9, a reputable third party.

Contrary arguments such as these might now be expected to hold sway in the United Kingdom, where by reason of the Human Rights Act, courts must not act in a way which is incompatible with the rights in the ECHR, and must in defamation actions pay particular regard to the Article 10 right to freedom of expression.[82] Where material is journalistic, literary, or artistic in nature, courts must have regard to the extent to which the material has or is about to become available to the public, the public interest in the publication of the material, and any relevant privacy code.[83]

In the case of the material relayed by Channel 7 in *Thompson*, it might be argued in the United Kingdom that:

- the material was journalistic in nature;
- the material had already become public by reason of it having been broadcast by Channel 9;

---

[80] *Auvil*, 800 F Supp 928 (ED Wa, 1992), 931.

[81] See eg *Weldon v 'The Times' Book Company (Ltd)* (1911) 28 TLR 143, 144 (Cozens-Hardy MR): 'It was quite impossible that distributing agents such as the respondents should be expected to read every book they had. There were some books as to which there might be a duty on the respondents or other distributing agents to examine them carefully because of their titles or the recognized propensity of their authors to scatter libels abroad. Beyond that the matter could not go. It was impossible to say there was a liability to examine the two in question, which were by authors of high character and related to a distinguished musician who had been dead for over a quarter of a century.' See also *Bottomley v FW Woolworth & Co, Ltd* (1932) 48 TLR 521 (Scrutton LJ): 'The remainders of American magazines were disposed of by Messrs Woolworth and Co, and they sold about 50,000 copies every week. The average weekly consignment might contain from 400 to 500 different magazines. The matter complained of was obviously defamatory unless it was justified, and it was not justified. Any one who read the table of contents would have seen that it included what was probably a defamatory article, but Messrs Woolworth and Co did not read every magazine that was sent to them. There was no evidence to justify a finding that there was in the nature of the magazine something which should have led the defendants to suppose that it contained a libel.'

Other authorities expressing similar points include *Sun Life Assurance Co of Canada v WH Smith & Son, Ltd* [1933] All ER Rep 432, 435, 437 (Scrutton LJ), 438 (Lawrence LJ), but cf 439–40 (Greer LJ); *Goldsmith v Sperrings Ltd* [1977] 1 WLR 478, 488–9 (Lord Denning MR).

[82] See paras 30.03–30.04.

[83] Human Rights Act 1998 (UK), s 12(4).

- the material concerned subjects of public interest, namely teenage pregnancy, drug abuse, and incest;
- the material was relayed instantaneously by Channel 7, which had no opportunity to review or censor the material before it went to air;
- the aggrieved party had a cause of action against the original publisher of the material, Channel 9, a major media outlet with deep pockets; and
- in those circumstances, imposing liability on Channel 7 amounted to a disproportionate curtailment of freedom of expression which served no pressing social need, in violation of Article 10 of the ECHR.[84]

Summary

In summary, therefore, it is suggested that *Thompson* was wrongly decided: **18.42** Channel 7 should not have been denied subordinate distributor status, and Channel 7 should have been entitled to the benefit of the innocent dissemination defence. It did not know and had no reason to know that the *Today Show* contained defamatory matter, and its lack of knowledge was not due to negligence on its part.

C. Applying the Defence of Innocent Dissemination to Internet Publications

Introduction

In cases involving Internet intermediaries in the United Kingdom, the defences **18.43** in regulations 17–19 of the Electronic Commerce Regulations,[85] and in section 1 of the Defamation Act 1996,[86] will be of much greater importance than the common law defence of innocent dissemination. To the extent that the common law defence survives, and has some residual operation in cases falling outside the scope of those other defences,[87] *Thompson* is likely to be treated as a persuasive authority. There are strong arguments, however, that the outcome in *Thomspon* is inconsistent with the guarantee of freedom of expression in Article 10 of the ECHR and ought not to be followed in the United Kingdom.[88]

In Australia, unless a lower court can be persuaded to distinguish *Thompson*, it will bind all lower courts when considering the application of the common law defence of innocent dissemination to Internet intermediaries.

---

[84] See also para 30.44.
[85] See chapter 17.
[86] See chapter 16.
[87] See para 18.06.
[88] See paras 18.39, 18.41.

18.44 Assuming that Internet intermediaries are 'publishers' of the material passing through their computer systems,[89] the reasoning in *Thompson* would be likely to apply to Internet intermediaries as follows:

Intermediaries who host or cache defamatory Internet content

Subordinate distributor status

18.45 In principle, the defence of innocent dissemination will be available to subordinate distributors of Internet publications.[90] Internet intermediaries who host or cache content on their computer systems are, however, unlikely in most cases to be categorized as subordinate distributors.[91] Although intermediaries such as ISPs, bulletin board operators, and the operators of business networks might not participate in any way in the production of material hosted or cached by them, the relevant question appears to be whether they have 'the ability to control and supervise the material' they host or cache.[92] This is a question of fact, to be determined in the circumstances of each case.

Intermediaries who host content on their computer systems will almost invariably have the technical ability to control and supervise the material they host or carry, by configuring their systems so as to prevent IP datagrams from being transmitted to another computer system without first having been reviewed. The same conclusion probably follows in relation to intermediaries who 'cache', or temporarily store, material on their servers for the purpose of ensuring that it is more efficiently available to subscribers.

Duty of care

18.46 The fact that it is not feasible for intermediaries who host or cache material to monitor everything which is stored on their computer systems is, on the authority of *Thompson*, not to the point; nor is the fact that they might arrange their affairs so that material is communicated instantaneously and without monitoring.[93] It

---

[89] See chapter 15.

[90] *Thompson* (1996) 186 CLR 574, 589, 594.

[91] Examples of intermediaries who hosted or cached content in the relevant sense include those in *Cubby, Inc v CompuServe Inc*, 776 F Supp 135 (SD NY, 1991) ('*Cubby*'), discussed in paras 31.12–31.22; *Stratton Oakmont, Inc v Prodigy Services Company*, 1995 WL 323710; 23 Media L Rep 1794 (SC NY, 1995) ('*Stratton Oakmont*'), discussed in paras 31.23–31.34; *Lunney v Prodigy Services Co*, 94 NY 2d 242 (CA NY, 1999), discussed in paras 31.35–31.45 (in so far as it concerned the transmission of allegedly defamatory bulletin board postings); *Zeran v America Online, Inc*, 129 F 3d 327 (4th cir, 1997), 331 ('*Zeran*'), discussed in paras 31.55–31.64; *Blumenthal v Drudge*, 992 F Supp 44 (D DC, 1998), discussed in paras 31.65–31.73.

[92] *Thompson* (1996) 186 CLR 574, 589 (Brennan CJ, Dawson, and Toohey JJ).

[93] ibid, 590 (Brennan CJ, Dawson, and Toohey JJ); cf *Auvil*, 800 F Supp 928 (ED Wa, 1992), 932; see paras 18.24–18.25; *Cubby*, 776 F Supp 135 (SD NY, 1991), 140, discussed in paras 31.12–31.22; *Lunney v Prodigy Services Co*, 94 NY 2d 242 (CA NY, 1999), discussed in paras

appears unlikely, at least in Australia,[94] that an intermediary could hide behind the sheer volume of material carried through its computer system, or the fact that, as a matter of practicality, it has configured its system so as to pass on material instantaneously. It also appears unlikely, at least in Australia, that an intermediary could avoid liability by incurring an obligation to pass on material instantaneously and without monitoring it by, for example, contracting with subscribers to do so. Any such contract would presumably be entered into voluntarily by the intermediary, and so, to adapt the words of Brennan CJ, Dawson, and Toohey JJ, amount to a decision which is understandable, but which is still its decision.[95]

If, as the majority judges in the Australian High Court held, current affairs **18.47** programmes carry a high risk of defamatory statements being made, it seems highly likely that the same could be said of Internet publications. It can scarcely be doubted that a significant quantity of the material communicated via the Internet contains defamatory content, in the sense apparently intended by the court. E-mail communications, bulletin board postings, and web pages are all fertile forums for making 'comments about persons'.[96]

Summary

For all these reasons, it seems likely that the Australian High Court judges **18.48** who decided *Thompson* would hold that intermediaries who host or cache Internet content on their computer systems, such as ISPs, bulletin board operators, and the operators of business networks, are not subordinate distributors. They appear to be more analogous to affiliate television stations than to newsagents, bookshops, or video libraries.[97] In terms of Gaudron J's test, they publish material by 'authorizing' its communication, albeit without regard to its contents, for without their authority, the material would not be communicated.[98]

Even if intermediaries who host or cache Internet content could be said to be **18.49** 'subordinate distributors', it is likely that in most cases they would be unable to prove the elements of the innocent dissemination defence as defined by Brennan CJ, Dawson, and Toohey JJ, who adopted in this regard the reasoning of

---

31.35–31.45; *Zeran*, 129 F 3d 327, 331 (4th cir, 1997), discussed in paras 31.55–31.64; but see also *Stratton Oakmont*, 1995 WL 323710; 23 Media L Rep 1794 (SC NY, 1995), 3–5, discussed in paras 31.23–31.34.

[94] cf the position in the United Kingdom: see para 18.41.
[95] *Thompson* (1996) 186 CLR 574, 590.
[96] *Thompson* (1994) 54 FCR 513, 520, cited in *Thompson* (1996) 186 CLR 574, 590, 620.
[97] *Thompson* (1994) 54 FCR 513, 519.
[98] *Thompson* (1996) 186 CLR 574, 595–6.

Burchett and Ryan JJ in the Full Federal Court.[99] It is difficult to see what precautions intermediaries who host or cache Internet content could put in place to discharge their duty of care, apart from employing staff to review manually every communication which is hosted or carried by them. The use of other forms of monitoring, such as software configured to identify certain kinds of communication, are not well adapted to identifying libels, as they cannot replace the exercise of human judgment involved in determining whether or not words, in their natural and ordinary meaning, or as a matter of true or legal innuendo, convey defamatory meanings, let alone in ascertaining whether there might be some defence available in respect of the words, such as justification, fair comment, or privilege.[100]

Mere conduit intermediaries

Subordinate distributor status

18.50   The position is likely to be different in relation to those intermediaries who are mere conduits of Internet communications, in the sense that they merely operate communications networks or computer systems through which Internet communications happen to pass en route from one computer to another. Because Internet communications travel as a series of IP datagrams, with the individual datagrams likely to travel via several different paths en route from sender to recipient, it will often not be possible at a technical level for the entire communication to be reconstituted by every computer or router along the route. In any event, the communication will usually only in fact be reconstituted on the recipient's computer.

Such intermediaries are thus much more likely, following the reasoning in *Thompson*, to be subordinate distributors.

Duty of care

18.51   Mere conduit intermediaries are also likely to be able to prove the other elements of the innocent dissemination defence as defined by the majority judges in

---

[99] ibid, 590, adopting *Thompson* (1994) 54 FCR 513, 520 (Burchett and Ryan JJ): '[Channel 7] took no precautions of any kind, knowing the programme was a current affairs programme, a programme which by its nature would be likely to involve comments about persons.'

[100] This point was well expressed in *Lunney v Prodigy Services Co*, 683 NYS 2d 557 (AD NY, 1998), 561 (Bracken JP): 'It may be true that Prodigy has devised a method by which certain epithets are automatically excluded from the messages sent via its network. But application of any unintelligent automated word-exclusion program of this type cannot be equated with editorial control. A highly offensive message can be composed in the most impeccable prose, just as the words often thought of as offensive can be used affectionately or humorously in certain contexts. Intelligent editorial control involves the use of judgment, and no computer program has such a capacity.'

the Australian High Court. These intermediaries will usually have no difficulty in pleading that they did not know, and had no reason to know, that material passing through their computer systems contained defamatory content. Lack of knowledge is unlikely to be due to negligence on their part, especially in cases where it would not have been technically possible for the intermediary to reconstitute the communication. Even where it would be technically possible for the intermediary to reconstitute the communication, it seems less likely that the intermediary would be obliged to do so in order to establish the proper exercise of due care. This conclusion is reinforced by the fact that it will generally be a criminal offence for a mere conduit intermediary to intercept a private Internet communication.[101]

Summary

It seems likely, therefore, that the defence of innocent dissemination would be available to intermediaries involved in the transmission of ordinary e-mail messages. The position may be different, however, in relation to e-mails sent to and from business networks. Those messages will typically be stored or backed up by the operator of the network on a temporary or permanent basis. The operator will usually have the ability to control and supervise material sent to and by employees.[102] The position may also be different in those rare cases where the mere conduit intermediary has actual knowledge of the existence of the material at the time of publication.[103]

18.52

---

[101] Regulation of Investigatory Powers Act 2000 (UK), s 1; Telecommunications (Interception) Act 1979 (Cth), s 7.

[102] In addition, employers may be vicariously liable for defamatory publications by their employees: see chapter 22.

[103] As in the facts of *Anderson v New York Telephone Company*, 361 NYS 2d 913 (CA NY, 1974); see paras 15.31–15.34.

19

STATUTORY DEFENCES IN AUSTRALIA

A. Introduction

In Australia, the Broadcasting Services Act 1992 (Cth) ('the BSA') provides **19.01** 'Internet content hosts' and 'Internet service providers' with a measure of protection from criminal and civil liability for defamatory material hosted, cached, or carried by them, but which they did not create. The defence takes a very different form from that in section 1 of the Defamation Act 1996 (UK), and in regulations 17 to 19 of the Electronic Commerce (EC Directive) Regulations 2002 (UK) ('Electronic Commerce Regulations'). Other statutory defences are potentially available to Internet intermediaries in Queensland and Tasmania.[1]

---

[1] See paras 19.39–19.43.

B. The Clause 91 Defence

The provision

19.02   Clause 91(1) of Schedule 5 to the BSA provides:

> A law of a State or Territory, or a rule of common law or equity, has no effect to the extent to which it:
>
> (a) subjects, or would have the effect (whether direct or indirect) of subjecting, an Internet content host to liability (whether criminal or civil) in respect of hosting particular Internet content in a case where the host was not aware of the nature of the Internet content; or
>
> (b) requires, or would have the effect (whether direct or indirect) of requiring, an Internet content host to monitor, make inquiries about, or keep records of, Internet content hosted by the host; or
>
> (c) subjects, or would have the effect (whether direct or indirect) of subjecting, an Internet service provider to liability (whether criminal or civil) in respect of carrying particular Internet content in a case where the service provider was not aware of the nature of the Internet content; or
>
> (d) requires, or would have the effect (whether direct or indirect) of requiring, an Internet service provider to monitor, make inquiries about, or keep records of, Internet content carried by the provider.

19.03   The Minister may exempt the operation of specified State or Territory laws, or specified rules of common law or equity, from the operation of clause 91(1).[2] No such laws or rules had been exempted by the Minister at the time of writing (March 2005).

Internet content hosts

19.04   Under the BSA, an 'Internet content host' is a person who hosts Internet content, or who proposes to host Internet content, in Australia.[3] 'Internet content' means information that is kept on a data storage device and is accessed, or available for access, using an Internet carriage service, but does not include ordinary electronic mail, or information that is transmitted in the form of a broadcasting service.[4]

Internet service providers

19.05   An 'Internet service provider' is a person who supplies, or proposes to supply, an Internet carriage service to the public.[5] An 'Internet carriage service' means a

---

[2] Broadcasting Services Act 1992 (Cth), Sch 5, cl 91(2).
[3] ibid, Sch 5, cl 3 (definition of 'Internet content host').
[4] ibid (definition of 'Internet content').
[5] ibid, Sch 5, cl 8(1). The Minister may declare specified persons who supply, or propose to supply, a specified Internet carriage service to be Internet service providers for the purposes of Sch 5: cl 8(2).

listed carriage service that enables end-users to access the Internet.[6] A 'listed carriage service' has the same meaning as in the Telecommunications Act 1997 (Cth).[7] Under that Act, a 'listed carriage service' means, in effect, a service for carrying communications by means of guided or unguided electromagnetic energy between two or more points, at least one of which is in Australia.[8]

No reported cases have yet been decided concerning the operation of the clause 91 defence. A number of points can, however, be made about the likely application of that provision to defamatory material published via the Internet.

The defence potentially applies to liability arising under civil defamation law

Intended effect of the clause 91 defence

The clause 91 defence was added to the BSA by the Broadcasting Services Amendment (Online Services) Act 1999 (Cth). The amending legislation was intended to provide a means for addressing complaints about certain Internet content, to restrict access to certain Internet content which is likely to cause offence to reasonable adults, and to protect children from exposure to Internet content which is unsuitable for children.[9] The material to which the legislation relates is generally limited to content which has been, or would be, classified RC (Refused Classification), X, or R by the Australian Classification Board.[10] Broadly speaking, the restricted content might be described as 'offensive material'.

19.06

The restrictions do not apply, other than incidentally, to defamatory Internet material. Notably, however, civil proceedings, including civil defamation proceedings, do not lie against Internet content hosts or Internet service providers in respect of various matters done by them pursuant to the amending legislation.[11] Nor do such proceedings lie against persons who make complaints to the Australian Broadcasting Authority in good faith about Internet content of concern to them, or who make statements or give documents or information to the Authority in the course of an investigation into such a complaint.[12]

19.07

The primary purpose underlying the clause 91 defence was to override any State or Territory legislation which exposed Internet content hosts or Internet service

19.08

---

[6] ibid, Sch 5, cl 3 (definition of 'Internet carriage service').
[7] ibid (definition of 'listed carriage service').
[8] Telecommunications Act 1997 (Cth), ss 7, 16.
[9] Broadcasting Services Act 1992 (Cth), s 3(k)–(m). (Paragraphs (k)–(m) were each added by the Broadcasting Services Amendment (Online Services) Act 1999 (Cth), Sch 1, cl 2.)
[10] A simplified outline of the regulatory regime is set out in the Broadcasting Services Act 1992 (Cth), Sch 5, cl 2.
[11] ibid, Sch 5, cl 37.
[12] ibid, Sch 5, cl 29.

providers to criminal or civil liability for unwittingly hosting or carrying offensive material.[13]

Breadth of the clause 91 defence

19.09   Nonetheless, there can be little doubt that the clause 91 defence is sufficiently broad to provide Internet content hosts and Internet service providers with a measure of protection from liability under civil defamation law. The provision expressly contemplates overriding civil liabilities arising under State and Territory laws, and under rules of common law and equity. The cause of action for defamation arises as a matter of common law in Victoria, South Australia, Western Australia, and the Australian Capital Territory. It arises as a matter of State legislation in New South Wales, Queensland, and Tasmania and as a matter of Territory legislation in the Northern Territory.[14]

19.10   The potential application of the clause 91 defence to liability arising under civil defamation law was noted by Professor David Flint, then Chair of the Australian Broadcasting Authority, in his appearance before the hearing of the Senate Select Committee on Information Technologies concerning the Broadcasting Services Amendment (Online Services) Bill 1999 (Cth). Professor Flint said:

> It is worth noting that the legislation is not only a burden but gives a distinct benefit to the hosts and the content [*sic*] providers in clause 87 [which became clause 91], which exempts the providers and the hosts from any civil or criminal liability under any state or federal [*sic*] law or the common law in relation to material of which they are not aware. For example, the unclear question as to liability and defamation is removed by section [*sic*] 87. So it is not an Act which only imposes obligations; it proposes to give benefits.[15]

---

[13] See eg Commonwealth, *Parliamentary Debates*, 21 April 1999 (Senator Ian Campbell, Parliamentary Secretary to the Minister for Communications, Information Technology and the Arts). Relevant State and Territory legislation include the Classification (Publications, Films and Computer Games) Enforcement Act 1995 (NSW); Classification of Publications Act 1991 (Qld); Classification of Films Act 1991 (Qld); Classification of Computer Games and Images Act 1995 (Qld); Classification (Publications, Films and Computer Games) Act 1995 (SA); Classification (Publications, Films and Computer Games) Enforcement Act 1995 (Tas); Classification (Publications, Films and Computer Games) (Enforcement) Act 1995 (Vic); Censorship Act 1996 (WA); Classification (Publications, Films and Computer Games) (Enforcement) Act 1995 (ACT); Classification of Publications, Films and Computer Games Act 1985 (NT).

[14] Defamation Act 1974 (NSW), s 9(2); Defamation Act 1889 (Qld), ss 7; Defamation Act 1957 (Tas), s 9; Defamation Act 1938 (NT), s 2.

[15] Commonwealth, *Senate Select Committee on Information Technologies: Broadcasting Services Amendment (Online Services) Bill 1999 Discussion*, 27 April 1999. Later on the same day, Mr Patrick Fair, a representative of the Internet Industry Association told the Committee that the Association was in favour of the proposed provision, and said: 'We would like to see exemptions included in the legislation which enable our members to monitor content services without picking up the civil liability for perhaps not being quick enough to take material off and prevent a defamation or other civil liability.'

The defence does not apply to all Internet publications

The clause 91 defence applies only to 'Internet content' hosted by Internet **19.11** content providers, or carried by Internet service providers. The definition of 'Internet content' in clause 3 of Schedule 5 expressly excludes 'ordinary electronic mail' and 'information that is transmitted in the form of a broadcasting service', as well as information that is not 'kept on a data storage device'.

Ordinary electronic mail

The intended meaning of the expression 'ordinary electronic mail' was **19.12** explained in the Supplementary Explanatory Memorandum to the Broadcasting Services Amendment (Online Services) Bill 1999 (Cth) as follows:

> The use of the term ordinary electronic mail is intended to make it clear that the exclusion only applies to what an ordinary user of the Internet would regard as being e-mail, and that the exclusion does not apply to other forms of postings of material, such as postings to newsgroups. The term is also intended to minimize the scope for technical arguments about the outer boundaries of the term e-mail within the Internet community.

Clause 3 of Schedule 5 to the BSA provides, relevantly, that 'ordinary electronic **19.13** mail does not include a posting to a newsgroup'.

It seems clear that e-mail messages sent in the usual way will therefore not satisfy **19.14** the definition of 'Internet content' for the purposes of the clause 91 defence. The clause 91 defence will therefore not protect Internet intermediaries in respect of e-mail messages hosted, cached, or carried by them. The liability of Internet intermediaries arising out of hosting, caching, or carrying defamatory e-mail messages will depend on the application of the ordinary rules of civil defamation law.[16]

It seems unlikely that communications such as instant messaging or private chat **19.15** room postings would fall within the expression 'ordinary electronic mail', although conceptually it makes little sense to distinguish between such communications for the purposes of the liability of Internet intermediaries. Instant messages and private chat room postings are analogous to ordinary electronic mail messages, in the sense that they are essentially private communications sent from one person to another, or from one person to a defined group.

It seems likely, however, that instantaneous forms of Internet communication **19.16**

---

[16] See esp chapters 15, 18. So eg the cl 91 defence would not have applied on the facts in *Lunney v Prodigy Services Co*, 94 NY 2d 242 (CA NY, 1999), discussed in paras 31.35–31.45, in so far as they concerned the transmission of an allegedly defamatory e-mail message.

such as instant messaging and chat room postings will ordinarily be excluded from the definition of 'Internet content' for other reasons.[17]

Information that is transmitted in the form of a broadcasting service

19.17 Under the BSA, a 'broadcasting service' is a service that delivers 'television programs or radio programs', but does not include a service that provides 'no more than data, or no more than text (with or without associated still images)', a service that makes 'programs available on demand on a point-to-point basis', or a service or class of services specifically excluded by the Minister.[18]

19.18 Most services delivering ordinary web pages and bulletin boards will not fall within the definition of a 'broadcasting service', because they do not deliver information in the nature of 'television programs or radio programs'.[19] Furthermore, many services delivering ordinary web pages and bulletin boards will provide 'no more than data, or no more than text (with or without associated still images)' and will be excluded from the definition of a 'broadcasting service' on that basis.[20]

19.19 Some Internet services do, however, deliver television programmes and radio programmes by means of video or audio streaming, or file transfer. By a determination gazetted on 27 September 2000 for the purposes of section 6(1) of the BSA, the Minister for Communications determined that services that deliver television programmes or radio programmes via the Internet, other than services that deliver such programmes using the broadcasting services bands,[21] are not 'broadcasting services' for the purposes of the BSA. Internet content hosts and Internet service providers are thus potentially entitled to the benefit of the clause 91 defence in respect of television and radio programmes delivered via the Internet.

Material kept on a data storage device

19.20 'Internet content' is limited to material 'kept on a data storage device'.[22] This limitation probably has the effect of excluding almost all forms of instantaneous

---

[17] See paras 19.20–19.22.
[18] Broadcasting Services Act 1992 (Cth), s 6(1), which is reproduced in full in para 4.14.
[19] See paras 4.14–4.23.
[20] Broadcasting Services Act 1992 (Cth), s 6(1).
[21] The 'broadcasting services bands' are that part of the radiofrequency spectrum that has been designated under s 31 of the Radiocommunications Act 1992 (Cth) as being primarily for broadcasting services and referred to the Australian Broadcasting Authority for planning: ibid.
[22] Broadcasting Services Act 1992 (Cth), Sch 5, cl 3 (definition of 'Internet content'). A 'data storage device' means 'any article or material (eg a disk) from which information is capable of being reproduced, with or without the aid of any other article or device': ibid.

Internet communication, such as instant messaging, chat services, and voice communications, from the definition of 'Internet content'.[23]

19.21 The limitation is probably effective, because instantaneous forms of Internet communication are generally not kept on an intermediary's data storage device for any period longer than is necessary for their transmission. Rather, they are instantaneously transferred as a series of IP datagrams from one computer to the next via the Internet. Once transferred, they are generally not stored by the Internet content host or Internet service provider for later access.

19.22 In particular cases, however, it is possible that instantaneous Internet communications will satisfy the definition of 'Internet content', where they are in fact kept on a data storage device by an Internet service provider or Internet content host and are available for later access by Internet users.

Summary

19.23 In summary, the definition of 'Internet content' in clause 3 of Schedule 5 to the BSA does not extend to all forms of material which can be published via the Internet. As a result, the protection potentially afforded by the clause 91 defence is limited. In those cases where material published via the Internet does not fall within the definition of 'Internet content', the clause 91 defence will have no application. In such cases, the potential liability of Internet content hosts and Internet service providers will be determined by the ordinary rules of civil defamation law.[24]

The defence potentially applies to most kinds of intermediaries

Hosting and caching

19.24 An Internet intermediary who hosts or caches web pages or bulletin boards on its computer system would ordinarily satisfy the description of an 'Internet content host' for the purposes of the BSA.[25] Such intermediaries 'host', in the relevant sense, the web pages and bulletin boards which are temporarily or permanently stored on their computer systems and which are accessible by Internet users.[26]

---

[23] See Explanatory Memorandum to the Broadcasting Services Bill 1999 (Cth) (definition of 'Internet content').
[24] See esp chapters 15 and 18.
[25] See Broadcasting Services Act 1992 (Cth), Sch 5, cl 3.
[26] Examples would include the intermediaries in *Cubby, Inc v CompuServe Inc*, 776 F Supp 135 (SD NY, 1991) ('*Cubby*'), discussed in paras 31.12–31.22; *Stratton Oakmont, Inc v Prodigy Services Company*, 1995 WL 323710; 23 Media L Rep 1794 (SC NY, 1995) ('*Stratton Oakmont*'), discussed in paras 31.23–31.34; *Lunney v Prodigy Services Co*, 94 NY 2d 242 (CA NY, 1999), discussed in paras 31.35–31.45 (in so far as it was involved in the transmission of allegedly

The definition of 'Internet content host' is broadly cast. It does not differentiate between providers who merely host content on their servers, and providers who, in addition to hosting content, operate bulletin boards or web sites from which that content is accessible.

Mere conduits

19.25 Internet intermediaries who merely operate computer systems through which Internet content passes en route from one Internet user to another would ordinarily satisfy the description of 'Internet service providers' for the purposes of the BSA. Most such intermediaries operate services that enable end-users to access the Internet, and carry communications by means of guided or unguided electromagnetic energy between two or more points.[27]

Where an Internet intermediary hosts, caches, or carries material which does not satisfy the definition of 'Internet content', however, that intermediary will not be an 'Internet content host' or an 'Internet service provider' in respect of that material for the purposes of the BSA.[28]

Operators of private networks

19.26 The operators of business networks which provide employees with Internet access, or networks maintained by schools or universities for the benefit of their staff and students, will not generally be 'Internet service providers' for the purposes of clause 91, because they do not provide their service 'to the public'.[29] The liability of the operators of such networks for defamatory material carried by them, such as e-mails sent to or by employees or students[30] or material posted to newsgroups by employees or students, will therefore depend on the ordinary principles of defamation law and in particular those discussed in chapters 15 and 18.

Where the operators of such networks host content on their computer systems, on the other hand, they will generally be Internet content hosts for the purposes of the clause 91 defence, even in respect of material created by their employees or students.

---

defamatory bulletin board postings); *Zeran v America Online, Inc*, 129 F 3d 327 (4th cir, 1997) ('*Zeran*'), discussed in paras 31.55–31.64; and *Blumenthal v Drudge*, 992 F Supp 44 (D DC, 1998), discussed in paras 31.65–31.73.

[27] An example would be the intermediary in *Lunney v Prodigy Services Co*, 94 NY 2d 242 (CA NY, 1999), discussed in paras 31.35–31.45, in so far as it was involved in the transmission of an allegedly defamatory e-mail message.

[28] See paras 19.11–19.23.

[29] Broadcasting Services Act 1992 (Cth), Sch 5, cl 8(1); see para 19.05.

[30] Note that, for other reasons, ordinary e-mail messages are excluded from the ambit of the cl 91 defence even in respect of persons who satisfy the definition of Internet service providers in the BSA: see paras 19.12–19.14.

One apparently anomalous consequence arising out of the breadth of the clause 91 defence is that ordinary principles of vicarious liability might not apply to an employer or principal who hosts defamatory 'Internet content'[31] created by an employee or agent, where the employer or principal is not aware of the nature of that material. Principles of vicarious liability are rules of common law. Where the application of those rules would have the effect of subjecting an employer or principal to liability for unwittingly hosting defamatory Internet content, the effect of the clause 91 defence may be to exclude the operation of those rules. It seems highly unlikely that the clause 91 defence was intended to have this effect.

It might perhaps be argued in appropriate cases that where an employee publishes defamatory Internet content via the Internet, the employer has actual knowledge of the nature of the content within the meaning of clause 91(a) or (c) of Schedule 5 to the BSA. In cases where the employer has actual knowledge of the nature of the content, the employer would not be able to rely on the clause 91 defence to exclude the operation of the rules relating to vicarious liability.

Vicarious liability rules are the subject of chapter 22.

Intermediaries who commission content

A related point is that 'Internet content hosts' and 'Internet service providers' **19.27** are entitled to the benefit of the clause 91 defence in respect of particular 'Internet content' so long as they are not aware of the nature of that content. Accordingly, it seems that hosts and providers who commission third parties to create content which then appears, for example, on the intermediary's own web site will not automatically be deprived of the benefit of the clause 91 defence.[32] For the purposes of the clause 91 defence, the only relevant question will be whether the host or provider had actual knowledge of the nature of the Internet content complained of. By contrast, intermediaries who commission third parties to create such content would almost certainly be deprived of the benefit of the section 1 defence in the United Kingdom, because they will be the 'publisher' of that content, as that term is defined in section 1(2) of the Defamation Act 1996 (UK).[33] The Electronic Commerce Regulations are to the same effect. The Regulations do not protect a service provider from liability where the provider of the content was acting under the authority or the control of the service provider.[34]

---

[31] See paras 19.11–19.23.
[32] See eg the facts in *Cubby*, 776 F Supp 135 (SD NY, 1991), discussed in paras 31.12–31.22 and *Blumenthal v Drudge*, 992 F Supp 44 (D DC, 1998), discussed in paras 31.65–31.73.
[33] See paras 16.03, 16.11.
[34] Electronic Commerce (EC Directive) Regulations 2002 (UK), reg 19(b); see para 17.21.

The defence only applies to content hosted or carried in Australia

Internet content hosts

19.28   The definition of 'Internet content host' in the BSA is confined to persons who host, or who propose to host, Internet content in Australia.[35] The protection potentially afforded by the clause 91 defence will therefore not be available to Internet intermediaries located outside Australia who host web pages and bulletin boards, even where those web pages and bulletin boards contain material that is published in Australia, or contain content created in Australia.

Internet service providers

19.29   The definition of 'Internet service provider' is, in effect, limited to providers of services for carrying Internet communications between two or more points, at least one of which is in Australia.[36] Internet intermediaries located outside Australia who do nothing more than operate computer systems through which Internet content happens to pass en route from one computer to another are therefore potentially able to avail themselves of the protection afforded by the clause 91 defence, provided that the relevant communication originated from, or is destined for, a point within Australia.

The defence is not available where the host or provider is aware of the nature of the Internet content

Actual knowledge defeats the defence

19.30   Where an Internet content host or Internet service provider is aware of the nature of the Internet content which it hosts or carries, the clause 91 defence has no operation.[37] It appears that actual knowledge on the part of the host or provider is required before the clause 91 defence ceases to be available. The clause 91 defence probably continues to be available even where the host or provider ought to be aware of the nature of the content, or is not aware of the nature of the content due to its own negligence.[38]

19.31   Where an Internet content host or Internet service provider knows that it is hosting, caching, or carrying unlawful defamatory material contained on a web

---

[35] Broadcasting Services Act 1992 (Cth), Sch 5, cl 3.
[36] See para 19.05.
[37] Broadcasting Services Act 1992 (Cth), Sch 5, cl 91(1)(a), (c).
[38] See Commonwealth, *Parliamentary Debates*, 21 April 1999 (Senator Ian Campbell, Parliamentary Secretary to the Minister for Communications, Information Technology and the Arts) (second reading speech relating to the Broadcasting Services Amendment (Online Services) Bill 1999 (Cth)): '[I]t is the intention that service providers not be liable for content hosted on, or accessed by means of, a service provider's system where the service provider is not responsible for the creation of the content, or has not committed a "positive act" in relation to that content.'

page, or in a bulletin board posting, it will therefore not be entitled to the benefit of the clause 91 defence.[39] In such cases, the potential liability of the host or provider will depend on the operation of the ordinary rules of civil defamation law.

'Nature' of the Internet content

The extent and quality of the knowledge which hosts or providers must have **19.32** before they cease to be entitled to the protection of the clause 91 defence is not entirely clear. Suppose, for example, that an Internet content host had actual knowledge that a particular web page was stored on its computer system. Suppose further that the web page contained defamatory material, but that the host did not appreciate, and had no means of knowing, that the content was defamatory, or whether any defence might be available in respect of the material, such as a defence of justification, fair comment, or privilege. In such a case, the defamed person would no doubt argue that the Internet content host was, in the relevant sense, 'aware of the nature of the Internet content' and therefore not entitled to the benefit of the clause 91 defence.

It could be argued, however, that a host or provider is only aware of the 'nature' **19.33** of Internet content, and so unable to take advantage of the clause 91 defence, if the host or provider is aware of facts or circumstances from which it is or ought to be apparent that the content is of a character capable of giving rise to liability. In other words, it might be argued that knowledge of the existence of Internet content is not the same as knowledge of the 'nature' of that content. Some support for this interpretation can be derived from dictionary definitions of the word 'nature'. *The Macquarie Dictionary*, for example, defines the word 'nature' as meaning, among other things, 'the particular combination of qualities belonging to a person or thing by birth or constitution' and 'character, kind, or sort'. These definitions suggest that hosts or providers will only be aware of the 'nature' of Internet content if they have some qualitative awareness of it beyond mere knowledge of its existence.

The latter interpretation seems desirable as a matter of policy. If hosts or providers are effectively compelled to remove or disable access to Internet content immediately upon becoming aware of its existence in order to ensure that they will be able to avail themselves of the clause 91 defence, then the clause 91 defence has the potential to chill online freedom of expression. Intermediaries will often be in no position to assess whether some defence might be available in relation to defamatory material hosted on their servers. Persons who are unhappy about material accessible via web sites or bulletin boards may be able

---

[39] See eg the facts in *Godfrey v Demon Internet Ltd* [2001] QB 201, discussed in paras 15.03–15.07 and *Zeran*, 129 F 3d 327, 331 (4th cir, 1997), discussed in paras 31.55–31.64.

to effect its removal simply by putting the relevant host on notice of its existence and making threats of legal action. Material which is true, and in the public interest, might be unjustifiably censored.

Knowledge or suspicion that material is unlawfully defamatory is necessary to defeat the operation of an analogous defence in the United Kingdom,[40] and probably also the common law defence of innocent dissemination.[41]

Attempts to remove offending material

19.34   Once an Internet content host or Internet service provider knows that it is hosting, caching, or carrying offending material, the clause 91 defence immediately ceases to provide protection. If the offending material continues to be accessible, then the host or provider is potentially liable under the ordinary rules of civil defamation law,[42] even if the host or provider has made all reasonable attempts to remove the offending material or to prevent it from continuing to be accessible. In this respect the clause 91 defence is more restrictive than regulations 18 and 19 of the Electronic Commerce Regulations, which protect service providers from liability for caching or hosting defamatory material provided that, upon obtaining actual knowledge or awareness of the material, they act expeditiously to remove or disable access to it.[43]

The defence discourages monitoring

Negligence is irrelevant

19.35   On the other hand, the fact that an Internet content host or Internet service provider is not aware of the nature of particular Internet content hosted, cached, or carried by it by reason of its own negligence will not deprive the host or provider of the potential benefit of the clause 91 defence. For example, suppose that a person defamed on a web page sends an e-mail message to the relevant Internet content host demanding the removal of the offending material, but that due to negligence on the part of the host, the aggrieved person's e-mail message is deleted before it is read, or not read for a significant period of time. In such a case, the Internet content host would presumably still be entitled to the benefit of the clause 91 defence, because it 'was not aware of the nature of the Internet content'.[44]

---

[40] Electronic Commerce (EC Directive) Regulations 2002 (UK), reg 19(a)(i): see para 17.25.
[41] See paras 18.04–18.06.
[42] See esp chapters 15, 18.
[43] Electronic Commerce (EC Directive) Regulations 2002 (UK), regs 18(b)(v), 19(a)(ii): see paras 17.16, 17.26.
[44] See also n 38 above.

Clause 91 therefore discourages Internet content hosts and Internet service **19.36** providers from monitoring or making inquiries about whether Internet content they host or carry might be defamatory, and even from putting in place procedures for handling complaints about allegedly defamatory content. Nor could courts or State or Territory legislatures impose monitoring requirements: any State or Territory law, or rule of common law or equity which, directly or indirectly, requires or has the effect of requiring a host or provider to monitor or make inquiries about Internet content hosted or carried by it is of no effect.[45]

Summary

The clause 91 defence does not cover the field

In summary, the clause 91 defence was not primarily intended to create a new **19.37** defence to civil defamation law. Rather, it was intended to exclude State and Territory Internet-specific laws which have the effect of regulating Internet content hosts and Internet service providers who host or carry offensive material. Civil defamation law has not been exempted, however, from the operation of the clause 91 defence. Unless it is exempted at some future time by the Minister, the clause 91 defence will have the effect, in many cases, of protecting Internet content hosts and Internet service providers from potential liability in civil defamation law.

As the clause 91 defence is of only limited application, the general rules of civil defamation law discussed in chapters 15 and 18 will remain of vital relevance in many cases involving Internet intermediaries.

Commonwealth laws not excluded

Finally, it should be noted that even where it operates, the clause 91 defence **19.38** only excludes laws of the States and Territories, and rules of common law or equity. Commonwealth legislation, such as the Trade Practices Act 1974, is not excluded. This could potentially give rise to anomalous outcomes.

C. Queensland and Tasmania

Statutory defences

In Queensland and Tasmania, the common law defence of innocent dissemin- **19.39** ation has been replaced by a statutory defence which protects sellers of books, pamphlets, print, writing, or other things containing defamatory matter from

---

[45] Broadcasting Services Act 1992 (Cth), Sch 5, cl 91(1)(b), (d).

liability except where, at the time of the sale, they have actual knowledge that the material contains defamatory matter.[46] In the case of periodicals, sellers are liable only if they actually know that the periodical contains defamatory matter, or that defamatory matter is habitually or frequently contained in that periodical.[47] 'Periodical' means 'any newspaper, review, magazine, or other writing that is published periodically'.[48]

The defences only apply to sellers of written material

19.40   Unlike the common law defence of innocent dissemination, the Queensland and Tasmanian defences apply only to the sellers of written material. The defences are therefore unlikely to apply to Internet intermediaries in most cases, because intermediaries cannot usually be described as the sellers of written material. Internet intermediaries are typically sellers only of access to the Internet.

Application of the defences to Internet intermediaries

19.41   There might be cases, however, where an Internet intermediary is, in the relevant sense, a seller of written material and therefore able to rely on the statutory defences. If an Internet intermediary made third-party content available electronically to subscribers upon the payment of a fee, then the intermediary might be a seller of that content, and able to rely on the statutory defences upon proving that the intermediary had no actual knowledge that it contained the defamatory matter and, in the case of a 'periodical', no actual knowledge that the periodical habitually or frequently contained defamatory matter.[49] There might be an argument, however, that the statutory defences should only apply to mere sellers of written material, and not to Internet intermediaries who have commissioned or otherwise adopted that material by incorporating it into their own Internet service.

19.42   In any event, the statutory defences would only be likely to be available where the intermediary charged a specific fee for the provision of the particular content, as opposed to a fee for access to the Internet. In the absence of a direct link between the fee charged and the provision of the text, it would seem unlikely

---

[46] Defamation Act 1889 (Qld), s 26; Defamation Act 1957 (Tas), s 26(2). Similar defences apply in criminal defamation cases in Western Australia: Criminal Code (WA), ss 365, 366.
[47] Defamation Act 1889 (Qld), s 25; Defamation Act 1957 (Tas), s 26(1).
[48] Definition of 'periodical': Defamation Act 1889 (Qld), s 3, Defamation Act 1957 (Tas), s 3.
[49] See eg the facts in *Cubby*, 776 F Supp 135 (SD NY, 1991), discussed in paras 31.12–31.22, and *Stratton Oakmont*, 1995 WL 323710; 23 Media L Rep 1794 (SC NY, 1995); 23 Media L Rep 1794, discussed in paras 31.23–31.34. As to whether online editions of newspapers and magazines are to be treated as analogous to their hard copy counterparts, see para 13.08 (n 32).

that the intermediary could be said to be a 'seller' of the text, any more than a library which charges an annual membership fee could be said to be a 'seller' of books borrowed by members.

Actual knowledge defeats the defences

Finally, it should be noted that the statutory defences in Queensland and Tasmania are only defeated by actual knowledge on the part of the seller. In this respect, the statutory defences are similar to the clause 91 defence.[50] By contrast, the common law defence of innocent dissemination is defeated by actual knowledge, or an absence of knowledge, where that absence of knowledge is due to negligence.[51]

19.43

---

[50] See paras 19.30–19.34.
[51] See para 18.01.

PART V

REMEDIES AND RELATED MATTERS

20

INJUNCTIONS AND RELATED REMEDIES

A. Interim Injunctions

Introduction

The primary objective of many persons upon being defamed, or being threat-   **20.01**
ened with being defamed, is to restrain publication or further publication of
the defamatory material. Defamation law will, however, only rarely enable a
claimant to achieve such an objective.

England

General principles

In England, at common law, interim injunctions[1] are only granted in defam-   **20.02**
ation actions in exceptional circumstances. To obtain interim relief, the claimant must establish that the material complained of is so clearly defamatory that
if a jury were to find that it was not defamatory, an appeal court would be

---

[1] An interim, or interlocutory, injunction is one which applies until further order of the court,
or until the final hearing of the case. Interim injunctions of more than a few days' duration are
invariably only granted after the defendant has had the opportunity to put material before the
court and to be heard. The applicable rules in England are the Civil Procedure Rules, Pt 25 and
Practice Direction 25.

obliged to set aside the jury's verdict as unreasonable.[2] Underlying the restrictive approach towards the availability of interim injunctions in defamation actions is 'the importance of leaving free speech unfettered'.[3]

20.03 Interim injunctive relief must therefore be refused in England if there is any real ground for supposing that the defendant might succeed in a defence. So, for example, if the defendant raises a defence of justification, no injunction will be granted unless the imputation is plainly untrue.[4] Where a defence of justification is raised, the motive of the defendant in making the publication is irrelevant.[5] If the defendant pleads a defence of qualified privilege, the injunction must be refused, unless the evidence of malice is so overwhelming that it would be 'perverse [for a jury] to acquit the defendant of malice'.[6] If the defendant indicates an intention to rely on a defence of fair comment, an application for an interim injunction will fail unless it is clear that the publication could not be in the public interest, or must have been actuated by malice.[7] Injunctive relief may also have to be refused in cases where the claimant, if successful, would be likely to recover only nominal damages.[8]

20.04 Even where it is established that the publication is unarguably defamatory, and that the defendant has no possible defence, the grant of interim injunctive relief is discretionary.[9] The claimant must establish that the defendant has threatened or intends to publish[10] or repeat the defamatory statement.[11] Even then, the

---

[2] *Bonnard v Perryman* [1891] 2 Ch 269, 284.
[3] ibid (Coleridge CJ).
[4] *Herbage v Pressdram Ltd* [1984] 2 All ER 769, 771; *Holley v Smyth* [1998] QB 726, 743. In one Australian case, it was said that the court may even, in appropriate cases, have regard to what is said as to possible defences tentatively from the bar table: *Church of Scientology of California Inc v Reader's Digest Services Pty Ltd* [1980] 1 NSWLR 344, 352–4. See also Patrick Milmo and WVH Rogers, *Gatley on Libel and Slander* (10th edn, 2003) ('Gatley') para 25.6: 'Where the defendant contends that the words complained of are true, and swears that he will plead and seek at trial to prove the defence of justification, the court will not grant an interlocutory injunction, unless, exceptionally, the court is satisfied that such a defence is one that cannot succeed.'
[5] *Holley v Smyth* [1998] QB 726, 744, 748–9; *Moran v Heathcote* (English High Court, Eady J, 15 January 2001).
[6] *Herbage v Pressdram Ltd* [1984] 2 All ER 769, 771 (Griffiths LJ); *William Coulson & Sons v James Coulson & Co* (1887) 3 TLR 846; *Holley v Smyth* [1998] QB 726.
[7] *Fraser v Evans* [1969] 1 QB 349, 360.
[8] *Bonnard v Perryman* [1891] 2 Ch 269, 284–5; *Stocker v McElhinney (No 2)* [1961] NSWR 1043, 1048–9.
[9] ie in accordance with the ordinary principles which apply in applications for interim injunctions: see *American Cyanamid Co v Ethicon Ltd* [1975] AC 396.
[10] A *quia timet* order is available in appropriate cases, where there is a reasonable certainty as to the words of the threatened publication: *British Data Management Plc v Boxer Commercial Removals Plc* [1996] 3 All ER 707.
[11] eg *Quartz Hill Consolidated Gold Mining Company v Beall* (1882) 20 Ch 501, 508–9.

fundamental public interest in maintaining freedom of expression may be sufficient to defeat an application for an interim injunction.[12]

European influences

The English position is, if anything, more protective of freedom of expression **20.05** than the jurisprudence of the European Court of Human Rights under Article 10 of the European Convention on Human Rights (ECHR).[13] The European Court of Human Rights has held that, although interim injunctions are not prohibited by Article 10,[14] the dangers inherent in their use 'are such that they call for the most careful scrutiny on the part of the Court', particularly in cases involving publications by the press.[15]

In *Attorney-General v Guardian Newspapers Ltd (No 2)*,[16] Lord Goff considered **20.06** the relationship between Article 10 of the ECHR and the common law rule limiting the circumstances in which an interim injunction might lie to restrain the disclosure of government secrets. Lord Goff concluded that there was no inconsistency between English law and Article 10 of the ECHR.[17]

Human Rights Act 1998 (UK)

In all United Kingdom defamation actions in which interim injunctions are **20.07** sought, regard must now be had to section 12 of the Human Rights Act 1998 (HRA), which provides:

(1) This section applies if a court is considering whether to grant any relief which, if granted, might affect the exercise of the Convention right to freedom of expression.

(2) If the person against whom the application for relief is made ('the respondent') is neither present nor represented, no such relief is to be granted unless the court is satisfied—

(a) that the applicant has taken all practicable steps to notify the respondent; or

---

[12] See eg *R v Central Independent Television Plc* [1994] 3 All ER 641, 652 (Hoffman LJ): 'It cannot be too strongly emphasized that outside the established exceptions . . . there is no question of balancing freedom of speech against other interests. It is a trump card which always wins'; cf *Douglas v Hello! Ltd* [2001] QB 967, 982 (Brooke LJ): 'Although the right to freedom of expression is not in every case the ace of trumps, it is a powerful card to which the courts of this country must always pay appropriate respect', 1005 (Sedley LJ), 1008 (Keene LJ).

[13] Convention for the Protection of Human Rights and Fundamental Freedoms ('European Convention on Human Rights' or 'ECHR'). Art 10 guarantees a right to freedom of expression, subject only to such limitations as 'are prescribed by law and are necessary in a democratic society'. See further chapter 30. Art 10 is reproduced in para 30.02.

[14] See eg *Sunday Times v United Kingdom* (1979) 2 EHRR 245; *Markt Intern Verlag GmbH and Beermann v Germany* (1989) 12 EHRR 161; *Wingrove v United Kingdom* (1996) 24 EHRR 1.

[15] *Observer and Guardian v United Kingdom* (1991) 14 EHRR 153, para 60.

[16] [1990] 1 AC 109.

[17] ibid, 283–4. See also *Holley v Smyth* [1998] QB 726, 744–5, but cf 734, 748.

     (b) that there are compelling reasons why the respondent should not be
         notified.

(3) No such relief is to be granted to restrain publication before trial unless the
    court is satisfied that the applicant is likely to establish that publication
    should not be allowed.

(4) The court must have particular regard to the importance of the Conven-
    tion right to freedom of expression and, where the proceedings relate to
    material which the respondent claims, or which appears to the court, to be
    journalistic, literary or artistic material (or to conduct connected with such
    material), to—

     (a) the extent to which—
        (i) the material has, or is about to, become available to the public; or
        (ii) it is, or would be, in the public interest for the material to be
           published;
     (b) any relevant privacy code.[18]

(5) In this section—

     'court' includes a tribunal; and
     'relief' includes any remedy or order (other than in criminal proceedings).

20.08   Section 12 of the HRA makes Article 10 of the ECHR applicable as between
private parties to litigation. In having regard to Article 10, courts must consider
not just the right to freedom of expression in Article 10(1), but also the qualifications to that right set out in Article 10(2). Those qualifications include the
reputation and rights of others, and the protection of information received in
confidence.[19]

In an interim injunction application, when assessing whether the applicant is
likely to establish at trial that publication should not be allowed, the court must
weigh the competing interests having regard to 'principles of legality and proportionality'.[20] The court must look at the merits of the case and be satisfied
that, at trial, 'the scales are likely to come down in the applicant's favour'.[21]

20.09   In *Greene v Associated Newspapers Ltd*,[22] the Court of Appeal considered the
interplay between the common law principles applicable to the granting of
interim injunctive relief in defamation actions and the HRA. The court com-
prehensively rejected the claimant's argument that the enactment of the HRA
had significantly weakened the inhibitions that judges should feel before
imposing prior restraint on the press.

---

[18] Such as topic 3 of the *Code of Practice* of the Press Complaints Commission (November 1997).

[19] *Douglas v Hello! Ltd* [2001] QB 967, 1003–5 (Sedley LJ).

[20] ibid, 1005: 'Neither element is a trump card.'

[21] ibid, 1008 (Keene LJ).

[22] [2005] 1 All ER 30. See also *Tillery Valley Foods v Channel Four Television* [2004] EWHC 1075.

The court observed that section 12(3) of the HRA is expressly concerned with the protection of freedom of expression and not with undermining it, and that accordingly Parliament could not be interpreted as having abrogated the rule in *Bonnard v Perryman* 'by a sidewind'.[23] The court said it had:

> no hesitation in holding that there is nothing in section 12(3) of the Human Rights Act 1998 that can properly be interpreted as weakening in any way the force of the rule in *Bonnard v Perryman*.[24]

The court also considered section 6(1) of the HRA, which provides that it is unlawful for a public authority, including a court, to act in a way which is incompatible with a Convention right. The court acknowledged that in defamation cases where interim injunctions are sought, the Convention right to freedom of expression, and other Convention rights such as the right to protect one's reputation, will often be in conflict.[25] The court concluded that in defamation actions, the damage that may be done to a claimant's reputation by refusing an injunction 'pales into insignificance compared with the damage which would be done to freedom of expression and the freedom of the press if the rule in *Bonnard v Perryman* was relaxed'.[26]

A different outcome may be mandated in cases where other competing interests **20.10** are involved, such as where publication would result in the disclosure of confidential documents or national secrets,[27] or serious physical injury to or the death of the claimant.[28] An intense focus on the comparative importance of the specific rights being claimed in the individual case is necessary.[29] While the primacy accorded to freedom of expression is not a mechanical rule, it will only be displaced by unusual or exceptional circumstances.[30]

Australia

General principles

In recent years, Australian courts have departed from the common law position **20.11** which obtains in England. The modern Australian cases treat the grant of

---

[23] [2005] 1 All ER 30, para 61. The rule in *Bonnard v Perryman* is dealt with in para 20.02.
[24] ibid, para 66.
[25] ibid, paras 68, 78.
[26] ibid, para 78.
[27] ibid, paras 78, 81; *Cream Holdings Ltd v Banerjee* [2004] 4 All ER 617; *Campbell v MGN Ltd* [2004] 2 AC 457; *A v B Plc* [2003] QB 195.
[28] *Douglas v Hello! Ltd* [2001] QB 967, 1004–7; *Venables v News Group Newspapers Ltd* [2001] 1 All ER 908, paras 82–87.
[29] *In re S (FC) (a child)* [2004] 4 All ER 683, para 17.
[30] ibid, para 18 (right of the press to report everything that takes place in a criminal court prevails over the right to privacy of the son of the defendant, who had been charged with murdering the son's older brother).

interim injunctions in defamation cases as being a matter generally within the discretion of the court. Bearing in mind the significant impact the granting of an injunction has on freedom of speech, however, such injunctions will only be granted in rare and very clear cases.[31]

To succeed in an application for an interim injunction in Australia, plaintiffs must prove that there is a serious question to be tried,[32] and that the balance of convenience favours the granting of the injunction.[33]

Serious question to be tried

20.12 In determining whether the plaintiff has established a serious question to be tried, it will be relevant to assess both the plaintiff's case and any defences pleaded by the defendant. The court needs only to be satisfied that the plaintiff has a prima facie case.[34]

Balance of convenience

20.13 In assessing whether the balance of convenience favours the granting of an interim injunction, the most significant factor will be the public interest in the free discussion of matters of public or general interest.[35] Other factors relevant to the balance of convenience include whether damages would be an adequate remedy, and whether it is otherwise just in all the circumstances for the interim injunction to be granted, having regard to matters such as any delay on the part of the plaintiff in applying for relief and any hardship to the defendant which might result from the granting of the interim injunction.[36] Where the defendant puts forward evidence which raises, prima facie, a real issue of fact as to some relevant matter which would give rise to a complete defence, or negates the existence of an element of the cause of action, then the balance of convenience

---

[31] *Chappell v TCN Channel Nine Pty Ltd* (1988) 14 NSWLR 153, 157–63; *National Mutual Life Association of Australasia Ltd v GTV Corporation Pty Ltd* [1989] VR 747, 764; *Meriton Apartments Pty Ltd v SBS Corporation* [2002] NSWSC 915.

[32] See *American Cyanamid Co v Ethicon Ltd* [1975] AC 396. There has been some controversy as to whether this is the test applicable in Australia. In *Beecham Group Ltd v Bristol Laboratories Pty Ltd* (1968) 118 CLR 618, 620, Kitto J had stated the Australian test in terms of whether the plaintiff had proved 'a probability of success', by which he meant 'a sufficient likelihood of success to justify in the circumstances the preservation of [the status quo]'. The *American Cyanamid* test has however been applied, although not consistently, in Australia: see RP Meagher, WMC Gummow, and JRF Lehane, *Equity: Doctrines and Remedies* (3rd edn, 1992) paras 2169–73. In *National Mutual Life Association of Australasia Ltd v GTV Corporation Pty Ltd* [1989] VR 747, 764, a defamation case, Fullagar, Hampel, and McDonald JJ described the test as 'whether there is a substantial question to be investigated at trial'.

[33] *National Mutual Life Association of Australasia Ltd v GTV Corporation Pty Ltd* [1989] VR 747, 764.

[34] ibid, 764–6.

[35] ibid, 754 (Ormiston J at first instance, with whom Fullagar, Hampel, and McDonald JJ expressed complete agreement).

[36] See generally Meagher, Gummow, and Lehane (n 32 above) paras 2174–5.

will usually be against the granting of an interim injunction, even if the balance of the evidence on that issue favours the plaintiff, rather than the defendant.[37]

Scotland

The strict English test has not been applied in Scotland. Interim interdict has   **20.14** generally been available in Scots law in defamation actions in accordance with the ordinary rules which apply to interim interdict applications; that is, where the pursuer establishes a prima facie case, and the balance of convenience favours restraining the defender.[38] The HRA is likely, however, to lead to a tightening of the Scottish test. By reason of section 12(3) of the HRA, courts must now be satisfied that the petitioner is likely to establish at trial that publication should not be allowed.[39] It is also difficult to see how the traditional Scottish test could be reconciled with section 12(4) of the HRA, which requires United Kingdom courts, when considering whether to grant relief which might affect the exercise of the right to freedom of expression in Article 10 of the ECHR, to have particular regard to that right.[40]

Application to the Internet

General principles

Where material is published, or threatened to be published, on the Internet, an   **20.15** interim injunction may lie against the author, assuming the author can be identified, to restrain publication or further publication in appropriate cases.[41] For the reasons just outlined, such cases are more likely to arise in Australia than in the United Kingdom. The English Court of Appeal appears to have assumed, however, without needing to decide the point, that in an appropriate case an English court might grant an injunction to restrain the publication of defamatory Internet material within England, where there is a threat or real risk of wider publication within England.[42]

---

[37] *Stocker v McElhinney (No 2)* [1961] NSWR 1043, 1049, expressly approved in *National Mutual Life Association of Australasia Ltd v GTV Corporation Pty Ltd* [1989] VR 747, 754 (Ormiston J at first instance, with whom Fullagar, Hampel, and McDonald JJ on appeal expressed complete agreement). See also the analysis undertaken by Hunt J in *Chappell v TCN Channel Nine Pty Ltd* (1988) 14 NSWLR 153, 164–71.

[38] eg *Boyd v British Broadcasting Corporation* 1969 SLT (Sh Ct) 17; *Fairbairn v Scottish National Party* 1980 SLT 149; *Kwik-Fit-Euro Ltd v Scottish Daily Record and Sunday Mail Ltd* 1987 SLT 226; *McMurdo v Ferguson* 1993 SLT 193.

[39] An application for interim interdict was refused on this ground in *Dickson Minto, WS v Bonnier Media Ltd* 2002 SLT 776.

[40] See paras 20.07–20.10.

[41] An Australian example is *Oxford Media Pty Ltd v Haynes* (Supreme Court of Queensland, White J, 18 April 1997).

[42] *Dow Jones & Co Inc v Jameel* [2005] EWCA Civ 75.

Interim injunctions would ordinarily not lie, however, against Internet intermediaries in either the United Kingdom or Australia. In both countries, the intermediary will generally be able to establish a strongly arguable defence, based on the defences discussed in Part IV.[43]

20.16   Suppose, however, that the plaintiff in *Godfrey v Demon Internet Ltd*[44] had sought an interim injunction to restrain the defendant intermediary from making the defamatory bulletin board posting concerning him available from its servers. Suppose further that the posting was unarguably defamatory, and that the defendant could not swear that it had any likely defence. The defence in section 1 of the Defamation Act 1996 (UK) was not available to the defendant, because it had actual knowledge of the content of the offending posting. The provisions of the Electronic Commerce (EC Directive) Regulations 2002 (UK) ('Electronic Commerce Regulations'), had they been in force at the time, would probably not have applied for the same reason.[45] In any event, the Electronic Commerce Regulations do not prevent courts from requiring Internet intermediaries to prevent or stop infringements.[46] For the purposes of section 12(3) of the Human Rights Act 1998 (UK), had it been in force at the time, the court could have been satisfied that the plaintiff would be likely to establish at trial that publication of the posting should not be allowed.[47]

In those circumstances, it is possible that an interim injunction might have been granted in the United Kingdom.

Defendant outside the jurisdiction of the Court

20.17   It seems, however, that courts will be less likely to grant injunctions to restrain the publication or further publication of defamatory Internet material where the defendant is outside the jurisdiction of the court.

In *Macquarie Bank Ltd v Berg*,[48] Simpson J of the New South Wales Supreme Court refused to grant an injunction restraining the publication of a web page by the defendant. The defendant was not present in New South Wales and all acts resulting in publication of the material in New South Wales were done by him from outside that state. The defendant did not appear in the proceedings and the matter proceeded on an *ex parte* basis.

20.18   In refusing to grant the relief sought by the plaintiff, Simpson J held:

---

[43] See chapters 16, 17, 18 and 19.
[44] [2001] QB 201; see paras 15.03–15.07.
[45] Electronic Commerce (EC Directive) Regulations 2002 (UK), reg 19; see para 17.22.
[46] ibid, regs 20(1)(b), 20(2); see para 17.28.
[47] See para 20.07.
[48] [1999] Aust Defamation Reports ¶53,035.

An injunction to restrain defamation in NSW is designed to ensure compliance with the laws of NSW, and to protect the rights of plaintiffs, as those rights are defined by the law of NSW. Such an injunction is not designed to superimpose the law of NSW relating to defamation on every other state, territory and country of the world. Yet that would be the effect of an order restraining publication on the Internet. It is not to be assumed that the law of defamation in other countries is coextensive with that of NSW, and indeed, one knows that it is not. It may very well be that, according to the law of the Bahamas, Tazhakistan [*sic*], or Mongolia, the defendant has an unfettered right to publish the material. To make an order interfering with such a right would exceed the proper limits of the use of the injunctive power of the court.

Simpson J was also concerned about the potential unenforceability of any injunction she might grant: **20.19**

It seems to me unsatisfactory to make orders the effectiveness of which is solely dependent upon the voluntary presence, at a time of his selection, of the person against whom the orders are made. The uncertainty of unenforceability is a factor adverse to the exercise of discretion in the plaintiff's favour.

Simpson J did not explore whether, if the defendant had been present within New South Wales, an injunction might have been granted restraining him from doing any acts in New South Wales which might result in the publication of the offending material. While such an injunction might have been of limited value to the plaintiffs, there would not appear to be any reason why such an injunction could not have been granted.[49]

The reasoning underlying Simpson J's judgment in *Macquarie Bank* was founded on a questionable assumption, namely that it is impossible to craft an injunction restraining a foreign defendant from publishing material via the Internet within the geographic jurisdiction of the court.

Nonetheless, injunctions are a discretionary remedy and Simpson J can scarcely be criticized for being concerned that the authority of the court might be undermined by granting an injunction which in all probability would have been ignored. The defendant was not present within the jurisdiction of the court and was not readily amenable to enforcement processes.[50]

---

[49] The injunction granted in *Oxford Media Pty Ltd v Haynes* (Supreme Court of Queensland, White J, 18 April 1997) eg restrained the defendant 'by himself, his servants and agents and every one of them . . . from publishing, further publishing, printing, copying, using or divulging [the offending] material or any of the information therein or derived therefrom or any part thereof or to the effect of that material'. Similarly broad injunctions have been granted in Canada: see *Ager v Canjex Publishing Ltd* (British Columbia Supreme Court, Shaw J, 6 June 2003), para 110; *Yaghi v WMS Gaming Inc* [2004] WWR 657 (Alberta Court of Queen's Bench), para 58; and *Barrick Gold Corporation v Lopehandia* (2004) 71 OR (3d) 416 (Ontario Court of Appeal), see esp paras 73–8.
[50] *Macquarie Bank Ltd v Berg* [1999] Aust Defamation Reports ¶53,035 (Simpson J): 'Any order made by this court would be enforceable only if the defendant were voluntarily to return to

20.20   *Macquarie Bank Ltd v Berg* can be contrasted with *Barrick Gold Corporation v Lopehandia*.[51] In that case, the Ontario Court of Appeal granted an injunction restraining the defendants, a resident of British Columbia and a British Columbian corporation, from posting defamatory statements concerning the plaintiff on the Internet. The defendants had posted a 'blizzard' of defamatory postings on bulletin boards, including bulletin boards operated by Yahoo Canada Inc in Ontario.

Blair JA, with whom Doherty and Laskin JJA agreed, said he was troubled by the 'marginal presence' of the defendants in the jurisdiction, and about the enforceability of any injunction.[52] On the other hand, Blair JA noted that the posting of messages via the Internet constituted an act that affects the plaintiff's 'reputation, goodwill, and personal property in Ontario, and arguably constitutes an act done' in Ontario.[53] Blair JA concluded that the courts in Ontario had jurisdiction to restrain the defendants. Blair JA thought there were two reasons why the injunction might be effective: it would operate to prevent Yahoo from continuing to post the defamatory messages; and any injunction might be enforceable in British Columbia, where the defendants were located.[54]

B. Permanent Injunctions

General principles

20.21   The considerations applicable to the granting of permanent injunctions—that is, injunctions which form part of the final relief awarded in a defamation action—are different from those which apply to the granting of interim injunctions.

The general rule is that where claimants succeed in defamation actions, they may be entitled to a permanent injunction, restraining the defendant, from the date of judgment, from further publication of the defamatory material or material to the same purport or effect, if they can establish that future publication is likely and that it will constitute an actionable wrong.[55] In cases of

---

NSW. He cannot be compelled to do so for the purpose of enforcement.' See also *Macquarie Bank Ltd v Berg* [2002] NSWSC 254.

[51] (2004) 71 OR (3d) 416.
[52] ibid, para 73.
[53] ibid, para 76.
[54] ibid, paras 76–7.
[55] See eg *Bonnard v Perryman* [1891] 2 Ch 269, 283; Gatley (n 4 above) para 9.27; Michael Gillooly, *The Law of Defamation in Australia and New Zealand* (1998) 320–2.

slanders which are not actionable per se,[56] however, it seems that a permanent injunction will not be granted unless the claimant has suffered special damage,[57] or unless such 'damage will necessarily or probably arise from the further publications threatened by the defendant'.[58]

Application to the Internet

Courts may be reluctant to award permanent injunctions with extraterritorial reach in cases involving Internet publications, however, for the same reasons as discussed in relation to interim injunctions; namely, because the effect of the injunction might be to restrain worldwide publication of the offending material, even in jurisdictions in which publication might be innocent.[59]   **20.22**

Where claimants have recovered damages, those damages compensate the claimant not only to the time of the trial, but also for damages likely to accrue in the future from the same words.[60] The claimant will be prevented by the doctrine of *res judicata* from bringing a later action to recover further damages from the same defendant in respect of the same material.   **20.23**

It will therefore be important for claimants in cases involving the publication of material via the Internet to seek permanent injunctions, wherever possible, to restrain the defendant from publishing or continuing to publish the same words. In the absence of such an injunction, it seems the defendant will not be required to take any action to prevent further publications of the same material, such as via online archives.

Where an intermediary is successfully sued in respect of defamatory material contained on its computer system, an order should be sought compelling the intermediary to remove or disable access to the offending material.

Human Rights Act 1998 (UK)

As already noted, whenever a United Kingdom court is considering whether to grant relief, including a permanent injunction, it must have particular regard to   **20.24**

---

[56] See para 4.01.

[57] *White v Mellin* [1895] AC 154, 163–4, 167, 170.

[58] *British Railway Traffic and Electric Company, Ltd v The CRC Company, Ltd* [1922] 2 KB 260, 273 (McCardie J); *White v Mellin* [1895] AC 154, 167–8.

[59] *Macquarie Bank Ltd v Berg* [1999] Aust Defamation Reports ¶53,035; cf *Barrick Gold Corporation v Lopehandia* (2004) 71 OR 3d 416 (Ontario Court of Appeal); see paras 20.17–20.20. See also *HH Sheikha Mouza Al Misnad v Azzaman Ltd* [2003] EWHC 1783, para 36: 'an English court should think long and hard before granting injunctions and giving directions having such extra-territorial effect' (Gray J).

[60] *Lord Townsend v Hughes* (1676) 2 Mod 150, 151; 86 ER 994, 994–5; *Ingram v Lawson* (1840) 6 Bing NC 212; 133 ER 84; *Gregory v Williams* (1844) 1 C & K 568; 174 ER 941; *Mallan v AM Bickford & Sons, Ltd* [1915] SALR 47, 93.

the importance of the right to freedom of expression in Article 10 of the European Convention on Human Rights.[61] The court must weigh the right to freedom of expression against the competing interests recognized in Article 10(2) of the ECHR, including the reputation and rights of others and the protection of information received in confidence, to determine whether the granting of a permanent injunction would be justified.[62] Where the proceedings involve journalistic, literary, or artistic material, the court must consider the extent to which the material has or is about to become public, the extent to which it would be in the public interest for the material to be published, and any relevant privacy code.[63] A permanent injunction may accordingly be more likely to be granted in a case involving material concerning the private details of an individual than in a case involving matters of broad public concern.

C. Corrections and Apologies

Introduction

20.25   Except where interim injunctions are awarded, defamation remedies are a blunt instrument in the sense that they are unlikely to achieve their objective of restoring the claimant's reputation to the level enjoyed before the offending publication. Publicity surrounding the awarding by a court of damages, or injunctive relief, may convince some of the falsity of a defamatory publication and restore the claimant's reputation in the minds of some people. It may, however, take many months or years for a defamation action to reach trial. The damage which is done by the publication of defamatory material can often not be reversed by the awarding of damages, or a restraint preventing repetition of the defamation.

20.26   Where defamatory material is published via the Internet, a damages award months or years after the original publication may be even less likely to restore the claimant's reputation in the eyes of those to whom the original material was published. The successful outcome of defamation proceedings in the United Kingdom or Australia will be most unlikely to attract publicity in all of the places around the world in which material on a bulletin board, or web page, has been published. Any publicity attracted by such proceedings might, in any event, be unlikely to come to the attention of all of the people around the world who saw the offending material.

---

[61] Human Rights Act 1998 (UK), s 12; see para 20.07.
[62] See paras 20.08–20.10.
[63] Human Rights Act 1998 (UK), s 12(4). An example of a relevant privacy code is topic 3 in the *Code of Practice* of the Press Complaints Commission.

It would therefore seem desirable for defamation law to provide an expedited **20.27**
remedy in appropriate cases, and for courts to have the power to compel unsuccessful defendants to publish some form of correction or apology, or a prominent report of the outcome of the proceedings. A prompt hearing, coupled with
such a correction, apology, or report would appear to offer claimants a better
prospect of vindication.

The summary disposal provisions in the Defamation Act 1996 (UK) are
intended to establish such a remedy.

United Kingdom: summary disposal procedure

The summary disposal procedure applies in England and Northern Ireland[64] in **20.28**
cases where it appears to the court that one or other of the parties has 'no
realistic prospect of success', and that there is no reason why the claim should be
tried.[65] The principal advantage of the summary disposal procedure is that it
offers a speedy and relatively cost-effective alternative to trial, in appropriate
cases.

In considering whether a claim should be tried, the court must have regard to **20.29**
whether all the persons who are or might be defendants in respect of the publication complained of are before the court, whether summary disposal of the
claim against another defendant would be inappropriate, the extent to which
there is a conflict of evidence, the seriousness of the content of the statement
and the extent of publication, and whether it is justifiable in the circumstances
to proceed to a full trial.[66] Summary disposal proceedings are heard and
determined without a jury.[67]

Where summary disposal is ordered, the court may grant only the limited relief **20.30**
prescribed in section 9(1) of the Defamation Act 1996. That relief includes
damages not exceeding £10,000 or such other amount as may be prescribed
by the Lord Chancellor,[68] and injunctive relief.[69] The court may also make a

---

[64] In Northern Ireland, the provisions apply only to proceedings in the High Court: Defamation Act 1996 (UK), s 11.
[65] ibid, s 8(2) (plaintiff's claim has no realistic prospect of success and there is no reason why it
should be tried), s 8(3) (defendant has no defence to the claim which has a realistic prospect of
success and there is no other reason why the claim should be tried). See eg *Clarke v Davey* [2002]
EWHC 2342; *Buffery v Guardian Newspapers Ltd* [2004] EWHC 1514.
[66] Defamation Act 1996 (UK), s 8(4).
[67] ibid, s 8(5).
[68] ibid, s 9(1)(c), (3).
[69] ibid, s 9(1)(d). It has been held that the summary disposal procedure does not affect the
principles governing the granting of interim injunctive relief: *Moran v Heathcote* (English High
Court, Eady J, 15 January 2001).

declaration that the statement was false and defamatory of the claimant,[70] or order that the defendant publish or cause to be published a suitable correction and apology.[71] Unless the claimant asks for summary relief, the court must only grant relief if satisfied that it will adequately compensate the claimant for the wrong suffered.[72]

Rules for the conduct of summary disposal proceedings are prescribed.[73] The summary disposal procedure operates as an alternative to the general right to apply for summary judgment.[74]

20.31   Summary disposal will be refused where the prospect of success of a defence is not unrealistic or fanciful,[75] where a defendant has unsuccessfully sought with reasonable diligence to obtain material evidence at the time of the application and there is some prospect that such evidence may emerge before trial,[76] where the relief sought on summary disposal includes injunctive relief and directions for the publication of a correction or apology which would have extraterritorial effect,[77] or where the relevant law is uncertain or in possible need of refinement.[78]

The summary disposal procedure should not be invoked where the defence advanced turns on the facts, and where there is reason to think that further facts may emerge or require investigation before a fair or final conclusion can be reached.[79] On the other hand, the court should not shy away from careful

---

[70]   Defamation Act 1996 (UK), s 9(1)(a).

[71]   ibid, s 9(1)(b). The content of any correction and apology, and the time, manner, form, and place of publication is for the parties to agree. If the parties cannot agree on the content, the court may direct the defendant to publish or cause to be published a summary of the court's judgment. If the parties cannot agree on the time, manner, form, or place of publication, the court may direct the defendant to take such reasonable and practicable steps as it considers appropriate: s 9(2).

[72]   ibid, s 8(3). See eg *Burstein v Times Newspapers Ltd* [2001] 1 WLR 579; *Ferguson v Associated Newspapers Ltd* (English High Court, Gray J, 15 March 2002); *Mawdsley v Guardian Newspapers Ltd* [2002] EWHC 1780.

[73]   Civil Procedure Rules, r 53.2 and Practice Direction 53, para 5; see also Defamation Act 1996 (UK), s 10.

[74]   Civil Procedure Rules, r 53.2(3). Note, however, that an application for summary judgment may not be made where an application for summary disposal has been made but not yet disposed of, or where summary relief has been granted on an application for summary disposal: ibid.

[75]   *HH Sheikha Mouza Al Misnad v Azzaman Ltd* [2003] EWHC 1783, paras 38–9, 48; *Clarke v Davey* [2002] EWHC 2342. The test is the same as the test under Civil Procedure Rules, r 24.2: see *Mosley v Focus Magazin Verlag GmbH* [2001] EWCA Civ 1030, para 10; *Swain v Hillman* [2001] 1 All ER 91.

[76]   *HH Sheikha Mouza Al Misnad v Azzaman Ltd* [2003] EWHC 1783, paras 34–5.

[77]   ibid, para 36.

[78]   *Chase v News Group Newspapers Ltd* [2002] EWHC 2209.

[79]   *Downtex v Flatley* [2003] EWCA Civ 1282, para 31; *Chase v News Group Newspapers Ltd* [2002] EWHC 2209.

consideration and analysis of the facts relied on by the parties in order to decide whether the line of defence advanced is no more than fanciful, at least where there is no reason to think that defendants will be in a position to advance their case to any significant extent at trial.[80]

The Court of Appeal held in *Loutchansky v Times Newspapers Ltd (Nos 4 and 5)* **20.32** that section 8 of the Defamation Act 1996 (UK) gives the court jurisdiction, even after liability has been determined at trial or admitted, to order that the issue of quantum be disposed of summarily.[81]

There may be an advantage for claimants in appropriate cases to seek to have quantum disposed of summarily because of the possibility of simultaneously obtaining an order for an apology; an option which is not otherwise available in a defamation action.[82]

An example of a case in which summary disposal was granted is *Green v Times* **20.33** *Newspapers Ltd*.[83] An article defamatory of the claimants had appeared in *The Sunday Times* newspaper and on *The Sunday Times* web site. Following a complaint by the claimants, the defendant made offers of amends in respect of the newspaper article, which were accepted by the claimants.[84] The offers did not relate to the web site article. The parties were unable to agree on the damages payable in relation to the newspaper article, and the matter was referred to a judge for damages to be assessed. Meanwhile, the claimants brought separate proceedings against the defendant in respect of the web site article. The claimants rejected an offer of amends in relation to the web site article, apparently on the basis that they thought they might obtain a higher award of damages from a jury.

Gray J held, despite the apparent absurdity, that the proceeding concerning the web site article was properly constituted, and related to causes of action which were 'at any rate notionally' distinct from those arising out of the newspaper article. The commencement of the proceedings was accordingly not an abuse of process. Gray J went on to hold, however, that it was an appropriate case for the court to order summary disposal. Gray J said:

> It appears to me that it is necessary to apply some common sense. The issue of *The Sunday Times* containing the article complained of was published to millions of readers. *The Sunday Times* is an influential publication, and I have no doubt that its business pages are taken seriously by those who read them. The seriousness of

---

[80] *Downtex v Flatley* [2003] EWCA Civ 1282, para 31.
[81] [2002] QB 783, 823–4.
[82] ibid.
[83] English High Court, Gray J, 17 January 2001.
[84] The offer of amends procedure is described in paras 13.01–13.02.

the libel would have been apparent upon its publication to those readers in the columns of the hard copy of *The Sunday Times*. I take the view that the damage to the claimants' reputations was done almost entirely by the publication of the article in the newspaper.

Gray J granted summary disposal and referred the question of what relief ought to be granted to the judge appointed to assess compensation in respect of the newspaper article under the offer of amends procedure.

20.34   The summary disposal procedure may prove an attractive option for claimants in appropriate defamation actions involving material published via the Internet. In many cases it is likely that claimants would be satisfied with a declaration that the material was false and defamatory, an order that the defendant publish a correction and apology on the Internet, an injunction restraining the defendant from publishing material to the same purport and effect, and a modest award of damages.

Where the defendant is located outside England and Northern Ireland, however, a court might be reluctant in particular cases to grant injunctions with extraterritorial effect, or to order the publication of corrections and apologies via the Internet, on the ground that the defendant's conduct might not be actionable under the laws of many places where the material in question might have been read, heard, or seen.[85]

Defendants might also apply for summary disposal of claims in appropriate cases involving material published via the Internet, either for the purpose of having the claim dismissed, or for the purpose of having the claim determined quickly and relatively inexpensively, and with the knowledge that if summary disposal is granted, the compensation payable will not exceed £10,000.

Australia

20.35   Although summary judgment procedures apply in all Australian jurisdictions, no Australian jurisdiction presently has the power to order the publication of apologies, corrections, or reports of proceedings in defamation cases.[86]

---

[85] *HH Sheikha Mouza Al Misnad v Azzaman Ltd* [2003] EWHC 1783, para 36. See also paras 20.17–20.20 where similar reservations to the granting of interim injunctions are discussed.

[86] 'Correction orders' were one of the reforms advocated by the Australian Law Reform Commission in 1979: Australian Law Reform Commission, *Unfair Publication*, Report No 11 (1979) 142–3, Draft Bill, cls 25–7. In 1995, the New South Wales Law Reform Commission recommended that plaintiffs be entitled to sue for a 'declaration of falsity', as an alternative to an action for general damages for defamation: New South Wales Law Reform Commission, *Defamation*, Report No 75 (1995) 87–112. Under the recommendation, the plaintiff would have had to elect whether to sue for a declaration of falsity, or for general damages for defamation: 90–1.

21

DAMAGES

A. Introduction

The primary means by which defamation law protects and vindicates reputation **21.01** is the award of damages following judgment being entered for the claimant at trial. Damages may be available under two broad heads:

- compensatory damages (including aggravated damages); and
- exemplary damages.[1]

B. Compensatory Damages

General principles

Compensatory damages are to compensate a claimant for the damage to his or **21.02** her reputation and to vindicate his or her good name. They include damages for the actual monetary consequences of the attitude adopted by other persons towards the claimant as a result of the defamatory publication, as well as, in the

---

[1] Exemplary damages are not available in Scotland or New South Wales: see para 21.13.

289

case of individuals, damages for the distress, hurt, and humiliation caused to the claimant by the defamatory publication.[2] In Scots law, where the defamatory material was communicated only to the pursuer, damages are available only under this latter head.[3]

Damages for distress, hurt, and humiliation are 'at large', to be assessed, in effect, as a solatium.[4] The damages should, however, be proportionate to the seriousness of the defamation and the extent of publication. Damages may be reduced by reason of a claimant's conduct in the course of the litigation, such as where a claimant attempts to pervert the course of justice, makes or procures false testimony, or makes damaging allegations of corruption or lying against innocent third parties.[5]

At common law, it is presumed that a defamatory publication causes damage to its victim.[6]

A successful claimant is entitled to recover the whole of the damages caused by a defamatory publication. The recoverable damages may include damages resulting from republications or partial republications of the offending material, provided that those republications flowed in the ordinary course of things from the original publication.[7]

The choice of the Internet as the medium for the publication of defamatory material may be an important factor in determining the extent of compensatory damages. As the Ontario Court of Appeal observed in *Barrick Gold Corporation v Lopehandia*:

> Internet defamation is distinguished from its less pervasive cousins, in terms of its potential to damage the reputation of individuals and corporations, by . . . its

---

[2] *McCarey v Associated Newspapers Ltd (No 2)* [1965] 2 QB 86, 107; *John v MGN Ltd* [1997] QB 586, 607; *Coyne v Citizen Finance Ltd* (1991) 172 CLR 211, 216.
[3] *Mackay v M'Cankie* (1883) 10 R 537; *Ramsay v MacLay & Co* (1890) 18 R 130. Elsewhere in the United Kingdom and in Australia, there is no cause of action unless the defamatory material is communicated to someone other than the defamed person: see para 5.02.
[4] *Broome v Cassell & Co Ltd* [1972] AC 1027, 1125; *Uren v John Fairfax & Sons Pty Ltd* (1966) 117 CLR 118, 150; *Amalgamated Television Services Pty Ltd v Marsden* [2002] NSWCA 419, para 1315.
[5] *Campbell v News Group Newspapers Ltd* [2002] EMLR 43, 996. See also *Godfrey v Demon Internet Ltd (No 2)* (English High Court, Morland J, 23 April 1999); *Cornelius v De Taranto* [2001] EMLR 12, 347.
[6] *Shevill v Presse Alliance SA* [1996] AC 959, 983; *Berezovsky v Michaels* [2000] 2 All ER 986, 993; *Selecta Homes and Building Co Pty Ltd v Advertiser-News Weekend Publishing Co Pty Ltd* [2001] SASC 140, para 142; *Herald & Weekly Times Ltd v Popovic* [2003] VSCA 161, para 379; *Jameel v Wall Street Journal Europe Sprl (No 2)* [2005] EWCA Civ 74, para 3; *Dow Jones & Co Inc v Jameel* [2005] EWCA Civ 75, paras 19–41; *Hill v Church of Scientology of Toronto* [1995] 2 SCR 1130, para 164.
[7] See para 5.18.

interactive nature, its potential for being taken at face value, and its absolute and immediate worldwide ubiquity and accessibility.[8]

Corporate claimants cannot recover damages for injury to feelings and reputa-   **21.03**
tion; their damages are limited to injuries which 'sound in money'.[9] Such damages include actual monetary loss, and damage to trading reputation or goodwill, in so far as it is capable of being assessed in monetary terms.[10] Corporations are, however, entitled to the presumption that they have been damaged by a defamatory publication, and are not obliged to prove special damage.[11]

In New South Wales, corporations may only sue in respect of a defamatory imputation about the corporation if, at the time of publication, the corporation employed fewer than ten persons and had no subsidiaries within the meaning of the Corporations Act 2001 (Cth).[12]

Damages are awarded by the jury, in jury cases, in the United Kingdom and in   **21.04**
all Australian jurisdictions except New South Wales, South Australia, and the Australian Capital Territory.[13]

Level of damages

General

Counsel and the judge may suggest to the jury the level of damages which it   **21.05**
should award.[14]

---

[8] (2004) 71 OR (3d) 416, paras 34, 44. See also *Markovic v White* [2004] NSWSC 37, para 21; *Reichmann v Berlin* (Ontario Superior Court of Justice, Sachs J, 8 July 2002), para 10; *Vaquero Energy Ltd v Weir* (2004) 352 AR 191 (Alberta Court of Queen's Bench), para 17; *Ross v Holley* (Ontario Superior Court of Justice, Low J, 9 November 2004), paras 7–8, 11: 'the use of e-mail is far more powerful than the sending out of a multiple of hard copy letters defaming the plaintiff, but on the other hand, the e-mail medium is far less powerful than a posting on a web site that has, as its initial audience, a substantially wider reach and therefore an exponentially greater potential for re-dissemination'. The correctness of this last statement as a general proposition is to be doubted: a defamatory e-mail message sent to people who know a claimant is likely to have a much more devastating effect than the same message posted on an obscure web site.
[9] *Lewis v Daily Telegraph Ltd* [1964] AC 234, 262 (Lord Reid); *Australian Broadcasting Corporation v Comalco Ltd* (1986) 12 FCR 510, 586 (a trading corporation does not have a reputation distinct from its reputation in the way of its trade or business); *Derbyshire County Council v Times Newspapers Ltd* [1993] AC 534, 547; *Selecta Homes and Building Co Pty Ltd v Advertiser-News Weekend Publishing Co Pty Ltd* [2001] SASC 140, paras 49, 158.
[10] *Lewis v Daily Telegraph Ltd* [1964] AC 234, 262; *Australian Broadcasting Corporation v Comalco Ltd* (1986) 12 FCR 510, 586; cf *Andrews v John Fairfax & Sons Ltd* [1980] 2 NSWLR 225, 254.
[11] *Jameel v Wall Street Journal Europe Sprl (No 2)* [2005] EWCA Civ 74, paras 113–17; cf *Steel and Morris v United Kingdom* (European Court of Human Rights, 15 February 2005); see para 21.15.
[12] Defamation Act 1974 (NSW), s 8A.
[13] In New South Wales, the judge determines the damages to be awarded: Defamation Act 1974 (NSW), s 7A(4)(b). Civil juries have been abolished in South Australia and the Australian Capital Territory: Juries Act 1927 (SA), s 5; Supreme Court Act 1933 (ACT), s 22.
[14] *John v MGN Ltd* [1997] QB 586, 615–16; *Coyne v Citizen Finance Ltd* (1991) 172 CLR 211, 235; *Carson v John Fairfax & Sons Ltd* (1993) 178 CLR 44, 59–60, 93.

Relevance of defamation awards

21.06 In England, there is authority for the proposition that juries should not be informed of the level of damages awarded by juries in other defamation actions.[15] They may, however, be told of awards of damages approved or substituted by the Court of Appeal.[16]

Relevance of personal injuries awards

21.07 Recent decisions in both England and Australia enable counsel or the court to give juries an indication as to the ordinary level of the general damages component awarded in different types of personal injuries cases.[17] The purpose of the comparison is to 'maintain a sense of proportion' between defamation awards and personal injuries awards, without 'seeking any precise correlation'.[18] The difficulties of equating reputational injury with severe personal injuries such as quadriplegia or very severe brain damage are obvious.[19]

In New South Wales, where damages are a matter for the judge rather than the jury, and in the Australian Capital Territory, where there is no provision for civil juries, judges are directed, in effect, to undertake comparisons with damages awards in personal injuries cases.[20]

C. Aggravated Damages

General principles

21.08 A claimant may recover aggravated damages in cases where the conduct of the defendant has increased the subjective hurt suffered by the claimant.[21]

---

[15] *Rantzen v Mirror Group Newspapers Ltd* [1994] QB 670, 694; *John v MGN Ltd* [1997] QB 586, 612; cf the position in Scotland: *Winter v News Scotland Ltd* 1991 SLT 828, 831.

[16] *Rantzen v Mirror Group Newspapers Ltd* [1994] QB 670, 694; *John v MGN Ltd* [1997] QB 586, 612.

[17] *John v MGN Ltd* [1997] QB 586; *Carson v John Fairfax & Sons Ltd* (1993) 178 CLR 44, 59. Comparisons with personal injuries cases have been held to be not appropriate, and 'not particularly helpful or useful' in Scotland: *Winter v News Scotland Ltd* 1991 SLT 828, 831; *Baigent v British Broadcasting Corporation* 2001 SC 281.

[18] *Jones v Pollard* [1997] EMLR 233, 257 (Hirst LJ).

[19] eg ibid; *John v MGN Ltd* [1997] QB 586, 614. The latter case marked a reversal of approach in England. As recently as 1994, the Court of Appeal had held that 'there is no satisfactory way in which the conventional awards in actions for damages for personal injuries can be used to provide guidance for an award in an action for defamation': *Rantzen v Mirror Group Newspapers Ltd* [1994] QB 670, 695.

[20] Defamation Act 1974 (NSW), s 46A; Civil Law (Wrongs) Act 2002 (ACT), s 136. As to the approach to be taken when making such comparisons, see *Rogers v Nationwide News Pty Ltd* (2003) 201 ALR 184, paras 71–6, 82 (Hayne J).

[21] *Rookes v Barnard* [1964] AC 1129, 1221; *David Syme & Co Ltd v Mather* [1977] VR 516, 518, 526, 534–5.

Aggravated damages will be available where the defendant has acted out of malevolence or spite,[22] or where the defendant's conduct has been improper, unjustifiable, or lacking in bona fides.[23] Aggravated damages are a form of compensatory damages: they are to compensate claimants 'when the harm done to [them] was aggravated by the manner in which the act was done'.[24]

Examples

Examples of situations in which claimants might be entitled to an award of aggravated damages include where the defendant has unjustifiably failed to retract or apologize,[25] where the defendant has repeated the offending allegations,[26] where the defendant failed to investigate the defamatory allegations before publishing them,[27] where the defendant's conduct prior to or during the trial,[28] or even after the verdict, was calculated to deter the claimant from proceeding,[29] and where a defence of justification or fair comment has been pleaded with reckless indifference as to its relevance,[30] provided in all cases that the defendant's conduct increased the harm suffered by the claimant. **21.09**

It has been held in Australia that persisting in a bona fide defence or putting claimants to their proof is not enough to aggravate a claimant's damages.[31] By contrast, in England, it is clear that persistence in a plea of justification or fair comment may suffice, even where the defendant has an honest belief in the availability of the defence.[32] **21.10**

---

[22] *Rookes v Barnard* [1964] AC 1129, 1221; *Stein v Beaverbrook Newspapers Ltd* 1968 SC 272, 278–9.

[23] *Triggell v Pheeney* (1951) 82 CLR 497, 514; *Mirror Newspapers Ltd v Fitzpatrick* [1984] 1 NSWLR 643, 653–4.

[24] *Uren v John Fairfax & Sons Pty Ltd* (1966) 117 CLR 118, 149; *Amalgamated Television Services Pty Ltd v Marsden* [2002] NSWCA 419, para 1316; *Herald & Weekly Times Ltd v Popovic* [2003] VSCA 161, para 380.

[25] *Sutcliffe v Pressdram Ltd* [1991] 1 QB 153, 184; *Rantzen v Mirror Group Newspapers Ltd* [1994] QB 670, 683; but cf *Morgan v Odhams Press Ltd* [1971] 1 WLR 1239, 1247, 1262. In Australia, a mere failure to apologize is not considered capable of aggravating a claimant's damages: *Carson v John Fairfax & Sons Ltd* (1993) 178 CLR 44, 66; cf earlier Australian decisions such as *Andrews v John Fairfax & Sons Ltd* [1980] 2 NSWLR 225, 243, 250–1; *Mirror Newspapers Ltd v Fitzpatrick* [1984] 1 NSWLR 643, 659.

[26] *Sutcliffe v Pressdram Ltd* [1991] 1 QB 153, 184.

[27] *Andrews v John Fairfax & Sons Ltd* [1980] 2 NSWLR 225, 244, 250.

[28] *Sutcliffe v Pressdram Ltd* [1991] 1 QB 153, 184.

[29] *Herald & Weekly Times Ltd v Popovic* [2003] VSCA 161, para 415.

[30] *Herald & Weekly Times Ltd v McGregor* (1928) 41 CLR 254, 262; *Hewitt v West Australian Newspapers Ltd* (1976) 17 ACTR 15, 26. See also *Sutcliffe v Pressdram Ltd* [1991] 1 QB 153, 184.

[31] *Coyne v Citizen Finance Ltd* (1991) 172 CLR 211, 237; *David Syme & Co Ltd v Mather* [1977] VR 516, 517–18, 527–8, 535.

[32] *Broome v Cassell & Co Ltd* [1972] AC 1027, 1125; *Rantzen v Mirror Group Newspapers Ltd* [1994] QB 670, 683–4.

Application to the Internet

21.11 Aggravated damages are likely to be available to claimants defamed by Internet publications in much the same circumstances as they would be available in relation to traditional forms of publication. For example, aggravated damages might be available where an ISP, sued in respect of a publication on a web page stored on the ISP's server, pleads and persists with an unmeritorious defence of justification or fair comment, and thereby increases the harm suffered by the claimant. The same ISP might be spared from an award of aggravated damages if pleading and persisting only with one of the statutory defences for intermediaries discussed in Part IV[33] or the common law defence of innocent dissemination.[34] In these latter situations, the ISP's conduct is unlikely to increase the injury to the claimant's feelings resulting from the defamation.

Aggravated damages might be appropriate where a defendant encourages others to forward, republish, or establish hyperlinks to defamatory material.[35]

D. Exemplary Damages

General principles

21.12 Exemplary damages are awarded in appropriate cases to punish defendants for 'particularly reprehensible conduct at the time of or subsequent to the defamatory publication'.[36] The purpose of exemplary damages is to punish the defendant for outrageous conduct, to mark disapproval of that conduct, and to deter the defendant from repeating that conduct.[37] Exemplary damages will only be awarded in England where the defendant has knowingly or recklessly published false defamatory material, with 'the motive that the chances of economic advantage outweigh the chances of economic, or perhaps physical penalty'.[38] Exemplary damages will be awarded if, and only if, compensatory damages are inadequate to punish the defendant for outrageous conduct, to deter the

---

[33] See chapters 16, 17, and 19.

[34] See chapter 18.

[35] *Ross v Holley* (Ontario Superior Court of Justice, Low J, 9 November 2004), para 14.

[36] Michael Gillooly, *The Law of Defamation in Australia and New Zealand* (1998) 302–3.

[37] *Rookes v Barnard* [1964] AC 1129, 1228.

[38] *Broome v Cassell & Co Ltd* [1972] AC 1027, 1079 (Lord Hailsham), 1088 (Lord Reid), 1094 (Lord Morris), 1130 (Lord Diplock); *John v MGN Ltd* [1997] QB 586, 618–19; cf the more liberal position which prevails in Australia: *Uren v John Fairfax & Sons Pty Ltd* (1966) 117 CLR 118, 138, 143, 154, 160; *Selecta Homes and Building Co Pty Ltd v Advertiser-News Weekend Publishing Co Pty Ltd* [2001] SASC 140, paras 87–8, 186; cf *Herald & Weekly Times Ltd v Popovic* [2003] VSCA 161, para 442.

defendant and others from engaging in similar conduct, and to mark the court's disapproval of the conduct.[39]

There is some doubt as to whether, for the purposes of exemplary damages, the state of mind of an employee or agent should be imputed to his or her employer or principal.

In *Thompson v Commissioner of Police of the Metropolis*,[40] a false imprisonment and malicious prosecution case, the Court of Appeal ordered the defendant, who was vicariously liable for the conduct of a number of police officers, to pay exemplary damages to the plaintiff.

In *Kuddus v Chief Constable of Leicestershire Constabulary*, however, the House of Lords reserved for future consideration whether exemplary damages should be available in cases where a defendant's liability is purely vicarious.[41] The only member of the House to give the matter detailed consideration, Lord Scott, opined provisionally that there was 'no room for an award of exemplary damages against an individual whose alleged liability is vicarious only and who has not done anything that constitutes punishable behaviour',[42] and that 'vicarious punishment, via an award of exemplary damages, is contrary to principle and should be rejected'.[43]

Scotland and New South Wales

Exemplary damages are not available under Scots law[44] or under the law of New South Wales.[45]

Application to the Internet

Exemplary damages awards might be made in appropriate cases where claimants are defamed in e-mail messages, bulletin board postings, or web pages, where the effect has been to cause substantial damage to their reputations in a number

21.13

21.14

---

[39] See eg *Broome v Cassell & Co Ltd* [1972] AC 1027, 1089 (Lord Reid), 1063 (Lord Hailsham), 1095 (Lord Morris), 1118 (Lord Wilberforce), 1121–2 (Lord Diplock); *John v MGN Ltd* [1997] QB 586; *Amalgamated Television Services Pty Ltd v Marsden (No 2)* (2003) 57 NSWLR 338.

[40] [1998] QB 498.

[41] [2002] 2 AC 122, 135, 140–1, 146, 153, 164.

[42] ibid, 162.

[43] ibid, 163. See also 153 (Lord Hutton): 'Lord Scott of Foscote has developed a powerful argument against the awarding of exemplary damages on the basis of vicarious liability.'

[44] *Stein v Beaverbrook Newspapers Ltd* 1968 SC 272, 278; *Winter v News Scotland Ltd* 1991 SLT 828.

[45] Defamation Act 1974 (NSW), s 46(3)(a). Damages are not to be affected by malice or other state of mind of the publisher at the time of publication, except so far as that malice or other state of mind affects the harm suffered by the defamed person: ibid, s 46(3)(b).

of countries, and where the defendant knew or ought to have known that the imputations published were false.[46] Exemplary damages will not be awarded in England, however, unless 'the defendant's conduct has been calculated by him to make a profit for himself which may well exceed the compensation payable to the claimant'.[47]

Exemplary damages will only be available against Internet intermediaries in the most extreme of cases. Ordinarily, even where an Internet intermediary knows that outrageous material is stored on its servers, and does nothing to disable access to or remove that material, it will be difficult or impossible to establish that the intermediary is motivated by a desire for profit.

E. Other Matters

Human Rights Act 1998 (UK)

21.15 Section 12 of the Human Rights Act 1998 (UK) ('the HRA') requires United Kingdom courts, in all defamation actions, to have particular regard to the importance of the right in Article 10 of the European Convention on Human Rights to freedom of expression.[48] The awarding of damages in a defamation action may affect the exercise of that right, if the amount awarded is disproportionate to the legitimate aim of compensating the claimant for a damaged reputation.[49] Where the claimant is a corporation which has not established that it suffered any financial loss by reason of the defamatory publication, even a modest award of damages may violate Article 10.[50]

Where defamation proceedings concern the publication of journalistic, literary, or artistic material, or conduct connected with such material, the court must also consider, among other things, the extent to which it would be in the public interest for the material to be published.[51] A large damages award will therefore be less justified in a case concerning the publication of material which is in the public interest, than in a case concerning the publication of an individual's private details, particularly where those details have not previously been made public.[52]

---

[46] See eg *Reichmann v Berlin* (Ontario Superior Court of Justice, Sachs J, 8 July 2002), paras 10, 18; *Vaquero Energy Ltd v Weir* (2004) 352 AR 191 (Alberta Court of Queen's Bench), paras 18, 26; *Barrick Gold Corporation v Lopehandia* (2004) 71 OR (3d) 416, paras 62, 64.

[47] *Rookes v Barnard* [1964] AC 1129, 1226.

[48] See para 20.07.

[49] eg *Tolstoy Miloslavsky v United Kingdom* (1995) 20 EHRR 442.

[50] *Steel and Morris v United Kingdom* (European Court of Human Rights, 15 February 2005). See para 30.28.

[51] Human Rights Act 1998 (UK), s 12(4)(a)(ii).

[52] ibid, s 12(4)(a)(i), (b); *Douglas v Hello! Ltd* [2001] QB 967, 994–5 (Brooke LJ).

Mitigation of damages

Apology

At common law, evidence of an apology by the defendant is admissible in mitigation of damages.[53]

21.16

The common law is also reflected by legislation in England and Northern Ireland, and in all Australian jurisdictions except New South Wales.[54] Where the statutory right is relied upon, however, the apology must have been made or offered before the commencement of the action or, in cases where the action was commenced before there was the opportunity of making or offering the apology, at the earliest opportunity afterwards.

In all cases, the apology must generally be a full and frank withdrawal of the defamatory imputations if it is to be effective in lowering the defendant's liability.[55] An immediate apology is more likely to reduce the extent of the injury to the claimant than an apology tendered at the door of the court.[56]

Damages already recovered

In the United Kingdom, and in all Australian jurisdictions except Western Australia, damages may also be mitigated where the claimant has already recovered damages, or has received or agreed to receive compensation, in respect of any other publication of matter to the same purport or effect.[57] In Victoria, Queensland, and Tasmania, this rule only operates in actions for defamatory material in a newspaper or periodical;[58] in South Australia it operates only in actions concerning libel.[59]

21.17

---

[53] *Smith v Harrison* (1856) 1 F & F 565; 175 ER 854; *Morrison v John Ritchie and Company* (1902) 4 F 645, 652; *David Syme & Co Ltd v Mather* [1977] VR 516, 528; *Fairbairn v John Fairfax and Sons Ltd* [1977] 21 ACTR 1, 5–7. The fact that a defendant made an offer of amends under the Defamation Act 1996 (UK), ss 2–4 may also be relied on in mitigation of damages in a case where the offer is not accepted, or where the defendant relies on some other defence, or pleads no defence at all: Defamation Act 1996 (UK), s 4(5); see para 13.01.

[54] Libel Act 1843, s 1; Defamation Act 1889 (Qld), s 21; Civil Liability Act 1936 (SA), s 9; Defamation Act 1957 (Tas), s 22; Wrongs Act 1958 (Vic), s 6; Libel Act 1843 (Imp) (applicable in WA); Civil Law (Wrongs) Act 2002 (ACT), s 131; Defamation Act 1938 (NT), s 8.

[55] *Risk Allah Beh v Johnstone* (1868) 18 LT 620, 621.

[56] *Kiam v Neil (No 2)* [1996] EMLR 493, 509.

[57] Defamation Act 1952 (UK), s 12 (England and Scotland); Defamation Act (Northern Ireland) 1955, s 12; Defamation Act 1974 (NSW), s 48; Defamation Act 1889 (Qld), s 24; Civil Liability Act 1936 (SA), s 11; Defamation Act 1957 (Tas), s 25; Wrongs Act 1958 (Vic), s 12; Civil Law (Wrongs) Act 2002 (ACT), s 135; Defamation Act 1938 (NT), s 10.

[58] Defamation Act 1889 (Qld), s 24 ('a periodical'); Defamation Act 1957 (Tas), s 25 ('a periodical'); Wrongs Act 1958 (Vic), s 12 ('any newspaper'). As to whether the rule might apply to online editions of newspapers and periodicals, see para 13.08 (n 32).

[59] Civil Liability Act 1936 (SA), s 11.

By legislation in the United Kingdom, and in all Australian jurisdictions except Western Australia, Victoria, and the Australian Capital Territory, evidence is also admissible in mitigation of damages that the claimant has brought other proceedings for damages in respect of any other publication of matter to the same purport or effect.[60]

Bad reputation

21.18 Evidence that the claimant had a bad general reputation at the time of publication is admissible in mitigation of damages.[61] The evidence must, however, relate to the claimant's general reputation and not to specific acts of misconduct. The evidence must relate to the relevant area or sector of the claimant's reputation.[62] Although evidence of specific acts of misconduct may not be adduced, evidence of relevant criminal convictions will be admissible, on the basis that they give 'the best guide to [the claimant's] reputation and standing'.[63] The English authorities are to the effect that post-publication evidence of a bad reputation or of subsequent criminal convictions is not admissible in mitigation of damages.[64] Evidence of rumours that the imputations borne by the offending publication are true is not admissible,[65] nor is evidence of other publications bearing the same imputations.[66]

In *Burstein v Times Newspapers Ltd*, the Court of Appeal took the view that English courts have a wide discretion to exclude admissible evidence tending to mitigate damages in the interests of efficient case management.[67]

---

[60] Defamation Act 1952 (UK), s 12 (England and Scotland); Defamation Act (Northern Ireland) 1955, s 12; Defamation Act 1974 (NSW), s 48; Defamation Act 1889 (Qld), s 24; Civil Liability Act 1936 (SA), s 11; Defamation Act 1957 (Tas), s 25; Defamation Act 1938 (NT), s 10.

[61] *Scott v Sampson* (1882) 8 QBD 491, 503.

[62] *Plato Films Ltd v Speidel* [1961] AC 1090, 1131, 1140; *Goody v Odhams Press Ltd* [1967] 1 QB 333, 341; *Morosi v Mirror Newspapers Ltd* [1977] 2 NSWLR 749, 801; *O'Hogan v Nationwide News Pty Ltd* (2001) 53 NSWLR 89; *Australian Broadcasting Corporation v McBride* (2001) 53 NSWLR 430, 435.

[63] *Goody v Odhams Press Ltd* [1967] 1 QB 333, 341; *Pamplin v Express Newspapers Ltd (No 2)* [1988] 1 All ER 282, 286–7; *Jones v Pollard* [1997] EMLR 233, 250–1; *Burstein v Times Newspapers Ltd* [2001] 1 WLR 579. See also *Plato Films Ltd v Speidel* [1961] AC 1090, 1023–4, 1140–2, 1147. The admissibility of criminal convictions is facilitated in England by s 13 of the Civil Evidence Act 1968 (UK), and in Australia by the Evidence Act 1995 (Cth), s 157 (which applies to proceedings in all Australian courts by reason of s 5).

[64] *Thompson v Nye* (1850) 16 QBD 175, 180; 117 ER 846, 847; *Associated Newspapers Ltd v Dingle* [1964] AC 371, 399; *Pamplin v Express Newspapers Ltd (No 2)* [1988] 1 All ER 282, 286–7. More recent authorities in Australia and New Zealand suggest that such evidence is admissible: *Television New Zealand Ltd v Quinn* [1996] 3 NZLR 24, 65–7; *Middendorp Electric Co Pty Ltd v Sonneveld* [2001] VSC 312, paras 338–9; *Australian Broadcasting Corporation v McBride* (2001) 53 NSWLR 430, 442–4, 447–8; cf *Rochfort v John Fairfax & Sons Ltd* [1972] 1 NSWLR 16, 23.

[65] *Scott v Sampson* (1882) 8 QBD 491, 503–4; *Plato Films Ltd v Speidel* [1961] AC 1090, 1136.

[66] *Associated Newspapers Ltd v Dingle* [1964] AC 371, 405–6, 412, 417–18; cf para 21.17.

[67] [2001] 1 WLR 579, applying Civil Procedure Rules, r 32.1.

It was alleged in *Godfrey v Demon Internet Ltd* that the plaintiff had provoked the posting of defamatory bulletin board messages of and concerning him by himself posting:

> deliberately provocative, offensive, obnoxious and frequently puerile comments about other countries, their citizens and cultures . . . with a view to provoking others to trade insults which he can then claim are defamatory and seek to use as the basis for bringing vexatious libel actions against them and against access or service providers.[68]

Morland J held that the fact of the allegedly provocative postings was relevant and able to be taken into account in assessing the damage suffered by the plaintiff. The postings did not fall within the prohibition on adducing evidence of specific acts of misconduct, because they were 'causally connected to the libel sued upon'. The defendant was entitled to assert that the action was not brought bona fide for the purpose of vindicating the plaintiff's reputation and recovering compensation for true injury to his reputation and feelings.

Appellate interference with jury awards

United Kingdom

In England, as a result of the decision in *Rantzen v Mirror Group Newspapers Ltd*, the Court of Appeal has lowered the previous standard for interference with the level of damages awarded by a jury.[69] The court will now subject large awards of damages to 'searching scrutiny' and substitute an award of damages of its own choosing where it concludes that no reasonable jury could have thought that the damages it awarded were necessary to compensate the claimant and to re-establish his or her reputation.[70]   **21.19**

In Scotland, where an award of damages is excessive, the usual remedy is the grant of a new trial limited to the question of damages.[71]

Australia

Appellate courts in Australia will be slow to interfere with the amount of   **21.20**

---

[68] *Godfrey v Demon Internet Ltd (No 2)* (English High Court, Morland J, 23 April 1999). Other aspects of this case are discussed in paras 15.03–15.07.

[69] [1994] QB 670.

[70] ibid, 692. See also *John v MGN Ltd* [1997] QB 586; *Campbell v News Group Newspapers Ltd* [2002] EMLR 43; *Kiam v MGN Ltd* [2003] QB 281; *Grobbelaar v News Group Newspapers Ltd* [2003] EMLR 1. As to the Court of Appeal's power to substitute an award of damages, see Courts and Legal Services Act 1990, s 8(2); Civil Procedure Rules, r 52.10(3).

[71] Court of Session Act 1988 (UK), ss 29, 30; *Boal v Scottish Catholic Printing Company, Ltd* 1908 SC 667; *Winter v News Scotland Ltd* 1991 SLT 828. See also *Baigent v British Broadcasting Corporation* 2001 SC 281.

damages awarded by juries,[72] although in the leading High Court authority, the court appeared to adopt the broader test of whether 'the amount awarded is so high or so low that it is outside the range of what could reasonably be regarded as appropriate to the circumstances of the case'.[73]

Contribution

21.21 By legislation in the United Kingdom and each Australian jurisdiction, a defendant to defamation proceedings may seek contribution against any other person who is also a publisher of the same material.[74] The extent of the contribution is to be such as the court considers just and equitable, having regard to the extent of the person's responsibility for the damage in question.[75] The court may exempt any person from liability to make contribution, or order that the contribution to be recovered from any person should amount to a complete indemnity.[76] In the United Kingdom, indemnity agreements from one publisher to another in respect of the same material are lawful, except where at the time of the publication the indemnified publisher knows that the matter is defamatory and does not reasonably believe there is a good defence to any action brought upon it.[77]

---

[72] *Coyne v Citizen Finance Ltd* (1991) 172 CLR 211, 228, 238–9; cf 215–16; cf also *Carson v John Fairfax & Sons Ltd* (1993) 178 CLR 44, 59.

[73] *Carson v John Fairfax & Sons Ltd* (1993) 178 CLR 44, 59 (Mason CJ, Deane, Dawson, and Gaudron JJ), quoting a passage from the dissenting judgment of Mason CJ and Deane JJ in *Coyne v Citizen Finance Ltd* (1991) 172 CLR 211, 215; cf *Rogers v Nationwide News Pty Ltd* (2003) 201 ALR 184, para 64 (Hayne J): 'the question for the appellate court is whether the result at which the trial judge [or jury] arrived *bespeaks* error'.

[74] Civil Liability (Contribution) Act 1978 (UK), s 1 (England and Northern Ireland); Law Reform (Miscellaneous Provisions) (Scotland) Act 1940, s 3; Law Reform (Miscellaneous Provisions) Act 1946 (NSW), s 5; Law Reform Act 1995 (Qld), s 6; Law Reform (Contributory Negligence and Apportionment of Liability) Act 2001 (SA), s 6(1); Tortfeasors and Contributory Negligence Act 1954 (Tas), s 3; Wrongs Act 1958 (Vic), s 23B; Law Reform (Contributory Negligence and Tortfeasors' Contribution) Act 1947 (WA), s 7; Law Reform (Miscellaneous Provisions) Act 1955 (ACT), s 11; Law Reform (Miscellaneous Provisions) Act 1956 (NT), s 12.

[75] Civil Liability (Contribution) Act 1978 (UK), s 2(1) (England and Northern Ireland); Law Reform (Miscellaneous Provisions) (Scotland) Act 1940, s 3; Law Reform (Miscellaneous Provisions) Act 1946 (NSW), s 5(2); Law Reform Act 1995 (Qld), s 7; Law Reform (Contributory Negligence and Apportionment of Liability) Act 2001 (SA), s 6(5); Tortfeasors and Contributory Negligence Act 1954 (Tas), s 3(2); Wrongs Act 1958 (Vic), s 24(2); Law Reform (Contributory Negligence and Tortfeasors' Contribution) Act 1947 (WA), s 7(2); Law Reform (Miscellaneous Provisions) Act 1955 (ACT), s 12; Law Reform (Miscellaneous Provisions) Act 1956 (NT), s 13.

[76] Civil Liability (Contribution) Act 1978 (UK), s 2(2) (England and Northern Ireland); Law Reform (Miscellaneous Provisions) Act 1946 (NSW), s 5(2); Law Reform Act 1995 (Qld), s 7; Law Reform (Contributory Negligence and Apportionment of Liability) Act 2001 (SA), s 6(7); Tortfeasors and Contributory Negligence Act 1954 (Tas), s 3(2); Wrongs Act 1958 (Vic), s 24(2); Law Reform (Contributory Negligence and Tortfeasors' Contribution) Act 1947 (WA), s 7(2); Law Reform (Miscellaneous Provisions) Act 1955 (ACT), s 12; Law Reform (Miscellaneous Provisions) Act 1956 (NT), s 13.

[77] Defamation Act 1952 (UK), s 11 (England and Scotland); Defamation Act (Northern Ireland) 1955, s 11.

In apportioning liability, the court will have regard to the extent to which each **21.22**
tortfeasor is culpable, and to the relative importance of the acts of each tortfeasor in causing the damage suffered by the claimant. Put another way, the court
will make an apportionment based on who is really to blame.[78]

In a case where a defamed person successfully sued both the author of defama- **21.23**
tory material and the intermediary on whose computer system the defamatory
material was stored,[79] the author's culpability would ordinarily be expected to
exceed that of the intermediary. It would be expected in such a case that the
intermediary's contribution would be limited, taking into account factors such
as when the intermediary discovered that its computer system was being used to
host, cache, or carry defamatory material, and what steps the intermediary took
to remove or disable access to the offending material.

As a general rule, the relative importance of the acts of a content host intermediary in causing the damage suffered by a defamed person would be expected to
exceed that of a mere conduit intermediary. In a case where both intermediaries
are liable, one would expect damages to be apportioned largely to the content
host.

Joint publishers are, however, jointly and severally liable to the claimant for **21.24**
the whole of the damage suffered by reason of a defamatory publication.[80]
Claimants may accordingly enforce the whole of their judgments against any
defendant found to be liable in respect of a particular publication.[81]

---

[78] *Croston v Vaughan* [1938] 1 KB 540, 565; *Davies v Swan Motor Co (Swansea) Ltd* [1949] 2
KB 291, 313, 326–7; *Stapley v Gypsum Mines Ltd* [1953] AC 663, 682; *Smith v Dyer* [1949]
SASR 187, 194–5; *Adams v Associated Newspapers Ltd* [1999] EMLR 325; *Rowan v Cornwall (No
7)* [2003] SASC 49.
[79] ie assuming that no defences were available to the intermediary of the kind outlined in Pt IV.
[80] *London Association for Protection of Trade v Greenlands, Ltd* [1916] 2 AC 15, 31; *Broome v
Cassell & Co Ltd* [1972] AC 1027, 1063–4; *Bryanston Finance Ltd v de Vries* [1975] QB 703, 730–
1; *XL Petroleum (NSW) Pty Ltd v Caltex Oil (Australia) Pty Ltd* (1985) 155 CLR 448, 459–60,
466; *Thompson v Australian Capital Television Pty Ltd* (1996) 186 CLR 574, 603–4; *Television
New Zealand Ltd v Ah Koy* [2002] 2 NZLR 616.
[81] cf, in Queensland, Civil Liability Act 2003 (Qld), s 30.

22

VICARIOUS LIABILITY

A. General Principles

Introduction

In accordance with usual tortious principles, employers are generally liable for **22.01** the publication of defamatory material by their employees, if the publication is made in the course of the employee's employment.[1] A principal is liable for the publication of defamatory material by an agent, if the agent has acted within the scope of his or her authority.[2] A stricter position appears to obtain in Scotland, where an employer is only liable for what an employee says on instructions, or as necessary for the proper discharge of his or her duties.[3]

In medieval times, English law held masters strictly responsible for the actions of **22.02** their servants.[4] By the first half of the nineteenth century, the common law had

---

[1] *Citizens' Life Assurance Company, Ltd v Brown* [1904] AC 423 (PC), 427–8; *Colonial Mutual Life Assurance Society Ltd v Producers and Citizens Co-operative Assurance Company of Australia Ltd* (1931) 46 CLR 41, 46–7, 50; *Coulthard v South Australia* (1995) 63 SASR 531, 536, 539–40.

[2] Patrick Milmo and WVH Rogers, *Gatley on Libel and Slander* (10th ed, 2003) ('Gatley') para 8.29; *Webb v Bloch* (1928) 41 CLR 331, 359, 364–6. An agent for these purposes means a person acting in right of another, with his or her authority: see *Colonial Mutual Life Assurance Society Ltd v Producers and Citizens Co-operative Assurance Company of Australia Ltd* (1931) 46 CLR 41, 50.

[3] *Mandelston v North British Railway Company* 1917 SC 442, 446.

[4] See generally PS Atiyah, *Vicarious Liability in the Law of Torts* (1967); OW Holmes, 'Agency' (1891) 4 *Harvard Law Review* 345, 364; John Wigmore, 'Responsibility for Tortious Acts: Its History' (1894) 7 *Harvard Law Review* 315, 383; RFV Heuston and RA Buckley, *Salmond and Heuston on the Law of Torts* (21st edn, 1996) ('Salmond') 430–1.

developed the more flexible concept of vicarious liability: the principle that employers are responsible for all torts committed by their employees in the course of their employment. The rationale underlying the concept is perhaps dimly revealed through the related maxims *respondeat superior*, the superior should answer, and *qui facit per alium facit* per se, those who act through others are deemed to act in person. More satisfying, however, is the honest admission of Lord Pearce in *Imperial Chemical Industries Ltd v Shatwell*, that '[t]he doctrine of vicarious liability has not grown from any very clear, logical or legal principle but from social convenience and rough justice'.[5]

22.03 Formulations of vicarious liability are broadly similar in English, Australian, and American law.[6] In each country the authorities fall mainly within two categories: cases concerning the outer limits of the relationship of employer and employee, and cases concerning whether unauthorized acts by an employee were nonetheless committed in the course of employment.

The employer–employee relationship

22.04 An employee is

> any person employed by another to do work for him on the terms that he, the servant, is to be subject to the control and direction of his employer in respect of the manner in which his work is to be done.[7]

A distinction is drawn between employees and independent contractors. As a general rule, vicarious liability applies where there is a contract *of* service, but not where there is a contract *for* services. Where in the eyes of the community the person would be regarded as a part of the employer's own working staff, he or she is likely to be an employee.

The principal indication of an employer–employee relationship is actual control by the employer, or the right to control the conduct of the employee in the performance of his or her duties. Also relevant are factors including the nature of the occupation, whether such work is customarily supervised by an employer,

---

[5] [1965] AC 656, 685. The competing rationales are exhaustively analysed in Gummow J's judgment in *Scott v Davis* (2000) 204 CLR 333. See also Lord Wilberforce's opinion in *Launchbury v Morgans* [1973] AC 127.

[6] Salmond (n 4 above) 430–66; W Page Keeton (ed), *Prosser and Keeton on the Law of Torts* (5th edn, 1984) ('Prosser and Keeton'), §§69–70; John Fleming, *The Law of Torts* (9th edn, 1998), 409–38.

[7] Salmond (n 4 above) 434, approved in *Hewitt v Bonvin* [1940] 1 KB 188, 191–2 as a definition which could 'hardly be bettered'. The American Law Institute, *Restatement (Second) of the Law of Agency* ('Second Agency Restatement'), §220(1), defines a servant as 'a person employed to perform services in the affairs of another and who with respect to the physical conduct in the performance of the services is subject to the other's control or right to control'.

the level of skill required, who supplies the place, materials, and equipment for the work, the duration of the work, and the method of payment.[8]

Scope of the employment

Most obviously, employers will be vicariously liable for the acts of their   **22.05** employees if those acts are authorized by the employer. Vicarious liability may still attach, however, even in relation to unauthorized and unlawful acts, if those acts are 'so connected with the authorized act as to be a mode of doing it'.[9] In American parlance, vicarious liability will attach to unauthorized acts of an employee if those acts:

> are so closely connected with what the servant is employed to do, and so fairly and reasonably incidental to it, that they may be regarded as methods, even though quite improper ones, of carrying out the objectives of the employment.[10]

The act is likely to be in the scope of the employee's employment if it 'is of the kind he is employed to perform', 'occurs substantially within the authorized time and space limits', and 'is actuated, at least in part, by a purpose to serve the master'.[11] Conversely, the conduct will not be within the scope of employment if it is 'different in kind from that authorized, far beyond the authorized time or space limits, or too little actuated by a purpose to serve the master'.[12]

One colourful Australian case illustrating the scope of the employment relation-   **22.06** ship is *Bugge v Brown*.[13] Brown was a cattle grazier. He supplied his employee, Winter, with raw meat each day for his lunch, and instructed Winter to cook the meat at a certain house on the land. Winter lit a fire elsewhere on the land, closer to where he was working, and negligently caused a fire which damaged the plaintiff's adjoining land. The High Court held that Brown was vicariously liable for Winter's negligence. Higgins J explained the basis for his decision as follows:

> The precise terms of the authority are not the criterion of liability: the function, the operation, the class of act to be done by the employee, is the criterion— whatever be the instructions as to the time, the place, or the manner of doing the act. In other words, the employer is liable for damage resulting from the negligent use of a fire on his land if he has sanctioned the lighting of the fire anywhere on his property for the occasion.

---

[8] Second Agency Restatement (n 7 above) §220(2); Prosser and Keeton (n 6 above) §70; Salmond (n 4 above) 435–8; Fleming (n 6 above) 413–20.

[9] Salmond (n 4 above) 443, approved in many cases, including *Keppel Bus Co Ltd v Ahmad* [1974] 1 WLR 1082, 1084.

[10] Prosser and Keeton (n 6 above) §70.

[11] Second Agency Restatement (n 7 above) §228(1).

[12] ibid, §228(2).

[13] (1919) 26 CLR 110. An American case with analogous facts, and reaching the same result, is *Ohio Farmers Insurance Co v Norman*, 594 P 2d 1026 (CA Az, 1979).

22.07   In short, as a general rule, where an unlawful act is performed by an employee during business hours, and has some connection with the employer's business, the employer will be vicariously liable for that act. It seems that the publication of defamatory material by an employee will not fall outside the scope of his or her employment solely by reason that the employee was actuated by malice.[14] The rule of thumb, however, is that the employer will not be vicariously liable for unlawful acts of employees who are not on the employer's business, but are 'going on a frolic of [their] own'.[15]

22.08   An example of such a frolic appears in *General Engineering Services Ltd v Kingston & St Andrew Corporation*.[16] Employees of the defendant, a fire service, delayed their journey to the scene of a fire for the purpose of pressuring the employer in connection with an industrial dispute. The plaintiff's building was destroyed as a result of the delay. The employer was held not to be vicariously liable, because the conduct of the employees 'was the very negation of carrying out some act authorized by the employer, albeit in a wrongful and unauthorized mode'.[17]

The effect of employer prohibitions

22.09   It is clear in each of the United Kingdom, Australia, and the United States that edicts by employers prohibiting employees from engaging in particular conduct may not protect the employer from being vicariously liable where the employee breaches the edict.

The leading example of this proposition is *Limpus v London General Omnibus Company*.[18] The defendant bus company had expressly prohibited its employee

---

[14] Gatley (n 2 above) para 8.32.

[15] The phrase derives from Parke B in *Joel v Morison* (1834) 6 C & P 501, 503; 172 ER 1338, 1339.

[16] [1989] 1 WLR 69.

[17] Another example of the same principle is *Harrison v Dean Witter Reynolds, Inc*, 715 F Supp 1425 (ND Il, 1989). In that case, two brokers had solicited money under false pretences from an investor. The investor sued the brokerage firm. The court held that the brokerage firm was not vicariously liable, because the illegal activities of the brokers were not specifically authorized by the firm and were not within the scope of their employment. The court noted in particular that the investor was not a customer of the firm itself, and had not dealt with the firm in the course of the transactions. The relationship with the brokers occurred primarily outside the firm's offices and there was no evidence that the brokers intended to benefit the firm through their illegal activities. See also *Rusnack v Giant Food, Inc*, 337 A 2d 445 (CA Md, 1975): the defendant business was sued for assault and battery committed by an employee security guard, as well as for false arrest and malicious prosecution. The court held that the business was not vicariously liable for the acts of its security guard, which on the facts were in no way actuated by a purpose of serving the defendant. The security guard was off-duty, not ordinarily employed at the particular store, and was shopping for personal items at the time of the incident.

[18] (1862) 1 H & C 526; 158 ER 993.

drivers from racing with or obstructing other buses. In defiance of that prohibition, an employee pulled across the road in front of a bus owned by one of the defendant's competitors, causing a collision which overturned the competitor's bus. The defendant was held vicariously liable for the driver's conduct, which was merely an unauthorized mode or method of performing that which he was employed to do, namely drive a bus.[19]

A defamation case illustrating the point that employer prohibitions may not be effective in avoiding vicarious liability is *Colonial Mutual Life Assurance Society Ltd v Producers and Citizens Co-operative Assurance Company of Australia Ltd.*[20] The defendant was an insurance company sued in respect of defamatory statements made by one of its representatives, a Mr Ridley, in the course of canvassing new customers. Ridley had a written agreement with the defendant by which he undertook that he would: **22.10**

> not in any circumstances whatsoever use language or write anything respecting any person or institution which may have the effect of reflecting upon the character, integrity or conduct of such person or institution, or which may tend to bring the same into disrepute or discredit.

A majority of the Australian High Court held that this prohibition did not operate to prevent the defendant from being vicariously liable for Ridley's defamatory statements. Gavan Duffy CJ and Starke J said:

> The class of acts which Ridley was employed to do necessarily involved the use of arguments and statements for the purpose of persuading the public to effect policies of insurance with the defendant, and in pursuing that purpose he was authorized to speak, and in fact spoke, with the voice of the defendant. Consequently the defendant is liable for defamatory statements made by Ridley in the course of his canvass, though contrary to its direction.[21]

Where an employee is authorized as part of his or her employment to publish material via the Internet, such as by sending e-mail messages or bulletin board postings, or by uploading material to web sites, it thus seems likely that his or her employer will be vicariously liable if the employee publishes defamatory material with some connection to the employer's business, even if the employer has expressly prohibited the publication of defamatory material by employees. The employer will be unlikely to be liable, however, in respect of material with   **22.11**

---

[19] See also *Rose v Plenty* [1976] 1 All ER 97; *Lister v Hesley Hall Ltd* [2002] 1 AC 215 (school vicariously liable for acts of sexual abuse against pupils by a warden of the boarding house); Salmond (n 4 above) 446–7; cf *Twine v Bean's Express Ltd* [1946] 1 All ER 202.
[20] (1931) 46 CLR 41.
[21] ibid, 46–7. See also ibid, 50 (Dixon J), cf 64 (Evatt J), 72 (McTiernan J). American cases to the same general effect include *McLeod v Dean*, 270 F Supp 855 (SD NY, 1967); *Carter v Willert Home Products, Inc*, 714 SW 2d 506 (SC Mo, 1986); and *Aversa v United States*, 99 F 3d 1200 (1st cir, 1996); cf *Craig v Inveresk Paper Merchants* 1970 SLT (Notes) 50.

no connection to the employer's business, particularly if the material was uploaded in defiance of the employer's policy concerning employee use of the Internet at work.

Indemnities from employees

22.12   Absent a statutory prohibition, an employer who is vicariously liable for some misconduct by an employee may be entitled to claim an indemnity from the employee. In *Lister v Romford Ice & Cold Storage Co Ltd*, the House of Lords held that an indemnity may be available in cases involving mere negligence by an employee, as well as in cases where the employee's misconduct was intentional or reckless.[22] The right to an indemnity may be available as a matter of contract,[23] or under legislation providing for rights of contribution and indemnity.[24] It seems, however, that no right of indemnity applies where the employee, although acting within the scope of employment, is not carrying out the duties for which he or she was employed.[25]

As a matter of practicality, indemnities are rarely claimed by employers from their employees, having regard to the risks of industrial retaliation, the incidence of insurance, and the likelihood that the employee would in any event be unable to meet the indemnity.

In Australia, legislation prohibits employers' insurers from being subrogated to the rights of the employer against the employee where the misconduct of the employee was not 'serious or wilful'.[26] In some Australian jurisdictions, employers are prohibited by legislation from seeking or claiming indemnities from employees, at least in cases where the employee does not hold insurance covering liability for the misconduct.[27]

Exemplary damages

22.13   The law is unsettled as to whether employers and principals whose liability is wholly vicarious are to be imputed with the state of mind of their employees or agents for the purposes of the awarding of exemplary damages.[28]

---

[22] [1957] AC 555; cf *Morris v Ford Motor Co Ltd* [1973] QB 792; *FAI General Insurance Co Ltd v AR Griffiths & Sons Pty Ltd* (1997) 71 ALJR 651.

[23] ibid. The contractual right arises because of an implied term of employment that employees will not intentionally or negligently cause damage to the employer.

[24] See paras 21.21–21.24.

[25] *Harvey v RG O'Dell Ltd* [1958] 2 QB 78.

[26] Insurance Contracts Act 1984 (Cth), s 66.

[27] See Employees Liability Act 1991 (NSW), s 3; *McGrath v Fairfield Municipal Council* (1985) 156 CLR 672; Civil Liability Act 1936 (SA), s 59; Law Reform (Miscellaneous Provisions) Act 1956 (NT), s 22A.

[28] See para 21.12.

Queensland and Tasmania

Vicarious liability principles have been modified by defamation legislation in Queensland and Tasmania.[29] In those jurisdictions, employers are not liable for defamatory matter contained in books, pamphlets, print, writing, or other things sold by a servant, unless the employer authorized the sale and:

22.14

- knew the book, pamphlet, print, writing, or other thing contained defamatory matter; or
- in the case of a number or part of a periodical, knew that defamatory matter was habitually or frequently published in that periodical.

'Periodical' means a newspaper, review, magazine, or other writing that is published periodically.[30]

The Queensland and Tasmanian provisions apply only to the sale by employees of written material. These provisions will have limited application to Internet publications, which do not ordinarily involve such sales.

B. Direct Liability

Even where employees or agents have engaged in frolics of their own, such that employers or principals would not be vicariously liable for their unlawful conduct, employers and principals may nonetheless be directly liable for that conduct, by reason of having provided employees or agents with the means of accessing the Internet. Employers and principals who provide their employees and agents with Internet access may be intermediaries in the communication of material via the Internet by their employees, akin in many respects to commercial Internet service providers or content hosts. They may have the ability to control and supervise the material which is sent to and from their computer systems. They will frequently have policies containing a broad right to do so.

22.15

The circumstances in which intermediaries might be directly liable as publishers of defamatory material hosted, cached, or carried by them, but which they did not create, is the subject of Part IV.

In Australia, the limited statutory defence for intermediaries in clause 91 of Schedule 5 to the Broadcasting Services Act 1992 (Cth) may have the anomalous

22.16

---

[29] Defamation Act 1889 (Qld), s 27; Defamation Act 1957 (Tas), s 27.
[30] Defamation Act 1889 (Qld), s 3; Defamation Act 1957 (Tas), s 3. As to whether online newspapers and periodicals might fall within this definition, see para 13.08 (n 32).

and apparently unintended consequence of excluding ordinary principles of vicarious liability to the extent that they apply to 'Internet content' created by employees or agents and hosted or carried by employers or principals.[31]

---

[31] See para 19.26.

23

RECOGNITION AND ENFORCEMENT OF JUDGMENTS IN FOREIGN COUNTRIES

A. General Principles

In many cases where defamatory material is published via the Internet, the **23.01**
claimant and possible defendants such as the author of the publication or
intermediaries involved in its communication may be located in different countries. For example, web pages maintained by English individuals or companies
will often be located on servers operated in the United States by American ISPs
or content hosts. Claimants contemplating the commencement of defamation
proceedings in the United Kingdom or Australia against foreign defendants may
need to consider not just the operation of jurisdiction and choice of law rules,[1]
but also whether any judgment obtained in a United Kingdom or Australian
court will be enforceable against the foreign defendant in a jurisdiction in which
that defendant has assets.

The usual mechanism for the enforcement of judgments in foreign jurisdictions **23.02**
is for the claimant to apply to register and then enforce the judgment in the
foreign jurisdiction, in accordance with the law of that jurisdiction.

Judgments of United Kingdom courts are readily registrable and enforceable in **23.03**

---

[1] See Part VI, chapters 25–29.

Member States of the European Union. Council Regulation 44/2001 of 22 December 2000 on jurisdiction and the enforcement of judgments in civil and commercial matters ('the Brussels Regulation')[2] contains detailed provisions on the recognition and enforcement of judgments as between all Member States other than Denmark.[3] United Kingdom judgments are registrable and enforceable in Denmark in accordance with the provisions of the Brussels Convention on jurisdiction and the enforcement of judgments in civil and commercial matters.

United Kingdom judgments can be registered and enforced in Iceland, Norway, and Switzerland in accordance with the provisions of the Lugano Convention on jurisdiction and the enforcement of judgments in civil and commercial matters.

The registration and enforcement of judgments of United Kingdom courts in other countries, and the registration and enforcement of Australian judgments outside Australia, is more complicated. The position will vary according to the law of each foreign jurisdiction.[4] Judgments of United Kingdom and Australian courts in defamation proceedings are, however, enforceable without any great difficulty in countries with which the United Kingdom and Australia have reciprocal arrangements.[5]

---

[2] [2001] OJ L12/1. Member States have their own domestic legislation governing the registration and enforcement of judgments. In the United Kingdom, see the Civil Jurisdiction and Judgments Act 1982 (UK).

[3] Brussels Regulation, Arts 32–56.

[4] By way of example, judgments of most United Kingdom courts are enforceable in Australia in accordance with the Foreign Judgments Act 1991 (Cth), s 6. Judgments of superior Australian courts may be registered in the United Kingdom in accordance with the Foreign Judgments (Reciprocal Enforcement) Act 1933 (UK), s 2.

[5] The United Kingdom has reciprocal arrangements for the enforcement of judgments with Australia, Austria, Canada, India, the Isle of Man, Israel, Italy, Germany, Guernsey, Jersey, the Netherlands, Norway, Pakistan, Suriname, and Tonga: see the Orders in Council made pursuant to the Foreign Judgments (Reciprocal Enforcement) Act 1933 (UK), s 1. Australia has similar arrangements: see Foreign Judgments Act 1991 (Cth), s 5(1); Foreign Judgments Regulations (Cth), reg 3, Sch. Typically, foreign countries with whom reciprocal arrangements exist reserve the right not to register foreign judgments where enforcement 'would be contrary to public policy' in the foreign jurisdiction: see eg Foreign Judgments (Reciprocal Enforcement) Act 1933 (UK), s 4(1)(a)(v); Foreign Judgments Act 1991 (Cth), s 7(2)(a)(xi); Reciprocal Enforcement of Judgments Act 1934 (New Zealand), s 6(1)(e). Judgments of United Kingdom and Australian superior courts in defamation proceedings would not ordinarily be contrary to public policy in those countries which continue to have defamation laws based on the English common law, such as Canada, Hong Kong, Ireland, Malaysia, New Zealand, and Singapore. For circumstances in which Canadian courts might decline to recognize foreign defamation judgments, see *Braintech, Inc v Kostiuk* (1999) 171 DLR (4th) 46.

B. Enforcement of Judgments in the United States

Introduction

Generally speaking, courts of the United States will, as a matter of discretion, **23.04** give recognition to and enforce judgments of foreign courts on the basis of the 'comity of nations', a concept arising out of international duty and convenience.[6] Comity will only require recognition and effect to be given, however, where the foreign laws and proceedings on which the judgment is based are consistent with American public policy.[7]

In two notable decisions, American courts refused to recognize judgments of English courts in defamation proceedings, on the basis of inconsistency between English defamation law and American public policy.

Bachchan v India Abroad Publications Inc

In *Bachchan v India Abroad Publications Inc*,[8] the Supreme Court of New York **23.05** County refused to recognize a judgment of the English High Court. The publication which gave rise to the English proceedings alleged that the plaintiff's bank account had been frozen by Swiss authorities because of a link between the plaintiff and a Swedish arms company. The Swedish arms company had previously been charged with paying kickbacks to obtain a large contract with the Indian government.

Fingerhood J noted that under English law, the plaintiff had not had to prove that the defamatory imputation borne by the publication was false. Rather, falsity of the defamatory imputation was presumed under English defamation law. By contrast, under American defamation law, the plaintiff would have had to establish, among other things, that the allegation in the publication was false.[9] According to Fingerhood J, the onus of proving falsity was on the plaintiff in American defamation law to avoid the 'chilling effect' which fear of liability might otherwise have on media defendants who publish speech on matters of public concern.[10] Fingerhood J concluded:

---

[6] *Hilton v Guyot*, 159 US 113 (1895), 163–4; *Laker Airways Ltd v Sabena, Belgian World Airlines*, 731 F 2d 909 (DC cir, 1984), 937–45; *Telnikoff v Matusevitch*, 702 A 2d 230 (CA Md, 1997), 236–7.

[7] See eg *Martens v Martens*, 31 NE 2d 489 (CA NY, 1940), 490; *Laker Airways Ltd v Sabena, Belgian World Airlines*, 731 F 2d 909 (DC cir, 1984), 937–8; *Telnikoff v Matusevitch*, 702 A 2d 230 (CA Md, 1997), 237. See also the Uniform Foreign-Money Judgments Recognition Acts of each American State.

[8] 585 NYS 2d 661 (SC NY, 1992).

[9] ibid, 664, citing *Philadelphia Newspapers, Inc v Hepps*, 475 US 767 (1986).

[10] ibid.

It is true that England and the United States share many common law principles of law. Nevertheless, a significant difference between the two jurisdictions lies in England's lack of an equivalent to the First Amendment to the United States Constitution. The protection to free speech and the press embodied in that amendment would be seriously jeopardized by the entry of foreign libel judgments granted pursuant to standards deemed appropriate in England but considered antithetical to the protections afforded the press by the US Constitution.[11]

Telnikoff v Matusevitch

23.06   *Bachchan v India Abroad Publications Inc* was followed by the Court of Appeals of Maryland in *Telnikoff v Matusevitch*.[12] Telnikoff had sued Matusevitch in the United Kingdom in relation to a letter published in the *Daily Telegraph* in which Matusevitch had, in effect, accused Telnikoff of spreading racialist views concerning the desirable ethnicity of broadcasters on the BBC's Russian Service.[13] Telnikoff was successful, and was awarded £240,000 by a jury in the English High Court.

A majority of the Maryland Court of Appeal noted that 'American and Maryland history reflects a public policy in favor of a much broader and more protective freedom of the press than ever provided for under English law.'[14] The court commented on a number of differences between Maryland defamation law and English defamation law, before noting:

> A comparison of English and present Maryland defamation law does not simply disclose a difference in one or two legal principles . . . Instead, present Maryland defamation law is totally different from English defamation law in virtually every significant respect. Moreover, the differences are rooted in historic and fundamental public policy differences concerning freedom of the press and speech.[15]

On the facts of the case, the majority concluded that in Maryland, 'Matusevitch's alleged defamatory language would, as a matter of law, be treated as "rhetorical hyperbole" in the course of rebuttal during a vigorous public debate.'[16] In the result, the majority held:

> The principles governing defamation actions under English law, which were applied to Telnikoff's libel suit, are so contrary to Maryland defamation law, and

---

[11]   585 NYS 2d 661 (SC NY, 1992), 665.

[12]   702 A 2d 230 (CA Md, 1997); affirmed without further reasons being given in *Matusevitch v Telnikoff*, 159 F 3d 636 (DC cir, 1998).

[13]   The United Kingdom proceeding reached the House of Lords: see *Telnikoff v Matusevitch* [1992] 2 AC 343.

[14]   *Telnikoff v Matusevitch*, 702 A 2d 230 (CA Md, 1997), 240 (Eldridge J).

[15]   ibid, 248.

[16]   ibid, 249.

to the policy of freedom of the press underlying Maryland law, that Telnikoff's judgment should be denied recognition under principles of comity.[17]

Yahoo!, Inc v LICRA

There have also been instances where defendants have sought declarations from American courts to the effect that foreign judgments are not or will not be enforceable in the United States on the grounds of incompatibility with American public policy.

23.07

A prominent example is *Yahoo!, Inc v LICRA*.[18] The case concerned a web site maintained by an American defendant, Yahoo, which offered Nazi memorabilia for sale. The sale of such memorabilia was prohibited in France by the Code Pénal, but was not prohibited by the law of the United States, or indeed the law of many other countries. In proceedings in France, Premier Vice-Président Gomez of the Tribunal de Grande Instance de Paris held that the French court had jurisdiction to grant an injunction to compel Yahoo and its French subsidiary to take any and all steps to prevent the web site from continuing to be accessible in France. The court was satisfied that the difficulties in preventing the web site from being accessed in France were not insurmountable.

23.08

Yahoo subsequently announced that it would cease all auctions of Nazi memorabilia and other material promoting 'hate groups' on its web sites, worldwide, and would enforce its ban using filtering software and a team of employees.

Despite that decision, Yahoo brought proceedings in California seeking a declaration that the French court's orders were 'neither cognizable nor enforceable' under the laws of the United States.

23.09

In granting the relief sought, Judge Fogel said:

> What is at issue here is whether it is consistent with the Constitution and laws of the United States for another nation to regulate speech by a United States resident within the United States on the basis that such speech can be accessed by Internet users in that nation. In a world in which ideas and information transcend borders and the Internet in particular renders the physical distance between speaker and audience virtually meaningless, the implications of this question go far beyond the facts of this case. The modern world is home to widely varied cultures with radically divergent value systems. There is little doubt that Internet users in the United States routinely engage in speech that violates, for example, China's laws against religious expression, the laws of various nations against advocacy of gender

---

[17] ibid.
[18] *Yahoo!, Inc v La Ligue Contre le Racisme et L'Antisémitisme*, 145 F Supp 2d 1168 (ND Ca, 2001) and ND Ca, Judge Fogel, 7 November 2001.

equality or homosexuality, or even the United Kingdom's restrictions on freedom of the press.[19]

Judge Fogel went on to say:

> Although France has the sovereign right to regulate what speech is permissible in France, this court may not enforce a foreign order that violates the protections of the United States Constitution by chilling protected speech that occurs simultaneously within our borders.

23.10 Judge Fogel added the following significant qualification:

> If a hypothetical party were physically present in France engaging in expression that was illegal in France but legal in the United States, it is unlikely that a United States court would or could question the applicability of French law to that party's conduct. However, an entirely different case would be presented if the French court ordered the party not to engage in the same expression in the United States on the basis that French citizens (along with anyone else in the world with the means to do so) could later read, hear or see it. While the advent of the Internet effectively has removed the physical and temporal elements of this hypothetical, the legal analysis is the same.

Dow Jones & Co, Inc v Harrods Ltd

23.11 Another example is *Dow Jones & Co Inc v Harrods Ltd*.[20] The British store Harrods had brought defamation proceedings against the American publisher Dow Jones in England arising out of a short article published in the *Wall Street Journal* and its online equivalent. The article was written and uploaded in the United States. Dow Jones sought a declaratory judgment against Harrods and its chairman in the United States to prevent them from prosecuting the English proceedings. Dow Jones contended that it should not be put to the trouble and inconvenience of defending the English proceedings, which would fall to be determined according to principles which are antithetical to the rules, traditions, and policies protecting free speech and freedom of the press in the United States, and which would be summarily dismissed under American defamation law.[21]

Marrero J refused to grant the declaratory judgment, primarily on the ground that there was no 'actual controversy' between the parties.[22] He observed that there was considerable doubt as to whether Dow Jones would be liable under English law.[23]

---

[19] ND Ca, Judge Fogel, 7 November 2001.
[20] 237 F Supp 2d 394 (SD NY, 2002).
[21] ibid, 402–3.
[22] See also *Basic v Fitzroy Engineering, Ltd*, 949 F Supp 1333 (ND Ill 1996).
[23] 237 F Supp 2d 394 (SD NY, 2002) 403, 442.

Marrero J observed that granting the declaratory relief sought by Dow Jones would confer upon his court 'a preemptive style of global jurisdiction branching worldwide and able to strike down offending litigation anywhere on Earth'.[24] Marrero J distinguished *Yahoo!, Inc v LICRA* on the grounds that in that case the French court had made orders explicitly extending to an American national's activities in the United States, and that the relief sought in that case in the United States did not involve an attempt to bar the French court from exercising jurisdiction or enforcing its orders in France.[25]

Marrero J went on to note, however, that if the English court gave judgment in Harrods' favour, and Harrods sought to execute the judgment in the United States, there was a 'substantial likelihood' that the judgment 'would not be cognizable under American jurisprudence governing freedom of expression, and hence would be unenforceable in United States jurisdictions'.[26] He said that if a judgment were entered against Dow Jones which incorporated 'legal principles inimical to prevailing American First Amendment jurisprudence and public policy', Dow Jones would not be without recourse in the United States.[27]

23.12 Some months after Marrero J delivered his ruling, Dow Jones applied to Eady J in the English High Court for, among other things, a stay of the English proceedings on the ground that the English court was a *forum non conveniens*. Eady J refused that application, observing that as the claim had been brought by an English company for the purpose of protecting its trading reputation in respect of publications which occurred in England, it was 'most conveniently dealt with in an English court'.[28]

Analysis

General

23.13 There can be little doubt that the courts in both *Bachchan v India Abroad Publications Inc* and *Telnikoff v Matusevitch* would have reached the same conclusions had the judgments in question been obtained in a Scottish or Australian court. Scots defamation law and Australian defamation law have much more in common with English defamation law than with American defamation law. It is also clear that the rules of New York and Maryland defamation law on which

---

[24] ibid, 411.
[25] ibid, 413–14.
[26] ibid, 432–3.
[27] ibid, 446–7.
[28] *Harrods Ltd v Dow Jones & Co Inc* [2003] EWHC 1162, paras 36–43. See para 26.30.

the courts relied in those cases are rules which apply generally throughout the United States.[29]

The position in relation to the enforcement of Anglo-Australian defamation judgments in American courts therefore appears to be that recognition and effect will only be available to successful claimants in cases where liability would have arisen under American defamation law.[30]

It seems that American defendants will not generally be able to obtain injunctions to prevent claimants from prosecuting defamation actions in the United Kingdom or Australia. Where American defendants are the subject of adverse foreign defamation judgments, however, they may be able to seek declaratory relief from American courts to the effect that the foreign judgment is neither cognizable nor enforceable in the United States.

Human Rights Act 1998 (UK)

23.14   It may be that American courts could be persuaded to reconsider the conclusions reached in *Bachchan v India Abroad Publications Inc* and *Telnikoff v Matusevitch* in view of the higher level of protection afforded to freedom of expression in the United Kingdom in the wake of the passage and commencement of the Human Rights Act 1998 (UK).[31] That Act has not, however, altered any of the fundamental differences between civil defamation law as it operates in the United States and the United Kingdom. The United Kingdom remains a much more friendly jurisdiction for defamation claimants than the United States. Falsity is still presumed in defamation actions in the United Kingdom, whereas it must be proved by the claimant in the United States.[32] Perhaps most

---

[29] See the discussion in *Bachchan v India Abroad Publications Inc*, 585 NYS 2d 661 (SC NY, 1992), 663–5; *Telnikoff v Matusevitch*, 702 A 2d 230 (CA Md, 1997), 244–8.

[30] See Derek Devgun, 'United States Enforcement of English Defamation Judgments: Exporting the First Amendment?' (1994) 23 Anglo-American Law Review 195, 210; Jeremy Maltby, 'Juggling Comity and Self-Government: The Enforcement of Foreign Libel Judgments in US Courts' (1994) 94 Columbia Law Review 1978, 1993–8; Kyu Ho Youm, 'Suing American Media in Foreign Courts: Doing an End-Run Around US Libel Law?' (1994) 16 Hastings Communications and Entertainment Law Journal 235, 259–63; Eric McCarthy, 'Networking in Cyberspace: Electronic Defamation and the Potential for International Forum Shopping' (1995) 16 University of Pennsylvania Journal of International Business Law 527, 561–3. For a compelling critique of the decision in *Bachchan v India Abroad Publications Inc*, see Craig Stern, 'Foreign Judgments and the Freedom of Speech: Look Who's Talking' (1994) 60 Brooklyn Law Review 999, 1036: '[T]o find . . . repugnance between an English libel judgment and the freedom of speech secured by the First Amendment requires a court to misconstrue the First Amendment, making the clause a universal declaration of human rights rather than a limitation designed specifically for American civil government. This enterprise is provincialism by universalization.'

[31] See chapter 30. Such an argument was put by the defendant in *Dow Jones & Co Inc v Harrods, Ltd*, 237 F Supp 2d 394 (SD NY, 2002), 403. Marrero J disposed of the matter without expressing any view on the issue.

[32] This factor was considered critical in *Bachchan v India Abroad Publications Inc*, 585 NYS 2d 661 (SC NY, 1992), 664.

importantly, the United Kingdom has rejected the introduction of a generic privilege for the communication of political information, or of an American-style 'public figure' defence.[33]

Application to the Internet

It seems likely that if a United Kingdom or Australian court were to give judgment in defamation proceedings against an American ISP because the ISP was a publisher of defamatory material on a web page,[34] and was not able to avail itself of one of the statutory defences discussed in Part IV,[35] or the common law defence of innocent dissemination,[36] then that judgment would not be enforceable in the United States. The American court would be likely to conclude that the judgment of the United Kingdom or Australian court was repugnant to American public policy, as embodied in section 230(c) of the Communications Decency Act,[37] and that accordingly the judgment was not entitled to recognition in accordance with principles of comity.[38]   **23.15**

Whether American courts might also decline to enforce judgments in cases involving material published via the Internet on the grounds that the foreign court had exceeded its jurisdiction remains to be resolved.[39] A Canadian court declined to recognize an American defamation judgment on this basis in *Braintech, Inc v Kostiuk*.[40]

Summary

Short of a change in American public policy, or the passage of an international treaty dealing with the issue,[41] it is difficult to see how any solution could be found to the problems which claimants are likely to encounter in seeking to have United Kingdom or Australian defamation judgments recognized in the United States. Claimants contemplating bringing defamation proceedings in the United Kingdom or Australia against American defendants should satisfy   **23.16**

---

[33] *Reynolds v Times Newspapers Ltd* [2001] 2 AC 127; see paras 11.14–11.21, 30.37–30.38.

[34] See chapter 15.

[35] See chapters 16, 17, and 19.

[36] See chapter 18.

[37] See para 31.51.

[38] The relevance of statutory requirements to the determination of public policy was recognized in *Telnikoff v Matusevitch*, 702 A 2d 230 (CA Md, 1997), 239.

[39] In eg circumstances such as those in *Ligue Contre le Racisme et L'Antisémitisme v Yahoo! Inc* (Tribunal de Grande Instance de Paris, Premier Vice-Président Gomez, 22 May 2000 and 20 November 2000): see generally paras 23.08–23.10. The differences between the circumstances in which American courts, and courts in the United Kingdom and Australia, will assert jurisdiction over foreign defendants in defamation actions are explored in paras 31.84–31.107.

[40] (1999) 171 DLR (4th) 46.

[41] See eg the Draft Convention on jurisdiction and foreign judgments in civil and commercial matters proposed by the Hague conference on private international law.

themselves that the intended defendants have sufficient assets in a country in which the judgment might be enforced, to enable recovery of any sum awarded by way of damages, unless it is obvious that the defendant would be liable under American defamation law.[42]

---

[42] See eg *Imagis Technologies Inc v Red Herring Communications Inc* (British Columbia Supreme Court, Pitfield J, 12 March 2003), paras 33–4: if fault and malice are proved in a Canadian defamation action, a United States court might be persuaded that the judgment should be enforced.

24

ALTERNATIVES TO DEFAMATION LAW

A. Introduction

Depending on the circumstances, claimants defamed by material published via **24.01**
the Internet may have a number of causes of action, other than defamation,
open to them. Some of the most important alternative causes of action are
briefly canvassed below. A detailed treatment of the alternatives is beyond the
scope of this text.

B. Malicious falsehood and Verbal Injury

General

The tort of malicious or injurious falsehood provides a remedy where a defend- **24.02**
ant maliciously publishes false material which causes special damage[1] to a claim-

---

[1] Special damage is not necessary in England where the publication is in writing or other
permanent form, or where the publication was calculated to cause pecuniary damage to the
claimant in respect of any office, profession, calling, trade, or business held or carried on at the
time of publication: see Defamation Act 1952, s 3.

ant, or to a claimant's property.[2] This tort is also sometimes known as disparagement (or slander) of goods, or disparagement (or slander) of title. Malicious falsehood may be proved in respect of false material which is not defamatory, and in respect of material which denigrates property, rather than the person. In other respects, however, the tort generally overlaps with, and offers no advantages over, that of civil defamation.

Scots law

24.03   Scots law recognizes a delict of 'verbal injury', which operates in respect of false, non-defamatory statements which are made with the intention of injuring the pursuer, and which in fact cause injury to the pursuer.[3] The onus is on the pursuer to prove that the statement was false, made with the intention of causing injury, and that it in fact caused injury. Malicious falsehood is an example of verbal injury.[4]

Scots law treats statements which expose the pursuer to hatred, contempt, or ridicule as falling outside the scope of defamation law.[5] Such statements are potentially actionable, however, as verbal injury, where the pursuer can prove the elements of the cause of action.[6]

The requirement that the pursuer must establish that the offending statement caused loss is somewhat alleviated by legislation which provides that the pursuer need not 'aver or prove special damage if the words on which the action is founded are calculated to cause pecuniary damage to the pursuer'.[7]

---

[2]   *Ratcliffe v Evans* [1892] 2 QB 524; *Joyce v Sengupta* [1993] 1 All ER 897, 901; *Palmer Bruyn & Parker Pty Ltd v Parsons* (2001) 208 CLR 388. See also Patrick Milmo and WVH Rogers, *Gatley on Libel and Slander* (10th edn, 2003) ('Gatley') paras 20.1–20.3; Michael Gillooly, *The Law of Defamation in Australia and New Zealand* (1998) 4–7.

[3]   *Paterson v Welch* (1893) 20 R 744, 749–50; *Steele v Scottish Daily Record and Sunday Mail Ltd* 1970 SLT 53.

[4]   See generally Kenneth Norrie, *Defamation and Related Actions in Scots Law* (1995) ch 4.

[5]   cf the position in England and Australia: see para 7.16. On whether Scots law recognizes a separate delict of '*convicium*', being a cause of action arising out of certain kinds of imputations for which *veritas* is not an absolute defence, see Norrie (n 4 above) 35–8. Norrie argues that 'there is no case in the law reports that unequivocally describes itself as one of *convicium* as an action different from defamation. It exists only in the writings of the commentators.' In *Quilty v Windsor* 1999 SLT 346, 357, however, Lord Kingarth, quoting from David Walker, *The Law of Delict in Scotland* (2nd edn, 1981) 738 seemed to accept that an action for *convicium* lies where 'the defender has (a) maliciously, (b) communicated of and concerning the pursuer an idea, which may be either true or false (the falsity not being an essential of the action and the truth no defence), (c) calculated to bring him into public hatred, contempt or ridicule, and has thereby caused him loss, injury or damage'.

[6]   See eg *Paterson v Welch* (1893) 20 R 744; *Steele v Scottish Daily Record and Sunday Mail Ltd* 1970 SLT 53.

[7]   Defamation Act 1952, ss 3, 14(b); but see Norrie (n 4 above) 54–5.

C. Negligence

In England, at least, the negligent publication of a misstatement may also give **24.04** rise to a cause of action which is capable of operating concurrently with civil defamation law in a case where there is a sufficient relationship of proximity between the claimant and the defendant publisher.[8] A negligent misstatement occurs where a defendant, who owes a duty of care to the claimant, breaches that duty of care by words which cause the claimant to suffer reasonably foreseeable, pure economic loss.[9] This alternative cause of action will generally be most attractive in cases where claimants would be deprived of a remedy in defamation law because false material was published of and concerning them without malice, on an occasion of qualified privilege. In such cases, provided a duty of care and causation can be proved, such claimants may be able to recover damages for negligence.[10]

D. Privacy

In recent times, English courts, informed by the incorporation into domestic **24.05** law of Article 8 of the European Convention on Human Rights by the Human Rights Act 1998, have extended the common law of breach of confidence to

---

[8] *Spring v Guardian Assurance Plc* [1995] 2 AC 296, 324, 325, 335–6, 349–53; *Cox v Sun Alliance Life Ltd* [2001] EWCA Civ 649; *Cornelius v London Borough of Hackney* [2002] EWCA Civ 1073; cf *JD v East Berkshire Community Health* [2004] QB 558, para 102. In Australia, Canada, and New Zealand, by contrast, it has been held that the potential availability of a cause of action for defamation generally excludes the operation of negligence: 'the law as to injury to reputation and freedom of speech is a field of its own. To impose the law of negligence upon it by accepting that there may be common law duties of care not to publish the truth would be to introduce a distorting element': *Bell-Booth Group Ltd v Attorney-General* [1989] 3 NZLR 148, 156. See also *Balfour v Attorney-General* [1991] 1 NZLR 519, 529; *South Pacific Manufacturing Co Ltd v New Zealand Security Consultants & Investigations Ltd* [1992] 2 NZLR 282, 302; *Sattin v Nationwide News Pty Ltd* (1996) 39 NSWLR 32, 43–5; *Fulton v Globe & Mail* (1997) 152 DLR (4th) 377; *Haskett v Trans Union of Canada Inc* (2003) 224 DLR (4th) 419; *Dinyer-Fraser v Laurentian Bank* (British Columbia Supreme Court, Ballance J, 18 February 2005); *Sullivan v Moody* (2001) 207 CLR 562, paras 54–5; *Cornwall v Rowan* [2004] SASC 384, paras 693–4; but cf *Wade v State of Victoria* [1999] 1 VR 121; *Warren v Tweed Shire Council* [2002] NSWSC 1105, paras 33–5; *Midland Metals Overseas Pte Ltd v The Christchurch Press Co Ltd* [2002] NZLR 289, paras 34, 39 (wherein Gault, Keith, and McGrath JJ of the New Zealand Court of Appeal recognized 'the desirability of providing a remedy' in cases such as *Spring v Guardian Assurance Plc* and accepted 'that such cases might justify imposing a duty of care in negligence'. They went on, however, to observe that '[s]o far as the media respondents are concerned, there is not the necessary special relationship or proximity between a newspaper publisher and persons who (or whose goods) are referred to in a news item' and that to 'impose such duties would be to fundamentally change the business of newspaper publishing').

[9] *Hedley Byrne & Co Ltd v Heller & Partners Ltd* [1964] AC 465.

[10] *Spring v Guardian Assurance Plc* [1995] 2 AC 296.

cases involving the publication of private information obtained by intrusion.[11] Claimants may have a cause of action, in appropriate cases, even where there is no confidential relationship between the claimant and the defendant.[12] The court must, however, subject the competing interests of freedom of expression and the right to respect for private life to a carefully focused and penetrating balancing exercise.[13] English law does not recognize a general tort of invasion of privacy.[14]

Although there is no necessary overlap between privacy and reputation, there may be cases in which defamatory material published via the Internet will concurrently amount to be a breach of confidence.

E. Data Protection Legislation

Data Protection Act 1998 (UK)

24.06   The Data Protection Act 1998 (UK) ('the DPA') regulates the processing of information relating to individuals in the United Kingdom.[15] At the heart of the DPA is the protection of the right to privacy, enshrined in Article 8 of the ECHR. In broad terms, the DPA imposes obligations on 'data controllers' in respect of the processing of personal data. Internet intermediaries and content providers will generally satisfy the definition of 'data controllers' in the DPA.[16]

---

[11] See eg *Douglas v Hello! Ltd* [2001] QB 967; *Venables v News Group Newspapers Ltd* [2001] 1 All ER 908; *A v B Plc* [2003] QB 195; *Wainwright v Home Office* [2004] 2 AC 406; *Campbell v MGN Ltd* [2004] 2 AC 457. In Australia, see *Australian Broadcasting Corporation v Lenah Game Meats Pty Ltd* (2001) 208 CLR 199. In New Zealand, see *Hosking v Runting* [2004] NZCA 34.

[12] *Douglas v Hello! Ltd* [2001] QB 967; *Wainwright v Home Office* [2004] 2 AC 406, 422; *Campbell v MGN Ltd* [2004] 2 AC 457; cf *A v B Plc* [2003] QB 195, 207.

[13] Human Rights Act 1998 (UK) ss 6, 12; European Convention on Human Rights, Arts 8 and 10; see also eg *A v B Plc* [2003] QB 195, 204–10 (Lord Woolf); *Campbell v MGN Ltd* [2004] 2 AC 457, 480, 489–93 (Lord Hope), 497–502 (Baroness Hale), 504–5 (Lord Carswell).

[14] *Wainwright v Home Office* [2004] 2 AC 406, 424; *Campbell v MGN Ltd* [2004] 2 AC 457.

[15] As to territorial limitations, see Data Protection Act 1998 (UK), s 5. The DPA implements Directive 95/46/EC of the European Parliament and of the Council on the protection of individuals with regard to the processing of personal data and on the free movement of such data [1995] OJ L281/31.

[16] Intermediaries will often be 'data controllers' on the basis that they determine the purposes for which and the manner in which information is processed, by means of equipment operating automatically in response to instructions given for that purpose: see the definitions of 'data' and 'data controller': Data Protection Act 1998 (UK), s 1(1). Internet content providers will generally satisfy the definition of 'data controllers' because they determine the purposes for which and the manner in which information is recorded as part of a 'relevant filing system': ibid. 'Processing', in relation to information or data, means 'obtaining, recording or holding the information or data or carrying out any operation or set of operations on the information or data, including . . . disclosure of the information or data by transmission, dissemination or otherwise making available': ibid. The recording of information in a web page or bulletin board posting would satisfy the definition of a 'relevant filing system': ibid. Note, however, that there are a large range of qualifications and exemptions in the DPA: see particularly Pt IV.

Depending on the circumstances, individuals may be entitled, among other matters, to have access to any personal data processed by a data controller[17] or to require a data controller to cease processing their personal data upon notice.[18] An individual may be entitled, by notice in writing to any data controller, to require the data controller to ensure that no decision taken by or on behalf of the data controller which significantly affects that individual is based solely on the processing by automatic means of personal data in respect of which that individual is the data subject for the purpose of evaluating matters relating to the individual such as, for example, his or her performance at work, credit-worthiness, reliability, or conduct.[19] Where a court is satisfied that a data controller has processed inaccurate personal data, it may order the data controller to rectify, block, erase, or destroy those data 'and any other personal data in respect of which he is the data controller and which contain an expression of opinion which appears to the court to be based on the inaccurate data'.[20] An individual who suffers damage by reason of a contravention of the DPA is entitled to compensation from the data controller.[21]

24.07

The DPA might protect a person who could show, for example, that a photograph published via the Internet was taken of him or her without consent on some private occasion.[22] There are broad exemptions in the DPA, however, for personal data which are processed with a view to the publication by any person of any journalistic, literary, or artistic material, or where the data controller reasonably believes that, having regard to the special importance of the public interest in freedom of expression, publication would be in the public interest.[23]

24.08

Where false, defamatory material is stored on the computer system of an Internet intermediary or user, therefore, the DPA may, subject to the operation of some exemption, give the subject of that material the right to seek rectification, erasure, or destruction of the material, or compensation for any damage suffered. Any such rights would be capable of operating concurrently with rights in civil defamation law.

24.09

---

[17] ibid, ss 7–9.
[18] ibid, s 10.
[19] ibid, s 12(1).
[20] ibid, s 14(1).
[21] ibid, s 13.
[22] ibid, s 4, Sch 1, Pt I, para 1(a), and Sch 2; see also *Douglas v Hello! Ltd* [2001] QB 967, 983–4 (Brooke LJ).
[23] Data Protection Act 1998 (UK), s 32(1)(a), (b). When considering whether the belief of a data controller that publication would be in the public interest was reasonable, regard may be had to compliance with any relevant code of practice, such as, presumably, the *Code of Practice* of the Press Complaints Commission: s 32(3).

Australia

24.10 In Australia, the processing of personal information is subject to the provisions of, among other legislation, the Privacy Act 1988 (Cth). The operation of that Act has been extended in some respects to the private sector.[24]

F. Misleading and Deceptive Conduct

Trade Practices Act 1974 (Cth)

24.11 In Australia, section 52 of the Trade Practices Act 1974 (Cth) prohibits corporations[25] from engaging in conduct, in trade or commerce, which is misleading or deceptive, or likely to mislead or deceive. Similar prohibitions apply to natural persons in State and Territory fair trading laws.[26]

24.12 This versatile cause of action is capable of applying concurrently with civil defamation law where a publication contains representations which are false, misleading, or deceptive.[27] Except where advertising and promotional material is concerned, however, the cause of action is not available in respect of publications by persons who carry on a business of providing information, such as newspaper, book, and magazine publishers and broadcasters,[28] where the publication occurs in the course of carrying on such a business.[29] Internet

---

[24] See Privacy Amendment (Private Sector) Act 2000 (Cth). See in particular Privacy Act 1988 (Cth), s 16A, Sch 3.

[25] 'Corporation' has an extended meaning: see Trade Practices Act 1974 (Cth), s 6(4).

[26] Fair Trading Act 1987 (NSW), s 42; Fair Trading Act 1989 (Qld), s 38; Fair Trading Act 1987 (SA), s 56; Fair Trading Act 1990 (Tas), s 14; Fair Trading Act 1999 (Vic), s 9; Fair Trading Act 1987 (WA), s 10; Fair Trading Act 1992 (ACT), s 12; Consumer Affairs and Fair Trading Act 1990 (NT), s 42.

[27] See eg *Typing Centre of NSW Pty Ltd v Northern Business College Ltd* [1989] ATPR ¶40–943; *FAI General Insurance Co Ltd v RAIA Insurance Brokers* (1992) 108 ALR 479; *Gianni Versace SpA v Monte* [2002] FCA 190, para 45; *Cassidy v NRMA Health Pty Ltd* (2002) ATPR ¶41–891, para 70.

[28] As to the scope of the exemption, see *Advanced Hair Studio Pty Ltd v TVW Enterprises Pty Ltd* (1987) 18 FCR 1; *Horwitz Grahame Books Pty Ltd v Performance Publications Pty Ltd* [1987] ATPR ¶40–764; *Krahe v Freeman* [1988] ATPR ¶40–871; *Sun Earth Homes Pty Ltd v Australian Broadcasting Corporation* (1993) 45 FCR 265; *Nixon v Slater & Gordon* (2000) 175 ALR 15.

[29] Trade Practices Act 1974 (Cth), s 65A, which was inserted to reverse the effect of decisions such as *Australian Ocean Line Pty Ltd v West Australian Newspapers Ltd* (1985) 58 ALR 549 and *Global Sportsman Pty Ltd v Mirror Newspapers Pty Ltd* (1984) 2 FCR 82. The equivalent provisions to s 65A in the State and Territory legislation are as follows: Fair Trading Act 1987 (NSW), s 60; Fair Trading Act 1989 (Qld), s 51; Fair Trading Act 1987 (SA), s 74; Fair Trading Act 1990 (Tas), s 28; Fair Trading Act 1999 (Vic), s 32; Fair Trading Act 1987 (WA), s 63; Fair Trading Act 1992 (ACT), s 31; Consumer Affairs and Fair Trading Act 1990 (NT), s 60. Note, however, that publishers of advertisements have a defence to proceedings under s 52 if they are in the business of publishing or arranging for the publication of advertisements, received the advertisement in the ordinary course of business, and did not know and had no reason to suspect that publication

intermediaries will be likely in many cases to be entitled to this exemption in respect of false, misleading, or deceptive material stored on their computer systems, on the grounds that they carry on a business of providing information, and publish material in the course of carrying on such a business. The exemption would also generally apply to commercial Internet content providers, other than in respect of advertising and promotional material.

G. Criminal Libel

Other than in Scotland,[30] it is a criminal misdemeanour at common law to publish a libel. Publication only to the defamed person is sufficient to found liability.[31] At common law, truth was no defence to a charge of criminal libel.[32] With those exceptions, the elements of the common law offence and the available defences are generally the same as those for the tort.[33]   **24.13**

The common law has been modified, and in some cases replaced, by legislation in England and Northern Ireland,[34] and in each Australian jurisdiction.[35] In England, for example, it is a statutory offence to publish a libel maliciously,[36] or to publish a libel maliciously with knowledge that it is false.[37] Truth is a defence if it was for the public benefit that the material was published.[38] Nothing in the Defamation Act 1952 or the Defamation Act 1996, however, affects the law relating to criminal libel.[39]   **24.14**

---

would amount to a contravention of the Act: s 85(3). The equivalent provisions in State and Territory legislation are Fair Trading Act 1987 (NSW), s 71(4); Fair Trading Act 1989 (Qld), s 97(4); Fair Trading Act 1987 (SA), s 88(4); Fair Trading Act 1990 (Tas), s 40(4); Fair Trading Act 1999 (Vic), s 155(4); Fair Trading Act 1987 (WA), s 83(4); Fair Trading Act 1992 (ACT), s 49(4); Consumer Affairs and Fair Trading Act 1990 (NT), s 94(4).

[30] See Norrie (n 4 above) 3.

[31] *R v Adams* (1888) 22 QBD 66; *R v Hardy* [1951] VLR 454, 456; cf the position in relation to civil defamation: see para 5.02.

[32] *R v Carden* (1879) 5 QBD 1, 6.

[33] See generally Gatley (n 2 above) ch 22; Gillooly (n 2 above) 18–20.

[34] Libel Act 1843, ss 4–7. These provisions do not apply in Scotland, and have a modified operation in Northern Ireland.

[35] Defamation Act 1974 (NSW), ss 49–53; Defamation Act 1889 (Qld), ss 8–9; Criminal Law Consolidation Act 1935 (SA), s 257 and Sch 11, cl 1(26); Criminal Code (Tas), ss 196–225; Wrongs Act 1958 (Vic), ss 9–11; Criminal Code (WA), ss 345–69; Defamation (Criminal Proceedings) Act 2001 (ACT); Criminal Code (NT), ss 203–8.

[36] Libel Act 1843, s 5.

[37] ibid, s 4.

[38] ibid, s 6. Guidance as to the meaning of the 'public benefit' requirement can be derived from the Australian authorities in jurisdictions where a 'public benefit' requirement is an element of the civil defamation defence of justification: see paras 8.15–8.18.

[39] Defamation Act 1952, s 17(2); Defamation Act 1996, s 20(2).

Prosecutions for criminal libel are increasingly rare.

24.15 It has been suggested that a criminal libel conviction in England or Northern Ireland might contravene the right to freedom of expression in Article 10 of the European Convention on Human Rights.[40] In *Worme v Commissioner of Police*, however, the Privy Council observed that 'criminal libel, in one form or another, is to be found in the law of many democratic societies, such as England, Canada and Australia'.[41] The Council rejected the proposition that criminal libel is not reasonably justifiable in a democratic society.

In a series of recent decisions the European Court of Human Rights has confirmed that in appropriate circumstances convictions for criminal defamation will not violate Article 10.[42]

H. Industry Self-regulation

Industry codes of practice

24.16 To many in the community, the availability of criminal content via the Internet, such as that depicting or encouraging child pornography, is of much more pressing concern than whether those defamed via the Internet have adequate means of redress. In both the United Kingdom and Australia, and a great many other countries, Internet industry associations have developed self-regulatory Codes of Practice primarily aimed at restricting the availability of such material. If those Codes refer to the availability of defamatory material via the Internet at all, they tend to do so only indirectly. The Codes of Practice currently on offer in the United Kingdom and Australia do not provide an alternative to the resolution of civil defamation disputes through the courts.

ISPA

24.17 The United Kingdom's Internet Services Providers Association (ISPA), for example, adopted a Code of Practice on 25 January 1999.[43] The Code binds all ISPA members. The Code contains no guidance for Internet intermediaries whose computer systems contain defamatory material created by third parties. Members are exhorted to 'use their reasonable endeavours' to ensure that 'Ser-

---

[40] eg *Gleaves v Deakin* [1980] AC 477, 482 (Lord Diplock); Richard Clayton and Hugh Tomlinson, *The Law of Human Rights* (2001) para 15.256.

[41] [2004] 2 AC 430, 455.

[42] See eg *Perna v Italy* (2004) 39 EHRR 28; *Chauvy v France* (European Court of Human Rights, 29 June 2004); *Cumpănă and Mazăre v Romania* (European Court of Human Rights, 17 December 2004); *Pedersen and Baadsgaard v Denmark* (European Court of Human Rights, 17 December 2004); cf *Nikula v Finland* (2004) 38 EHRR 45.

[43] See <http://www.ispa.org.uk>.

vices[44] (excluding Third Party Content[45]) and Promotional Material[46] do not contain anything which is in breach of UK law, nor omit anything which UK law requires'.[47] Members are also to comply with data protection laws[48] and are not to 'encourage anything which is in any way unlawful'.[49] The Code establishes a complaints procedure to deal with alleged breaches of the Code by members.[50]

The ISPA Code binds members to adhere to the procedures of the Internet **24.18** Watch Foundation (IWF) for the removal of illegal material from web sites and newsgroups.[51] The IWF receives and investigates complaints from members of the public, and sends notices to its members to remove or disable access to material depicting child pornography hosted anywhere in the world, and criminally obscene or criminally racist content hosted in the United Kingdom. The IWF does not appear ever to have issued a notice requiring its members to remove or disable access to any material solely on the grounds that it was defamatory.

LINX

The London Internet Exchange (LINX), another association of Internet inter- **24.19** mediaries, has published 'Best Practice' guidelines for the handling by its members of 'illegal material', including defamatory material. In its current form, however, the guidelines simply advise intermediaries 'to balance the rights of the customer and the person allegedly defamed, and their own risks by continuing to carry the material', and to consider requesting indemnities from their subscribers.[52] The guidelines advise intermediaries that the innocent dissemination defence in section 1 of the Defamation Act 1996 (UK) 'might not apply once they have been notified' that they are hosting a defamatory publication.[53]

IIA

A more detailed Code of Practice has been adopted by the Internet Industry **24.20** Association of Australia (IIA). Version 7 of the Code was registered with the ABA in May 2002. The Code has legislative backing: the Australian

---

[44] Defined as 'services provided by any Member'.
[45] Defined as 'material accessible via a Member's Service, which originates from and/or is owned by one or more third parties (including, for the avoidance of doubt, that Member's Customers)'.
[46] Defined as 'material promoting any Services'.
[47] ISPA, *Code of Practice*, cl 2.2.1.
[48] ibid, cl 4.
[49] ibid, cl 2.2.2.
[50] ibid, cl 8.
[51] ibid, cl 5.
[52] <http://www.linx.net/noncore/bcp/illegal-material-bcp.html>.
[53] ibid.

Broadcasting Authority may issue warnings or written notices requiring intermediaries to comply with the Code.[54] A failure to comply with a direction is a
criminal offence.[55] Where an intermediary fails to comply with a direction, the
ABA may apply to the Federal Court for an order that the intermediary cease
supplying an Internet carriage service, or hosting Internet content.[56]

As with its United Kingdom counterparts, however, the IIA Code offers no
guidance to Internet intermediaries in relation to defamatory material hosted or
stored on their computer systems, but which they did not create. The Code is
aimed at restricting the availability of material which has been classified RC or X
by the Classification Board, or unclassified material which, if it were classified,
would be likely to be classified RC or X. Underlying the Code is a principle of
'electronic equivalence'; namely that, as far as possible, behaviour and transactions that can take place in the 'real world' should be permissible over the
Internet without additional requirements or restrictions.[57]

---

[54] Broadcasting Services Act 1992 (Cth), Sch 5, cls 66–7; see also cls 83–4.
[55] ibid, Sch 5, cl 82.
[56] ibid, cl 85.
[57] ibid, cl 3.1(a).

PART VI

JURISDICTION AND CHOICE OF LAW

25

GROUNDS OF JURISDICTION

A. Introduction

Multi-jurisdictional defamation in the pre-Internet age

Until recently, cross-jurisdictional questions, although difficult, presented a **25.01** limited range of practical problems in defamation cases in the United Kingdom. Although for the purposes of private international law England (including Wales), Scotland, and Northern Ireland are distinct jurisdictions, the defamation law of each of those places is largely the same.[1] Leaving aside short-wave radio transmissions, television and radio broadcasts from the United Kingdom were not generally received, until recently, in other countries. If newspapers and

---

[1] Although there are a number of substantive differences between the defamation laws of England and Scotland, those differences have spawned remarkably few legal controversies: see generally Kenneth Norrie, *Defamation and Related Actions in Scots Law* (1995) ch 13. For a recent example see *Lennon v Scottish Daily Record and Sunday Mail Ltd* [2004] EMLR 18.

magazines were available overseas, their circulation was generally limited to a small number of copies.

25.02 More difficult questions have traditionally arisen in the Australian context. Each Australian State and Territory is a different jurisdiction, with different defamation laws. The law of defamation is codified in Queensland and Tasmania, substantially modified by legislation in New South Wales and the Australian Capital Territory, and a matter mostly of common law in Victoria, South Australia, Western Australia, and the Northern Territory. Courts have long grappled with the issues arising in cases of intra-Australian defamation. Australia's geographic isolation, however, meant that until recently Australian publications were mostly available only on the Australian continent.

25.03 In more recent times, the potential for international defamation has increased with the establishment of international cable and satellite television networks. The prohibitive start-up and ongoing costs of operating such networks means that the number of major international players is unlikely to increase to more than a handful.

The advent of the Internet

25.04 The Internet represents a communications revolution. It makes instantaneous global communication available cheaply to anyone with a computer and an Internet connection. It enables individuals, institutions, and companies to communicate with a potentially vast global audience. It is a medium which does not respect geographical boundaries. Concomitant with the utopian possibility of creating virtual communities, enabling aspects of identity to be explored, and heralding a new and global age of free speech and democracy, the Internet is also potentially a medium of virtually limitless international defamation.

Issues

25.05 The revolutionary impact of the Internet on communications, and in particular the ability to publish material instantaneously in a vast number of jurisdictions, thus raises the following complex issues of private international law:

- When does a court have jurisdiction to determine the legal consequences of the publication of defamatory material by foreign publishers?
- In what circumstances will a court, seized of such jurisdiction, nonetheless decline to exercise it on *forum non conveniens* grounds?
- When a court has jurisdiction, and resolves to exercise it, which law or laws will be applied to determine the legal consequences?
- How does a party seeking to rely on foreign law prove the content of that law?

This chapter is concerned with the circumstances in which courts have jurisdiction to deal with defamation actions with a foreign element. Chapter 26 is concerned with the circumstances in which courts will decline to exercise jurisdiction on *forum non conveniens* grounds. Chapters 27 and 28 deal with choice of law rules in the United Kingdom and Australia, respectively. Chapter 29 deals with proof of foreign law.

B. Sources of Law

Traditional rules

Traditionally, courts developed their own principles governing the circum-   **25.06**
stances in which they assumed jurisdiction over a dispute. At common law, subject to principles of *forum non conveniens*,[2] courts will exercise jurisdiction where the defendant has been served within the jurisdiction of the court, where the defendant has voluntarily submitted to the jurisdiction of the court, or where service outside the jurisdiction is authorized by the rules of the court.[3]

Brussels Regulation and the Brussels and Lugano Conventions

Application

The application of the common law rules has been partly displaced in the   **25.07**
United Kingdom by reason of its accession to the Brussels and Lugano Conventions on jurisdiction and the enforcement of judgments in civil and commercial matters ('the Conventions'),[4] and by reason of Council Regulation 44/2001 of 22 December 2000 on jurisdiction and the recognition and enforcement of judgments in civil and commercial matters ('the Brussels Regulation').[5] As the jurisdictional bases in the Brussels Regulation and the Conventions are substantially the same, it is convenient to deal with them simultaneously.

The Brussels Regulation governs jurisdiction whenever a defendant is domiciled   **25.08**
in a Member State of the European Union other than Denmark. The Brussels Regulation generally supersedes the Conventions. The Brussels Convention continues to govern jurisdiction, however, where a defendant is domiciled in

---

[2] See chapter 26.
[3] See paras 25.21–25.30.
[4] The Conventions have the force of law in the United Kingdom: Civil Jurisdiction and Judgments Act 1982 (UK), ss 2(1), 3A(1).
[5] [2001] OJ L12/1. The Brussels Regulation is directly applicable in the United Kingdom: Art 76.

Denmark.[6] The Lugano Convention continues to govern jurisdiction where a defendant is domiciled in Iceland, Norway, or Switzerland.[7] It seems the Conventions are also capable of applying in cases with other international elements against defendants domiciled in the United Kingdom.[8]

For simplicity, in this Part, a 'Regulation State' means a State in respect of which the Brussels Regulation applies, and a 'Convention State' means, in relation to the Brussels Convention, Denmark, and in relation to the Lugano Convention, Iceland, Norway, or Switzerland.

'Domicile'

25.09 **General principle.** Courts of Regulation States and courts of Convention States apply their own internal law in order to determine whether a party is domiciled in that State.[9] If a party is not domiciled in that State, then in order to determine whether the party is domiciled in another Regulation State or Convention State, courts apply the law of that Regulation State or Convention State.[10]

25.10 **Natural persons.** Natural persons are domiciled in the United Kingdom or some part thereof if they are resident there, and the nature and circumstances of their residence indicates that they have a substantial connection with the United Kingdom or that part of the United Kingdom.[11] A person who has been resident in the United Kingdom for at least three months is presumed to have a substantial connection with the United Kingdom, in the absence of proof to the contrary.[12] A person who is domiciled in the United Kingdom, but has no substantial connection with any particular part of the United Kingdom, is treated as domiciled in the part in which he or she is resident.[13]

25.11 **Companies, associations, and other legal persons.** For the purposes of the Brussels Regulation, companies, associations, and other legal persons are domiciled at the place where they have their 'statutory seat', central administration, or principal place of business.[14] For the purposes of the United Kingdom, a

---

[6] Denmark is a Contracting State to the Brussels Convention and is a Member State of the European Union, but is excluded from the operation of the Brussels Regulation: see Brussels Regulation, Art 68(1).
[7] Iceland, Norway, and Switzerland are Contracting States to the Lugano Convention, but not Member States of the European Union.
[8] Case C–281/02, *Owusu v Jackson* (European Court of Justice, 1 March 2005): Brussels Convention held to apply in a case against a defendant domiciled in the United Kingdom, but concerning events which occurred in Jamaica. See para 26.03.
[9] Brussels Regulation, Art 59(1); Conventions, Art 52.
[10] Brussels Regulation, Art 59(2); Conventions, Art 52.
[11] Civil Jurisdiction and Judgments Act 1982 (UK), s 41(2), (3).
[12] ibid, s 41(6).
[13] ibid, s 41(5).
[14] Brussels Regulation, Art 60(1).

'statutory seat' means 'the registered office or, where there is no such office anywhere, the place of incorporation or, where there is no such place anywhere, the place under the law of which the formation took place'.[15]

Under the Conventions, companies, associations, and other legal persons are **25.12** domiciled in the place where they have their 'seat'.[16] They have their seat in the United Kingdom if they are incorporated or were formed under the law of any part of the United Kingdom and have their registered office or some other official address there,[17] or if their 'central management and control' is exercised there.[18] Companies, associations, and other legal persons domiciled in the United Kingdom may be treated as domiciled in that part or those parts of the United Kingdom in which they have their registered office, they exercise their central management and control, or they have places of business.[19] United Kingdom courts will treat a company, association, or other legal person as being domiciled in another state if it was incorporated or formed under the law of that State and has its registered office or some other official address there,[20] or if its central management and control is exercised in that State,[21] unless it is shown that the courts of that State would not regard it as having its seat there.[22]

Civil Jurisdiction and Judgments Act 1982 (UK)

The traditional rules as to jurisdiction have also been partly displaced by the **25.13** Civil Jurisdiction and Judgments Act 1982. That Act has implications, in particular, for jurisdiction in intra-United Kingdom cases, and in cases before Scottish courts.

The rules as to jurisdiction in intra-United Kingdom matters—that is, where the issue is whether the courts of a part of the United Kingdom have jurisdiction in relation to a dispute with some connection to another part of the United Kingdom—are set out in Schedule 4 to the Civil Jurisdiction and Judgments Act 1982 (UK). Schedule 4 is a modified version of the jurisdiction rules in the Brussels Regulation.[23]

The circumstances in which a person may be sued in civil proceedings in the **25.14**

---

[15] ibid, Art 60(2).
[16] Conventions, Art 53.
[17] Civil Jurisdiction and Judgments Act 1982 (UK), s 42(3)(a).
[18] ibid, s 42(3)(b).
[19] ibid, s 42(4).
[20] ibid, s 42(6)(a).
[21] ibid, s 42(6)(b).
[22] ibid, s 42(7). A corporation may have seats in a number of states: *The Deichland* [1990] 1 QB 361, 375, 379.
[23] See para 25.42.

Scottish Court of Session or in a Scottish sheriff court are prescribed in Schedule 8 to the Civil Jurisdiction and Judgments Act 1982 (UK).[24]

Overview

25.15   There will be no great difficulty in finding a basis for the assertion of jurisdiction by a United Kingdom or Australian court in most cases involving defamation via the Internet. The publication of defamatory material within the jurisdiction of the court is a basis for jurisdiction under the traditional rules,[25] the Brussels Regulation,[26] the Conventions,[27] and Schedules 4 and 8 to the Civil Jurisdiction and Judgments Act 1982 (UK).[28]

25.16   For the purposes of defamation law, material is published at the place or places where it is read, heard, or seen, rather than the place from which the material originated or was uploaded. A separate publication occurs, and a separate cause of action accrues, each time defamatory material is read, heard, or seen.[29]

25.17   Where a web page or bulletin board posting is published to a global audience, United Kingdom and Australian courts will therefore almost always have a basis for asserting jurisdiction, because publication will have occurred within the jurisdiction of the court. The claimant has only to prove that someone other than the defamed person has accessed the material in question within the jurisdiction of the court.[30] The more important question in Internet defamation proceedings in the United Kingdom and Australia will be whether the court should decline to exercise jurisdiction on the basis that it is a *forum non conveniens*.[31]

25.18   A more detailed explanation of the major bases for jurisdiction under the traditional rules, the Brussels Regulation, and the Conventions is set out below.[32]

United States

25.19   A very different approach towards jurisdiction is taken in the United States. Courts there generally exercise jurisdiction in defamation actions over defend-

---

[24] See para 25.43.
[25] See para 25.27 (United Kingdom), 25.30 (Australia).
[26] See paras 25.33–25.36.
[27] ibid.
[28] See paras 25.42–25.43.
[29] See para 5.10.
[30] See para 5.04. Note that communication to a third party is not required in Scots law: see para 5.02.
[31] See chapter 26.
[32] See paras 25.21–25.30 (traditional rules); 25.31–25.41 (Brussels Regulation and the Conventions).

ants domiciled outside the jurisdiction of the court only where the defendant intended to and did cause damage in the forum; that is, where the defendant's conduct in some way targeted the forum.[33]

Further, in most American States, a 'single publication' rule applies, so that only one cause of action arises out of:

> any single publication or exhibition or utterance, such as any one edition or issue of a newspaper or book or magazine or any one presentation to an audience or any one broadcast over radio or television or any one exhibition of a motion picture.[34]

Future reforms

For the sake of completeness, two matters should be noted. First, issues of   **25.20**
jurisdiction are also the subject of a draft Convention on jurisdiction and foreign judgments in civil and commercial matters, proposed by the Hague Conference on Private International Law.[35] The future of the draft Hague Convention is uncertain.

Under the draft Hague Convention, a plaintiff would be able to recover the whole of the damages suffered by reason of a defamatory Internet publication by suing in the courts of the State in which either the defendant[36] or the plaintiff[37] is habitually resident. The plaintiff could also sue in the courts of any other State in which publication or damage occurred, but only in respect of such damage as was suffered in that State.[38] Courts would also have jurisdiction where the defendant voluntarily submitted to the jurisdiction of the court, by proceeding on the merits without contesting jurisdiction.[39]

Secondly, there is a school of thought, particularly emanating from the United States, to the effect that entirely new concepts of jurisdiction may be necessary if the law is to cope adequately with the advent of the Internet, and if jurisdictional disputes are to be minimized. The issues are exhaustively canvassed in a report of the American Bar Association.[40] That report describes the conceptual challenge facing those formulating jurisdictional rules as depending on whether the Internet is viewed 'as a place, a means of communication, or a technological

---

[33] See paras 31.84–31.107.
[34] See para 13.22.
[35] Draft Convention on jurisdiction and foreign judgments in civil and commercial matters, proposed by the Hague Conference on Private International Law adopted by the Special Commission on 30 October 1999 ('draft Hague Convention').
[36] ibid, Art 3.
[37] ibid, Art 10(1), (4).
[38] ibid.
[39] ibid, Art 5.
[40] American Bar Association, *London Meeting Draft: Achieving Legal and Business Order in Cyberspace* (2000).

state of mind'.[41] It goes on to advocate a series of 'jurisdictional default rules',[42] and to recommend the establishment of a multi-national Global Online Standards Commission with the aim of developing 'uniform principles and global protocol standards'.[43]

The adoption of international jurisdictional standards of the kind advocated by the American Bar Association is remote. The merits of adopting such standards and the form those standards might take are matters beyond the scope of this text.

C. Traditional Rules

Application

25.21   The following jurisdictional rules apply:

- in proceedings in England and Northern Ireland,[44] except where the Brussels Regulation or the Conventions apply;[45] and
- in proceedings in Australia.

Presence within the jurisdiction

25.22   English and Australian courts have jurisdiction to hear and determine cases brought before them where the defendant has been validly served, within the jurisdiction of the court, with the claim form, writ, or other process which originated the proceeding, and the court is competent to hear and determine the case.[46]

The defendant needs only to be temporarily present within the jurisdiction for service to be validly effected and jurisdiction conferred. An English court will have jurisdiction, for example, where an Australian defendant is served with an English claim form during a temporary visit to London. The same court would not necessarily have jurisdiction, however, if the same claim form were served on the defendant at his or her home in Melbourne. In such a case, some other basis for jurisdiction would have to be found.

---

[41] American Bar Association, (n 40 above), 6.
[42] ibid, 17–21.
[43] ibid, 22.
[44] cf Scotland: see para 25.43.
[45] See paras 25.08, 25.31–25.41.
[46] *Colt Industries Inc v Sarlie* [1966] 1 WLR 440; *Adams v Cape Industries Plc* [1990] Ch 433, 518–19; Lawrence Collins (ed), *Dicey and Morris on Conflict of Laws* (13th edn, 2000) ('Dicey and Morris'), 291–301; David McLean, *Morris: The Conflict of Laws* (5th edn, 2000) 73–4; Peter Nygh, *Conflict of Laws in Australia* (6th edn, 1995) 41–3.

In Australia, process validly issued out of any State or Territory court may   **25.23**
be served on a defendant located anywhere in Australia, even if only on a
temporary visit.[47]

Voluntary submission to jurisdiction

Defendants may voluntarily submit to the jurisdiction of a competent court to   **25.24**
hear and determine a defamation action brought against them.[48] A defendant
typically submits to the jurisdiction of a court by filing an acknowledgement of
service (appearance), and then not contesting the jurisdiction of the court
within the time limited by the rules of the court.[49]

Service authorized by rules of court

General principles

English and Australian courts will also have jurisdiction to hear and determine   **25.25**
defamation actions against foreign defendants where the claim form, writ, or
other originating process of the court has been served on the defendant in
circumstances authorized by the applicable rules of court. In England, other
than in cases governed by the Brussels Regulation or the Conventions,[50] leave of
the court is required before service outside the jurisdiction can occur.[51] Leave
will ordinarily be granted where the claimant satisfies the court[52] that:

- service outside the jurisdiction is authorized by the rules of the court; and
- the jurisdiction is the proper place to bring the claim, in that if leave is
  granted, the proceeding would not subsequently be stayed on *forum non
  conveniens*[53] or other grounds.[54]

In most Australian jurisdictions, service outside the jurisdiction may occur

---

[47] Service and Execution of Process Act 1992 (Cth), s 15.
[48] Dicey and Morris (n 46 above) 301–5; McLean (n 46 above) 77, 108; Nygh (n 46 above) 64–5.
[49] See eg Civil Procedure Rules, Pts 10–11 (England).
[50] ibid, r 6.19.
[51] ibid, rr 6.20 and 6.21, and Practice Direction 6b. In Australia, prior leave is required in the Supreme Courts of Western Australia and the Australian Capital Territory. Prior leave should ordinarily be sought in the Federal Court, although leave can be sought after service in some circumstances. In the remaining Australian jurisdictions, service outside the jurisdiction may take place without prior leave.
[52] In an application for leave to serve proceedings outside the jurisdiction of the court, the onus is on the claimant: *Spiliada Maritime Corporation v Cansulex Ltd* [1987] 1 AC 460, 480.
[53] eg *King v Lewis* [2005] EMLR 4, para 2. *Forum non conveniens* principles are the subject of chapter 26.
[54] Dicey and Morris (n 46 above) 330–1; McLean (n 46 above) 78–9; Nygh (n 46 above) 47–8.

without leave.[55] In those jurisdictions, leave to proceed is generally required if the defendant fails to appear.

Rules of court: England

25.26 The Civil Procedure Rules authorize the service of claim forms on foreign defendants who are not domiciled in a Regulation State or a Convention State in a number of circumstances.

25.27 **Place of publication.**   Most importantly, claim forms may be served with leave on foreign defendants in respect of claims in tort where damage was sustained within England or Wales, or where the damage sustained resulted from an act committed within England or Wales.[56] In the case of defamation, damage is sustained, and the act resulting in damage committed, in the place or places in which the offending material is published; that is, in the place where the material is read, heard, or seen.[57]

Courts in England and Wales may, therefore, authorize service abroad provided that someone has read, heard, or seen the offending publication within England or Wales. This requirement will be unlikely to cause any difficulties where material is published to a global audience via the Internet.[58] In such cases, the more important question will be whether the court should refuse leave, or decline to exercise its jurisdiction, on the grounds of *forum non conveniens*.[59]

Claimants seeking leave to serve a claim form outside England and Wales on this basis must, however, limit their claim to publications of the offending material within England and Wales.[60]

25.28 **Other grounds.**   Courts in England and Wales may also authorize service abroad where the defendant is domiciled within the jurisdiction of the court,[61] where a claim is made for an injunction to restrain the defendant from doing an act

---

[55] Prior leave is not required in the High Court, or the Supreme Courts of Victoria, New South Wales, Queensland, South Australia, Tasmania, or the Northern Territory. Prior leave should ordinarily be sought in the Federal Court, although prior service without leave can be confirmed by the court in limited circumstances.

[56] Civil Procedure Rules, r 6.20(8).

[57] See para 5.10.

[58] See the authorities cited in paras 26.16–26.31.

[59] See chapter 26.

[60] *Diamond v Sutton* (1866) LR 1 Ex 130, 132; *Berezovsky v Michaels* [2000] 2 All ER 986, 994; *King v Lewis* [2004] EWHC 168, para 18.

[61] Civil Procedure Rules, r 6.20(1). 'Domicile' is determined in accordance with ss 41–6 of the Civil Jurisdiction and Judgments Act 1982 (UK), discussed in paras 25.09–25.12: see r 6.18(g).

within the jurisdiction,[62] and where the defendant is a necessary or proper party to a claim over which the court otherwise has jurisdiction.[63]

This last basis for jurisdiction may be important in some cases involving Internet defamation. Suppose, for example, that a claimant wished to bring defamation proceedings against the English author of a defamatory web page, and the Australian ISP who hosted the offending page. In such a case, the Australian ISP might well be a necessary and proper party to the claimant's claim. This basis for jurisdiction is similar to that in Article 6(1) of the Brussels Regulation and Article 6(1) of the Conventions.[64]

Discretion. The granting of leave to serve proceedings outside the jurisdiction is discretionary.   **25.29**

In an application for leave, the claimant must satisfy the court 'that England and Wales is the proper place in which to bring the claim'.[65] The claimant must show a serious issue to be tried; that is, 'a substantial question of fact or law or both, arising on the facts disclosed by the affidavits, which the [claimant] bona fide desires to try'.[66] This requirement calls for a judgment of the kind which arises in *forum non conveniens* inquiries,[67] which will be considered in chapter 26. Where leave is sought to serve proceedings in Scotland or Northern Ireland, the court must consider whether it would be more cost-effective and convenient for the proceedings to be held there, rather than in England or Wales.[68]

Rules of court: Australia

Service outside Australia is authorized by the rules of court in all Australian jurisdictions where the proceedings are founded on a tort committed within the   **25.30**

---

[62] Civil Procedure Rules, r 6.20(2). This rule is cast in broad terms. Leave could presumably be obtained under this rule to serve defendants located outside England or Wales with proceedings seeking an injunction to restrain the publication of defamatory material accessible via the Internet in England or Wales. Such an injunction would only be granted in a very rare case, however: see chapter 20. The claim for injunctive relief must be made in good faith, and not merely to attract the benefit of the rule. Leave will usually not be granted if damages are sought by the claimant: *De Bernales v The New York Herald* (1893) 68 LT 658 (appeal on other grounds subsequently dismissed); *Watson & Sons v Daily Record (Glasgow), Ltd* [1907] 1 KB 853. As to the circumstances in which injunctions might be granted to restrain the publication of defamatory material via the Internet, see chapter 20.

[63] Civil Procedure Rules, r 6.20(3).

[64] See paras 25.37–25.40.

[65] Civil Procedure Rules, r 6.21(2A).

[66] *Seaconsar Far East Ltd v Bank Markazi Jomhouri Islami Iran* [1994] 1 AC 438, 452 (Lord Goff). See also *Amin Rasheed Shipping Corporation v Kuwait Insurance Co* [1984] AC 50, 72; *Chadha v Dow Jones & Co Inc* [1999] EMLR 724.

[67] *Seaconsar Far East Ltd v Bank Markazi Jomhouri Islami Iran* [1994] 1 AC 438, 455; see also *Amin Rasheed Shipping Corporation v Kuwait Insurance Co* [1984] AC 50, 72; *Spiliada Maritime Corporation v Cansulex Ltd* [1987] 1 AC 460, 478–82; *Berezovsky v Michaels* [2000] 2 All ER 986.

[68] Civil Procedure Rules, r 6.21(3).

jurisdiction of the court, or where proceedings are brought for damage suffered wholly or partly within the jurisdiction of the court and caused by a tortious act or omission wherever occurring.[69] Service outside Australia of proceedings issued by an Australian court will therefore be authorized by the rules in all cases where publication has occurred within the jurisdiction of the Australian court, or where damage has been suffered by reason of the publication within the jurisdiction of the court.[70]

Similar discretionary considerations apply in Australia as in England, in those jurisdictions in which leave to serve proceedings outside the jurisdiction is required.

D. Brussels Regulation and the Conventions

Application

25.31   The traditional rules just discussed do not apply in the United Kingdom where defendants are domiciled in Regulation States or Convention States.[71] In such cases, leave of the court to serve proceedings outside the jurisdiction is not required.[72] The principal bases for jurisdiction under the Brussels Regulation and the Conventions are as follows.

Domicile in the United Kingdom

25.32   Under Article 2 of the Brussels Regulation, persons domiciled in a Regulation State may be sued in the courts of that State, regardless of their nationality. Similarly, under Article 2 of each of the Conventions, persons domiciled in a Convention State may be sued in the courts of that State.

Defamation proceedings with an international element may therefore be

---

[69] High Court Rules 2004, r 9.07.1 (circumstances authorized by the Federal Court Rules); Federal Court Rules, O 8, r 1(a), (ac), (ad); Supreme Court Rules 1970 (NSW), Pt 10, r 1A(1)(a), (d), (e); Uniform Civil Procedure Rules 1999 (Qld), r 124(1)(a), (k), (l); Supreme Court Rules 1987 (SA), r 18.02(f), (fa); Supreme Court Rules 2000 (Tas), r 147A(1)(b), (c), (d); Supreme Court (General Civil Procedure) Rules 1996 (Vic), r 7.01(i), (j); Rules of the Supreme Court 1971 (WA), O 10, r 1(k); Supreme Court Rules 1937 (ACT), O 12, r 2(e)(ii); Supreme Court Rules (NT), r 7.01(j), (k).

[70] Note, however, that leave to serve outside the jurisdiction of the court is required for proceedings before the Supreme Courts of Western Australia and the Australian Capital Territory, and is usually required for proceedings in the Federal Court.

[71] See para 25.08.

[72] Civil Procedure Rules, r 6.19, Practice Direction 6b. As to service in Member States of the European Union, see Council Regulation 1348/2000 of 29 May 2000 on the service in the Member States of judicial and extrajudicial documents in civil or commercial matters [2000] OJ L160/37.

brought in the United Kingdom under both the Brussels Regulation and the Conventions against defendants who are domiciled in the United Kingdom.[73]

Place where the harmful event occurred

Article 5(3) of the Brussels Regulation provides: **25.33**

A person domiciled in a Member State may, in another Member State, be sued . . .

3   in matters relating to tort, delict or quasi-delict, in the courts for the place where the harmful event occurred or may occur.

Article 5(3) of each of the Conventions provides:

A person domiciled in a Contracting State may, in another Contracting State, be sued . . .

3   in matters relating to tort, delict or quasi-delict, in the courts for the place where the harmful event occurred.

In defamation actions, the 'harmful event' occurs both in the place or places **25.34** where the defamatory publication is distributed, and in the place where the publisher is established.[74]

Defendants domiciled in a Regulation State may therefore be sued in the courts of any Regulation State in which they are established, or in the courts of any Regulation State in which the defamatory material was distributed or in which distribution has been threatened. Defendants domiciled in a Convention State may be sued in the courts of any Convention State in which they are established, or in the courts of any Convention State in which the defamatory material was distributed.[75]

Where material is published by a defendant domiciled in a Regulation State or a **25.35** Convention State to a global audience via the Internet, and it can be proved that the material has been read, heard, or seen in the United Kingdom, Article 5(3) of the Brussels Regulation and Article 5(3) of each of the Conventions will therefore permit a United Kingdom court to exercise jurisdiction over that defendant.

Where a defamation action is brought in the place where the publisher is estab- **25.36** lished, the court has jurisdiction to award damages for all the harm caused by the defamatory publication. Where a defamation action is brought in a place in

---

[73] The circumstances in which a defendant will be domiciled in the United Kingdom are dealt with in paras 25.09–25.12.

[74] *Shevill v Presse Alliance SA* [1995] 2 AC 18, 62–3.

[75] It has been held in Scotland that such courts have jurisdiction even in respect of threatened wrongs that are likely to produce a harmful event within Scotland: *Bonnier Media Ltd v Smith* [2002] ETMR 87, 1060–1; cf Dicey and Morris (n 46 above) 354–5.

which the publication was merely distributed, however, the courts of that place may only award damages in respect of the harm caused by the offending publication in that State; that is, by reason of the distribution of the offending publication in that State.[76]

Joint tortfeasors

25.37 Under Article 6(1) of the Brussels Regulation, joint defendants domiciled in different Regulation States may be sued in the courts of the place where any one of the defendants is domiciled, provided the claims are so closely connected that it is expedient to hear and determine them together to avoid the risk of irreconcilable judgments resulting from separate proceedings. Article 6(1) of each of the Conventions is to the same effect as regards joint defendants domiciled in different Convention States.[77]

25.38 In practice, where multiple defendants domiciled in different Regulation States are sued in respect of the same Internet publication, it seems likely that Article 6(1) of the Brussels Regulation would operate to enable them to be sued in the courts of the place where any one of them is domiciled. The same result would be likely under Article 6(1) of each of the Conventions in respect of multiple defendants domiciled in different Convention States.

Suppose, for example, that a French claimant is defamed by material posted on a web page by a person who is domiciled in England, and that the web page is hosted on the computer system of an Internet intermediary domiciled in Germany. Suppose further that the claimant sues both the English author and the German intermediary in England. It would seem likely that in such a case the English court would have jurisdiction over both defendants under Article 6(1) of the Brussels Regulation. In such a case the claims against the author and the intermediary are 'so closely connected' that it must surely be expedient for them to be heard and determined together to avoid the risk of irreconcilable judgments resulting from separate proceedings.

25.39 It may be that where the Brussels Regulation applies, Article 6(1) will encourage forum shopping in cases involving defamatory publications with multiple defendants domiciled in different Regulation States. The claimant is not required by Article 6(1) to sue in the courts of the place with the closest and most substantial connection with the offending publication. It seems the claim-

---

[76] *Shevill v Presse Alliance SA* [1995] 2 AC 18, 62–3.

[77] The Conventions do not expressly require a close connection between the claims against the joint defendants. Article 6(1) of the Conventions has been interpreted, however, as imposing such a requirement: Case 189/87 *Kalfelis v Bankhaus Schröder, Münchmeyer, Hengst & Co* [1988] ECR 5565.

ant could elect to sue in the courts of a place in which any defendant is domiciled, regardless of the extent of that defendant's involvement in the publication of the offending material, for the purpose of taking advantage of the substantive or procedural laws of that place.[78]

Where a court has jurisdiction by reason of Article 6(1) of the Brussels Regulation or the Conventions, the claimant will, if successful, be entitled to damages in respect of all publications of the offending material, not just those occurring within the forum. **25.40**

Submission to jurisdiction

Under the Brussels Regulation, courts of Regulation States also have jurisdiction in cases where the defendant enters an acknowledgement of service (appearance), provided that the acknowledgement of service was not entered for the sole purpose of contesting jurisdiction.[79] The same principle applies under each of the Conventions.[80] **25.41**

E. Civil Jurisdiction and Judgments Act 1982 (UK)

By section 16 of the Civil Jurisdiction and Judgments Act 1982 (UK), the provisions of Schedule 4 to that Act determine, for each part of the United Kingdom, whether the courts of that part have jurisdiction in defamation proceedings. Schedule 4 contains a modified version of the jurisdiction provisions of the Brussels Regulation. A court in England, for example, will have jurisdiction in defamation actions where a defendant is domiciled in England.[81] Where a defendant is domiciled in some other part of the United Kingdom, English courts will have jurisdiction if, for example: **25.42**

- the defamatory publication has been distributed or threatened in England;[82]
- the defendant submits to the jurisdiction of the court;[83] or

---

[78] The applicable law will depend on the operation of the choice of law rules of the forum. The choice of law rules applicable to defamation actions in the United Kingdom are the subject of chapter 27.

[79] Brussels Regulation, Art 24. Acknowledgements of service in English proceedings, and the mechanism for disputing the jurisdiction of English Courts, are dealt with in the Civil Procedure Rules, Pts 10, 11.

[80] Conventions, Art 18.

[81] Civil Jurisdiction and Judgments Act 1982 (UK), s 16, Sch 4, para 1. In relation to joint defendants each domiciled in different parts of the United Kingdom, see Sch 4, para 5(a).

[82] ibid, s 16, Sch 4, para 3(c); *Shevill v Presse Alliance SA* [1995] 2 AC 18, 62–3. Where the defendant is not established in England, the English court may only award damages in respect of the harm caused by reason of the distribution of the publication in England.

[83] Civil Jurisdiction and Judgments Act 1982 (UK), s 16, Sch 4, para 13.

- the defendant is one of a number of defendants, at least one of whom is domiciled in England, provided the claims are so closely connected that it is expedient to hear and determine them together to avoid the risk of irreconcilable judgments resulting from separate proceedings.[84]

25.43   Schedule 8 to the Civil Jurisdiction and Judgments Act 1982 prescribes the circumstances in which a person may be sued in civil proceedings in the Court of Session or in a sheriff court.[85] For the purposes of civil defamation law, those circumstances are the same as those in the Brussels Regulation, although they apply even where a defender is not domiciled in a Regulation State or another part of the United Kingdom.

---

[84] ibid, s 16, Sch 4, para 5.
[85] ibid, s 20.

26

FORUM NON CONVENIENS

A. General Principles

United Kingdom

In defamation cases not governed by the Brussels Regulation,[1] or the Brussels **26.01**
and Lugano Conventions,[2] United Kingdom courts will decline to exercise
jurisdiction, even though it has been regularly invoked, if some other court is a
'clearly more appropriate' forum for the resolution of the dispute.[3] The court
seeks to identify the 'natural forum'; that is, the court 'with which the action has

---

[1] Council Regulation 44/2001 of 22 December 2000 on jurisdiction and the recognition and
enforcement of judgments in civil and commercial matters, [2001] OJ L12/1. See paras 25.07–
25.12, 25.31–25.41.

[2] Brussels and Lugano Conventions on jurisdiction and the enforcement of judgments in civil
and commercial matters ('the Conventions'). See paras 25.07–25.12, 25.31–25.41.

[3] eg *Spiliada Maritime Corporation v Cansulex Ltd* [1987] 1 AC 460, 477 (Lord Goff);
Cumming v Scottish Daily Record and Sunday Mail Ltd [1995] EMLR 538; *Shell UK Exploration and Production Ltd v Innes* 1995 SLT 807; *Berezovsky v Michaels* [2000] 2 All ER 986.
See also Supreme Court Act 1981 (UK), s 49(3); Civil Jurisdiction and Judgments Act 1982
(UK), s 49.

the most real and substantial connection'.[4] In a case where the court so declines to exercise its jurisdiction, it is said to be a *forum non conveniens*.

26.02   It seems, however, that United Kingdom courts may not decline to exercise jurisdiction on the grounds that the courts of some other country are a clearly more appropriate forum in cases governed by the Brussels Regulation or the Conventions.

It has been held, for example, that where jurisdiction under the Brussels Convention has been properly invoked against a defendant who is domiciled in one of the Convention States,[5] United Kingdom courts do not have the discretion to decline to exercise jurisdiction on the grounds of *forum non conveniens* where the alternative forum is a court in another Convention State,[6] or in another part of the United Kingdom.[7] By parity of reasoning, where the Brussels Regulation applies, United Kingdom courts would have no discretion to decline to exercise jurisdiction on *forum non conveniens* grounds where the defendant is domiciled in one of the Regulation States[8] and the alternative forum is a court in another Regulation State, or in another part of the United Kingdom.

26.03   More controversially, in *In re Harrods (Buenos Aires) Ltd*, the Court of Appeal held that proceedings brought in England against a defendant domiciled in a Convention State may be stayed on *forum non conveniens* grounds where some court in a non-Convention State was a clearly more appropriate forum.[9] In *Owusu v Jackson*, the Court of Appeal, in effect, referred the correctness of that conclusion to the European Court of Justice for a preliminary ruling.[10] While that ruling was pending, single judges of the English High Court reached

---

   [4] *Spiliada Maritime Corporation v Cansulex Ltd* [1987] 1 AC 460, 477–8 (Lord Goff), adopting *The Abidin Daver* [1984] AC 398, 415 (Lord Keith). A similar approach has been taken in Canada: see eg *Dickhoff v Armadale Communications Ltd* (1992) 103 Sask R 307, reversed on other grounds (1993) 108 DLR (4th) 464; the authorities discussed in paras 26.27–26.28; cf *Olde v Capital Publishing Ltd Publishing* (1998) 108 OAC 304, affirming (1996) 5 CPC (4th) 95.
   [5] See para 25.08.
   [6] *In re Harrods (Buenos Aires) Ltd* [1992] Ch 72, 93, 103. See generally Lawrence Collins (ed), *Dicey and Morris on Conflict of Laws* (13th edn, 2000) ('Dicey and Morris'), 391–5 and the authorities cited therein at n 50. Note, however, that s 49 of the Civil Jurisdiction and Judgments Act 1982 (UK) provides that nothing in that Act is to prevent any United Kingdom court from staying proceedings on the grounds of *forum non conveniens* where 'to do so is not inconsistent with' the Conventions.
   [7] *Cumming v Scottish Daily Record and Sunday Mail Ltd* [1995] EMLR 538, 541.
   [8] That is, a Member State of the European Union other than Denmark. See para 25.08.
   [9] [1992] Ch 72 (overruling *S & W Berisford v New Hampshire Insurance* [1990] 2 QB 631 and *Arkwright Mutual Insurance v Bryanston Insurance* [1990] 2 QB 649); *Ace Insurance SA-NV v Zurich Insurance Company* [2001] 1 Lloyd's Rep 618. See also Dicey and Morris (n 6 above) 392–4.
   [10] [2002] EWCA Civ 877.

conflicting conclusions as to the applicability of that conclusion to cases governed by the Brussels Regulation.[11]

In its ruling in *Owusu v Jackson*, a Grand Chamber of the European Court of Justice held, contrary to the view taken by the Court of Appeal in *In re Harrods (Buenos Aires) Ltd*, that:[12]

- the Brussels Convention applies to proceedings with an international element against defendants domiciled in the United Kingdom, even if the jurisdiction of no other Convention State is in issue or the proceedings have no connecting factors to any other Convention State;[13] and
- the Brussels Convention precludes courts of Convention States from declining the jurisdiction conferred on them by the Brussels Convention in relation to defendants domiciled in that State on the ground that a court in a non-Convention State would be a more appropriate forum for the trial of the action.[14]

The position thus now seems to be that courts of the United Kingdom may not decline to exercise jurisdiction on the grounds that the courts of some other country are a more appropriate forum in actions involving defendants domiciled in a Regulation State or a Convention State, or actions with an international element involving defendants domiciled in the United Kingdom.[15]

Suppose, for example, that a French defendant published a web page defamatory of an English claimant. Suppose further that although the web page was overwhelmingly accessed by persons in America, it could be proved that it has been accessed in England. In those circumstances, English courts would have jurisdiction over the French defendant pursuant to Article 5(3) of the Brussels Regulation in respect of the harm suffered by reason of publications of the web page occurring in England. The effect of the European Court of Justice's ruling in *Owusu v Jackson* seems to be that the English court would be obliged to accept jurisdiction, and could not decline to exercise jurisdiction on the ground that an American (or French) court would be a clearly more appropriate forum.

---

[11] *DSM Anti-Infectives BV v SmithKline Beecham Plc* [2004] EWHC 1309; cf *Travelers Casualty and Surety Company of Europe Ltd v Sun Life Assurance Company of Canada (UK) Ltd* [2004] EWHC 1704. The Court of Appeal declined to express a view on the controversy: *DSM Anti-Infectives BV v SmithKline Beecham Plc* [2004] EWCA Civ 1199, para 46.

[12] Case C–281/02, *Owusu v Jackson* (European Court of Justice, 1 March 2005).

[13] ibid, para 35.

[14] ibid, para 46.

[15] Note, however, that the European Court of Justice declined to say whether the application of *forum non conveniens* rules were excluded in cases where identical or related proceedings were pending before the courts of a Convention State and the courts of a non-Convention State: ibid, paras 47–52.

26.04   Where, however, a defamation action is brought in England against a person
who is not domiciled in the United Kingdom, a Regulation State, or a Convention State, but the court of a Regulation State or Convention State is a clearly
more appropriate forum, it has been held that English courts retain a discretion
to stay the action.[16]

26.05   It has also been held that a discretion to stay proceedings on *forum non conveniens* grounds may be exercised where a United Kingdom court concludes that a
court in some other part of the United Kingdom is a clearly more appropriate
forum for the determination of a defamation action brought against a defendant domiciled in the United Kingdom. In *Cumming v Scottish Daily Record and
Sunday Mail Ltd*, this conclusion was said to be justified on the basis that in
intra-United Kingdom cases, the jurisdiction of the court derives exclusively
from the Civil Jurisdiction and Judgments Act 1982 (UK).[17] In *Lennon v
Scottish Daily Record and Sunday Mail Ltd*, Tugendhat J reached the same
conclusion, reasoning that 'no legislation within the United Kingdom will be
inconsistent with the Brussels Convention, or the Lugano Convention or the
[Brussels] Regulation, because those instruments allocate jurisdiction between
Member States', not jurisdiction between different parts of the United
Kingdom.[18]

Those conclusions would appear to be likely to withstand the ruling of the
European Court of Justice in *Owusu v Jackson*.[19] For the Brussels Convention
(or, by analogy, the Brussels Regulation and the Lugano Convention) to apply at
all, 'the existence of an international element is required'.[20]

26.06   Finally, the European Court of Justice has ruled that the Brussels Convention
precludes national courts from granting injunctions which have the effect of
preventing a party to proceedings from commencing or continuing proceedings
before a court of another Convention State, even where that party is acting in
bad faith with a view to frustrating the existing proceedings.[21] That conclusion
would appear to apply equally to the Lugano Convention and the Brussels
Regulation.

---

[16] *Sarrio SA v Kuwait Investment Authority* [1997] 1 Lloyd's Rep 113, 124 (subsequently
reversed on other grounds); *Haji-Ioannou v Frangos* [1999] 2 Lloyd's Rep 337, 346.

[17] [1995] EMLR 538, 541 (Drake J), departing from his earlier contrary decision in *Foxen v
Scotsman Publications Ltd* [1995] EMLR 145.

[18] [2004] EMLR 18, para 15.

[19] C–281/02, *Owusu v Jackson* (European Court of Justice, 1 March 2005); see para 26.03.

[20] ibid, para 25, citing P Jenard, 'Report on the Convention on jurisdiction and the enforcement of judgments in civil and commercial matters', [1979] OJ C59/1, 8. See also Civil Jurisdiction and Judgments Act 1982 (UK), s 49: 'Nothing in this Act shall prevent any court in the
United Kingdom from staying, sisting, striking out or dismissing any proceedings before it, on the
grounds of *forum non conveniens* or otherwise, where to do so is not inconsistent with the 1968
[Brussels] Convention or, as the case may be, the Lugano Convention.'

[21] *Turner v Grovit* [2004] 3 WLR 1193.

Australia

A different test has been adopted in Australia. Australian courts will not **26.07** decline to exercise jurisdiction on the grounds of *forum non conveniens* simply because some other place is a more appropriate forum; rather, an Australian court will decline to exercise jurisdiction only where satisfied that it is a 'clearly inappropriate' forum for the hearing and determination of the proceeding.[22]

B. *Forum Non Conveniens* Inquiries

Circumstances

Questions of *forum non conveniens* generally arise in one of two ways:[23] on an **26.08** application by the claimant for leave to serve proceedings outside the jurisdiction, or on an application by the defendant to have service of proceedings outside the jurisdiction set aside. In the former case, the onus is on the claimant to satisfy the court that it is the proper place in which to bring the claim;[24] in the latter case, the onus is on the defendant.[25]

Relevant factors

Where a court has jurisdiction to hear and determine a defamation action **26.09** because material has been published within the jurisdiction of the court, there is an initial presumption that it is the natural or appropriate forum for the trial of the action.[26]

In determining whether a court should decline to exercise its jurisdiction because the forum is a *forum non conveniens*, the court next has regard to the 'connecting factors' between the forum and the parties or subject matter. Those factors will include matters affecting convenience and expenses, such as the domicile of the parties, the place where the relevant events occurred, and the

---

[22] *Voth v Manildra Flour Mills Pty Ltd* (1990) 171 CLR 538, 559 (Mason CJ, Deane, Dawson, and Gaudron JJ), following Deane J in *Oceanic Sun Line Special Shipping Company Inc v Fay* (1988) 165 CLR 197, 241–57. See also *Dow Jones & Co Inc v Gutnick* (2002) 210 CLR 575, para 9; *BHP Billiton Ltd v Schultz* [2004] HCA 61, para 11.

[23] That is, in cases where the court has a discretion to decline to hear proceedings on *forum non conveniens* grounds: see paras 26.01–26.06.

[24] See para 25.25.

[25] *Spiliada Maritime Corporation v Cansulex Ltd* [1987] 1 AC 460, 476–7; *Voth v Manildra Flour Mills Pty Ltd* (1990) 171 CLR 538, 564–5.

[26] *Cordoba Shipping Co Ltd v National State Bank, Elizabeth, New Jersey (The 'Albaforth')* [1984] 2 Lloyd's Rep 91, 96; *King v Lewis* [2005] EMLR 4, para 24. The circumstances in which courts have jurisdiction to hear and determine defamation actions are the subject of chapter 25.

location of witnesses.[27] Another relevant factor is whether the substantive law of the forum is applicable in determining the rights and liabilities of the parties.[28] The court seeks to identify whether 'the case may be tried more suitably for the interests of all the parties and the ends of justice' in some other available forum.[29] The more tenuous the claimant's connection with the jurisdiction, the more likely the forum is a *forum non conveniens*.[30]

26.10 If some other forum has the closest connection with the proceeding, the court may nonetheless refuse to stay the proceeding, if to do so is in the interests of justice.[31] Relevant factors include any 'legitimate personal or juridical advantage' available to the claimant in the forum which would not be available in an alternative forum.[32] Such advantages might include the availability of damages on a higher scale, a more complete disclosure procedure, a power to award interest, or a more generous limitation period.[33] In complicated cases calling for highly professional representation, the fact that legal aid would be available in the forum, but not in the more appropriate forum, might justify refusing a stay.[34]

26.11 Such advantages will not ordinarily be decisive.[35] Where, having regard to the connecting factors, some other forum is 'clearly more appropriate' (United Kingdom) or the existing forum is 'clearly inappropriate' (Australia), claimants must generally take the foreign forum as they find it and accept, for example, lower damages or a less complete disclosure.[36] A stay will only be refused if 'substantial justice cannot be done in the [foreign] forum'.[37]

---

[27] *Spiliada Maritime Corporation v Cansulex Ltd* [1987] 1 AC 460, 478; *Oceanic Sun Line Special Shipping Company Inc v Fay* (1988) 165 CLR 197, 245 (Deane J), adopted in *Voth v Manildra Flour Mills Pty Ltd* (1990) 171 CLR 538, 564–5.

[28] *Spiliada Maritime Corporation v Cansulex Ltd* [1987] 1 AC 460, 478; *Voth v Manildra Flour Mills Pty Ltd* (1990) 171 CLR 538, 566.

[29] *Spiliada Maritime Corporation v Cansulex Ltd* [1987] 1 AC 460, 476.

[30] *King v Lewis* [2005] EMLR 4, para 27.

[31] *Spiliada Maritime Corporation v Cansulex Ltd* [1987] 1 AC 460, 482–4. The Court of Appeal expressed misgivings about this staggered approach towards *forum non conveniens* inquiries in *King v Lewis* [2005] EMLR 4, paras 38–9, before concluding that such an approach nonetheless represents the present state of the law.

[32] *Spiliada Maritime Corporation v Cansulex Ltd* [1987] 1 AC 460, 482.

[33] ibid, approved in *Voth v Manildra Flour Mills Pty Ltd* (1990) 171 CLR 538, 564–5.

[34] *Connelly v RTZ Corporation Plc* [1998] AC 854, 873–4; cf *Lubbe v Cape Plc* [2000] 1 Lloyd's Rep 139.

[35] *Connelly v RTZ Corporation Plc* [1998] AC 854, 872.

[36] ibid, 872–3.

[37] *Spiliada Maritime Corporation v Cansulex Ltd* [1987] 1 AC 460, 482 (Lord Goff); *Connelly v RTZ Corporation Plc* [1998] AC 854, 872.

C. Application to Defamation Cases and to the Internet

Connecting factors in defamation actions

Where material is published to a global audience via the Internet, it may be **26.12**
read, heard, or seen by, and thereby published to, persons in the United Kingdom or Australia, even though the subject matter of the publication and the
parties otherwise have no links at all to those countries.

The place of publication—that is, the place where material is read, heard, or **26.13**
seen—is at the very heart of the cause of action for defamation, and is consequently a highly relevant factor in determining the appropriate forum for the
hearing and determination of defamation actions.[38] Where material is published
to a global audience via the Internet, however, publication will have occurred,
and the cause of action for defamation will have accrued, in multiple jurisdictions. In those circumstances, the place where the tort is committed may cease
to be a 'potent limiting factor'.[39] On the other hand, it will generally be possible
to lead evidence about the extent of publication in various jurisdictions.

Other important factors will be whether the claimant has a reputation to protect
in the forum, whether the claimant's claim is limited to publications occurring
in the forum, the extent to which publications occurred in other countries in
which the claimant has a substantial reputation, and the location of the parties
and witnesses.[40]

In Australia, the fact of publication within the jurisdiction of the court may be
enough to justify the exercise of jurisdiction: in such a case, the court might be
unlikely to conclude that it is a 'clearly inappropriate' forum.[41]

Juridical advantages

Where some publications of defamatory material have occurred in a jurisdiction **26.14**

---

[38] *Schapira v Ahronson* [1999] EMLR 735, 745; *Berezovsky v Michaels* [2000] 2 All ER 986,
994–5, each relying in part on *Cordoba Shipping Co Ltd v National State Bank, Elizabeth, New
Jersey (The 'Albaforth')* [1984] 2 Lloyd's Rep 91, 96; cf *Kroch v Rossell et Compagnie Société des
Personnes à Responsabilité Limitée* [1937] 1 All ER 725.

[39] *King v Lewis* [2005] EMLR 4, para 28. As the Court of Appeal went on to observe, however,
in practice there will often only be a finite number of jurisdictions in contention: ibid, para 31.

[40] *Schapira v Ahronson* [1999] EMLR 735, see para 26.16; *Berezovsky v Michaels* [2000] 2 All
ER 986, see paras 26.17–26.22; cf *Chadha v Dow Jones & Co Inc* [1999] EMLR 724, see paras
26.23–26.24; *Dow Jones & Co Inc v Gutnick* (2002) 210 CLR 575, see paras 26.25–26.26;
Bangoura v Washington Post (2004) 235 DLR (4th) 564 (Ontario Superior Court of Justice), see
paras 26.27–26.28; *King v Lewis* [2005] EMLR 4, see para 26.29. See also *Braintech, Inc v Kostiuk*
(1999) 171 DLR (4th) 46 (British Columbia Court of Appeal).

[41] *Dow Jones & Co Inc v Gutnick* (2002) 210 CLR 575; see paras 26.25–26.26.

other than that in which proceedings have been brought, the substantive law of that jurisdiction may be relevant in determining the rights and liabilities of the parties in respect of those publications.[42] In Australia, however, it has been held that the fact that choice of law rules require the application of foreign substantive law is of itself insufficient to render the court a clearly inappropriate forum.[43]

26.15   There may be a number of advantages to claimants in bringing defamation proceedings arising out of Internet publications in the United Kingdom or Australia.

In general, for example, American public figures are more likely to have a remedy under United Kingdom or Australian law than under American law where defamatory material of and concerning them has been published.[44] To take another example, claimants might choose to issue proceedings in the United Kingdom or Australia because the defendant has assets in those countries against which a judgment could be enforced. A third reason for issuing in the United Kingdom or Australia might be that a damages award in a defamation action in those countries is likely to be more generous than in alternative jurisdictions.

It is unlikely, however, that such matters would sway a court to refuse a stay in a case where some other court had the closest connection with the proceeding.[45]

Illustrations

Shapira v Ahronson

26.16   In *Schapira v Ahronson*[46] Peter Gibson LJ refused to stay proceedings brought by an Israeli citizen, domiciled in London, in respect of allegedly defamatory material published in an Israeli newspaper with a very small circulation in England. The plaintiff limited his claim to publications of the newspaper within England. Peter Gibson LJ said:

> Where the tort of libel is allegedly committed in England against a person resident and carrying on business in England by foreigners who were aware that their publication would be sent to subscribers in England, that English resident is entitled to bring proceedings here against those foreigners and to limit his claim to publication in England, even though the circulation of the article alleged to be

---

[42]   See chapters 27–28.
[43]   *Regie Nationale des Usines Renault SA v Zhang* (2002) 210 CLR 491, para 81 (Gleeson CJ, Gaudron, McHugh, Gummow, and Hayne JJ).
[44]   See paras 31.04–31.06.
[45]   cf *King v Lewis* [2005] EMLR 4, paras 40–2.
[46]   [1999] EMLR 735.

defamatory was extremely limited in England and there was a much larger publication elsewhere.[47]

Berezovsky v Michaels

A similar outcome occurred in *Berezovsky v Michaels*.[48] That case concerned **26.17** allegations against the plaintiffs, two prominent Russian citizens, in *Forbes*, a business magazine primarily circulated in the United States. The magazine had a circulation of around 785,710 copies in North America, 13 copies in Russia, and 1,915 copies in England and Wales. The plaintiffs confined their claim for damages to publications of the magazine in England and Wales, including distributions of hard copies of the magazine, and publications of the offending material in England and Wales via the Internet. By a majority, the House of Lords refused to stay the action.

Lord Steyn, with whom Lord Hobhouse agreed, delivered the leading opinion. **26.18** Lord Steyn held:

> The present case is a relatively simple one. It is not a multi-party case: it is, however, a multi-jurisdictional case. It is also a case in which all the constituent elements of the torts occurred in England. The distribution in England of the defamatory material was significant. And the plaintiffs have reputations in England to protect. In such cases it is not unfair that the foreign publisher should be sued here.[49]

Lord Steyn went on to find that Russia was not a more appropriate forum, because 'on the evidence adduced by *Forbes* about the judicial system in Russia, it is clear that a judgment in favour of the plaintiffs in Russia will not be seen to redress the damage to the reputations of the plaintiffs in England'.[50] Lord Steyn also rejected the United States as a more appropriate forum, on the basis that the plaintiffs did not have reputations which needed protecting there.[51]

Lord Steyn declined to discuss specific issues arising out of the publication of **26.19** the offending magazine via the Internet, concluding that there had been insufficient evidence before the House to enable that 'important issue' to be considered satisfactorily.[52]

Lord Nolan reached the same conclusion, holding that: **26.20**

> This case is solely concerned with the plaintiffs' reputations in England. They seek to have their reputations judged by English standards. The Court of Appeal

---

[47] ibid 735, 748–9, see also 749 (Phillips LJ).
[48] [2000] 2 All ER 986.
[49] ibid, 994.
[50] ibid, 995–6.
[51] ibid, 996.
[52] ibid.

thought for this purpose England was the natural forum, and I agree with them. I do not follow the relevance of the [first instance] judge's remark that the article has 'no connection with anything which has occurred in this country'. A businessman or politician takes his reputation with him wherever he goes, irrespective of the place where he has acquired it.[53]

26.21   In a strong dissent, Lord Hoffman held that the plaintiffs were 'forum shoppers in the most literal sense'.[54] Lord Hoffman said the plaintiffs were seeking to avoid having to litigate in the United States, because the decision in *New York Times Company v Sullivan*[55] made it too likely that they would lose. At the same time, they did not want to sue in Russia 'for the unusual reason that other people might think it was too likely' that they would win.[56] Lord Hoffman would have stayed the English proceedings.

26.22   Lord Hope also dissented, observing that it would be regrettable if defamation actions could be brought in England against foreign publishers in respect of things said or done elsewhere by persons with established international reputations who have formed no long-standing or durable connections with England, and who are unable to demonstrate that the publication has had any material effect upon business or other transactions by them in England.[57]

Chadha v Dow Jones & Co Inc

26.23   A different result was reached in *Chadha v Dow Jones & Co Inc*,[58] an appeal from a decision refusing leave to serve defamation proceedings against a magazine publisher in the United States.[59] The first appellant was a resident of the United States and the chief executive of the second appellant, a company incorporated in California. The second appellant had acquired another American company and its United Kingdom subsidiary in January 1996. The name of the subsidiary was changed to a name similar to that of the second appellant in April 1997. The offending article was published in an edition of *Barrons Magazine* in August 1997, which had a total circulation of 294,346 copies, of which 283,520 were sold in the United States, and 1,257 in the United Kingdom.

The first appellant claimed that he had many contacts in the United Kingdom. The second appellant claimed that sales in the United Kingdom were an important and growing aspect of its business. It is not clear from the report of

---

[53]   [2000] 2 All ER 986, 998.
[54]   ibid, 1005.
[55]   376 US 254 (1964); see para 31.04.
[56]   *Berezovsky v Michaels* [2000] 2 All ER 986, 1005.
[57]   ibid, 1013.
[58]   [1999] EMLR 724.
[59]   ie under the predecessor to Civil Procedure Rules, r 6.21: see para 25.25.

the case whether the appellants had confined their claim to damages for publications of the offending article in the United Kingdom.[60]

The Court of Appeal held that there was ample material to justify the conclusion that it would be inappropriate for the action to be tried in the United Kingdom, rather than the United States. Roch LJ, with whom Otton and Pill LJJ agreed, said:

26.24

> Whereas the appellants in 1997 had reputations worthy of vindication in the United States, the evidence that they had such a reputation in this country in August 1997, a mere four months after the name of their English subsidiary was changed to include the word 'Osicom' is in my view vague and imprecise. Still more problematical is the evidence that such reputations as the appellants had at that time within the jurisdiction was [*sic*] harmed by such publication of the article as occurred in this country.[61]

Dow Jones & Co Inc v Gutnick

Another decision in line with those already discussed is that of the Australian High Court in *Dow Jones & Co Inc v Gutnick*.[62] In October 2000, *Barron's* magazine and its online cousin, *Barron's Online*, published a feature article about Australian businessman Mr Joseph Gutnick. It traversed a range of issues, accusing Gutnick of exploiting religious charities in the United States, of involvement in share manipulation and tax evasion, and of improper dealings with a gaoled tax evader and money launderer. Gutnick brought defamation proceedings against the American publisher of *Barron's* and *Barron's Online*, Dow Jones, in the Supreme Court of his home State, Victoria. Gutnick undertook to sue in respect of the article only in Victoria and only in respect of publication of the article occurring in Victoria.

26.25

Dow Jones sold 305,563 copies of the relevant print edition of *Barron's* magazine. Only fourteen of those copies were sold in Victoria. Access to *Barron's Online* is restricted to persons who have applied for and obtained a user name and password from Dow Jones. At the relevant time, *Barron's Online* had some 550,000 subscribers, including 1,700 in Australia and about 300 in Victoria. Dow Jones had its editorial offices in New York. The servers on which *Barron's Online* is stored were located in New Jersey.

The core conclusion of the High Court can be simply stated: material accessible via the Internet is published, for the purposes of defamation law, at the time

26.26

---

[60] It would have been an abuse of process for the appellants to seek leave to serve the proceedings in the United States without limiting or undertaking to limit their claim in this way: see para 25.27.

[61] [1999] EMLR 724, 734. See also *Kroch v Rossell et Compagnie Société des Personnes à Responsibilité Limitée* [1937] 1 All ER 725.

[62] (2002) 210 CLR 575.

when and place where it is downloaded in comprehensible form. The tort of defamation is committed each time and in each place where defamatory material is downloaded in comprehensible form, provided that the defamed person has a reputation in that place which is thereby damaged.[63] As Gutnick had sued only in respect of publication of the article occurring in Victoria and had limited his claim to damage to his reputation in that State, his claim related entirely to causes of action accruing in Victoria and fell to be determined according to Victorian defamation law. Although the article had been written and edited in New York, and uploaded to web servers located in New Jersey, those matters were not relevant to locating the place of the tort. No choice of law question thus arose. There was no basis for concluding that Victoria was a clearly inappropriate forum.[64]

Bangoura v Washington Post

26.27 There have been a number of first instance Canadian decisions exploring the circumstances in which courts will exercise jurisdiction over foreign defendants in relation to defamatory material published via the Internet. A representative illustration of the Canadian approach is *Bangoura v Washington Post*.[65]

The plaintiff was an 'international public servant' employed by the United Nations who had lived in various countries including Austria, the Ivory Coast, and Kenya. He moved to Ontario in 1997. He had never lived in the United States.

Articles allegedly defamatory of the plaintiff were published in the *Washington Post* and on its web site in early 1997, while the plaintiff was still working in Kenya.

The plaintiff brought defamation proceedings in Ontario against the publisher of the *Washington Post* and three of its reporters. The publisher of the *Washington Post* was a company incorporated in Delaware, with its head office in the District of Columbia. The reporters were residents of the United States, but were located at relevant times in Washington, the Ivory Coast, and Kenya. The *Washington Post's* only presence in Ontario consisted of leased office space in Toronto for newsgathering purposes. There were seven paid subscribers to the print edition of the *Washington Post* in Ontario at the relevant time.

---

[63] (2002) 210 CLR 575, paras 44, 151, 184, 197.
[64] ibid, paras 48, 64–5, 163.
[65] (2004) 235 DLR (4th) 564 (Ontario Superior Court of Justice). At the time of writing (March 2005) an appeal to the Ontario Court of Appeal had been heard but not determined. See also *Kitakufe v Oloya* (Ontario Court of Justice, Himel J, 2 June 1998); *Imagis Technologies Inc v Red Herring Communications Inc* (British Columbia Supreme Court, Pitfield J, 12 March 2003); *Wiebe v Bouchard* (British Columbia Supreme Court, Melvin J, 14 January 2005).

Pitt J held that it was appropriate for the Ontario Superior Court of Justice to assume jurisdiction, observing among other things that: **26.28**

- the plaintiff was a resident of Ontario who had found a home and work there;
- Ontario was the place where the damage to the plaintiff's reputation would have the greatest impact;
- the *Washington Post* was 'a major newspaper in the capital of the most powerful country in a world now made figuratively smaller by, *inter alia*, the Internet';
- the defendants 'should have reasonably foreseen that the story would follow the plaintiff wherever he resided';
- the *Washington Post* was 'a newspaper with an international profile, and its writers influence viewpoints throughout the English speaking world', and which either had, or should have, insurance for damages for defamation anywhere in the world;
- the plaintiff had no connection with any of the jurisdictions where the defendants reside;
- there was a 'clear juridical advantage' to the plaintiff in Ontario (presumably, because the plaintiff was more likely to succeed under Canadian defamation law than under United States' law);
- the fact that an American court might not recognize or enforce a Canadian defamation judgment, and that therefore the plaintiff might have to re-litigate in the United States, was not determinative;
- there would be 'problems whether this action is tried in Ontario or the District of Columbia';
- either Ontario or the District of Columbia would be appropriate fora; and
- in circumstances where there was no clearly more appropriate forum, the plaintiff's choice of forum should not be disturbed.

King v Lewis

In *King v Lewis*,[66] the English Court of Appeal considered two online publications allegedly defamatory of the well-known boxing promoter Don King. King resided in Florida. By the time the Court of Appeal decided the matter, there was one remaining defendant, Judd Burstein, a New Yorker. The publications were stored on servers based in California. King sought and was granted leave by a Master to serve a claim form, seeking damages confined to publications occurring in England and Wales. Eady J declined to set aside the Master's order.[67] The Court of Appeal dismissed an appeal from Eady J's decision, emphasizing that the 'strands in the learning' concerning *forum non conveniens* inquiries 'are really   **26.29**

---

[66] [2005] EMLR 4.
[67] *King v Lewis* [2004] EWHC 168.

matters of practical reasoning, and not legal rules'.[68] The court said that the relative importance of all the factors which must be examined 'are matters which will inform the judge who must decide where the balance of convenience lies' and expressed dismay that 'there is so much learning about them'.[69]

Harrods Ltd v Dow Jones & Co Inc

26.30 In *Harrods Ltd v Dow Jones & Co Inc*,[70] Eady J of the English High Court had to decide whether to permit the operator of a well-known English department store to maintain a defamation action against an American publisher in England arising out of a short item which appeared in the American edition of the *Wall Street Journal*. Only ten copies had been sent to subscribers in the United Kingdom. The same edition of the *Wall Street Journal* had a distribution of about 1.8 million copies in the United States. The item had also appeared in the online edition of the *Wall Street Journal*. The evidence was that the online publication had received only a 'very small number' of hits. Eady J concluded that although the publications occurring in England were 'limited and technical', they were nonetheless conveniently dealt with by an English court.[71]

Dow Jones & Co Inc v Jameel

26.31 Finally, the English Court of Appeal in *Dow Jones & Co Inc v Jameel*[72] held that jurisdiction had to be declined in a case brought by a Saudi national in respect of an online article by an American defendant that had been published to only five individuals in England, and that had apparently caused no more than minimal harm to the claimant's reputation.[73] The Court of Appeal took the view that the proceeding involved an inappropriate and disproportionate use of judicial and court resources,[74] and that in order to keep a proper balance between the right to freedom of expression in Article 10 of the European Convention on Human Rights and the protection of individual reputation it was necessary to stop the proceeding as an abuse of process.[75] The court concluded that the five publications that had taken place in England 'did not, individually or collectively, amount to a real and substantial tort'.[76]

---

[68] *King v Lewis* [2005] EMLR 4, para 36.
[69] ibid.
[70] [2003] EWHC 1162.
[71] ibid, para 43. The American publisher brought proceedings in the United States in an attempt to restrain the claimant and its chairman from prosecuting the English proceedings. That action failed. See *Dow Jones & Co, Inc v Harrods Ltd*, 237 F Supp 2d 394 (SD NY, 2002); see paras 23.11–23.12.
[72] [2005] EWCA Civ 75.
[73] ibid, para 38.
[74] ibid, paras 54–6.
[75] ibid, para 55. The role of Art 10 of the European Convention on Human Rights in defamation actions in the United Kingdom is the subject of chapter 30.
[76] ibid, para 70.

Summary

While exercises in comparing the facts of one case with those of another are **26.32** perhaps antithetical to the exercise of discretion at the heart of the *forum non conveniens* inquiry,[77] in a text of this kind an attempt to extract statements of principle from the authorities for the edification of readers seems both unavoidable and desirable.

The key principles, in cases where the *forum non conveniens* discretion is **26.33** available,[78] appear to be:

- Where material is published by a foreign defendant to a global audience via the Internet, claimants will generally be able to sue in the United Kingdom if they limit their claims to publications occurring and harm suffered in the United Kingdom, provided there is evidence that they have reputations worthy of protection there.[79] The court will be likely to permit the proceeding to continue where the claimant resides in the United Kingdom.[80]
- United Kingdom courts will be more likely to decline to exercise jurisdiction on *forum non conveniens* grounds in cases where:
  - claimants reside outside the United Kingdom;
  - claimants have no reputation worthy of vindication in the United Kingdom;
  - there is scant evidence that such publications as occurred in the United Kingdom caused any harm to the reputation of the claimant there;
  - claimants do not limit their claims to damages to publications occurring in the United Kingdom; or
  - the claimant's decision to sue in the United Kingdom is forum shopping in the literal sense.[81]

- Similar principles will apply in Australia, although by reason of the 'clearly inappropriate forum' test which prevails there, it might be expected that

---

[77] *Spiliada Maritime Corporation v Cansulex Ltd* [1987] 1 AC 460, 465 (Lord Templeman); *Berezovsky v Michaels* [2000] 2 All ER 986, 1002 (Lord Hoffmann); *King v Lewis* [2005] EMLR 4, paras 35–6.

[78] See paras 26.01–26.06.

[79] As in *Shapira v Ahronson* [1999] EMLR 735, see para 26.16; *Berezovsky v Michaels* [2000] 2 All ER 986, see paras 26.17–26.22 and *King v Lewis* [2005] EMLR 4, see para 26.29.

[80] As in *Shapira v Ahronson* [1999] EMLR 735, see para 26.16 and *Harrods Ltd v Dow Jones & Co Inc* [2003] EWHC 1162, see para 26.30. See also *Bangoura v Washington Post* (2004) 234 DLR (4th) 564 (Ontario Superior Court of Justice), discussed in paras 26.27–26.28; *Kitakufe v Oloya* (Ontario Court of Justice, Himel J, 2 June 1998); *Imagis Technologies Inc v Red Herring Communications Inc* (British Columbia Supreme Court, Pitfield J, 12 March 2003).

[81] See *Chadha v Dow Jones & Co Inc* [1999] EMLR 724, see paras 26.23–26.24; *Dow Jones & Co Inc v Jameel* [2005] EWCA Civ 75; see para 26.31. See also *Reuben v Time Inc* [2003] EWCA Civ 6, para 14: proceedings not based on publications occurring in England would 'almost certainly' be stayed.

courts will be more reluctant to stay proceedings on *forum non conveniens* grounds than in the United Kingdom.[82]

26.34 In the United States courts generally exercise jurisdiction in respect of defamatory publications originating outside the forum only where the defendant has targeted—that is, intentionally directed—the publication towards the forum.[83] The relevance of the intention of the defendant to *forum non conveniens* inquiries was rejected 'out of hand' by the Court of Appeal in *King v Lewis*, albeit without any analysis of the American authorities, on the basis that when material is published on the web, the defendant has targeted every jurisdiction where the material may be downloaded.[84]

D. Australia: Staying and Transferring Proceedings

Cross-vesting legislation

26.35 Defendants may apply to have proceedings in an Australian superior court[85] transferred to another Australian superior court[86] under the Jurisdiction of Courts (Cross-Vesting) Acts of the Commonwealth, States, and Territories ('the Cross-Vesting Acts').[87] The Cross-Vesting Acts allow proceedings to be transferred between different Australian superior courts in three circumstances, the most important of which is 'in the interests of justice'.[88]

The expression 'in the interests of justice' requires the court to ascertain whether the proposed transferee court is a 'more appropriate forum' for the hearing and determination of the proceeding, taking into account the same sort of factors

---

[82] See para 26.07; *Dow Jones & Co Inc v Gutnick* (2002) 210 CLR 575; see paras 26.25–26.26.

[83] See paras 31.84–31.107.

[84] [2005] EMLR 4, paras 33–4; cf *Dow Jones & Co Inc v Gutnick* (2002) 210 CLR 575, para 54.

[85] That is, the Supreme Courts of the States and Territories, the Federal Court of Australia, and the Family Court of Australia.

[86] Note, however, that to the extent that the Cross-Vesting Acts purport to confer State jurisdiction on federal courts, they are invalid: *Re Wakim, ex p McNally* (1999) 198 CLR 511.

[87] Jurisdiction of Courts (Cross-Vesting) Acts (Cth, States, and Territories) ('the Cross-Vesting Acts'), s 5.

[88] Cross-Vesting Acts, s 5(2)(a), (b)(iii). Transfers are also possible where a proceeding is pending in an Australian Supreme Court, and a second, related proceeding is pending in another Australian Supreme Court, if it is 'more appropriate' that the first proceeding be determined by that court: see Cross-Vesting Acts, s 5(2)(a), (b)(i); and where another court is 'more appropriate', having regard to whether, but for the Cross-Vesting Acts, the proceeding or a substantial part of the proceeding would have been incapable of being instituted in the first court, the extent to which the matters for determination are matters arising under or involving questions as to the application, interpretation, or validity of a law of the forum of the other court, and the interests of justice: see Cross-Vesting Acts, s 5(2)(a), (b)(ii).

which are relevant to a *forum non conveniens* inquiry.[89] The court is not concerned with whether it is justified in refusing to exercise jurisdiction. Rather, the court is required to ensure that cases are heard in the forum dictated by the interests of justice.[90] It follows that no onus applies in an application to transfer under the Cross-Vesting Acts and that no regard may be paid to the plaintiff's choice of forum.[91] If, in a particular respect, a plaintiff's assumed advantage and a defendant's assumed disadvantage are 'commensurate, the one simply being the converse of the other, then that does not advance the matter'.[92]

A forum which could not be described as 'clearly inappropriate' for the purposes of an Australian *forum non conveniens* application may thus have to yield to another 'more appropriate' forum in an application to transfer defamation proceedings from one Australian court to another 'in the interests of justice'. **26.36**

In tort cases, the most appropriate forum will usually be the place where the tort was committed.[93] As the tort of defamation is committed in each place where defamatory material is published—that is, read, heard, or seen[94]—and as, in Internet defamation cases, those places may be myriad, the place of commission of the tort will often be a neutral factor in Internet defamation cases. Other connecting factors, such as the place where most of the parties and likely witnesses reside, may be of greater significance.[95] **26.37**

Other factors which are relevant in balancing the interests of justice include comparative cost,[96] and possibly also the speed with which the proceeding could be heard in each jurisdiction.[97] **26.38**

---

[89] See eg *Bankinvest AG v Seabrook* (1988) 14 NSWLR 711, 730; *BHP Billiton Ltd v Schultz* [2004] HCA 61, para 27. The factors relevant to a *forum non conveniens* inquiry are discussed in paras 26.09–26.11.

[90] *BHP Billiton Ltd v Schultz* [2004] HCA 61, para 14.

[91] ibid, para 25. To the extent that the following decisions in defamation cases suggest to the contrary, they can no longer be considered good law: *Waterhouse v Australian Broadcasting Corporation* (1989) 86 ACTR 1; *Baffsky v John Fairfax & Sons Ltd* (1990) 97 ACTR 1; *Arrowcrest Group Pty Ltd v Advertiser News Weekend Publishing Company Pty Ltd* (1993) 113 FLR 57; *Dawson v Baker* (1994) 123 FLR 194; *O'Connor v Nationwide News Pty Ltd* (1995) 128 FLR 61; *Carrey v ACP Publications Pty Ltd* (Supreme Court of Victoria, Hedigan J, 26 September 1997); *National Road and Motorists' Association Ltd v Nine Network Australia Pty Ltd* [2002] ACTSC 9; *Windschuttle v ACP Publishing Pty Ltd* [2002] ACTSC 64.

[92] *BHP Billiton Ltd v Schultz* [2004] HCA 61, para 26 (Gleeson CJ, McHugh, and Heydon JJ).

[93] ibid, paras 170, 259.

[94] See para 5.10.

[95] See eg *Waterhouse v Herald & Weekly Times Ltd* (Supreme Court of New South Wales, Levine J, 10 June 1997); *Hayward v Barratt* [2000] NSWSC 708.

[96] *Hunter v West Australian Newspapers Ltd* (Supreme Court of New South Wales, Levine J, 12 May 1995); *Laing-Peach v The Cairns Post Pty Ltd* (Supreme Court of New South Wales, 20 October 1989); *McPhersons Ltd v Rudzki* (Supreme Court of New South Wales, Levine J, 17 May 1995).

[97] *Hunter v West Australian Newspapers Ltd* (Supreme Court of New South Wales, Levine J, 12 May 1995); *Carrey v ACP Publications Pty Ltd* (Supreme Court of Victoria, Hedigan J, 26

Substantive differences in the laws of different Australian States and Territories are not, however, reasons for withholding from the parties the neutral application of the policy to which the Cross-Vesting Acts give effect.[98]

Service and Execution of Process Act 1992 (Cth)

26.39 Finally, under section 20 of the Service and Execution of Process Act 1992 (Cth) ('the SEPA'), Australian courts, other than Australian Supreme Courts, may stay proceedings if satisfied that a court of another State that has jurisdiction to determine all the matters in issue between the parties is the appropriate court to determine those matters.[99] In determining whether to grant a stay, the court must take into account various factors, including the places of residence of the parties and the witnesses likely to be called in the proceeding, the financial circumstances of the parties, and the law that would be most appropriate to apply in the proceeding.[100] The court may not take into account the fact that the plaintiff chose to issue in the court.[101] The court may grant a stay on such conditions as may be just and appropriate in order to facilitate determination of the matter in issue without delay or undue expense.[102]

The power to grant a stay under section 20 of the SEPA operates as an alternative to the power to stay a proceeding on the grounds of *forum non conveniens*.[103] An application under section 20 will often be more attractive to defendants than a *forum non conveniens* application. In a *forum non conveniens* application in Australia, the defendant must prove that the court is a 'clearly inappropriate forum'.[104] By contrast, under section 20 of the SEPA, the defendant has only to prove that some other Australian court is 'the appropriate court' to determine the matters in issue.

September 1997). In *Aopi v Rapke* [2000] NSWSC 1195, Levine J declined to transfer a proceeding to Victoria 'in the interests of justice' in a case with no real connection to New South Wales at all. The plaintiff resided in Papua New Guinea and the defendant in Victoria. The offending publication appeared in a national newspaper. Levine J at paras 19–21 seemed to base his decision on the (perceived) superiority of the mechanisms for case management of defamation actions in New South Wales; cf *National Road and Motorists' Association Ltd v Nine Network Australia Pty Ltd* [2002] ACTSC 9, paras 21–2; *Stalyce Holdings (Aust) Pty Ltd v Cetec Pty Ltd* [2002] FCA 278, paras 11, 12. See also *BHP Billiton Ltd v Schultz* [2004] HCA 61, para 15.

[98] *BHP Billiton Ltd v Schultz* [2004] HCA 61, paras 79–80, 171, 258, cf 26.
[99] Service and Execution of Process Act 1992 (Cth), s 20(1), (3).
[100] ibid, s 20(4)(a), (c), (e). The other relevant matters are the place where the subject matter of the proceeding is situated, any agreement between the parties about the court or place in which the proceeding should be instituted, and whether a related or similar proceeding has been commenced against the person served or another person: ibid, s 20(4)(b), (d), (f).
[101] ibid, s 20(4).
[102] ibid, s 20(5).
[103] ibid, s 20(9).
[104] See para 26.07.

Applications under section 20 of the SEPA are not available in cases before Australian Supreme Courts,[105] or in cases where some court outside Australia is the appropriate court for the determination of the matters in issue.

---

[105] In such cases, a *forum non conveniens* application (see paras 26.07–26.34), or a transfer application under the Cross-Vesting Acts (see paras 26.35–26.38), are the relevant mechanisms.

27

CHOICE OF LAW IN THE
UNITED KINGDOM

A. Introduction

Where a United Kingdom court has jurisdiction to entertain defamation pro- **27.01**
ceedings arising out of material published in another jurisdiction—that is,
material which is read, heard, or seen in another jurisdiction—and the court
proposes to exercise that jurisdiction, it must then determine which law or laws
to apply to determine the legal consequences of the publication or publications.
The applicable laws are determined by applying common law choice of law
rules.

The common law choice of rules for torts have largely been replaced by legislative rules in the United Kingdom.[1] The legislative reforms do not apply,
however, to defamation actions.[2]

---

[1] Private International Law (Miscellaneous Provisions) Act 1995 (UK), Pt III (especially
ss 11–12).
[2] ibid, s 13.

369

Choice of law rules for torts are likely to form the subject of a European Regulation in the not too distant future.[3]

27.02 The test applicable in defamation cases in the United Kingdom involving material published abroad is markedly different, at least in form, from the approach favoured in Australia,[4] Canada,[5] and the United States.[6]

B. The Double Actionability Test

Phillips v Eyre

27.03 The starting point for a consideration of the traditional choice of law test for torts committed abroad is *Phillips v Eyre*.[7]

Eyre was governor of Jamaica. During a time of rebellion, he declared a state of martial law over the island. While the state of martial law was in place, Phillips was assaulted and imprisoned by Jamaican authorities, who apparently believed Phillips was part of a conspiracy to overthrow the Government. Eyre caused legislation to be enacted which, in effect, granted him an indemnity in respect of any liability which might have arisen as a result of acts done in furtherance of martial law. Phillips brought proceedings for assault and false imprisonment against Eyre in England.

27.04 The court held that Phillips was not entitled to succeed. Willes J said:

> As a general rule, in order to found a suit in England for a wrong alleged to have

---

[3] A proposal for a Council Regulation on the law applicable to non-contractual obligations, known as 'Rome II', was released by the Commission of the European Communities on 22 July 2003. The relevant provisions for defamation actions are Arts 3 and 6. See also the accompanying explanatory memorandum, 17–18; cf the preliminary draft proposal, Art 7.

[4] See chapter 28.

[5] In *Tolofson v Jensen* [1994] 3 SCR 1022, the Supreme Court of Canada held that the law of the place of the tort was the applicable law in all intra-Canadian tort cases. In cases with a foreign element, La Forest J, 307–8 (obiter dictum) favoured the operation of the law of the place of the tort, subject to a discretion permitting courts to apply Canadian law in appropriate cases. In *Society of Composers, Authors & Music Publishers of Canada v Canadian Association of Internet Providers* (2004) 240 DLR (4th) 193, the Canadian Supreme Court, citing *Tolofson*, applied Canadian copyright law in a case involving music downloaded in Canada from servers located outside Canada. It seems, however, that in defamation cases involving publications in multiple jurisdictions a proper law of the tort approach might prevail in Canada: see eg *Olde v Capital Publishing Ltd Partnership* (1996) 5 CPC (4th) 95, para 15 (applicable law in a defamation case might be the law of the place where a majority of sales of the publication take place); *Direct Energy Marketing Ltd v Hillson* (1999) 247 AR 48 (Alberta Court of Queen's Bench), paras 43–5, 56 (applicable law in a defamation case is the law of the place where the reputation of the plaintiff was most injured).

[6] See para 31.108–31.110.

[7] (1870) LR 6 QB 1.

been committed abroad, two conditions must be fulfilled. First, the wrong must be of such a character that it would have been actionable if committed in England. Secondly, the act must not have been justifiable by the law of the place where it was done.[8]

As Eyre could not be liable to Phillips under the law of Jamaica, the second condition in the passage just cited was not satisfied and, accordingly, Phillips' action failed.

Refinements of the *Phillips v Eyre* test: double actionability

The meaning of the second element of the *Phillips v Eyre* test was considered by the Court of Appeal in *Machado v Fontes*.[9] That case concerned a defamatory publication in the Portuguese language in Brazil. The publication gave rise to criminal, but not civil, liability under the law of Brazil. As the publication was not 'innocent' under Brazilian law, the court held that the publication was 'not justifiable' for the purposes of the second element of the *Phillips v Eyre* test. Accordingly, the defendant was not able to avoid liability by contending that he would not have been liable to pay damages had the action been heard and determined in Brazil.   **27.05**

Machado v Fontes has since been overruled in England[10] and Canada.[11] It has not been followed in Scotland,[12] and its correctness has been doubted in Australia.[13]

In *Boys v Chaplin*,[14] the House of Lords considered the application of the *Phillips v Eyre* test in a case concerning a road accident in Malta involving two English residents. Under Maltese law, the plaintiff would have been entitled to recover only special damages. Under English law, the plaintiff would have been entitled to recover additional damages for pain and suffering. The court held that the plaintiff was entitled to recover both special damages and damages for pain and suffering assessed according to English law. The opinions of the members of the House of Lords are, however, somewhat difficult to reconcile.[15]   **27.06**

---

[8] ibid, 28–9.

[9] [1897] 2 QB 231.

[10] *Boys v Chaplin* [1971] AC 356, 377, 381, 388, cf 383, 400–1.

[11] *Tolofson v Jensen* [1994] 3 SCR 1022; overruling *McLean v Pettigrew* [1945] 2 DLR 65.

[12] *Joseph Evans & Sons v John G Stein & Company* 1904 12 SLT 462; *Naftalin v The London, Midland and Scottish Railway Company* 1933 SC 259; *M'Elroy v M'Allister* 1949 SC 110.

[13] *Koop v Bebb* (1951) 84 CLR 629, 643. See also *Varawa v Howard Smith & Co Ltd (No 2)* [1910] VLR 509, 528–34.

[14] [1971] AC 356.

[15] As Lord Slynn noted in *Red Sea Insurance Co Ltd v Bouygues SA* [1995] 1 AC 190, 198 (PC): the reasons 'varied to such an extent that both academic writers and judges in other cases have expressed doubt as to whether there can be extracted from the speeches one binding ratio decidendi'.

For present purposes it is sufficient to note that a majority of the House recast the *Phillips v Eyre* test as one of 'double actionability'. Lords Hodson, Guest, and Wilberforce each held that to recover in respect of a foreign tort in England, it was essential that the act the subject of the claim gave rise to civil actionability by the law of the place where the act was done.[16]

27.07 The *Phillips v Eyre* test had also been judicially considered extensively in Australia prior to its abolition there.[17] It had been authoritatively restated in Australia as a 'double actionability' test, for practical purposes to the same effect as that which presently applies in the United Kingdom.[18]

27.08 The double actionability test has been applied or considered in a number of English cases,[19] and is now, subject to the important qualifications to be discussed shortly, the test which prevails in defamation actions involving foreign publications in England. The broad effect of the double actionability test is that, subject to the operation of what might be termed a 'flexibility exception',[20] and the substance–procedure distinction,[21] claimants can only succeed to the extent that the defendant is liable under both the law of the forum (the *lex fori*) and the law of the place of the tort (the *lex loci delicti*).

27.09 In Scots law, the double actionability requirement has been interpreted somewhat more strictly than in England. Pursuers may recover in Scots law only to the extent that the defender is liable in respect of the same cause of action and liable to the same remedy under both the *lex fori* and the *lex loci delicti*.[22]

27.10 The authors of *Dicey and Morris on Conflict of Laws*[23] state the current English test in the following terms:

---

[16] [1971] AC 356, 377, 381, 389; cf 383, 405.

[17] *John Pfeiffer Pty Ltd v Rogerson* (2000) 203 CLR 503; *Regie Nationale des Usines Renault SA v Zhang* (2002) 210 CLR 491. See chapter 28. The earlier Australian cases 'are still of interest where issues arise under the common law' in England: *Kuwait Airways Corporation v Iraqi Airways Company (Nos 4 and 5)* [2002] 2 AC 883, 1113 (Lord Hope).

[18] *Breavington v Godleman* (1988) 169 CLR 41, 110–11 (Brennan J); followed by a majority of the High Court in two cases, *McKain v RW Miller & Company (South Australia) Pty Ltd* (1991) 174 CLR 1, 39 and *Stevens v Head* (1993) 176 CLR 433, 453.

[19] See eg *Church of Scientology of California v Commissioner of Metropolitan Police* (1976) 120 SJ 690; *Metall und Rohstoff AG v Donaldson Lufkin & Jenrette Inc* [1990] 1 QB 391, 439–40; *Johnson v Coventry Churchill International Ltd* [1992] 3 All ER 14; *Red Sea Insurance Co Ltd v Bouygues SA* [1995] 1 AC 190 (PC); *University of Glasgow v The Economist Ltd* [1997] EMLR 495; *Pearce v Ove Arup Partnership Ltd* [2000] Ch 403; *Loutchansky v Times Newspapers Ltd (Nos 4 and 5)* [2002] QB 783, 819–21; *Kuwait Airways Corporation v Iraqi Airways Company (Nos 4 and 5)* [2002] 2 AC 883; *Komarek v Ramco Energy Plc* (English High Court, Eady J, 29 October 2002). See also Lawrence Collins (ed), *Dicey and Morris on Conflict of Laws* (13th edn, 2000) ('Dicey and Morris') 1511 (n 41), 1565 (n 35).

[20] See paras 27.11–27.16.

[21] See paras 27.30–27.36.

[22] *M'Elroy v M'Allister* 1949 SC 110.

[23] Dicey and Morris (n 19 above).

As a general rule, an act done in a foreign country which is alleged to give rise to a liability such as is mentioned in clause (1) of this Rule[24] is actionable as such in England, only if it is both

(a) actionable as such according to English law (or in other words is an act which, if done in England, would give rise to such a claim) and

(b) actionable according to the law of the foreign country where it was done.[25]

C. Flexibility

England

In the House of Lords' decision in *Boys v Chaplin*, Lords Hodson and Wilber-   **27.11**
force thought that the time had come to allow greater flexibility to admit or exclude extraterritorial torts claims in the interests of public policy.[26] Lords Hodson and Wilberforce concluded that the law of the place of the tort should ordinarily govern substantive issues,[27] except where that law, because of the weakness of its relationship with the occurrence and the parties, should not be applied as a matter of policy.[28] Lord Pearson also favoured permitting flexibility in the operation of choice of law rules.[29]

A flexibility exception was applied in *Johnson v Coventry Churchill International Ltd*,[30] a case concerning an injury sustained by an English worker in Germany in the course of his employment with an English company. West German law,

---

[24] Namely, claims 'under the law of England for libel or slander or for slander of title, slander of goods or other malicious falsehood, any claim under the law of Scotland for verbal injury, and any claim arising under the law of any country corresponding to or otherwise in the nature of any of the foregoing claims, hereinafter referred to as a defamation claim'.

[25] Dicey and Morris (n 19 above) 1560, r 205(2). Rule 205(3) then describes a flexibility exception: see paras 27.11–27.16. An earlier formulation to substantially the same effect as this rule but applicable to torts generally was approved by the Privy Council in *Red Sea Insurance Co Ltd v Bouygues SA* [1995] 1 AC 190, 198, a case dealing with the application of the *Phillips v Eyre* test prior to the commencement of the Private International Law (Miscellaneous Provisions) Act 1995 (UK).

[26] [1971] AC 356, 378, 389–92.

[27] ibid, 379, 389.

[28] ibid, 392 (Lord Wilberforce); see also 380 (Lord Hodson): where some other law 'has the greater concern with the specific issue raised in the litigation'. By contrast, Lord Guest, 381–3, thought that the law of the place of the tort invariably governed the extent of liability. Lord Donovan, 383, and Lord Pearson, 398–400, each thought that under English law, once the two conditions in *Phillips v Eyre* had been satisfied, the law of the forum was the substantive law to be applied to determine the extent of liability. Lord Donovan, 383, considered that there was no need to depart from that view of the law, and rejected the call for flexibility in the application of choice of law rules.

[29] ibid, 406. Lord Pearson saw no reason to discard or modify the existing rules, although he thought that, as a matter of public policy, it might be desirable in some cases to apply 'the law of the natural forum' as a means of discouraging forum shopping.

[30] [1992] 3 All ER 14.

unlike English law, did not provide for an employer to be liable for personal injuries suffered by an employee as a result of the employer's negligence. JW Kay QC, sitting as a deputy judge of the English High Court, held that England was the country with the most significant relationship with the occurrence and the parties and that it was appropriate in the circumstances to apply English law to the exclusion of West German law.

27.12   The Privy Council has since held that a flexibility exception may also be applied in appropriate cases to exclude entirely the law of the forum. In *Red Sea Insurance Co Ltd v Bouygues SA*, the Council held that, in appropriate cases, the law of the place of the tort can be applied to determine the whole of a claim, even where no liability arises under the law of the forum.[31] That approach was also taken by the Court of Appeal in *Pearce v Ove Arup Partnership Ltd*.[32]

27.13   The flexibility of the exception was extended further in *Kuwait Airways Corporation v Iraqi Airways Company (Nos 4 and 5)*.[33] A majority of the House of Lords held that the law of the forum may be applied without regard to the law of the place of the tort if it would be contrary to public policy to permit application of some repugnant foreign law.[34] The law in question was a decree made in the circumstances of Iraq's 1990 invasion of Kuwait purporting to seize assets belonging to the claimant and to transfer those assets to the defendant.

27.14   The trend disclosed in cases such as *Johnson, Red Sea Insurance, Pearce*, and *Kuwait Airways* is, in effect, to treat the double actionability test as merely a starting point for a more broad-ranging inquiry into which law ought to apply to any particular issue between the parties to litigation, having regard to the place with the most significant relationship to the occurrence and the parties. In particular, in all cases where an act is not actionable by either the law of the forum or the law of the place of the tort, there will be scope for argument that an exception to the double actionability test should apply. It may be that, in practice, the English test is not all that different from a 'proper law of the tort' approach of the kind which prevails in the United States.[35]

27.15   The authors of *Dicey and Morris on Conflict of Laws* describe the flexibility exception to the double actionability test as follows:

---

[31] [1995] 1 AC 190, 206; see also Andrew Dickinson, 'Further Thoughts on Foreign Torts: *Boys v Chaplin* explained?' [1994] Lloyds Maritime and Commercial Law Quarterly 463; PB Carter, 'Choice of Law in Tort: The Role of the *Lex Fori*' (1995) 54 Cambridge Law Journal 38; Pippa Rogerson, 'Choice of Law in Tort: A Missed Opportunity?' (1995) 44 International and Comparative Law Quarterly 650.

[32] [2000] Ch 403 (action in England for infringement of Dutch copyright).

[33] [2002] 2 AC 883.

[34] ibid, paras 33 (Lord Nicholls), 117 (Lord Steyn), 148, 168 (Lord Hope); cf 198 (Lord Scott).

[35] See paras 31.108–31.110.

By way of exception to clause (2) of this Rule,[36] a particular issue between the parties which arises in a defamation claim[37] may be governed by the law of the country which, with respect to that issue, has the most significant relationship with the occurrence and the parties.[38]

Scotland

In the leading Scottish decision, the double actionability test was expressed in unqualified terms.[39]

27.16

D. Choice of Law in Defamation Cases

Apart from *Machado v Fontes*,[40] choice of law questions have been the subject of remarkably few recent reported defamation cases in the United Kingdom.[41] The potential application of the test was considered, however, in *Church of Scientology of California v Commissioner of Metropolitan Police*.[42] In that case, the defendant Commissioner had published an allegedly defamatory report concerning the plaintiff's activities in England to the West German Criminal Police Authority. On an interlocutory appeal, the Court of Appeal held that it was arguable that the *Boys v Chaplin* flexibility exception to the double actionability test might apply, having regard to the fact that the plaintiff was most closely related to and resident in England, the plaintiff had as its aim the propagation of its beliefs in the United Kingdom and the world, and the defendant was an English police officer.

27.17

The application of the double actionability test was also considered in *University of Glasgow v The Economist Ltd*.[43] In that case, the plaintiffs sought to amend their statement of claim to allege publication of a book in a number of foreign places, including Australia, Canada, and the United States. The amendment sought simply to allege that the publication 'is and was actionable by the law of those countries'. Popplewell J allowed the amendment, noting:

27.18

---

[36] See para 27.10.

[37] 'Defamation claim' is defined broadly: see n 24 above.

[38] Dicey and Morris (n 19 above) 1560, r 205(3).

[39] *M'Elroy v M'Allister* 1949 SC 110; see also Kenneth Norrie, *Defamation and Related Actions in Scots Law* (1995) 190.

[40] See para 27.05.

[41] For two older Scottish examples, see *Longworth v Hope* (1865) 3 M 1049; *Joseph Evans & Sons v John G Stein & Company* 1904 12 SLT 462. See also *Loutchansky v Times Newspapers Ltd (Nos 4 and 5)* [2002] QB 783: see para 27.36; *Komarek v Ramco Energy Plc* (English High Court, Eady J, 29 October 2002): see n 65 below.

[42] (1976) 120 SJ 690.

[43] [1997] EMLR 495.

> There is no dispute now as to the law relating to a tort committed abroad. It has to be actionable by the law of this country and actionable by the law of the country where the tort is committed.[44]

27.19   Popplewell J went on to conclude that, while it was open to the plaintiffs to set out affirmatively the law of foreign countries in support of their plea, they did not have to do so. The plaintiffs were entitled to rely on the presumption that the law of the foreign countries was the same as the law of England. It was then for the defendants to rebut that presumption, by pleading and proving that the foreign law was different from English law.[45]

E. Application to the Internet

Availability of foreign law defences

27.20   Where defamatory material is published abroad, the effect of applying the double actionability test is to limit liability to the extent that the defendant is liable under both the law of the forum and the law of the place of publication. The test enables defendants to rely on defences available in the forum to avoid liability in respect of publications, wherever they occur. It enables defendants to rely on defences available in any other jurisdiction in which publication occurred to avoid liability in respect of publications in that jurisdiction.

27.21   Most obviously, applying the double actionability test would limit the extent to which claimants could recover damages in the United Kingdom in respect of material published via the Internet in countries such as the United States.

For example, suppose that a claimant sues an American intermediary, such as an ISP or content host, in England in relation to defamatory material stored on that intermediary's computer system in the United States. Suppose further that the intermediary would be liable under English substantive law because the intermediary has actual knowledge of the existence and nature of the offending material but has failed to remove or disable access to it,[46] and no other defence is available in respect of the material. In such a case, the intermediary would not be liable under the substantive law of the United States, by reason of the operation of section 230(c)(1) of the Communications Decency Act.[47]

Subject to the availability of a flexibility exception, the operation of the double

---

[44] [1997] EMLR 495, 498.

[45] ibid, 502; see also *Goh Chok Tong v Tang Liang Hong* [1997] 2 SLR 641; cf *Yorke v British & Continental Steamship Co Ltd* (1945) 78 Lloyd's LR 181 (a negligence case); *Mother Bertha Music Ltd v Bourne Music Ltd* [1997] EMLR 457 (a copyright case). See also chapter 29.

[46] In such a case, none of the defences for intermediaries discussed in chapters 16–18 would be available.

[47] See para 31.51.

actionability test in such a case would have the effect of making the defendant liable in respect of publications of the defamatory web page or bulletin board posting occurring within England, but not the United States.

The application of the double actionability test potentially gives rise to huge practical difficulties in cases involving defamatory Internet publications. A defendant seeking to avoid liability in respect of the worldwide publication of a defamatory web page might be compelled to plead and prove defences under the laws of each place in which the defamatory material has been published; that is, read, heard, or seen. A failure to plead and prove foreign defences may result in liability being determined according to the law of the forum[48] which, in the case of the United Kingdom, will often be less favourable to the defendant than the law of other places in which the material was published. There are thus obvious tactical implications. While it is a relatively simple matter for the claimant to allege damage arising out of the worldwide publication of defamatory material, for the defendant, proving the availability of defences in multiple foreign jurisdictions will often be complicated, time-consuming, and expensive.

27.22

Application of the flexibility exception

These complexities may be reduced in some cases by the application of the flexibility exception to the double actionability test. That exception may constitute an important curb on the operation of the double actionability test in cases involving multi-jurisdictional, defamatory publications via the Internet.

27.23

Suppose, for example, that a claimant sues in England in respect of defamatory material in a posting on a special-purpose bulletin board for staff, students, and alumni of a British university. Suppose further that, although overwhelmingly viewed by persons within England, it can be proved that the posting has been viewed by alumni of the university all around the world. In such a case, the claimant might argue that English law should be applied to resolve all questions of liability in respect of the foreign publications. Although publication has occurred outside England, the occurrence and the parties have no substantial connection with any foreign jurisdictions. If the court accepted the application of a flexibility exception, and liability were proved, the claimant would be entitled to recover damages in England in respect of the foreign publications. The defendant would be denied the benefit of any defences available under the laws of the foreign places of publication in answer to the claimant's claim in respect of publications occurring outside England.[49]

27.24

---

[48] See chapter 29.

[49] eg *Boys v Chaplin* [1971] AC 356; *Church of Scientology of California v Commissioner of Metropolitan Police* (1976) 120 SJ 690; *Johnson v Coventry Churchill International Ltd* [1992] 3 All ER 14; see para 27.11.

27.25   To take a further example, suppose that a defendant who is resident in the United States is sued in England by an American public figure who has a substantial reputation worthy of protection in England. Assume that the claimant has been defamed on a web page created and stored on a computer in America, but that the offending page is accessible throughout the world. Suppose further that the claimant would be unable to succeed in defamation proceedings in the United States, because he or she would be unable to prove actual malice on the part of the defendant.[50] Finally, suppose that the material was unarguably defamatory, and that no defence would be available to the defendant under English defamation law.

Under the double actionability test, the claimant in such a case would not be able to recover damages in respect of the publication of the material in the United States, because although liability arises under English defamation law, no liability arises under American law. Assuming that the English court had jurisdiction,[51] and was not a *forum non conveniens*,[52] the claimant would, however, be able to recover damages in respect of the publication of the defamatory material in England.

In such a case, however, the defendant might be able to argue that American law should be applied by the English court to prevent the claimant from recovering damages, even in respect of publications occurring in England. It might be argued that the United States has the most significant relationship with the occurrence and the parties, and that American law should be applied to the exclusion of English law. Such an argument would only be likely to succeed in an extreme case.[53] Further, it is likely that in such a case the court would conclude that it was a *forum non conveniens*.[54]

27.26   There is little guidance in the authorities as to the matters which should be taken into account in a defamation action for the purpose of determining the court with the most significant connection to the occurrence and the parties. In the case of Internet defamation, where identical publications occur in a number of jurisdictions, there are obviously a number of potentially relevant factors, including the place where most publications occurred, the place of domicile of the claimant, the place of origin of the publication, and the place where the claimant predominantly enjoys a reputation.

---

[50] See para 31.04.
[51] See chapter 25.
[52] See chapter 26.
[53] eg *Red Sea Insurance Co Ltd v Bouygues SA* [1995] 1 AC 190; *Pearce v Ove Arup Partnership Ltd* [2000] Ch 403; see para 27.12.
[54] See chapter 26.

In the absence of a body of multi-jurisdictional defamation cases to draw upon, **27.27** it is somewhat difficult to predict what law or laws a United Kingdom court might apply in Internet cases with a complicated series of foreign elements. Complexities will be heightened, for example, in cases where the claimant sues multiple defendants, each of whom is domiciled in a different country, in a bid to recover damages in respect of publications occurring in a number of places.

Practical matters

The difficulties with the application of the double actionability test, and the **27.28** flexibility exception to that test, are likely however to be more theoretical than real in many cases involving the publication of defamatory material in multiple jurisdictions via the Internet.

In the first place, complexities will often be reduced by the application of jurisdictional principles. In those cases where proceedings can be stayed on the grounds of *forum non conveniens*, for example, claimants may be compelled to limit their claims to damages to publications occurring within the jurisdiction of the forum, or perhaps within a defined number of foreign jurisdictions.[55] In cases where claimants need to seek leave to serve a claim form outside the jurisdiction of the court, they necessarily must so limit their claims to avoid abusing the process of the court.[56] In cases governed by the Brussels Regulation[57] or the Brussels and Lugano Conventions,[58] the claimant is generally[59] limited to recovering damages in respect of harm suffered by reason of distributions of the offending publication occurring within the jurisdiction of the court, except where proceedings are brought in the place where the publisher is established.[60] Where a claimant sues in England, for example, in respect of material published by a defendant domiciled in Italy, the claimant will generally be restricted to recovering damages in respect of publications occurring within England. Only English law is relevant in such a case.[61] In other words, the jurisdictional rule in such a case has the effect of prescribing the applicable law.

Even where claimants are not, for jurisdictional reasons, limited to claiming **27.29**

---

[55] See chapter 26.
[56] See para 25.27.
[57] Council Regulation 44/2001 of 22 December 2000 on jurisdiction and the recognition and enforcement of judgments in civil and commercial matters, [2001] OJ L12/1. See paras 25.07–25.12, 25.31–25.41.
[58] Brussels and Lugano Conventions on jurisdiction and the enforcement of judgments in civil and commercial matters. See paras 25.07–25.12, 25.31–25.41.
[59] ie unless one or other of the circumstances described in paras 25.37–25.41 applies.
[60] See paras 25.34–25.36.
[61] See eg *Szalatnay-Stacho v Fink* [1947] KB 1; *Dow Jones & Co Inc v Gutnick* (2002) 210 CLR 575, 608 (Gleeson CJ, McHugh, Gummow, and Hayne JJ).

damages in respect of publications occurring in a single country, or a small number of defined countries, there may be other reasons why it is unnecessary to inquire into the substantive laws of a wide range of foreign jurisdictions. Claimants may, for example, elect not to make claims in respect of publications occurring in particular places because, for example, they do not have a reputation in those places, or know that the defendant has a good defence under the law of those places. Claimants may decide not to pursue a defendant domiciled in a particular country because any judgment they obtain might not be recognized and enforced there.[62] Defendants may elect not to plead and prove foreign defences in all places in which publication occurred. Defendants might, for example, ignore those jurisdictions where the claimant has no reputation, or plead and prove defences only in those jurisdictions which are most likely to assist their case, or simply rely on legal presumptions as to the content of foreign law.[63] In some cases there will be double actionability; that is, the publication will be actionable under both the law of the forum and the law of each place of publication. In cases where the publication is not actionable under both laws, the weight of connections with a particular jurisdiction may be so overwhelming that the application of the flexibility exception to the double actionability test will be tolerably certain.

F. The Substance–Procedure Distinction

General principles

27.30 An important exception to the principles already discussed is that matters of procedure are always governed by the law of the forum. Drawing the line between matters of substance and matters of procedure can be difficult. In *Phillips v Eyre*, Willes J explained the distinction in these terms:

> [T]he law is clear that, if the foreign law touches only the remedy or procedure for enforcing the obligation, as in the case of an ordinary statute of limitations, such law is no bar to an action in this country; but if the foreign law extinguishes the right it is a bar in this country equally as if the extinguishment had been by a release of the party, or an act of our own legislature.[64]

The substance–procedure distinction raises particular difficulties in relation to limitation periods, and the availability of heads of damages.[65]

---

[62] See chapter 23.
[63] See chapter 29.
[64] (1870) LR 6 QB 1, 29.
[65] See also *Komarek v Ramco Energy Plc* (English High Court, Eady J, 29 October 2002): the operation of any bar against a remedy based on diplomatic considerations, whether of personal immunity or the inviolability of archives, documents, or correspondence, is to be classified as procedural, rather than substantive, and therefore governed by the law of the forum.

Limitation periods

At common law, it has long been held in the United Kingdom that statutes of limitation which take away claimants' remedies, but do not otherwise extinguish their rights, are procedural in nature. Statutes of limitation which extinguish a cause of action, on the other hand, are substantive.[66]

27.31

In England, the Foreign Limitation Periods Act 1984 overrides the common law, by providing that where in any action or proceeding the law of any other country is to be taken into account, the court must apply the limitation rules of that country,[67] regardless of whether they are substantive or procedural,[68] except where to do so would conflict with public policy.[69] Where the law of England and the law of a foreign country must be taken into account, as where the double actionability test is applied in defamation actions involving foreign publications, both limitation rules are to be applied, so that the action will be barred upon the expiry of either the English limitation period or the foreign limitation period.[70]

27.32

A foreign limitation period will conflict with public policy if its application would cause 'undue hardship' to a person who is or might be a party.[71] Depending on the individual circumstances of the parties or prospective parties to an action, an unduly short, or unduly long limitation period might satisfy this test.[72]

In Scotland, legislation provides that where the substantive law of a country other than Scotland governs an obligation, Scottish courts must, subject to a public policy exception, apply the limitation laws of that country, whether substantive or procedural in character, 'to the exclusion of any corresponding rule of Scots law'.[73] Where the double actionability test applies, however, the legislative rule has no application, as there are two governing substantive laws. It would seem, therefore, that the common law test continues to apply in defamation actions in Scotland.[74]

27.33

---

[66] *Phillips v Eyre* (1870) LR 6 QB 1, 29; *Huber v Steiner* (1835) 2 Bing NC 203; 132 ER 80; *Leroux v Brown* (1852) 12 CB 801; 138 ER 1119; *Harris v Quine* (1869) LR 4 QB 653; *Alliance Bank of Simla v Carey* (1880) 5 CPD 429; *M'Elroy v M'Allister* 1949 SC 110; *Black-Clawson International Ltd v Papierwerke Waldhof-Aschaffenburg AG* [1975] AC 591, 630–1; *Yew Bon Tew v Kenderaan Bas Mara* [1983] 1 AC 553, 558 (PC). The common law position is different in Australia: see paras 28.07–28.09, and in Canada: see *Tolofson v Jensen* [1994] 3 SCR 1022.

[67] Foreign Limitation Periods Act 1984 (UK), s 1(1).

[68] ibid, s 4(2).

[69] ibid, s 2(1).

[70] ibid, s 1(1)(b), (2).

[71] ibid, s 2(2).

[72] Dicey and Morris (n 19 above) 175–6.

[73] Prescription and Limitation (Scotland) Act 1973, s 23A.

[74] See also Norrie (n 39 above) 188; *M'Elroy v M'Allister* 1949 SC 110, 125–6, 127–8.

Availability of heads of damages

27.34 In *Boys v Chaplin*, Lords Hodson, Wilberforce, and Pearson held that questions such as whether pain and suffering was an admissible head of damages were questions of substantive law, governed by the double actionability test, while questions going only to the quantification of damages were procedural in nature and governed by the law of the forum.[75] Lords Guest and Donovan dissented on this issue. Lord Guest held that a claim for pain and suffering was merely an element in the quantification of the total compensation payable to a claimant, and was therefore governed by the law of the forum.[76] Lord Donovan said only that an English court 'should award its own remedies'.[77]

27.35 The application of the substance–procedure distinction to damages issues has been addressed more recently in some detail by the Court of Appeal in *Harding v Wealands*.[78] The claimant sought damages in England for injuries sustained in a motor vehicle accident in New South Wales. The proceedings were served on the defendant, an Australian national, in England. The issue before the Court of Appeal concerned the characterization of a New South Wales statute which, among other things, capped the amount of non-economic loss recoverable by motor accident victims, required courts to disregard certain losses, prescribed a 'discount rate' to be applied to future economic losses, and contained prescriptions in relation to the calculation of interest on different heads of loss.

Arden LJ held that a foreign law which imposes a restriction on the right to recover damages is to be regarded as substantive.[79] The statutory cap on non-economic loss and the requirement that certain losses be disregarded were thus matters of substance.[80] Given 'the precision of the directions' in the New South Wales statute, Arden LJ thought the prescribed discount and interest rates were also limitations on the substantive right to recover damages.[81] Arden LJ distinguished those matters from questions going to the form of the remedy, such as whether damages can be paid by instalments, whether subsequent damages for the same injury can be claimed in a fresh action, and the conversion of sums from one currency to another. Arden LJ said that such matters would more probably be questions of procedure.[82]

Sir William Aldous agreed with Arden LJ's conclusion. He articulated a broader proposition of principle, however, namely that:

---

[75] [1971] AC 356, 379, 384–5, 393.
[76] ibid, 382–3.
[77] ibid, 383.
[78] [2005] 1 All ER 415.
[79] ibid, paras 54–5.
[80] ibid, para 55.
[81] ibid.
[82] ibid, paras 57–8.

matters that affect the existence, extent or enforceability of the rights or duties of the parties to an action are matters that, on their face, appear to be concerned with issues of substance, not with issues of procedure.

To put it another way, he said that:

rules which are directed to governing or regulating the mode or conduct of court proceedings are procedural and all other provisions or rules are to be classified as substantive.[83]

Waller LJ dissented. He took the view that the New South Wales statute reflected New South Wales policy and that it was 'clear' that the statute would be applied by a New South Wales court, whatever the substantive law might be.[84] Waller LJ thought the limitations in the New South Wales statute went to the assessment of damages, rather than the availability of particular heads of damages, and concluded that each of the relevant matters was procedural.[85]

Harding v Wealands thus stands as authority for the proposition that foreign **27.36** laws which impose a restriction on the right to recover damages, such as statutory caps and exclusions, are to be regarded as substantive. The prohibitions on awards of exemplary damages in defamation actions in Scots law and New South Wales law[86] are examples. An English court applying the double actionability test in a case involving publications occurring in Scotland or New South Wales would not be expected to award exemplary damages in respect of those publications, even if an award of exemplary damages would be justified applying principles of English defamation law.

Matters such as the extent to which foreign courts require claimants in defamation actions to prove that they suffered damage by reason of a libel, on the other hand, go to the mode or conduct of proceedings, and so give rise to procedural, rather than substantive, questions.[87]

---

[83] ibid, para 99. Sir William Aldous drew on the test which prevails in Australia in cases involving intra-Australian torts: see para 28.11. Whether that test also applies in Australia in cases concerning foreign torts is unresolved: see para 28.12.

[84] That correctness of that conclusion is to be doubted: see paras 28.11–28.12.

[85] [2005] 1 All ER 415, paras 35, 39.

[86] See para 21.13.

[87] *Loutchansky v Times Newspapers Ltd (Nos 4 and 5)* [2002] QB 783, paras 80–7.

28

CHOICE OF LAW IN AUSTRALIA

A. Governing Law

The double actionability test[1] was abolished in respect of intra-Australian torts **28.01** in *John Pfeiffer Pty Ltd v Rogerson* ('*John Pfeiffer*'),[2] and in respect of torts committed abroad in *Regie Nationale des Usines Renault SA v Zhang* ('*Zhang*').[3] In all proceedings before Australian courts the substantive law for the determination of rights and liabilities in respect of interstate and foreign torts is the *lex loci delicti* (the law of the place of the tort).

In settling on the *lex loci delicti* as the governing law for intra-Australian torts in **28.02** *John Pfeiffer*, Gleeson CJ, Gaudron, McHugh, Gummow, and Hayne JJ evaluated and rejected alternatives such as adopting a 'proper law of the tort' approach,[4] or the *lex fori*.[5] They said that applying the *lex loci delicti* promoted certainty, all but eliminated the potential for forum shopping, and gave effect to the reasonable expectations of most people in a federation.[6] Against these advantages, however, had to be weighed the disadvantage that in some cases, it may be difficult to determine the place of the tort, or the place of the tort may be fortuitous.[7]

---

[1] See paras 27.03–27.10.
[2] (2000) 203 CLR 503.
[3] (2002) 210 CLR 491.
[4] (2000) 203 CLR 503, para 79.
[5] ibid, paras 81–6.
[6] ibid, paras 83–7.
[7] ibid, para 82.

28.03 Gleeson CJ, Gaudron, McHugh, Gummow, and Hayne JJ held that the double actionability test should be discarded,[8] primarily because they thought that, within a federation, questions of public policy which in international cases might militate against giving effect to a law which was contrary to the law of the forum could have no application.[9] Secondly, they considered that giving effect to laws of the forum in cases where a tort was committed in some other place was to give to that law an unjustifiable extraterritorial operation.[10]

28.04 In *Zhang*, an identically constituted court abolished the double actionability test for foreign torts, and held that the *lex loci delicti* is the governing law in Australia in all cases involving torts committed outside Australia. In farewelling the double actionability test, Kirby J observed that it was:

> a rule inappropriate to a time of global and regional dealings, technological advances that increase international conflictual situations and attitudinal changes that reject, or at least reduce, xenophobic opinions about the worth and applicability of the law of other jurisdictions.[11]

B. Flexibility

28.05 The High Court held in *John Pfeiffer* that there was no room for the operation of any flexibility exception of the kind which was applied in decisions such as *Boys v Chaplin*[12] and *Red Sea Insurance Co Ltd v Bouygues SA*[13] in cases involving intra-Australian torts.[14]

28.06 In *Zhang*, the court held that no general flexibility exception would be available in foreign tort cases.[15] The majority judges, however, reserved for future decision the circumstances in which public policy considerations might direct that an action not be maintained in Australia.[16]

---

[8] (2000) 203 CLR 503, para 96. See also para 155 (Kirby J). Callinan J dissented.
[9] ibid, para 91.
[10] ibid, para 92.
[11] (2002) 210 CLR 491, para 132.
[12] [1971] AC 356. See para 27.11.
[13] [1995] 1 AC 190. See para 27.12.
[14] *John Pfeiffer Pty Ltd v Rogerson* (2000) 203 CLR 503, paras 79–80 (Gleeson CJ, Gaudron, McHugh, Gummow, and Hayne JJ), 157 (Kirby J). See also *McKain v RW Miller & Company (South Australia) Pty Ltd* (1991) 174 CLR 1, 38–9. The flexibility exception which applies in the United Kingdom is discussed in paras 27.11–27.16.
[15] (2002) 210 CLR 491, para 75 (Gleeson CJ, Gaudron, McHugh, Gummow, and Hayne JJ), cf para 122 (Kirby J).
[16] ibid, para 60 (Gleeson CJ, Gaudron, McHugh, Gummow, and Hayne JJ). See also para 122 (Kirby J). A decision in which public policy concerns were determinative in the United Kingdom is *Kuwait Airways Corporation v Iraqi Airways Company (Nos 4 and 5)* [2002] 2 AC 883.

C. The Substance–Procedure Distinction

Limitation periods

28.07
In *McKain v RW Miller & Company (South Australia) Pty Ltd* ('*McKain*'), a majority of the High Court held that limitation statutes which bar a remedy, but permit the plaintiff to apply for an order extending the time for bringing an action, are procedural. Only statutes of limitation which bar the plaintiff's right of action were to be treated as substantive.[17]

28.08
Following that decision, each Australian jurisdiction enacted legislation which had the effect of deeming the limitation periods of each State and Territory and of New Zealand to be substantive.[18]

28.09
In *John Pfeiffer*, the High Court reversed the effect of *McKain*, unanimously holding that limitation periods, of all kinds, should be considered substantive, rather than procedural, at common law,[19] thereby bringing the common law into line with the legislation referred to in the previous paragraph. In *Zhang*, the majority judges extended that conclusion to foreign limitation periods.[20] As a result, in an action in one Australian State concerning a publication in another Australian State, the court will apply only the interstate limitation period to determine whether the cause of action is statute-barred. A defamation action in Australia in respect of a foreign publication will be statute-barred only if the foreign limitation period has expired.[21]

Availability of heads of damages

Intra-Australian cases

28.10
In *Stevens v Head*, Brennan, Dawson, Toohey, and McHugh JJ held that statutory limitations affecting the measure of damages recoverable by a plaintiff were procedural in character. Limitations affecting recoverable heads of liability, on the other hand, were to be treated as substantive.[22]

---

[17] (1991) 174 CLR 1, 44, cf 27–9, 46–53, 62.

[18] Choice of Law (Limitation Periods) Act 1993 (NSW), s 5; Choice of Law (Limitation Periods) Act 1996 (Qld), s 5; Limitation of Actions Act 1936 (SA), s 38A; Limitation Act 1974 (Tas), s 32C; Choice of Law (Limitation Periods) Act 1993 (Vic), s 5; Choice of Law (Limitation Periods) Act 1994 (WA), s 5; Limitation Act 1985 (ACT), s 56; Choice of Law (Limitation Periods) Act 1994 (NT), s 5.

[19] (2000) 203 CLR 503, paras 100, 161, 192–3.

[20] (2002) 210 CLR 491, para 76. See also *John Pfeiffer Pty Ltd v Rogerson* (2000) 203 CLR 503, paras 98–100, 161, 192–3.

[21] Subject, perhaps, to public policy considerations: see para 28.06.

[22] (1993) 176 CLR 433, 459–60. See also *Boys v Chaplin* [1971] AC 356, 379, 384–5, 393, discussed in para 27.34.

28.11   In *John Pfeiffer*, the High Court reached a different view, concluding that all laws which bear upon 'the existence, extent or enforceability of remedies, rights and obligations should be characterized as substantive and not as procedural laws'.[23] All laws governing heads of damages and measures of damages are therefore to be treated as substantive, rather than procedural. Only laws which are directed to governing or regulating the mode or conduct of court proceedings are to be considered procedural.[24]

Torts with a foreign element

28.12   In *Zhang*, Gleeson CJ, Gaudron, McHugh, Gummow, and Hayne JJ reserved for future consideration whether questions about the kinds of damage, or amount of damages that may be recovered in places outside Australia should be treated as substantive issues governed by the *lex loci delicti*, or as procedural issues governed by the law of the forum.[25]

D.   Application to Defamation Cases

28.13   *John Pfeiffer* and *Zhang* were not defamation cases. In the course of their reasons for judgment in *John Pfeiffer*, however, Gleeson CJ, Gaudron, McHugh, Gummow, and Hayne JJ observed that the tort of libel may be committed in many States when a national publication defames a person.[26] The observation was made in the context of the relative merits of the *lex loci delicti* and the *lex fori* as potential governing laws for intra-Australian torts. Gleeson CJ, Gaudron, McHugh, Gummow, and Hayne JJ did not go on to consider the implications for defamation actions of adopting the *lex loci delicti* as the governing law for intra-Australian or foreign tort cases. They did say, however that:

> for every hard case that can be postulated if one form of universal rule is adopted, another equally hard case can be postulated if the opposite universal rule is adopted.[27]

28.14   In a similar vein, Kirby J noted in *John Pfeiffer* that the problem where acts or omissions occur in more than one single Australian law area is 'tricky'. Although not specifically adverting to defamation actions, Kirby J said:

> It may be appropriate to solve [the problem] by applying the substantive law of the law area within Australia with which the proceedings have the predominant terri-

---

[23] *John Pfeiffer Pty Ltd v Rogerson* (2000) 203 CLR 503, para 102; see also paras 161, 193–200.
[24] ibid, paras 99, 161, 192.
[25] (2002) 210 CLR 491, para 76. There is recent authority on this issue in England: *Harding v Wealands* [2005] 1 All ER 415. See paras 27.35–27.36.
[26] (2002) 210 CLR 491, para 81.
[27] ibid, para 82.

torial connection. No final conclusion on this aspect of the matter need be stated in the present proceedings.[28]

The decisions in *John Pfeiffer* and *Zhang* have wide-ranging implications for the conduct of defamation actions in Australia.

28.15

Interstate and foreign defences. Most obviously, the adoption of the *lex loci delicti* as the governing law for intra-Australian and foreign torts means that where defamatory material has been published[29] in another State or Territory or abroad, the liability of the defendant is to be determined in accordance with the law of that other place.[30]

28.16

Where material is published to a global audience via the Internet, then subject to questions of jurisdiction and *forum non conveniens*,[31] a defendant might wish or be compelled to plead and prove a vast number of diverse defences from a myriad of different places. Proof of foreign defences, in particular, may prove cumbersome and costly where a plaintiff seeks to recover damages for publications of defamatory material occurring outside Australia.[32]

In *Dow Jones & Company Inc v Gutnick*,[33] Kirby J expressed misgivings about the effect of the decision in *Zhang* on Internet defamation cases. Kirby J observed that it was arguable that, as a matter of comity, 'no jurisdiction should ordinarily impose its laws on the conduct of persons in other jurisdictions in preference to the laws that would ordinarily govern such conduct where it occurs', unless perhaps that jurisdiction 'can demonstrate that it has a stronger interest in the resolution of the dispute in question'.[34] Kirby J opined that perhaps the applicable law in Internet defamation cases should be law of the place that has the strongest connection with, or is in the best position to control or regulate, the conduct that is to be influenced.[35] Ultimately, however, Kirby J concluded that such matters called for national legislative attention and international discussion, rather than judicial intervention.[36]

The risk of defamation actions becoming bogged down in debates about the

---

[28] ibid, para 158.
[29] That is, read, heard, or seen: see para 5.10.
[30] See eg *National Road and Motorists' Association Ltd v Nine Network Australia Pty Ltd* [2002] ACTSC 9, para 17.
[31] See chapters 25 and 26.
[32] As to proof of foreign law and related matters, see chapter 29.
[33] (2002) 210 CLR 575.
[34] ibid, para 114.
[35] ibid; cf the possible application of the flexibility exception to the double actionability test in the United Kingdom: see paras 27.24–27.29.
[36] (2002) 210 CLR 575, paras 137–8, 164–6.

defences available under the laws of every country on Earth, however, should not be overstated.[37]

28.17 **Forum shopping.** The abolition of the double actionability test means that, in cases involving intra-Australian torts, the same substantive result should occur regardless of the court in which an action is heard and determined. Suppose, for example, that a defendant publishes nationally material conveying an imputation which is true, but whose publication is not for the public benefit, which does not relate to any matter of public interest, and is not published under qualified privilege. Under the double actionability test, it was to the plaintiff's advantage to sue in those places where a public benefit or public interest requirement applies to the defence of justification, because the application of the test meant that defendants could not succeed in a defence of justification, even in respect of publications occurring in those jurisdictions where truth *simpliciter* is a defence.[38] The abolition of the double actionability test means that wherever proceedings are brought, the defendant will fail in a defence of justification in respect of publications occurring in those jurisdictions where a public benefit or public interest requirement applies, but succeed in a defence of justification in respect of publications occurring in each other jurisdiction.

The implications of the abolition of the double actionability test for forum shopping in cases involving foreign publications will depend on the substantive defamation laws of, and the jurisdiction and choice of law rules applied in, the alternative fora.

28.18 **Exemplary damages.** Section 46(3)(a) of the Defamation Act 1974 (NSW) abolishes exemplary damages in defamation actions. In the pre-*John Pfeiffer* decision of *Costello v Random House Australia Pty Ltd*,[39] Higgins J held that section 46(3)(a) was procedural in nature. The effect of Higgins J's view was that plaintiffs suing outside New South Wales would be entitled to exemplary damages, in appropriate circumstances, even in relation to publications occurring within New South Wales.[40]

Different views about the proper characterization of section 46(3)(a) were expressed by Hunt CJ in *Waterhouse v Australian Broadcasting Corporation*,[41] and

---

[37] Many of the matters identified in paras 27.28–27.29 are equally applicable in the Australian context. See also *Dow Jones & Co Inc v Gutnick* (2002) 210 CLR 575, paras 53–4 (Gleeson CJ, McHugh, Gummow, and Hayne JJ), 165 (Kirby J).
[38] See paras 8.01–8.02.
[39] (1999) 137 ACTR 1.
[40] ibid, paras 386–7.
[41] (1992) 27 NSWLR 1, 3.

by Crispin J in *Steiner Wilson & Webster Pty Ltd v Amalgamated Television Services Pty Ltd.*[42]

One effect of the decision in *John Pfeiffer* was to resolve that conflict in the authorities. As a result of the conclusion that Australian laws governing heads of damages and measures of damages are substantive,[43] it is clear that exemplary damages are available in defamation actions in New South Wales in respect of publications occurring outside New South Wales, despite section 46(3)(a) of the Defamation Act 1974 (NSW). In defamation proceedings in courts outside New South Wales, it is clear that exemplary damages will not be available in respect of publications occurring in New South Wales.[44]

Cross-vested proceedings. Finally, the decision in *John Pfeiffer* removes a   **28.19**
potential anomaly when defamation actions are transferred from one jurisdiction to another under the Jurisdiction of Courts (Cross-Vesting) Acts of the Commonwealth and each State and Territory.[45] Under section 11 of those Acts, where proceedings are transferred from one court to another, the applicable substantive law is prescribed. Where the right of action arises out of a written law of another State or Territory, section 11(1)(b) requires the court to apply the written and unwritten law of that State or Territory.[46] In other words, section 11(1)(b) directed the court in such cases not to apply the double actionability test, and to apply the *lex loci delicti*. The right of action for defamation arises as a matter of written law in Queensland, Tasmania, New South Wales, and the Northern Territory.[47] In all other matters, section 11(1)(a) requires the court to apply the written and unwritten law in force in the forum, including the choice of law rules in the forum.[48] Prior to *John Pfeiffer*, therefore, section 11(1)(a) required the court in defamation actions which had been transferred to apply the double actionability test in respect of publications occurring in Victoria, South Australia, Western Australia, and the Australian Capital Territory. Now that the *lex loci delicti* is the governing law for all intra-Australian torts, however,

---

[42] [1999] ACTSC 123, paras 219–21. See also *Waterhouse v Australian Broadcasting Corporation* (1989) 86 ACTR 1, 19.

[43] See para 28.11.

[44] *Randwick Labor Club Ltd v Amalgamated Television Services Pty Ltd* [2000] NSWC 906; *Jarratt v John Fairfax Publications Pty Ltd* [2001] NSWSC 739; *Jackson v TCN Channel Nine Pty Ltd* [2002] NSWSC 1229; see also *Amalgamated Television Services Pty Ltd v Marsden* [2002] NSWCA 419, para 1472.

[45] See paras 26.35–26.38.

[46] Jurisdiction of Courts (Cross-Vesting) Act (Cth, States, and Territories), s 11(1)(b).

[47] The Defamation Act 1889 (Qld) and the Defamation Act 1957 (Tas) each codify the law of defamation. In NSW, see Defamation Act 1974 (NSW), s 9(2); *Australian Broadcasting Corporation v Waterhouse* (1991) 25 NSWLR 519, 524. In the Northern Territory, see Defamation Act 1938 (NT), s 2.

[48] Jurisdiction of Courts (Cross-Vesting) Act (Cth, States and Territories), s 11(1)(a).

section 11(1)(a) will no longer have that effect. The *lex loci delicti* will govern the substantive rights and obligations of the parties in defamation actions, regardless of whether they have been transferred under the cross-vesting legislation.[49]

---

[49] Note that s 11(1)(c) of the Jurisdiction of Courts (Cross-Vesting) Acts provides that in all transferred cases, the rules of evidence and procedure to be applied are those which the court considers appropriate in the circumstances, being rules which are applied in an Australian superior court.

29

PROOF OF FOREIGN LAW

A. General Principles

Where a United Kingdom or Australian court has to determine whether conduct is actionable under the law of a foreign jurisdiction,[1] the law of that place must be proved. In some circumstances, courts may take judicial notice of the law of foreign places. Otherwise, proof of the law of the foreign place is a question of fact.[2] The two main methods by which foreign law is proved are by expert evidence, or by production of legislation or judgments in circumstances permitted by statute.   **29.01**

Where foreign law is not proved, the court generally presumes that the relevant foreign law is the same as the law of the forum, and applies the law of the forum.[3] The burden of pleading and proving the foreign law is on the party   **29.02**

---

[1] For this purpose, England (including Wales), Scotland, and Northern Ireland are distinct jurisdictions.

[2] eg *Lazard Brothers & Co v Midland Bank Ltd* [1933] AC 289, 297–8; *Lloyd v Guibert* (1865) LR 1 QB 115, 129.

[3] See eg *Lloyd v Guibert* (1865) LR 1 QB 115, 129; *Stuart v Potter, Choate & Prentice* 1911 1 SLT 377, 382; *Dynamit Actien Gesellschaft v Rio Tinto Company Ltd* [1918] AC 292, 301; *Szechter v Szechter* [1971] P 286, 296; *Bumper Development Corporation Ltd v Commissioner of Police of the Metropolis* [1991] 4 All ER 638, 644; *Allsop v Incorporated Newsagencies Co Pty Ltd* (1975) 26 FLR 238, 242; *University of Glasgow v The Economist Ltd* [1997] EMLR 495; cf *Shaker v Mohammed Al-Bedrawi* [2002] 4 All ER 835.

seeking to rely on it.[4] In an Internet defamation action, this burden will favour the claimant. A defendant seeking to avoid liability in respect of the publication of defamatory Internet material in foreign jurisdictions will have to plead and prove the content of the defences available to it under the laws of those jurisdictions.[5] A failure to do so will mean that the defendant is able to rely only on the defences available in the forum.

In *HH Sheikha Mouza Al Misnad v Azzaman Ltd*,[6] Gray J said that he would be reluctant to dispose summarily of a defamation action concerning publications occurring in foreign jurisdictions on the basis of that presumption.[7]

B. Judicial Notice

United Kingdom

29.03　The House of Lords may take judicial notice of the law of any part of the United Kingdom. In an appeal from the Inner House, for example, the House of Lords applies Scots law, and may take judicial notice of the law of England and Northern Ireland.[8]

29.04　In England, where some question of foreign law has been the subject of a finding or decision by various courts, including the High Court, the Court of Appeal, the House of Lords, or the Privy Council, section 4(2) of the Civil Evidence Act 1972 permits that finding or decision to be admitted in evidence in any subsequent civil proceeding.[9] The content of the foreign law is to be taken to be in accordance with that finding or decision in the absence of proof to the contrary.[10]

Australia

29.05　Australian courts may take judicial notice of and apply the law of each other

---

[4] *King of Spain v Machado* (1827) 4 Russ 225, 239; 38 ER 790, 795.
[5] *University of Glasgow v The Economist Ltd* [1997] EMLR 495; cf *Yorke v British & Continental Steamship Co Ltd* (1945) 78 Lloyd's LR 181, 184 (a negligence case); *Mother Bertha Music Ltd v Bourne Music Ltd* [1997] EMLR 457 (copyright). See also Lawrence Collins (ed), *Dicey and Morris on Conflict of Laws* (13th edn, 2000) ('Dicey and Morris') 1568–70; *Goh Chok Tong v Tang Liang Hong* [1997] 2 SLR 641, 666–7.
[6] [2003] EWHC 1783.
[7] ibid, para 37. The summary disposal procedure is discussed in paras 20.28–20.34.
[8] eg *Cooper v Cooper* (1888) 13 App Cas 88, 101; *Elliot v Joicey* [1935] AC 209, 213, 236; *Rockware Glass Ltd v MacShannon* [1978] AC 795, 815, 821.
[9] There are various qualifications to this right: see Civil Evidence Act 1972 (UK), s 4(2), (3), (5).
[10] ibid, s 4(2).

Australian jurisdiction.[11] As a consequence, formal proof in any Australian court of the law applicable in any other Australian jurisdiction is not required.

C. Expert Evidence

Foreign law may be proved by leading evidence from an expert witness skilled in the content of the relevant foreign law,[12] such as a legal practitioner or academic.[13] Where there is a conflict in the expert evidence, the judge must decide between the competing evidence.[14] **29.06**

Procedures are available in the United Kingdom for the ascertainment of some foreign laws by the reference of cases stated to foreign courts.[15] These procedures are cumbersome and little used.[16] **29.07**

D. Production of Legislation or Judgments

Legislation may permit foreign law to be proved by the simple production of relevant legislation or judgments. **29.08**

---

[11] This power derives principally from the Constitution (Cth), s 118, the State and Territorial Laws and Records Recognition Act 1901 (Cth), ss 3, 18, the Evidence Act 1995 (Cth), s 143, and specific powers in the Evidence Acts of each Australian jurisdiction. See generally Patrick Lane, *Lane's Commentary on the Australian Constitution* (2nd edn, 1997) 812–20.

[12] eg *Nelson v Bridport* (1845) 8 Beav 527, 536; 50 ER 207, 211; *Lazard Brothers & Co v Midland Bank Ltd* [1933] AC 289, 298; *Bumper Development Corporation Ltd v Commissioner of Police of the Metropolis* [1991] 4 All ER 638, 644.

[13] eg Civil Evidence Act 1972 (UK), s 4(1): 'a person who is suitably qualified . . . on account of his knowledge or experience'; see also *Clyne v Federal Commissioner of Taxation (No 2)* (1981) 57 FLR 198, 202–4.

[14] eg *Bumper Development Corporation Ltd v Commissioner of Police of the Metropolis* [1991] 4 All ER 638, 644. Although questions of fact are ordinarily matters for the jury in jury trials, legislation in England and in most Australian States makes determining the content of foreign law a matter for the judge: Administration of Justice Act 1920 (UK), s 15 (England); Supreme Court Act 1981 (UK), s 69(5) (England); County Courts Act 1984 (UK), s 68 (England); Evidence Act 1995 (Cth), s 176; Evidence Act 1995 (NSW), s 176; Evidence Act 1929 (SA), s 63A; Evidence Act 2001 (Tas), s 176; Supreme Court Civil Procedure Act 1932 (Tas), s 36; Supreme Court Act 1986 (Vic), s 39; Supreme Court Act 1935 (WA), s 172. There are no equivalent provisions in Queensland, the Australian Capital Territory, or the Northern Territory. The content of foreign law was a matter for the judge in Queensland until s 13 of the Reciprocal Enforcement of Judgments Act 1959 (Qld) was repealed by the Statute Law Revision Act (No 2) 1995 (Qld), s 5(3) and Sch 9, with effect from 29 November 1995.

[15] eg British Law Ascertainment Act 1859 (generally Commonwealth countries); European Convention on Information on Foreign Law (signed by most Member States of the Council of Europe, but not the subject of any legislation or court rules in the United Kingdom).

[16] Dicey and Morris (n 5 above) 231–2.

United Kingdom

29.09 The Evidence (Colonial Statutes) Act 1907 permits authorized copies[17] of laws of the legislatures of 'British possessions' and former colonies[18] to be produced and received in evidence in United Kingdom courts.[19]

Australia

29.10 Much more liberal statutory provisions apply in Australia. Generally speaking, evidence of foreign law may be adduced by the simple production of legislation or judgments in most Australian jurisdictions with little difficulty.[20]

E. Application to the Internet

29.11 Where, for example, defamation proceedings are brought against American defendants in the United Kingdom, and the claimant seeks damages in respect of publication in, among other places, the United States, it is thus for the defendants to plead and prove any differences between the relevant United Kingdom and American law of advantage to them, in order to defeat the claimant's claim in respect of publications occurring in America. Failure to do so would ordinarily be expected to result in the United Kingdom court applying its own law and denying the defendants the benefit of the defamation laws of the United States,[21] which are generally more advantageous to defendants than the defamation laws of the United Kingdom.[22]

---

[17] ie copies purporting to have been made by the government printer: s 1(1).

[18] Generally, Commonwealth countries. See also *Jasiewicz v Jasiewicz* [1962] 1 WLR 1426; Dicey and Morris (n 5 above) 230–1.

[19] Evidence (Colonial Statutes) Act 1907 (UK), s 1(1).

[20] Evidence Act 1995 (Cth), ss 174–6; Evidence Act 1995 (NSW), ss 174–6; Evidence Act 1929 (SA), s 63; Evidence Act 2001 (Tas), ss 174–6; Evidence Act 1906 (WA), ss 70–1; Evidence Act 1971 (ACT), Pt VIII; Evidence Act 1939 (NT), ss 27, 63. The law in Queensland is less liberal: Evidence Act 1977 (Qld), ss 68, 72. In Victoria, judicial notice may be taken of Acts of the United Kingdom: Evidence Act 1958 (Vic), s 76. All other foreign law must be proved in Victoria by expert testimony.

[21] *University of Glasgow v The Economist Ltd* [1997] EMLR 495; cf *HH Sheikha Mouza Al Misnad v Azzaman Ltd* [2003] EWHC 1783, para 37.

[22] See chapter 31.

PART VII

OTHER SOURCES OF LAW

Part VII

OTHER AREAS OF LAW

30

JURISPRUDENCE OF THE EUROPEAN COURT OF HUMAN RIGHTS

A. Introduction

Sources of law

Until the commencement of the Human Rights Act 1998 (UK) ('the HRA') on 1 October 2000, the rights and freedoms in the European Convention on Human Rights (ECHR) did not form a direct part of the law of the United Kingdom, in the sense that they did not confer substantive rights capable of being enforced in the courts of the United Kingdom between private citizens.[1] The HRA introduces the rights and freedoms in the ECHR into the law of the United Kingdom.[2] **30.01**

Most importantly, Article 10 of the ECHR guarantees a right to freedom of expression, in the following terms: **30.02**

> (1) Everyone has the right to freedom of expression. This right shall include freedom to hold opinions and to receive and impart information and ideas without interference by public authority and regardless of frontiers. This Article shall not prevent States from requiring the licensing of broadcasting, television or cinema enterprises.

---

[1] *The Parlement Belge* (1879) 4 PD 129.
[2] HRA, ss 1(2), 6.

(2) The exercise of these freedoms, since it carries with it duties and responsibilities, may be subject to such formalities, conditions, restrictions or pen-
alties as are prescribed by law and are necessary in a democratic society, in
the interests of national security, territorial integrity or public safety, for the
prevention of disorder or crime, for the protection of health or morals, for
the protection of the reputation or rights of others, for preventing the
disclosure of information received in confidence, or for maintaining the
authority and impartiality of the judiciary.

Articles 6 and 8 of the ECHR are also of importance. Article 6 guarantees the
right to a fair and public hearing within a reasonable time by an independent
and impartial tribunal established by law. Article 8 guarantees the right to
respect for private and family life.[3]

30.03 Section 6(1) of the HRA makes it unlawful for public authorities, including
courts and tribunals,[4] to act in a way which is incompatible with ECHR rights.[5]
In determining questions arising in connection with ECHR rights and freedoms, courts and tribunals must take into account various matters, including
relevant judgments, decisions, declarations, and advisory opinions of the European Court of Human Rights, certain opinions and decisions of the European
Commission on Human Rights, and certain decisions of the Committee of
Ministers.[6] United Kingdom courts must read and give effect to legislation, as
far as possible, in a way which is compatible with the rights and freedoms in the
ECHR.[7]

Where a party to litigation claims that an adverse verdict would contravene or
has contravened a Convention right, that party may rely on the Convention
right concerned at first instance or on appeal.[8]

30.04 Further, by section 12 of the HRA, where a court is considering whether to
grant any relief which might affect the exercise of the Article 10 right to freedom

---

[3] Art 8 provides:

   (1) Everyone has the right to respect for his private and family life, his home and his
   correspondence.
   (2) There shall be no interference by a public authority with the exercise of this right except
   such as is in accordance with the law and is necessary in a democratic society in the
   interests of national security, public safety or the economic well-being of the country,
   for the prevention of disorder or crime, for the protection of health or morals, or for the
   protection of the rights and freedoms of others.

The implementation of Art 8 has already led to changes to the common law of breach of
confidence: see para 24.05.

[4] HRA, s 6(3)(a).

[5] By ibid, s 1(1), the rights implemented by the HRA are those set out in Arts 2–12 and 14 of
the ECHR, Arts 1–3 of the First Protocol to the ECHR, and Art 1 of the Thirteenth Protocol, as
read with Arts 16–18 of the ECHR.

[6] HRA, s 2(1).

[7] ibid, s 3(1).

[8] ibid, ss 7, 9.

of expression,[9] the court must have particular regard to the importance of that right.[10] It must also have regard, where the material is journalistic, literary, or artistic in nature, to the extent to which the material has or is about to become available to the public, the public interest in the publication of the material, and any relevant privacy code.[11]

The Article 10 right to freedom of expression will invariably be affected where relief is granted, including damages,[12] in a defamation action.

Relevance of the jurisprudence of the European Court of Human Rights

Relevance to United Kingdom courts

The HRA is likely to have two main effects on defamation actions in the United Kingdom. First, although courts will not apply the articles of the ECHR as if they created new causes of action, section 12 may give impetus to the incremental development of the principles of civil defamation law.[13] Secondly, in all cases where a court is considering whether to grant relief which might affect the exercise of the right to freedom of expression in Article 10 of the ECHR, section 12 requires United Kingdom courts to pay particular regard to Article 10.[14] In all such cases, the jurisprudence of the European Court of Human Rights will inform the court's assessment of whether there is any inconsistency between the granting of a defamation law remedy and the Article 10 right to freedom of expression, or any of the other rights protected by the ECHR.

30.05

The European Court of Human Rights

The ECHR is relevant to defamation actions in the United Kingdom in a further way. Persons, non-governmental organizations, and groups of individuals who believe that an adverse defamation verdict constitutes a violation of the ECHR may apply to the European Court of Human Rights for relief against the United Kingdom itself.[15] The court may only accept applications from parties who have exhausted their domestic remedies, within six months of the final decision being taken.[16] The admissibility of applications is determined by a committee of three judges sitting as the Commission of Human Rights.[17] If the

30.06

---

[9] ibid, s 12(1).
[10] ibid, s 12(4).
[11] ibid. See also para 24.05.
[12] See eg *Tolstoy Miloslavsky v United Kingdom* (1995) 20 EHRR 442.
[13] See paras 30.35–30.45.
[14] See also paras 20.07–20.10 (interim injunctions), 20.24 (permanent injunctions), 21.15 (damages).
[15] ECHR, Art 34.
[16] ibid, Art 35(1).
[17] ibid, Arts 27 and 28.

case is admissible, it is then heard and determined by a Chamber of seven judges,[18] or by a Grand Chamber of seventeen judges in a case which:

> raises a serious question affecting the interpretation of the Convention or the protocols thereto, or where the resolution of a question before the Chamber might have a result inconsistent with a judgment previously delivered by the Court.[19]

Adverse decisions of the court are almost invariably respected by the United Kingdom.

B. An Overview of the Authorities

Freedom of expression

30.07 Most of the cases decided by the European Court of Human Rights concerning the compatibility of defamation laws with the rights and freedoms protected by the ECHR have involved publications by journalists and traditional media outlets, and have focused on the Article 10 right to freedom of expression.

The court has repeatedly emphasized the pre-eminent role of the press in societies governed by the rule of law. The press has an obligation to impart information and ideas on political questions and on other matters of public interest, and the public has a reciprocal interest in receiving that information. Article 10 protects journalists where they are reporting on matters of general interest, provided that they act 'in good faith in order to provide accurate and reliable information in accordance with the ethics of journalism'.[20] A degree of exaggeration or provocation, or a polemical or aggressive tone, may be allowed. The freedom of the press is subject, however, to limits, including limits based on protecting the reputation of others and preventing the disclosure of confidential information.[21] In addition, journalists may be required to offer defamed persons a right of reply, and may be criticized for failing to undertake adequate research before publish-

---

[18] ECHR, Art 29.

[19] ibid, Art 30.

[20] *Bergens Tidende v Norway* (2001) 31 EHRR 16, para 53, citing *Goodwin v United Kingdom* (1996) 22 EHRR 123 and *Fressoz and Roire v France* (2001) 31 EHRR 2. See also *McVicar v United Kingdom* (2002) 35 EHRR 22, paras 72–3; *Pedersen and Baadsgaard v Denmark* (European Court of Human Rights, 17 December 2004), para 78; *Busuioc v Moldova* (European Court of Human Rights, 21 December 2004), para 59.

[21] See eg *Sunday Times v United Kingdom* (1979) 2 EHRR 245, para 65; *Observer and Guardian v United Kingdom* (1991) 14 EHRR 153, para 59(b); *Castells v Spain* (1992) 14 EHRR 445, para 43; *Jersild v Denmark* (1994) 19 EHRR 1, para 31; *Prager and Oberschlick v Austria* (1995) 21 EHRR 1, para 38; *De Haes and Gijsels v Belgium* (1998) 25 EHRR 1, para 37; *Bladet Tromsø and Stensaas v Norway* (1999) 29 EHRR 125, para 59; *Bergens Tidende v Norway* (2001) 31 EHRR 16, para 49; *Selistö v Finland* (European Court of Human Rights, 16 November 2004), para 48; *Pedersen and Baadsgaard v Denmark* (European Court of Human Rights, 17 December 2004), para 71; *Busuioc v Moldova* (European Court of Human Rights, 21 December 2004), paras 56, 59.

ing damaging allegations.[22] On the other hand, investigative journalists should inform and alert the public about undesirable phenomena in society as soon as the relevant information comes into their possession.[23]

The press is not, however, the only guardian of freedom of expression. A high level of protection must also be afforded to 'groups and individuals outside the mainstream' who 'contribute to the public debate by disseminating information and ideas on matters of general public interest'.[24] While a degree of hyperbole and exaggeration may be expected and tolerated, they too must act in good faith and provide accurate and reliable information, particularly when presenting statements of fact, rather than value judgments.[25]

Limits must be prescribed by law

By Article 10(2), limitations on the right to freedom of expression are only justifiable where they 'are prescribed by law and are necessary in a democratic society'.

30.08

In *Zana v Turkey*,[26] the court restated the principle, established in a series of earlier cases, that the exceptions to freedom of expression in Article 10(2) must be 'construed strictly'.[27] Freedom of expression should only be curtailed where the need to do so has been 'established convincingly', having regard to a 'pressing social need'.[28] National courts of Member States nonetheless have a 'margin of appreciation' in assessing the need for any restriction on freedom of expression, but subject always to the supervisory jurisdiction of the European Court of Human Rights.[29] In exercising its supervisory jurisdiction, the court determines, in particular, whether the interference with freedom of expression was

30.09

---

[22] *Prager and Oberschlick v Austria* (1995) 21 EHRR 1, para 37; *Selistö v Finland* (European Court of Human Rights, 16 November 2004), para 67; *Pedersen and Baadsgaard v Denmark* (European Court of Human Rights, 17 December 2004), para 90.

[23] *Cumpănă and Mazăre v Romania* (European Court of Human Rights, 17 December 2004), para 96.

[24] *Steel and Morris v United Kingdom* (European Court of Human Rights, 15 February 2005).

[25] ibid, para 90.

[26] (1997) 27 EHRR 667.

[27] ibid, para 51. See also *Pedersen and Baadsgaard v Denmark* (European Court of Human Rights, 17 December 2004), para 71.

[28] ibid. See also *Handyside v United Kingdom* (1976) 1 EHRR 737, para 49; *Barthold v Germany* (1985) 7 EHRR 383, para 55; *Sunday Times v United Kingdom* (1979) 2 EHRR 245, para 62; *Lingens v Austria* (1986) 8 EHRR 407, para 41; *Groppera Radio AG v Switzerland* (1990) 12 EHRR 321, para 71; *Autronic AG v Switzerland* (1990) 12 EHRR 485, paras 61–2; *Thorgeirson v Iceland* (1992) 14 EHRR 843, para 63; *Jersild v Denmark* (1994) 19 EHRR 1, para 37; *Bergens Tidende v Norway* (2001) 31 EHRR 16, para 48; *Chauvy v France* (European Court of Human Rights, 29 June 2004), para 64.

[29] *Zana v Turkey* (1997) 27 EHRR 667, para 51. See also *Lingens v Austria* (1986) 8 EHRR 407, para 39; *Groppera Radio AG v Switzerland* (1990) 12 EHRR 321, para 72.

'proportionate to the legitimate aims pursued' and whether the reasons given by the national court to justify the interference were 'relevant and sufficient'. In doing so the court has to satisfy itself that the national court based its decision on an acceptable assessment of the relevant facts and applied standards in conformity with the principles embodied in Article 10.[30]

30.10 The court does not merely scrutinize the statements taken into account by the national court in reaching its decision. The court will instead look to the whole publication, so as not 'to lose sight of its overall content and its very essence'.[31]

30.11 To be a valid restriction on freedom of expression, the law authorizing the restriction must be formulated so as to be sufficiently foreseeable and accessible.[32] Generally, the court has held restrictions imposed on freedom of expression by the common law of the United Kingdom to be sufficiently foreseeable. In *Sunday Times v United Kingdom*,[33] for example, the court accepted that a reformulation of the principles of contempt of court by the House of Lords was foreseeable, to a degree that was reasonable in the circumstances.[34] In *Tolstoy Miloslavsky v United Kingdom*,[35] the court held that awards of damages by juries in defamation cases were sufficiently foreseeable. The court accepted that juries needed to have a considerable degree of flexibility in awarding damages, because of the infinite variety of factual circumstances which could arise in defamation cases.[36] The court paid regard to the fact that juries were instructed to take various matters into account when determining an award of damages, including injury to feelings, the anxiety and uncertainty undergone in the litigation, the absence of an apology, any aggravation of the defamation, and the need to vindicate reputation.[37] Reference was also made to the supervisory role of the

---

[30] *Zana v Turkey* (1997) 27 EHRR 667, para 51. See also *Sunday Times v United Kingdom* (1979) 2 EHRR 245, para 62; *Lingens v Austria* (1986) 8 EHRR 407, para 40; *Barfod v Denmark* (1989) 13 EHRR 493, para 28; *Barthold v Germany* (1985) 7 EHRR 383, para 55; *Marônek v Slovakia* (2004) 38 EHRR 5, paras 52–3; *Chauvy v France* (European Court of Human Rights, 29 June 2004), para 70; *Cumpănă and Mazăre v Romania* (European Court of Human Rights, 17 December 2004), para 90; *Pedersen and Baadsgaard v Denmark* (European Court of Human Rights, 17 December 2004), paras 68–70.

[31] *Perna v Italy* (2004) 39 EHRR 28, para 47.

[32] See eg *Markt Intern Verlag GmbH and Beermann v Germany* (1989) 12 EHRR 161, paras 29–30; *Barthold v Germany* (1985) 7 EHRR 383, paras 47–9; *Sunday Times v United Kingdom* (1979) 2 EHRR 245, para 62; *Groppera Radio AG v Switzerland* (1990) 12 EHRR 321, paras 65–8; *Autronic AG v Switzerland* (1990) 12 EHRR 485, para 57; *Müller v Switzerland* (1988) 13 EHRR 212, para 29; *Tolstoy Miloslavsky v United Kingdom* (1995) 20 EHRR 442, paras 37–44; *Goodwin v United Kingdom* (1996) 22 EHRR 123, paras 29–34; *Busuioc v Moldova* (European Court of Human Rights, 21 December 2004), paras 52–4.

[33] (1979) 2 EHRR 245.

[34] ibid, para 52.

[35] (1995) 20 EHRR 442.

[36] ibid, para 41.

[37] ibid, para 42.

Court of Appeal in reviewing irrational damages awards.[38] The court has acknowledged that defamation laws are inevitably couched in terms which are, to a greater or lesser extent, vague and whose interpretation and application are questions of practice.[39]

A law may still satisfy the requirement of foreseeability even if a person has to take legal advice to assess, to a degree that is reasonable in the circumstances, the consequences which a given action may entail.[40] Journalists and publishers, in particular, are used to having to proceed with a high degree of caution when pursuing their occupation and can accordingly be expected to take special care in assessing risks.[41] **30.12**

Generally speaking, it seems that the court considers that English defamation law is not so complex as to require a defendant to have legal assistance,[42] although in a case of exceptional complexity and length a denial of legal aid to defamation defendants may contravene the right in Article 6(1) of the ECHR to a fair hearing.[43]

Types of protected expression

The decisions of the court differentiate between different kinds of expression. The court has emphasized, in particular, the importance in a democratic society of limiting restrictions on the ability of the press to publish material concerning political matters and subjects of public interest.[44] **30.13**

Political expression

Generally speaking, the decisions of the court afford the greatest level of protec- **30.14**

---

[38] ibid. Note that, in the result, the court concluded that an award of damages of £1.5m violated Art 10, as it was disproportionate to the legitimate aim of compensating the defamed plaintiff for the damage to his reputation.

[39] *Sunday Times v United Kingdom* (1979) 2 EHRR 245, para 49; *Hertel v Switzerland* (1999) 28 EHRR 534, para 35.

[40] See eg *Tolstoy Miloslavsky v United Kingdom* (1995) 20 EHRR 442, para 37; *Grigoriades v Greece* (1999) 27 EHRR 464, para 37; *Chauvy v France* (European Court of Human Rights, 29 June 2004), para 44.

[41] See eg *Chauvy v France* (European Court of Human Rights, 29 June 2004), paras 45–6.

[42] *McVicar v United Kingdom* (2002) 35 EHRR 22.

[43] *Steel and Morris v United Kingdom* (European Court of Human Rights, 15 February 2005): defamation proceedings by McDonalds against two defendants involving 28 interlocutory applications, a first instance trial lasting 313 court days, an appeal lasting 23 days, 40,000 pages of documentary evidence, 130 oral witnesses, and more than 20,000 pages of transcript.

[44] See eg *Lingens v Austria* (1986) 8 EHRR 407, para 42; *Oberschlick v Austria (No 1)* (1991) 19 EHRR 389, paras 58–9; *Castells v Spain* (1992) 14 EHRR 445, para 43; *Thorgeirson v Iceland* (1992) 14 EHRR 843, paras 63–4; *Jersild v Denmark* (1994) 19 EHRR 1, para 31; *Bladet Tromsø and Stensaas v Norway* (1999) 29 EHRR 125, para 59; *Bergens Tidende v Norway* (2001) 31 EHRR 16, paras 48–9; *Busuioc v Moldova* (European Court of Human Rights, 21 December 2004), para 57.

tion to political speech,[45] on the basis that the discussion of political matters is vital to the operation of democratic systems of government.[46] National laws which restrict the freedom to discuss political matters are most likely to contravene Article 10.[47] There is 'little scope' under Article 10(2) of the Convention for restrictions on political speech or on debate on questions of public interest.[48]

30.15 Freedom of expression, although important for everybody, is particularly important in the case of elected politicians, who represent the people by drawing attention to their preoccupations and defending their interests. Interferences with the freedom of expression of elected politicians therefore calls for the closest scrutiny. The absolute privilege accorded to statements made in Parliament is justifiable, despite its potential to undermine other protected rights.[49]

30.16 The limits of acceptable criticism of politicians are wider than the limits of acceptable criticism of civil servants exercising their powers, or of private individuals.[50] Politicians must display a greater degree of tolerance, especially when they themselves make public statements that are susceptible to criticism.[51] Private individuals and associations lay themselves open to a higher level of scrutiny when they enter the arena of a political or public debate. Although they may not have to accept the high level of tolerance expected of politicians, their decision to enter the political fray is a relevant factor in assessing whether any defamatory criticism of them is protected by Article 10.[52]

30.17 The court has developed a broad concept of political expression, extending it to the discussion by a journalist of a German politician's activities during World War II,[53] serious allegations about the role of the government and police in the murder of political activists,[54] allegations of police brutality,[55] allegations of bias

---

[45] See eg *Castells v Spain* (1992) 14 EHRR 445; *Cumpănă and Mazăre v Romania* (European Court of Human Rights, 17 December 2004), paras 94–5.

[46] eg *Handyside v United Kingdom* (1976) 1 EHRR 737, para 49; *Lingens v Austria* (1986) 8 EHRR 407, para 42.

[47] eg *Wingrove v United Kingdom* (1996) 24 EHRR 1, para 58; *Jerusalem v Austria* (2003) 37 EHRR 25.

[48] eg *Feldek v Slovakia* (European Court of Human Rights, 12 July 2001), para 74.

[49] *A v United Kingdom* (2003) 36 EHRR 51.

[50] *Feldek v Slovakia* (European Court of Human Rights, 12 July 2001), para 74; *Nikula v Finland* (2004) 38 EHRR 45, para 48; *Hrico v Slovakia* (European Court of Human Rights, 20 July 2004), para 40(g).

[51] eg *Jerusalem v Austria* (2003) 37 EHRR 25, paras 36–8.

[52] eg *Nilsen and Johnsen v Norway* (2000) 30 EHRR 878, para 52; *Jerusalem v Austria* (2003) 37 EHRR 25, para 38.

[53] *Lingens v Austria* (1986) 8 EHRR 407.

[54] *Castells v Spain* (1992) 14 EHRR 445.

[55] *Thorgeirson v Iceland* (1992) 14 EHRR 843, para 62.

against the judiciary,[56] and allegations concerning the conduct in court of a judge who was about to enter political life.[57]

The court has not, however, recognized an unfettered right of political expres- **30.18**
sion, or gone so far as to articulate a 'public figure' defence of the kind which prevails in the United States.[58]

Matters of public concern

Speech concerning matters of broad public concern, but not amounting to **30.19**
political expression, has also been recognized by the court as deserving of a high level of protection. In *Bergens Tidende v Norway*,[59] for example, a pub- lisher claimed that a substantial award of damages against it in a defamation action breached its right to freedom of expression. The publisher had made serious allegations of medical malpractice by a cosmetic surgeon. While acknowledging that the publication in question had damaged the surgeon's reputation, the court held that the judgment of the national court contra- vened Article 10. There was 'no reasonable relationship of proportionality between the restrictions placed by the measures applied by the [national court] on the applicants' right to freedom of expression and the legitimate aim pursued'.[60] In *Steel and Morris v United Kingdom*,[61] the court held that leaflets containing very serious allegations against the fast food chain McDonalds, namely abusive and immoral farming and employment practices, deforest- ation, the exploitation of children and their parents through aggressive advertising, and the sale of unhealthy food, were entitled to a 'high level of protection' under Article 10, and observed that large public companies and the people who manage them must expect and tolerate a high level of scrutiny and criticism.[62]

On the other hand, some narrow restrictions on freedom of expression directed

---

[56] *Barfod v Denmark* (1989) 13 EHRR 493.

[57] *Hrico v Slovakia* (European Court of Human Rights, 20 July 2004).

[58] See eg Eric Barendt, 'Human Rights Act 1998 and Libel Law: Brave New World?' (2001) 6 Media and Arts Law Review 1, 7. An overview of the 'public figure' test in the United States is set out in paras 31.04–31.06.

[59] (2001) 31 EHRR 16; see also *Thorgeirson v Iceland* (1992) 14 EHRR 843, para 64; *Feldek v Slovakia* (European Court of Human Rights, 12 July 2001), para 74.

[60] *Bergens Tidende v Norway* (2001) 31 EHRR 16, para 60. See also *Selistö v Finland* (European Court of Human Rights, 16 November 2004) (article discussing aspects of health care and patient safety raised serious issues affecting the public interest); *Marônek v Slovakia* (2004) 38 EHRR 5 (open letter to the Prime Minister posted at several tram and bus stops concerning state housing raised matters of general interest and was not published excessively).

[61] European Court of Human Rights, 15 February 2005.

[62] *Steel and Morris v United Kingdom* (European Court of Human Rights, 15 February 2005), paras 88, 94.

to maintaining public confidence in the administration of justice and the dignity of the legal profession may be permitted.[63]

30.20 In some circumstances the publication of allegations concerning aspects of the private lives of public figures or their spouses may be in the public interest.[64] The publication of photographs depicting aspects of the private lives of well-known persons, however, will not be in the public interest if the sole purpose is to satisfy the curiosity of a particular readership, without contributing to any debate of general interest to society.[65]

Commercial and artistic speech

30.21 Commercial and artistic speech, while certainly entitled to protection under Article 10, has not been accorded the same level of protection as political speech or speech on matters of general public concern.

30.22 **Artistic speech.** In *Müller v Switzerland*,[66] for example, the court upheld the ruling of a Swiss court convicting the applicants of obscenity, and confiscating certain paintings displaying sodomy, fellatio, bestiality, and erect penises. The paintings had been exhibited publicly, and had been seen by minors and others. The court held that national authorities are in the best position to judge the necessity of restricting the right to freedom of expression in the interests of protecting public morals.[67] A similar restriction on freedom of expression was allowed in *Otto-Preminger Institute v Austria*,[68] a case concerning the seizure and forfeiture of a film mocking and abusing the Roman Catholic religion.[69]

30.23 **Commercial speech.** In *Markt Intern Verlag GmbH and Beermann v Germany*,[70] the court held that an injunction restraining a trade magazine from publishing certain allegations did not contravene Article 10. The court held that 'commercial speech' was not entitled to the same degree of protection as political speech, and could be restricted in the interests of respecting the privacy of

---

[63] *Nikula v Finland* (2004) 38 EHRR 45, paras 45–6; *Amihalachioaie v Moldova* (European Court of Human Rights, 20 April 2004), paras 27–8; *Hrico v Slovakia* (European Court of Human Rights, 20 July 2004), para 40(f).

[64] *Karhuvaara and Iltalehti v Finland* (European Court of Human Rights, 16 November 2004), para 45.

[65] *Von Hannover v Germany* (2005) 40 EHRR 1, paras 61–6. See also *Peck v United Kingdom* (2003) 36 EHRR 41 (disclosure of closed circuit television footage to the media).

[66] (1988) 13 EHRR 212.

[67] ibid, paras 35–6.

[68] (1994) 19 EHRR 34.

[69] See also *Wingrove v United Kingdom* (1996) 24 EHRR 1.

[70] (1989) 12 EHRR 161.

others or the confidentiality of commercial information.[71] Similarly, restrictions on advertising by professionals have been upheld.[72]

Fact and opinion

The court distinguishes between expressions of opinion, and statements of fact. **30.24** National laws which require a publisher to prove the truth of the former contravene Article 10, because opinions represent value judgments which are not susceptible of proof.[73] Publishers may be required, however, to demonstrate that there was some sufficient factual basis to support the opinion expressed.[74] Whether a statement is one of fact or opinion is, in the first instance, a matter falling within the ambit of the margin of appreciation afforded to national courts.[75] Ultimately, it is to be determined by examining the imputations in issue in the light of the publication as a whole.[76] In *Feldek v Slovakia*, the court rejected the proposition that a value judgment can only be considered as such if it is accompanied by the facts on which that judgment is based.[77] While each case must be assessed individually, it will not be necessary to state the facts supporting the value judgment if they are well known.[78]

By contrast, the court ordinarily requires a publisher to have verified seriously defamatory factual allegations prior to publication.[79] In particular, 'special grounds are required before the media can be dispensed from their ordinary obligation to verify factual statements that are defamatory of private individuals'.[80] Whether such grounds exist will depend on the nature and degree of

---

[71] Although the deciding factor in the case may have been the 'margin of appreciation' left by the court to national authorities: see ibid, paras 33–8.

[72] *Casado Coca v Spain* (1994) 18 EHRR 1. While stressing that the balance between freedom of expression and the regulation of advertising by professionals was largely a matter within Member States' 'margins of appreciation', the court noted that there was a growing tendency towards the relaxation of restrictions on advertising in most Member States: ibid, paras 54–5. See also *Colman v United Kingdom* (1993) 18 EHRR 119, para 12 (Commission).

[73] *Lingens v Austria* (1986) 8 EHRR 407, para 46; *Fressoz and Roire v France* (2001) 31 EHRR 2; *Jerusalem v Austria* (2003) 37 EHRR 25; *Busuioc v Moldova* (European Court of Human Rights, 21 December 2004), para 61.

[74] *De Haes and Gijsels v Belgium* (1998) 25 EHRR 1, para 47; *Oberschlick v Austria (No 2)* (1997) 25 EHRR 357, para 33; *Jerusalem v Austria* (2003) 37 EHRR 25; *Busuioc v Moldova* (European Court of Human Rights, 21 December 2004), para 61; *Steel and Morris v United Kingdom* (European Court of Human Rights, 15 February 2005), para 87.

[75] *Pedersen and Baadsgaard v Denmark* (European Court of Human Rights, 17 December 2004), para 76.

[76] *Cumpănă and Mazăre v Romania* (European Court of Human Rights, 17 December 2004), para 100.

[77] European Court of Human Rights, 12 July 2001, para 86.

[78] ibid.

[79] *Bladet Tromsø and Stensaas v Norway* (1999) 29 EHRR 125, paras 66–7; *Cumpănă and Mazăre v Romania* (European Court of Human Rights, 17 December 2004), paras 101–2.

[80] *Pedersen and Baadsgaard v Denmark* (European Court of Human Rights, 17 December 2004), para 78.

the defamatory allegations and the extent to which the sources of the allegations are reliable.[81] The more serious the allegation, and the wider the audience, the more solid the factual basis has to be.[82] In relation to less serious defamatory allegations, it will suffice that the publisher had some reasonable basis for making the allegations, such as reliance on an official report.[83]

The presumption of falsity

30.25 The fact that a defendant seeking to rely on the defence of justification bears the onus of proving the substantial truth of a publication[84] was held not to violate Article 10 of the ECHR in one case involving the publication of serious allegations with potentially very grave consequences.[85]

In *Steel and Morris v United Kingdom*,[86] on the other hand, the court held that English defamation law did not strike the correct balance between freedom of expression and the right to reputation by requiring two unrepresented defendants of modest means to bear the burden of proving the truth of very serious allegations they had published concerning the environmental and employment practices of McDonalds. The English court had failed to address the 'inequality of arms' between the defendants and McDonalds, or to protect adequately the 'general interest in promoting the free circulation of information and ideas about the activities of powerful commercial entities'.[87]

In *Castells v Spain*, the court held that Spanish law contravened Article 10 of the ECHR because it denied the author the right to prove the truth of the allegations he had made.[88]

Protection of reputation

30.26 Defamation verdicts against journalists and others in relation to publications concerning the conduct of governments and politicians will occasionally contravene Article 10.[89]

30.27 In balancing the right to reputation against the public interest in freedom of

---

[81] ibid. See also *Bladet Tromsø and Stensaas v Norway* (1999) 29 EHRR 125, para 66; *McVicar v United Kingdom* (2002) 35 EHRR 22, para 84.

[82] *Pedersen and Baadsgaard v Denmark* (European Court of Human Rights, 17 December 2004), paras 78–9.

[83] *Bladet Tromsø and Stensaas v Norway* (1999) 29 EHRR 125, paras 66, 68.

[84] See para 8.01.

[85] *McVicar v United Kingdom* (2002) 35 EHRR 22, paras 85–7.

[86] European Court of Human Rights, 15 February 2005.

[87] ibid, para 95.

[88] (1992) 14 EHRR 445, para 48. See also *Jerusalem v Austria* (2003) 37 EHRR 25, paras 42–6.

[89] eg *Lingens v Austria* (1986) 8 EHRR 407, para 42; *Castells v Spain* (1992) 14 EHRR 445, para 46.

expression, the extent of the damage suffered by the defamed person is relevant, but not determinative. In *Bladet Tromsø and Stensaas v Norway*,[90] for example, a defamation verdict against the applicant publishers was held to have contravened Article 10, even though the subjects of the offending publication had suffered relatively serious damage to their reputations. The court held that the subject of discussion, seal hunting, was of sufficient importance that it outweighed the plaintiffs' private interests.[91]

Similar results have been reached by the court in other cases.[92] In *Tolstoy Miloslavsky v United Kingdom*, for example, the court held that an award of damages by a jury of £1.5 million to the plaintiff in a defamation action contravened Article 10, as the sum awarded was disproportionate to the legitimate aim of compensating the plaintiff for his damaged reputation.[93] In *Steel and Morris v United Kingdom*, the court held that awards of damages against two defendants totalling £76,000 were disproportionate to the aim of vindicating the reputation of McDonalds, in circumstances where McDonalds had not established that it had suffered any financial loss by reason of the defendants' publications.[94]

30.28

A permanent injunction prohibiting the repetition of allegations which a defendant cannot prove on the balance of probabilities to be substantially true will not violate Article 10, at least where the injunction is not unduly wide and the allegations are serious.[95]

30.29

It seems likely that the court would not consider an order that a defendant publish a correction and apology under section 9(1)(b) of the Defamation Act 1996 (UK)[96] to be a violation of Article 10.[97]

30.30

Application to the Internet

It can be seen, then, that defamation verdicts in favour of the claimant may contravene Article 10 of the ECHR in a variety of circumstances. Most importantly, Article 10 distinguishes between the level of protection to be afforded to

30.31

---

[90] (1999) 29 EHRR 125, paras 61–73.

[91] ibid, para 73.

[92] *Nilsen and Johnsen v Norway* (2000) 30 EHRR 878; *Tolstoy Miloslavsky v United Kingdom* (1995) 20 EHRR 442; *Bergens Tidende v Norway* (2001) 31 EHRR 16; *Karhuvaara and Iltalehti v Finland* (European Court of Human Rights, 16 November 2004); cf *Wabl v Austria* (2001) 31 EHRR 51; *Chauvy v France* (European Court of Human Rights, 29 June 2004).

[93] (1995) 20 EHRR 442, para 51. The court was also influenced by the fact that, at the time, the Court of Appeal had no power to set aside damages awards on the basis that they were excessive: ibid, para 50. The test for intervening to lower damages awards by juries has since changed: see *Rantzen v Mirror Group Newspapers Ltd* [1994] QB 670; see para 21.19.

[94] European Court of Human Rights, 15 February 2005, paras 96–8.

[95] *McVicar v United Kingdom* (2002) 35 EHRR 22, paras 80–1.

[96] See paras 20.28–20.34.

[97] cf *Chauvy v France* (European Court of Human Rights, 29 June 2004), para 78.

different kinds of expression, giving most weight to political expression, and least weight to pure commercial expression. Competing rights, such as the right to a reputation, may restrict the right to freedom of expression, but only where there is a pressing social need which has been established convincingly. Even in the case of political expression, however, the right to freedom of expression is not absolute.

30.32 There is no reason to doubt that the court would apply these principles in a case involving the publication of information and ideas via the Internet. The Internet is particularly suited to the publication of material containing political content, or discussing matters of general public concern; indeed, it is the first medium which truly offers to members of the public at large the possibility of disseminating their views to a potentially unlimited global audience.

30.33 It would be wrong to think that Article 10 would invariably protect persons who publish unsubstantiated, defamatory allegations on bulletin boards or web pages. The right to freedom of expression is not unlimited. Whether Article 10 has been contravened will depend on a wide range of matters, including the nature of the content and extent of the publication, the extent to which the publisher attempted to verify or is able to substantiate any factual allegations, the state of mind of the publisher, and whether the defamed person has been offered a right of reply.

30.34 Where political material, or material of general public concern is published on a bulletin board or a web page by ordinary members of the public, however, it is difficult to see why those responsible for its publication should not be afforded the same level of protection as journalists and traditional media outlets. In both cases, the publication of such material serves the general social purpose of imparting information and ideas on matters of public concern.[98]

C. Incremental Changes to Defamation Law

General principles

30.35 The ECHR had influenced United Kingdom law even before the passage and commencement of the HRA.[99] Although it is clear that the HRA will enhance

---

[98] See para 30.07.

[99] *Attorney-General v Guardian Newspapers Ltd (No 2)* [1990] 1 AC 109 (common law rule that an order restraining the disclosure of government secrets could only be made if it was shown that the information was confidential and that it was in the public interest that it not be disclosed held to be consistent with Article 10); *Derbyshire County Council v Times Newspapers Ltd* [1992] QB 770 (CA) (no pressing social need for public authorities to have the right to sue for defamation); cf [1993] AC 534, 551 (HL) (same conclusion, without relying on Article 10); *Rantzen v*

that influence, the extent to which United Kingdom courts will modify or develop new principles of defamation law so as to give effect to or secure conformity with the rights and freedoms in the ECHR is difficult to predict.

The most significant decisions of United Kingdom courts concerning the compatibility of common law principles with the ECHR since the commencement of the HRA have related to invasions of privacy and the common law of breach of confidence.[100] It is clear from those decisions that United Kingdom courts will be prepared in appropriate cases to pronounce incremental changes to the common law where the application of existing common law rules does not adequately protect ECHR rights.

Where it is necessary to consider the interplay between two (or more) competing ECHR rights, Lord Steyn has said that there are four propositions to be borne in mind: **30.36**

> First, neither article has as such precedence over the other. Secondly, where the values under the two articles are in conflict, an intense focus on the comparative importance of the specific rights being claimed in the individual case is necessary. Thirdly, the justifications for interfering with or restricting each right must be taken into account. Finally, the proportionality test must be applied to each.[101]

Application in defamation cases

In three decisions all pre-dating the commencement of the HRA, *Attorney-General v Guardian Newspapers Ltd (No 2)*,[102] *Derbyshire County Council v Times Newspapers Ltd*,[103] and *Reynolds v Times Newspapers Ltd* ('*Reynolds*'),[104] the House of Lords rejected the argument that existing common law principles provide insufficient protection to freedom of expression. In *Reynolds*, the court expressly contemplated the implications of the HRA for the defamation law defence of qualified privilege. The opinions in that case effected a liberalization of the circumstances in which the common law defence of qualified privilege will be available in cases involving the discussion of political information, but   **30.37**

Mirror Group Newspapers Ltd [1994] QB 670 (appellate intervention to reduce damages awards by juries required if a reasonable jury could not have thought the damages awarded were necessary to compensate the plaintiff and re-establish her reputation); *Reynolds v Times Newspapers Ltd* [2001] 2 AC 127, 203–5 (Lord Nicholls), 215 (Lord Steyn) (liberalized form of the common law defence of qualified privilege accords with human rights jurisprudence).

[100] *Douglas v Hello! Ltd* [2001] QB 967; *Venables v News Group Newspapers Ltd* [2001] 1 All ER 908; *A v B Plc* [2003] QB 195; *Wainwright v Home Office* [2004] 2 AC 406; *Campbell v MGN Ltd* [2004] 2 AC 457; *In re S (FC) (a child)* [2004] 4 All ER 683. See para 24.05.

[101] *In re S (FC) (a child)* [2004] 4 All ER 683, para 17. The proportionality test is the 'ultimate balancing test' between each competing right: ibid.

[102] [1990] 1 AC 109.

[103] [1993] AC 534.

[104] [2001] 2 AC 127.

fell well short of adopting a generic privilege for political information, or 'public figure' style defence.[105] In the leading opinion, Lord Nicholls said that the common law accorded with the present state of European human rights jurisprudence.[106]

30.38   In view of the House's clear conclusion in *Reynolds* that common law qualified privilege properly balances the right to freedom of expression against the protection and vindication of reputation, and is sufficiently elastic to enable interference with freedom of speech to be confined to what is necessary in the circumstances of each case, it is difficult to imagine any United Kingdom court concluding that the HRA requires the common law to develop new and broad-ranging defences to civil defamation law.[107]

30.39   Since the commencement of the HRA, appellate courts in the United Kingdom have regularly found existing principles of defamation law to be compatible with the ECHR.

In *Berezovsky v Forbes Inc*,[108] the Court of Appeal held that requiring a defendant to be able to establish the truth of the essence or substance or sting of a damaging assault on a claimant's reputation in order to succeed in a defence of justification did not amount to a disproportionate invasion of the right to freedom of expression, because it met the legitimate purpose of protecting claimants from the publication of damaging and unjustified falsehoods, and because separate defences of fair comment and qualified privilege were available to test exaggeration and error and thereby give adequate weight and liberty to press freedom.[109]

In *Chase v News Group Newspapers Ltd*,[110] the Court of Appeal found various aspects of the defence of justification to be compatible with the Article 10 right to freedom of expression. The court held, among other things, that the common law rule that publishers who repeat allegations made by others must prove the substantial truth of the allegations to succeed in a defence of justification, rather

---

[105] See paras 11.14–11.20.

[106] [2001] 2 AC 127, 203. See also ibid, 215 (Lord Steyn); *McCartan Turkington and Breen v Times Newspapers Ltd* [2001] 2 AC 277, 297.

[107] It has been argued, however, that the approach of the House of Lords in *Reynolds* leaves the law so uncertain for media organizations publishing material relating to matters of public interest as to amount to an unacceptable restriction on freedom of expression: Richard Clayton and Hugh Tomlinson, *The Law of Human Rights* (2001) para 15.249. The availability of the common law defence of qualified privilege in such cases depends on an investigation of the whole of the background to the publication, which may be inconsistent with the approach articulated in *Bergens Tidende v Norway* (2001) 31 EHRR 16.

[108] [2001] EMLR 45.

[109] ibid, para 12; cf *Steel and Morris v United Kingdom* (European Court of Human Rights, 15 February 2005); see para 30.25.

[110] [2003] EMLR 11.

than merely the fact that the allegations had been made, was unobjectionable on ECHR grounds.[111] The common law rule that in justifying an imputation that there were reasonable grounds to suspect a claimant was guilty of an offence a publisher is restricted to relying on matters occurring before publication was also found to be unobjectionable.[112]

The Court of Appeal has also held that the following aspects of English common law do not amount to disproportionate restrictions on the Article 10 right to freedom of expression: **30.40**

- the highly restricted circumstances in which interim injunctions will be granted to restrain the publication of defamatory material;[113] and
- the rule that each separate publication of defamatory material gives rise to a separate cause of action.[114]

While the common law presumption that a defamatory publication caused some damage to its victim[115] is consistent with the Article 10 guarantee of freedom of expression,[116] a claimant might be prevented from prosecuting a defamation action having regard to the need to keep 'a proper balance between the Article 10 right to freedom of expression and the protection of individual reputation' if the allegedly defamatory publication had been seen by only a handful of people and had caused minimal damage to the claimant's reputation.[117]   **30.41**

Section 12 of the HRA invites arguments concerning whether an adverse defamation verdict would contravene Article 10 of the ECHR. Such arguments have become increasingly commonplace in the United Kingdom. It seems likely that publishers will attempt to persuade courts to liberalize further the circumstances in which a defence of qualified privilege will be available where false, defamatory material is published on matters of public interest, or concerning public figures.[118] There may also be attempts to persuade courts to alter long-standing principles of defamation law which have the effect of imposing liability on unintentional publishers, and on publishers who unwittingly or inadvertently identify or defame a person.   **30.42**

---

[111] ibid, para 64; see also *Mark v Associated Newspapers Ltd* [2002] EMLR 38, 853–6. The repetition rule is discussed in para 8.05.
[112] [2003] EMLR 11, para 64.
[113] *Greene v Associated Newspapers Ltd* [2005] 1 All ER 30. See paras 20.09–20.10.
[114] *Loutchansky v Times Newspapers Ltd (Nos 4 and 5)* [2002] QB 783, 817. See para 13.22.
[115] See para 21.02.
[116] *Dow Jones & Co Inc v Jameel* [2005] EWCA Civ 75, paras 32–41; *Vassiliev v Amazon.com Inc* [2003] EWHC 2302; cf *Steel and Morris v United Kingdom* (European Court of Human Rights, 15 February 2005); see para 30.28.
[117] *Dow Jones & Co Inc v Jameel* [2005] EWCA Civ 75, paras 40, 55, 70; see also *Wallis v Valentine* [2003] EMLR 8.
[118] See eg Barendt (n 58 above) 10–11.

30.43   The first case in which an argument of this last kind found favour was *O'Shea v MGN Ltd*.[119] In that case, the claimant alleged that she had been defamed by a photograph in an advertisement in a newspaper for a pornographic Internet web site. The advertisement did not name or otherwise identify the claimant. It seems that the photograph was not of the claimant, but looked so like her that persons who knew her reasonably thought it was her.

Morland J of the English High Court noted that applying the traditional common law authorities,[120] it was irrelevant that the publisher did not intend to identify the claimant in the photograph; the publisher was liable if a hypothetical sensible reader knowing the claimant could infer that the advertisement depicted her. Morland J held, however, that such strict liability principles placed an impossible burden on publishers. No pressing social need could be demonstrated for imposing liability on the publisher in the circumstances. Accordingly, the common law rule violated, and had to yield to, the Article 10 guarantee of freedom of expression.

30.44   In light of the decision in *O'Shea v MGN Ltd*, analogous arguments will no doubt be raised in relation to a number of the traditional rules of civil defamation law which have the effect of imposing strict liability on publishers, without regard to the circumstances or content of the publication. It would seem to be open to argument that each of the following rules may have the effect, in particular cases, of imposing onerous or impossible burdens on publishers:

- the presumption of falsity, at least in extreme cases;[121]
- the liability of original authors of defamatory material for the unauthorized republication or repetition of that material by others;[122]
- the liability of original authors in an Internet context for publications arising out of others linking to or framing defamatory material on their web sites;[123]
- the rule that defendants are responsible for all defamatory meanings conveyed by a publication, even meanings which they did not intend to convey, and which were conveyed only by reason of extrinsic facts not known to them;[124]
- the ascertainment of the meaning of a publication by reference only to the standards of the ordinary person;[125]

---

[119] [2001] EMLR 40.

[120] Such as *E Hulton & Co v Jones* [1910] AC 20 and *Morgan v Odhams Press Ltd* [1971] 1 WLR 1239; see also para 6.06.

[121] *Steel and Morris v United Kingdom* (European Court of Human Rights, 15 February 2005), para 95; cf *McVicar v United Kingdom* (2002) 35 EHRR 22, paras 85–7 (see para 30.25); *Berezovsky v Forbes Inc* [2001] EMLR 45 (see para 30.39).

[122] See paras 5.18–5.23.

[123] See paras 5.24–5.32.

[124] See para 7.10.

[125] See paras 7.07–7.17.

- the ascertainment of defamatory meaning by reference only to the standards of society generally;[126]
- the rule that a defendant may not establish a defence by reference to true imputations borne by a publication, except where those imputations, or imputations with a common sting to those imputations, have been sued on by the claimant;[127] and
- the operation of the common law defence of innocent dissemination, to the extent that it exposes intermediaries in the publication of defamatory material to the risk of liability in respect of material which they did not create and of which they have no actual knowledge.[128]

It seems highly unlikely, however, that there will be a massive overhaul of long-standing principles of defamation law. The growing body of appellate decisions concluding that existing principles of defamation law are compatible with the ECHR has already led one judge to caution against seeking to apply and interpret the ECHR afresh with every defamation case that comes along and to observe that '[i]f one applies the English law of defamation properly, there should be no reason to think that the principles underlying the Convention are infringed'.[129]   **30.45**

---

[126] See para 7.20.
[127] See paras 8.08, 8.12; cf *Perna v Italy* (2004) 39 EHRR 28, para 47.
[128] See paras 18.39, 18.41.
[129] *Galloway v Telegraph Group Ltd* [2004] EWHC 2786, para 132 (Eady J). See also *Branson v Bower* [2001] EMLR 32, para 8; *W v Westminster City Council* [2004] EWHC 2866, paras 96–8.

31

ASPECTS OF UNITED STATES LAW

A. Introduction

There are a number of reasons for including an overview of American defam- **31.01** ation law, and a more detailed treatment of those aspects of American law most relevant in cases involving multi-jurisdictional defamation, in a book dealing with defamation and the Internet in the United Kingdom and Australia. First, circumstances will frequently arise where persons in the United Kingdom or Australia are defamed by material written or edited in the United States, or hosted on the computer system of an Internet intermediary located in the United States. In such cases, the rights of the defamed person against the inter- mediary may depend in part on American substantive law.[1] Secondly, American

---

[1] See chapters 27–28.

law will also be relevant where successful claimants in the United Kingdom or Australia seek to enforce their judgments in the United States, or conversely where defendants apply to American courts to seek to prevent cases in the United Kingdom or Australia from proceeding, or to have United Kingdom or Australian judgments declared unenforceable in the United States.[2] Thirdly, the American cases provide useful examples to illustrate the operation of the principles of United Kingdom and Australian law already discussed. Finally, the extent to which principles derived from the American Internet defamation cases might be capable of being adapted or applied in analogous circumstances in the United Kingdom or Australia cannot be assessed without an appreciation of the uniquely American approach towards defamation law, intermediary liability, jurisdiction over foreign publishers, and choice of law in multi-state defamation cases.

B. Overview of American Defamation Law

Introduction

31.02 By reason of the First Amendment to the United States' Constitution, which guarantees freedom of speech and of the press,[3] the cause of action for defamation in the United States has developed in radically different ways from the United Kingdom and Australia.

31.03 Many differences between Anglo-Australian and American principles have been highlighted in the preceding chapters, such as:

- the circumstances in which orders might be made to uncover the identity of anonymous publishers of defamatory material;[4]
- the standards by which defamatory meaning is assessed;[5]
- the potential liability of mere conduit intermediaries such as telephone companies,[6] Internet service providers involved in the carriage of e-mail messages,[7] and affiliate television stations;[8]

---

[2] See chapter 23.
[3] United States' Constitution (1787), Amendment I (1791): 'Congress shall make no law respecting an establishment of religion, or prohibiting the free exercise thereof; or abridging the freedom of speech, or of the press . . .'.
[4] See para 5.41.
[5] See para 7.21.
[6] See paras 15.30–15.34.
[7] See para 15.35. See also paras 31.35–31.45.
[8] See paras 18.20–18.28.

- the circumstances in which foreign defamation judgments will be recognized and enforced;[9] and
- the 'single publication' rule.[10]

The most striking differences between American defamation law and Anglo-Australian defamation law, however, lie in the matters which must be proved by a plaintiff to succeed in a defamation action in the United States.

Public figure plaintiffs

General principles

Where the plaintiff is a 'public figure', such as a public official, candidate for public office, or well-known celebrity, defendants will only be liable for damages in a defamation action against a media defendant in the United States where the plaintiff proves that the defendant published false, defamatory material with actual malice, that is with knowledge of its falsity or with reckless disregard for its truth or falsity.[11] The burden of proving falsity and actual malice is on the plaintiff.[12]

31.04

Non-media defendants

Whether the 'actual malice' requirement applies where a public figure sues a non-media defendant has not been resolved by the United States Supreme Court,[13] although it seems unlikely that the court would apply a different standard to media and non-media defendants.[14]

31.05

The Internet

It is not at all clear whether, if a distinction is to be drawn, Internet publishers should be treated as media or non-media defendants. While, on the one hand, Internet users have the ability to publish material to a vast global audience, on the other hand much of the material published via the Internet may in fact reach only a tiny or well-defined audience. Most Internet publishers, such as individuals, interest groups, government departments, and companies are a world away from traditional mass media outlets, such as newspaper publishers and television or radio broadcasters. In one case to consider the point, it was held

31.06

---

[9] See paras 23.04–23.16.
[10] See para 13.22.
[11] *New York Times Company v Sullivan*, 376 US 254 (1964), 279–80; *Curtis Publishing Company v Butts*, 388 US 130 (1967).
[12] eg *Philadelphia Newspapers, Inc v Hepps*, 475 US 767 (1986), 775.
[13] *Hutchinson v Proxmire*, 443 US 111 (1979), 134 (n 16); *Philadelphia Newspapers, Inc v Hepps*, 475 US 767 (1986), 779 (n 4); *Milkovich v Lorain Journal Co*, 497 US 1 (1990), 20 (n 6).
[14] See eg *Dun & Bradstreet, Inc v Greenmoss Builders, Inc*, 472 US 749 (1985).

that an Internet content provider which made information technology reports available via the Internet to subscribers who paid US$19,000 per year was a 'member of the mass media'. The court attached significance to the fact that the provider had over 28,000 individual clients and more than 7,400 organizational clients.[15]

Other plaintiffs

31.07   Where plaintiffs are purely private individuals, they are generally able to recover damages where the material defaming them is false, and the defendant was negligent as to the truth or falsity of the material.[16]

Where the publication concerns the discussion of a matter of public concern, however, the damages recoverable by private plaintiffs are limited to damages for actual injury, unless the plaintiff proves actual malice on the part of the defendant.[17]

The burden of proving falsity and negligence is on the plaintiff, at least in cases involving media defendants, where the publication concerns the discussion of a matter of public concern.[18] Whether the common law presumption of falsity survives in cases where private plaintiffs sue non-media defendants, or where private plaintiffs sue in respect of matters of only private concern, has not been addressed by the United States Supreme Court.

Policy differences

31.08   The burden on the plaintiff in a defamation action in the United States is therefore considerably more onerous than that which prevails in Anglo-Australian law. The burden varies, depending on the nature of the plaintiff and the character of the publication.

31.09   The differences between American defamation law and Anglo-Australian defamation law are so great that American courts have refused to accord automatic recognition to English defamation judgments, on the grounds that the principles of English defamation law are 'antithetical to the protections afforded the press by the US Constitution',[19] or so contrary to American

---

[15]   *Metastorm, Inc v Gartner Group, Inc,* 28 F Supp 2d 665 (D DC, 1998).
[16]   *Gertz v Robert Welch, Inc,* 418 US 323 (1974), 349–52; *Dun & Bradstreet, Inc v Greenmoss Builders, Inc,* 472 US 749 (1985), 763.
[17]   *Gertz v Robert Welch, Inc,* 418 US 323 (1974), 349–50; *Dun & Bradstreet, Inc v Greenmoss Builders, Inc,* 472 US 749 (1985), 751.
[18]   *Philadelphia Newspapers, Inc v Hepps,* 475 US 767 (1986), 776–7.
[19]   *Bachchan v India Abroad Publications Inc,* 585 NY 2d 661 (SC NY, 1992), 665 (Fingerhood J); see para 23.05.

principles that they 'should be denied recognition under principles of comity'.[20]

C. The Liability of Internet Intermediaries under American Common Law

Introduction

Many more cases have been decided in the United States concerning the liability of Internet intermediaries who host, cache, or carry defamatory content which they did not create than in either the United Kingdom or Australia. As with the general principles of American defamation law just discussed, however, a very different approach has been favoured in the United States.

31.10

The American Congress legislated in 1996 in relation to the liability of Internet intermediaries[21] against the backdrop of two seminal cases: *Cubby, Inc v CompuServe Inc* and *Stratton Oakmont, Inc v Prodigy Services Company*.

31.11

Cubby, Inc v CompuServe Inc[22]

Background

CompuServe operated a computerized library and bulletin board service, known as the CompuServe Information Service (CIS). Subscribers paid a fee for access to CIS. Information on CIS was divided into, among other things, special interest 'forums', including a Journalism Forum, which contained material likely to be of particular interest to those involved in the media. CompuServe contracted with an independent company, Cameron Communications, Inc (CCI), to manage the Journalism Forum. CCI's contractual obligations included obligations to 'manage, review, create, delete, edit or otherwise control the contents' of the Journalism Forum, 'in accordance with editorial and technical standards and conventions of style as established by CompuServe'.[23]

31.12

CCI had a contract with Don Fitzpatrick Associates (DFA) for the provision of a daily 'newsletter' to the Journalism Forum known as Rumorville USA, which contained, among other things, gossip about broadcast journalism and journalists. Rumorville USA was available to users of the Journalism Forum who had made membership arrangements with DFA. Under the contract between CCI

---

[20] *Telnikoff v Matusevitch*, 702 A 2d 230 (CA Md, 1997), 249 (Eldridge J); see para 23.06.
[21] See para 31.51.
[22] 776 F Supp 135 (SD NY, 1991) ('*Cubby*').
[23] ibid, 137.

and DFA, DFA accepted 'total responsibility for the contents' of Rumorville USA.[24]

CompuServe had no direct relationship with DFA. The only remuneration CompuServe received for making Rumorville USA available was through membership fees and online time fees charged to CIS subscribers. CIS was configured such that CompuServe had no opportunity to review Rumorville USA before it was made available to subscribers. CompuServe contended that it had not received any complaints about the contents of Rumorville USA or DFA.[25]

CompuServe played no part in the preparation of Rumorville USA, yet it was only possible to obtain access to Rumorville USA via CompuServe's computer network. CompuServe had the opportunity of monitoring the content of Rumorville USA and could have prevented its publication or continuing publication.

31.13   The plaintiffs in the proceeding were the creators of Skuttlebut, a computer database which was designed to compete with Rumorville USA. The plaintiffs claimed that they had been defamed by the contents of several editions of Rumorville USA in April 1990. The material complained of included allegations that Skuttlebut was a 'scam' and that the plaintiffs obtained information for Skuttlebut 'through some back door'.[26]

Proceedings were brought in the United States District Court in New York. CompuServe applied for summary judgment before Leisure J.

31.14   Under the applicable civil procedure rules, summary judgment could be granted only if, on the basis of the papers filed in the proceeding, there was 'no genuine issue as to any material fact and . . . the moving party is entitled to a judgment as a matter of law'.[27]

Under New York defamation law, plaintiffs must prove that defendants are publishers of the material complained of. A distinction is drawn between 'publishers' and 'distributors' of material. Distributors are not liable 'if they neither know nor have reason to know of the defamation'.[28]

The decision

31.15   Citing a number of authorities interpreting the First Amendment to the United States' Constitution, Leisure J noted that it would be unreasonable for mere

---

[24]   *Cubby*, 137.
[25]   ibid.
[26]   ibid, 138.
[27]   Federal Rule of Civil Procedure 56(c); see 776 F Supp 135, 138.
[28]   *Cubby*, 776 F Supp 135 (SD NY, 1991), 139, citing *Lerman v Chuckleberry Publishing, Inc*, 521 F Supp 228 (SD NY, 1981), 235.

distributors of defamatory material to be liable as publishers; among the effects would be to restrict the material available in bookshops and periodical stands 'to material of which their proprietors had made an inspection'.[29] To impose a duty on distributors to monitor all the material they distribute would place an impermissible burden on free speech.[30]

Leisure J concluded that CIS was an 'electronic, for-profit library', much like a public library, book store, or news-stand, and that CompuServe was thus a distributor for the purposes of New York defamation law.[31] Leisure J thought it significant that once CompuServe had decided to carry a given publication, it had little or no editorial control over its contents, especially where the publication was managed by a company unrelated to CompuServe. Leisure J also considered that it was no more feasible for CompuServe to examine every publication it carried than it would be for a public library, book store, or news-stand to do so.[32]

The plaintiffs had not contended that there was any evidence to suggest that CompuServe knew, or had reason to know, that Rumorville USA contained the allegedly defamatory statements.[33] Leisure J thus granted summary judgment in CompuServe's favour.

Analysis

Several points can be made about the decision in *Cubby*. First, Leisure J thought that Internet intermediaries were more like public libraries, book stores, or news-stands, than editors. He thus had no difficulty characterizing Internet intermediaries as distributors, rather than publishers.   **31.16**

Secondly, Leisure J was concerned about the implications for freedom of speech under the First Amendment which would result from holding CompuServe to the standard of a publisher, rather than a distributor.[34] There is no discussion in the judgment of a need to balance the rights of the plaintiffs to vindication and protection of their reputations against the public interest in free speech.

Thirdly, there is no discussion in the judgment about whether the distributor of a publication such as Rumorville USA should be on notice that, by its name and nature, it is the very kind of publication likely to contain controversial and defamatory material. Rather, Leisure J simply accepted the affidavit evidence filed by CompuServe to the effect that it did not know the particular issues of

---

[29] *Smith v California*, 361 US 147 (1959), 153.
[30] *Lerman v Flynt Distributing Co*, 745 F 2d 123 (2d cir, 1984), 139.
[31] *Cubby*, 776 F Supp 135 (SD NY, 1991), 140.
[32] ibid.
[33] ibid, 141.
[34] ibid, 139.

Rumorville USA complained of contained the allegedly defamatory statements.[35]

Fourthly, Leisure J accepted as fact that CompuServe had 'in reality' little or no editorial control over the contents of the publication.[36] There was no discussion about whether CompuServe had the right to exert editorial control over material available on CIS. The judgment is thus influenced by the feasibility of CompuServe exerting editorial control, rather than the ability to do so.

Finally, because neither CCI nor DFA were parties to the proceeding, there was no analysis of whether those companies might have been liable to the plaintiffs.

How Cubby *might have been decided in the United Kingdom*

31.17   **Section 1 of the Defamation Act 1996.**   Had Rumorville USA been hosted by CompuServe in the United Kingdom, and proceedings been brought against CompuServe in that country, then the statutory defence in section 1 of the Defamation Act 1996 would probably not have operated to protect Compu-Serve from liability.

In the first place, CompuServe was almost certainly a 'publisher' of CIS, as that term is defined in section 1(2) of the Act:

> 'publisher' means a commercial publisher, that is, a person whose business is issuing material to the public, or a section of the public, who issues material containing the statement in the course of that business.

Secondly, CompuServe would not have been able to prove that its conduct in the publication of Rumorville USA was limited to that described in one or more of the paragraphs under section 1(3) of the Defamation Act 1996.[37] Compu-Serve operated the CIS, and had entered into a contract with CCI to manage the Journalism Forum part of the CIS. CCI had, in turn, contracted with DFA to provide the Rumorville USA section of the Journalism Forum. CompuServe's conduct thus exceeded that described in section 1(3)(c) of the Act, namely 'operating or providing any equipment, system or service by means of which the statement is retrieved, copied, distributed or made available in electronic form'. Its role was also greater than that described in section 1(3)(e) of the Act, namely:

> the operator of or provider of access to a communications system by means of which the statement is transmitted, or made available, by a person over whom he has no effective control.

Thirdly, the defence in section 1 of the Defamation Act 1996 (UK) may not

---

[35] *Cubby*, 141.
[36] ibid, 140.
[37] See paras 16.04, 16.07–16.12.

have succeeded in the United Kingdom because CompuServe failed to exercise reasonable care in relation to the publication of Rumorville USA.[38] Courts are required by section 1(5)(b) of the Act to have regard to 'the nature or circumstances of the publication' in determining whether a person has taken reasonable care for the purposes of the section 1 defence. A United Kingdom court might well take the view that a publication such as Rumorville USA is the very kind of publication likely to contain defamatory material.[39] Furthermore, CompuServe had the ability to monitor and censor material on its servers, but did not do so. It had imposed editorial standards on CCI in relation to the material posted on the CIS, but had apparently not enforced those standards.

Electronic Commerce (EC Directive) Regulations 2002.   In the terms of the   **31.18**
Electronic Commerce (EC Directive) Regulations 2002 (UK) ('Electronic Commerce Regulations'),[40] CompuServe was the 'host' of Rumorville USA. Regulation 19(a) of the Electronic Commerce Regulations excludes hosts from liability for information provided by users of the service, provided that the host:

   (i)   does not have actual knowledge of unlawful activity or information or, where a claim for damages is made, is not aware of facts or circumstances from which it would have been apparent that the activity or information was unlawful; or

  (ii)   upon obtaining such knowledge or awareness, acts expeditiously to remove or disable access to the information.

By regulation 19(b), however, the exclusion from liability does not apply where the user was acting 'under the authority or the control' of the host.

On the facts in *Cubby*, the author of the material appearing on Rumorville USA, DFA, may have been acting under the authority or the control of CompuServe. CompuServe had entered into a contract with CCI for it to manage the Journalism Forum. CCI had contracted with DFA for the provision of the Rumorville USA section of the Forum. If that analysis is correct, CompuServe would not have been entitled to the benefit of the defence in regulation 19 of the Electronic Commerce Regulations.

Common law.   Applying common law principles, CompuServe was almost   **31.19**
certainly a 'publisher' of Rumorville USA. Its role in the publication of Rumorville USA was at least as significant as the role of Demon Internet in the

---

[38] Defamation Act 1996, s 1(1)(b); see paras 16.13–16.16.
[39] See eg *Thompson v Australian Capital Television Pty Ltd* (1994) 54 FCR 513, 520; (1996) 186 CLR 574, 589–90; see esp paras 18.13, 18.17, 18.40; cf *Auvil v CBS '60 Minutes'*, 800 F Supp 928 (ED Wa, 1992), discussed in paras 18.20–18.28.
[40] See chapter 17.

publication of the bulletin board postings which were the subject of Morland J's decision in *Godfrey v Demon Internet Ltd.*[41]

In so far as the common law defence of innocent dissemination is concerned, it is unlikely that CompuServe would have been categorized as a subordinate distributor.[42] It is likely, on the authority of *Thompson v Australian Capital Television Pty Ltd* ('*Thompson*'), that Internet intermediaries such as CompuServe would be treated as original publishers of the material stored on their computer systems. The approach in *Cubby*, however, is to be preferred: Internet intermediaries like CompuServe are much more like the traditional categories of subordinate distributors, such as public libraries, book stores, and news-stands than the traditional categories of original publishers, such as authors and editors.[43]

Even if CompuServe was a subordinate distributor of CIS, a court applying *Thompson* would be likely to deny it the benefit of the defence of innocent dissemination. Bulletin boards such as CIS carry a high risk of containing libels.[44] CompuServe could, despite the difficulties, have arranged its affairs so that each message posted on the bulletin board was monitored and, if necessary, censored. It could have prevented the publication, or continuing publication, of Rumorville USA. A United Kingdom court might conclude that if CompuServe did not actually know that CIS was carrying the libel complained of, then its lack of knowledge was due to negligence on its part.

An intermediary such as CompuServe might, however, plausibly argue that imposing liability in circumstances where it had no knowledge of, and no practical means of monitoring or censoring, material posted on its bulletin boards would violate Article 10 of the European Convention on Human Rights.[45]

How Cubby *might have been decided in Australia*

31.20   **The clause 91 defence.**   Had Rumorville USA been hosted by CompuServe in Australia, and proceedings been brought against CompuServe in Australia, the clause 91 defence would probably have operated to exclude the operation of the rules of civil defamation law.[46] Rumorville USA would constitute 'Internet content' for the purposes of the clause 91 defence.[47] As there was no evidence that CompuServe was aware of the nature of the offending content, any rule of civil defamation law which would have subjected CompuServe to liability

---

[41] [2001] QB 201; see paras 15.03–15.07.
[42] cf para 18.39.
[43] See para 18.45.
[44] See *Thompson* (1996) 186 CLR 574, 590; see paras 18.46–18.47.
[45] See para 18.41.
[46] ie the defence in the Broadcasting Services Act 1992 (Cth), Sch 5, cl 91; see chapter 19.
[47] See paras 19.11–19.23.

would be of no effect. The clause 91 defence would thus have operated to protect CompuServe from liability.

Common law. If, on the other hand, proceedings had been brought in Aus-   **31.21**
tralia against CompuServe in respect of its hosting of Rumorville USA in the
United States, then CompuServe would not have been entitled to the benefit of
the clause 91 defence, because it would not be an 'Internet content host' for the
purposes of that defence.[48] In such a case, CompuServe's liability in Australia
would depend on the operation of the rules of civil defamation law, as well as
the application of jurisdiction and choice of law rules. The application of the
common law rules as they apply in Australia suggests that CompuServe was a
'publisher' of Rumorville USA, and that CompuServe would not have succeeded in a defence of innocent dissemination in respect of publications of
Rumorville USA occurring in Australia.[49]

Queensland and Tasmania. It is possible that CompuServe would have been   **31.22**
entitled to the benefit of the statutory defences of innocent dissemination which
apply in respect of publications occurring in Queensland and Tasmania.[50]
CompuServe was arguably a 'seller' of Rumorville USA, because CompuServe's
subscribers paid a fee for access to the CIS. Rumorville USA was probably a
'periodical' for the purposes of the statutory defences: in both Queensland and
Tasmania a periodical means 'any newspaper, review, magazine or other writing
that is published periodically'.[51] If those assumptions are correct, then Compu-
Serve would be entitled to the benefit of the statutory defences, unless it had
actual knowledge that Rumorville USA contained defamatory matter, or that
defamatory matter was habitually or frequently contained in Rumorville USA.[52]

It could perhaps be argued, however, that the statutory defences in respect of
publications occurring in Queensland and Tasmania ought not to protect
CompuServe, because its role was really in the nature of a commercial publisher,
rather than a mere seller of Rumorville USA.

Stratton Oakmont, Inc v Prodigy Services Company[53]

Background

Prodigy was the host for a special-purpose financial bulletin board, 'Money   **31.23**
Talk'. Money Talk was only available to subscribers through Prodigy's computer

---

[48] See para 19.28.
[49] See para 31.19.
[50] Queensland: Defamation Act 1889 (Qld), ss 25–6; Tasmania: Defamation Act 1957 (Tas), s 26; see paras 19.39–19.43.
[51] Definition of 'periodical': Defamation Act 1889 (Qld), s 3; Defamation Act 1957 (Tas), s 3.
[52] Defamation Act 1889 (Qld), s 25; Defamation Act 1957 (Tas), s 26(1).
[53] 1995 WL 323710; 23 Media L Rep 1794 (SC NY, 1995) ('*Stratton Oakmont*').

network. The plaintiffs alleged that they had been defamed by statements posted on Money Talk in October 1994 to the effect that they were involved in criminal fraud and were liars.

The plaintiffs prepared and filed affidavit material in support of a partial summary judgment application seeking, among other things, judgment to the effect that Prodigy was a 'publisher' of the statements complained of.

31.24 The affidavit material filed by the plaintiffs was aimed squarely at establishing a basis to enable the court to differentiate Prodigy from CompuServe in *Cubby*. It set out in detail:

- Historical public statements by Prodigy representatives, and extracts from Prodigy's policies, to the effect that Prodigy was a service which exercised editorial control over messages posted on its bulletin boards. Included were statements by Prodigy's Director of Market Programs and Communications likening Prodigy's service to a newspaper. The latest such material relied on by the plaintiffs was dated February 1993, some eighteen months prior to the posting of the allegedly defamatory statements.[54]
- Relevant extracts from Prodigy's Content Guidelines, which warned users that Prodigy would remove insulting or harassing messages, or messages which were in bad taste, grossly repugnant to community standards, or harmful to maintaining a harmonious online community, upon those messages coming to Prodigy's attention.[55]
- The use by Prodigy of software screening programs, which prescreen messages for the use of offensive language.[56]
- The use by Prodigy of 'Board Leaders' to enforce the Content Guidelines, and the availability to Board Leaders of an 'emergency delete' function which enabled rapid deletion of messages from Prodigy's system.[57]

Prodigy contended that it had changed its policies since February 1993, in part because of the increased volume of messages posted on its bulletin boards. Prodigy also argued that, although Board Leaders were able to remove messages from Prodigy's system, they did not function as editors.[58]

31.25 Ain J of the Supreme Court of New York was critical of the material put before him by Prodigy, noting that documentation and detailed explanations had not

---

[54] 1995 WL 323710, 2.
[55] ibid.
[56] ibid.
[57] ibid.
[58] ibid, 3.

been submitted, and that some of Prodigy's assertions were put in 'conclusory manner'.[59]

The decision

Ain J held that Prodigy was a publisher, not a distributor, for the purposes of **31.26** New York defamation law. Ain J held that Prodigy was distinguishable from CompuServe for two reasons. First, it was significant that Prodigy had held itself out as exercising editorial control over the contents of its service. Secondly, Prodigy in fact exercised such control by using automatic software screening programs, Content Guidelines, and Board Leaders. The fact that Prodigy's editorial control was not complete was irrelevant, because Prodigy had 'uniquely arrogated to itself the role of determining what is proper for its members to post and read on its bulletin boards'.[60]

Ain J also thought that Prodigy was distinguishable from the affiliate stations in *Auvil*, noting that, unlike the affiliate stations, Prodigy had taken it upon itself to create 'an editorial staff of Board Leaders who have the ability to continually monitor incoming transmissions and in fact do spend time censoring notes'.[61]

Ain J asserted that his decision was consistent with *Cubby* and *Auvil*. It is Prodigy's own policies, technology and staffing decisions which have altered the scenario and mandated the finding that it is a publisher.[62]

On the policy issues identified in *Cubby* and *Auvil*, Ain J had this to say:

> For the record, the fear that this Court's finding of publisher status for Prodigy will compel all computer networks to abdicate control of their bulletin boards, incorrectly presumes that the market will refuse to compensate a network for its increased control and the resulting increased exposure . . . Presumably Prodigy's decision to regulate the content of its bulletin boards was in part influenced by its desire to attract a market it perceived to exist consisting of users seeking a 'family-oriented' computer service. This decision simply required that to the extent computer networks provide such services, they must also accept the concomitant legal consequences. In addition, the Court also notes that the issues addressed herein may ultimately be preempted by federal law if the Communications Decency Act of 1995, several versions of which are pending in Congress, is enacted.[63]

Some time after Ain J delivered his judgment in *Stratton Oakmont*, Prodigy **31.27** sought leave to re-argue or 'renew' the case, contending that by oversight, it had

---

[59] ibid.
[60] ibid, 4.
[61] ibid, 5. *Auvil*, 800 F Supp 928 (ED Wa, 1992) is discussed in paras 18.20–18.28.
[62] ibid.
[63] ibid.

failed to put before the court evidence which would have satisfied it that Prodigy did not possess and exercise significant editorial control over the content of its bulletin boards.[64] Stratton Oakmont did not oppose Prodigy's application, apparently because the parties had agreed to settle their dispute on terms which included applying to have the orders made by Ain J vacated.[65]

Ain J dismissed Prodigy's motion, noting that Prodigy had failed to give any 'acceptable excuse' for the failure to include the new evidence in its original application.[66] Ain J also noted that it was important that his original decision stand, because to:

> vacate that precedent on request because these two parties (or the Plaintiff) has [sic] lost interest or decided that the litigation would be too costly or time con-suming would remove the only existing New York precedent in this area leaving the law even further behind the technology.[67]

Analysis

31.28   Four main points can be made about the decision in *Stratton Oakmont*. First, it arose out of a partial summary judgment application. Its outcome did not render Prodigy liable to the plaintiffs under defamation law; it simply deter-mined that Prodigy was a publisher for the purposes of that law.

Secondly, the court appeared to be influenced by the imminent passage of the Communications Decency Act,[68] which it thought would protect publishers such as Prodigy from liability for defamatory statements of the kind in issue in the proceeding. Free speech concerns were dealt with only cursorily by the court in the passage cited in paragraph 31.26 above.

Thirdly, Ain J's assertion that his decision was consistent with *Auvil* suggests that he thought there was a point at which the partial exercise of editorial control converts a distributor into a publisher for the purposes of New York defamation law. In *Auvil*,[69] it was clear that the affiliate stations had the ability to censor programmes, and had in the past occasionally exercised that ability, although not in relation to the *60 Minutes* programme. The affiliate stations did thus exercise partial editorial control over national programming, but not enough control to render them publishers of that programming. Ain J must have thought that the degree of partial editorial control exercised by Prodigy, and Prodigy's public statements in relation to the extent to which it exercised

[64] *Stratton Oakmont, Inc v Prodigy Services Company*, 1995 WL 805178 (SC NY), 2.
[65] ibid, 1.
[66] ibid, 2–3.
[67] ibid, 1.
[68] See para 31.50–31.83.
[69] See paras 18.20–18.28.

editorial control, made Prodigy qualitatively different from the affiliate stations in *Auvil*, but he gives little guidance as to why he formed this conclusion. In other words, Ain J felt that the facts in *Stratton Oakmont* were sufficiently different from those in *Auvil* to enable him to reach an opposite conclusion without applying inconsistent logic.

Finally, Ain J rejected much of the affidavit evidence filed by Prodigy because it was not backed up by sufficient documentation, and because it made claims in a 'conclusory manner', even though Prodigy voiced its concern that such an important decision should not be reached 'without the benefit of a full record'.[70] Ain J therefore must have rejected Prodigy's assertions that it had changed its policies, was unable to review every posting manually, and that its Board Leaders did not function as editors. The decision may thus be capable of being confined narrowly to its facts; that is, to bulletin board operators and Internet service providers which hold themselves out as exercising editorial control over content, have guidelines to give effect to that policy, and actually utilize software and staff to censor postings with sufficient regularity.

How Stratton Oakmont *might have been decided in the United Kingdom*

Section 1 of the Defamation Act 1996.   Had *Stratton Oakmont* been deter- **31.29** mined in the United Kingdom, and Money Talk been hosted by Prodigy in the United Kingdom, Prodigy would almost certainly not have been entitled to the benefit of the defence in section 1 of the Defamation Act 1996 (UK). Prodigy was probably both an 'editor' and a 'publisher' of Money Talk, as those terms are defined in section 1(2) of the Act.[71] In addition, its conduct went well beyond that described in paragraphs (c) and (e) of section 1(3) of the Act.[72] Thirdly, for much the same reasons as discussed in relation to *Cubby*, Prodigy probably failed to exercise reasonable care in relation to the publication of Money Talk, as required by section 1(1)(c) of the Act.[73]

Electronic Commerce Regulations.   The benefit afforded by regulation 19 of **31.30** the Regulations to 'hosts' would not have protected Prodigy if it could be said that the contributors to Money Talk were acting under 'the authority or the control' of Prodigy.[74] That expression, however, is probably apt only to describe employees and agents of service providers, and not third parties in arm's length relationships such as subscribers and contributors. Prodigy, presumably, was not in a position to issue instructions or directions in relation to the content

---

[70] *Stratton Oakmont*, 1995 WL 323710 (SC NY) 3.
[71] See paras 16.03, 16.10, 16.11.
[72] See paras 16.04, 16.07, 16.08.
[73] See para 31.17.
[74] Electronic Commerce Regulations, reg 19(b); see para 17.21.

submitted by its contributors to Money Talk. Contributors were not, in that sense, acting under Prodigy's authority or control in relation to their contributions.

It is not clear from the available information whether, if the facts in *Stratton Oakmont* had occurred in the United Kingdom, it might have been argued that Prodigy could not rely on the regulation 19 defence because it was 'aware of facts or circumstances from which it would have been apparent' that 'unlawful information' was being contributed by subscribers.[75]

31.31   **Common law.**   It is unlikely that Prodigy would have been entitled to the benefit of the common law defence of innocent dissemination, had the facts in *Stratton Oakmont* arisen and been determined in the United Kingdom. Prodigy was, for common law purposes, a 'publisher' of Money Talk.[76] Prodigy would probably have been treated by a United Kingdom court as an 'original publisher', rather than a 'subordinate distributor', of the statements posted on Money Talk. It had the 'ability to control and supervise' those statements.[77] Even if Prodigy was a subordinate distributor of the offending statements, it seems strongly arguable that the common law defence of innocent dissemination would not have been available to it. Although Prodigy had taken some precautions in relation to messages posted on its bulletin boards, those precautions may have been inadequate for a service with some two million subscribers,[78] having regard to the high risk that many of those messages would contain libels.[79]

How Stratton Oakmont *might have been decided in Australia*

31.32   **The clause 91 defence.**   Had *Stratton Oakmont* been determined by an Australian court, and Money Talk been hosted by Prodigy in Australia, then the clause 91 defence[80] would probably have applied to protect Prodigy from liability in respect of publications of Money Talk occurring in Australia. Prodigy was an 'Internet content host' for the purposes of the clause 91 defence.[81] The rules of civil defamation law do not apply to such hosts except where they are actually aware of the nature of the content complained of.[82]

31.33   **Common law.**   If, however, the clause 91 defence did not apply for any of the reasons outlined in chapter 19, then an Australian court applying *Thompson* would almost certainly have concluded that the defence of innocent dissemin-

---

[75] ibid, reg 19(a)(i); see paras 17.23–17.25.
[76] *Godfrey v Demon Internet Ltd* [2001] QB 201; see esp para 15.04.
[77] *Thompson* (1996) 186 CLR 574, 589 (Brennan CJ, Dawson, and Toohey JJ).
[78] *Stratton Oakmont*, 1995 WL 323710 (SC NY) 1.
[79] *Thompson* (1996) 186 CLR 574, 590–1, adopting *Thompson* (1994) 54 FCR 513, 520; cf paras 18.39, 18.41.
[80] See chapter 19.
[81] See para 19.04.
[82] Broadcasting Services Act 1992 (Cth), Sch 5, cl 91(1)(a); see para 19.02.

ation was not available in respect of publications of Money Talk occurring in Australia.[83]

Queensland and Tasmania.   It is possible that the statutory defences of inno-   **31.34**
cent dissemination which apply in Queensland and Tasmania would have protected Prodigy from liability in respect of publications of Money Talk occurring
in those States. Prodigy was arguably a 'seller' of Money Talk for the purpose of
those defences. Money Talk was only available to Prodigy subscribers, who paid
a fee for access to Prodigy's bulletin boards, including Money Talk. There was
no suggestion that Prodigy knew that Money Talk contained the allegedly
defamatory postings. It is not clear whether Money Talk habitually or frequently
contained defamatory matter.[84] It might be argued, however, that Prodigy was
more than a mere 'seller' of Money Talk, having regard to the fact that it had held
itself out as exercising, and had in fact exercised, editorial control over its bulletin
boards.

Lunney v Prodigy Services Company

Facts and decision

Stratton Oakmont was criticized in *Lunney v Prodigy Services Company*,[85] a case   **31.35**
concerning the transmission of an allegedly defamatory e-mail message and two
allegedly defamatory bulletin board postings.

An unknown impostor had opened a number of accounts with Prodigy in the
name of the plaintiff, Alexander Lunney. The impostor had then sent a vulgar e-
mail message to a local scoutmaster. The e-mail came to Prodigy's attention, and
after some internal investigation Prodigy notified Lunney that it was terminat-
ing one of his accounts 'due to the transmission of obscene, abusive, threaten-
ing, and sexually explicit material through the Prodigy service and providing
inaccurate profile information'.[86] Lunney informed Prodigy that the message
had been sent by an impostor, who had opened the account in his name and
without his authority. Prodigy accepted this explanation, apologized to Lunney,
and conducted an investigation which revealed that a further four accounts had
been opened in Lunney's name. Prodigy promptly closed all of those accounts.

Lunney brought proceedings against Prodigy for a range of causes of action,
including defamation arising out of Prodigy's carriage of the vulgar e-mail message which had been sent by the impostor. In the course of discovery in the
proceeding, Prodigy produced two bulletin board messages which had been
posted on one of Prodigy's bulletin boards in Lunney's name during the period

---

[83] See para 31.31.
[84] See para 19.39.
[85] 683 NYS 2d 557 (AD NY, 1998) ('*Lunney*'), affirmed in 94 NY 2d 242 (CA NY, 1999).
[86] 94 NY 2d 242 (CA NY, 1999), 247.

while the false accounts were active. Lunney expanded his case to make similar claims against Prodigy in relation to its hosting and carriage of those messages.

31.36 As noted earlier, the decision of the Court of Appeals of New York in *Lunney* stands as authority for the proposition that Internet intermediaries, at least in so far as they are involved in the transmission of e-mail messages, are analogous to telephone carriers.[87] Under American law, telephone carriers are mere conduits, rather than publishers, of the messages they carry.[88]

31.37 In relation to the allegedly defamatory bulletin board postings hosted by Prodigy, the court held that, even though some editorial control had been exercised by Prodigy over the content of some of the messages posted on its bulletin boards, Prodigy had been entirely passive in relation to millions of other postings. It was, as a result, not a 'publisher' of the offending postings. The court expressly declined to express a view as to whether there might be circumstances in which an Internet intermediary playing a more active role in the transmission of bulletin board postings might qualify as a 'publisher'.

31.38 The intermediate appeal court in *Lunney* was critical of the decision in *Stratton Oakmont*, and ultimately held itself not bound by it.[89] Several bases for distinguishing *Stratton Oakmont* were given, including that the decision in *Stratton Oakmont* was made in a different factual context. Prodigy had abandoned the efforts at editorial control which swayed the court against it in *Stratton Oakmont* in January 1994, before the communications complained of in *Lunney*. The intermediate appeal court in *Lunney* also noted that *Stratton Oakmont* was bad as a matter of policy, as it 'discourages the very conduct which the plaintiff in *Stratton Oakmont* argued should be encouraged'.[90]

31.39 The United States Supreme Court refused to hear an appeal from the decision of the Court of Appeals of New York in *Lunney*, without giving reasons.

How Lunney *might have been decided in the United Kingdom*

31.40 **Section 1 of the Defamation Act 1996.** The same result would probably have been reached by a United Kingdom court, in so far as the case concerned the transmission of allegedly defamatory e-mail messages, had the facts in *Lunney* arisen and fallen for determination there.

Prodigy was almost certainly not an 'author, editor or publisher' of the allegedly defamatory e-mail message. Its role in the transmission of that message was

---

[87] See para 15.35.
[88] *Anderson v New York Telephone Company*, 361 NYS 2d 913 (CA NY, 1974); see paras 15.30–15.34.
[89] 683 NYS 2d 557 (AD NY, 1998), 561–2.
[90] ibid, 562.

probably limited to 'operating or providing [a] . . . service by means of which the statement was . . . made available in electronic form': section 1(3)(c).[91] Alternatively, Prodigy acted only as 'the operator or provider of access to a communications system by means of which the statement is transmitted, or made available, by a person over whom he has no effective control': section 1(3)(e).[92]

Even if Prodigy was an author, editor, or publisher of the allegedly defamatory e-mail message, it probably took reasonable care in relation to its publication for the purposes of section 1(1)(b), particularly having regard to the nature of e-mail messages as private, and instantaneous forms of communication.[93] At the time the message was transmitted, there was no reason for Prodigy to believe that the account had been opened fraudulently, or that the account would be used for the transmission of defamatory material.[94]

In so far as the facts in *Lunney* concerned the transmission of allegedly defamatory bulletin board postings, the position is not quite so clear. It is arguable that, as in relation to *Stratton Oakmont*,[95] Prodigy was an 'editor' of the bulletin board postings for the purposes of section 1(1)(a) of the Defamation Act 1996.[96] Prodigy had reserved the right to exercise, and in fact had exercised, editorial control over some of the postings on its bulletin boards by screening them for vulgarities. The better view would appear to be, however, that Prodigy's role in the publication of the offending bulletin board postings was limited to that described in section 1(3)(c) of the Act,[97] particularly having regard to the evidence that it had been 'passive' in relation to the overwhelming number of posted messages.

Electronic Commerce Regulations. The Electronic Commerce Regulations would probably have protected Prodigy from liability in circumstances such as those which fell for determination in *Lunney*.

31.41

In so far as Prodigy had transmitted an allegedly defamatory e-mail message, it was almost certainly a 'mere conduit' for the purposes of the Regulations.[98] Under regulation 17, mere conduits are not liable for the transmission of information where they did not initiate the transmission, select the receiver of the transmission, or select or modify the information contained in the transmis-

---

[91] See para 16.07.
[92] See para 16.08.
[93] Defamation Act 1996 (UK), s 1(5)(b); see para 16.14.
[94] ibid, ss 1(1)(c), 1(5)(c); see para 16.15.
[95] See para 31.29.
[96] See paras 16.03, 16.10.
[97] See para 16.07.
[98] See para 17.07.

sion.[99] An intermediary's status as a mere conduit is not affected by reason only of the fact that it stored the information on an automatic, intermediate, and transient basis for the sole purpose of carrying out the transmission, provided that the information was not stored for any period longer than was reasonably necessary for the transmission.[100]

In so far as Prodigy had transmitted allegedly defamatory bulletin board postings, it was a 'host' for the purposes of the Electronic Commerce Regulations.[101] There did not appear to be any evidence that Prodigy had actual knowledge of unlawful activity or information on its bulletin board, or that it was aware of facts or circumstances from which it would have been apparent that the activity or information was unlawful, at the time the bulletin board messages were posted. In those circumstances, regulation 19 of the Electronic Commerce Regulations would operate so as to prevent Prodigy from being liable for transmitting the allegedly defamatory bulletin board postings.

31.42   Common law.   At common law, Prodigy was almost certainly a 'publisher' of the allegedly defamatory bulletin board postings.[102] It was arguably also a 'publisher' of the allegedly defamatory e-mail message.[103]

Prodigy would probably be entitled to the benefit of the common law defence of innocent dissemination in respect of the transmission of the allegedly defamatory e-mail message. In so far as that message was concerned, Prodigy was probably a 'subordinate distributor',[104] with no knowledge, or reason to believe, that the message contained a libel.[105]

In relation to the allegedly defamatory bulletin board postings, the application of the common law defence of innocent dissemination is less clear. It is likely that Prodigy would be denied the benefit of that defence in the United Kingdom if a court appled the principles in *Thompson*, for the reasons discussed in relation to *Cubby*[106] and *Stratton Oakmont*.[107] Although Prodigy played a less substantial role in the publication of the bulletin board postings than the intermediaries in either of those cases, it was probably still an 'original publisher' rather than a 'subordinate distributor' of them in the sense discussed in *Thompson*: it plainly did have the 'ability to control and supervise' the material posted

---

[99] Electronic Commerce Regulations, reg 17(1).
[100] ibid, reg 17(2).
[101] ibid, reg 19; see paras 17.20–17.27.
[102] *Godfrey v Demon Internet Ltd* [2001] QB 201; see esp para 15.04.
[103] See paras 15.07, 15.43.
[104] See para 18.50.
[105] See para 18.51.
[106] See para 31.19.
[107] See para 31.31.

on its bulletin boards,[108] even if it was scarcely feasible for it to monitor and censor that material. Even if it was a subordinate distributor, Prodigy may not have been able to prove the other elements of the defence. A court applying the principles in *Thompson* might hold that Prodigy was under an obligation to take greater precautions to monitor and censor the material appearing on its bulletin boards, which by its nature was likely to contain comments about persons.[109]

There would, however, be obvious scope for arguing that to impose liability on an intermediary such as Prodigy on the facts in *Lunney* is to impose an impossibly onerous burden serving no pressing social need, in violation of Article 10 of the European Convention on Human Rights.[110]

How Lunney *might have been decided in Australia*

The clause 91 defence. Had the offending bulletin board postings been   **31.43**
hosted by Prodigy in Australia, the clause 91 defence would have operated to protect Prodigy from liability in respect of such publications of the bulletin board postings as occurred in Australia. Prodigy would in those circumstances have been an 'Internet content host' in relation to the postings.[111] As Prodigy had no actual knowledge of the content of the postings, apparently until the discovery phase of the proceedings brought by *Lunney*, clause 91(1)(a) of Schedule 5 to the Broadcasting Services Act 1992 (Cth) would have operated to protect Prodigy from liability for defamation.[112]

The clause 91 defence would not have applied in relation to the allegedly defamatory e-mail message, however, because 'ordinary e-mail' is excluded from the definition of 'Internet content' in clause 3 of Schedule 5 to the Broadcasting Services Act 1992 (Cth).[113] Prodigy's potential liability in relation to the publication of such an e-mail message in Australia would therefore have depended on the application of the ordinary rules of civil defamation law.

Common law. The common law defence of innocent dissemination would   **31.44**
probably apply to protect Prodigy from liability in relation to publication in Australia of the allegedly defamatory e-mail message, but not the allegedly defamatory bulletin board postings.[114]

Queensland and Tasmania. The statutory defences of innocent dissemination   **31.45**
would not have applied to protect Prodigy from liability in respect of publica-

---

[108] *Thompson* (1996) 186 CLR 574, 589.
[109] ibid, 590, citing *Thompson* (1994) 54 FCR 513, 520; see esp paras 18.13, 18.17, 18.40–18.41, 18.46–18.47, 18.49.
[110] See paras 18.39, 18.41, 30.44.
[111] See para 19.04.
[112] See para 19.02.
[113] See paras 19.12–19.14.
[114] See para 31.42.

tions occurring in Queensland or Tasmania. Prodigy was not a 'seller' of either the allegedly defamatory e-mail message or the bulletin board postings.[115]

Prodigy would, however, probably have been able to avoid liability in respect of publication of the allegedly defamatory e-mail message in Tasmania, because it was not a 'publisher' of that message. By section 7(b) of the Defamation Act 1957 (Tas), a person only 'publishes' material where he or she knows or has the opportunity of knowing the contents or nature of that material. The same argument would not have protected Prodigy from liability in respect of publication of the allegedly defamatory bulletin board postings in Tasmania, because Prodigy had the opportunity of knowing the contents of those postings.[116]

Conclusions about the American common law

31.46 On the basis of the authorities so far reviewed, the position under American common law is that intermediaries involved in the transmission of e-mail messages are akin to telephone carriers, and therefore entirely outside the reach of American defamation law.[117]

In relation to other Internet content, such as bulletin board postings and web pages, intermediaries who do not exercise editorial control over content, and who do not hold themselves out as exercising such control, are characterized as distributors, and so are liable for defamatory content only if they know, or have reason to know, of the defamation.[118]

31.47 Intermediaries who hold themselves out as exercising editorial control, and who do in fact exercise such control, however, are potentially liable as publishers under American common law, whether or not they know of the defamation in question.[119] The degree of editorial control actually exercised by the intermediary is a relevant factor. The point at which a partial exercise of editorial control makes an intermediary liable as a publisher, rather than a distributor, is uncertain.

31.48 The uncertainty in the cases, and in particular the outcome in *Stratton Oakmont*, probably had the effect of discouraging ISPs and bulletin board operators from exercising any editorial control over content available via their computer services.[120]

31.49 First Amendment concerns tend to weigh heavily in the American common law

---

[115] See paras 19.39–19.41.
[116] See para 15.28 (n 39).
[117] *Lunney v Prodigy Services Co*, 94 NY 2d 242 (CA NY, 1999); see paras 31.35–31.45.
[118] *Cubby*, 776 F Supp 135 (SD NY, 1991); see paras 31.12–31.22.
[119] *Stratton Oakmont*, 1995 WL 323710 (SC NY); see paras 31.23–31.34.
[120] See eg *Lunney v Prodigy Services Co*, 93 NY 2d 809 (CA NY, 1999).

decisions. In particular, great weight is attached to the adverse consequences for free speech which would be likely to flow from holding intermediaries liable as publishers. These consequences are generally not balanced in any detail in the cases against the interests of the plaintiffs in protecting and vindicating their reputations. Notably, the American decisions do not consider the nature of the publication in question to be a relevant consideration: no store was placed on the fact that the publication in *Cubby* was a gossip-laden bulletin board, or on the fact that the publication in *Auvil*[121] was a current affairs programme renowned for its controversial content. To be liable, an intermediary who is a distributor has to know, or have reason to know, that the particular publication complained of contains defamatory content.

Decisions taken by intermediaries not to exercise editorial control, or to configure their technology so as to make it difficult or impossible to exercise such control, were accepted uncritically by the courts in both *Cubby* and *Auvil*. No weight was given in either case to the fact that both CompuServe and the affiliate stations had the ability, if they so chose, to exert editorial control over content.

D. The Communications Decency Act 1996

Introduction

In 1996, Congress enacted the Communications Decency Act (CDA),[122] which was primarily designed to prohibit the transmission of obscene and indecent communications by means of telecommunications devices, and the sending of patently offensive communications through the use of interactive computer services, to persons under the age of eighteen years.[123] **31.50**

Section 230(c) of the CDA provides, under the heading, 'Protection for "Good Samaritan" Blocking and Screening of Offensive Material': **31.51**

(1) TREATMENT OF PUBLISHER OR SPEAKER
No provider or user of an interactive computer service shall be treated as the publisher or speaker of any information provided by another information content provider.
(2) CIVIL LIABILITY
No provider or user of an interactive computer service shall be held liable on account of—

---

[121] See paras 18.20–18.28.
[122] Communications Decency Act, 47 USC (USA), s 230(c) (1996). The CDA is Title V of the Telecommunications Act (1996) (USA).
[123] 47 USC, ss 223(a)(1)(B), 223(d)(1).

(A) any action voluntarily taken in good faith to restrict access to or avail-ability of material that the provider or user considers to be obscene, lewd, lascivious, filthy, excessively violent, harassing, or otherwise objectionable, whether or not such material is constitutionally pro-tected; or

(B) any action taken to enable or make available to information content providers or others the technical means to restrict access to material described in paragraph (1).

31.52 Section 230(c)(2) was intended to enable intermediaries to remove offensive material from their computer systems, without fear of being sued by the pro-viders of that material, even where the removed material was otherwise consti-tutionally protected.[124] Section 230(c)(1) was intended to overcome the effects of *Stratton Oakmont*, by encouraging intermediaries to exercise editorial control over material available via their computer systems, without fear of being liable as publishers.[125]

31.53 The CDA prohibitions against the transmission of obscene and indecent com-munications, and the sending of patently offensive communications, to minors were declared unconstitutional in *Reno v American Civil Liberties Union*.[126] That case did not, however, affect the validity of section 230(c).

31.54 Section 230(c)(1) is considerably broader than the statutory defences in the United Kingdom and Australia. In the first place, section 230(c)(1) applies to all providers and users of interactive computer services. The section 1 defence in the United Kingdom, by contrast, applies only to persons other than 'the author, editor or publisher of the statement complained of', as those terms are defined.[127] The Electronic Commerce Regulations apply only to mere conduits, hosts, and Internet intermediaries who cache content, in the circumstances outlined in regulations 17–19 of the Regulations.[128] The clause 91 defence in Australia applies only to 'Internet content hosts' and 'Internet service providers', as those terms are defined in the Broadcasting Services Act 1992 (Cth).[129]

Secondly, the application of section 230(c)(1) is, unlike the Australian clause 91 defence, not limited to 'Internet content', as that term is defined in clause 3 of Schedule 5 to the Broadcasting Services Act 1992 (Cth). The definition of 'Internet content' significantly limits the operation of the clause 91 defence, and gives rise to potential anomalies.[130]

---

[124] *Zeran v America Online, Inc*, 958 F Supp 1124 (ED Va, 1997), 1131, 1134.
[125] ibid, 1134.
[126] 521 US 844 (1997).
[127] Defamation Act 1996 (UK), s 1(1)(a); see paras 16.03, 16.07–16.12.
[128] See chapter 17.
[129] See paras 19.04, 19.05.
[130] See paras 19.11–19.23.

Thirdly, section 230(c)(1) operates even where the provider or user of the inter-active computer service is aware of the nature of the content it is hosting or carrying. By contrast, the protection afforded by the section 1 defence in the United Kingdom only applies where intermediaries did not know, and had no reason to believe, that what they did caused or contributed to the publication of a defamatory statement.[131] The Electronic Commerce Regulations do not pro-tect hosts who have actual knowledge of unlawful activity or information, or who are, in respect of claims for damages, aware of facts or circumstances from which it would have been apparent that the activity or information was unlaw-ful, except where upon obtaining such knowledge or awareness the host acts expeditiously to remove or disable access to the information.[132] In Australia, the clause 91 defence has no operation where an Internet content host or Internet service provider is aware of the nature of the Internet content.[133]

Zeran v America Online, Inc

Facts and decision

The meaning of section 230(c)(1) was considered in *Zeran v America Online, Inc*.[134] The plaintiff sued America Online (AOL) for the negligent distribution of defamatory material linking him with the sale of items glorifying the Oklahoma City bombing of 1995. The material appeared on a bulletin board operated by AOL. It consisted of advertisements for various tasteless items. The plaintiff's first name and telephone number were attached to the advertise-ments. The plaintiff was not involved in the creation or posting of the material. **31.55**

The plaintiff brought the material to AOL's notice shortly after it came to his attention and AOL arranged for its removal the next day. Similar material reappeared, however, on AOL's bulletin boards on several occasions over a period of about one week. Efforts made by AOL to stop the re-emergence of the material were unsuccessful.

The plaintiff argued that AOL was liable to him as a distributor, because it knew and had reason to know that its service contained the allegedly defamatory material.

Before the United States District Court at Virginia, AOL successfully argued that the plaintiff's action had been 'pre-empted' by the enactment of section 230(c)(1) of the CDA. Ellis J held that, although the CDA did not pre-empt all **31.56**

---

[131] Defamation Act 1996 (UK), s 1(1)(c); see paras 16.17–16.18.
[132] See paras 17.20, 17.23–17.27.
[133] See paras 19.30–19.34.
[134] 958 F Supp 1124 (ED Va, 1997) ('*Zeran*').

State laws concerning interactive computer services,[135] the plaintiff's attempt to impose distributor liability on AOL was, in effect, an attempt to have AOL treated as a publisher of defamatory material. Such treatment was pre-empted by section 230(c)(1) of the CDA.[136] Secondly, Ellis J concluded that a finding that AOL was liable to the plaintiff would frustrate one of the purposes of the CDA, namely to encourage Internet service providers to engage in editorial control over material posted on their bulletin boards, without fear of being liable for defamatory content as publishers.[137]

Finally, Ellis J observed that, in the absence of section 230(c), it would be simple for Internet service providers to escape liability as publishers by refraining from exercising editorial control over content, and thereby eliminating any basis for having 'reason to know' of any defamation.[138] This observation leaves Ellis J at odds with Ain J in *Stratton Oakmont*, who considered that there would be commercial reasons for Internet service providers to exercise editorial control and market themselves to the public as doing so, notwithstanding the concomitant legal risks.[139]

31.57 Ellis J's decision was affirmed by the Fourth Circuit Court of Appeals.[140] Chief Judge Wilkinson, who delivered the opinion of the court, noted:

> By its plain language, s 230 creates a federal immunity to any cause of action that would make service providers liable for information originating with a third-party user of the service. Specifically, s 230 precludes courts from entertaining claims that would place a computer service provider in a publisher's role. Thus, lawsuits seeking to hold a service provider liable for its exercise of a publisher's traditional editorial function—such as deciding whether to publish, withdraw, postpone or alter content—are barred.[141]

Chief Judge Wilkinson went on to note that there were a number of purposes underlying the statutory immunity conferred by section 230(c), including removing the 'threat that tort-based lawsuits pose to freedom of speech in the new and burgeoning Internet medium',[142] avoiding the 'restrictive effect' which potential liability would impose on the number and type of messages which could be posted on interactive computer services,[143] and removing the 'disincentives to self-regulation created by the *Stratton Oakmont* decision'.[144]

---

[135] *Zeran*, 1131.
[136] ibid, 1133.
[137] ibid, 1135.
[138] ibid.
[139] See para 31.26.
[140] *Zeran v America Online, Inc*, 129 F 3d 327 (4th cir, 1997).
[141] ibid, 330.
[142] ibid.
[143] ibid, 331.
[144] ibid.

Special leave to appeal to the United States Supreme Court was unanimously   **31.58**
denied.[145]

How Zeran *might have been decided in the United Kingdom*

Section 1 of the Defamation Act 1996.   The section 1 defence would not have   **31.59**
been available to AOL had *Zeran* been decided according to United Kingdom
law, at least in respect of publications of the offending postings occurring after
AOL learned of their existence.[146] The fact that AOL had unsuccessfully attempted
to remove the notices is not relevant to the operation of the section 1 defence.

Separate publications occurred, however, each time the notices reappeared after
having been removed by AOL. Assuming, as appears likely, that AOL exercised
reasonable care to prevent the reappearance of the offending postings, the section 1 defence would have protected AOL in respect of the reappearing postings
until such time as AOL learned, or ought with reasonable diligence to have
learned, of their existence.[147]

Electronic Commerce Regulations.   The application of the Electronic Com-   **31.60**
merce Regulations to the facts in *Zeran* is not entirely clear. AOL was a 'host' of
the bulletin board notices. It seems most likely that regulation 19 would not
provide intermediaries such as AOL with protection from liability. AOL had
actual knowledge of the offending notices, and had not succeeded in removing
or disabling access to them.

It is at least arguable, however, that AOL's attempts to remove or disable access
to the postings complained of would be sufficient to attract the protection of
regulation 19.[148] Regulation 19(2) might be interpreted only as requiring hosts
to 'act' expeditiously, rather than to 'remove or disable access' expeditiously.
This interpretation leads to the better outcome.[149]

Common law.   At common law, AOL would probably not have succeeded in a   **31.61**
defence of innocent dissemination in the United Kingdom. It was a 'publisher'
of the offending bulletin board postings.[150] Even if it was a subordinate

---

[145] *Zeran v America Online, Inc*, 118 S Ct 2341 (1998). The hapless plaintiff also failed in
defamation proceedings against a radio station which broadcast the comments attributed to him
in the offending postings, together with his telephone number, and urged listeners to call him:
Zeran v Diamond Broadcasting, Inc, 203 F 3d 714 (10th cir, 2000).
[146] Defamation Act 1996 (UK), s 1(1)(c), see paras 16.02, 16.17; *Godfrey v Demon Internet Ltd*
[2001] QB 201; see para 16.19.
[147] Defamation Act 1996, s 1(1)(b); see para 16.02.
[148] See paras 17.26–17.27.
[149] cf *Carter v British Columbia Federation of Foster Parents Association* (2004) 27 BCLR (4th)
123 (British Columbia Supreme Court), paras 106–9.
[150] *Godfrey v Demon Internet Ltd* [2001] QB 201; see esp para 15.04.

distributor, the common law defence would probably not have been available, because it knew that each posting contained a libel.[151]

How Zeran *might have been decided in Australia*

31.62 **The clause 91 defence.** Had AOL hosted the offending bulletin board notices in Australia, it would not have been entitled to the benefit of the clause 91 defence from the time it learned of the existence of each posting. The clause 91 defence fails where the Internet content host or Internet service provider is aware of the nature of the Internet content, regardless of the extent of the efforts made by it to prevent the continued accessibility of that content.[152]

31.63 **Common law.** For the same reasons as discussed in relation to the law of the United Kingdom, the common law defence of innocent dissemination would probably not have been available to AOL in respect of publications of the bulletin board postings occurring in Australia.[153]

31.64 **Queensland and Tasmania.** The statutory defences of innocent dissemination which apply in Queensland and Tasmania would probably not have been available to AOL in respect of publications of the bulletin board postings occurring in those States. AOL was in reality a seller of access to the Internet, rather than a seller of the material posted on its bulletin boards. In any event, AOL had actual knowledge of the content of the offending postings.[154]

Applications of *Zeran*

Introduction

31.65 Section 230(c)(1) of the CDA, as interpreted in *Zeran*, has since been applied in a number of American cases to excuse Internet intermediaries from liability in relation to third-party content passing through or hosted on their computer systems. Perhaps the most significant of the post-*Zeran* cases is *Blumenthal v Drudge*.[155] More recently, however, *Zeran* has not been followed in two appellate decisions in California.[156]

Blumenthal v Drudge

31.66 Matt Drudge was a gossip columnist who had allegedly defamed the plaintiffs, an Assistant to the President of the United States and his wife, in his Internet column, the *Drudge Report*. Drudge had a contractual arrangement with AOL

---

[151] See paras 18.01, 18.46–18.47, 18.49.
[152] Broadcasting Services Act 1992 (Cth), Sch 5, cl 91(1)(a) and (c); see esp para 19.34.
[153] See para 31.61.
[154] See paras 19.39–19.43.
[155] 992 F Supp 44 (D DC, 1998).
[156] *Barrett v Rosenthal*, 9 Cal Rptr 3d 142 (CA Ca, 2004); *Grace v eBay, Inc*, 16 Cal Rptr 3d 192 (CA Ca, 2004). See paras 31.76–31.78.

to create, update, and manage editions of the *Drudge Report*. The *Drudge Report* was available to all AOL subscribers. Shortly after publishing the offending report, Drudge retracted it and apologized.

The plaintiffs sued both Drudge and AOL in the United States District Court for the District of Columbia. AOL applied to Friedman J for summary judgment, on the basis that section 230(c)(1) conferred on it an absolute immunity from suit.

Friedman J expressed the view that, had Congress not enacted section 230(c)(1) **31.67** of the CDA, he would have held AOL to be a publisher of the *Drudge Report*. Friedman J said:

> AOL has certain editorial rights with respect to the content provided by Drudge and disseminated by AOL, including the right to require changes in content and to remove it; and it has affirmatively promoted Drudge as a new source of unverified instant gossip on AOL . . . Because it has the right to exercise editorial control over those with whom it contracts and whose words it disseminates, it would seem only fair to hold AOL to the liability standards applied to a publisher or, at least, like a book store or library, to the liability standards applied to a distributor. But Congress has made a different policy choice by providing immunity even where the interactive service provider has an active, even aggressive role in making available content prepared by others.[157]

Friedman J considered himself bound, however, to grant AOL's application for summary judgment, noting that:

> Congress has conferred immunity from tort liability as an incentive to Internet service providers to self-police the Internet for obscenity and other offensive material, even where the self-policing is unsuccessful or not even attempted.[158]

The plaintiffs later settled with Drudge, reportedly paying him US$2,500 to 'make him go away and deprive him of his sort of oxygen'.[159]

How Blumenthal v Drudge *might have been decided in the United Kingdom*

AOL would probably not have been entitled to the benefit of the defence in **31.68** section 1 of the Defamation Act 1996. In the first place, AOL was both an 'editor' and a 'publisher' of the *Drudge Report*, as those terms are defined in section 1(2) of the Act.[160] Secondly, AOL knew that the *Drudge Report* habitually contained unverified gossip. In those circumstances, it seems likely that AOL had not exercised reasonable care in relation to the publication of the

---

[157] ibid, 51–2.
[158] ibid, 52.
[159] 'Clinton Aide Settled with Matt Drudge', *The New York Times*, 4 May 2001.
[160] See paras 16.03, 16.10–16.11.

Drudge Report, having regard to the nature of the publication and the previous conduct of its author.[161]

31.69 The Electronic Commerce Regulations probably do not protect intermediaries from liability in cases such as *Blumenthal v Drudge*. In compiling the *Drudge Report*, Matt Drudge was probably acting under the authority or the control of AOL. Regulation 19 does not protect hosts of Internet content in those circumstances.[162]

31.70 The common law defence of innocent dissemination would probably not have operated to protect AOL from liability in the United Kingdom. AOL was almost certainly an 'original publisher', rather than a 'subordinate distributor' of the *Drudge Report*. The *Drudge Report* was prepared pursuant to a contract between AOL and Matt Drudge. Under that contract, AOL reserved to itself certain editorial rights. In those circumstances, AOL was a world away from the kinds of secondary distributor ordinarily entitled to the benefit of the defence of innocent dissemination, such as newspaper vendors, booksellers, and public libraries.[163] Even if AOL was a secondary distributor of the *Drudge Report*, the defence of innocent dissemination would probably fail because AOL knew or should have known that the *Drudge Report* was the very kind of publication which was likely to contain a libel.[164]

How Blumenthal v Drudge *might have been decided in Australia*

31.71 If AOL had hosted the *Drudge Report* in Australia, the clause 91 defence would probably have operated to exclude the operation of the rules of civil defamation law in respect of publications occurring in Australia. AOL would, in those circumstances, satisfy the definition of an 'Internet content host' in clause 3 of Schedule 5 to the Broadcasting Services Act 1992 (Cth), namely a person who hosts Internet content, or who proposes to host Internet content, in Australia.[165] The Broadcasting Services Act does not distinguish between Internet content hosts who play no role at all in the preparation of the material they host, and Internet content hosts who, like AOL, commission that content. Under the Act, the only relevant question is whether the Internet content host is aware of the nature of the particular content complained of.[166] In addition, the clause 91

---

[161] Defamation Act 1996 (UK), ss 1(1)(b), 1(5)(b) and (c); see paras 16.14–16.15.

[162] Electronic Commerce Regulations, reg 19(b); see para 17.21.

[163] See paras 18.12, 18.16, 18.30–18.37, 18.45; cf *Auvil*, 800 F Supp 928 (ED Wa, 1992), discussed in paras 18.20–18.28.

[164] See paras 18.13, 18.17, 18.40, 18.46–18.47; cf *Auvil*, 800 F Supp 928 (ED Wa, 1992), discussed in paras 18.20–18.28.

[165] See paras 19.04, 19.28.

[166] Broadcasting Services Act 1992 (Cth), Sch 5, cl 91(1)(a); see paras 19.02, 19.24.

defence appears to exclude the operation of common law vicarious liability rules.[167]

The common law defence of innocent dissemination would not have been available to AOL in respect of publications of the *Drudge Report* occurring in Australia, for the same reasons as discussed in relation to the United Kingdom.[168] **31.72**

The statutory defences of innocent dissemination which apply in respect of publications occurring in Queensland and Tasmania would probably not have been available to AOL. AOL was not a mere 'seller' of the *Drudge Report*. Rather, it was an Internet service provider which provided subscribers with access to the Internet. Its role in the publication of the *Drudge Report* was much more than that of the usual seller of written material. AOL was, in effect, the editor and commercial publisher of that material.[169] **31.73**

Other progeny of Zeran

The broad interpretation of section 230(c) of the CDA in *Zeran* and *Blumenthal v Drudge* has been applied in a number of other decisions involving ISPs and content hosts,[170] and has been extended to other providers and users of interactive computer services in a range of circumstances. **31.74**

In *Schneider v Amazon.com, Inc*,[171] for example, the State Court of Appeals of Washington held that section 230(c) immunized an online bookseller from liability in relation to negative book reviews submitted by Internet users and posted on the bookseller's web site.

In *Patentwizard, Inc v Kinko's, Inc*,[172] the United States District Court in South Dakota held that the defendant, who provided access to the Internet by renting computers to individual users, could not be liable by reason of section 230(c) in respect of material posted by those users. A similar conclusion was reached by a State appellate court in California in relation to a city which provided

---

[167] See para 19.26.
[168] See para 31.70.
[169] See paras 19.39–19.43.
[170] See eg *Ben Ezra, Weinstein, and Company, Inc v America Online, Inc*, 206 F 3d 980 (10th cir, 2000) (certiorari denied by United States Supreme Court, 2 October 2000); *Doe v Oliver*, 755 A 2d 1000 (SC Ct, 2000); *Dow v Franco Productions*, Case 99C7885 (ND Il, 2000); *Doe v America Online, Inc*, 783 So 2d 1010 (SC Fl, 2001); *Green v America Online*, 318 F 3d 465 (3d cir, 2003); *Noah v AOL Time Warner, Inc*, 261 F Supp 2d 532 (ED Va, 2003); *Novak v Overture Services, Inc*, 309 F Supp 2d 446 (ED NY, 2004); cf *Sabbato v Hardy*, Case 2000CA00136 (CA Oh, 18 December 2000).
[171] 31 P 3d 37 (CA Wa, 2001).
[172] 163 F Supp 2d 1069 (D SD, 2001).

unrestricted Internet access to members of the public through computers at a public library.[173]

31.75 In *Gentry v eBay, Inc*, a State appellate court in California held that section 230(c) protected the operator of a web site that describes goods for sale by third-party sellers from liability arising out of false descriptions supplied by those sellers.[174]

In *Batzel v Smith*, the Ninth Circuit Court of Appeals held that the moderator of a newsgroup would be protected by section 230(c) in relation to information which was submitted to him, but which he edited before posting to members of the newsgroup and on a web site, provided that the information had been submitted to him for that purpose.[175]

In *Carafano v Metrosplash.com, Inc*,[176] the Ninth Circuit Court of Appeals held that an online matchmaking service was entitled to the protection of section 230(c) in relation to a profile which purported to be from the plaintiff, an actor from the series Star Trek. The profile included the plaintiff's home and e-mail address, and a number of photographs, and had been automatically generated as a result of an unknown person responding to an online questionnaire on the defendant's web site without the knowledge or consent of the plaintiff. The court held that the defendant was not an 'information content provider' because the selection of the content of each profile was left exclusively to users, and 'no profile has any content until a user actively creates it'.[177] Even if the defendant had been an 'information content provider', it would not have been liable in respect of the offending profile because it did not create or develop the particular information in issue.[178]

Limitations of *Zeran*

31.76 Despite those decisions, however, State appellate courts in California have declined to follow *Zeran* in two recent decisions, on the basis that section 230(c) excludes the liability of 'publishers', but not 'distributors'.

31.77 In *Barrett v Rosenthal*,[179] the issue was whether section 230(c) protected a defendant who 'reposted' material originally posted to a newsgroup by another

---

[173] *Kathleen R v City of Livermore*, 104 Cal Rptr 2d 772 (CA Ca, 2001).
[174] 121 Cal Rptr 2d 703 (CA Ca, 2002); cf *Grace v eBay, Inc*, 16 Cal Rptr 3d 192 (CA Ca, 2004); see para 31.78.
[175] 333 F 3d 1018 (9th cir, 2003); cf 351 F 3d 904 (9th cir, 2003).
[176] 339 F 3d 1119 (9th cir, 2003).
[177] ibid, 1124.
[178] ibid, 1125.
[179] 9 Cal Rptr 3d 142 (CA Ca, 2004).

person. The court held that section 230(c) did not apply in those circumstances. The defendant was a 'distributor', not a 'publisher' of the postings. The court said that section 230(c)(1) operated to prevent providers and users of interactive computer services from being treated as 'publishers' of information provided by others, but did not prevent providers and users from being treated as 'distributors', who at common law are liable if they know or have reason to know of the defamatory nature of the material they disseminate. The court said that section 230(c)(1) 'should not be interpreted as having abrogated the common law principle of distributor or knowledge-based liability'.[180]

A differently constituted court reached the same conclusion in *Grace v eBay, Inc*.[181] The plaintiff had purchased a number of items on eBay. One of the persons from whom the plaintiff had bought items posted feedback as to the plaintiff on eBay, accusing him of being dishonest. eBay refused to remove the offending feedback. The court held that section 230(c) was not 'intended to preclude liability where the provider or user knew or had reason to know that the matter was defamatory, that is, common law distributor liability'. The court went on:

    31.78

> [W]e disagree with the *Zeran* court's conclusion that because the term 'publication' can encompass any repetition of a defamatory statement, use of the term 'publisher' in section 230(c)(1) indicates a clear legislative intention to abrogate common law distributor liability.

Arguments to the same effect as those which found favour in *Barrett v Rosenthal* and *Grace v eBay, Inc* were, however, rejected by the Appellate Court of Illinois, Second District, in the earlier decision of *Barrett v Fonorow*. In that case the court observed that to that time section 230 had 'enjoyed perfectly uniform application in published decisions'.[182]

    31.79

Summary

Until the recent Californian decisions in *Barrett v Rosenthal* and *Grace v eBay, Inc*, the position with respect to the liability of intermediaries involved in the provision of interactive computer services under American defamation law had seemingly been resolved by section 230(c)(1) of the CDA, as interpreted in *Zeran* and its progeny.[183] The position was that Internet intermediaries were not

    31.80

---

[180] ibid, 166.
[181] 16 Cal Rptr 3d 192 (CA Ca, 2004).
[182] 799 NE 2d 916 (AC Il, 2003).
[183] Many commentators had, however, expressed doubt about the correctness of *Zeran*: for two influential critiques, see David Sheridan, '*Zeran v AOL* and the Effect of Section 230 of the Communications Decency Act upon Liability for Defamation on the Internet' (1997) 61 Albany Law Review 147, 151, 162, 168–71; Steven Cordero, 'Damnum Absque Injuria: *Zeran v AOL* and Cyberspace Defamation Law' (1999) 9 Fordham Intellectual Property, Media and Entertainment Law Journal 775.

liable under the law of the United States for the defamatory content of others made available via their computer services, regardless of whether the intermediaries were mere conduits, distributors, or publishers in relation to that content.

31.81 In the State courts of California, at least, Internet intermediaries who distribute defamatory material created by others are now potentially liable, despite section 230(c), if they know or have reason to know of the defamation.[184] As the decision in *Cubby* demonstrates, however, the threshold for distributor liability in the United States is relatively high.[185]

31.82 The interpretation of section 230(c) favoured in cases such as *Zeran* led to the exceptionally broad immunity conferred in *Blumenthal v Drudge*,[186] a decision which is difficult to defend from an Anglo-Australian perspective. In that case the intermediary, AOL, commissioned the offending material. It knew that the *Drudge Report* habitually contained unverified gossip. Its role in the publication of the offending material went well beyond that of an Internet intermediary who merely hosts, caches, or carries content which it did not create.

31.83 AOL would not, on the facts in *Blumenthal v Drudge*, have been able to avail itself of the defence in section 1 of the Defamation Act 1996 (UK),[187] regulation 19 of the Electronic Commerce Regulations,[188] the common law defence of innocent dissemination,[189] or the statutory defences of innocent dissemination which operate in Queensland and Tasmania.[190] Of the available defences in the United Kingdom and Australia, only the Australian clause 91 defence would have been likely to protect AOL from liability, and even then only because of apparently unintended anomalies in the operation of that defence.[191]

E. Jurisdiction in Internet Defamation Actions in the United States

General principles

31.84 Many cases have arisen in the United States in which courts have had to consider whether to assert jurisdiction over non-residents in relation to allegedly

---

[184] See para 31.14.
[185] See paras 31.12–31.22.
[186] See paras 31.65–31.73.
[187] See para 31.68.
[188] See para 31.69.
[189] See paras 31.70, 31.72.
[190] See para 31.73.
[191] See para 31.71. The apparently unintended anomalies are the exclusion of ordinary vicarious liability rules (see para 19.26), and the absence of an exception for cases where Internet content hosts have commissioned the preparation of the defamatory content (see para 19.27).

defamatory publications available in the forum. The approach adopted in the American cases is very different from that adopted by courts in the United Kingdom and Australia.[192]

American courts will exercise jurisdiction over conduct occurring outside the forum only where jurisdiction is proper under the applicable 'long-arm' statute[193] and consistent with the Fourteenth Amendment to the United States Constitution, which guarantees due process.[194] The long-arm statutes of most American States, in substance, permit jurisdiction to the extent permitted by the Fourteenth Amendment, so that 'the statutory inquiry ... merges with the constitutional inquiry, and the two inquiries essentially become one'.[195]

31.85

The Fourteenth Amendment has been interpreted as permitting a court to exercise jurisdiction over conduct occurring outside the forum where:

31.86

• the defendant has purposefully availed himself or herself of the benefits and protections of the forum State by establishing 'minimum contacts' with that State; and
• the exercise of jurisdiction over the defendant does not offend 'traditional notions of fair play and substantial justice'.[196]

Where the 'contacts' between a defendant and a State are extensive, wide-ranging, substantial, continuous, and systematic, 'general' jurisdiction may exist in respect of all causes of action against the defendant arising out of conduct

31.87

---

[192] See chapters 25–26.

[193] Long-arm statutes prescribe the circumstances in which courts may assert jurisdiction against non-residents. Each State has its own long-arm statute. In some States, the long-arm statute permits State courts to exercise jurisdiction 'on any basis not inconsistent with the Constitution of [the] state or of the United States': see eg Code of Civil Procedure (California), §410.10. In other States, jurisdiction is dependent on proof of one or more prescribed matters, including (typically, and among other things) that the non-resident has transacted business within the State or committed a tortious act within the State: see eg Code of Civil Procedure (Illinois), 735 ILCS 5/2–209; Florida Statutes, §48.193. Narrower bases for jurisdiction are prescribed in some other States; see eg Civil Practice Law and Rules (New York), §302: relevantly, the non-defendant must have transacted business within the State or contracted anywhere to supply goods or services in the State; cf District of Columbia Code, §13–423.

[194] United States Constitution (1787), Amendment XIV (1868), section 1: 'All persons born or naturalized in the United States, and subject to the jurisdiction thereof, are citizens of the United States and of the state wherein they reside. No state shall make or enforce any law which shall abridge the privileges or immunities of citizens of the United States; nor shall any state deprive any person of life, liberty, or property, without due process of law; nor deny to any person within its jurisdiction the equal protection of the laws.'

[195] *Stover v O'Connell Associates, Inc*, 84 F 3d 132 (4th cir, 1996), 135–6.

[196] The most important United States Supreme Court decisions establishing and explaining these principles include *Milliken v Meyer*, 311 US 457 (1941), 463; *International Shoe Company v Washington*, 326 US 310 (1945), 316; *World Wide Volkswagen Corporation v Woodson*, 444 US 286 (1980), 295; *Keeton v Hustler Magazine, Inc*, 465 US 770 (1984), 774; *Burger King Corporation v Rudzewicz*, 471 US 462 (1985), 475.

occurring outside the forum, even if there is no connection between those contacts and the particular claim asserted against the defendant.[197]

In cases where general jurisdiction does not exist, 'specific' jurisdiction may be exercised in respect of conduct occurring outside the forum if the particular claim asserted against the defendant arises out of his or her contacts with the forum State.[198]

31.88 The American cases concerning the circumstances in which courts will assert jurisdiction in respect of Internet publications by defendants who are not residents of the forum are legion and cannot all be reconciled. Broadly speaking, however, American courts assess jurisdiction in such cases by applying an 'effects test', a 'sliding scale test', or both.

The effects test

31.89 The leading Supreme Court decision concerning jurisdiction in a defamation action in respect of conduct occurring outside the forum is *Calder v Jones*.[199] Jones was a professional entertainer who lived and worked in California. She claimed that she was defamed by an article published in 1979 in *The National Enquirer*, a Florida publication with a higher circulation in California than in any other American State. The article was written and edited in Florida. The journalist made a number of phone calls to sources in California in the course of preparing the article.

Rehnquist J delivered the opinion of the United States Supreme Court. Rehnquist J said that as 'the brunt of the harm, in terms both of [Jones'] emotional distress and the injury to her professional reputation, was suffered in California', jurisdiction was 'therefore proper in California based on the "effects" of [the] Florida conduct in California'. Rehnquist J noted that the conduct of the defendants had been intentional and expressly aimed at California, and that the defendants knew that the article would have a potentially devastating impact on Jones in that State, where she lived and worked and where *The National Enquirer* had its largest circulation. Rehnquist J said that the defendants 'must "reasonably anticipate being haled into court there" to answer for the truth of the statements made in their article'. The test applied by the Supreme Court in *Calder v Jones* has come to be known as the 'effects test'.

31.90 The 'effects test' has been considered in a number of defamation actions arising

---

[197] See eg *International Shoe Company v Washington*, 326 US 310 (1945), 316; *Mansour v Superior Court*, 38 Cal App 4th 1750 (1995), 1758; *Mink v AAAA Development LLC*, 190 F 3d 333 (5th cir, 1999), 336.
[198] ibid.
[199] 465 US 783 (1984).

out of Internet publications. In almost all such cases, the mere fact that the plaintiff resided in the forum and that the brunt of the harm from the defamatory publication would be felt there was insufficient to justify the forum court asserting jurisdiction.[200]

A more expansive application of the effects test, however, occurred in *Planet Beach Franchising Corporation v C3ubit, Inc*, a decision of the United States District Court for the Eastern District of Louisiana.[201] Pennsylvania-based defendants had posted an article on a web site which was critical of the financial viability and practices of the Louisiana-based plaintiff and its president. The court held that it had jurisdiction to hear and determine the action. The defendants had 'published a controversial, allegedly defamatory article about a corporation that [the] defendants knew to be based in Louisiana'. The defendants had obtained information from persons in Louisiana before publication. The court said that the article was directed towards a specialized audience that was very likely to include franchisees of the plaintiff corporation. In the circumstances, Louisiana was a convenient forum for the hearing and determination of the dispute.[202]

The sliding scale test

The approach adopted in *Planet Beach Franchising Corporation v C3ubit, Inc* is **31.91** difficult to reconcile, however, with the prevailing trend in American cases concerning jurisdiction in respect of online conduct occurring outside the forum.[203] That trend involves courts distinguishing between different forms of Internet conduct based on a 'sliding scale' of interactivity.[204]

---

[200] See eg *Naxos Resources (USA) Ltd v Southam, Inc*, 1996 WL 662451 (CD Ca); *Copperfield v Cogedipresse*, 26 Media L Rep 1185 (CD Ca, 1997); *Jewish Defense Organization, Inc v Superior Court of Los Angeles County*, 72 Cal App 4th 1045 (CA Ca, 1999); *Barrett v The Catacombs Press*, 44 F Supp 2d 717 (ED Pa, 1999); *Bailey v Turbine Design, Inc*, 86 F Supp 2d 790 (WD Tn, 2000); *Griffis v Luban*, 646 NW 2d 527 (SC Mn, 2002); *English Sports Betting, Inc v Tostigan*, 2002 WL 461592 (ED Pa); *Hy Cite Corporation v Badbusinessbureau.com, LLC*, 297 F Supp 2d 1154 (WD Wi, 2004). Cases in which the effects test resulted in jurisdiction being asserted include *Blakey v Continental Airlines, Inc*, 751 A 2d 538 (AD NJ, 2000) (defendants published messages with knowledge that they would be published in the forum and could influence the plaintiff's efforts to seek a remedy under a forum law); *Atkinson v McLaughlin*, 343 F Supp 2d 868 (D ND, 2004) (defendants' web site deliberately and knowingly targeted the forum and the plaintiffs and was meant to foster debate in the forum).
[201] 2002 WL 1870007 (ED La).
[202] It should be noted that the court relied, in part, on the first instance decision in *Young v New Haven Advocate*, 184 F Supp 2d 498 (WD Va, 2001), which was subsequently overturned on appeal: *Young v New Haven Advocate*, 315 F 3d 256 (4th cir, 2002), discussed below.
[203] A Maine court rejected the reasoning in *Planet Beach Franchising Corporation v C3ubit, Inc* as 'unpersuasive' in *The Gentle Wind Project v Garvey*, 2005 WL 40064 (D Me).
[204] See eg *Hy Cite Corporation v Badbusinessbureau.com, LLC*, 297 F Supp 2d 1154 (WD Wi, 2004): 'Courts across the country have adopted the sliding scale approach, at least nominally, in personal jurisdiction cases involving internet contacts' (Chief Judge Crabb, who went on to decline to adopt the sliding scale test as a substitute for the effects test).

31.92 The 'sliding scale' approach was articulated in an Internet domain name case, *Zippo Manufacturing Company v Zippo Dot Com, Inc.*[205] The plaintiff in that case was a Pennsylvanian corporation. The defendant was a Californian corporation. The plaintiff sued the defendant in Pennsylvania, alleging that the defendant had infringed its trade mark through the registration and use of certain domain names. The evidence was that the defendant offered access to newsgroups to some 140,000 paying subscribers, including 3,000 subscribers in Pennsylvania. The defendant had entered into seven contracts with Internet access providers to furnish its services to customers in Pennsylvania. The question for the court was whether those contacts with Pennsylvania were sufficient to found jurisdiction.

31.93 The court established a 'sliding scale' test for assessing whether jurisdiction existed in cases involving online conduct occurring outside the forum:

> The cases are scant. Nevertheless, our review of the available cases and materials reveals that the likelihood that personal jurisdiction can be constitutionally exercised is directly proportionate to the nature and quality of commercial activity that an entity conducts over the Internet. This sliding scale is consistent with well developed personal jurisdiction principles. At one end of the spectrum are situations where a defendant clearly does business over the Internet. If the defendant enters into contracts with residents of a foreign jurisdiction that involve the knowing and repeated transmission of computer files over the Internet, personal jurisdiction is proper. At the opposite end are situations where a defendant has simply posted information on an Internet Web site which is accessible to users in foreign jurisdictions. A passive Web site that does little more than make information available to those who are interested in it is not grounds for the exercise of personal jurisdiction. The middle ground is occupied by interactive Web sites where a user can exchange information with the host computer. In these cases, the exercise of jurisdiction is determined by examining the level of interactivity and nature of the exchange of information that occurs on the Web site.[206]

31.94 The court held that the defendant's activities in and in respect of Pennsylvania were sufficient to found jurisdiction:

> Dot Com [the defendant] repeatedly and consciously chose to process Pennsylvania residents' applications and to assign them passwords. Dot Com knew that the result of these contracts would be the transmission of electronic messages into Pennsylvania. The transmission of these files was entirely within its control. Dot Com cannot maintain that these contracts are 'fortuitous' or 'coincidental' . . .

---

[205] 952 F Supp 1119 (WD Pa, 1997). The Third Circuit Court of Appeals recently called the decision 'a seminal authority regarding personal jurisdiction based upon the operation of an Internet web site': *Toys 'R' Us, Inc v Step Two, SA*, 318 F 3d 446 (3d cir, 2003). See also *Cybersell, Inc v Cybersell, Inc*, 130 F 3d 414 (9th cir, 1997); *Mink v AAAA Development LLC*, 190 F 3d 333 (5th cir, 1999).

[206] 952 F Supp 1119 (WD Pa, 1997), 1124 (footnotes and references omitted).

When a defendant makes a conscious choice to conduct business with the residents of a forum state, 'it has clear notice that it is subject to suit there.' Dot Com was under no obligation to sell its services to Pennsylvania residents. It freely chose to do so, presumably in order to profit from those transactions. If a corporation determines that the risk of being subject to personal jurisdiction in a particular forum is too great, it can choose to sever its connection to that state. If Dot Com had not wanted to be amenable to jurisdiction in Pennsylvania, the solution would have been simple—it could have chosen not to sell its services to Pennsylvania residents.[207]

The sliding scale test has come to be a convenient rule of thumb for predicting the circumstances in which American courts will exercise jurisdiction over online conduct occurring outside the forum. It has been applied in a number of defamation actions, not all of which are reconcilable. Some notable examples include *Copperfield v Cogedipresse*,[208] *Blumenthal v Drudge*,[209] *Barrett v The Catacombs Press*,[210] *Jewish Defense Organization, Inc v Superior Court of Los Angeles County*,[211] *Bochan v La Fontaine*,[212] *Bailey v Turbine Design, Inc*,[213] *Wagner v Miskin*,[214] and *Best Van Lines, Inc v Walker*.[215]   **31.95**

---

[207] ibid, 1126–7.

[208] 26 Media L Rep 1185 (CD Ca, 1997): Californian court declined to assert specific jurisdiction over a French defendant in respect of an essentially passive web site.

[209] 992 F Supp 44 (D DC, 1998): District of Columbia court held that it was able to assert personal jurisdiction over a Californian defendant. The defendant's web site was interactive because it allowed users to e-mail the defendant and request subscriptions online. Additional factors justifying jurisdiction included the subject matter of the site (political gossip and rumour), the fact that the defendant had solicited contributions of $250 from District of Columbia residents, and the fact that the defendant had had a number of non-Internet related contacts with the jurisdiction, including visits and participation in media interviews.

[210] 44 F Supp 2d 717 (ED Pa, 1999): Pennsylvanian court held it would not assert specific jurisdiction over a non-resident in relation to a passive web site and bulletin board postings allegedly defamatory of the plaintiff. The court held that bulletin board postings are to be equated with passive web sites for the purposes of the sliding scale test.

[211] 72 Cal App 4th 1045 (CA Ca, 1999): Californian court declined to assert specific jurisdiction over a New York organization and its founder in relation to material on a passive web site.

[212] 68 F Supp 2d 692 (ED Va, 1999): Virginian court held it had specific jurisdiction in relation to bulletin board postings by residents of Texas and New Mexico. The Texan defendants had posted the offending messages using a Virginia based ISP. The fact that the postings were stored in Virginia and transmitted from Virginia around the world was sufficient to justify jurisdiction. Jurisdiction over the New Mexico defendant was justified because he operated a business which solicited business via an interactive web site which was 'accessible to Virginia Internet users 24 hours a day'.

[213] 86 F Supp 2d 790 (WD Tn, 2000): Tennessee court declined to assert specific jurisdiction over material posted on a Florida corporation's passive web site.

[214] 660 NW 2d 593 (SC ND, 2003): North Dakota court asserted jurisdiction over a non-resident in relation to material on a web site concerning issues and staff at the University of North Dakota.

[215] 2004 WL 964009 (SD NY): New York court declined to exercise specific jurisdiction over a resident of Iowa in relation to an essentially passive web site containing material allegedly defamatory of a New York company.

Recent trends

31.96   The recent trend in the American authorities concerning jurisdiction in defamation actions can be illustrated by reference to two decisions of federal appellate courts.

Revell v Lidov[216] is a decision of the Fifth Circuit Court of Appeals. It concerned an article posted on an Internet bulletin board hosted by Columbia University in New York by an academic at Harvard University in Boston, Massachusetts. The article alleged, among other things, that the plaintiff, a Texan resident who was formerly the Associate Deputy Director of the FBI, had been complicit in a conspiracy whereby the United States Government had failed to stop the terrorist attack on Pan Am Flight 103 over Lockerbie, Scotland in 1988, despite having clear advance warnings. The plaintiff sued in Texas.

The court held that the Columbia University bulletin board was interactive, and thus within the middle category described in *Zippo Manufacturing Company v Zippo Dot Com, Inc.* It was interactive because it involved an 'open forum' in which any visitor to the site could participate.

In assessing whether personal jurisdiction existed, the court then went on to consider the application of the effects test in *Calder v Jones*, ultimately concluding that the test did not support a finding of personal jurisdiction. Among other things, the article did not contain any references to Texas or to the Texan activities of the plaintiff and was not specifically directed at Texan readers.

31.97   The approach of the court in *Revell v Lidov* was thus to treat the effects test as being relevant because the site in question was interactive, and therefore within the 'middle ground' of the sliding scale. Viewed in this way, the court said it saw no 'tension' between the sliding scale test and the effects test. The court expressly declined to decide whether a 'passive' web site 'could still give rise to personal jurisdiction under *Calder*'.[217]

---

[216] 317 F 3d 467 (5th cir, 2002).

[217] A similar approach was taken in *Zidon v Pickerell*, 344 F Supp 2d 624 (D ND, 2004). A North Dakota court held that it had specific jurisdiction against Pickerell, a resident of Colorado, who had set up a web site and sent e-mails which were allegedly defamatory of her former boyfriend, Zidon, a resident of North Dakota. Chief Judge Hovland assessed the web site as interactive for the purposes of the sliding scale test because, among other things, it had a bulletin board permitting users to exchange information. Chief Judge Hovland concluded that the interactive nature of the web site, coupled with the fact that 'Pickerell deliberately and knowingly directed the Web Site, e-mail, and Internet comments at the State of North Dakota because North Dakota is Zidon's residence', justified the court exercising jurisdiction; cf *Atkinson v McLaughlin*, 343 F Supp 2d 868 (D ND, 2004), a decision of the same judge: web site with a hyperlink to an e-mail address held to be passive, not interactive; jurisdiction nonetheless justified applying the effects test.

Another instructive recent American case concerning jurisdiction in respect of   **31.98**
online defamation is *Young v New Haven Advocate*.[218] Two Connecticut newspapers published online articles discussing that State's policy of housing its
prisoners in correctional facilities in Virginia. Defamation proceedings were
brought in Virginia by a warden of a Virginian prison, who alleged that the
articles had imputed that he was a racist and an advocate of racism, and that he
had encouraged the abuse of inmates by guards. The articles were written
entirely in Connecticut. Some telephone calls were made by reporters to
Virginia for the purpose of gathering information for the articles. Neither newspaper solicited subscribers from Virginia or had any offices, employees, assets, or
business relationships there. One of the newspapers had eight subscribers in
Virginia, while the other had none at all.

The Fourth Circuit Court of Appeals held that the Virginian court did not have
jurisdiction to hear and determine the action. The court said:

> [T]he fact that the newspapers' web sites could be accessed anywhere, including
> Virginia, does not by itself demonstrate that the newspapers were intentionally
> directing their web site content to a Virginia audience. Something more than
> posting and accessibility is needed . . . The newspapers must, through the Internet
> postings, manifest an intent to target and focus on Virginia readers.

The court concluded that the articles had been aimed at a Connecticut
audience, in circumstances where the newspapers could not have reasonably
anticipated being haled into court[219] in Virginia to answer for the truth of the
statements made in their articles.[220]

Summary

There are a number of key differences between the way in which American   **31.99**
courts, and courts in the United Kingdom and Australia, approach questions of
jurisdiction in respect of Internet conduct occurring outside the forum.

First, in the United Kingdom, courts seized of jurisdiction by reason of the
Brussels Regulation[221] or the Conventions[222] have no discretion to decline to
exercise jurisdiction on *forum non conveniens* grounds.[223] No such constraints
apply in the United States.

---

[218] 315 F 3d 256 (4th cir, 2002).
[219] See *Burger King Corporation v Rudzewicz*, 471 US 462 (1985), 474.
[220] See also *Falwell v Cohn*, 2003 WL 751130 (WD Va).
[221] Regulation 44/2001 of 22 December 2000 on jurisdiction and the enforcement of judgments in civil and commercial matters [2001] OJ L12/1.
[222] Brussels and Lugano Conventions on jurisdiction and the enforcement of judgments in
civil and commercial matters.
[223] See paras 26.02–26.05.

31.100   Secondly, jurisdictional inquiries in the United Kingdom and Australia focus on the weight of connections between the parties and occurrences, and the forum.[224] The intentions and expectations of the defendant are irrelevant.[225] Jurisdiction may be exercised even where the defendant has no connection to the forum, apart from having published material which is incidentally accessible there.[226] Jurisdictional inquiries in the United States, by contrast, are informed by the guarantee of due process in the Fourteenth Amendment, and so concentrate on the weight of connections between the defendant and the forum. The intention and expectations of the defendant, the extent of the defendant's business or other contacts with the forum, and the geographic focus of the offending material, are the critical factors. The weight of connections between the claimant and the forum are largely irrelevant.

31.101   Thirdly, courts in the United Kingdom and Australia have consistently held that foreign publishers must anticipate the risk of being haled into courts in the United Kingdom and Australia to answer for defamatory material they publish affecting the reputations of claimants in those countries. As Kirby J of the Australian High Court put it in *Dow Jones & Co Inc v Gutnick*,[227] an Internet defamation case arising out a publication written, edited, uploaded, and overwhelmingly read in the United States, but which was of and concerning a resident of the State of Victoria:

> Where a person or corporation publishes material which is potentially defamatory of another, to ask the publisher to be cognisant of the defamation laws of the place where the person resides and has a reputation is not to impose on the publisher an excessive burden. At least it is not to do so where the potential damage to reputation is substantial and the risks of being sued are commensurately real. Publishers in the United States are well aware that few, if any, other jurisdictions in the world observe the approach to the vindication of reputation adopted by the law in that country.[228]

Callinan J, in the same case, was more blunt:

> If a publisher publishes in a multiplicity of jurisdictions it should understand, and must accept, that it runs the risk of liability in those jurisdictions in which the publication is not lawful and it inflicts damage.[229]

---

[224] See the grounds of jurisdiction discussed in chapter 25, and the factors relevant to *forum non conveniens* enquiries discussed in chapter 26.

[225] eg *King v Lewis* [2005] EMLR 4, paras 33–4. See also the authorities discussed in paras 26.16–26.31.

[226] See eg *Schapira v Ahronson* [1999] EMLR 735 (see para 26.16); *Berezovsky v Michaels* [2000] 2 All ER 986 (see paras 26.17–26.22); *Dow Jones & Co Inc v Gutnick* (2002) 210 CLR 575 (see paras 26.25–26.26); *King v Lewis* [2005] EMLR 4 (see para 26.29); *Harrods Ltd v Dow Jones & Co Inc* [2003] EWHC 1162 (see para 26.30).

[227] (2002) 210 CLR 575; see paras 26.25–26.26.

[228] ibid, para 151.

[229] ibid, para 192.

Similar statements have been made in English cases.[230]

American courts take an entirely different approach. In *Revell v Lidov*, for example, the court said:

> Lidov must have known that the harm of the article would hit home wherever Revell resided. But that is the case with virtually any defamation. A more direct aim is required than we have here.[231]

Putting the American approach towards jurisdiction in context

Generally speaking, the authorities bear out the proposition that courts in the United Kingdom and Australia have a more expansive approach towards the circumstances in which jurisdiction may be exercised over defamatory publications originating outside the forum than American courts. The marked differences in approach between the jurisdictions, however, make it dangerous to generalize, particularly in cases involving commercial contacts between a foreign defendant and the residents of a forum state. **31.102**

For example, the decision of the Australian High Court in *Dow Jones & Co Inc v Gutnick*,[232] enabling a resident of the State of Victoria to maintain a defamation action against an American publisher in the Supreme Court of Victoria, attracted widespread criticism in the United States. An editorial in the late edition of *The New York Times* on 11 December 2002, for instance, expressed the view that the High Court decision 'could strike a devastating blow to free speech online'. **31.103**

It is, however, by no means clear that an American court would have reached a different conclusion from the Australian High Court on the facts in *Dow Jones & Co Inc v Gutnick*. **31.104**

While the *Barron's Online* web site under examination in that case was essentially a 'passive' web site with little or no interactivity within the meaning of the sliding scale test described in *Zippo Manufacturing Company v Zippo Dot Com, Inc*, it was a subscription site; that is, a site on which most content was available only to persons who had applied to Dow Jones for a username and password, generally by providing a name, address, and credit card number. Dow Jones

---

[230] *Berezovsky v Michaels* [2002] 2 All ER 986, 994 (Lord Steyn): see para 26.18; *Harrods Ltd v Dow Jones & Co, Inc* [2003] EWHC 1162, para 43: 'I also take the view that these English publications relating to an English corporation, however limited and technical, are most conveniently dealt with in an English court' (see also para 26.30); *King v Lewis* [2005] EMLR 4, para 31: 'a global publisher should not be too fastidious as to the part of the globe where he is made a libel defendant' (see also para 26.29).
[231] 317 F 3d 467 (5th cir, 2002).
[232] (2002) 210 CLR 575; see paras 26.25–26.26.

chose to process subscription applications from some 300 Victorian residents and to assign them passwords. By accepting their applications, Dow Jones formed a contractual relationship with each of those subscribers. Dow Jones knew that the result of accepting their applications would be the transmission of the content of *Barron's Online* into the State of Victoria. Dow Jones was under no obligation to accept subscriptions from residents of Victoria. The transmission of *Barron's Online* into Victoria was within Dow Jones' control.

31.105 The nature and quality of commercial activity conducted by Dow Jones in Victoria via the *Barron's Online* site was thus analogous in many respects to that conducted by the defendant in Pennsylvania in the *Zippo* case.[233]

31.106 An interesting decision analogous in some respects to *Dow Jones & Co Inc v Gutnick* in which a Californian court held that it had jurisdiction in respect of a foreign defendant is *Metro-Goldwyn-Mayer Studios v Grokster, Ltd.*[234] A corporation incorporated in Vanuatu but with its business principally based in Australia, Sharman Network Ltd (Sharman), had distributed file sharing software which enabled Internet users to search through and download files from the computers of other Internet users, including music and video files. The software had been downloaded some 143 million times worldwide, including around two million times in California. The defendant did not charge for the software, although it derived income from advertising bundled with it. The plaintiffs alleged that Sharman was liable for contributory and vicarious copyright infringement. The court held that it had jurisdiction:

> Sharman has not denied and cannot deny that a substantial number of its users are California residents, and thus that it is, at a minimum, constructively aware of continuous and substantial commercial interaction with residents of this forum. Further, Sharman is well aware that California is the heart of the entertainment industry, and that the brunt of the injuries described in these cases is likely to be felt here. It is hard to imagine on these bases alone that Sharman would not reasonably anticipate being haled into court in California.

31.107 While a court in the United States might have reached the same conclusion as the Australian High Court, had the facts in *Dow Jones & Co Inc v Gutnick* arisen and fallen for determination there, different conclusions will ordinarily be reached in cases involving publications originating outside the forum appearing

---

[233] See paras 31.92–31.94. For other examples of the application of the sliding scale test based on commercial contacts with the forum, see eg *CompuServe, Inc v Patterson*, 89 F 3d 1257 (6th cir, 1996); *Edias Software International, LLC v Basis International Ltd*, 947 F Supp 413 (D Az, 1996); *Telco Communications v An Apple a Day*, 977 F Supp 404 (ED Va, 1997); *Gator.com Corporation v LL Bean, Inc*, 341 F 3d 1072 (9th cir, 2003).

[234] 243 F Supp 2d 1073 (CD Ca, 2003). Similar cases to the same effect include *Motown Record Co, LP v iMesh.com, Inc*, 2004 WL 503720 (SD NY); *Autodesk, Inc v R K Mace Engineering, Inc*, 2004 WL 603382 (ND Ca).

on 'passive' web sites. American courts tend not to assume jurisdiction in such cases, because the publication cannot be said to have been deliberately and knowingly targeted at the forum. Courts in the United Kingdom and Australia, on the other hand, treat the intention of the publisher as utterly irrelevant, and will generally exercise jurisdiction where claimants have reputations to protect in the forum and are prepared to limit their claims to publications occurring there, without paying regard to the place where the publication originated.[235]

F. Choice of Law in Defamation Actions in the United States

The choice of law test applied in most American jurisdictions in respect of defamatory publications occurring in more than one place is also fundamentally different, at least in form, from the approach which prevails in the United Kingdom[236] and Australia.[237]

31.108

Most American jurisdictions have adopted a 'proper law of the tort' approach towards choice of law in multi-jurisdictional defamation actions. That approach can be described broadly as follows:[238]

31.109

- where material is published in only one jurisdiction, rights and liabilities in defamation law are to be determined by applying the local law of the State where the publication occurs 'unless, with respect to the particular issue, some other state has a more significant relationship . . . to the occurrence and the parties, in which event the local law of the other state will be applied';[239]
- in cases of 'multi-State' defamation, rights and liabilities in defamation law are to be 'determined by the local law of the state which, with respect to the particular issue, has the most significant relationship to the occurrence and the parties';[240]
- where a natural person has been defamed, 'the state of most significant relationship will usually be the state where the person was domiciled at the time, if the matter complained of was published in that state';[241]
- where a corporation or other legal person has been defamed, 'the state of most

---

[235] See para 26.33.
[236] See chapter 27.
[237] See chapter 28.
[238] The approach derives from a motor vehicle negligence case, *Babcock v Jackson*, 12 NY 2d 473 (CA NY, 1963). The application of the proper law of the tort approach to multi-jurisdictional defamation actions has been authoritatively stated in the American Law Institute, *Restatement of the Law, Second, Conflict of Laws 2d* (1971) §§149, 150.
[239] American Law Institute, *Restatement of the Law, Second, Conflict of Laws 2d* (1971) §149.
[240] ibid, §150(1).
[241] ibid, §150(2).

significant legal relationship will usually be the state where the corporation, or other legal person, had its principal place of business at the time, if the matter complained of was published in that state'.[242]

31.110   The application of the proper law of the tort approach may be unpredictable in defamation cases involving publications occurring in many jurisdictions, parties and witnesses domiciled in different places, and plaintiffs with national or international reputations.

The key advantage of the proper law of the tort approach, however, is that it leads in all cases to a court applying a single substantive legal standard, regardless of the number of jurisdictions in which defamatory material has been published. By contrast, the double actionability test which applies in the United Kingdom,[243] and the *lex loci delicti* test which applies in Australia, require courts to have regard to and apply, potentially, the defamation laws of every place where defamatory material has been read, heard, or seen.[244]

---

[242]   ibid, §150(3).
[243]   At least where a flexibility exception is not applied: see para 27.14.
[244]   See chapters 27 and 28.

GLOSSARY OF INTERNET TERMS*

3G	'Third Generation' standard enabling Internet content to be sent wirelessly to, and displayed on, mobile telephones or computers at a faster rate than WAP or GPRS.
AARNET	The original Australian backbone WAN for connections to the Internet.
ActiveX	A tool developed by Microsoft Corporation which enables the creation of highly dynamic web pages, typically incorporating animation and sound. *See also* **Java**
ADSL	Asymmetric digital subscriber line: a form of broadband Internet connection and a variant of DSL. ADSL is asymmetrical because the rate at which data are received downstream exceeds the rate at which data are sent upstream.
Advanced Research Projects Agency	*See* **ARPA**
ANS	Advanced Networks and Services: a company formed by International Business Machines Corporation (IBM), MCI, Inc, and Merit Network, Inc in 1990.
AOL	America Online, Inc. Reputedly the world's largest ISP.
AOL Instant Messenger	An instant messaging system.
Applet	A program contained on a Java web page which is capable of being activated by an Internet user.
ARPA	Advanced Research Projects Agency: an agency funded by the United States Department of Defense from the early 1960s to research the interconnection of different types of computer network.

---

* Assistance was derived in compiling this glossary from many sources including Douglas Comer, *The Internet Book* (2nd edn, 1997), Preston Gralla, *How the Internet Works* (4th edn, 1998), Alan Freedman, Alfred Glossbrenner, and Emily Glossbrenner, *The Internet Glossary and Quick Reference Guide* (1998); James Gillies and Robert Cailliau, *How the Web was Born* (2000); Berny Goodheart and Frank Crawford, *Oz Internet* (1995); Geoff Ebbs and Jeremy Horey, *The Australian Internet Book* (1995), and the Webopedia Dictionary located at <http://www.webopedia.com>.

ARPANET	The WAN developed by ARPA in the late 1960s. ARPANET became known as the Internet project.
Asymmetric digital subscriber line	*See* **ADSL**
auDA	.au Domain Administration Ltd: the Australian organization which regulates domain names with the suffix '.au'.
.au Domain Administration Ltd	*See* **auDA**
Backbone WAN	A WAN to which many computer networks are connected.
Bandwidth	The capacity of a link between networks. Bandwidth measures the amount of information which can be transferred between networks, usually in bits per second.
BBS	Bulletin Board System/Bulletin Board Service: an American term which was originally used to describe computer network services which enable subscribers to exchange messages with other subscribers. Most BBSs later expanded to become ISPs, by allowing subscribers access to the Internet.
BITNET	The Because It's Time Network: a system developed in the early 1980s for the exchange of e-mail messages and files between IBM computers.
Broadband	A high speed Internet connection.
Browser	Software which enables computer users to access the web.
Bulletin board	A service which enables computer users to exchange messages with other users, by viewing messages posted for others to read, and by contributing messages of their own. Some bulletin boards are 'moderated', because control is exercised over what messages are posted on or accessible via the bulletin board. Other bulletin boards are 'unmoderated', because no such control is exercised. *See also* **BBS**
Bulletin Board System/Bulletin Board Service	*See* **BBS**
Caching	The temporary storage of information in a computer or server for the purpose of making the future transmission or display of that information more efficient.

CGI	Common Gateway Interface: technology which enables Internet users, by following a hyperlink, to submit information to, and activate computer programs on, remote computers.
Chat room	A service permitting computer users to exchange messages in much the same way as IRC. Some chat room services allow the exchange of messages which incorporate sound, pictures, and video, as well as text.
Client	An application that runs on a computer in conjunction with a server located on a remote computer. An e-mail client eg is an application that enables an Internet user to send e-mail to a remote mail server, and to receive e-mail from a remote mail server.
Convergence	The merging of, or interaction between, different technologies such as the Internet, telecommunications, and broadcasting.
CSNET	Computer Science Network: a network funded by the NSF in the late 1970s. It was designed to reach and connect all computer scientists in the United States.
Cyberspace	A term coined by William Gibson in his novel *Neuromancer* (1984). The term has no agreed meaning, although it is commonly used interchangeably with 'Internet'. Its use is best reserved to describe the artificial human and computer enhanced interactions which the convergence of the Internet with virtual reality technologies promises to facilitate.
Deep linking	The inclusion of a hyperlink on a web page which, when followed, transports the Internet user to a web page deep in the heart of a third party's web site; that is, to a web page other than the third party's homepage. *Cf* **shallow linking, framing**
Digital subscriber line	*See* **DSL**
DNS	Domain Name Server: a computer containing a directory of domain names, and the routes to those domain names.
Domain name	The name by which computer users know a computer or computer network's address or a part of such an address eg 'ispb.co.uk'.
Domain name server	*See* **DNS**
DSL	Digital subscriber line: a method of broadband Internet connection using copper telephone lines. *Cf* **ADSL**

eBay	A web-based auction site operated by eBay, Inc, enabling Internet users to post items for sale, and bid for items posted by other Internet users.
EBONE	A major European backbone WAN for connections to the Internet.
Electronic mail	*See* **e-mail**
E-mail	Electronic mail: a facility which enables computer users to exchange messages, which can incorporate text, sound, and pictures.
E-mail address	The name which identifies the destination for an e-mail message sent via the Internet eg 'jack@networka.co.uk'.
Emoticon	A typed symbol used in Internet communication to simulate tone of voice or facial expression. The symbol ':-)' eg represents a smiling face, and might be used to convey that a message is not to be taken seriously. Some common emoticons are set out in Table 3 on page 100.
File transfer protocol	*See* **FTP**
Flaming	The sending of e-mail messages or bulletin board postings which are deliberately insulting, provocative, or defamatory.
Framing	A form of linking, involving the inclusion on a web page of a hyperlink which, when followed by an Internet user, causes another web page to be displayed within a 'frame' on the original web page. Unlike ordinary linking, the Internet user remains connected to the original web page, rather than being transported entirely to the framed site, and may not even be aware that the framed content comes from another site. Framing can also be automatic; that is, a web page might be constructed so that content from different web sites is simultaneously displayed, in separate frames, on the user's screen.
FTP	File Transfer Protocol: the system used to transfer computer programs and files from one computer to another via the Internet.
General Packet Radio Service	*See* **GPRS**
Gopher	An Internet service which connects menu-driven indexes of various Internet addresses. Gophers have become for all practical purposes obsolete because of the popularity of the web and search engines.

GPRS	General Packet Radio Service: a standard enabling Internet content to be sent wirelessly to, and displayed on mobile telephones or computers at a faster rate than WAP. *Cf* **3G**
Header	Information attached to a packet by computer software to identify the sending computer, and the intended recipient computer.
Hit	A measure of the number of times a particular web page has been visited by Internet users eg 'this web page has recorded 200 hits'. This measure does not usually differentiate between new and repeat visitors, and cannot measure how many people have seen a single hit, and so is a crude measure of the number of people who have displayed and seen an Internet publication.
Homepage	The nominated web page to which a browser first connects a user. Also used to describe the main web page of a web site.
Host	The computer on which particular Internet content is stored. *See also* **Internet content host**
HTML	Hypertext Markup Language: the computer language which enables hypertext documents to be created. The most significant aspect of HTML is its ability to embed hyperlinks in hypertext documents.
HTTP	Hypertext Transport Protocol: the system by which hyperlinks permit users to access different hypertext documents.
Hyperlink	A link in a hypertext document which enables a computer user to transfer to another hypertext document or to activate a program located on another computer connected to the Internet, anywhere in the world. Hyperlinks typically appear on a user's screen as graphics, or bold, coloured, or underlined text, and are activated by clicking a mouse pointer on the hyperlink. *See also* **linking, framing**
Hypertext document	The term for information which has been constructed using HTML and posted on the web. A hypertext document can incorporate text, sound, pictures, and hyperlinks. *See also* **web page**
Hypertext mark-up language	*See* **HTML**
Hypertext transport protocol	*See* **HTTP**

ICANN	Internet Corporation for Assigned Names and Numbers: the organization responsible for managing and coordinating domain names to ensure that every Internet address is unique and that all users of the Internet can find all valid addresses. ICANN is also responsible for accrediting domain name registrars.
ICQ	A popular instant messaging system.
IIA	The Internet Industry Association (Australia).
Information superhighway	A term coined by then American Vice President Al Gore and used, mainly by the popular press, to describe the aim of the American National Information Infrastructure (NII) initiative. Colloquially, this term is also used to refer to the Internet itself.
Instant messaging service or system	A variant on e-mail. Subscribers are able to identify whether particular persons are logged onto the Internet and, if so, send messages to them instantly, with the knowledge that those messages are likely to be read more quickly than traditional e-mail.
Interactive web site	A web site with which Internet users can interact by eg exchanging information with the site operator or other users.
Intermediary	An operator of a computer system on which Internet content is hosted or cached, or via which Internet content is carried en route from one computer to another. Internet intermediaries include Internet service providers, Internet content hosts, and mere conduits.
Internet	A global network of interconnected computer networks, which communicate using common software protocols.
Internet content host	An Internet intermediary who stores on its computer system Internet content created by other parties, typically in the nature of web pages and bulletin board postings, and makes that content available to Internet users.
Internet protocol	*See* **IP**
Internet relay chat	*See* **IRC**
Internet service provider	*See* **ISP**
IP	Internet Protocol: software which enables basic communication between incompatible computer networks. *See also* **TCP/IP**
IP address	The unique number assigned to a computer which is connected to the Internet eg '123.45.67.89'.

470

IP datagram	A packet which is in a form capable of being transferred via the Internet.
IRC	Internet Relay Chat: a service which enables participants to send and receive messages in relay. IRC simulates a conversation in which there can be any number of participants. Each participant joins an IRC 'channel' of interest to them, and receives a copy of each message sent to that channel as it is posted. IRC can also be used for private 'conversations' between two or more Internet users. *See also* **chat room**
ISP	Internet Service Provider: the operator of a WAN with a connection to the Internet. Individuals or computer networks wanting access to the Internet can do so by subscribing to an ISP.
ISPA	The Internet Service Providers Association (United Kingdom).
IWF	The Internet Watch Foundation (United Kingdom).
Java	A tool developed by Sun Microsystems, Inc which enables the creation of highly dynamic web pages, typically incorporating animation and sound. *See also* **ActiveX, applet**
LAN	Local Area Network: a network of interconnected computers, usually within close proximity to one another in an individual government or university department, or business. Each computer in the network is usually connected by cable.
Linking	The inclusion on a web page of a hyperlink which, when followed, transports Internet users to another web page.
LINX	The London Internet Exchange.
Local area network	*See* **LAN**
Mailing list	A list of e-mail addresses.
Mere conduit	An intermediary operating a computer system through which a particular Internet communication passes en route from one computer to another, without being stored other than on an automatic and transient basis.
Mirror/mirror site	A web site that contains the same content as another site. Mirror sites may be set up eg in different geographic locations to improve efficient transmission of data.
Modem	Modulator-demodulator. A device which enables digital data to be transmitted along, and received from, an analogue transmission line, such as a telephone line.

MSN Messenger	A popular instant messaging system.
MUD	Multiple User Domain or Dungeon: a form of chat room, with a defined theme or environment. Other similar forms of chat room include MUSEs (multiple user social environment), MUSHes (multiple user social hosts), and MOOs (multiple object-oriented).
Multiple user domain or dungeon	*See* **MUD**
Narrowband	A low speed Internet connection.
National information infrastructure	*See* **NII**
Netnews	*See* **network news**
Network	The generic term for any configuration of connected computers.
Network news	An Internet bulletin board service. Also known as netnews. *See also* **USENET**
Network packet	A packet which is in a form capable of being transferred within a single computer network.
Newsgroup	The collective name for subscribers to a particular topic of netnews discussion.
NII	National Information Infrastructure. An American initiative which had as its aim making Internet access affordable and available to schools and homes. *See also* **information superhighway**
Nominet UK	The organization with responsibility for assigning domain names with the suffix '.uk': see <http://www.nominet.org.uk>.
NSF	The National Science Foundation (United States).
NSFNET	A WAN developed by the NSF, International Business Machines Corporation (IBM), MCI, Inc, and Merit Network, Inc which replaced ARPANET as the backbone WAN for the Internet in 1988.
Packet	A unit of data. Signals transferred over computer networks, including the Internet, are divided into packets. *See also* **network packet, IP datagram**
Packet switching	A technique which ensures that all computers in a network that want to transfer packets at the same time have fair access to the available resources. Packet switching technology effectively forces each computer on the network to take turns in transferring packets.
Passive web site	A web site which is a mere repository of information, permitting little or no interaction with Internet users who visit the site.

Route	The path taken by IP datagrams which are transferred via the Internet.
Router	Each network connected to the Internet has a router. The network router is a dedicated device whose primary purpose is to send packets from one network to another, and to receive packets destined for a computer within the router's network.
Search engine	A service, usually provided via a web site, which contains extensive indexes of the contents of other web pages. Users ask the search engine to display a summary of all the web pages within its index which contain words specified by the user. The summary will contain a hyper-link to the indexed web pages.
Server	A computer program which offers some service. An e-mail server eg is a program which holds e-mail messages until the recipient is ready to receive them. Also used to refer to a computer dedicated to performing some such function. Web pages eg are stored on web servers.
Shallow linking	The inclusion of a hyperlink on a web page which, when followed, transports the Internet user to a third party's homepage. *Cf* **deep linking, framing**
Spam	Unsolicited, 'junk' e-mail messages sent indiscriminately or to large mailing lists of recipients.
Streaming	A process whereby a sound or video file stored on a server commences playing on a remote computer in a 'stream', without having been fully transferred to that computer.
TCP	Transmission Control Protocol: software which regulates the order in which packets of information are sent and reassembled via the Internet. Sometimes called Transfer Control Protocol. *See also* **TCP/IP**
TCP/IP	Formally known as the TCP/IP Internet Protocol Suite, TCP/IP is the software which enables computer networks which are connected to the Internet to communicate and exchange signals. *See also* **TCP** and **IP**
Transmission control protocol	*See* **TCP**
Uniform resource locator	*See* **URL**
URL	Uniform Resource Locator: a web address. The (fictional) URL 'http://www.networka.co.uk/' eg might refer to the homepage for the Network A web site.

USENET	Originally a network of computers dedicated to exchanging network news, USENET is a term still used to describe services which enable the exchange of network news messages via the Internet.
vBNS	Very high speed Backbone Network System: a backbone WAN developed by MCI, Inc in 1995.
Virtual reality	A computer generated environment in which participants simulate activities in the 'real' world. Virtual reality technology varies from simple computer games to sophisticated environments in which all the human senses are stimulated, and otherwise impossible human interactions are facilitated.
Voice over Internet Protocol	*See* **VoIP**
VoIP	Voice over Internet Protocol: a method of converting sounds into digital data for transmission via the Internet.
WAN	Wide Area Network: a network of interconnected computers, usually spread over a large geographic distance. Each computer in the network is connected to a server. The connection will usually be achieved using a modem which sends signals along a telephone line or fibre-optic cable. Connections within a WAN may, however, be achieved using cables, satellites, or a range of other wired and wireless technologies.
WAP	Wireless Application Protocol: a standard which enables Internet content to be sent wirelessly to, and displayed on mobile telephones or computers. *Cf* **GPRS, 3G**
Web	Short for world wide web (www). A service which interconnects information stored on many Internet servers in a user-friendly way, by incorporating text, sound, pictures, and hyperlinks.
Webcam	A special purpose camera which connects to a computer to facilitate video communications via the Internet.
Web page	A hypertext document. A web page forms part of a web site.
Web site	The term for the combination of all interconnected web pages maintained by a single Internet user or entity.
Wide area network	*See* **WAN**

Wi-Fi	Wireless Fidelity. A service enabling users in a limited geographic area, known as a 'hot spot', to connect to the Internet via specified radiofrequencies, without being physically connected to any network.
Wireless application protocol	*See* **WAP**
Wireless broadband	Services that deliver high speed Internet access using the radiofrequency spectrum.
World wide web	*See* **www, web**
www	world wide web. *See* **web**

APPENDIX
SELECTED LEGISLATION

A.1 Defamation Act 1996 (UK), section 1*

(1) In defamation proceedings a person has a defence if he shows that—

    (a) he was not the author, editor or publisher of the statement complained of,

    (b) he took reasonable care in relation to its publication, and

    (c) he did not know, and had no reason to believe, that what he did caused or contributed to the publication of a defamatory statement.

(2) For this purpose 'author', 'editor' and 'publisher' have the following meanings, which are further explained in subsection (3)—

    'author' means the originator of the statement, but does not include a person who did not intend that his statement be published at all;

    'editor' means a person having editorial or equivalent responsibility for the content of the statement or the decision to publish it; and

    'publisher' means a commercial publisher, that is, a person whose business is issuing material to the public, or a section of the public, who issues material containing the statement in the course of that business.

(3) A person shall not be considered the author, editor or publisher of a statement if he is only involved—

    (a) in printing, producing, distributing or selling printed material containing the statement;

    (b) in processing, making copies of, distributing, exhibiting or selling a film or

---

* Crown Copyright 1996.

sound recording (as defined in Part I of the Copyright, Designs and Patents Act 1988) containing the statement;

(c) in processing, making copies of, distributing or selling any electronic medium in or on which the statement is recorded, or in operating or providing any equipment, system or service by means of which the statement is retrieved, copied, distributed or made available in electronic form;

(d) as the broadcaster of a live programme containing the statement in circumstances in which he has no effective control over the maker of the statement;

(e) as the operator of or provider of access to a communications system by means of which the statement is transmitted, or made available, by a person over whom he has no effective control.

In a case not within paragraphs (a) to (e) the court may have regard to those provisions by way of analogy in deciding whether a person is to be considered the author, editor or publisher of a statement.

(4) Employees or agents of an author, editor or publisher are in the same position as their employer or principal to the extent that they are responsible for the content of the statement or the decision to publish it.

(5) In determining for the purposes of this section whether a person took reasonable care, or had reason to believe that what he did caused or contributed to the publication of a defamatory statement, regard shall be had to—

(a) the extent of his responsibility for the content of the statement or the decision to publish it,

(b) the nature or circumstances of the publication, and

(c) the previous conduct or character of the author, editor or publisher.

(6) This section does not apply to any cause of action which arose before the section came into force.

A.2 Electronic Commerce (EC Directive) Regulations 2002 (UK) ('Electronic Commerce Regulations'), regulations 17–20, 22

Regulation 17: Mere conduit

(1) Where an information society service[1] is provided which consists of the transmission in a communication network of information provided by a recipient of the service or the provision of access to a communication network, the service provider[2] (if he otherwise would) shall not be liable for damages or for any other pecuniary remedy or for any criminal sanction as a result of that transmission where the service provider—

---

[1] An 'information society service' means 'any service normally provided for remuneration, at a distance, by electronic means and at the individual request of a recipient of services': Electronic Commerce Regulations, reg 2(1), incorporating Art 2(a) of the Directive on Electronic Commerce. Article 2(a) of the Directive on Electronic Commerce incorporates the definition in Directive 98/34/EC laying down a procedure for the provision of information in the field of technical standards and regulations and of rules on information society services, as amended by Directive 98/48/EC.

[2] 'Service provider' means any person providing an information society service: Electronic Commerce Regulations, reg 2(1).

(a) did not initiate the transmission;

(b) did not select the receiver of the transmission; and

(c) did not select or modify the information contained in the transmission.

(2) The acts of transmission and of provision of access referred to in paragraph (1) include the automatic, intermediate and transient storage of the information transmitted where:

(a) this takes place for the sole purpose of carrying out the transmission in the communication network; and

(b) the information is not stored for any period longer than is reasonably necessary for the transmission.

Regulation 18: Caching

Where an information society service[3] is provided which consists of the transmission in a communication network of information provided by a recipient of the service, the service provider[4] (if he otherwise would) shall not be liable for damages or for any other pecuniary remedy or for any criminal sanction as a result of that transmission where—

(a) the information is the subject of automatic, intermediate and temporary storage where that storage is for the sole purpose of making more efficient onward transmission of the information to other recipients of the service upon their request, and

(b) the service provider—

(i) does not modify the information;

(ii) complies with conditions on access to the information;

(iii) complies with any rules regarding the updating of the information, specified in a manner widely recognized and used by industry;

(iv) does not interfere with the lawful use of technology, widely recognized and used by industry, to obtain data on the use of the information; and

(v) acts expeditiously to remove or to disable access to the information he has stored upon obtaining actual knowledge of the fact that the information at the initial source of the transmission has been removed from the network, or access to it has been disabled, or that a court or an administrative authority has ordered such removal or disablement.

Regulation 19: Hosting

Where an information society service[5] is provided which consists of the storage of information provided by a recipient of the service, the service provider[6] (if he otherwise would) shall not be liable for damages or for any other pecuniary remedy or for any criminal sanction as a result of that storage where—

(a) the service provider—

(i) does not have actual knowledge of unlawful activity or information and, where a claim for damages is made, is not aware of facts or circumstances from which it would have been apparent to the service provider that the activity or information was unlawful; or

---

[3] See n 1 above.

[4] See n 2 above.

[5] See n 1 above.

[6] See n 2 above.

    (ii) upon obtaining such knowledge or awareness, acts expeditiously to remove or to disable access to the information, and

  (b) the recipient of the service was not acting under the authority or the control of the service provider.

Regulation 20: Protection of rights

(1) Nothing in regulations 17, 18 and 19 shall—

    (a) prevent a person agreeing different contractual terms; or

    (b) affect the rights of any party to apply to a court for relief to prevent or stop infringement of any rights.

(2) Any power of an administrative authority to prevent or stop infringement of any rights shall continue to apply notwithstanding regulations 17, 18 and 19.

Regulation 22: Notice for the purposes of actual knowledge

In determining whether a service provider has actual knowledge for the purposes of regulations 18(b)(v) and 19(a)(i), a court shall take into account all matters which appear to it in the particular circumstances to be relevant and, among other things, shall have regard to—

  (a) whether a service provider has received a notice through a means of contact made available in accordance with regulation 6(1)(c),[7] and

  (b) the extent to which any notice includes—

    (i) the full name and address of the sender of the notice;

    (ii) details of the location of the information in question; and

    (iii) details of the unlawful nature of the activity or information in question.

A.3 Directive 2000/31/EC of the European Parliament and of the Council on certain legal aspects of information society services, in particular electronic commerce, in the internal market ('Directive on Electronic Commerce'), Articles 12–15

Article 12: 'Mere conduit'

(1) Where an information society service[8] is provided that consists of the transmission in a communication network of information provided by a recipient of the service, or the provision of access to a communication network, Member States must ensure that the service provider[9] is not liable for the information transmitted, on condition that the provider:

---

    [7] That is, received in accordance with the details of the service provider made available to recipients of the service and any relevant enforcement authority. Those details must be easily, directly, and permanently accessible, and include the service provider's electronic mail address, so as to enable the provider to be contacted rapidly, directly, and effectively: Electronic Commerce Regulations, reg 6(1)(c).

    [8] An 'information society service' means 'any service normally provided for remuneration, at a distance, by electronic means and at the individual request of a recipient of services': see Art 2(a), which incorporates the definition in Directive 98/34/EC, as amended by Directive 98/48/EC.

    [9] 'Service provider' means 'any natural or legal person providing an information society service': see Art 2(b).

(a) does not initiate the transmission;

(b) does not select the receiver of the transmission; and

(c) does not select or modify the information contained in the transmission.

(2) The acts of transmission and of provision of access referred to in paragraph 1 include the automatic, intermediate and transient storage of the information transmitted in so far as this takes place for the sole purpose of carrying out the transmission in the communication network, and provided that the information is not stored for any period longer than is reasonably necessary for the transmission.

(3) This Article shall not affect the possibility for a court or administrative authority, in accordance with Member States' legal systems, of requiring the service provider to terminate or prevent an infringement.

Article 13: 'Caching'

(1) Where an information society service[10] is provided that consists of the transmission in a communication network of information provided by a recipient of the service, Member States shall ensure that the service provider[11] is not liable for the automatic, intermediate and temporary storage of that information, performed for the sole purpose of making more efficient the information's onward transmission to other recipients of the service upon their request, on condition that:

(a) the provider does not modify the information;

(b) the provider complies with conditions on access to the information;

(c) the provider complies with rules regarding the updating of the information, specified in a manner widely recognized and used by industry;

(d) the provider does not interfere with the lawful use of technology, widely recognized and used by industry, to obtain data on the use of the information; and

(e) the provider acts expeditiously to remove or to disable access to the information it has stored upon obtaining actual knowledge of the fact that the information at the initial source of the transmission has been removed from the network, or access to it has been disabled, or that a court or an administrative authority has ordered such removal or disablement.

(2) This Article shall not affect the possibility for a court or administrative authority, in accordance with Member States' legal systems, of requiring the service provider to terminate or prevent an infringement.

Article 14: Hosting

(1) Where an information society service[12] is provided that consists of the storage of information provided by a recipient of the service, Member States shall ensure that the service provider[13] is not liable for the information stored at the request of a recipient of the service, on condition that:

---

[10] See n 8 above.

[11] See n 9 above.

[12] See n 8 above.

[13] See n 9 above.

(a) the provider does not have actual knowledge of illegal activity or information and, as regards claims for damages, is not aware of facts or circumstances from which the illegal activity or information is apparent; or

(b) the provider, upon obtaining such knowledge or awareness, acts expeditiously to remove or to disable access to the information.

(2) Paragraph 1 shall not apply when the recipient of the service is acting under the authority or the control of the provider.

(3) This Article shall not affect the possibility for a court or administrative authority, in accordance with Member States' legal systems, of requiring the service provider to terminate or prevent an infringement, nor does it affect the possibility for Member States of establishing procedures governing the removal or disabling of access to information.

Article 15: No general obligation to monitor

(1) Member States shall not impose a general obligation on providers, when providing the services covered by Articles 12, 13 and 14, to monitor the information which they transmit or store, nor a general obligation actively to seek facts or circumstances indicating illegal activity.

(2) Member States may establish obligations for information society service providers promptly to inform the competent public authorities of alleged illegal activities undertaken or information provided by recipients of their service or obligations to communicate to the competent authorities, at their request, information enabling the identification of recipients of their service with whom they have storage agreements.

A.4 Broadcasting Services Act 1992 (Cth), Schedule 5, clause 91

(1) A law of a State or Territory, or a rule of common law or equity, has no effect to the extent to which it:

(a) subjects, or would have the effect (whether direct or indirect) of subjecting, an Internet content host[14] to liability (whether criminal or civil) in respect of hosting particular Internet content[15] in a case where the host was not aware of the nature of the Internet content; or

---

[14] 'Internet content host' means 'a person who hosts Internet content in Australia, or who proposes to host Internet content in Australia': Broadcasting Services Act 1992 (Cth), Sch 5, cl 3.
[15] 'Internet content' means information that:
(a) is kept on a data storage device; and
(b) is accessed, or available for access, using an Internet carriage service;
but does not include:
(c) ordinary electronic mail; or
(d) information that is transmitted in the form of a broadcasting service.
See Broadcasting Services Act 1992 (Cth), Sch 5, cl 3. 'Data storage device' means 'any article or material (for example, a disk) from which information is capable of being reproduced, with or without the aid of any article or device'. 'Ordinary electronic mail' is defined so as not to include 'a posting to a newsgroup'. 'Internet carriage service' means a listed carriage service that enables end-users to access the Internet'. 'Listed carriage service' has 'the same meaning as in the Telecommunications Act 1997'. Under the Telecommunications Act 1997 (Cth) ss 7, 16, 'listed carriage service' means, in effect, a service for carrying communications by means of guided or unguided electromagnetic energy between two or more points, at least one of which is in Australia.

(b) requires, or would have the effect (whether direct or indirect) of requiring, an Internet content host to monitor, make inquiries about, or keep records of, Internet content hosted by the host; or

(c) subjects, or would have the effect (whether direct or indirect) of subjecting, an Internet service provider[16] to liability (whether criminal or civil) in respect of carrying particular Internet content in a case where the service provider was not aware of the nature of the Internet content; or

(d) requires, or would have the effect (whether direct or indirect) of requiring, an Internet service provider to monitor, make inquiries about, or keep records of, Internet content carried by the provider.

(2) The Minister may, by written instrument, exempt a specified law of a State or Territory, or a specified rule of common law or equity, from the operation of subclause (1).

(3) An exemption under subclause (2) may be unconditional or subject to such conditions (if any) as are specified in the exemption.

(4) The Minister may, by written instrument, declare that a specified law of a State or Territory, or a specified rule of common law or equity, has no effect to the extent to which the law or rule has a specified effect in relation to an Internet content host.

(5) The Minister may, by written instrument, declare that a specified law of a State or Territory, or a specified rule of common law or equity, has no effect to the extent to which the law or rule has a specified effect in relation to an Internet service provider.

(6) A declaration under subclause (4) or (5) has effect only to the extent that:
(a) it is authorized by paragraph 51(v) of the Constitution (either alone or when read together with paragraph 51(xxxix) of the Constitution); or
(b) both:
(i) it is authorized by section 122 of the Constitution; and
(ii) it would have been authorized by paragraph 51(v) of the Constitution (either alone or when read together with paragraph 51(xxxix) of the Constitution) if section 51 of the Constitution extended to the Territories.

(7) An instrument under subclause (2), (4) or (5) is a disallowable instrument for the purposes of section 46A of the *Acts Interpretation Act 1901.*

A.5 Communications Decency Act, 47 USC (1996) (USA), section 230(c)

(1) TREATMENT OF PUBLISHER OR SPEAKER

No provider or user of an interactive computer service shall be treated as the publisher or speaker of any information provided by another information content provider.

(2) CIVIL LIABILITY

No provider or user of an interactive computer service shall be held liable on account of—

---

[16] 'Internet service provider' means a person who supplies, or proposes to supply, an Internet carriage service to the public, or a person declared by the Minister by written instrument to be an Internet service provider for the purposes of the Schedule: Broadcasting Services Act 1992 (Cth), Sch 5, cl 8. A written instrument by the Minister under this clause is a disallowable instrument for the purposes of the Acts Interpretation Act 1901 (Cth): ibid, cl 8(3).

(A) any action voluntarily taken in good faith to restrict access to or availability of material that the provider or user considers to be obscene, lewd, lascivious, filthy, excessively violent, harassing, or otherwise objectionable, whether or not such material is constitutionally protected; or

(B) any action taken to enable or make available to information content providers or others the technical means to restrict access to material described in paragraph (1).

INDEX